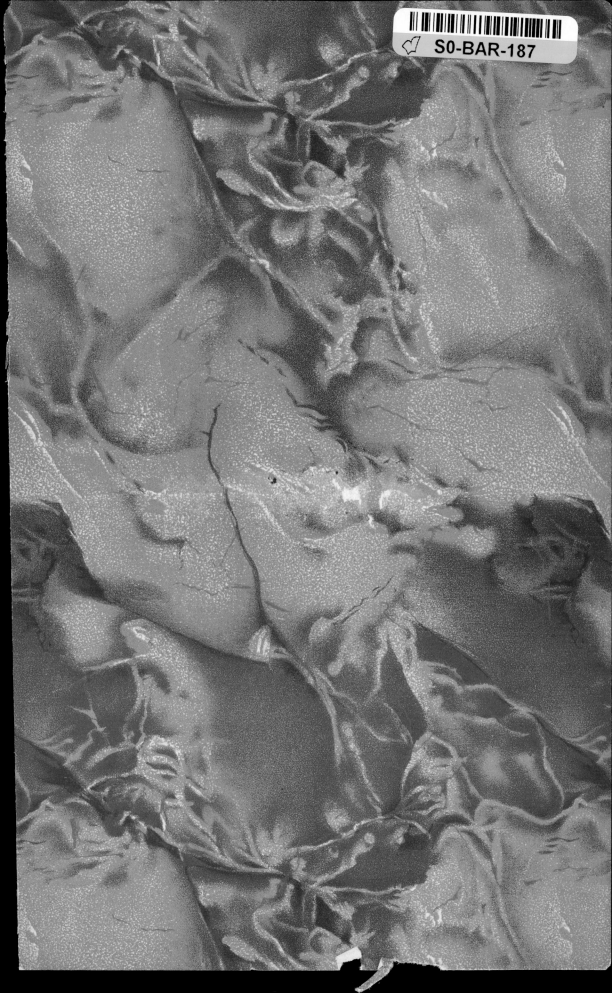

Copyright, 1929
The Lewis Publishing Company

VIRGINIA

REBIRTH OF THE OLD D[O]

VIRGINIA BIOGRAPHY
By Special Staff of Writers

Issued in Five Volumes

VOLUME IV

ILLUSTRATED

THE LEWIS PUBLISHING COMPANY
CHICAGO AND NEW YORK

1929

HISTORY *of* VIRGINIA

GOODRICH HATTON, attorney-at-law at Portsmouth, has lived in that Virginia community all his life. He is a scholarly lawyer, has enjoyed success in his profession, is deeply interested in his native state and at different times has rendered valuable service of a public nature.

He was born in Norfolk County May 8, 1862. The Hatton family in Virginia was founded by John Hatton, who arrived in Virginia in 1613 and settled in Elizabeth City County. Mr. Hatton's father, Edward Alexander Hatton, was a son of John Goodrich and Emmeline (Leckie) Hatton and a grandson of, Edward and Mary (Jones) Hatton. The mother of Goodrich Hatton was Susan Rebecca Nash, a daughter of Dempsey and Elizabeth Nash and granddaughter of Cornelius and Susan Nash. Mr. Hatton is a direct descendant in the sixth generation from Capt. John Hatton, who was one of the deputies of the County Court of Norfolk County in 1686 and 1692.

Mr. Hatton was educated in Norfolk Academy under Rev. Robert Gatewood, and received the degree of B. L. from the University of Virginia. He has practiced law at Portsmouth for over forty years.

In his home city he served as president of the Board of School Trustees and represented Portsmouth in the Constitutional Convention of 1901-02. For eight years he was a member of the Board of Visitors of the University of Virginia. In 1896 he was a delegate to the National Democratic Convention at Indianapolis which repudiated the free silver doctrines of William J. Bryan and pledged that portion of the party to the sound money ticket headed by Palmer and Buckner. When America entered the World war in 1917 Mr. Hatton offered his services to the President in any way he could be useful. He was not accepted for military duty but became a member of the Legal Advisory Board in connection with the Selective Service Act.

He married in 1893 Mary Reed Watts, daughter of Legh Richmond and Mattie P. Watts. There are two daughters, Mary Watts, who married Augustine S. Mason, of Hagerstown, Maryland, and has one daughter, Mary Watts Hatton; and Susan Rebecca, who married George H. Lewis, Jr., of Norfolk, Virginia.

JUNIUS BLAIR FISHBURN, veteran banker, newspaper publisher and man of affairs at Roanoke, is a member of a family that has been in Virginia for seven generations.

He was born in Franklin County, Virginia, September 27, 1865, son of James Addison and Louise H. (Boon) Fishburn, and a grandson of Samuel Fishburn and Fleming and Susan (Kinsey) Boon. He received his early educational advantages at Danville, Kentucky, and Roanoke, Virginia.

In 1915 the directors of the National Exchange Bank of Roanoke presented him a loving cup in appreciation of the important services he had rendered during the twenty-five years

3

of his active association with the bank. He entered that institution as cashier, for many years was its president, and finally became chairman of the Board of Directors. Mr. Fishburn has also been honored in banking circles by the office of vice president of the Virginia Bankers Association and vice president of the American Bankers Association of Virginia.

Mr. Fishburn has large interests in two of Virginia's most influential newspapers, the *Roanoke Times* and *Roanoke World-News*, published by the Times-World Publishing Corporation. He has been an officer or director in many industrial organizations of his home city.

He has traveled widely, having been around the world, and his cultivated mind, sound standards of taste, broad sympathies and interests have made him a delightful companion, interesting to others as well as intensely interested in people and things. For about forty years he has been a steward of the Greene Memorial Methodist Church at Roanoke, is a Democrat, member of the Shenandoah Club, Roanoke Country Club, University Club, Century Club, Roanoke Library, Masonic fraternity, and has a life membership in the Virginia Historical Society, the National Geographic Society, Wisconsin Historical Society, New England Genealogical and Historical Society and Pennsylvania Historical Society.

He married at Cleveland, Tennessee, in 1893, Grace Theresa Parker, daughter of John H. and Mary K. Parker. They have three children: Junius Parker Fishburn, a graduate of Princeton University; Mary Evelyn Fishburn, who was educated in Hollins College and Columbia University; and Ernest Louise Fishburn, a graduate of the Ogontz School in Pennsylvania. The son after his university career became editor of the *Roanoke World-News*.

ELBERT LEE TRINKLE, who was governor of Virginia from 1922 to 1926, has been both a lawyer and business man, and while there was no sectionalism in his administration he might be said to have represented the great and progressive district of Southwest Virginia, since his home for many years has been at Roanoke.

In fact he is a native of Southwest Virginia, born in the old community of Wytheville March 12, 1876, son of Elbert S. and Letitia M. Trinkle. His father was a business man. Governor Trinkle was educated at Hampden-Sidney College, where he took the Bachelor of Arts and Bachelor of Science degrees in 1896. He graduated from the law department of the University of Virginia in 1898. He has practiced law with success and distinction over Southwest Virginia, and during his active connection with the bar from 1899 to 1922 was connected with many notable cases. However, he brought more than the viewpoint of a lawyer to public life. For many years he has been interested in insurance, in agriculture, manufacturing and general business, and since 1926 has been vice president of the Shenandoah Life Insurance Company of Roanoke.

Governor Trinkle is an outstanding member of the Virginia Democracy. He was at one time Democratic candidate for Congress from the Ninth Congressional District. He was elected and served as a member of the Virginia Senate from 1916 to 1922. In 1922 he was nominated in the Democratic primaries for governor, defeating Hon. Harry St. George Tucker. In the

Cuuon G. Williams

general election he was accorded a majority of 75,000 votes over his Republican opponent, this being the largest majority ever given in a state election in Virginia. While a review of his administration is the part of the general historian, it may be noted here that as governor he inaugurated the "pay as you go" plan for building public roads in the state, and the satisfactory results obtained from that plan have given Virginia a wonderful system of hard roads, linking the state with the roads program of other eastern states. In 1925 he was chosen president of the Governor Conference, comprising the governors of all of the states. He was awarded the prize by the national committee of prisons and prison labor for practical humanitarian effort in eliminating some of the abuses of prisons in his state. Governor Trinkle has made many speeches on public questions all over the South.

He is a member of the Sigma Chi social fraternity, Phi Delta Phi legal fraternity, Omicron Delta Kappa honorary society, is a Knight Templar and Scottish Rite Mason and Shriner, member of the Knights of the Court of Honor, Independent Order of Odd Fellows, Knights of Pythias, B. P. O. Elks, and Junior Order United American Mechanics. He is a member of the Shenandoah Club of Roanoke, the Rotary Club and the Presbyterian Church.

Governor Trinkle married at Houston, Texas, February 24, 1910, Miss Helen Ball Sexton, daughter of Rev. James W. and Susan (Ball) Sexton. She is a direct descendant of the distinguished Ball family of Virginia. They have three children, E. Lee, Jr., Helen Sue and William S. Trinkle.

ENNION GIFFORD WILLIAMS, commissioner of the Virginia State Board of Health, has had a career of many distinctions and important service in his profession.

Doctor Williams was born at Richmond, January 31, 1874, son of John Langbourne and Maria Ward (Skelton) Williams. His ancestry includes many famous names in Virginia Colonial and state history, his earliest American ancestors having settled in this country in the latter half of the seventeenth century. His father was a Master of Arts graduate from the University of Virginia, spent an active career as a banker and broker, and held many positions of trust and civic responsibility, though never elected to a political office. He was first a Whig and later a Democrat, and a member of the Episcopal Church. Doctor Williams' mother was a daughter of Dr. John Gifford Skelton, a physician who at one time was lecturer on obstetrics at the Medical College of Virginia.

Doctor Williams was educated in the McGuire Preparatory School at Richmond, had two years in the academic department of the University of Virginia and graduated from that institution with the M. D. degree in 1897. While he was studying medicine he became interested in the recently announced discovery of the Roentgen or X-Ray, and he was a pioneer in study and experimentation in the work of adapting the X-Ray to medicine and surgery, and wrote many articles on the prinicples governing its use and the results of treatment. Doctor Williams served his internship in the Willard's Hospital at New York and the Polyclinic Hospital at Philadelphia. During the past thirty years he has devoted a large part of his time to study and research. He did post-graduate work at Johns Hopkins University, Harvard, University of Pennsylvania, Tulane Uni-

versity of New Orleans, and abroad in Munich. From 1901 to
1908 he held the chair of histology, bacteriology and pathology
in the Medical College of Virginia, and from 1916 to 1923 was
professor of preventive medicine in that institution. Doctor
Williams has given twenty years to the duties of state health
commissioner, having been first appointed in 1908, and since
then has held office continuously by four reappointments. In
addition to his administrative responsibilities he has written
many articles on public health subjects and is a member of many
medical and public health societies. He was president of the
Richmond Academy of Medicine in 1906-07, of the Medical Society of Virginia in 1917-19, and of the Conference of State and
Provincial Boards of Health of North America in 1915-16.
He is a member of the American Public Health Association and
American Medical Association. He took a leading part in the
investigation of the Health Department of the City Home at
Richmond, resulting in a complete reorganization of both. He
was a member of the State Council of Defense in 1917-18, and
was a member of the Naval Reserve Corps in 1918. Doctor
Williams is a Democrat, was a member of the Richmond City
Council in 1906-08, has served several terms on the vestry of
the Episcopal Church and is a member of the Delta Psi
fraternity.

He married, October 21, 1902, Miss Anna Heath Lassiter,
daughter of Dr. William Daniel and Anna Rives (Heath) Lassiter, of Petersburg. Her father was a distinguished physician
and citizen of Virginia and Mrs. Williams had three brothers
who achieved eminence: Francis Rives Lassiter, at one time
United States district attorney and a member of Congress from
Virginia at the time of his death; William Lassiter, a major
general in the United States Army; and Charles T. Lassiter,
Petersburg attorney. Doctor and Mrs. Williams have a family
of eight children: Virginia Lassiter, Ennion Skelton, Anna
Heath, Daniel Lassiter, John Randolph, Charles Lassiter, Elizabeth Rives and Edmund Randolph.

GARDNER LLOYD BOOTHE. A number of advantages result
from the constantly increasing tendency of men learned in the
science of the law to embark in occupations outside their
immediate sphere of activity. This is the natural result of a
profession which equips its members for successful participation
in more lines of business than perhaps any other wage-earning
medium, causing it justly to be regarded as a means rather
than an end, and as an adjunct rather than an entirety. The
result is necessarily an elevation of commercial and financial
standards, an avoidance of complications, an adjustment out of
courts and a general simplifying of conditions through a knowledge of underlying principles and penalties. An illustration of
this modern phase of law is found in Gardner Lloyd Boothe, who
is a leading member of the Alexandria City bar, and also president of the First National Bank of Alexandria, the oldest
national bank in Virginia.

Mr. Boothe was born at Alexandria, June 1, 1872, and is a
son of William J. and Mary G. (Leadbeater) Boothe, natives
of Alexandria, where his father, who was for many years
superintendent of the American Coal Company, died in 1894,
his mother being also deceased. Gardner L. Boothe was reared
at Alexandria, where he acquired his early education in the
private schools and at Potomac Academy, and then entered the

Gardner L. Boothe.

University of Virginia, from which he was graduated with the degree Bachelor of Laws as a member of the class of 1893. At that time he entered the practice of his profession, and for thirty-five years has maintained his position among the leaders of the bar in Alexandria. He has been interested in many large cases and has a general practice, being equally well informed in all departments of his profession, of which he has never ceased being a student. He maintains offices at 108 N. St. Asaph Street, and is a member of the American Bar Association and the Virginia State Bar Association and president of the Alexandria Bar Association. For seven years Mr. Boothe served as city attorney of Alexandria, during which period he gained and held the full confidence of the people for the manner in which he discharged the responsibilities of his office. In July, 1909, Mr. Boothe was elected president of the First National Bank of Alexandria, the oldest national bank in Virginia, and has held that position ever since, directing its activities with rare judgment and sound ability and keeping it on a sound and prosperous footing. His fellow-officials are M. B. Harlow, vice president; George E. Warfield, cashier and trust officer; and A. K. Warfield, assistant cashier and assistant trust officer; and Robert G. Whitton, assistant cashier, the Board of Directors being composed of Benoit Baer, Jr., Harry Hammond, Mr. Boothe, William A. Moore, Jr., M. B. Harlow, Albert V. Bryan and George E. Warfield. A statement at the close of business December 31, 1928, showed the following: Resources—Loans and Investments $3,196,673.05; U. S. Bonds and Certificates, $274,200.00; Banking House, $57,320.70; Cash and Due from Banks, $417,967.11; 5% Fund $5,000.00. Liabilities—Capital, $200,000.00; Surplus and Profits, $533,109.68; Reserved for Interest and Taxes, $10,129.61; Circulation, $98,650.00, and Deposits, $2,959,271.64; Bills Payable, $150,-000.00. Mr. Boothe is widely and favorably known in banking circles as a man of conservatism, ability and good judgment as to local and general conditions. A stanch Democrat in his political allegiance, Mr. Boothe has been a member of the State Democratic Committee for the past twenty-five years and is chairman of the Eighth Congressional District Democratic Committee. He belongs to the Belle Haven Country Club, the Westmoreland Club of Richmond, the Racquet Club of Washington, D. C., the Kiwanis Club, the Alexandria Chamber of Commerce, the Alpha Tau Omega fraternity, and the Sons of the American Revolution. His pleasant and attractive home is at 711 Princess Street. An active member of the Episcopal Church, he is a member of the Standing Committee of the Diocese and a member of the Board of Trustees of the Protestant Episcopal Theological Seminary and the Protestant Episcopal High School in Virginia. As will be seen, his life has been an active and useful one, and at all times he has maintained high standards of morality and good citizenship.

On February 7, 1906, Mr. Boothe was united in marriage with Miss Eleanor Harrison Carr, a daughter of Joseph and Frances (Harrison) Carr, natives of Petersburg, Virginia, the former of whom fought in the Confederate army during the war between the states. He died some years ago, while his widow survived him until April, 1927. To Mr. and Mrs. Boothe there have come two children: Armistead Lloyd, born September 23, 1907, who graduated from the University of Virginia and is now a Rhodes Scholar of Oxford, England; and

Gardner Lloyd, Jr., born November 13, 1912, who is attending St. James Episcopal School near Hagerstown, Maryland. Mrs. Boothe is one of the active figures in the work of the Episcopal Church at Alexandria, and also is a popular and influential member of the Daughters of the American Revolution and the Society of Colonial Dames.

ROBERT WALTON MOORE, of Fairfax, who has represented the Eighth Virginia District in Congress since 1919, was born at Fairfax, February 6, 1859, son of Thomas and Hannah (Morris) Moore. Mr. Moore is a distinguished Virginia lawyer and for many years has been a recognized authority on transportation matters. He was educated at the University of Virginia, was admitted to the bar in 1880, and in 1907 became assistant to Edmund Baxter, representing numerous railway and steamship companies in matters relating to interstate commerce. In 1910 he succeeded Mr. Baxter as counsel in cases before the Interstate Commerce Commission. During 1918-19 he was assistant general counsel for the United States Railroad Administration.

He was elected to Congress to fill a vacancy May 27, 1919, entering the Sixty-sixth Congress, and has served consecutively, being now a member of the Seventieth Congress and a member of the committee on foreign affairs. He served as president of the Virginia State Bar Association in 1911, and is a member of the American Bar Association.

Mr. Moore was a member of the Virginia State Senate from 1887 to 1890. He was a presidential elector in 1892, member of the Virginia Constitutional Convention of 1901-02, has served on the Board of Visitors of the University of Virginia and William and Mary College, and is a former president of the General Alumni Association of the University of Virginia. He has been a regent of the Smithsonian Institute at Washington. Mr. Moore is a Phi Beta Kappa, member of the Chi Phi, and the Episcopal Church.

GEORGE L. BROWNING, lawyer and former judge of the Circuit Court at Orange, is a member of some of the distinguished families of this section of Virginia.

He was born in Rappahannock County April 3, 1867, son of John Armistead and Mary L. (Willis) Browning. The Brownings have lived in Rappahannock County for nearly two centuries, the title to the old estate in that county having been signed by Lord Fairfax in 1735. Judge Browning's mother was a great-great-granddaughter of Bettie Washington, sister of Gen. George Washington. John Armistead Browning was born at the Greenfield estate of the family, and lived there until his death at the age of seventy-six. He was a farmer and blooded stock breeder, and served two terms in the Legislature. His wife died in 1868, and of their family of children the only two now living are John A., Jr., owner of the family estate in Rappahannock County, and George L.

George L. Browning grew up in Rappahannock County, and for nine years was in the Government service at Washington as an employe of the House of Representatives. While in Washington he graduated in 1895 from Georgetown University, and later took a special law course at the University of Virginia. In 1899 he formed a law partnership with Judge James Hay at Madison, Virginia. Judge Hay is now judge of the United States Court of Claims. After locating at Orange he was a partner for four years with the late John G. Williams, and then was associated with Alexander T. Browning, a distant cousin, until 1922. He is now in practice with S. M. Nottingham.

He was appointed by the judge of Madison County to serve an unexpired term as commonwealth attorney in 1908, but refused to become a candidate to succeed himself in that office. He was a member of the State Legislature from 1912 to 1916, representing Orange County, and during the World war was chairman of the Liberty Loan committee, the Savings Stamp campaign, and chairman of the Four-Minute Men. While in the State Legislature he was a member of the economy and efficiency committee in 1914, having been appointed by Richard Byrd, father of the present Governor Byrd.

Judge Browning married, February 27, 1905, Mrs. Eva B. (Hill) Ranson, of Culpeper County, daughter of Henry Hill, who was a captain in the Confederate army and died shortly after the close of the war. Judge and Mrs. Browning have three children: Willis, born February 17, 1907, a graduate of Virginia Military Institute; George L., Jr., born November 6, 1909, a student of medicine at the University of Virginia; and Francis Henry, born February 5, 1911.

JOHN WIMBISH CRADDOCK as chairman of the Craddock-Terry Company of Lynchburg is and has been for years one of the eminent figures in Virginia's industrial and commercial affairs.

He is a native Virginian, born at Halifax Court House August 14, 1858, son of Dr. Charles J. and Fannie Y. (Easley) Craddock. His father died January 1, 1866. John W. Craddock was then eight years of age, and the death of his father combined with the general impoverishment of the people and the state following the war acted on the one side in limiting his educational and cultural opportunities, and on the other spurred him to effort in the line of self achievement. Mr. Craddock at the age of sixteen was working in a country store, subsequently was employed in Lynchburg business houses, and his abilities and energies brought him at the age of twenty-six to membership in the wholesale shoe house at Baltimore.

The Craddock-Terry Company gives the date of its founding as 1888. It was in that year that Mr. Craddock returned to Lynchburg and organized the wholesale shoe house of Craddock-Terry & Company. The Craddock-Terry Company was incorporated in 1898. It was the second wholesale shoe house in Lynchburg. Many years ago it passed out of the class of a local manufacturing and jobbing concern. The Craddock-Terry Company does a nation-wide business and is a Virginia institution that ranks well up among the great organizations in the same field elsewhere. With the executive offices at Lynchburg, the company has factories in that city, three in the State of Missouri, including one at Saint Louis, and two in Wisconsin. The company has manufacturing, wholesale and other distributing branches and agencies in Saint Louis, Milwaukee, Baltimore and Portland, Oregon.

Mr. Craddock has found his chief satisfaction in building up a great business that contributes to Virginia's prestige among the southeastern states. He has had no ambition for political service, but has been deeply interested in educational affairs, serving on the Lynchburg school board and for a number of

years as a member of the Board of Vistors of the University of
Virginia. During the World war he was chairman for Lynchburg and Campbell County of three loan campaigns and was
one of the Nation's conspicuous business men called into the
service of the Government as specialist in their particular field.
From February to August, 1918, he was assigned by General
Goethals to the position of chief of the shoe, leather and rubber
goods branch of the Quartermaster's Corps, a branch having
charge of all purchases for the army both at home and abroad of
shoes, rubber goods, raincoats and similar supplies. Mr. Craddock had to leave the duties of this responsible position because
of a breakdown in health, and received from General Goethals
a certificate commending him for the successful conduct of the
affairs of the department.

Mr. Craddock married, December 6, 1886, Miss Mary
Peachy Gilmer, and after her death he married Mrs. Elza Deane
Baker, daughter of Frank Deane and widow of Dr. W. H. Baker.
By his first marriage Mr. Craddock had four children: Gilmer
G., Charles G., Elise and John W., Jr.

DAVID RANDOLPH PHELPS, Doctor of Dental Surgery, has
enjoyed the relationship of a successful professional man and
an active citizen of his community of Lynchburg since 1908.

Doctor Phelps was one of a large family of children of an
Episcopal clergyman, and grew up under those peculiarly stimu-
lating conditions where the atmosphere of the home is of an
elevated character but where the income permits no luxuries or
extravagance. Doctor Phelps early learned to rely upon him-
self, and his work and individual efforts provided him with a good
education of a literary character as well as a thorough professional training. He was born in Hyde County, North Carolina,
July 30, 1880, son of William Girard and Mary (Randolph)
Phelps. His mother was a daughter of Edward and Charlotte
(Stockdale) Randolph and was related to the Meades and other
Colonial families of old Virginia. She was born at Petersburg,
Virginia, and now resides at Victoria of this state. William
Girard Phelps was born in Washington County, North Carolina,
was educated at Asheville in that state, served as a chaplain in
the Seventeenth North Carolina Regiment in the Civil war and
devoted his active life to the Episcopal ministry, serving various
churches in Virginia and North Carolina. He was the father of
thirteen children, nine of whom are living.

David Randolph Phelps was educated in an academy at
Houston, Virginia, and in 1903 graduated with the A. B. degree
from Washington and Lee University at Lexington, Virginia.
During 1903-04 he taught school, then entered the Atlanta
Dental College at Atlanta, Georgia, was graduated in 1907, and
for six months practiced at Tifton, Georgia.

Doctor Phelps located at Lynchburg May 1, 1908. He has
had a large general practice, and the profession has come to
know him as a specialist in bridge and crown and gold inlay
work. He also does dental-X-Ray work. Doctor Phelps is a
member of the Lynchburg, Virginia and American Dental Societies. He was one of the organizers of Saint John's Episcopal
Church at Lynchburg and has been a vestryman.

He married, in 1909, Florence Juliette Schirmacher. She
was born at LaGrange, Georgia, was educated in the Woman's
College there and in Hardin College at Mexico, Missouri. Her
father, Herman Schirmacher, was a graduate from the Leipsic

Walter Blair.

Conservatory of Music of Leipsic, Germany, and became a well known teacher of music in the South and West.

WALTER BLAIR, A. M. D. L., was a distinguished Virginia scholar and educator. The most fruitful years of his life were spent in Hampden-Sidney College, where he held the chair of Latin for over forty years. Through the hundreds of his pupils and by his broader contact with organizations of scholars he exercised a highly important influence in raising the standards of education and general culture throughout the South.

He was in a manner born to the profession which he served so well. He was a descendant of John Blair, who was born in Ireland in 1720, a younger brother of Rev. Samuel Blair, who was born in 1712. Both became distinguished pioneer clergymen of the Presbyterian Church in America. Samuel Blair is buried at Fagg's Manor, having died July 5, 1751. John Blair was licensed to preach and was ordained December 27, 1742, was pastor in Cumberland County, Pennsylvania, and while he was there he made two visits to Virginia, preaching and organizing several congregations. On account of his location on the frontier exposed to Indian hostilities he resigned December 28, 1748, and in 1757 accepted a call to the church at Fagg's Manor, where his brother had previously been pastor. He remained there nearly ten years and also became head of the school which his brother had established. In 1767 he was elected professor of divinity at Nassau Hall at New Jersey College, now Princeton University, and was appointed vice president of the college, and was acting president until Doctor Witherspoon entered upon the duties of that office. He resigned his chair in 1769, and during the last three years of his life was pastor of a church in Orange County, New York, where he died December 8, 1771. He married a daughter of John and Sarah E. Heron Durburrow, of Philadelphia.

His son, Rev. John Durburrow Blair, born at Fagg's Manor, Pennsylvania, October 15, 1759, died in January, 1823. He was known in Virginia as Parson Blair. He labored for years as a teacher and preacher in Hanover County, and afterwards became the first Presbyterian pastor at Richmond. Parson Blair was the father of Walter D. Blair, a prominent Richmond citizen and father of Professor Walter Blair, who was born at Richmond November 10, 1835, and died at Atlantic City, New Jersey, September 12, 1909. Walter Blair had his early educational advantages in Richmond, at the age of fifteen, became a pupil under Dr. Robert L. Dabney, and at the age of seventeen entered the junior class at Hampden-Sidney College, from which he graduated with honors in 1855. He served two sessions as tutor and teacher of the grammar school and was then appointed assistant professor of ancient languages in the college. Two years later, in 1860, he was elected professor of Latin language with leave of absence to study abroad. He spent a year or two at Berlin and Leipsic Universities, and then returned to Virginia, enlisting in the Richmond Howitzers. Later he was made sergeant major in Colonel Cabell's Artillery Battalion, and with that organization served throughout the war. Though in many battles with the Army of Northern Virginia he was never wounded.

After the war he resumed his work at Hampden-Sidney and for some time was professor of German as well as Latin. He was active in his department until 1896, when, on account of impaired eyesight, he resigned and was then elected professor emeritus. In 1899 he reestablished his home in his native city of Richmond.

The resolutions of the faculty of Hampden-Sidney adopted at the time of his death contain a paragraph reading as follows: "For forty years filling with distinguished ability the chair of Latin, and from its establishment until his retirement that of the German language, a master of either tongue, he always with the utmost modesty stood a perfect exemplar of the courtly gentleman and cultured scholar, and we desire to place on record our appreciation of his character and services, to tender our heartfelt sympathy to his widow and daughter in their great bereavement, and to express our regret that the announcement of his death reached us too late to have representatives of the Faculty join in his native city other friends and mourners in the last sad rites of honor and affection."

Doctor Blair contributed several articles to reviews and was author of a small work on Latin pronunciation. He is credited, with the distinguished Latin scholar of Johns Hopkins, B. L. Gildersleeve, with having done most to introduce the Roman method of pronunciation of Latin in the schools of the South.

An old friend and associate, Richard McIlwaine, writing in the Hampden-Sidney magazine expressed this tribute to him as a scholar and gentleman: "As a scholar Professor Blair stood in the front rank, having been more than once called to take up work with institutions of large endowment and wider reputation than Hampden-Sidney. Early in his professional career he published a little book on Latin pronunciation, which received wide approval, exerted a large influence and brought its author into touch with many of the most scholarly men in the country. Not long after he received the honorary degree of Doctor of Literature from Washington and Lee University. As a teacher he was punctual, regular, careful, considerate and thorough, demanding of his students an adequate standard of attainment. As a member of the college faculty, while independent in the formation and expression of his opinions, he was always sympathetic with the judgments of his colleagues, and ever ready to concur in the maintenance of law and order and in the adoption of such measures as appeared to conduce to the production of manly character and studious habits on the part of the youth entrusted to our care. As a gentleman he was unobtrusive, and at first somewhat restrained, but easily approached and evincing every element that goes to make up the high-born and well-bred social instinct, and to foster whatever is adapted to evoke purity, integrity and happiness. As a Christian he was regular in attendance on the ordinances of divine worship, generous in ministering to the poor and other benevolent objects which attracted his attention, but wholly distrustful of himself for any ground of salvation and resting alone on the grace of God as revealed in the Gospel of our Lord Jesus Christ for the hope of eternal life. Altogether it appears to me that he is an admirable model to set before young men for imitation. I do not mean to say that he had attained perfection, but for strength and purity of character, for allegiance and steadfastness to what he believed to be right, for noble accomplishment of what he set out and attempted to do in life, few have equalled and perhaps fewer still, if any, have excelled him."

Professor Blair married, April 27, 1874, Miss Ellen Donnell Smith, of Baltimore, daughter of Simon W. and Ellen (Donnell)

Smith. He was survived by Mrs. Blair and one daughter, Ellen Donnell Codrington Blair. Miss Blair resides at 609 South Davis Avenue in Richmond. She was educated chiefly under the direction of her parents and is a member of the Richmond's Woman's Club and the Presbyterian Church.

RICHARD BOOTH, Doctor of Dental Surgery, has been engaged in practice at Lynchburg nearly a quarter of a century.

He was born in Charlotte County, Virginia, November 7, 1880, son of James Edward and Fannie Whitehead (Coleman) Booth, his father a native of Charlotte County and his mother of Lunenburg County. His grandfathers were John Booth and John Lewis Coleman, both Virginia farmers and planters. James Edward Booth was a soldier in the Confederate army throughout the war between the states, spent his active career as an agriculturist, his farm still being owned by the family, and for twenty-six years he held the office of magistrate in his county. He was a Democrat, and both parents were members of the Methodist Episcopal Church, South. Of their eight children two are living: John Coleman, a druggist at Drakes Branch, Virginia, and Richard. Sallie Rowlett, who was the wife of John W. Howard, a farmer and poultry man at Sykes, Virginia, died January 7, 1928.

Dr. Richard Booth grew up on a farm, had the advantages of the public schools of Charlotte County, and after leaving public school began the study of dentistry in the Medical College of Virginia at Richmond. He took his degree in 1902 and for two years practiced at Buena Vista. In 1904 he located at Lynchburg, and for many years has enjoyed a reputation as one of the most skillful members of his profession in the city, with a large practice. He is a member of the Piedmont, Lynchburg and Virginia and also the National Dental Associations. Doctor Booth is a member of the Masonic fraternity and is a steward in the Court Street Methodist Episcopal Church, South.

He married, in 1904, Miss Louise Harris Zimmerman, of Rockbridge County, who was educated at Buena Vista. They have four children, all receiving opportunities for a liberal education: Dorothy Louise, now an art student in New York City; Frances Major, a kindergarten student at the Normal College at Farmsville; Mary Clare, now a student at the Randolph-Macon Woman's College at Lynchburg, Virginia; and Richard, Jr., attending the public schools of Lynchburg.

JAMES ALBERT REESE, Doctor of Dental Surgery at Lynchburg, represents an old family of Bedford County. He was reared and educated there, and had several years of general commercial experience before he took up his profession.

He was born in Bedford County on a farm, December 29, 1875, son of William Nicholas and Hester Mary (Parker) Reese, both natives of Bedford County. His paternal grandfather, William Washington Reese, established one of the first tanneries in Bedford County and followed that occupation all his life. His maternal grandfather, Amon H. Parker, was a native of Bedford County, a farmer and slave owner. The Parkers were among the pioneers of Bedford County. William Nicholas Reese grew up on a farm, learned the tanning business from his father and during his active life conducted a tannery, a store and also looked after his farm. He was a soldier in the Confederate army, always a staunch Democrat, was church clerk of the Baptist

Church and sang in the church choir, was a member of the Masonic fraternity and the Independent Order of Odd Fellows. He and his wife had a family of twelve children, nine of whom are living.

James Albert Reese had the opportunities of a country boy in Bedford County, attending the common schools and the New London Academy. After this education he clerked in a store in West Virginia for several years. He then entered the Medical College of Virginia, taking his degree, Doctor of Dental Surgery, in 1905. Doctor Reese practiced at Norton, Virginia, from 1905 to 1909 and since the latter year has had a general practice at Lynchburg. His offices are in the Medical Arts Building. He is a member of all the dental societies, including the National Dental Association. Doctor Reese has a beautiful home in the country about six miles from his office. He has served as a deacon of the Baptist Church at Lynchburg and is now treasurer of missions. He is affiliated with the Independent Order of Odd Fellows and Woodmen of the World. Mrs. Reese is a Methodist and is active in the Daughters of the American Revolution and Daughters of the Confederacy. He married, in 1907, Miss Mallie Witten, a native of Tazewell County, Virginia, where she was educated, finishing her schooling in the Martha Washington Academy at Abingdon.

GEORGE GARLAND RHUDY, physician and surgeon, formerly of Bluefield, West Virginia, is now engaged in his work as an eye, ear, nose and throat specialist at Roanoke, with offices in the Colonial Bank Building.

Doctor Rhudy, who was a medical officer overseas during the World war, was born at Elk Creek, Grayson County, Virginia, in 1888, son of William Freel and Julia Caroline (Cornett) Rhudy, and grandson of William Rhudy and Alexander Cornett, all natives of Grayson County. The Rhudy family came from Holland. Doctor Rhudy's father and grandfathers were Grayson County farmers, and his father also conducted a mercantile business at Elk Creek. He was honored with several county offices, and he and his wife were very active members of the Methodist Episcopal Church, South. He was a Confederate soldier in the Civil war.

Doctor Rhudy was the Twelfth in a large family of thirteen children, eleven of whom are living. He attended the high school at Elk Creek, and was graduated in medicine from the University of Virginia in 1915. After one year in the Moore Hospital of Richmond he practiced two years in Wise County, and then answered the call to the colors.

He had several weeks of training in the Army Medical School at Washington, and went overseas as a casual, being assigned duty with the British Army Medical Corps. He was with the colors altogether twenty-three months, and eighteen months of this time were spent overseas. He was commissioned a lieutenant and came out with the rank of captain, and while with the British Army was awarded a British Military Cross and several times was cited for special service. He received his honorable discharge in 1919, and while abroad had three months of special training in eye, ear, nose and throat work. Subsequently he spent portions of two years in Chicago, taking work in his special line, and in 1927-28 was in Philadelphia pursuing a course in bronchoscopy. Mr. Rhudy practiced four years at Bluefield and in May, 1927, located at Roanoke, where he con-

WILLIAM A. HINES

fines his practice to eye, ear, nose and throat. He is a member of the Roanoke Academy of Medicine, the Medical Society of Virginia, Southwest Virginia Medical Society and the American Medical Association.

Mr. Rhudy is unmarried. He is a member of the Methodist Episcopal Church, South, is a York Rite Mason and Shriner, member of the American Legion and the Roanoke Country Club. His skill and abilities and personal character have gained him a very popular place among the professional men of Roanoke.

WILLIAM ALONZO HINES. While many worthy civilian efforts characterized the usefulness of the late William Alonzo Hines, it is, perhaps, as a gallant naval officer of the Confederacy during the war between the states that those nearest and dearest to him like best to remember him. Certain it is that the traits of courage and faithfulness with which Mr. Hines was so richly endowed found no more direct avenue of expression than in the great struggle between the North and the South, although in later years he became a substantial agriculturist and well known business man of Norfolk, where he was the owner of the first machinery operated wood yard in the city.

Mr. Hines was born in Isle of Wight County, Virginia, April 4, 1837, and was a son of William and Martha Jane (Smith) Hines. His father, who was a man of excellent education, was a private school teacher and planter. During the war between the states he was arrested by the Federal authorities because of his son's activities in destroying Federal shipping, and did not live to see the outcome of the war.

William Alonzo Hines acquired his education under the instruction of his father, and when still a youth went to sea and learned navigation. He then secured the position of keeper of the White Shoal Lighthouse, which, at the outbreak of the war in 1861, was seized by the Federal troops. Mr. Hines then enlisted in the Confederate navy and at first was identified with the quartermaster's department, but subsequently was commissioned by General Hager to destroy the Federal shipping in the James River. He led his expedition of men and boats to success in this perilous venture, but was captured in the uniform of a dead Federal soldier and was to be sent to Washington, D. C., to be tried for his life. At Hampton, Virginia, he escaped from his captors and made his way back into the Confederate lines in Warwick County, whence he returned to the Confederate navy. Later he became a bold and successful blockade runner of note, and continued to render valuable service to the Confederacy, and his exploits are mentioned frequently in histories of the war.

At the close of the great struggle Mr. Hines went back to the home farm of his mother, known as "Smith Neck," which had been a land grant to his mother's ancestors early in the history of the colonies. After a few years he moved to Norfolk, where he entered the wood business and installed the first machinery in a yard of this kind in the city. A man of progressive spirit and ability, he continued to conduct this enterprise with success until his retirement in 1894, when he again returned to the ancestral home. There he resided until his final illness, when he was taken to Baltimore, Maryland, for treatment, and died there in October, 1899. Mr. Hines was a member of the Masonic fraternity and of the Episcopal Church, and was held in great esteem for his many sterling qualities of mind and heart.

On November 18, 1874, Mr. Hines was united in marriage
with Miss Sarah M. Matthews at St. Paul's Church, Norfolk.
Her great-grandfather, Dr. John Tankard, a direct descendant
of a former King of Sicily, served as a surgeon with the Continental troops during the War of the Revolution. Mrs. Hines
was born in Northampton County, Virginia, a daughter of Louis
N. Matthews, a farmer of that county, where he was a captain
of militia prior to the war between the states, and later a trucker
in Norfolk County. Mrs. Hines' mother was Mariah H. Wyatt,
a direct descendant of Sir Francis Wyatt, first governor of the
American colonies. The three children born to Mr. and Mrs.
Hines are living: Alvin Paul, an attorney and Government employe of Washington, D. C., who married Sadie Chapman, now
deceased, and had two children, Alvin Paul, Jr., who married a
Maryland girl and has one child, Alva, and Sadie Pauline, a
student at William and Mary College; Stella May, who married
Ollie S. King, of Isle of Wight, and has three children, Lloyd
N., May Evelyn and Ollie S., Jr.; and Leroy O., civil engineer
of Princess Anne County, Virginia, who married Louise Mosher,
of Roanoke, and has one child, Mabel. As a young man Leroy O.
Hines entered the employ of the Churchfield Coal and Coke Company, with which he continued to be identified as a civil engineer
until the entrance of the United States into the World war,
when he resigned his position and volunteered his service. He
was accepted and sent to France, where he saw hard service in
the front line trenches for a number of months, and subsequently
accompanied his command into Germany with the Army of
Occupation. He then returned to the United States and received
his honorable discharge, and for several years served under the
civil engineer of Norfolk, Virginia. He later was appointed
engineer of Princess Anne County. Mrs. Hines, who survives
her husband and is a resident of Norfolk, at 431 Maryland
Avenue, is active in the enterprises and charities of the Episcopal Church, of which she has been a member for many years.

RANDOLPH HARRISON exemplified the character of a scholarly
lawyer, a gifted gentleman and a man of affairs, and his individual career was fully in keeping with the illustrious records of
his ancestry. Mr. Harrison was of the James River family of
Harrisons. He was born in Augusta County, Virginia, January
25, 1858, and died on February 16, 1928. He was a son of
Henry and Jane Sinclair (Cochran) Harrison. He was educated at the Virginia Polytechnic Institute, graduated from the
University of Virginia in 1881, and in 1882 located at Lynchburg, where for forty-five years he kept his home and had his
offices as a lawyer, though his professional connections made
him well known throughout the state. In December, 1892, he
formed a partnership with A. R. Long, and they were associated
until Mr. Harrison's death. In later years the firm was Harrison, Long & Williams. Samuel H. Williams had been associated
with the firm from 1914 and became a member in 1923. Mr.
Harrison's firm had been counsel for the Chesapeake & Ohio
Railway since 1902, for the Southern Railway since 1916, and
also for the American Telephone & Telegraph Company and the
Chesapeake & Potomac Telephone Company.

Randolph Harrison was honored with election as president
of the Virginia State Bar Association for the year 1919-20. He
was also a member of the American Bar Association. Among
his services as an attorney vested with a public interest was

that of acting as chief counsel for Virginia in the Virginia-West Virginia debt settlement. He was continuously identified with that notable litigation from 1894 until the settlement was reached in 1919. He was a member of the Legislature in 1893-94 and 1895-96, and for a number of years was an alderman of Lynchburg.

Randolph Harrison was survived by three brothers, E. C. Harrison of Staunton, William B. Harrison of Colorado, and Beverly Harrison of Fredericksburg, and one sister, Mrs. Carter Page Johnson of Staunton, Virginia. Among his brothers who died before him was the late Judge George M. Harrison, of the Virginia Supreme Court of Appeals, and was at one time president of Mount Airy, Shenandoah County. Randolph Harrison married Julia Halsey Meem, daughter of John G. Meem, Jr. There were three children: Randolph, Jr., Aurelia Halsey and Julia Meem Harrison, Randolph, Jr., is Vice Consul at Havana, Cuba.

EDWARD H. HANCOCK is a son of the veteran Lynchburg contractor, C. W. Hancock, concerning whom a full account is given on other pages. Edward H. Hancock has for many years been associated with his father in the contracting business, being a member of the well known firm of that name.

He was born at the home of his parents in Appomattox County, Virginia, April 14, 1886. Mr. Hancock finished his education in the Virginia Military Institute, graduating from that honored institution in 1908. For one year after leaving school he was commandant of the Augusta Military Academy. He then joined his father, and for twenty years has been associated with the widespread activities of the firm C. W. Hancock & Sons, Incorporated, of which he is vice president, secretary and treasurer. Mr. Hancock also is well known in banking circles at Lynchburg, being a director of the First National Bank and president of the Mutual Bank & Trust Company.

He married, February 25, 1911, Miss Cordelia Hamner, a native of Lynchburg. Her father, Walker G. Hamner, was a prominent banker and manufacturer of Lynchburg. Mrs. Hancock attended high school in her native city. They have one son, C. W. Hancock II. The family are members of the Rivermont Baptist Church. Mr. Hancock is affiliated with the B. P. O. Elks, members of the Rotary Club, and is a past president of the Lynchburg Rotary Club.

DAVID C. SMITH, chief of police of Lynchburg, has had a rather remarkable career of service in the police department. For over thirty-five years he has been on the police force at Lynchburg, and his experience as an officer has made him familiar with almost the entire growth and expansion of one of the most rapidly growing cities of commerce and trade in the entire State of Virginia.

Mr. Smith was born at Brookneal, Virginia, June 16, 1868, son of John Daniel and Chestina (Price) Smith, and grandson of John Daniel Smith and William Price, all natives of Virginia. His grandfather John Daniel Smith was a mechanic and blacksmith and a Baptist minister. The parents of Chief Smith were born in Charlotte Court House and his father was a Confederate soldier under Captain Bruce for four years. He followed the trade of his father, mechanic and blacksmith, and after retiring from business moved to Lynchburg. He was a Democrat in politics and member of the First Baptist Church. There were six sons and one daughter in the family and the four now living are: P. P. Smith, of Brookneal; David C.; Robert L., in the automobile business at Lynchburg; and Samuel E., of Lynchburg.

David C. Smith acquired his early schooling at Brookneal and Leesville, and he satisfied his inheritance of mechanical disposition by two years of service as a locomotive fireman. Mr. Smith on March 4, 1890, joined the police department of Lynchburg and has given a consecutive service ever since, earning a record of fidelity, accomplishments and performance of duty that has become a matter for pride of the entire force. During this time Mr. Smith has seen the police department grow from a few men to a force of fifty-five. He entered the department in the rank of private, later was promoted to sergeant, and since 1921 has been chief of the department. He is a member of the International Chiefs of Police.

Mr. Smith married, October 15, 1903, Miss Bertie Ogden, who was born in Amherst County, Virginia, and was reared and educated there. Her father, Silas Ogden, was a farmer. They have three children: Lloyd Terrell, who graduated from the Virginia Polytechnic Institute in 1927 and is now connected with the Appalachian Power Company; Randolph Lewis, attending high school; and Helen Paxton, in the grade schools at Lynchburg. Chief Smith and family are members of the Presbyterian Church and he is affiliated with the Masonic fraternity and Lions Club.

WILLIAM R. DOOLEY as banker, business man and public official is one of the outstanding citizens of Bedford County, admired for the success he has made in material affairs as well as the integrity and public spirit of his citizenship and personal character.

He was born February 15, 1867, on a farm near Bedford, son of James A. and Saluda (Jeter) Dooley, and grandson of William Dooley, who came from Ireland and settled in Bedford County, where he spent the rest of his life as a farmer. The Jeter family were in Bedford County from Colonial times. James A. Dooley began his career as a contractor and builder, later taking up the tobacco business and that of commission merchant. He was a soldier in the Confederate army for four years and an active member of the Baptist Church. He died in 1917, at the age of eighty-three, and his widow still lives on the old farm at the age of eighty-eight.

William R. Dooley was third in a family of seven children. He attended a private school while a boy on the farm, and at the age of seventeen began work in his father's tobacco warehouse. Mr. Dooley spent over thirty years in the tobacco business. He was the man chiefly responsible for founding and building up the Bedford Rubber Tire Company at Bedford, of which he is president and general manager. He is also a director of the Peoples National Bank of Bedford, and his business and financial experience have been called upon for important service to the county as county treasurer, an office he has held continuously since 1915.

He married, in 1893, Miss Laura Ferguson, a native of Bedford, daughter of James A. Ferguson, a Bedford County farmer. She died in 1905, mother of five children. The three now living are: Paul W., Ruth, wife of a Chicago broker, and Warren W. Mr. Dooley married in 1917 Florence M. Sampson, who was born

at Easton, Pennsylvania, and was educated in her native state and at Lynchburg, Virginia. They have two children, Jack, born in 1918, and Beth. Mrs. Dooley is a member of the Methodist Church, while he is a Baptist. Mr. Dooley is affiliated with the United Commercial Travelers and the B. P. O. Elks, and for many years has been a local leader in the Democratic party. He served some time as member of the City Council of Bedford.

JAMES W. COMER. The leading business men who have left the impress of their genius on the commercial and industrial history of Virginia have been in the main men of affairs with little instruction in science. They have stepped from the workshop or counter to the office, demonstrating their fitness to be leaders by soundness of judgment and skill in management. Such a man the generation of business men now engaged in the scenes of active business recognized in James W. Comer when he took his proper place among the leaders. From that time to the present he has developed a capacity for business management, including those opposite qualities of boldness and caution, enterprise and prudence, which stamp him as a born engineer of trade.

Mr. Comer was born in Roanoke County, Virginia, January 18, 1875, and is a son of Francis and Ellen Rebecca (Bishop) Comer. His father, who was born at Petersburg, Virginia, was a young man at the outbreak of the war between the states, in which he enlisted as a soldier of the Confederacy, and during four years of valiant service narrowly escaped death on two occasions, being shot through the body just before the close of the war. These wounds undoubtedly hastened his death, which occurred in 1888, at the age of sixty-three. Mrs. Comer, also a native of Petersburg, passed away three years before, at the age of fifty. They were the parents of eleven children, of whom five are living, James W. being the youngest.

James W. Comer was only ten years of age at the time of the death of his mother, and thirteen when his father died, so that he had few of the advantages of youth, either as to recreation or education. However, he attended the public schools of Roanoke County whenever the opportunity offered, but was still only a youth when he secured employment in the N. & W. Railway Shops, where he worked for five years, and in the meanwhile took a business course with the National Business College. With this preparation he was able to obtain a position as stenographer in a wholesale grocery business, and during the ten years he was employed by that concern neglected no opportunity of making himself thoroughly familiar with every detail of the business. Thus he was ready to take part in the reorganization of the Patterson-Palmer Company, the name of which was changed to the Hix-Palmer Company, Incorporated, of which Mr. Comer is now president, C. L. Palmer, vice president, and J. C. Peters, secretary and treasurer. Later Mr. Comer was the leading factor in the establishment of the Rex Manufacturing Company, manufacturers of gloves, and these companies now do a large business in jobbing in hats, caps and notions, with seven traveling men on the road throughout Virginia, West Virginia and North Carolina. Mr. Comer devotes the principal part of his time to these two concerns, but also has other interests and is a member of the directorate of the Allegany Finance Corporation. He has established himself firmly in the confidence of his associates as a business man of sound and substantial quali-

ties and the highest integrity and probity, and at the same time
has been an ardent supporter of all civic measures and an enthusiastic member of the Roanoke Chamber of Commerce, belonging also to the Rotary Club. A stanch Democrat in his political
views, in 1922 he was elected a member of the City Council, in
which body he has proved to be a constructive and hard working
member. He belongs to the Methodist Episcopal Church, South,
and is a member of the Board of Stewards.

In 1897 Mr. Comer was united in marriage with Miss Ella
Ruth Smith, who was born in Henrico County, Virginia, and
educated at Roanoke. Her father, Benjamin R. Smith, was for
many years a merchant at Vinton and a man who was held in
esteem and respect. Mrs. Comer has been very active in church
and club work and is one of Roanoke's socially popular matrons.
She and her husband have had five children: James Edward, a
graduate of Roanoke College, now identified with the First National Exchange Bank of Roanoke; Elizabeth Jennings, a graduate of Randolph-Macon College, now Mrs. Irad B. Lower, having
been married November 8, 1927; Robert Percy, a graduate of
Virginia Polytechnic Institute; Virginia Ruth, a graduate of
Hollins College; and Ella Rebecca, who is attending the public
schools.

ALPHEUS V. CONWAY is an old resident of Charlottesville, and
his sturdy qualities enabled him to rise from an obscure position
to one of the city's leading business men.

Mr. Conway was born in Fauquier County, Virginia, April
30, 1867, son of Edward Henry and Sallie J. (Strother) Conway.
His maternal grandfather was A. W. Strother, a well-to-do Fauquier County farmer. The paternal grandfather was a physician in Stafford County. Edward Henry Conway was born in
Stafford County and his wife in Fauquier County. He was educated in Randolph-Macon College and spent many years as a
teacher. He died in 1870 and his wife in 1912, and of their five
children, two sons and three daughters, Alpheus is the only
survivor. Alpheus V. Conway was only three years of age when
his father died. He attended Bethel Military Academy and as a
boy clerked in a store at Upperville, Virginia. In 1883 he moved
to Charlottesville, being then a youth of sixteen, and for two
years continued his work as a store clerk, was with J. W.
Marshall and Company as clerk, for a time worked in the freight
office of the Chesapeake & Ohio Railway, and in 1887 acquired an
interest in the Marshall business, selling out January 21, 1890.
For seven years following he was in the grocery and confection-
ery business, and has also been interested at different times in
banking and the loan business. One of his chief activities at
Charlottesville was the printing and publishing business. He
had charge of the office of the *Charlottesville Progress* two years.
In 1902 he organized the Michie Grocery Company, a wholesale
business, with which he was connected for two years. He then
resumed his connection with the *Progress,* and in 1904 took over
the job printing end of the business, organizing the Conway
Printing Company.

Mr. Conway in 1912 was elected mayor of Charlottesville,
and in 1913 was chosen the first business manager of the city,
serving in that capacity until 1916. For several years he was
associated with the Irving, Way, Hill Company, and from 1916
to 1918 was again identified with the *Charlottesville Progress.*
He was a director of the Jefferson National Bank of Charlottes-

ville from 1912 to 1916, and since 1916 has been a member of the board of the Peoples National Bank.

Mr. Conway married, April 25, 1892, Fannie Fitz-Hugh Lee Eubank, daughter of Alexander Eubank, of Bedford County, Virginia, who was a Baptist minister and proprietor of a private school in Bedford County. Mrs. Conway was educated in the Albemarle Institute, and taught music for several years. She is a member of the Baptist Church, while he is a Methodist. Mr. Conway is affiliated with the Masonic fraternity, Independent Order of Odd Fellows, B. P. O. Elks, and is a Democrat.

EDWIN G. LEE is secretary and treasurer of the Monticello Dairy Company, an organization serving the City of Charlottesville, and one of the most successful of a number of companies operating modern plants for the production and supply of pure milk products, comprising one of the large and growing industries of Virginia.

Mr. Lee is a native of Charlottesville and represents an old and well known family in this section of the state. He was born November 7, 1890, son of Rev. H. B. and Lucy Johnston (Marshall) Lee. His grandfather and great-grandfather were named Edmund Jennings Lee. His great-grandfather lived at Seminary Hill, Alexandria, Virginia. H. B. Lee was born in Jefferson County, West Virginia, in 1849, was educated in Washington and Lee University, and practiced law at Shepherdstown, West Virginia, several years. Later he studied for the Episcopal ministry, attending Washington and Lee University and the Theological Seminary, and had a distinguished career as a minister, serving Christ Episcopal Church at Charlottesville as rector for about thirty years. He was also well known in Masonic circles, having at one time been grand chaplain of the Grand Lodge of the State of Virginia. Rev. H. B. Lee died in 1921. His wife, Lucy Johnston Marshall, was born in Fauquier County in 1857, and now resides at Culpeper. Her father, James Keith Marshall, was a grandson of Chief Justice John Marshall, and before the Civil war was a merchant at Alexandria.

Edwin G. Lee was the fourth in a family of eight children, seven of whom are living. He was educated in the public schools of Charlottesville and finished at the University of Virginia in 1908. For some seven or eight years after leaving university he was with the J. N. Waddell shoe business, and for four years had experience in the lumber business in connection with the Albemarle mills. Mr. Lee in 1921 acquired an active interest in the management of the Monticello Dairy Company, of which he has since been secretary and treasurer. The other officers of the company are A. F. Howard, president, and S. A. Jessup, vice president. Mr. Lee gives his full time to the management of this modern dairy industry.

He married, in 1910, Estelle Marshall Behrendt, who was born at "Colle," a property once owned and developed by Thomas Jefferson in Albemarle County. She attended schools in Charlottesville. Her father, Thomas G. Behrendt, was born in New Orleans, was educated in a French school, and spent his active life as a professional accountant. Mr. and Mrs. Lee have five children: Frances Ambler, Estelle Behrendt, Nancy Gray, Edwin G., Jr., and Jaqueline Ambler Lee. Mr. Lee and family are members of the Episcopal Church, and he is secretary of the Charlottesville Rotary Club.

CHRISTIAN S. HUTTER has been active in the business life of Lynchburg more than forty years. Mr. Hutter among other interests is owner of the historic homestead "Poplar Forest" in Bedford County, where he was born and reared. This at one time was part of the property owned by Thomas Jefferson. Jefferson erected there a mansion almost a duplicate of his "Monticello" near Charlottesville. Poplar Forest went to Jefferson's son-in-law, Epps, and the Hutter family bought it from the Epps family.

The Hutter family since coming to America has won many distinctions in military and naval affairs. The founder of the American branch of the family was Col. Christian Jacob Hutter, who was born in Germany May 17, 1771, son of Johann Ludwig and Anna Maria (Kuntze) Hutter. His father was a leather manufacturer. It was on a mission for the Moravians that Christian Jacob Hutter came to America in 1789, locating at Bethlehem, Pennsylvania. He engaged in business, was an apothecary, and in July, 1817, founded and began the publication of the *Easton Sentinel* at Easton, Pennsylvania, a newspaper that has continued through more than a century. Colonel Hutter was a lieutenant colonel of militia in the War of 1812, was a member of the Pennsylvania Legislature from 1822 to 1825, and was one of the founders and the first worshipful master of Easton Lodge of Masons. He was three times married. A son of his first wife, Maria Magdalen Huber, was George Christian Hutter, who became an officer in the Regular Army, served in the Indian wars and the war with Mexico, and was paymaster with the rank of major at Charleston, South Carolina, and made the last payment before the bombardment of Fort Sumter in April, 1861. He resigned his commission, but declined a commission in the Confederate army, and spent the rest of his life at the Sandusky plantation near Lynchburg. His two brothers, Edward S. and James R., made distinguished records in the service of the Confederacy during the Civil war.

The second wife of Colonel Christian Jacob Hutter was Maria Charlotte Bauer, who was born April 1, 1774, and died August 10, 1829. Her son, Edward Sixtus Hutter, was born at Bethlehem, Pennsylvania, September 6, 1812, attended Mount Airy College at Germantown, Pennsylvania, and was commissioned a midshipman in the United States Navy by President Andrew Jackson February 24, 1832. In 1844 he resigned his commission to look after his extensive landed interests in Virginia, Kentucky and Missouri, including the Poplar Forest estate in Virginia, where he lived until his death, November 7, 1875. His wife died on the same day. Her maiden name was Emma Williams Cobbs, whose father, William Cobbs, had previously owned Poplar Forest. Several of their children died young. The oldest son, William C., attended the Naval Academy, resigned as midshipman in 1861 to become a lieutenant in the Confederate States Navy, and was killed during the battle between the *Monitor* and the *Merrimac*, March 8, 1862. A daughter, Ann R., married Samuel Griffin, who was a Virginia soldier in the Civil war. George Edward graduated from the United States Naval Academy in 1874, and retired from the navy in 1882 on account of disability caused by the Asiatic fever. The three surviving children are: Emma C., wife of James A. Logwood, of Sandusky, Virginia; Mrs. J. Risque Hutter, of Sandusky; and Christian Sixtus Hutter.

H E Jones—M.A.—E.R.A.

Christian Sixtus Hutter was born at Poplar Forest October 19, 1862. He attended the Bellevue Preparatory School and at the age of eighteen came to Lynchburg, and since 1887 has been a prominent coal and lumber merchant of that city, and is also a director of the Peoples National Bank. He has been a member of the City Council, was one of the charter members of the Oakwood Country Club, member of the Piedmont Club, and is a vestryman in St. Paul's Episcopal Church.

He married, January 21, 1885, Miss Ernestine Booker, who was born January 11, 1866, daughter of James M. Booker. She finished her education in the Patapsco Academy at Baltimore. Mr. and Mrs. Hutter have a family of ten children: Miss Claudine, at home; James Booker, in the wholesale lumber business; Christian S., Jr., who was educated for the law at the University of Virginia, served in France during the World war with Base Hospital No. 41; Edward W. Booker, who was also overseas in France, has followed a literary and journalistic career; Ernestine, wife of Capt. Marshall McDonald, who served in the Engineering Corps in France; Emily C., wife of Pierce Stewart, an ex-service man, now located at Chattanooga, Tennessee; Caroline E., wife of Capt. Cranston Williams, who was a captain in France, and is now general manager of the Southern Newspaper Publishers Association at Chattanooga, and for a time after the World war was private secretary to Senator Harris of Georgia; Beverly S., associated with his father in the lumber and coal business at Lynchburg; Quintus, a student at the University of Virginia, formerly of the University of North Carolina, where he made an outstanding record as full-back on the Varsity Football Team; and Malcolm, a student in the Augusta Military Academy.

HERMAN EVANT JONES, M. D., E. R. A. One of the most progressive members of the medical profession in Roanoke, Dr. Herman E. Jones is enjoying a very large and constantly augmenting practice, and is rendering a valuable service to humanity. Thoroughly abreast of the latest discoveries in his calling, he is quick to take advantage of them and his office is one of the best equipped in this section. He is a firm believer in the efficacy of the use of electricity, and has installed some of the best appliances so that he may give his patients the benefit of electrical treatments. Doctor Jones was born in Appomattox County, Virginia, September 20, 1860, a son of J. C. and Annie Olivia (Williams) Jones, he born in Campbell County, Virginia, and she in Appomattox County, Virginia. A man of prominence, J. C. Jones was a farmer, merchant and lumberman, and for two years represented his county in the State Legislature. During the war between the states he gave the South a devoted service, and was four times wounded, one of the bullets passing through his body, and another injury resulting in the loss of an arm. However, he recovered and was spared to live into an honored old age, dying in 1916, respected by all who knew him, although it was only his rugged constitution that saved him, for some of his wounds never fully healed, and his death came from their effect upon his system. Both he and his wife were active factors in the Baptist Church. For some years he served as supervisor of Appomattox County. Of the five children born to the parents three survive, namely: Doctor Jones; Miss Nina E. Jones, who resides in Appomattox; and Miss Mary Anna Jones, who also resides in Appomattox.

Doctor Jones attended several excellent private schools of Appomattox County and Appomattox Court House, and later became a student of the Virginia Polytechnic Institute, from which he was graduated in agriculture and engineering in 1884. While there he had also taken chemistry and physics, and he supplemented his studies in these last two branches in the University of Virginia, from which he was graduated in 1886, with the degree of Doctor of Medicine. Subsequently he took postgraduate work in New York City, and he is a close student and reader. In 1886 he located in Lowesville, Virginia, but not finding quite the environment he desired, he only remained there for two years, then closed his practice and returned home. While visiting with his family he investigated different neighborhoods, and decided that Roanoke best suited him, so came here June 19, 1888, and here he has since remained, carrying on a general practice until 1907, when he began specializing in treating germ diseases. In 1923 he graduated in Electronic Medicine at the College of Electronic Medicine at San Francisco California, after which he began the practice of Electronic diagnosis treatment to be correlated with orthodox medicine. His equipment is most elaborate, and fills two floors of the building at 506 South Jefferson Street. For years he has been noted for his ability in diagnosis. His success in treatment of cancer has been marked, and it is his theory that the disease is divided into four stages. The first and second stages he has always been able to cure; about twenty per cent of the cases in the third stage are curable, and some of the fourth stage. He is concentrating on malignant growths and germ diseases, and his patients come to him from all parts of the United States.

On December 17, 1890, Doctor Jones married Miss Eva Yates, of Roanoke County. They have no children. Fraternally Doctor Jones is a Mason, Odd Fellow and Knight of Pythias. Twice Doctor Jones has served as a member of the Board of Health of Roanoke, and he is pension examiner for this locality, which latter office he has held for many years. In both the Spanish-American and World wars he was a member of the examining boards, and it can be truly said that no public service has ever been asked of him in vain. His charities are many and he cheerfully contributes from his wealth to relieve those less fortunate, and his character is of the highest type.

GEORGE WILLIAM PARROTT, physician and surgeon, since 1920 has had a large private practice in his profession at Charlottesville, and is one of the ablest representatives of medicine and surgery in Albemarle County.

He is a native of that section of Virginia, born on a farm in Albemarle County May 29, 1881, son of Bernard T. and Sallie Amanda (Brown) Parrott, natives of the same county. His great-grandfather, Horace Brown, acquired several thousands of acres of land at what is now known as Browns Cove. During the Civil war he erected a large hospital on his plantation, and this hospital furnished treatment and service for both the Confederate and Union soldiers. Bernard T. Parrott was a farmer, and died at the age of seventy-six. He was the father of ten children. He devoted a great deal of time promoting the civic welfare and religious activities of his community. He was a steward in the Methodist Episcopal Church, Wesley Chapel, at Free Union, Virginia, for a period of sixty-one years. His widow still lives in Albemarle County, being an active member of the Methodist Episcopal Church, South. Bernard T. Parrott served as supervisor for a number of years and also on the school board, and was a member of the Democratic Executive Committee. He was affiliated with the Independent Order of Odd Fellows.

Dr. George William Parrott was the fourth in the family of ten children. For a time he attended Millers School. For five years he had a position as a traveling salesman on the road, and largely through this secured the modest capital that enabled him to enter the Medical College of Virginia at Richmond. While a student there he continued working and paying part of his way. He was graduated in medicine in 1912 and had additional training as an interne in the Johnston Willis Hospital at Richmond for one year. For five years he engaged in practice at Fork Union, Virginia, and after two years of post-graduate work in the New York Hospital, where he specialized in stomach and intestinal diseases, he located at Charlottesville in 1920, and has a busy practice with offices in the Y. M. C. A. Building. He is local surgeon for the Chesapeake & Ohio Railway, is a member of the Chesapeake & Ohio Railway Surgeons Association, is a member of the Medical Society of Virginia, the Southern and American Medical Associations, is a fellow of the American College of Physicians, and a member of the Phi Beta Pi medical fraternity.

Doctor Parrott married in 1908 Emmie Lucille Watkins, who was born in Charlotte County, Virginia, and was educated at Richmond. She is a member of the Episcopal Church, while Doctor Parrott has remained true to the church of his parents, the Methodist Episcopal.

GEORGE T. O'MOHUNDRO. It would be difficult to find a more satisfying type of good citizenship than George T. O'Mohundro, merchant, banker and promoter of Scottsville, who from his early manhood has demonstrated his admirable qualities in different channels of activity. Always a leading citizen, he exercises a wide influence for good not only in business affairs, in which he holds great prominence, but in public activities, and at all times he stands for good government and honesty in politics. Virginia is indeed fortunate in having men of his caliber at the head of its different enterprises.

George T. O'Mohundro was born in Buckingham County, Virginia, June 19, 1870, a son of Richard Calvin and Mary (Hopkins) O'Mohundro, natives of Virginia, he was born in Charlottesville. After his death in 1908 she was married to William C. Hughes, and they reside in Albemarle County. Richard Calvin O'Mohundro was early in life a hotel man and later a lumberman, and of the three children born to him and his wife two are living: George T., whose name heads this review; and Andrew Douglas O'Mohundro, superintendent of the waterworks of Charlottesville, Virginia. During the war between the states the father served Wise's Brigade, and he was a brave soldier and honorable man. While he was not a member of any religious organization he assisted in supporting the local Methodist Episcopal Church, of which his wife was a member. He was a son of George C. O'Mohundro, a native of Charlottesville, where he owned considerable property, including three hotels as well as farming land in the vicinity. He also owned and operated a stage line prior to the building of the railroads through that region, and was one of the leading men of his period. The maternal grandfather, Tipton Turner O'Mohundro, reared George T. O'Mohundro. He was a wealthy farmer of the James River section, and prominent in local affairs. As the name indicates, the family originated in Ireland, from whence two brothers O'Mohundro came to this country, settling in Norfolk, Virginia.

George T. O'Mohundro attended the Miller school of Albemarle County, from which he graduated with the class of 1888. In 1890 he began working for the Virginia-Albemarle Corporation, and remained with it until he reached his majority, when he went on the road for a time. Returning home, he was deputy sheriff of Albemarle County for four years, and then was appointed commissioner of revenue, which office he continued to hold for twenty-six consecutive years, but then resigned, as his private affairs required all of his time. In January, 1927, he, with others, bought the Scottsville National Bank, of which he is active vice president. He owns two large farms in the county and a beautiful home in Scottsville; and is president of the Scottsville Hardware Company, of which he is the majority stockholder, and his son, George T., Junior, is its secretary and treasurer and a director. He is a director in the Charlottesville National Bank, a director of the Albemarle Home Mutual Insurance Company, and is deeply interested in the Scottsville-Braid Corporation, and is its treasurer. The latter has just been organized in Scottsville, he being one of the organizers, and he has great confidence in its future.

On October 23, 1901, Mr. O'Mohundro married Miss Carrie Clay Page, of Greenfield, Nelson County, Virginia, who was born in Albemarle County, and educated in private and public schools, and completing the work of the Roanoke High School. She is a daughter of Henry Clay Page, now deceased, for many years a prosperous farmer of Nelson County. Mr. and Mrs. O'Mohundro have two sons, George T., Junior, who is a graduate of the Scottsville High School; and Henry Page, who is attending the National Business College, Roanoke, Virginia. The family belong to the Scottsville Methodist Episcopal Church, South, of which Mr. O'Mohundro is a steward.

RUSSELL CAMMACK CRANK, cashier and a director of the Bank of Louisa, is one of the substantial business men and financiers of Louisa County, and one who holds the full confidence of his community. Whenever there is any need of his cooperation in civic affairs his fellow citizens find him ready and helpful; he is an earnest church worker, and zealous in behalf of fraternal life, so that all in all he is representative of the best element, and one whose example and influence are constructive in character and effect.

The birth of Mr. Crank took place in Dinwiddie County, Virginia, June 6, 1896, and he is a son of John Henry and Willie E. (Cammack) Crank, both natives of Louisa County. The father was engaged in the lumber business most of his life. His death occurred February 5, 1928, and he is survived by the mother. In addition to his lumber interests he had others, and was vice president of the Bank of Louisa. Of the seven children born to him and his wife five are living: Ina Gladys, who married Percy B. Spicer, with the Pennsylvania Railroad; Henry F., who is with the American Can Company in Richmond, Virginia; Russell C., whose name heads this review; Willie Frances, who married Goodwin W. Turner, a traveling salesman for

D. L. Brooks, D. D. S.

Charles E. Brown, and is a resident of Richmond, Virginia; and Charles E., who resides in Richmond, in the employ of the Richmond, Fredericksburg & Potomac Railroad Company. The Baptist Church held the membership of the father. A Democrat, he was active in local and county politics. Although he began life as a poor boy, he died a man of means and prestige. The paternal grandfather of Russell Cammack Crank was John R. Crank; and the maternal grandfather was Horace Cammack, born in Spotsylvania County, Virginia, a farmer by occupation.

Russell Cammack Crank was educated in local schools and Massey Business College, Richmond, and when he had completed his course in the latter he entered the Bank of Louisa and in October, 1923, was made its cashier. When he entered the bank it was as clerk, but in 1918 he was made assistant cashier, holding the latter position until he was advanced to his present one. Associated with Mr. Crank in the bank are S. D. Crenshaw, president; John S. Purcell, vice president, and John Q. Rhodes, Junior, vice president. This is one of the solid financial institutions of Louisa County, and is patronized by the business men and farmers of the region, its conservative policies and strong connections, combined with the strength of the officials and directorate sustaining public confidence.

In 1918 Mr. Crank married Miss Mamie C. Rosson, born in Louisa County, and educated in Blackstone College. She is a daughter of Lee and Cora Rosson, natives of Louisa County, where he is a well known merchant. Mr. and Mrs. Crank have one son, Russell Cammack, Junior, who was born in April, 1923. Mrs. Crank belongs to the Baptist Church and Mr. Crank to the Christian Church, and both are active in religious work. He served as clerk of the church for a time, and is now its treasurer. His fraternal relations are those which he maintains with the Masonic fraternity. As his duties at the bank are heavy he devotes all of his time to them and so has no outside business interests.

BENJAMIN LEE BROOKS is a doctor of dental surgery, practicing at Lynchburg, and through his individual attainments and his work with organizations has become one of the outstanding representatives of his profession in Virginia.

He was born in Pittsylvania County, Virginia, March 23, 1885, son of Benjamin F. and Sallie Ann (Snead) Brooks, both natives of Halifax County and now living at South Boston, retired farmers. His father still owns the old homestead. Both grandfathers were Confederate soldiers, his maternal grandfather being Gordon Snead. Benjamin F. Brooks was well educated for his time, has been active in the work of the Methodist Church, and is a Democrat in politics. Of the seven children five are living, Dr. Benjamin L. being the second in age.

Doctor Brooks attended public schools in Halifax County, had a business college course at Richmond, and spent four years in railroad work in North and South Carolina. He prepared for the work of his profession in the Medical College of Virginia, graduating in dentistry in 1910. For several years he practiced in Southampton County and in 1913 located at Lynchburg. Doctor Brooks has had a large practice involving all the skill and resources of the modern dental surgeon, and has been unusually successful in handling cases of pyorrhea and is regarded as an authority in that special branch of dentistry. For four years he was an associate editor of the *American Dentist*, published at

Chicago, and he is former vice president of the American Academy of Applied Dental Science, has been president of the Lynchburg Dental Society, is a member of the Virginia, Piedmont and American Dental Societies and a member of the American Academy of Periodontology.

Doctor Brooks married, in 1910, Miss Grace Showalter, a native of Rockingham County, Virginia, daughter of Franklin P. and Margaret (Scott) Showalter, of Port Republic, a well known contractor of that town, who took the nurses' training course in the Memorial Hospital at Richmond. She studied art at the University of Virginia and is one of the cultured women in social circles at Lynchburg. Both she and her husband are active members of the Court Street Methodist Episcopal Church, South. Doctor Brooks is a member of the B. P. O. Elks, and is a charter member of the Lynchburg Lions Club, the first club of that organization established in Virginia. He is a member of the Oakwood Club. They have four children, Ben Lee, Jr., Winston Scott, Helen, and Peggy Hanna. All the children are attending school at Lynchburg.

W. DAN HADEN is a physician and surgeon who graduated from the University of Virginia and after special training and experience elsewhere eventually returned to Charlottesville, where he has a front rank standing among members of his profession, and is also prominent in business affairs.

Doctor Haden was born in Fluvanna County, Virginia, October 15, 1884, member of a Haden family which came from England to Virginia in Colonial times. Members of the family served as soldiers of the Revolution. The Hadens for several generations lived in Fluvanna County, where Doctor Haden's grandfather, William Haden, was born. The grandmother, Anna Haden, was a native of Hanover County, Virginia. William Haden was a farmer, lived to be eighty-four years of age, and had six sons who were Confederate soldiers, Joel, Edward, Richard, Nicholas, Socrates and Obey. E. G. Haden was born in Fluvanna County, was liberally educated and for many years has been a leading real estate man at Charlottesville, and for twelve years was mayor of that city. He is a Presbyterian and a Democrat. His wife, Martha Douglas Early, was a daughter of Abner Early, a native of Campbell County, Virginia, of Irish ancestry.

Doctor Haden was the second in a family of six children, five of whom are living. He graduated from the Charlottesville High School and took his medical degree at the University of Virginia in 1910. For one year after leaving the university he was engaged in work under the auspices of the New York State Board of Health, and then spent a year in post-graduate study at the Johns Hopkins University Hospital at Baltimore. Doctor Haden began practice at Charlottesville in 1912. He was engaged in general practice until 1916, when after special work in Johns Hopkins he specialized as an urologist. He is a member of the Albemarle County, Piedmont Medical Society, Medical Society of Virginia and American Medical Association.

Doctor Haden married in 1912 Sallie Cameron Pugh, a native of Louisiana. Her father, Llewellyn Pugh, is a retired sugar planter. Mrs. Haden finished her education in Eden Hall at Philadelphia. They have four children: Sallie Pugh, attending school in Philadelphia; Llewellyn Pugh, in the Woodbury Forest

School; W. Dan, Jr., and Elizabeth Catharine, pupils in the Stonefield Private School at Charlottesville.

Mrs. Haden is a Catholic. Doctor Haden is a member of the Pi Mu medical fraternity, Pi Kappa Alpha, the Redland Club, B. P. O. Elks, University Club of Richmond.

He is vice president and a director in the National Bank of Charlottesville and has his professional offices in the National Bank Building. He is also vice president and a director of the Theatrical Corporation of Charlottesville, director of the Piedmont Telephone Company, president and director of the Standardsville and Buckingham Telephone Company, and also vice president and a director of the Jackson Park Hotel Company, operating the Monticello Hotel at Charlottsville, Virginia.

JOHN S. EGGLESTON, Lawyer. Born in Powhatan County, Virginia, in 1880. B. L. Richmond College. Law offices, Mutual Building, Richmond, Virginia; residence, 3802 Seminary Avenue. Counsel for Bell Telephone System in Virginia and the Imperial Tobacco Company (of Great Britain and Ireland) Limited. Member of Board of Directors of the Chesapeake and Potomac Telephone Company of Virginia and State-Planters Bank and Trust Company of Richmond. Member and ex-president Westmoreland Club of Richmond. Married; one child, Grace.

LEMUEL F. SMITH, commonwealth attorney of Albemarle County, is an alumnus of the law school of the University of Virginia, and went out from that school with a promise of successful performance which has been amply fulfilled during the past decade.

Mr. Smith was born at Shadwell, April 21, 1890, son of Downing and Willie (Marshall) Smith, both natives of the same county. His grandfather, Downing Smith, was born in Greene County, Virginia, was a farmer and Confederate soldier. The maternal grandfather, James T. Marshall, was of the famous Marshall family which gave to Virginia and the Nation Chief Justice John Marshall. James T. Marshall was a farmer, was captain of muster when the Civil war broke out, and though past military age served a short time in the field. He was a lumber operator after the war. The father of Lemuel F. Smith spent his active life as a farmer in Albemarle County, and he succeeded in realizing his ambition of giving all his children collegiate training. There were nine sons and daughters and seven of them graduated from college. He and his wife were active members of the Methodist Episcopal Church, South, and he was a member of the Masonic fraternity. At one time he served as deputy sheriff of Albemarle County. His widow is still living.

Lemuel F. Smith was educated in public schools and graduated with the A. B. degree from Randolph-Macon College in 1910. He then went to Randolph-Macon Academy as an instructor for three years and in 1913 entered the University of Virginia School of Law, graduating in 1916. He has practiced at Charlottesville since 1917, and is now senior member of the law firm Smith & Walker, his law partner being Capt. E. V. Walker. Mr. Smith has been honored with various official responsibilities, giving time to these in addition to looking after his increasing law practice. He has been a member of the City Council of Charlottesville, for four terms represented Albemarle

County in the House of Delegates, and in 1926 was appointed commonwealth attorney and in 1927 elected for a regular term of four years in that office.

He married, in 1916, Miss Grace Stulting, who was born in Pocahontas County, West Virginia, and finished her education at Lewisburg and in Leipsic, Germany. Her father, Cornelius John Stulting, was a native of Holland and was a farmer and school teacher. Mr. and Mrs. Smith have three children: Downing Lemuel, Doyle and Minor Marshall. Mr. Smith is a steward in the Methodist Episcopal Church, South, is a Royal Arch Mason, member of the Kappa Sigma college fraternity and the honorary university club, The Raven Society.

JENNIE SMITH YATES is a well qualified dental surgeon who has practiced at Charlottesville for over twenty years.

He was born in Culpeper County, Virginia, in 1882, son of Andrew Jackson and Mertice (Browning) Yates. His mother was born in Rappahannock County, daughter of James N. Browning. Andrew Jackson Yates was a native of Culpeper County, and while in the service of the Confederate government during the Civil war was twice wounded. He gave his active life to farming, and was a member of the Baptist Church.

Doctor Yates was the ninth in a large family of children and acquired a good education, partly by his own efforts and earnings. He attended the Culpeper High School and in 1905 graduated in dentistry at Richmond. Since that year he has practiced in Charlottesville and has been one of the busy men of his profession there. He is a member of the Shenandoah Valley and Charlottesville Dental Societies.

He married, in 1913, Miss Lillie Gleason, a native of Charlottesville, where her father, H. M. Gleason, was in the grocery business. She attended the Charlottesville High School and was an active member of the Methodist Episcopal Church, South. Doctor Yates is a past exalted ruler of Charlottesville Lodge No. 389, B. P. O. Elks.

MATTHEW LAWMAN is founder and president of the Albemarle Grocery Company, a wholesale organization at Charlottesville which has been rapidly and vigorously growing during the past decade and is a worthy expression of the business career of Mr. Lawman.

Mr. Lawman was born at Charlottesville, February 1, 1889. His people were early settlers in Amherst County, where his parents, Edward and Mollie (Lucado) Lawman, were born. His grandparents were John and Mary (Mays) Lawman, the former a farmer in Amherst County, who during the Civil war served in the Confederate army and was wounded and for some time was in a northern prison. Edward Lawman was for some time a manufacturer of men's garments at Mount Vernon, Ohio, and is now in the real estate business at Detroit, Michigan. He is a member of the Christian Church and a Democrat in politics, and while living at Charlottesville served on the City Council. There were five children, three of whom are living: Matthew; Edgar, of Chattanooga, Tennessee; and Frances, wife of H. L. Bodamer, a lawyer at Buffalo, New York.

Matthew Lawman was educated at Charlottesville and in 1906, at the age of seventeen, entered the wholesale grocery business, a business he has learned from the ground up. For several years he was on the road as a salesman and in 1916 he utilized

J. C. Hudgins

his experience and connection to organize the Albemarle Grocery
Company, which he incorporated and which he served as secretary and treasurer until 1922, when he became president.   The
business now employs six traveling salesmen and the company
supplies a large retail trade throughout central and western
Virginia and West Virginia.

Mr. Lawman is a member of the United Commercial Travelers and the Presbyterian Church.   He married, October 29,
1914, Miss Nellie Blye Surber, who was born at Longdale, Alleghany County, Virginia, daughter of James W. Surber, a well-
to-do farmer in that vicinity.   Mrs. Lawman finished her education at Clifton Forge, Virginia.   They have three children, Margaret Frazer, Matthew, Junior, and William Edward.

JOHN CALVIN HUDGINS.   During the ten years that John
Calvin Hudgins has been engaged in the undertaking business,
he has gained a recognized position in his calling, and at present
is the owner of an establishment of his own at Claremont, Virginia, which is operated by a manager, and is secretary-
treasurer and general manager of the firm of W. D. Dinguid,
Incorporated, the oldest firm of funeral directors in the United
States, established in 1817, and now located at Lynchburg.   Mr.
Hudgins is also an ex-president of the Virginia Funeral Directors Association, and a member of the Virginia State Board of
Embalming.

Mr. Hudgins was born in Mathews County, Virginia, June
20, 1891, and is a son of John Roser and Lucy (Respess)
Hudgins.   He is connected with several families which have won
distinction, among them the Diggs family, which came from
Scotland in 1785 and settled in the eastern part of Virginia and
North Carolina, where they followed merchandising and the seaman's calling.   The mother of John Roser Hudgins was a Small-
wood, and a member of a family which fought with General
Washington during the Revolutionary war, several accompany-
ing him when he crossed the Delaware.   The original progenitor
had come from France with the French troops which assisted
the colonists in their struggle, and by his gallantry won high
rank.   Following the war he received a land grant in Ohio,
where he spent the rest of his life, and where a monument was
recently erected to his memory.

Hazel Hudgins, the paternal grandfather of John Calvin
Hudgins, was a ship carpenter by trade, and at the outbreak of
the war between the states was residing at Washington, D. C.,
but enlisted in the Confederate Navy, with which he fought
until the close of the struggle.   Following the war he settled in
Mathews County, where he was born and where he spent the
rest of his life.   There was born John Roser Hudgins, who has
passed his career as a merchant and farmer in Mathews County,
where he continues to make his home.   He is a member of the
Baptist Church and a Democrat in his political views.   Mr.
Hudgins married Lucy Respess, who was born in Mathews
County, and died in 1901, and they became the parents of four
children: John Calvin, of this review; Etta, the wife of John
Sparrow, a member of the old Virginia family of that name, who
is now engaged in the oyster and fish business in Mathews
County; Lucy, the wife of Melvin H. Callis, also of an old family
of Virginia, who is captain of a steamship running from the
Philippine Islands to Cuba, but makes his home at Baltimore,
Maryland; and Rhoda, the wife of Frederick H. Hope, of Nor-

folk, Virginia, a member of the board of trustees of the Virginia Pilots Association, who is engaged in piloting steamships into port. The maternal grandfather of John Calvin Hudgins, Washington Respess, was born in Virginia and was a descendant of a family which came from England about 1739 and settled on land in Mathews and Gloucester counties, Virginia, which had been given as a Crown grant for government services. One of the direct ancestors of John C. Hudgins was Richard Henry Respess, who donated ground to Mathews County in 1801 on which the first court house was erected.

John C. Hudgins attended the public schools of Mathews County, including two years at high school, and then took a two-year commercial course and did home extension work. His first employment was as a bookkeeper and stenographer at Claremont, and he was thus engaged when appointed postmaster by President Wilson. While serving in that capacity for two terms, he took up the study of undertaking and embalming, and at the end of his term as postmaster embarked in this business at Claremont, where he still continues in the same line, although having been a resident of Lynchburg since 1924, in which year he purchased an interest in the old-established business of W. D. Dinguid, Incorporated, of which he is secretary and treasurer and also the manager of the entire business. This is one of the most modern establishments of its kind, and includes a beautiful chapel and funeral home, with all the equipment for the reverent and dignified care of the dead. As before noted Mr. Hudgins has the full confidence of his associates in the business, and in 1926 served capably in the capacity of president of the Virginia Funeral Directors' Association. As a member of the Virginia State Board of Embalming he has been constructive in his work and has given full support to those measures which will be generally beneficial. Mr. Hudgins is a member of the Episcopal Church. Fraternally, he is a York Rite Mason and a member of the Independent Order of Odd Fellows, the Woodmen of the World and the Lions Club.

In 1914 Mr. Hudgins was united in marriage with Miss Margaret Stewart, who was born in Virginia and educated at Claremont and at a private school for girls. They have no children. Mrs. Hudgins is a daughter of Thomas A. Stewart, a native of Edinboro, Scotland, who married Elsie Stuart, connected with the famous Stuart family of English history. Mr. Stewart, who was a banker in Scotland, brought his bride to the United States on their honeymoon trip, and, becoming attached to the country, never returned to his native land. He first purchased a farm in the state of Missouri, but finally settled in Virginia, and for many years was engaged in the mercantile business at Claremont, where he was held in great esteem and where his death occurred.

CUTHBERT TUNSTALL, physician and surgeon, was in the air service during the World war, completed his professional training after returning home, and is a popular and talented member of the professional community at Charlottesville, where in addition to general practice he specializes in ear, nose and throat work.

Doctor Tunstall was born at Norfolk, Virginia, November 28, 1892. The Tunstalls were Colonial settlers in Virginia, and his grandfather, Robert B. Tunstall, a native of Norfolk, was an able physician in that community until his death in 1883.

The Tunstalls on coming to Virginia settled in King and Queen County. Doctor Tunstall's maternal grandfather, Henry A. Heiser, was born in New York State, and was a merchant and also operated a line of ships engaged in ocean trade. He had the degree of fortune which frequently attends men in that business, sometimes being wealthy and at other times on the verge of bankruptcy. Doctor Tunstall's parents were Richard B. and Isabelle Mercein (Heiser) Tunstall, his mother a native of New York State and his father born at Norfolk. Richard B. Tunstall was a lawyer, was educated at the University of Virginia, and at the age of sixteen was one of the boys who participated in the battle of New Market. He served many years as senior warden, vestryman and treasurer of St. Paul's Episcopal Church at Norfolk. Of his five children two are living: Robert B., who was educated in the University of Virginia, is a lawyer by profession, was on the Norfolk City Council for a time and is now member of the legal department of the Chesapeake & Ohio Railway at Richmond.

Dr. Cuthbert Tunstall attended the Norfolk Academy, the Episcopal High School at Alexandria, and graduated with the B. A. degree from the University of Virginia in 1913. When America declared war on Germany he trained for the infantry at Fort Myer near Washington, entered the air service and trained in Canada and Texas, went to England and reached the front just before the armistice was signed. He held the rank of first lieutenant. Doctor Tunstall graduated with the M. D. degree from the University of Virginia in 1921, following which he had three years of experience and training as an interne in the New York Post Graduate Hospital. Since 1925 he has specialized in ear, nose and throat at Charlottesville, and is a member of the Virginia Eye, Ear, Nose and Throat Society, and also the Albemarle County and Medical Society of Virginia, and American Medical Association. He belongs to the Delta Psi fraternity and St. Paul's Episcopal Church.

Doctor Tunstall married in December, 1920, Mrs. Mary (Wood) Moore, who was born at Rockfish, Virginia. Her father, O. O. Wood, was a railway man. Doctor and Mrs. Tunstall have one daughter, Mary Mercein Tunstall, born October 14, 1921.

WILLIAM WIRT WADDELL, physician and surgeon, was the first member of his profession to practice in the special field of pediatrics at Charlottesville. Doctor Waddell was born at the old university center of Virginia, and is one of the talented graduates from the university who have remained in that community.

He was born at Charlottesville in 1894, son of William W. and Martha (Payne) Waddell. His grandfather, Lyttelton Waddell, was born in Augusta County, Virginia, and for many years was well known as an editor at Charlottesville, conducting the *Tuckahoe Chronicle*. He was a vigorous writer, and in his writings and scholarship preserved a great deal of valuable history. William W. Waddell, father of Doctor Waddell, was born at Churchville, Augusta County, was educated at Charlottesville, and at the age of seventeen entered the Peoples Bank of that city and has been continuously in its service ever since, being now active vice president. His wife was born in Louisa County, Virginia, and both are active members of the Presbyterian Church. He is affiliated with the Masonic fraternity and B. P. O. Elks. Of their five children four are living: William Wirt; Mary Walker, wife of Fred L. Watson, a Charlottesville insurance man; Lyttelton, a lawyer at Charlottesville, who took his Master of Arts and Bachelor of Laws degrees at the University of Virginia; and Nancy Elizabeth, who was educated in the Mary Baldwin Seminary at Staunton.

William Wirt Waddell attended the Charlottesville High School, the Jefferson School for Boys, and was graduated in medicine at the University of Virginia in 1918. Then followed a period of service with the Naval Medical Corps, and he became a passed assistant surgeon. He was on duty until honorably discharged in 1919. For fourteen months he was an interne in a hospital at Philadelphia, practiced fourteen months in general medicine and surgery at White Sulphur Springs, following which he spent a year in residence at New York, giving special attention to pediatrics in Bellevue Hospital. After completing this special preparation he returned to Charlottesville, where he has largely limited his work to his special field. For several years he has been assistant professor of pediatrics in the University of Virginia School of Medicine. He is a member of the Nu Sigma Nu medical fraternity, the Albemarle County Medical Society of Virginia and the Virginia Pediatric Society. While at the university he was also a member of the Eli Banana Society and the Kappa Sigma fraternity. Doctor Waddell is a Presbyterian.

He married in June, 1921, Miss Barbara Belle Flock, who was born at Williamsport, Pennsylvania, and was educated there and in the Ossining School for Girls at Ossining, New York. They have two children: William Wirt III, born in June, 1922; and Ann Lyttelton, born in July, 1925.

HUGH H. KERR, commonwealth attorney of Augusta County, has been a member of the Staunton bar nearly thirty-five years, and more than half of that time has been spent in the performance of the duties of commonwealth attorney.

Mr. Kerr was born in Augusta County August 13, 1873, son of Samuel H. and Mary E. (Bondurant) Kerr, and grandson of D. Bell Kerr and John Bondurant, both of whom were identified with the early life of Augusta County and Prince Edward County, John Bondurant being descended from a pioneer French family. Samuel H. Kerr was born on the old Kerr homestead in Augusta County, and gave his active life to cultivating the land and maintaining it as one of the fine old country homes of Virginia. He was a Confederate soldier, enlisting April 11, 1861, and was in the service until Appomattox, almost exactly four years later. He served in Company E of the First Virginia Cavalry under General Stuart. He and his wife were active members of the Presbyterian Church. They had four children: Hugh H.; E. B. Kerr, a retired citizen of Staunton; Jenetta K., wife of W. F. Jones, of Staunton; and Elizabeth B., who is private secretary to Doctor Wilmer of Baltimore.

Hugh H. Kerr spent his boyhood days on the old homestead, which he now owns, the deed to this property having been given to the Kerr family by Robert Beverly. Mr. Kerr attended the Fishburne Military School and took his law degree at the University of Virginia in 1894. He began practicing law at Staunton in October of the same year, and his individual abilities have contributed notably to the success of several law partnerships. At different times he has been a law partner of Richard S. Kerr, John D. White, F. S. Crosby and Charles J. Churchman. Mr. Kerr was first elected commonwealth attorney of Augusta County

C. L. Dickens. D.D.S.

in 1911.   He has been regularly reelected in 1915, 1919, 1923 and 1927, now serving in his fifth consecutive term.

Mr. Kerr married in May, 1900, Miss Sarah E. Rock, a native of Augusta County, daughter of P. H. Rock.   She was educated at the Virginia Female Institute at Staunton.   They have two children.   Elizabeth, who attended Stuart Hall at Staunton and Miss Duval's School at Charles Town, West Virginia, is the wife of Maj. E. Walton Opie, manager and one of the owners of the Leader Publishing Company of Staunton.   The second child, Hugh H. Kerr, Jr., is attending school at Staunton.   Mrs. Kerr is a member of the Episcopal Church, while he is a deacon in the Presbyterian denomination.

CLEM L. DICKENS, Doctor of Dental Surgery, who has practiced his profession at Lynchburg for twenty years, is a native of Halifax County, Virginia, and his people have been honored as farmers and planters and good citizens of that locality for a number of generations.

He was born February 28, 1887, son of John N. and Lottie Jane (Hawkins) Dickens.   His grandfather, Abner Dickens, was a Confederate soldier and spent his life on a farm in Halifax County.   John N. Dickens died in 1908, having spent many years in the retail hardware business at Halifax Court House, where his widow still resides.   He was a Democrat, and both parents were active members of the Baptist Church.   Doctor Dickens was the fifth in a family of twelve children, ten of whom are living.

He was educated in public schools in Halifax County, and in 1906, at the age of twenty, graduated in dentistry from the Medical College of Virginia.   Doctor Dickens practiced two years in Charlotte County and in 1908 located at Lynchburg, where he has rendered a fine service in a professional capacity. He is a member of the Lynchburg, Virginia State and National Dental Societies.

He married, in 1912, Miss Vera Taylor, who was born in Giles County, Virginia, and was educated in the Southwest Virginia Female Academy.   They have two daughters, Elizabeth Jane and Vera Taylor, both attending school at Lynchburg. Doctor Dickens is a Baptist, while his wife is a Methodist.   He is a member of the Piedmont Club and Rotary Club, and is affiliated with the Masonic fraternity and Benevolent and Protective Order of Elks.

FRANK CYRUS MCCUE, physician and surgeon, has been a well known member of his profession in Charlottesville for a number of years, most of his active connections there having been with hospital service and work.

Doctor McCue was born in Albemarle County, April 24, 1874. The McCues came from Ireland and were early settlers in Virginia.   The McCue ancestry runs back to the time of King Heremon, who was the first Monarch of Ireland, and according to the traditional records reigned many years before the birth of Christ.   Doctor McCue's grandfather, James C. McCue, was born in Virginia.   James Cyrus McCue, father of Doctor McCue, was born near Afton, was well educated for his time, spent his life as a farmer, and owned 1900 acres near Afton, devoting this large estate to the raising of thoroughbred cattle and hogs.   For years he shipped regularly cattle and hogs to the Baltimore and Richmond markets.   As a very young man he volunteered and served in the Confederate army during the Civil war. His wife, Sarah Jane Moon, was born at Batesville, Virginia. Both were active members of the Presbyterian Church. Of their eleven children, one daughter and ten sons, five are now living: Will, who lives on the old homestead at Afton; Leslie, of Charlottesville; Edward, of Charlottesville; Frank C., of Charlottesville; and Harry, on the old home place. The maternal grandfather of Doctor McCue was Samuel O. Moon, an Englishman, who achieved a great deal of wealth as a tobacco merchant and left each of his five children property to the value of a hundred thousand dollars.

Dr. Frank Cyrus McCue was educated at Greenwood, Virginia, in high school, attended high school at Charlottesville as well, and took his M. D. degree at the University of Virginia in 1898. For two years he had further training as an interne in New York City, and still later went back to New York for postgraduate work in hospitals and clinics. For two years he practiced medicine at Strasburg, and then returned to Charlottesville, where for twenty-two years he has been connected with the Martha Jefferson Hospital.

While practicing at Strasburg he married Miss Mary Lyle Francisco, who was born at Warm Springs, Virginia, in Bath County, and was educated in private schools, the Belmont Female Institute and the school at Waynesboro taught by Colonel Winston. She died in 1908, and later Doctor McCue married her first cousin, Willie Glendye Erwin, who was born in Bath County and was educated in the Lewisburg Female Institute. Doctor McCue has three children by his first marriage: Frank Cyrus, Jr., who is employed by a construction firm at Lewisburg, West Virginia; Sarah Jane, at home; and James Cameron, a high school graduate, now employed by a book concern.

Doctor McCue's wife is a member of the Presbyterian Church. He is a Phi Gamma Delta, member of the Medical Society of Virginia, the Albemarle County Medical Society, of which he has been secretary and treasurer for over eleven years, and the Piedmont Medical Society. He is a Democrat in politics. Doctor McCue enjoys a very high standing as a gynecologist and obstetrician, and teaches a nurses class in obstetrics in his hospital.

PERCY HARRIS, M. D. The medical profession is for mankind, and its greatest problem is to secure honest and faithful performance of professional obligation. Whatever may be the favorite line of professional work, the physician cannot overlook the fact that he and his associates are a body of organized men laboring for the common good of humanity. Because so many of the most eminent of the world's physicians and surgeons recognize this fact, progress is constantly being made. The discoveries of one are shared by all for the common good of the human race, and thus it has been that remedies have been discovered for diseases formerly deemed incurable. One of these noble, self-sacrificing men of Virginia who is adding luster to his profession and to the city in which his activities are centered is Dr. Percy Harris of Scottsville, born in Nelson County, Virginia, March 18, 1881.

Doctor Harris is a son of Frederick J. and Roberta C. (Drummond) Harris, natives of Virginia, now living at Radford, Virginia, where he is serving as judge of the Police and Juvenile Courts. Frederick J. Harris's father was Willis Harris, who married Martha Horsley, who descended from Mary Cabell (see the Cabells and their kin by Alex Brown). Judge Harris was graduated from the University of Virginia, and was engaged in the practice of law at Amherst, Virginia, for a time, later becoming cashier of an Amherst bank. Leaving Amherst, he moved to Scottsville, Virginia, and was there for several months. Still later he moved to Radford, and there, as elsewhere, has been very successful. Eight children have been born to him and his wife: Percy, whose name heads this review; Mary Elizabeth, who married O. B. Bynum, of Rogersville, Tennessee; Sallie, who married William Ingles, Junior, of Radford, cashier of the First National Bank of that place; Elberta, who married Amos Miller, of Pocahontas, Virginia; and four who are deceased. Both parents are Presbyterians, and he is an elder in the Radford church, and he is also a Mason. The paternal grandfather of Doctor Harris was Willis Harris, also a native of Virginia, and he married Martha Horsley, also a native of Virginia. He was an educator of note, an instructor in the high schools of his period. Both the Harris and Horsley families are of English origin. The maternal grandparents, Henley and Elizabeth (Henley) Drummond, were born in Virginia, and were settlers of York County, where their families were pioneers.

Doctor Harris attended the local high school of Amherst, and Kenmore University High School and Brown University High School. He studied medicine in the Medical College of Virginia, Richmond, from which he was graduated in 1905, with the degree Doctor of Medicine, and he interned in Richmond Hospital. For seven years following his graduation Doctor Harris was engaged in a general practice in Nelson County and then came to Albemarle County, and since that time has continued in Scottsville. In addition to handling his very large general practice he owns and operates a valuable farm near Scottsville, on which he raises cattle.

In 1904 Doctor Harris married Innes Randolph, who was born at Alexandria, Virginia, and graduated from Randolph-Macon Woman's College at Lynchburg, class of 1904. Her father, Maj. Payton Randolph, was general manager of the Southern Railroad for many years, and a leading civil engineer of the state. He served as major in the Confederate army during the entire conflict. His was one of the oldest and most aristocratic families of the South, he being a direct descendant of Payton Randolph, president of the First Continental Congress. Her mother was Miss Mary Fisher, daughter of George D. Fisher, of Richmond, Virginia, who was president of the Gallego Mills at Richmond, which was destroyed during the invasion of the Northern troops. Four children have been born to Doctor and Mrs. Harris: Innes Roberta, who married John Adkins Moulton, of Scottsville, manager of the Jefferson Mills; Mary Payton, now attending the University of Alabama; Percy Harris, Junior, who is attending high school; and Susan Randolph, who is also attending high school. Doctor Harris was reared a Presbyterian and still holds to that creed, but Mrs. Harris and the children are Episcopalians. He is a past master of Scottsville Lodge, A. F. and A. M., of which he was master for two successive years. He belongs to Phi Chi medical Greek letter fraternity, and to the Piedmont, Albemarle Medical Society, the Southern Medical Society and the American Medical Association.

A man who has always lived up to high ideals in his profession, Doctor Harris is now reaping the rewards of faithful serv-

ice. Standing high among his associates, he earnestly strives to
prove worthy of the great trust reposed in his skill and ability,
and the success which attends his practice proves that the confidence he inspires is well merited. Broad in his sympathies, he
has always given liberally to aid worthy charities, and his support can be depended upon in the furtherance of measures he
believes will work for the advancement of the majority.

FRANK BOUDE KENNEDY is one of the veteran members of
the Staunton bar, having practiced law there over thirty-five
years.

He was born in Augusta County May 23, 1867, son of Isaac
and Virginia A. (Bartley) Kennedy, and grandson of Robert
Scott Kennedy, who came to Virginia with his parents from the
north of Ireland, and Oliver W. Bartley, who was born and
reared in Orange County, Virginia, and was a descendant of the
Washington family. Isaac Kennedy was born in Augusta
County, his wife in Orange County, and he was a farmer all his
active career except for the four years he served with the cavalry
in the Confederate army during the Civil war. He was always
a staunch Democrat, and both he and his wife were members of
the Methodist Episcopal Church, South. Of their five children
only one is now living.

Frank B. Kennedy grew up on the home farm, attended public schools, the Augusta Military Academy, and graduated in
law from Washington and Lee University in June, 1891. In
July following he started practice at Staunton, and in every session of the Circuit Court his name has been associated with some
cases and business, and his record throughout has been that of a
high minded and honorable lawyer. He is a Democrat in politics, an elder in the Presbyterian Church, and has taken part in
many civic and public spirited enterprises in Staunton.

He married, July 12, 1894, Martha Julia Spears, who was
born in Staunton, daughter of William Spears. Mr. and Mrs.
Kennedy had one daughter, Virginia, wife of Turner W. Marcus,
a traveling representative of the National Biscuit Company.
Mrs. Kennedy passed away February 11, 1928.

HERBERT JACKSON TAYLOR, Staunton attorney, with offices in
the Echols Building, is a member of a family that has lived in
Augusta County for generation after generation, and he is one
of the exceptions to a general line of agricultural people.

Mr. Taylor was born in Augusta County June 24, 1869, son
of Samuel K. and Sarah (Heiskell) Taylor, and grandson of
John Taylor and Porterfield A. Heiskell, all of whom were born
and spent their lives in Augusta County, following the occupations of farming. His parents were active members of the
Presbyterian Church. There were five children, the two now
living being Fannie K. and Herbert J. Fannie is a graduate of
Mary Baldwin Seminary and is now a teacher in North Carolina.

Herbert J. Taylor was educated in public schools, in a school
at Staunton, graduated from the law department of Washington
and Lee University at Lexington in 1894, and from George Washington University at Washington, D. C., in 1895. He has been
engaged in a steadily increasing law practice at Staunton since
1896. His reputation as a lawyer is also joined with a commendable interest in politics and public affairs. In 1914 he was
elected a member of the State Legislature from Augusta County
and represented that county continuously through the session of

1924. He also served as city attorney two years. He is a member of the Virginia State Bar Association, is a member of the Delta Tau Delta college fraternity, has been chancellor commander of the Knights of Pythias, is a member of the Masonic fraternity and the Presbyterian Church.

He married, in 1902, Charlotte Ranson, who was born in Staunton, Augusta County, and was educated in Mary Baldwin Seminary. Her father, Thomas D. Ranson, was a well known attorney. They have three children: Alfred Fontaine graduated from Washington and Lee University, had one year of law, and is now at Saint Louis, Missouri, with the Saint Louis Life Insurance Company, Mary Garland Taylor is a student in Mary Baldwin Seminary, and Charlotte Alexander Taylor is attending high school.

ROBERT M. GARRETT, president of the Roanoke Drug Company, is not only one of the prominent factors in the wholesale drug industry of his section, but is a man of unbounded capacity for hard work, the ability to see opportunities and the courage to take advantage of them. From the start he has had faith in Roanoke, here he has invested his money, and while he has been making money for himself he has been contributing to the development of the city. He was born in Bedford County, Virginia, November 11, 1873, a son of Robert M. and M. Clay (Saunders) Garrett, both of whom were also born in Bedford County, but are now deceased. All his life the father was a farmer, and he was also interested in merchandising. During the war between the states he served in the Virginia Cavalry, and after the close of hostilities he displayed equal courage in handling the difficult problems of the reconstruction period. A stalwart Democrat, he held some of the local offices, including that of constable, and in the latter he served for a number of years. He was a Baptist and his wife was a Methodist. Of the six children born to them three are now living: Robert M., whose name heads this review; Mrs. Charles Robey, who resides in East Radford, Virginia; and E. H., who is a farmer.

Growing to manhood in Bedford County, Robert M. Garrett began his business career as a clerk in a store and for eight years gained a knowledge of merchandising in that capacity in connection with a general store. Then for one year he was a clerk in a drug store, and was so well pleased with that business that he went into a drug business of his own in Keystone, West Virginia, and operated it for eight years; after which for twelve years he conducted a similar store in Bluefield, West Virginia, and in the meanwhile branched out, bought others, and when he sold in 1917 he owned five retail drug stores. He then came to Roanoke, established the Roanoke Drug Company, and has been its president and active head ever since. Five traveling salesmen are kept busy representing the company on the road in Virginia, Tennessee, North Carolina and West Virginia. The company is incorporated, and the original stock of $100,000 has been increased until today there is a capitalization of $200,000 of common stock and $100,000 of preferred stock. At one time Mr. Garrett was deeply interested in banking, being president of the Liberty National Bank and a director of the Colonial National Bank and of the Mountain Trust & Savings Bank, but is now devoting himself to his drug business. While he is a strong Democrat, he does not aspire to office. He is a York Rite and Shriner Mason and belongs to the Benevolent and

Protective Order of Elks, the Independent Order of Odd Fellows, going through the chairs in that order, and the Knights of Pythias. Both he and his wife are members of the Baptist Church, and he has served on the finance committee of the church.

In September, 1901, Mr. Garrett married Miss Cleo S. Thaxton, who was born in Bedford County, Virginia, and there educated. She is a daughter of John A. Thaxton, a merchant and farmer of Bedford County, and a veteran of the war between the states. Three children have been born to Mr. and Mrs. Garrett: Frances Lucile, who is at home; Marion Anthony and Robert Metteau, Jr., who are also at home. Mr. Garrett does not antagonize, he moves quietly and surely, understanding men and their motives, and has proven himself competent to meet all situations which arise, bringing into harmony opposing factions with a tact which amounts to power.

FITZHUGH ELDER, lawyer and banker at Staunton, is a son of Thomas C. Elder, and no two names in the legal profession have been associated with finer reputations and have connoted more sound legal talents.

Fitzhugh Elder was born in Lunenburg Courthouse, Virginia, September 30, 1865, son of Thomas C. and Anna Fitzhugh (May) Elder, and a grandson of Brooken Elder, also a native of Lunenburg County, where he followed farming and planting. The maternal grandfather, Dr. Henry May, graduated in medicine from the Philadelphia Medical College and practiced for many years in Lunenburg County. He was a son of George and Anna (Fitzhugh) May, an old Virginia family. Dr. Henry May died at the home of his daughter Sallie May Dooley in Richmond. She was the wife of James H. Dooley, a man of wealth and prominence in Richmond. Mrs. Dooley gave the Maymont Park to the City of Richmond.

Thomas C. Elder was born in Lunenburg County, Virginia, in June, 1834, and died in November, 1904. He was educated in Randolph-Macon College, finished his law course at the University of Virginia, practiced at Lunenburg Courthouse, then at Petersburg, where he had as a partner Gen. Roger A. Prior, and after 1870 his professional career was identified with Staunton as his place of residence, though his reputation extended all over Western Virginia. For many years he held the office of commonwealth attorney for the City of Staunton, finally resigning that position. In 1902, he was honored by election to the office of president of the Virginia Bar Association, an honor that reflected his high standing among the lawyers of the state. He was a gifted leader in the Democratic party, and had served with the rank of major in the commissary department of the Confederate army. He was also for many years a vestryman in the Trinity Episcopal Church at Staunton and at one time was a delegate to the General Church Conference at San Francisco. His wife, Anna Fitzhugh May, was born in 1834 and died in April, 1904, and of their eight chidlren six are living.

Fitzhugh Elder, the third child, was educated at Staunton, attending the Hoover Select High School there, studied law at the University of Virginia during 1890-91 and was admitted to the bar in the latter year. Since being licensed to practice he has looked after the interests of a large clientage. For many years he has been attorney for the Augusta National Bank, is one of the directors of this institution, one of the oldest and strongest banks in Staunton, and is also acting as its trust officer.

He married, September 23, 1905, Miss Sophia Luttgen, who was born in Pennsylvania and was educated in that state and in Boston. Her father, Rudolph Luttgen, was a railway man, long associated with the Erie Railway. His brother, Walther Luttgen, was for many years associated with the banking firm of August Belmont and Company of New York City. Mr. and Mrs. Elder have two children: Nancy Morris Elder, born May 23, 1910, now attending St. Catherine's Episcopal School at Richmond; and Fitzhugh Elder, Jr., born January 29, 1916, a student in Staunton public schools. Mr. Elder has served on the vestry and as junior warden of the Trinity Episcopal Church of Staunton.

CHARLES J. CHURCHMAN shared in the record of the Marine Corps as one of the most aggressive units of the American Expeditionary Forces, and after his return from overseas completed his law course, practiced at Richmond for seven years, and then returned to Augusta County, his native locality, and is one of the leaders of the Staunton bar, with offices in the Echols Building.

Captain Churchman is owner of the Chapel Hill Farm, which has been the home of the Churchman family for four generations. It was established by his great-grandfather, John Knight Churchman. John Knight Churchman was born in Augusta County and built the house on the Chapel Hill Farm. He was a descendant of ancestors who came from England in 1688, and from Delaware moved to Pennsylvania and thence to Virginia. John Knight Churchman was high sheriff of Augusta County and one of the founders of the Virginia Female Institute, subsequently known as Stuart Hall.

His son, John S. Churchman, was born at Chapel Hill farm, and lived the life of a wealthy planter. He was a soldier in the Civil war in Company A, Tenth Virginia Cavalry, and married Frances Crawford, a native of Staunton.

Their son, John W. Churchman, was born at Staunton September 12, 1857, and spent practically his entire life on Chapel Hill Farm, where he died February 24, 1909. He was a graduate of Hampden-Sidney College, a leader among the agricultural forces of Augusta County, and for a number of years was chairman of the Virginia State Board of Agriculture and represented his home county in the House of Delegates from 1898 until his death. For some years before his death he was a deacon in the Tinkling Spring Presbyterian Church. John W. Churchman married Annie Goodwin Johnston, who was born in Botetourt County, Virginia, and now lives at Richmond. Her father, George H. Johnston, was a captain in the Confederate army. John W. Churchman and wife had four children, two of whom died young. The two survivors are Charles J. and Frances, the latter the wife of Simon Seward, an attorney at Petersburg, Virginia.

Charles J. Churchman was educated in public schools in Augusta County, attended the Augusta Military Academy at Fort Defiance, graduated with the Bachelor of Science degree from the University of Virginia in 1913, following which he taught as an instructor in the Augusta Military Academy two years.

Mr. Churchman was a student of law at the University of Virginia when America entered the World war. In July, 1917, he was commissioned a second lieutenant of the Marine Corp

Reserves, and after training at Quantico, near Washington, was commissioned a second lieutenant of the Marine Corps in 1917. In October of that year he went overseas, with the Sixth Marine Regiment, and during the following twelve months his participation in the war can be followed by the localities and sectors of Toulon-Troyon, defensive sector; Belleau Wood and Chateau Thierry, defensive sector; Aisne-Marne offensive at Soissons; Marbach defensive sector; Saint Mihiel offensive, Champagne offensive; Argonne, where he was severely wounded in action November 1, 1918. After a period in the Base Hospital he joined his regiment, part of the second Division, in Germany, in January, 1919, and was with the Army of Occupation until July 28, 1919. He received a division citation, the Croix de Guerre, based on his service at Belleau Wood, and another division citation at Soissons. He was promoted to first lieutenant to date from June 15, 1918, and to captain to date July 1, 1918.

Captain Churchman returned home and received his honorable discharge on August 15, 1919. He then resumed his law studies at the university, being given his diploma in 1920. From 1920 to 1927 he practiced at Richmond with two of his classmates in the firm Parrish, Butcher & Churchman. In 1927 he returned to Staunton and has since practiced with H. H. Kerr. He is a member of the scholarship honorary fraternity Phi Beta Kappa, the Phi Kappa Sigma fraternity and the Phi Delta Phi legal fraternity, and is a member of the Tinkling Spring Presbyterian Church. He belongs to the Virginia State Bar Association. He married, November 9, 1921, Miss Elizabeth Vance Gilkeson, who was born in Virginia, daughter of Edwin M. and Cora (Finley) Gilkeson. Her father was a banker at Parkersburg, West Virginia. Captain and Mrs. Churchman have three children: Elizabeth Gilkeson, Anne Warren and Margaret Finley Churchman.

CHARLES WALKER PUTNEY as a surgeon has won recognition and connections that establish him definitely as one of the leaders in his profession in Western Virginia.

Doctor Putney, whose home is at Staunton, was born at Darlington Heights, Virginia June 1, 1893, son of Ellis W. and Virginia Alice (Putney) Putney. His grandfathers were first cousins, his paternal grandfather being William Ellis Putney. Three brothers of the name came from England, and two of them settled in the Virginias and the other in New England. Doctor Putney's parents were both born in 1858, in Buckingham County, Virginia. The mother is now deceased. The father, whose home is at Darlington Heights, has been a merchant and farmer, and since 1922 has lived retired. He is a member of the Baptist Church and is a Democrat in politics. Of nine children two are living: James Hansford, who owns and operates the old homestead, and Dr. Charles W.

Charles W. Putney attended high school at Darlington Heights, being one of the first graduating class of five members. After his high school work he depended upon his own earnings and exertions to get a higher education and complete his professional training. While a student in the Massey Business College of Richmond he worked as a salesman. He took his pre-medical course at Hampden-Sidney College, and every summer while in university and medical school he did farm work as a means of securing the funds for the next year. He was graduated from the Medical College of Virginia at Richmond in 1921,

and during his senior year was interne at the Soldiers Home Hospital, and another year at Grace Hospital at New Haven, Connecticut. For four months he was with the Norfolk & Western Railway, relief and pension department at Norfolk, practiced one year at Covington, and since 1923 has been at Staunton, where his offices are in the Professional Building. He is in general practice, but the main emphasis of his work has been in general surgery. He has attended the Post-Graduate School of Philadelphia. Doctor Putney is on the medical staff of the Kings Daughters Hospital, is secretary and treasurer of the Staunton Academy of Medicine, and is one of the consulting surgeons for the Western State Hospital.

He married, in 1921, Miss Louise Gathright, of Richmond. Mrs. Putney is a woman of unusual education and professional experience. She taught for six years at Richmond and was educated in the John Marshall High School there and the Richmond City Normal School. Doctor Putney is a deacon in the Baptist Church, is physician to the Order of Eagles, is a member of the Omega Epsilon Phi medical fraternity, and belongs to the Augusta County and Valley Medical Societies, Medical Society of Virginia, and is a fellow of the American Medical Association.

HON. CHARLES D. FOX, mayor of Roanoke, and president of the Savings Loan Corporation, is one of the substantial business men and political leaders of this region, and formerly was engaged in the practice of pharmacy, for twenty-two years owning and operating a drug store, but since 1918 he has been in his present corporation. He was born in Roanoke County, Virginia, January 31, 1869, a son of John C. and Sarah (Peck) Fox, both natives of Virginia, now deceased. All his life the father owned and conducted a tannery, and was in that line of business at the time of his death. Of the seven children born to him and his wife three survive, namely: Mrs. G. W. Kern, who resides in Danville, Virginia; Mrs. Minnie Eubank, who is a resident of Vinton, Virginia; and Mayor Fox. The parents were active members of the Baptist Church, and were highly esteemed by their fellow members. During the war between the states the father served in the Confederate army during the latter part of the conflict but in the earlier part of it tanned leather for the government of the South.

Reared in his native county, Mayor Fox attended its common and high schools, and his first work was done as a clerk in a general store, in which connection he was employed for five years. He then read medicine under the preceptorship of Dr. George T. Walker of Gish's Mill, but did not complete his medical studies, instead entered a drug store in Roanoke, and in the course of time succeeded his employer as the owner of it, and for the succeeding twenty-two years practiced in Roanoke, rising to considerable importance in that profession, and for twelve years he had the honor of belonging to the Virginia State Board of Pharmacy. He is licensed to practice pharmacy in every city of the United States, but, as already stated, does no more professional work. Selling his drug store he and M. J. Patsel established the Savings Loan Corporation in 1918, since which time he has been its president. During the years which followed this has been built up to large proportions, and is one of the sound financial concerns of this part of Virginia. For eight years Mayor Fox served most capably as a member of the Roanoke City Council, and in September, 1926, was elected mayor of the city. Under his wise administration the affairs of Roanoke have shown the effects of his good judgment and enterprise, and he is regarded as one of the best chief executives the city has ever possessed.

In March, 1889, Mayor Fox married Miss Carrie Bass, born in Petersburg, Virginia, where she was reared and educated. Four children have been born to them, namely: Edward C. Fox, who was graduated in electrical engineering from the Virginia Polytechnic Institute, is now engaged on construction work at Tokio, Japan; Charles D. Fox, Junior, who was graduated from the law department of the University of Virginia, is engaged in the practice of law in Roanoke; John C. Fox, who is an electrical engineer, is in the employ of the Virginia Railway Company at Narrows, Virginia; and Mary Dodd Fox, who married Edgar D. Hellweg, resides in Garden City, Long Island, where her husband is in the employ of Doubleday, Page & Company, and she is an alumnus of Hollis College. Mayor Fox is a member of the Baptist Church, but Mrs. Fox and the children belong to the Methodist Episcopal Church, South. He belongs to the Ancient, Free and Accepted Masons, the Knights of Pythias, being a past chancellor commander of the local lodge and grand chancellor commander of Virginia, and is now supreme representative of the state; he is past grand of the Independent Order of Odd Fellows of the Grand Lodge of Virginia, and has represented the state lodge in the Sovereign Grand Lodge; he is a member of the Improved Order of Red Men, and a past sachem; and is a member of the Woodmen of the World and the Maccabees. He is a past prince of the Knights of Khorassan, and was chairman of the transportation committee for the annual convention of that order held in Fort Worth in August, 1927. The Benevolent and Protective Order of Elks also holds his membership. In all of these orders, and in the country club, he is deservedly popular and he has many warm personal friends all over the state. No man can spend his life in one community, carrying on several different lines of business successfully, and also be accorded high honors both politically and fraternally without he possesses characteristics that are admirable and dependable, and Mr. Fox has proven the truth of this in his career and continued advancement. He and his wife have reared a family of fine children, given them the advantage of collegiate training, and now have the satisfaction of having them well established in the world.

WALTER B. WILSON, sheriff of Augusta County, is known over a wide section of Western Virginia through his many years of active work and experience as a traveling salesman.

He is a native of Augusta County, where his people have lived for several generations. Mr. Wilson was born March 14, 1873, son of Joseph and Margaret (Brownlee) Wilson, both natives of Augusta County. His grandfather, James Wilson, was born in Augusta County, of parents who were natives of Virginia. The maternal grandfather, Alexander Brownlee, was an Augusta County farmer and cabinet maker who owned a large amount of land and slaves, and was rated as one of the wealthy men of the county. Joseph Wilson spent his active life as a farmer, and in the closing scenes of the Civil war was enrolled in the service of the Confederate government and was at Lynchburg with a train when the final scene was enacted at Appomattox. Three of his brothers were soldiers, and one of them, James, was killed.

Joseph Wilson and wife were members of the Tinkling Spring Presbyterian Church. He made his start after the war and gained a reasonable degree of material prosperity, providing well for his family of children, who were four sons and one daughter. The surviving children are Bessie L., of Staunton, Walter B. and Harry W., the latter operating a farm and filling station in Augusta County.

Walter B. Wilson attended private and public schools in Augusta County, grew up on a farm and lived there until he was twenty years of age, and then had some experience in a commissary department of a coal company in West Virginia. On returning to Staunton he entered the service of the Erskine Miller Company, wholesale grocers, and for twenty-five years covered an extensive territory for this firm, and was one of the men who contributed a heavy volume of trade to his organization. After leaving the wholesale grocery house he spent eight years traveling for a tobacco firm.

Mr. Wilson was elected sheriff of Augusta County November 8, 1927, and has more than satisfied the wishes and expectations of his large following of personal friends who voted for him. Several years ago he was a candidate for commissioner of revenue. He is a member of the United Commercial Travelers and the First Presbyterian Church. Mr. Wilson owns an interest in one of the apple orchards in this wonderful horticultural section of Virginia.

He married, in 1907, Miss Bessie Johnson, a native of Augusta County, daughter of W. H. Johnson, a farmer. To their marriage were born nine children: Margaret, Katherine E., Elizabeth B., Frances C., Walter B., Jr., Joseph J., Thomas P., Nancy Ann and Charlotte L. The six older children are all in school, Margaret taking a special course in business training.

COL. HENRY C. FORD, professor of history in the Virginia Military Institute at Lexington, has for many years been a prominent leader in the educational affairs of Virginia as well as the great institution at Lexington.

He was born in Charlotte County, Virginia, December 12, 1867, son of Luther Rice and Pernette (Smith) Ford, natives of the same county, where his father lived out his life as a farmer. His father served four years in the Confederate army as a non-commissioned officer. Both were members of the Presbyterian Church, and he belonged to the Masonic fraternity. Of their six children four are living: Henry C.; Bessie, widow of Charles O. Finch, living in North Carolina; Mary, wife of William A. Finch, a lawyer at Wilson, North Carolina; and Emma, wife of Thaddeus A. Adams, a lawyer at Charlotte, North Carolina.

Col. Henry C. Ford received his education in private schools, was a student in the Virginia Polytechnic Institute in 1884-85, and in the Virginia Military Institute from 1885 to 1889, graduating with the Bachelor of Science degree. During the following year he remained at the institute as an instructor, and in 1890-93 taught in the Wentworth Military Academy at Lexington, Missouri. After further study at the University of Virginia he returned to the Virginia Military Institute in 1895, leaving there to become Master of St. Albans' School at Radford during 1896-98. In 1899 he was awarded the Doctor of Philosophy degree at the University of Virginia, and resumed his place on the faculty of the Virginia Military Institute as adjunct professor, during 1901-03 was commandant of cadets, and since 1902 has held the chair of history in the institute.

Colonel Ford was a member of Governor Tyler's staff with the rank of colonel in 1898. He served on the State Board of Education from 1911 to 1923, and in 1927 was again appointed for a four-year term. He is a Phi Beta Kappa, member of the Tilka Society of the University of Virginia, and the Kappa Alpha social fraternity. He and his family are Episcopalians.

Colonel Ford married, January 10, 1900, Miss Agnes Palmer, a native of Richmond, who died in 1902, leaving one daughter, Mary Lewis Ford. On July 12, 1905, he married Elizabeth Walker, who was born in North Dakota, daughter of Captain Walker, a regular army officer. Colonel and Mrs. Ford have three children: Virginia Easton attended Sweet Brier College, Henry Clinton, Jr., and Medora Beall. Henry C. is a cadet in the Virginia Military Institute, and Medora is attending Saint Mary's School at Raleigh, North Carolina.

FRANK M. LEECH, surgeon, is a native of Rockbridge County, and has won enviable distinction in his profession in the City of Lexington.

He was born on a farm in Rockbridge County, December 27, 1894, son of J. Henry and Nellie (McMaster) Leech, both natives of Rockbridge County, where they still reside. His paternal grandfather, William A. Leech, and his maternal grandfather, Samuel McMaster, were born in the same county and both of them were on the Confederate side in the Civil war. William A. Leech had a leg shot off in battle. J. Henry Leech has been a farmer and live stock man all his life, and is a Democrat in politics. His wife has been very active as a member of the Presbyterian Church.

Doctor Leech, oldest in a family of six children, attended the County High School, and after graduating A. B. from Washington and Lee University in 1916 entered the Medical College of Virginia at Richmond, where he took his diploma of graduation in 1920. Doctor Leech spent three years in the Gouverneur Hospital of New York, and when he opened his office at Lexington in 1923 he was exceptionally well qualified for his chosen work as a surgeon. He has confined his attention exclusively to surgery and is the outstanding man in that line in Lexington. He is a member of the Rockbridge County, Virginia State and American Medical Associations. During the World war he was enrolled with the Naval Reserve Militia. Doctor Leech is a member of the Presbyterian Church, a York Rite Mason and Shriner, member of the Knights of Pythias and the Omicron Upsilon Phi medical fraternity.

He married, in 1925, Miss Bessie Dunlap, a native of Rockbridge County and daughter of M. P. Dunlap.

DONALD CALLAR, Doctor of Dental Surgery at Staunton, is a native of Pennsylvania, and was reared and educated in the City of Washington.

He was born at Smithport, Pennsylvania, June 21, 1892, son of William Thomas and Addie (Cross) Callar. His paternal grandfather, Thomas Callar, was born in England, settled in Pennsylvania and became a prosperous business man. The maternal grandfather, Ambrose Cross, was born in Maryland, and became a gun designer for the United States Army and at one time had charge of the armory at Harpers Ferry. His

daughter, Addie Cross, was born at Harpers Ferry. William Thomas Callar was born in Allegheny County, Pennsylvania, and for many years was in the drug business in Pennsylvania and at Little Rock, Arkansas. He was a Methodist, while his wife was a Presbyterian, and he was a York and Scottish Rite Mason. There were two sons, Vernon Callar, an interior decorator at Philadelphia, and Donald.

Dr. Donald Callar spent many of his boyhood years in Fairfax County, Virginia, graduated from high school at Washington and took his dental course in George Washington University, graduating in 1914. He has practiced at Staunton since 1915, and has kept himself in touch with the rapidly advancing improvements in dental methods by post-graduate work in Columbia University, New York, and elsewhere. Doctor Callar is a member of the Virginia State, Shenandoah Valley and American Dental Societies.

He married, in 1915, Blanche Detwiler, who was born in Fairfax County, Virginia, and was educated in the Winchester Female Institute and the Randolph-Macon Woman's College. Her father, Benjamin D. Detwiler, was a dentist at Herndon, Virginia. Doctor and Mrs. Callar have two sons, Donald Evan and William Benjamin, both attending school at Staunton. The family are members of the Episcopal Church, and Doctor Callar is a vestryman. He is a York Rite Mason and Shriner, member of the Kiwanis Club, and gives his support to all worthy movements in his community.

JOHN P. PETTYJOHN, of Lynchburg, is a veteran contractor, and has been in business at Lynchburg for over half a century. He is founder of the widely known firm of John P. Pettyjohn & Company.

Mr. Pettyjohn was born on the James River in Amherst County, Virginia, February 8, 1846, son of George W. and Ann Taylor (Reynolds) Pettyjohn, his father a native of Amherst County, while his mother was born in Botetourt County. George W. Pettyjohn spent his life as a Virginia farmer and was a resident of Amherst County except during the years of the Civil war when he lived in Washington County. Three of his sons were Confederate soldiers. Of their ten children John P. is the last survivor.

John P. Pettyjohn was reared on a farm until twenty-one years of age, but in the meantime had at the age of fifteen enlisted in the service of the Confederate army and was with the southern forces about one year. He attended school in his native county and at Lynchburg, helped operate the home farm for his mother and learned the trade of carpenter. From working as a journeyman he began taking contracts, and at the outset of his business career his capital was only about fifteen dollars. He did some of the first work for the Norfolk and Western Railway at Lynchburg when that railroad was built to Roanoke, and as a contractor his firm has handled construction work for this railway system continuously for over forty years without a break. He has also been a contractor for the Chesapeake and Ohio, the Southern and Seaboard Air Line Railway Companies.

Mr. Pettyjohn at one time was a member of the Lynchburg City Council. He is a Democrat and has been a steward in the Court Street Methodist Episcopal Church, South.

He married, in 1870, Miss Nannie Rebecca Old, a native of Amherst County. She died in 1883, the mother of four children: Walker, of the firm of John P. Pettyjohn & Company; Mamie, wife of R. T. Watson, president of a bank at Warrenton, North Carolina; Oten R., a farmer in Amherst County; and Henrietta May, wife of J. C. Burwell, a tobacconist in North Carolina.

Mr. Pettyjohn married, August 27, 1884, Alice Bell Watts, also a native of Amherst County. She died in August, 1927. The four children of this marriage were: Albert D., in the real estate business at Tampa, Florida; Miss Martha W., at home; Archie P., proprietor of a men's furnishing goods store at Lynchburg; and Miss Ruth.

ALEXANDER TOBIE MOORE is a noted hotel man of Virginia, and for many years has been in that business at Staunton, where he is proprietor and manager of the Stonewall Jackson Hotel, one of the best of the modern hotels in point of service and facilities in the great valley.

Mr. Moore was born October 1, 1877, son of James W. and Tixie O. (Holland) Moore and grandson of William P. Moore and Joseph W. Holland. William P. Moore was a native of Virginia and served four years in the Confederate army, being wounded in one battle. Joseph W. Holland, a native of Southhampton County, Virginia, was a farmer there and was himself a soldier in the Confederate army and had three sons fighting for the cause of the South. James W. Moore was born at Southhampton, and during his active life was a merchant at Suffolk, Franklin and Newport News and died in Staunton. His wife was born in Southhampton County and died at Franklin, where both of them are buried. They were members of the Baptist Church and he was a Democrat and Mason. Of their six children three are living: Alexander T.; Henrietta, who lives with her brother at Staunton; and Bertha, wife of Joseph H. Holland, of Staunton.

Alexander Tobie Moore attended public schools in Suffolk and has been making his own way in the world since an early age. For four years he was employed by the Chesapeak & Ohio Elevator Company at Newport News, spent one year working in a ship yard and office, and for five years was connected with the Old Dominion Company at Newport News.

He had his first experience in the hotel business at Newport News, conducting the Hotel Warrick for eleven years. From there he came to Staunton, buying the Beverley Hotel and subsequently acquired the Virginia Building and erected the Stonewall Jackson, which was formally opened to the public in 1924. An incorporated company owns this fine hotel, Mr. Moore being its president as well as general manager of the hotel. The vice president is Julous L. Witz. Mr. Moore has acquired ground three miles north of Staunton where a fine golf course has been laid out by a competent architect to be operated for the benefit of the hotel guests. Mr. Moore is president of the Capital Tours Association, an organization made up of hotel men and other agencies in many cities and communities from New York to North Carolina.

Mr. Moore married, in 1903, Miss Elizabeth Baker, a native of Portsmouth, Virginia. After the common schools she attended Randolph-Macon College at Lynchburg and Saint Mary's School at Raleigh, North Carolina. Mr. and Mrs. Moore had one child, Ann Elizabeth, who is now the wife of Morton Neifert, a newspaper man of New York City, and they have a daughter,

Ann Elizabeth Neifert. After the death of his first wife Mr. Moore married, in 1923, Elizabeth Clemmer, a native of Augusta County, Virginia, who was educated in Stuart Hall. Mrs. Moore is a member of the Episcopal Church. He is a Presbyterian and is affiliated with the Masonic fraternity, and is a member and director of the Swannanoa Club. He served six years on the City Council of Staunton, in 1928 was again a candidate for the Council and through all the years has been active in the Chamber of Commerce, serving it as a director. He is president of the local Rotary Club.

REV. FRANK CARSON RILEY is pastor of the Orange Baptist Church at Orange. He is a gifted minister, thoroughly devoted to the work, and has found a most congenial field for his efforts and talents in Orange County. The Orange Baptist Church was organized in May, 1858, having twelve charter members. The first pastor was Rev. Mr. Quarles. When Rev. Mr. Riley took charge of the church its membership was 226. By 1927 the membership had increased to 450, and the Sunday School now has enrolled 330 students. Rev. Mr. Riley has also organized home department and foreign missions, cradle roll, home roll, and the Baptist Young People's Union.

He was born at Baltimore, Maryland, September 27, 1888, son of Joseph C. and Alice M. (Brewer) Riley. The Rileys originated in Normandy, France, went to England with William the Conqueror, and some of their descendants came to America in 1621, settling in New England. Many of the pioneers of the family were seafaring men. One of the family was Capt. James J. Riley, who had a thrilling adventure in Africa, and on returning to America wrote his experience in a book entitled *What he saw and did in Africa*. Captain Riley was a member of the New York State Historical Society.

The parents of Rev. Mr. Riley live near Baltimore. His father has been a building contractor for many years. The children were: Frank C.; Milton, who died in infancy; Thomas Dillard and Joseph Chapman, twins; Margaret Irma, wife of Sidney McConnell, of Baltimore; and Howard Lee, of Elk Ridge, Maryland.

Frank C. Riley attended public schools in Howard County, Maryland, and after those advantages he contrived opportunities through his own efforts and earnings for a higher education. For four years he was employed in a hat factory, and after the day's work was done attended a private school at night. For one year he studied in the Conway Hall Preparatory School at Carlisle, Pennsylvania, was graduated with the A. B. degree in 1913 from Richmond College, and completed his theological work in the Crozer Seminary at Chester, Pennsylvania. The seminary made him a Bachelor of Divinity and in 1915 he received his Master's degree from the University of Pennsylvania. He had also attended the Southern Baptist Theological Seminary during 1908-09. He is a member of the Phi Kappa Sigma fraternity.

Rev. Mr. Riley's ministry began as a supply to churches in Montgomery and other counties in Maryland. On December 1, 1915, he accepted the call to the Orange Baptist Church, and his ministry there covers a period of thirteen years. Rev. Mr. Riley has entered actively into the life of the community, being assistant chief of the Orange Volunteer Fire Department, probation officer of the Juvenile Court, and for twelve years was

scout master of the Boy Scouts. He is a Democrat in politics
and at Orange belongs to the Independent Order of Odd Fellows
and the patriotic order Sons of America. During the World
war he enlisted, was commissioned chaplain with the rank of
first lieutenant, was in training at Camp Taylor, Louisville,
Kentucky, with the Second Battalion, Three Hundred and Eighteenth Infantry, United States Army, and went overseas with
the Eightieth Division, serving in France from July, 1918, to
May, 1919. Prior to that he had acted as chairman in local
drives for the Y. M. C. A. and Red Cross.

Rev. Mr. Riley during 1922-27 served as moderator of the
Goshen Virginia Baptist Association, a district comprising
forty-nine churches. For several years he has spent his Sunday
afternoons preaching at country churches. Some of these rural
churches were organized as long ago as 1774.

Rev. Mr. Riley married, September 14, 1915, Miss Ethel
Pierpont, of Baltimore, daughter of Charles M. and Hannah
(Seaborn) Pierpont. Her mother died December 17, 1927. Her
father is a miller by occupation. Mrs. Riley has a sister, Hazel,
wife of L. W. Porter, of Catonsville, Maryland. The children
of Rev. Mr. and Mrs. Riley are: Nancy Lee, born June 14, 1916;
Betty Carson, born June 30, 1920; and Frank Carson, Jr., born
November 1, 1923.

RICHARD S. KER, judge of the Corporation Court of Staunton,
has been a practicing lawyer in that city forty years. He is a
scholarly lawyer, exemplifies the culture of a Virginia family
with traditions running back in this state for two centuries, and
has discharged his responsibilities as a lawyer and public official
with a high degree of credit.

Judge Ker was born in Staunton August 4, 1866, son of Heber
and Mary E. (Kinney) Ker. The founder of the Ker family in
America was Edward Ker, who settled in Virginia, where his
oldest son was born in 1721. Judge Ker's grandfather, Dr. John
Ker, of Eastville, Virginia, practiced medicine for many years
and married Miss Mary Jacobs. Heber Ker was born in Northampton County, Virginia, in 1836, was a graduate of the Virginia Military Institute, was in the insurance business for many
years, and at the time of his death in 1905 was serving as a
deputy United States marshal. He was a Republican in politics
and a member of the Episcopal Church. His wife, Mary E. Kinney, was born in Staunton and died in 1872. Her father, Chesley Kinney, was a Staunton attorney. Heber Ker and wife had
a family of six children, and the three now living are: Heber,
Jr., a retired steel man at Bellevue, Pennsylvania; Severn P.,
who is in the steel business at Youngstown, Ohio; and Richard S.

Richard S. Ker was educated in public schools at Staunton,
in the Hoover Military Academy there, and was graduated from
Washington and Lee University at Lexington in 1885. After
his university career he taught school two years, took his law
course at the University of Virginia, and was admitted to the
bar in 1888. Since that year he has been a member of the
Staunton bar, and in addition to handling a large volume of private practice he served thirteen years as commonwealth attorney
of Augusta County. In 1912 he was elected judge of the Corporation Court and by reelection has held that office for the past
sixteen years. Judge Ker is a veteran of the Spanish-American
war, having been captain in a Virginia regiment which spent
most of its time in training in Florida. Judge Ker is a Demo-

crat in politics, and for twenty years served as vestryman in the Emanuel Episcopal Church.

He married, May 11, 1898, Miss Jessie Shephard McNeill, who was born at Fayetteville, North Carolina, and was educated there and in Mary Baldwin Seminary at Staunton. Her father, George P. McNeill, was in the insurance business. Judge and Mrs. Ker have three children: George McNeill Ker was educated at Staunton and is now in the steel business at Youngstown, Ohio; Howard Ker graduated from West Point Military Academy in 1924, and as a second lieutenant of the United States Army is located in Hawaii; Charles Douglas Ker attended school at Staunton, for three years continued his education at the University of Virginia, and is now a student of architecture at Staunton.

WALTER C. BEASLEY. Prominent among the energetic and enterprising business men of the younger generation who have recognized the exceptional opportunities for success made possible by the advent and marvelous growth of the automobile industry, is found Walter C. Beasley, head of the Beasley Motor Company, Incorporated, of Lynchburg. Prior to entering this line of enterprise, Mr. Beasley had been identified with a successful shoe business, but with the continued growth of the motor car business he decided to change his line, and although he has been engaged in selling automobiles for only a comparatively short period, he has had no reason to regret the change he made.

Mr. Beasley has won his success in the midst of friends and neighbors, as he was born at Lynchburg, April 25, 1896, and is a son of Robert P. and Willie (McConville) Beasley. His father, who was born, reared and educated in Amherst County, Virginia, did not care for the agricultural life which his progenitors had followed, instead turning his attention to mercantile lines. Eventually he founded a modest wholesale shoe business, which through great industry and good business management he developed into one of the large and important enterprises of Lynchburg, the Beasley Shoe Company, Inc., manufacturers and wholesale dealers. He continued at the head of this business until 1922, when he turned over the presidency to his son, although he continued to have an interest in the concern until 1926 when it was sold. He is still a resident of Lynchburg, living in retirement from business cares, and is one of the highly esteemed men of his community, where he has an enviable reputation for integrity, straightforward dealing and good citizenship. He is a consistent member of the Court Street Methodist Episcopal Church, in which he served as a member of the board of stewards. He has never cared for public honors and maintains an independent stand upon political questions, voting rather for the man than the party. Mrs. Beasley, who also survives, is a native of Lynchburg, and she and her husband are the parents of four children: Robert Parker, Jr., a retired business man of Lynchburg; Walter C., of this review; Mrs. J. W. Grimes, a resident of Lynchburg; and Lee Hall, a student at Randolph-Macon College, at Ashland, Virginia.

Walter C. Beasley attended the public schools of Lynchburg and after his graduation from high school entered the University of Virginia, where he pursued a business law course and was graduated in 1917. He at once entered his father's business where he made himself familiar with every detail, and in 1922 succeeded the elder man in the presidency. During this time he entered the United States Army, and during the three months of his service was in training at Camp Joseph E. Johnston, at Jacksonville, Florida. This business was sold, as before noted, in May, 1926, and in August of that year Mr. Beasley became the organizer of the Beasley Motor Company, Incorporated, making a specialty of handling Hudson and Essex cars, and having the sales rights in several counties around Lynchburg. This concern has a commodious salesroom at Fifth and Federal streets, with a fully equipped service and filling station in connection, and also handles all kinds of automobile parts and accessories. Mr. Beasley is known as a young man of great business energy and good judgment, and devotes his entire time to his enterprise, having few outside interests, although he is a genial man and fond of the companionship of his fellows. With his family, he belonged to the Court Street Methodist Episcopal Church.

In 1919 Mr. Beasley was united in marriage with Miss Kathryn Harms, who was born at Chambersburg, Pennsylvania, and educated at Randolph-Macon Woman's College. Mr. and Mrs. Beasley are the parents of two children: Kathryn Harms, born September 21, 1922; and Betty Virginia, born November 19, 1927.

CHESLEY D. SHULTZ since early manhood has been identified with the printing and publishing business, and is president of one of the largest commercial printing establishments in Western Virginia, the McClure Company, Incorporated, at Staunton.

He was born at Greenville, Augusta County, Virginia, January 25, 1879, son of Frank G. and Emma Elizabeth (Steele) Shultz, both natives of Augusta County. The Shultz family was established in Pennsylvania in 1740 by German ancestors, and some of the family moved on into the Shenandoah Valley of Virginia about 1765. Mr. Shultz' grandfather, Henry Shultz, was born at Greenville, Virginia, served in the last year of the Civil war, being forty-five years of age at the time, and after the surrender he walked all the way home from Richmond. He followed the milling business. Frank G. Shultz lived for many years on his farm, and later became a rural mail carrier and did that work until he retired. He and his wife live in Augusta County and recently celebrated their golden wedding anniversary. They are members of the Methodist Episcopal Church. Emma Elizabeth Steele is a daughter of Isaac Steele, who was a farmer in Rockingham County. Her great-grandfather, Col. Robert Doak, was an officer in the Revolutionary war. Frank G. Shultz and wife had five sons: Chesley D.; W. H. Shultz, a traveling passenger agent for the Norfolk & Western Railway, with headquarters at Winston-Salem, North Carolina; E. M. Shultz, in the real estate business at Greenville; Dr. F. S. Shultz, a dentist at Roanoke; and James W., a telegraph operator at Wadesboro, North Carolina.

Chesley D. Shultz grew up on his father's farm and attended schools at Staunton, including business college. When he left school he learned the printing trade, and has been engaged in the printing business for thirty years. In 1911 he was one of the founders of the McClure Company, Incorporated, and since 1913 has been its president and general manager. The company owns and operates a modern establishment with all modern facilities for general job and book printing, and has handled printing contracts from all over the western part of the state.

Mr. Shultz married, in 1904, Miss Leonora C. Parker, daughter of John A. Parker, who died at the age of ninety years, after many years of service as a school teacher. Mrs. Shultz was born and educated at Brownsburg, Virginia. They have two children, Beverly Parker, a graduate of the Staunton High School, now attending the Dunsmore Business College, and Emma Jane, a student in the Junior High School. The family are members of the First Presbyterian Church. Mr. Shultz is a member of the Rotary Club and Chamber of Commerce, and is serving as registrar of the Second Ward of the City of Staunton.

BARTON H. CAMERON is a Richmond manufacturer, but for a number of years has made his permanent home at his beautiful country estate in Gordonsville, Orange County, where he finds occupation for his energies and taste in the management of a farm and a home property which is perhaps unsurpassed in beauty in all this section of Virginia.

Mr. Cameron was born at Richmond, October 31, 1871, son of Alexander and Mary (Haxall) Cameron. His maternal grandfather Haxall was in the milling business at Richmond and before the Civil war exported a large amount of flour to South America. The Haxalls came originally from Suffolk, England, and members of the family have had holdings in Orange County, Virginia, for about seventy-five years. Alexander Cameron was born in Scotland, and as a young man settled at Richmond, where he became a tobacco manufacturer and built up a business that in volume of trade and importance ranks among the large tobacco organizations in Virginia. During the Civil war he did a great deal of blockade running for the Confederacy, carrying supplies out of the harbor at Charleston, South Carolina, to Nassau, in the Bahama Islands, bringing back goods so badly needed by the Confederates. He gave his active supervision to the tobacco business until his death in February, 1915. His wife died in October, 1915. Alexander Cameron was a life long Democrat, but never sought the honors of a public office.

It was in 1875 that Alexander Cameron bought 500 acres at Gordonsville, in Orange County. He built a home, and for many years the family regarded this as a summer residence. Later the property was divided among the children and six of them have homes on the original 500 acres. However, Barton H. Cameron is the only one who regards it as a permanent place of residence. Barton Cameron's home sets on a high hill overlooking Gordonsville and the surrounding country side, and probably no property in that locality has been more generally admired. The children of Alexander Cameron and wife were: Mary H.; Alexander, Jr.; Barton H.; Janet J.; James B.; Flora M., who married G. W. Zinn; Elizabeth G., wife of J. H. Crosman; and E. Donald.

Barton H. Cameron attended school in Richmond and received the training of an engineer, graduating from the Stevens Polytechnic Institute at Hoboken, New Jersey, in 1894. He also took summer work in the University of Virginia. Mr. Cameron followed his profession for several years and then engaged in the stove manufacturing business at Richmond. To this industry he devoted his time and energies for a number of years, became president and general manager of the company, but lately has retired from the active management and is vice president of the company. Mr. Cameron is a Democratic voter, and holds membership in an Episcopal Church at Richmond.

He married, October 25, 1899, Miss Mary R. Newman, daughter of R. M. and Catherine (Taylor) Newman, of Hanover County, Virginia. Her father was a planter, who died in 1905, and her mother in 1907. Mrs. Cameron was the oldest child of her parents, the others being: Frances, wife of Graham Thomas; Page, who married Dr. M. B. Rudd; Elizabeth; Catherine, wife of A. B. Taliaferro; and Herbert. Mr. and Mrs. Cameron have one son, M. Graham, born March 20, 1913.

CARL H. NOLTING was reared and educated at Richmond, still has business interests in that city, but many years ago made a definite choice of the life of a Virginia country gentleman and has found ample satisfaction for his tastes in that direction as owner of a splendid stock farm and country home near Trevilians, Louisa County, located on Rural Route No. 2.

Mr. Nolting was born at Richmond, July 31, 1874, son of Emil O. and Susanne C. (Horn) Nolting. His father was born in Germany, and when a small boy was brought to America by the family, which located at Richmond. Emil O. Nolting was for many years one of the recognized leaders among the tobacco merchants who made their home and had their industrial interests at Richmond. He was one of the biggest men in the business. He was also president of the National Bank of Virginia at Richmond, and during the early '70s was chosen president of the Richmond Chamber of Commerce, said to be one of the first of such organizations in the country. During the Civil war he acted as consul for the Belgian government at Richmond and was always interested in civic affairs. He died in 1893, and his wife in June, 1915. They had a family of twelve children: Emil O., Jr., who died in infancy; Helen, who married F. H. McGuire, of Richmond; Luly, of Richmond; Emily, of Howardsville, Virginia; George, who died in infancy; Florine, who died in 1914, the wife of E. B. Thomason; W. Otto, who died in 1908; Frederick E., of Richmond; Carl H.; Susie, wife of L. M. Williams, of Richmond; Roberta, wife of R. Tate Irvine, of Richmond; and Dr. Margaret, of Richmond.

After attending a private school in Richmond, Carl H. Nolting entered the University of Virginia as a student and was graduated in 1895. His general business education came to him during the five years he clerked in banks at Richmond. He also spent considerable time in travel in Old Mexico. City life has never made a strong appeal to him, though he has business in Richmond and is treasurer of the Virginia Central Railway and active in several other organizations. He is a director of the Bank of Louisa and the National Bank of Gordonsville.

Mr. Nolting accepted the opportunity presented to him in 1903 to purchase a farm of 1,500 acres in Louisa County, a place that for many years had been known as "Bracketts." During the past quarter of a century Mr. Nolting has made this one of the famous centers for production of purebred live stock in Virginia. Up to 1918 he raised blooded Shetland and Welsh ponies. He has specialized in Hereford cattle and Cheviot and Hampshire sheep, all purebred, and his farm also produces large quantities of grain, hay and other crops. It is a real farm, operated on a businesslike basis, and it is also a maginficent country estate. The home is a large and fine house, surrounded

J. T. Eames

by many buildings used by the helpers on the farm   There is
a large lake stocked with game fish and furnishing duck hunting
in season.   Mr. Nolting for many years was chairman of the
County Democratic Executive Committee of Louisa County, and
he was elected and served in the State Legislature in 1908-10.
He has been a member of the Commission on State Fisheries and
he is president of the Louisa County Chamber of Commerce.
Mr. Nolting is a vestryman in the Episcopal Church at Louisa.

JOHN T. EANES.   While it is oftentimes desirable that the
substantial men of a community give a portion of their time and
attention to civic matters, their real service to their fellow citizens lies in their work in building up large industrial or commercial institutions that give employment to many and bring
into the place outside capital that can be invested in other enterprises.   No community however well conducted rises to importance with the outside world that has not within its confines some
industrial plants, for production is the very breath of progress.
The man or city that does not produce something is practically
useless, and this becomes more true with every year.   The demand for everything increases in proportion with the increase
in population, the changes in housing conditions and consequently the work of the household, and the ability of the wage
earner to secure for himself and his family what were once considered the luxuries of the rich, but which he and his have come
to regard as the necessities of a well-ordered existence.   Particularly is this true with regard to the great and rapidly expanding laundry industry.   Today there are but a small proportion of the housewives who have their laundry work done at
home, realizing as they do the quality of the service they can
secure at a very reasonable price.   The greater portion of the
laundry work of the country is cared for in a highly satisfactory
and sanitary manner in the great plants of the industry, and one
of them in Roanoke worthy of special mention is the Ideal Laundry, Dry Cleaners and Dyers, of which John T. Eanes, one of the
city's solid citizens, is proprietor.

John T. Eanes was born in New Swansonville, in Pittsylvania County, Virginia, March 5, 1878, a son of Mat and Jennie
(Merriecks) Eanes, both of whom were born in the same county
as their son.   The mother died when John T. Eanes was eighteen
months old, and the father when he was five years old, the latter
having been a millwright and wheelwright all his life, but gave
special attention to manufacturing boxes for tobacco.   The parents had three children: Delia A., who is deceased; James M.,
who is a merchant of Roanoke; and John T., who was the last
born.   The father was a Baptist and a good churchman.   His
political convictions made him a strong Democrat.   During the
close of the war between the states he enlisted in the Confederate army, and served until peace was declared.   The paternal
grandfather of John T. Eanes was Holbrook Eanes, a native of
Virginia and a minister of the Baptist Church.   The maternal
grandfather, Hop Merriecks, also a Virginian, was a farmer.

Left an orphan at so tender an age, John T. Eanes did not
have very good educational advantages, but he made the most of
what he was able to secure, and has learned much from contact
with men and participation in affairs of importance.   In 1905
he came to Roanoke, and afterward for a few years was a salesman in different mercantile establishments.   He then established
an office toilet and towel service, beginning in a small way, and

expanding his business as he felt he was justified in doing, and
in 1915 he branched out and established a general laundry business.   In the meanwhile he had established a small laundry in
the rear of a grocery store, and this growing, in 1916 he bought
a city block with railroad frontage located at the corner of
Eighth Street and Church Avenue, Southeast, on which he put
up a building.   To this first one he has added other buildings
until he now has the entire block covered with a two-story fireproof building, 450 feet by 110 feet, which he operates under
the name of the Ideal Laundry, Dry Cleaners and Dyers, and
here he employs 125 persons, his payroll aggregating $2,000 a
week.   His present plant is thoroughly modern, and compares
very favorably with his initial one, the equipment of which was
two zinc washtubs which he bought for $1.25 each.   He and his
wife did all of the washing at the opening of what later has
become so important a business.   They did the very best grade
of work possible with their equipment, and that policy is still
continued, and is responsible for much of their constantly augmenting patronage.   The plant is equipped with an up-to-date
cafeteria, where the best of food is furnished the employes at
cost, it being the only establishment of its kind in Virginia.

On August 31, 1905, Mr. Eanes married Miss Pearl Greenway, a daughter of W. S. Greenway, a pioneer auctioneer of
Roanoke City and County.   Mrs. Eanes was born near Roanoke
and educated in her home neighborhood.   There are no children,
but Mr. and Mrs. Eanes are caring for two orphans, giving to
them a tender parental care, and the advantages attendant upon
residing in their comfortable home in Roanoke.   They belong
to Raleigh Court Methodist Episcopal Church, South, and he is
chairman of its Board of Stewards and a teacher in the Sunday
School.   A Mason, Mr. Eanes has been advanced in the Scottish
Rite, and he also belongs to the Shrine.   He is a member of the
Benevolent and Protective Order of Elks, the Knights of Pythias
and the Kiwanis Club.   However, his chief interest is his business, which is his exclusive property, and he is devoting himself
to it with most gratifying results.

HENRY CREWE WARREN, a native of Richmond, where the
Warren and Crewe families have been prominent in commercial
affairs for many years, is a business man of Orange, being one
of the owners and managers of the Orange Mills.

Mr. Warren was born in Richmond, July 3, 1879, son of
George W. and Annie E. (Crewe) Warren.   The Crewe family
came to America from England in 1623, settling at Norfolk,
and were prominent in the Colonial history of Virginia.   George
W. Warren was a banker and broker, for many years a member
of the firm Warren & Quarles at Richmond, and was also in the
insurance business.   For a number of years he was a member
of the Richmond City Council, and while a Democrat, was not
especially active in politics.   He died in 1890, and his wife in
1914.   They had three children, George W., Allen B., and Henry
Crewe.   George W. is head of the Davenport Insurance Agency
at Richmond, while Allen B. is an insurance man at Orange and
is president of the Orange Mills and director of the National
Bank.

Henry Crewe Warren attended the McGuire Boys School at
Richmond, also the Woodbry Forest School at Orange, and spent
one year in college at Bedford, Virginia.   He was graduated in
1898 from Randolph-Macon College at Ashland, Virginia.   **Mr.**

Warren for thirty years has been active in commercial life. For several years he was employed by the Southern Bell Telephone Company of Richmond. His home has been at Orange since 1904. He was in insurance and other lines until 1918, when he helped organize the Orange Mills, of which his brother Allen is president, while he holds the post of vice president and manager. Mr. Warren is also director of the National Bank of Orange, is a former president of the Chamber of Commerce and in every sense a progressive leader in the commercial and civic life of the community. He votes as a Democrat and is a vestryman of the Episcopal Church at Orange. During the World war he was chairman of the third and fourth Liberty Loan drives and chairman of the Orange County Red Cross.

Mr. Warren married, November 12, 1902, Miss Fannie Conway, daughter of Dr. C. G. and Elizabeth (Jones) Conway. Her father died in 1903. He was a Confederate soldier under General Pickett at Gettysburg and in other battles, while Mr. Warren's father enlisted in Missouri under General Price and took part in such great battles of the war as Lookout Mountain, Missionary Ridge and others. Mrs. Warren was the third in a family of four children, the others being: Elizabeth, wife of Albert G. Kirkland, of Richmond; Edwin, of Orange County; and Margaret, Mrs. S. P. Regester. Mr. and Mrs. Warren have three children: Marianne G., now Mrs. L. W. Eshelman; Frances C., wife of Philip L. Thwing; and Miss Annie C.

MRS. FRANK MERIWETHER RANDOLPH, occupant and proprietor of "Cloverfield," was Charlotte Nelson Macon before her marriage. The Meriwethers and Macons are families so well known in Virginia history as to require no identification marks. The Meriwethers, originating in Wales, came to this country in 1824.

Particular interest attached to Cloverfield as one of the historic places occupied continuously by members of one family for generation after generation. The present Cloverfield is a quaint country estate in Albemarle County, consisting of 352 acres. It is a portion of a grant of land originally comprising 17,652 acres which was given to the Meriwether family by King George II. A copy of the original grant is on file at Richmond. This has been the home of Mrs. Randolph practically all her life, and many of her ancestors as well were born here.

She was born December 10, 1859, daughter of George W. and Mildred Nelson Macon. Her father was a planter, and because of his value in growing foodstuffs for the Confederate army he was required to remain at home and conduct the plantation rather than become a soldier at the time of the Civil war. He held a number of offices in his county, including those of magistrate and member of the board of the Miller School. He grew up near Monticello, the home of Thomas Jefferson. George W. Macon died May 26, 1884, and his widow survived him until March, 1904. They had a family of eight children: Thomas S., born December 18, 1858; Charlotte Nelson, born December 10, 1859; George, born in 1863, and died October 17, 1923; Lyttleton, born March 21, 1865; William Douglas, born April 17, 1868; and three others who died in infancy.

Charlotte Nelson Macon was educated in a private school at Keswick, Virginia. On January 17, 1883, she became the wife of Frank Randolph. They were married at Grace Church, Cismont, Virginia. The late Mr. Randolph was of the famous family of Randolphs connected by intermarriage with the Page, Bland, Byrd, Walker, Pendleton, Meriwether and other noted Virginia families. Mr. Randolph died September 8, 1922. Mrs. Randolph had four children: Margaret Douglas, born March 17, 1884; Mildred Nelson, born October 27, 1885, died in infancy; Caroline R., born October 28, 1886; and Charlotte N., born May 5, 1887. The daughter Caroline was married in 1906 to Edward H. Joslin, of Keene, New Hampshire. Charlotte Nelson was married January 25, 1919, to Gilbert T. Rafferty, of Pittsburgh, Pennsylvania. Mr. and Mrs. Rafferty reside with Mrs. Randolph at Cloverfield. The Rafferty children, members of the Cloverfield household, are: Caroline R., born in 1919; Anne, born September 16, 1920; Frances Douglas, born April 13, 1922; and Doris, born June 9, 1925. Mrs. Randolph is a member of the Episcopal Church at Cismont, in Albemarle County.

HARRY LEWIS BAPTIST, physician and surgeon, is practicing his profession in the interesting rural community of Ivy, in Albemarle County, where he has found opportunity for extended usefulness and service, being the leading physician in that locality.

Doctor Baptist was born in Spotsylvania County, Virginia, January 9, 1874, son of Rev. Edward G. and Sarah Lewis (Duerson) Baptist. Both his father and grandfather were ministers of the Baptist Church, and his grandfather preached all over Southern Virginia, and also was active in promoting the founding and maintenance of institutions of higher education. Rev. Edward G. Baptist was in the ministry more than forty-five years, having a number of pastorates in Central Virginia. He died in 1896. His first wife, whom he married in 1857, was Maria Duerson. She died in 1870, mother of five children. In 1871 he married her cousin, Sarah Lewis Duerson, who died in 1908. She was the mother of four children: Maude, who died in 1906, wife of Dr. B. L. Dillard; Dr. Harry Lewis; Noel, who died in infancy; and Maurice, of Winchester, Virginia.

Harry Lewis Baptist attended local schools and went to Baltimore to complete his professional education in the University of Maryland. He graduated from the School of Medicine in 1897. For a short time he was associated with a brother-in-law in practice, but has been settled in the community of Ivy for over thirty years, and still carries a large weight of burdens and responsibilities in a professional way. He has served as president of the Piedmont Medical Society and of the Albemarle Medical Society, and is a member of the Virginia and American Medical Associations.

Doctor Baptist was a member of the local school board from 1914 to 1917. As a busy professional man he has had little time for politics beyond voting as a Democrat.

He married, April 22, 1902, Miss Margaret E. Boyle, daughter of John B. and Agnes (Morton) Boyle. Her people were identified with the Colonial settlement of Virginia, and some of her ancestors participated in Indian wars. Her family came to America in 1619. Mrs. Baptist was born in Brazil, South America, where her father had gone as a missionary of the Presbyterian Church. He died, and when she was a small girl she was brought to the United States by her mother, who died soon afterward. Doctor and Mrs. Baptist have a family of six children: Agnes Morton, born October 23, 1904, now a teacher at Winston-Salem, North Carolina; Harry Lewis, Jr., born Sep-

tember 5, 1906, a resident of Nashville, Tennessee; Maude Glanville, born October 17, 1907; Woodson Boyle, born February 5, 1909; Margaret Esther, born December 21, 1912; and Sarah Eggleston, born October 30, 1916.

ROBERT HENDERSON ANGELL. In a state of ancient glories and traditions running back more than three centuries, Roanoke is a city without claim to age, but its history has been significant of the expression of the intense modern industrial development of Western Virginia. In that comparatively young community a man whose individual life has run step by step with the progress of the city has been Robert Henderson Angell.

Mr. Angell was born on a farm near Callaway, Franklin County, Virginia, January 25, 1868. His grandfather, Taylor Angell, moved to Franklin County from Cumberland County. Marshall Jefferson Angell was born in Franklin County, was a carpenter by trade, also a farmer, and served throughout the Civil war in the Confederate army. He was twice wounded at the second battle of Manassas, but in spite of the severity of his wounds reached the age of seventy-nine. He had two brothers, Anderson and Woodson, who were also in the war, Anderson being a member of Pickett's Division in the great charge at Gettysburg. Marshall Jefferson Angell married Emma Noel, who was born in Bedford County, Virginia, daughter of Caleb Noel. She died at the age of twenty-eight, leaving five sons, Eugene, Joseph, John A., Robert Henderson and Caleb Taylor.

Robert Henderson Angell lived on his father's farm in Franklin County, attended rural schools there, and came to Roanoke County when he was sixteen. He did farm work, attended school at Salem, and in the Village of Roanoke in 1886 began his experience working in a brick yard, and from that comparatively humble beginning has become one of the city's foremost men of affairs. In three months he was a partner in the brick yard, later managed and was admitted to partnership in a lumber business, bought the interests of his associates, and he laid the basis of his fortune as a lumber dealer and manufacturer of lumber and mill work. In 1910 he organized the Virginia Lumber Manufacturing Company, with headquarters at Roanoke, and the Lynchburg Manufacturing Company at Lynchburg, and practically owned and controlled both companies. Mr. Angell still has large interests in the lumber business, but for the past fifteen years much of his time has been taken up with banking and life insurance. He was elected president of the Colonial National Bank of Roanoke in 1912, and since 1913 has been president of the Shenandoah Life Insurance Company, an organization that in its volume of business has done much to establish Roanoke as an insurance center in Southwest Virginia. Mr. Angell since 1920 has been president of the Liberty Trust Company of Roanoke, is president of the Home Furniture Company, the Roanoke Glass Company, is vice president of the Roanoke Iron & Bridge Works, and no man in the city has a heavier load of responsibilities vital to the commercial advancement and welfare of Roanoke.

Mr. Angell is a Republican in politics and has been a delegate to a number of states and also to national conventions of his party. He was representative of Roanoke City and County in the House of Delegates from 1901 to 1904, and became a member of the State Board of Agriculture in 1914 by appointment of Governor Stuart. He served four years on the first

Board of Commissioners of Roanoke after the adoption of the commission form of government. Mr. Angell has been given the thirty-third honorary supreme degree in Scottish Rite Masonry, and was the first potentate of Kazim Temple of the Mystic Shrine. He is a member of the Independent Order of Odd Fellows, Knights of Pythias, B. P. O. Elks, Red Men, the Kiwanis Club, Shenandoah Club.

He married, in 1896, Miss Mary J. Barlow, who was born in Phillipsburg, Pennsylvania, daughter of Andrew and Mary Barlow, who came to Virginia when she was a child. The children of Mr. and Mrs. Angell are Robert, Joseph, Franklin, Randolph, Henry Clay, Hughes Thurston, Arthur and Virginia May.

MANLEY W. CARTER. The Carter family has had many prominent relationships with Orange County. They are of old Southern stock, were loyal supporters of the Confederacy, but for many years in politics they have affiliated with the Republican party.

Manley W. Carter, who is the present postmaster of Orange, was born in that county March 26, 1885, son of Thomas W. and Betty B. (Fletcher) Carter, natives of Virginia. His father during the last two years of the Civil war was in the Confederate army in Mosby's Rangers. He spent his early years as a farmer, later developed a nursery, and always kept in touch with the agricultural situation. For years he was the only Republican in Orange County, and did much to make the party respected there. For four terms he was postmaster of Orange, serving under the administrations of Harrison, McKinley, Roosevelt and Taft. He finally resigned the office in 1911. He died January 7, 1924, and his wife in 1910. There were four children: Lucile, wife of Tom F. P. Henderson, who served with the rank of captain in the World war and is a lawyer by profession; Manley W.; Ruth, wife of Elston Johnson, of Franklin, Tennessee; and Roy W., located at Washington, D. C.

Manley W. Carter graduated from the Locust Dale Military Academy in 1900, and from the time he left school to the present a large part of his energies and thought have been directed to farming and stock raising. His country estate is the fine farm known as Shadows, comprising about 287 acres and located a short distance from Orange. To this farm he has given more than local reputation as a center for the breeding of blooded race and hunting horses. The farm has provided him a satisfying occupation and source of revenue, but since 1922 he has divided his time between its management and the supervision of the postoffice at Orange. He was appointed postmaster that year. Mr. Carter, like his father, is a Republican. He is a Knight Templar Mason and Shriner, member of the Independent Order of Odd Fellows, and the Episcopal Church.

He married, May 2, 1915, Miss Sarah E. Bennett, of Culpeper, Virginia, daughter of William A. and Betty (Campbell) Bennett. Her father, who was a real estate man and race horse breeder, died in 1918, and her mother is still living, Mrs. Carter being one of five children. Mrs. Carter is a Virginia woman who has been interested in educational and literary matters. For years she served as a member of the high school board. She is a graduate of Maryland College at Luthersville, Maryland, and has also taken courses at the University of Virginia. Mrs. Carter wrote a history of Virginia counties.

JACOB HEVENER, city clerk of Staunton, represents an old and honored family of the Valley of Virginia, his people having been steady and industrious pioneers who came into the Valley at a time when the settlements were constantly threatened by Indian attacks.

Mr. Hevener was born in Highland County, Virginia, December 29, 1878, son of William and Lavina (Jordan) Hevener, both natives of the same county. His grandfather was Jacob Hevener, a native of Highland County, and the maternal grandfather was Samuel Jordan. Agriculture has been the staple occupation of the family for many generations. William Hevener spent all his life on his farm in Highland County and died January 20, 1893. He was a Democrat, represented his county in behalf of delegates one term and during the Civil war was a county justice. He and his wife were active members in the Methodist Episcopal Church, South. Of their five children three are living: Uriah, a farmer in Pennsylvania; Jacob; and Mary, wife of R. H. Crummett, a Highland County farmer.

Jacob Hevener was well educated, finishing his training in Randolph-Macon Academy at Front Royal, Virginia. After completing his school work he engaged in farming, and was on the farm until 1912, when he moved to Staunton. In Staunton he became identified with the insurance business, and carries on a line of general insurance. In 1923 he was appointed city clerk, and most of his time has been taken up with his official duties. He is a member of the Knights of Pythias, is a York Rite Mason and member of the Methodist Episcopal Church, South.

He married, in 1900, Miss Ocie McNeil, who was born in Pocahontas County, West Virginia, and was educated at Staunton and in the Valley Female College at Winchester. Her father, Rev. J. W. McNeil, was a Methodist minister in the Baltimore Conference. Mr. and Mrs. Hevener have two children: Harold McNeil, associated with his father's insurance agency; and Jacob, attending high school. Mr. Hevener is a steward in the Methodist Episcopal Church at Staunton.

REV. FREDERICK W. NEVE, D. D., has given a life and service to the people of the Blue Ridge Mountains in Western Virginia, and for many years has held the official title of "Archdeacon of the Blue Ridge Mountains." His home is at Ivy, in Albemarle County, and from that point he supervises the work which has grown to be one of such beneficence under his direction, affecting the spiritual and material well being of thousands in the mountains and valleys of the Blue Ridge.

Rev. Dr. Neve was born in Kent, England, December 8, 1855. He attended a boys' boarding school, and studied law two years, giving that up to prepare for the ministry. He graduated from Oxford University with the Bachelor of Arts degree in 1879, three years later was awarded the Master of Arts degree, and in 1880 was ordained a deacon in the Church of England, and in 1881 the Orders of Priesthood were conferred upon him in England.

Doctor Neve's work for forty years has been in Western Virginia. In 1888, on coming to the United States, he took charge of St. Paul's Church at Ivy, in Albemarle County, and also Emanuel Church at Greenwood. He might have found here a quiet routine of the country minister, but instead he recognized the great opportunity for extension of the influence of the church far beyond the borders of his immediate parish. He undertook establishing missions in the mountain districts, and that has been the great task to which he has devoted all the energies of his heart and mind for forty years. In 1904, in recognition of his efforts and as an official sanction for his service, he was made archdeacon of the Blue Ridge Mountains. In 1921 the Virginia Theological Seminary at Alexandria conferred upon him the Doctor of Divinity degree. Many visitors have written of the great value of his work, and he has himself described the manifold influences sent out under the auspices of the church over this region in a small volume called *The Church of the Living Waters*.

Doctor Neve married, June 21, 1893, Miss Fannie Taylor. She died in 1911, leaving two children: Pauline Mary, who married Allen M. White; and Frederica F. Both these daughters were educated in Stuart Hall at Staunton, Virginia. Doctor Neve married Miss Helen A. Cooch on March 25, 1913. By this marriage one daughter, Helen Cooch, was born.

WILLIAM FLETCHER PAULETT, of Scottsville, is descended from one of the oldest Virginia Colonial families. He is a man who has made his way by his own efforts and talents rather than by family influence, and for twenty years has been in business at Scottsville, handling building material and other commodities.

He was born in Fluvanna County, March 23, 1870, his birthplace being the old family homestead, known as "Refugee Home." The family name was originally Paulette, indicating its French origin. Another branch of the American descendants are known as Powletts. The first Virginia Paulett is mentioned in the book entitled *History of the First Legislative Assembly Ever Convened in America*. In this first Legislature one of the two delegates from "Argall's Guifte" was Capt. Thomas Paulette. Many of these first delegates or burgesses became noted men of Virginia. In 1623 Capt. Thomas Paulette received a grant for the famous estate on the James River known as "Westover," which later became the property of Col. William Byrd, an ancestor of the present governor of Virginia. There have been Pauletts of prominence locally or in the state in every generation since that time. Mr. Paulett's uncle, John W. Paulett, was at one time state superintendent of public instruction for Tennessee.

William Fletcher Paulett is a son of Fletcher and Mary (Porterfield) Paulett. His mother's father was one of the pioneer dentists who traveled about the country after the manner of the early members of that profession. When Fletcher Paulett was fourteen years old he enlisted in the Confederate army and served as a gunner throughout the entire war, and his gun was one that was used to fire the salute at the surrender at Appomattox, he firing the last shot. He farmed after the war, later operated a general store, and died at an early age, in 1870, a few months before his son, William Fletcher, was born. The mother died in November, 1918. The only other child, Angia Virginia, is the wife of G. L. Spencer, of Buckingham, Virginia, and has eleven children, nine living.

When William Fletcher Paulett was a small child his mother moved to Buckingham County, where he attended local schools and learned the mechanics of building contracting. He has been a hard worker and his success has been well earned. He has

G N Flowers

been established at Scottsville since 1907. He has been dealing in building material since that date, and as his business enlarged he installed planing mill machinery for the manufacture of interior finish and also deals in automobile supplies. Mr. Paulett is a Democrat, and all the family are members of the Baptist Church. His son Forrest belongs to the Masonic Order.

Mr. Paulett married, August 21, 1894, Olivia Haden, daughter of James A. and Anna (Bledso) Haden, and also related to Dr. W. D. Haden, a prominent physician and citizen of Charlottesville. Her father was a farmer, a Republican in politics, and died in 1917, while her mother passed away in 1914. Her mother's family were early settlers of Albemarle County. An uncle, Adam Bledso, was widely known over Virginia as a Methodist minister. Mrs. Paulett was one of eleven children, four of whom are now living. The children of Mr. and Mrs. Paulett are: Mary Anna, wife of R. D. Jones, of Charleston, West Virginia, and mother of a daughter, Cornelia Ann; Earl, a twin brother of Mary, died in 1898; Lena B. is the wife of Earl McEwen, of Richmond; Forrest Evert, associated in business with his father, is married and has a son, Forrest Evert, Jr.; and Ruby is the wife of G. T. O'Mohundro, of Scottsville.

GEORGE HORACE FLOWERS, manager of Liggett & Myers Tobacco Company, one of the largest exclusive cigarette manufacturing plants in the world, is a man whose entire business life has been spent in the tobacco industry. Mr. Flowers is a son of George Washington and Sally (Haynes) Flowers, the former a native of North Carolina, and held the rank of colonel in the Confederate army. The mother also was a native of North Carolina. Mr. Flowers of this review is one of a family of eight boys and one girl, as follows: Robert Lee, Charles Eugene, William Washington, Arthur Ellis, John McTyre, Fred, Claude and Estelle. He was born in Taylorsville, Alexander County, North Carolina, May 23, 1881, and he was graduated from Trinity College, now Duke University, Durham, North Carolina, in 1902.

Immediately upon leaving the university Mr. Flowers entered the employ of the American Tobacco Company at Durham, with which he was associated for a number of years in an executive capacity. He came to Richmond in 1911, and has continued to reside here ever since. He had been connected with the British American Tobacco Company and was sent to Richmond to establish Southern headquarters of the company in Richmond, Virginia. He retained this connection until 1916, at which time this corporation business was very much curtailed on account of the World war.

It was in 1917 that Mr. Flowers formed his present connection as executive manager for Liggett & Myers Tobacco Company's plant at Richmond. This plant manufactures cigarettes exclusively, the principal brands being the Chesterfield and Fatima, although a few others are manufactured, including the Richmond Straight Cut, one of the oldest brands of cigarettes in the history of the industry. The Richmond plant of Liggett & Myers, in addition to paying an enormous sum annually to the Federal Government in internal revenue taxes, employs steadily about 1,800 people and constitutes one of the basic industries of Richmond. The buildings are of modern industrial construction, and from an engineering and architectural standpoint represent the best features in industrial efficiency. The working conditions in the plant are as near ideal as it is possible to make them. Every modern convenience is furnished for the employee, including a high-class cafeteria.

Mr. Flowers is a man well fitted for his position, both because of his experience and also on account of his genuine liking for the work. He is a member of the Commonwealth Club, the Country Club of Virginia, and similar organizations, and he is identified generally with the civic affairs of Richmond.

In 1913 Mr. Flowers married Miss Blanche Patton, of Danville, Virginia, and they have two children: George Horace, Jr., and Elizabeth Lacy Flowers. Mrs. Flowers is a daughter of J. Allen and Miss Henry (Crew) Patton, of Danville, and is one of a family of three, Kate Ross Patton, now Mrs. Dr. James Irvin of Danville, Virginia, and Henry Crew Patton, of Danville.

ROBERT BACON WINSTON, JR., is postmaster at Pendletons, in Louisa County. The Winstons and the Bullocks are prominent Virginia families of Colonial ancestry and have been highly influential people in several sections of the state.

Mr. Winston was born at Pendletons, son of Robert Bacon and Sally M. (Bullock) Winston and grandson of William Chamberlayne and Sarah S. (Pollard) Winston. William C. Winston was a planter in Hanover County, owning 845 acres of land in Martin's Parish. The Winstons originally came from Wales and were in America long before the Revolution. William C. Winston died in 1884, and his wife in 1874. Of their eleven children, Robert Bacon Winston, Sr., is the only survivor. He was born September 21, 1842, and was a soldier in the Confederate army, being in the artillery under General Jackson and later under Col. William Nelson. He was badly wounded at the second battle of Cold Harbor. For sixteen years he served as commissioner of revenue of Louisa County, having located in that county in 1876, making his home on the farm of his wife. He now resides with his daughter Nancy. He is a member of the Episcopal Church and a life long Democrat. His wife died in 1906. They were married in March, 1872, and their children were: Harry, who died in 1886; Mrs. Nancy W. Goodwin; Alice P., deceased; Mrs. Norville Pendleton; Sarah C., deceased; Frank Meade, of New York City; and Robert B., Jr.

Robert B. Winston, Jr., was reared and educated in Louisa County, and after leaving school took up merchandising. In 1917 he was appointed postmaster of Pendletons.

Mr. Winston married Miss Elise Trice, of Louisa County, daughter of Robert E. and Mattie (Powell) Trice, and granddaughter of Anderson M. and Elizabeth (Wyatt) Trice. Her grandparents lived in Richmond and her grandfather was a Virginia farmer and planter, served in the Confederate army under General Lee, was active in the Christian Church. He died in 1904, and her grandmother in 1908. Mrs. Winston's father, Robert E. Trice, was born in Louisa County, August 20, 1864, and at an early age took charge of the home plantation. Later he was elected deputy tax collector of Louisa County and for nineteen years was land assessor and for fifteen years deputy sheriff. In connection with his work as a public official he has dealt in real estate and insurance. He is affiliated with the Independent Order of Odd Fellows and the Christian Church. The children in the Trice family were: Inez, wife of Charles Woolfolk; Mrs. Elise Winston; Vivian, Mrs. J. A. Duke, Jr.;

Hazel, Mrs. V. L. Phillips; Robert E., Jr.; Marjorie, wife of E. S. Goodman; Miss Iris; Anderson, who died in 1908; Clarrie, Melvin and Bernice. Mr. and Mrs. Winston have four children: Mattie Larease, born June 28, 1918; Nancy Roberta, born February 10, 1920; Rosalia Mae, born March 18, 1922; and Dorothy Anne, born March 5, 1924.

ELMO G. ALEXANDER. Probably nothing has done so much to give Waynesboro distinction among the cities of Virginia as the church furniture factory, which has just rounded out an existence of a century and has been continuously conducted by one family, four generations of whom have participated in the mechanical skill and artistic taste that have always character-ized the ecclesiastical furniture produced in the Alexander plant.

The business was started in 1828 by Moses Alexander, an old time cabinetmaker, who turned his skill to the making of the simpler forms of church furniture. From that beginning the plant has steadily grown and enlarged until it is one of the largest of its kind in the East. Moses Alexander sold the busi-ness to his brother, William V., about 1834. William V. Alex-ander had located at Waynesboro in 1825. Following William V. came his two sons, Charles W. and Thomas W., as active heads of the firm. Charles W. died in 1919. Thomas W. Alexander many years ago took his son, Elmo G., into the business. A son of Elmo represents the fourth generation of the family in the institution. Thomas Woodard Alexander was identified with the factory from early boyhood until death, taking a great personal interest in every detail of the plant. He was a Demo-crat and in early days active in town affairs, being chief of the fire department and serving on the City Council. He was a Presbyterian. Thomas Woodard Alexander died January 1, 1924, at the age of seventy-eight. He was for four years a Confederate soldier in the Fifty-second Virginia Infantry, and was captured and spent thirteen months in Fort Delaware Prison. While in prison he turned his mechanical ingenuity and skill to account in carving useful articles from bone. Some of these have been preserved by the family, including six knives and forks, six spoons and four pocket knives. Thomas Woodard Alexander married Emma J. Bateman, and they had three chil-dren: Lulu B., wife of Fred C. Jesser, of Covington, Virginia; Elmo G.; and Clarence B., who died in 1912.

Elmo G. Alexander was born at Waynesboro, August 20, 1875. He was educated in local schools, and in 1890, when only fifteen years of age, went to work for his father and has given more than thirty-five years to the Alexander Church Furniture Factory. Mr. Alexander is not only dominated by the standards of good taste and honest workmanship that have been inherit in the institution since it was started, but also possesses the modern spirit of business push and energy, and a constantly enlarging demand has come in recent years for the Alexander output. From 1924 to 1928 the business doubled in volume each year. In a radius of more than a hundred miles around Waynes-boro some of the finest churches exemplify in the furnishings the product of the Alexander factory. At Washington, D. C., two such churches are the Emery Methodist Episcopal and the Tacoma Park Presbyterian. At Richmond churches equipped and furnished by the Alexander Company are the West End Methodist Episcopal, Woodland Heights Methodist Episcopal, and Highland Park Christian. Several other fine churches at

Staunton, Charlottesville, Roanoke and other cities of the state were furnished from the Alexander plant.

Mr. Alexander and family are members of the Waynesboro Presbyterian Church. He has been affiliated since 1896 with Lee Lodge of Masons at Waynesboro, and his son is also a Mason. Elmo G. Alexander married, November 26, 1902, Miss Lula A. Michael, of Rockingham County, daughter of William A. and Molly (Pence) Michael. She was one of a family of four sons and two daughters, five of whom are now living. Mr. and Mrs. Alexander's son, William W., born August 20, 1904, attended the Fishbourne Military School at Waynesboro, completing his work there in 1922, and since then has been connected with the Alexander furniture business.

WILLIAM W. ACKERLY, commonwealth attorney of Rockbridge County, was born in this section of Virginia, and returned here after the World war, in which he had a part overseas, and has enjoyed a very successful career as a practicing attorney at Lexington. He was born at Summers Postoffice, June 15, 1890, son of John P. and Conna Blount (White) Ackerly, and grandson of William Ackerly. His father was born in Rockbridge County, and his mother in Bedford County. John P. Ackerly was a dealer in live stock, well known over Rockbridge County, and served as postmaster during the administration of President McKinley. He died August 4, 1927, at the age of seventy-seven, and his widow now lives in Lexington. She is a member of the Methodist Church, while he was a Presbyterian and belonged to the Independent Order of Odd Fellows. They had a family of seven children, five of whom are living: Mary D., who was reared and educated at Lexington and is now deputy commissioner of revenue; William W.; Lucy P., a teacher in public schools; John P., Jr., in the insurance business; and Eugene. The maternal grandfather of these children was John Milton White, a farmer and tobacco grower of Bedford County.

William W. Ackerly attended local schools and in 1912 was graduated from the law department of Washington and Lee University at Lexington. Instead of beginning practice, he accepted the opportunity to join the editorial staff of the Lawyers Cooperative Publishing Company at Rochester, New York, and spent five years in that work, which was a valuable experience and training, familiarizing him with many points of the law and legal literature that do not ordinarily come within the scope of the average lawyer's experience. While at Rochester he enlisted in the New York National Guard in 1915. He went with the First New York Cavalry to the Mexican border, and in 1917 organized an ammunition train company in New York State. He was with the Twenty-seventh Division overseas, was promoted to captain and took part in all the battles of his division.

After the war Mr. Ackerly returned to Lexington and began the practice of law there June 1, 1921. He was elected commonwealth attorney in November, 1927, and began his term January 1, 1928. His time is fully taken up with his official duties and his general law practice. Captain Ackerly is scout master of the Boy Scouts and served as land assessor of Rockbridge County from 1920 to 1925. He still holds a reserve commission in the Officers Reserve Corps and is prominent in the American

Legion, being a past commander of the post at Lexington and department judge advocate of the American Legion Department of Virginia for three years. He is an honorary member of the Square and Compass fraternity and the Sigma Delta Kappa law fraternity, is a charter member of the Kiwanis Club, a Democrat in politics, is a past master of Mountain City Lodge No. 67, A. F. and A. M., at Lexington, a Royal Arch Mason and member of Lexington Lodge No. 66, Knights of Pythias. Captain Ackerly is a Presbyterian.

LAWRENCE S. DAVIS. Banking institutions of any community are its greatest assets, exercising a tremendous influence in the business and industrial life of its people. The stock is generally held by the influential and solid citizens of the immediate vicinity, and directors are usually outstanding business men locally.

It is because of these facts, and others quite as important, that election to the executive head of a bank is always regarded as a signal honor, because such action sets the seal of approval upon a man as to his business capacity and standing in the community.

Therefore, the election of Lawrence S. Davis as active vice president of the State and City Bank of Roanoke, after his twenty years' service as treasurer of Roanoke, Virginia, is, in itself, a tribute to his ability, integrity and high standing in the community in which he has lived practically his entire life.

Lawrence S. Davis, active vice president of the State and City Bank of Roanoke, Virginia, now resides at 1525 Franklin Road, S. W., Roanoke, Virginia, in the old Lewis homestead, comprising five acres in the city. The original house was built over one hundred fifty years ago and is one of the oldest houses in Southwest Virginia. There are only three links in the chain of title—King George to Tosh family; Tosh to Lewis and Lewis to Sarah Blanche Rorer, wife of Mr. Davis. Mr. Davis was born in Hanover County, Virginia, on December 1, 1873.

His parents, the late Dr. James Waddy Davis and Ann Elizabeth Davis (nee Apperson), were both born in Richmond, Virginia. Doctor Davis attended Richmond College, and after graduation from the Medical College of Virginia, Richmond, at the age of nineteen he was appointed resident physician of Richmond Hospital and at the outbreak of the Civil war volunteered and was made an assistant surgeon in the Confederate army. After the war Doctor Davis moved to Missouri, and later, on account of his health, entered the newspaper business and removed to Roanoke in 1888 as editor of the *Roanoke Daily Times*, the first daily paper published in that city. He remained in this business until he retired. His death occurred in 1924, aged eighty-one years. Mrs. Davis still lives, aged eighty-four years.

There are three children living: Lawrence S., Marshall H. and Mary Emily (wife of James P. Hart, attorney-at-law, Roanoke, Virginia). Doctor Davis was a member of the First Presbyterian Church of the city and Mrs. Davis is a member of the First Baptist Church of Roanoke.

Before coming from Missouri to Roanoke Lawrence S. Davis attended Saint Charles College at Saint Charles, Missouri, and later Allegheny Institute, Roanoke, Virginia. His first work was with Charles Lyle, druggist, then with the *Roanoke Daily*

Times, and then with the Roanoke Trust, Loan and Safe Deposit Company, a leading banking institution at that time. Succeeding to the bank's insurance agency, he entered the general insurance business, which agency was established in 1896 and is now conducted in the name of Davis and Stephenson, Incorporated, at 112 Kirk Avenue, owning one of the most modern insurance office buildings in the South and operating one of the leading agencies in the city.

In 1901 he married Sarah Blanche Rorer, daughter of Patterson Hannah and Nannie McClanahan Rorer, her two grandfathers, Ferdinand Rorer and Elijah McClanahan, owning most of the land upon which Roanoke now stands, Mr. McClanahan owning the famous "Crystal Spring" which supplies Roanoke with water. The old McClanahan homestead (Mountain Home) has recently been razed and the First Presbyterian Church now stands thereon. The old site of the First Presbyterian Church was donated by Ferdinand Rorer. Mrs. Davis is a member of this church.

In 1905 Lawrence S. Davis was elected city treasurer of Roanoke, which position he held continuously, through successive reelections, for twenty years, assuming office January 1, 1906, and retiring January 1, 1926. Upon retirement he was elected vice president of the State and City Bank, which position he now holds.

Mr. Davis is president of Davis and Stephenson, Incorporated, general insurance; vice president of the National Theatre Corporation; secretary-treasurer of the Southwest Virginia Building and Loan Association of Roanoke, Virginia; secretary-treasurer of the Impactograph Corporation of Roanoke, Virginia; director of the Colonial National Bank, Liberty Trust Company, Shenandoah Life Insurance Company and Shenandoah Hotel Corporation, a member of the First Baptist Church and Finance Committee, and the following fraternal orders: Kazim Temple (Shrine), Dokkies, Elks, Knights of Pythias, Independent Order of Red Men.

He is a staunch and loyal Democrat, a member of the Democratic State Central Committee and chairman of the Sixth Congressional District Committee. He was a delegate to the National Democratic Convention at Houston, Texas, and cast one of Virginia's six votes for Hon. Alfred E. Smith.

JOSEPH MALCOLM SAMUELS, farmer, stock raiser and real estate man at Orange, was educated both in technical schools and by practical experience for a career of usefulness in connection with the agricultural life of his home state.

He was born in Rockingham County, Virginia, December 17, 1885. His parents were Joseph W. T. and Elizabeth (Shuler) Samuels. His paternal grandmother was a Taylor, related to the Orange County family of Taylors, one member of which was President Zachary Taylor. Joseph W. T. Samuels graduated in civil engineering from the University of Virginia and gave his active life to the supervision of his extensive farming and planting interests. He died in 1895, and his wife in 1896. They had three children: Ethel M., who married Dr. Ashby Turner; Joseph M.; and Leonidas, who died in infancy.

Joseph M. Samuels was liberally educated. For a year or so he attended the University of Virginia, and left there to take the work of the State Agricultural College, the Virginia Polytechnic Institute at Blacksburg. His father owned a large amount of land and Mr. Samuels took this training with the view to becoming a breeder of blooded stock. Since early manhood he has specialized in the breeding of Holstein and Jersey cattle and Berkshire hogs, and is one of the recognized authorities on these strains in his district. He owns and operates the old homestead, and since 1913 has been a dealer in real estate, specializing in the handling of farm land in the rich agricultural section of which Orange is the center. Mr. Samuels is a Royal Arch Mason, is secretary of the Orange County Chamber of Commerce, and a member of the Rotary Club.

He married, May 26, 1916, Miss Reba E. Crumpacker, of Montgomery County, Virginia, daughter of Charles A. and Ella (Byerly) Crumpacker. Her parents are still living on their farm in Montgomery County. They had three children: Mary, wife of A. A. Fletcher, of Washington; Mrs. Samuels; and Charlsie, wife of Dr. J. B. Lester, of Richmond. Mr. and Mrs. Samuels have four children: Joseph Taylor, born September 11, 1917; Jaquelin Earl, born January 27, 1920; Reba Elizabeth, born February 1, 1923; and Dorothy, born December 20, 1925.

GEORGE MCDUFFIE BLAKE is one of the old and honored residents of Louisa County, living at the Louisa Courthouse, where he is in the farm and insurance business and devotes his time to the editorial management of the *Central Virginian*.

Mr. Blake was born in Mathews County, Virginia, February 10, 1859. His parents, John H. and Emily A. (Lumpkin) Blake, were residents of Mathews County. His father was a country gentleman, was educated at William and Mary College, and during the '50s represented Mathews and Gloucester counties in the State Legislature. He was a Confederate soldier three years, and was captured and was a prisoner of war for some time. He was an ardent Democrat and member of the Masonic fraternity. Of his four sons, the two now living are James Polk, a merchant at Richmond, and George M. Rev. Eugene was a minister of the Methodist Episcopal Church, South, and died in Tennessee in 1926, and the other son, John D., was an eminent surgeon and practiced many years at Baltimore.

George McDuffie Blake attended public schools in Baltimore, to which city the family moved in 1870. For two sessions he attended a private school conducted by Rev. George Frazier in Russell County, Virginia. Mr. Blake spent many years as a business man at Richmond, developing a very prosperous grocery establishment. When he sold out in 1917 he bought a farm near Louisa, and since the World war has lived in the town engaged in fire insurance and real estate business. Later he bought the *Central Virginian,* the only newspaper in the county, and is its editor and owner. Through his newspaper and individually he takes a prominent part in Democratic politics. Mr. Blake is a member of the Royal Arcanum. He was a member of the Board of Aldermen in Richmond for four years.

Mr. Blake married, in 1882, Miss Emma Walters, of Richmond. She is a graduate of the Richmond High School. Her father, William A. Walters, was a Richmond merchant. Of the same family was James A. Walters, a local editor of the *Richmond Whig,* and who acted as second to Col. William C. Elam, a prominent Whig, in his duel with Col. Thomas Smith of Fauquier County. Mr. and Mrs. Blake have one daughter, Emily, wife of Emmett C. Cottrell, a coal merchant at Richmond. Mr.

and Mrs. Cottrell have a daughter, Ann, born in 1917. All of the family are members of the Episcopal Church.

HENRY FRANCIS PRIEST. Since Colonial times members of the Priest family have lived in Orange County. They have been planters and business men, solid and substantial citizens, home owners and upholders of the best social traditions of the locality.

The cashier of the Citizens National Bank of Orange, Henry Francis Priest, is a representative of the fourth generation of the family. He was born in Orange County, March 28, 1883, son of Henry Clark and Ida (Irving) Priest. His grandfather, Augustus G. Priest, at one time owned Clark Mountain in Orange County, and it was there that Henry Clark Priest was born. Henry Clark Priest is still living on his old homestead on the Rapidan River, and has spent his life as a farmer and planter. Augustus G. Priest was a soldier in the Confederate army under General Longstreet. The five children of Henry Clark Priest and wife are: William G., Henry Francis, Lena Payton, Blanche and Ethel. All are unmarried and all reside at home except Henry Francis and Blanche, the latter of whom is a school teacher.

Henry Francis Priest, after completing the work of the home schools, attended a business college at Richmond, and gained his early practical commercial training in a dry goods store at Orange. Following that he was in the freight department of the Southern Railway at Orange, and since 1911 all his business time has been devoted to the Citizens National Bank. He became bookkeeper, later assistant cashier and teller, and in 1917 was elected cashier by the Board of Directors. Mr. Priest is a Knight Templar Mason and an elder in the Presbyterian Church.

JAMES AUBREY KENT, county treasurer of Louisa County, has been a figure in the business and political life of that section for a quarter of a century.

He was born in Fluvanna County, Virginia, January 8, 1865, son of James M. and Elizabeth F. (Parrish) Kent. His mother was born in Louisa County. James M. Kent was a farmer and in 1845 organized a general store. That store became a community center in Fluvanna County and has ever since been known as Kents Store. James M. Kent was a soldier in the Confederate army under General Pickett. He was an influential Democrat, and while never holding office did a great deal of work to build up the party and secured organized support for the movement for the refunding of the state debt in early days. He died in 1883, at the age of sixty-five, and his wife passed away March 21, 1917, aged ninety-seven. They had nine children, but seven of them died during a diphtheria epidemic in 1873. The two survivors are James Aubrey and George H., the latter still a resident of Kents Store.

James Aubrey Kent attended local schools, and graduated from the Loisdale Academy in 1883. For twenty years he was associated with his father's business. In 1903 he located at Louisa and was in the drug business with Doctors Barrett and Woolfolk until 1920, when he sold his mercantile interests. Mr. Kent has been identified with several banks, beginning with the Farmers and Merchants Bank of Mineral, and later with its offshoot, the Farmers and Merchants Bank of Louisa. He is

now a director in the Bank of Louisa and has handled a considerable business in real estate.

Mr. Kent was elected county treasurer of Louisa County in 1923, and is now serving his second term in that office, having been reelected in 1927. He is a Democrat, member of the Independent Order of Odd Fellows and Methodist Episcopal Church, South. Mr. Kent married, in 1902, Miss Cora Bell, daughter of Ashley J. and Hardenia (Leslie) Bell, of Charlottesville. Her father, a Confederate veteran and for many years a merchant, died in 1896. Her mother died in 1902. Mrs. Kent was one of a family of six children, five of whom are living.

JOHN C. HALEY. The railroad industry created a calling entirely unknown a century ago. Its early members learned their art not in school or from books, but in the office and workshop or out on the road, in daily contact with the problems they had to face. So with them who followed the pioneers. They have had no precedents to guide them, but have worked out the problems which their employments brought in the school of experience. The railroad contractors deal with values of many figures and dispose of stupendous interests. The learned professions, as they are recognized by immemorial custom, attached a certain dignity to their practitioners from the nature and difficulty of the subjects with which they deal. The railroad contractor of modern times rises above these professions, perhaps, in the value of the interests which he conducts, as well as in the grasp of intellect and varied and high accomplishments which his calling exacts. The outside public accepts the results of his genius, it learns from time to time of his attainments, with little conception of the vast problems and intricate relations which these grand results involve.

John C. Haley, of the firm of W. W. Boxley & Company of Roanoke, belongs to this difficult profession, and by his skill and energy has placed himself among its leaders. In the school of practical experience he has wrought out its complex problems, and through his own efforts has gained recognition and position. He was born in Louisa County, Virginia, June 5, 1872, and is a son of Littleberry James and Mary (Long) Haley. Littleberry James Haley was born in Kentucky, where he received good educational advantages, later attending Richmond College and the University of Virginia, and being prepared for the Baptist ministry, of which he was a member for more than half a century. He was still a youth when the war between the states came on, and enlisted in the Confederate army, in which he became a chaplain. At the close of the struggle he returned to his ministerial duties in Louisa County, where he became one of the leading and prominent men of his community. A Democrat in his political convictions, he took an active part in public life, and at one time represented his county in the State Legislature. He likewise was an earnest and helpful friend of the cause of education, and for some years served in the capacity of superintendent of public instruction. He lived a long, full and useful life, and died in Louisa County, the funeral services being conducted under the auspices of the Masons, of which order he had long been a member. Mrs. Haley, who was born in Virginia, died in Louisa County. They were the parents of eight children, of whom four are living, John C. having been the seventh in order of birth.

John C. Haley attended Haley High School at Louisa Court House, Virginia, following which he pursued a business course at Eastman's National Business College, Poughkeepsie, New York. His first employment was as a bookkeeper at the stockyards in West Virginia, but he left that position to become identified with the old firm of Boxley, Carpenter & Haley, who were among the early concerns engaged in railway construction. He has been with this concern ever since, and is now a member of the firm which is known as W. W. Boxley & Company, having been admitted in 1910. The business is that of railroad contracting and stone crushing, and the business extends all over the State of Virginia and into other communities, having constructed many miles of railroad and also having furnished the crushed stone for long stretches of highways, etc. Mr. Haley occupies a prominent position among the capable and energetic business men of Roanoke, where he has other interests, being secretary and treasurer of the Roanoke Webster Brick Company and chairman of the Board of Directors of the State and City Bank. He is a self-made man in all that the expression implies, and his success is thus all the more impressive. Mr. Haley is a member of the First Baptist Church of Roanoke and of the Board of Deacons thereof, and also a member of the Board of Trustees. He is a Scottish Rite Mason and member of the Mystic Shrine, and belongs also to the Shenandoah Club and the Country Club. He votes the Democratic ticket, but takes only a good citizen's interest in political affairs and elections.

In 1895 Mr. Haley was united in marriage with Miss Flossie Chisholm, who was born in Louisa County, Virginia, and to this union there has been born one son, Edward Allen, who was educated in the Virginia Military Institute and the University of Virginia, and is now engaged in railway construction work with his father's firm. He married Elizabeth Ambler, and they are the parents of one son, Edward Allen, Jr. He is a member of the First Baptist Church, and Mr. Haley belongs to the local lodge of the Masonic fraternity.

ELIJAH D. DURRETTE is a native son of Greene County, has been long identified with the agricultural interests of that section, and his activity in politics has brought him several official honors and responsibilities. He is the present county treasurer of Greene County, with home at Standardsville.

He was born in Greene County, July 23, 1858, son of Elijah C. and Mariah (Miller) Durrette, natives of the same county. He was their only child. His father was a farmer, owning a splendid place of 700 acres, which is still in the family. He cultivated a large area in tobacco, and during the Civil war managed his farm in intensive production of foodstuff for the Confederate government. He was a Democrat and member of the Baptist Church, and died in 1899, while the mother of Elijah D. Durrette passed away in 1860, when he was two years old.

Mr. Durrette attended school at Standardsville, and since early manhood his time has been taken up with the duties of the home farm. Mr. Durrette for several years served as land assessor. In 1927 he was elected county treasurer, succeeding W. B. Cole in that office. Mr. Durrette is a Democrat, member of the Independent Order of Odd Fellows, and in the Baptist Church at Standardsville is clerk of the church and a teacher in the Sunday School.

He married, November 26, 1884, Miss Addie Beazley, of Greene County. Her father, Wyatt S. Beazley, was for many years judge of the Greene County Circuit Court and one of the eminent men of the county. He died in 1881, and her mother in 1895. Mrs. Durrette was the oldest of four children. Her sister Carrie Lee is Mrs. Carneal, of Richmond; Mary Jane married Thomas Durrette, of Richmond, and Dr. Wyatt S. Beazley also lives at Richmond.

Mr. and Mrs. Durrette have a family of five children. Mary Lee is the wife of R. B. Alport, of Richmond, and has two children, Robert and Marion. Dolly is the wife of F. Miller Garman, and her four children are Miletus, Addie Lee, Elizabeth, and E. D. The son Davis Durrette lives in Oakland, California, Frank is at Richmond, and Wyatt is on the home farm.

CAPT. MONTGOMERY BEVERLEY CORSE is an alumnus of the Virginia Military Institute who has been closely identified with that great school for many years and in different capacities. Captain Corse is a Lexington business man and has long been a community leader there.

He was born at Alexandria, Virginia, May 8, 1866, son of Montgomery D. and Elizabeth (Beverley) Corse. On both sides he represents old and honored family names in Virginia. The Corse family is of French origin, the name originally being spelled DeCoursey. Elizabeth Beverley was born in Fauquier County. Montgomery D. Corse was also a native of Alexandria, and lived a life replete with experience and achievement, and was greatly beloved by a wide circle of friends. He went out to California in 1849, having prior to that time been a captain in the Mexican war. When he returned from California in 1856 he engaged in the banking business at Alexandria with his father, John M. Corse. Not long afterward Virginia seceded and on account of his previous war experience he was commissioned a major in command of the Alexander Battalion and later was colonel of the Seventeenth Virginia Infantry, and after that he commanded Corse's Brigade in General Pickett's Division. He participated in some of the great battles of the war. He was three times wounded, and a short time before Appomattox he was captured and was held in Warren Prison in Boston Harbor until paroled. After the war he resumed banking. His firm was styled the Corse Brothers, Bankers and Brokers, a prominent financial institution in Northern Virginia. General Corse lived retired for a number of years before his death, which occurred in December, 1894. He survived his wife only a few weeks. He was born in 1815 and was nearly eighty years of age when he passed away. His children were: Montgomery B.; Virginia and William, both deceased; and Elizabeth, wife of Dr. Reid White, a prominent physician of Lexington.

Capt. Montgomery Beverley Corse was graduated from the Virginia Military Institute in 1885. During the following four years he was an instructor in the Fishbourne Military School at Waynesboro. For two years he pursued a special course in chemistry under Doctor Mallet at the University of Virginia, finishing in 1891. For three years he practiced as analytical chemist at Roanoke. In 1894, returning to Lexington, he was an instructor in the Virginia Military Institute until 1898. Captain Corse then bought the McCrum Drug Store interests, which was later incorporated into the McCrum Drug Company, and has been its president since its foundation. He is also president of the McCrum Creamery. He was for a number of years a director of the Rockbridge National Bank, and in addition he is a director of the Huger Davidson Sale Company, wholesale grocers.

While he was a teacher in the Virginia Military Institute he held the commission of captain of engineers, conferred by the governor of Virginia. He was appointed a member of the Board of Visitors of the Virginia Military Institute by three governors, Governors Mann, Trinkle and Byrd. He is secretary of the V. M. I. Alumni Association, is a past president of the local Rotary Club, served sixteen years as a member of the City Council, and during the World war was chairman of Liberty Loan campaigns and also chairman of the Rockbridge County Red Cross. He is president of the Chamber of Commerce, member of the Episcopal Church, a Democrat, and belongs to the Kappa Alpha college fraternity.

Captain Corse married, December 10, 1897, Miss Elise Semmes, daughter of Thomas M. and Louisa (Brockenborough) Semmes. Her grandfather, Judge John M. Brockenborough, was responsible for founding the law department of the Washington and Lee University. Her father, Thomas M. Semmes, was for many years a professor in the Virginia Military Institute. Captain and Mrs. Corse have one son, Thomas Semmes, born July 3, 1911.

CEYLON GREY QUESENBERY is practicing law in his native town of Waynesboro, Augusta County, and when he returned to that community after graduating from law school he found a busy routine of opportunities for useful service awaiting him.

He was born at Waynesboro, September 12, 1901. His parents, Thomas W. and Willie Lee (Barger) Quesenbery, are residents of Waynesboro, where his father for many years has been in the grocery business, conducting the Standard Grocery Company. The family of Mr. Quesenbery has been in Virginia since Colonial times, and there were representatives of it in the War of the Revolution as well as in the Confederate army. Thomas W. Quesenbery is a Democrat and has filled various offices in Waynesboro, having been a member of the council for many years. There were three children: Erceldean, who died in 1902; William D., a furniture merchant at Waynesboro; and Ceylon Grey.

Ceylon Grey Quesenbery attended school at Waynesboro as a boy and took his law course at the University of Virginia. He was graduated in 1923 and was licensed to practice law September 12, 1922. In half a dozen years he has proven his abilities as a capable and resourceful attorney and has had a very fine general practice. He is a director of the Citizens-Waynesboro Bank and Trust Company, has served as secretary of the local Chamber of Commerce, and later as a director of that organization, and is the present mayor of Waynesboro, having been elected June 7, 1926. Mr. Quesenbery is a Democrat, is a member of the Masonic Lodge at Waynesboro and the First Presbyterian Church.

He married, September 12, 1924, on his twenty-third birthday, Miss Esther Porter, of Rochester, New York. Her parents, George J. and Ada (Garland) Porter, now reside at Chester, Pennsylvania. Her father was in the planing mill business at

Rochester for many years, and after selling out retired and lives with his son Paul at Chester, Pennsylvania. His other son, William H., also lives at Chester. Mr. and Mrs. Quesenbery have one son, Ceylon G., Jr., born August 24, 1925.

L. J. BOXLEY. Prominently identified with the business life of Roanoke as a member of one of its old, enterprising and reliable establishments is L. J. Boxley, of W. W. Boxley & Company, railroad contractors and stone crushers. While his career has been passed entirely with one concern, and therefore is not as varied as those of men who have been identified with various lines of activity in far separated cities and in diversified occupations, it has been sufficiently engaging and interesting to entertain his entire thoughts and to develop inherent business talents. In spite of this engrossment, however, Mr. Boxley has found the time and opportunity to devote to civic affairs, and is accounted one of the constructive and public spirited men of the city of his adoption.

Mr. Boxley was born December 25, 1887, in Louisa County, Virginia, and is a son of W. W. Boxley, for many years a well-known citizen of Roanoke, a review of whose career appears elsewhere in this work. L. J. Boxley was given good educational advantages in his youth, including a course at Fishburne Military School in Augusta County, following his graduation from which he entered Washington and Lee University, from which institution he was graduated as a member of the class of 1909. Immediately thereafter he joined his father in the old firm of Carpenter and Boxley, who were among the early concerns of Virginia engaged in railway construction. In 1910 the name of the firm was changed to W. W. Boxley & Company, its present style, its offices being located in the Boxley Building. The business is that of railroad construction and rock crushing, and the activities of the concern extend all over the State of Virginia and into adjoining communities, the firm having constructed many miles of railroads and furnished crushed stone for countless miles of highways, etc. L. J. Boxley at this time is in full charge of all of the stone crushing activities of the company, and has made a close and careful study of this subject. He is conversant with the working of every piece of machinery and equipment used in this important branch, and is accounted one of the best informed men in the state on matters pertaining to his line of work. Mr. Boxley has various other business interests and is a member of the Board of Directors of the Colonial National Bank and the Liberty Trust Company. With his family he belongs to St. John's Episcopal Church, and he also belongs to the Shenandoah Club and Country Club of Roanoke, the Commonwealth Club of Richmond and the Pi Kappa Alpha fraternity. He has charge of four great stone crushers, one each at Pembroke, Blue Ridge, Pounding Mill and Emporia, Virginia.

In 1914 Mr. Boxley was united in marriage with Miss Margaret Waddey, who was born at Richmond, Virginia, and educated in the schools of that city and at Sweet Briar, this state, and to this union there have been born four children: Margaret Francis, who is attending public school; Caroline; L. J., Jr., and William W. II. Mr. and Mrs. Boxley occupy a pleasant modern home at Roanoke, which is the scene of numerous social gatherings. Mrs. Boxley is active in club and civic work and in the movements and enterprises of St. John's Episcopal Church.

REID WHITE, M. D. The university community of Lexington
for many years has cherished the name White as representative of some of the best citizenships, intellectual ideals and personal character. One member of the family at the present time
is Dr. Reid White, a talented physician and surgeon, who has
combined with his profession an active leadership in all matters
pertaining to the growth and progress of his home city.

Doctor White, whose offices are at 22 West Washington
Street, was born at Lexington, March 28, 1868, son of James
Jones and Mary Louisa (Reid) White and grandson of Dr.
William Spottswood White and Samuel McDowell Reid. Dr.
William Spottswood White was a minister of the Presbyterian
Church and for many years was pastor of what is known as
Stonewall Jackson's Church at Lexington. That was his last
charge. He was also prominent in the Hanover District Pres-
bytery. Doctor White died in 1875. His wife was Jane Watt,
of Hanover County. The maternal grandfather of Doctor White,
Samuel McDowell Reid, was born at Lexington, descended from
Samuel McDowell, one of the first settlers of Rockbridge County.
Samuel McDowell Reid was clerk of the County Court thirty
years, succeeding in that office his father, Andrew Reid, who
had been clerk of the county for fifty years. Samuel McDowell
Reid married Sally Hare, connected with the distinguished
Cabell family of Virginia.

James Jones White was for forty years professor of Greek
at Washington and Lee University. He was a graduate of the
University of Virginia with the class of 1851 and the following
year took up his duties at the old Washington College, serving
that institution up to the time of the war and afterwards during the presidency of General Lee and after it became Washington and Lee University. In 1861 he organized a company
of soldiers from students at the college, was elected its captain,
became a member of Stonewall Jackson's Brigade, but owing
to physical disability had to retire before the close of the war.
He died in 1893. He and his wife had the following children:
Sally Hare, widow of Helm Bruce, an attorney; Isabell, widow
of W. G. Brown, who was professor of chemistry at the University of Missouri at Columbia; Agnes, wife of Joel W. Golsby,
a judge of Mobile, Alabama; McDowell, who died in infancy;
William C., who died when thirty years old; and Doctor Reid.

Dr. Reid White was educated at Washington and Lee University and took his medical course at the University of Pennsylvania at Philadelphia, graduating in 1892. After eighteen
months of service as an interne in the Saint Agnes Hospital at
Philadelphia he returned to Lexington, and has been going about
in the performance of his duties in that community since 1893,
a period of thirty-five years. Doctor White for many years has
served as college physician to Washington and Lee University.
He is a member of the Rockbridge County Medical Society,
Medical Society of Virginia, the Southern and American Medical
Associations. During the World war he was a major in the
Army Medical Corps, and had charge of the medical members
of the Draft Board of Virginia with the designation of Medical
Aide to the Governor of Virginia.

Doctor White from 1908 to 1919 served as a member of the
Virginia Board of Health. He was a member of the Lexington
City Council seventeen years and has given his time and in-

fluence generously in behalf of the community's educational and public health interests.

Doctor White married, October 22, 1895, Lucy Waddell Preston, daughter of Dr. Thomas Louis and Lucy (Waddell) Preston. Her father was a Doctor of Divinity and for many years pastor of the Lexington Presbyterian Church, and died in 1894. Doctor Preston and wife had seven children, three of whom are now living. Mrs. White passed away in 1912. Her children were: Thomas Preston, a practicing physician at Charlotte, North Carolina; James Jones, who died March 5, 1927; Reid, Jr., a physician at Lexington, who served as an interne at the Philadelphia Hospital; and Lucy Preston, a student in the University of Pennsylvania Hospital Nurses School. Two of the sons, Thomas and James, were in the Tank Corps during the World war, being sent overseas to France. James J. was taken ill while overseas but died a number of years after returning home. The son Thomas P. White married Henrietta Tucker, daughter of Congressman Tucker from this district, and their son, James J. White, is a grandson of Doctor White.

In 1916 Doctor White married Mrs. Elizabeth Beverly Murdaugh, of Delaplane, Virginia, daughter of Gen. Montgomery Corse and a sister of Capt. M. B. Corse, of Lexington. By her first marriage she had two children: Albert C. Murdaugh, a graduate of the Annapolis Naval Academy, now a lieutenant in the United State Navy; and Montgomery B. Murdaugh, whose home is at Memphis, Tennessee.

MARSHALL TATE VADEN is a physician and surgeon, a professional man of thorough training and exceptional accomplishments, who has made himself an indispensable factor in the community of Buena Vista, in Rockbridge County.

Doctor Vaden was born at Chatham, Virginia, September 29, 1887, son of Giles Henry and Carrie (Tate) Vaden and grandson of Robert W. and Mary Reaves (Adams) Vaden and William Carrington and Maria Louise (Whitehead) Tate. Robert W. Vaden was born April 6, 1828, in Halifax County, was in the commissary department of the Confederate government during the war and died September 18, 1874.

Giles Henry Vaden, who died January 15, 1926, became one of the largest lumber operators in Virginia. He was active in that business for over thirty years. For two terms he was county treasurer of Pittsylvania County and was accorded well earned leadership in the Democratic party and in civic affairs. His widow is still living. Their ten children were: Ella Katherine, born January 16, 1881; Robert Carrington, born October 5, 1882; Irene White, born October 5, 1884; Marshall Tate, born September 29, 1887; Giles Henry, Jr., born October 29, 1889; Herbert Wentworth, born April 22, 1892; Harold Elmo, born December 24, 1894, and died February 16, 1928; Carrie Louise, born March 7, 1898; Thomas Hunt, born June 5, 1900; and Madaline, born July 13, 1902. In the paternal ancestry the Easley family is related to the Stone family, the founder of which was Col. John Stone, a London banker, who formed a little colony of his own and brought it out to Virginia, settling on the James River in 1620.

Mr. Marshall Tate Vaden was educated in high school, the Fork Union Military Academy, and the Chatham Training School, a military institution, where he graduated in 1909. He

then entered the University of Michigan and received his pre-
medical training at Richmond College, now the University of
Richmond. He received his M. D. degree at the Medical Col-
lege of Virginia at Richmond with the class of 1915. Doctor
Vaden was an interne in the Virginia Hospital in 1915-16, prac-
ticed about a year at Fairfield, and since then has given Buena
Vista the full benefit of his professional services. He is surgeon
for the Chesapeake & Ohio Railway, assistant surgeon to the
Norfolk & Western Railway, and during the World war was a
member of the Volunteer Medical Corps. Doctor Vaden is a
Phi Kappa Sigma and Phi-Chi, member of Buena Vista Lodge
No. 186, A. F. and A. M., and the Baptist Church.

He married, August 26, 1915, Miss Ellen Byrd Polland,
daughter of Chapman Taylor and Jerusha Jane (Carlton) Polland. Her father spent many years in the service of the Chesapeake & Ohio Railway at Richmond. He died in 1916, and her
mother in 1898. Mrs. Vaden has only one living sister, Mary,
who resides with Doctor and Mrs. Vaden, who have no children.

RICHARD OLIN BAGBY, of Buena Vista, is an educator and
school man whose qualifications include beside his natural gift a
long experience and contact with schools in both the West and
Middlewest.

Mr. Bagby is a native of North Carolina, born at Jonesville
January 17, 1882, son of Zack Taylor and Roxana (Mastin)
Bagby. The Bagby family is of English ancestry, and he is
descended from one of three brothers who came to America and
landed at Norfolk in Colonial times. Zack Taylor Bagby was
in early life a teacher, a farmer, engaged in raising beef cattle,
and sheep, and for over forty years conducted a photographic
studio at Jonesville. He was a member of the school board there
and always a staunch Democrat. His death occurred February
19, 1918, and the widowed mother now makes her home at
Laurens, Iowa. Their children were: Lillian, wife of G. C.
Smith, of Portsmouth, Virginia; Richard O.; Dr. William A.,
deceased; Nellie, wife of W. R. Ward, of Forest Hill, Maryland;
Zack T., Jr., of Antigo, Wisconsin; Mabel, wife of Edward
Whannel, of Laurens, Iowa; Sina, wife of Taylor Johnson, of
Bluefield, West Virginia; Paul T., of Sioux City, Iowa; Ella May,
wife of John Cowan, of Laurens, Iowa; and Ralph, also of
Laurens.

Richard Olin Bagby has had the benefit of educational opportunities in many institutions of learning. He first attended
school at Jonesville, North Carolina, in 1905 was graduated from
Trinity Park High School, now Duke University, at Durham,
North Carolina. He spent one year at the University of Indiana,
and three years in the State Teachers College at Cedar Falls,
Iowa, where he took his A. B. Degree. During 1911-13 he was a
graduate student at the University of Chicago, and after one
year at Columbia University in New York obtained his Master's
Degree. Among other schools he attended were those at Clarksville and Hartley, Iowa, Fulda and Long Prairie, Minnesota.
Mr. Bagby during these years has been a teacher, principal and
superintendent of schools in various states from North Carolina
to Iowa. He was assistant professor of education in the College
of William and Mary at Williamsburg, Virginia, and also had
charge of the public schools there.

F. W. Kling

He has been at Buena Vista since 1923, superintendent of the grade and high schools. In 1924 Buena Vista completed a handsome school building providing twenty-five rooms and other facilities for modern school work.

Mr. Bagby married, August 15, 1912, Myrtha Smith, of North Carolina, daughter of Dr. James Buchanan and Emma (Reisson) Smith. The other children of her parents were: James R., of Pilot Mountain, North Carolina; Gertrude, wife of Bud Hiatt, of Miami, Florida; Minnie, wife of Benjamin Hoggard, of Aulander, North Carolina; and Warren, now deceased. Mr. and Mrs. Bagby have two children, Frances Weston, born January 21, 1915, and James Taylor, born December 24, 1919.

FREDERICK W. KLING. While Frederick W. Kling has been a resident of Roanoke for more than thirty years, and among the city's most enterprising and substantial citizens, his business interests have been so extensive and widespread as to entitle him to claim identity with the great state of Virginia. He has been for twenty-three years identified with the lumber interests of the state, and as vice president and treasurer of the Adams, Payne & Gleaves Company is one of the most extensive manufacturers and largest dealers in lumber and supplies among the many enterprising men whose vigor and energy have made that one of the leading industries of the state.

Mr. Kling was born at Philadelphia, Pennsylvania, in 1876, and is a son of Francis and Kate A. (Benning) Kling. His paternal grandfather was Francis Kling, who was born at Kaiserlauten, Germany, and immigrated to the United States soon after his marriage, settling at Philadelphia, Pennsylvania, where he spent the remainder of an honorable life working as a mechanic. Francis Kling was born at Philadelphia, where he received a public school education, and inherited his father's love of mechanics. Throughout his career he has been engaged in mechanical work, and is now practically retired and makes his home at Roanoke. Mrs. Kling, who also survives, was born in Philadelphia, a daughter of Julius Benning, who was born in Prussia. Mr. and Mrs. Kling are faithful and active members of the Lutheran Church, and have been the parents of five children, of whom three survive: Frederick W., of this review; Mrs. Samuel I. Glasser, the wife of a mechanic of Allentown, Pennsylvania; and George L., an accountant of Rocky Mount, North Carolina.

The educational training of Frederick W. Kling was acquired in the public schools of Philadelphia and Allentown, Pennsylvania, and his first employment was as a clerk in a store. His position did not seem to offer much chance for advancement, and accordingly he came to Roanoke to serve a three-year apprenticeship to the patternmaker's trade. When this was completed he entered the employ of Robert H. Angell as a bookkeeper in the Central Manufacturing Company, a concern with which he was identified for ten years, or until 1906, when the Adams, Payne & Gleaves Company came into existence. Mr. Kling at that time joined the new concern in the capacity of bookkeeper, and has remained with it ever since, winning well merited promotion through integrity, ability and fidelity to his present position as vice president and treasurer. His career adds another to the thousands of illustrations that Virginia has furnished to the

world of the grand results which are attained by intelligence,
tact and perseverance when applied to the building up of a
great business under the favoring conditions which have
attended the state's enterprises. It is true that during this
period unusual opportunities have opened to business men, but
they have only yielded the meed of great success to those who
have the sagacity to perceive them and the boldness to push
them to their best results. The high position which Mr. Kling
occupies in business circles and in the esteem and confidence
of his associates is shown in the fact that he was president of
the Virginia State Retail Lumber, Building and Supply Merchants Association, and is a past president of the Retail
Merchants Association of Roanoke. He is a Scottish Rite Mason
and Shriner, and a past master of Virginia Heights Lodge No.
324, A. F. and A. M., and likewise belongs to the United Commercial Travelers. He takes a keen interest in all civic affairs
and for several years has been a director of the Chamber of
Commerce. With his family he belongs to the Lutheran Church.

In 1905 Mr. Kling was united in marriage with Miss Anna
Carrier, who was born at Marion, Smyth County, Virginia, and
educated at Marion Female College, and to this union there have
been born five children: Frederick W., Jr., a gradaute of Roanoke High School and Roanoke College, where he was a member
of the varsity football team, now a teacher in the high school at
Buena Vista, Virginia; Mildred, a graduate of high school, who
spent three years at the State Normal School, and is now a
teacher in the public schools of Roanoke; Lois, a graduate of
high school, who is attending the State Normal School; and
David and Wiley, at school.

GEORGE WILSON POE was a veteran official in the service of
the Chesapeake & Ohio Railway at Richmond and lived in that
city practically all of his life.

He was born at Richmond September 8, 1850, son of Major
John and Cornelia (Williams) Poe. His father was for many
years prominent in the civic affairs of Richmond, serving as
chief of police of that city for many years. He held the rank
of major in the Confederate army during the Civil war.

George Wilson Poe was the oldest in a family of fourteen
children. He was reared and educated at Richmond, attending
the public schools and also a private school, and was first
engaged in work as a clerk for the Lottier Tobacco Company.
He resigned because of the effect on his health, and on April
7, 1874, entered the service of the Chesapeake & Ohio Railway
Company. In 1880 he was promoted to chief clerk in charge
of passenger accounts, and subsequently became auditor of passenger traffic, the position he filled from November 15, 1897,
until December 31, 1916. At his own request he was retired
with a pension, but for a number of years had a desk and spent
several hours daily at his old office.

Mr. Poe died September 25, 1922, at the age of seventy-two
years. While he found his work as a railroad man the chief
medium for the expression of his energy and spirit of service,
he also cultivated other interests. He was a great home man,
was for fifty years identified with the various Masonic bodies,
being master of Temple Lodge No. 9, A. F. and A. M., in 1880-81,
held honorary posts in the Masonic bodies, was high priest of
Washington Chapter No. 9, Royal Arch Masons, in 1888-89,

eminent commander of Commandery of St. Andrew, Knights Templar, in 1886-87, was a member of the Mystic Shrine and was grand high priest of the Grand Royal Arch Chapter of Virginia in 1894-95. He voted as a Democrat, but was never a seeker for public office.

Mr. Poe was a loyal churchman and a thorough Christian in his daily activities as well as in his profession. For forty years he was a member of the Broad Street Methodist Episcopal Church, South, and served his church as a steward.

Mr. Poe married November 19, 1879, Miss Lucy Keesee. They were married in the Broad Street Methodist Church by Rev. Mr. Van Derslice. Her father for forty years was secretary and treasurer of Gallego Mills, now the Dunlap Mills, at Richmond. The late Mr. Poe found the finest rewards of a long life in the shelter of his own home. He was a host of boundless grace and courtesy. He loved his home with a passion. Upon his strong arm and heart his devoted wife leaned with complete trust and dependence. Their lives were complements. There was in each a response to the deepest in the nature of the other. Complete unity and affection reigned in their home. They walked arm in arm, companions of a perfect understanding. They lived each for the other. In the home he lived to make fuller and completer the heart and life of his companion of many years.

REV. ROBERT WILBUR COUSAR is one of the prominent younger ministers of the Presbyterian Church in Virginia, and has found a congenial field of usefulness for his talents and abilities in the church at Waynesboro, Augusta County.

He was born in South Carolina, December 31, 1897, son of James E. and Lenora (Muldrow) Cousar. His mother's family came from Scotland to America in 1790. His grandfather, James A. Cousar, was a Presbyterian minister and during the Civil war was a chaplain in the Confederate army. The maternal grandfather, William J. Muldrow, was in the commissary department of the Confederacy, and a great-uncle, John Bradley, held the rank of colonel in the armies of the South. Rev. Mr. Cousar's parents are living in South Carolina, where his father is a cotton planter. There were four sons, James E. Jr., George Richard, Robert W. and John B., all of whom have trained for professional careers. John is now a student in the medical department of the University of Virginia. James E., Jr., a Presbyterian minister, now located at St. Albans, West Virginia, was a missionary to Japan during 1923-24. George Richard Cousar was in the Aviation Corps during the World war, training at Camp Dix, New Jersey, and at Kelly Field, Texas, and is now a medical missionary located at Lubondi, in the Belgian Congo of Africa.

Robert Wilbur Cousar graduated from Davidson College, in North Carolina, in 1918. He completed his work in the Union Theological Seminary at Richmond in 1922, and shortly after graduation was called as pastor to the Presbyterian Church at Cradock, Virginia. He remained there until June, 1926, and since that date has been pastor of the First Presbyterian Church of Waynesboro, which is prospering and broadening its service as a community center in every way.

Rev. Mr. Cousar married, October 10, 1923, Miss Irving Blanton, of Farmville, Virginia. Her mother, Martha King Bugg, died many years ago. Her father is a retired merchant

and farmer, Charles William Blanton, of Farmville, Virginia.
Mrs. Cousar is one of a family of three sons and four daughters.
Rev. Mr. and Mrs. Cousar have two sons, Robert W., Jr., born
December 4, 1924, and John Burton, born November 16, 1926.

CLINTON WEBB IV was an insurance man at Richmond and
rounded out a successful career in that city. He was a native
of Georgia, born at Atlanta June 16, 1869. He established his
home at Richmond in 1901, and lived there until his death in
July, 1916.

His parents were Clinton and Matilda Webb, both natives
of Atlanta, Georgia. His father was prominent in Georgia politics and was a Confederate soldier at the time of the war between the states.

Clinton Webb IV, one of a family of three sons and two
daughters, was educated in Georgia and had business experience
in several lines before he permanently connected himself with
insurance, a field in which his abilities found most successful
expression. For a number of years he had his main offices in
Richmond, but did business over the entire State of Virginia.
He was a Democrat and a member of the Baptist Church, and
a liberal contributor to charities and public movements.

Mr. Webb married, June 22, 1904, Mrs. William Scott Young.
Mrs. Webb, who resides at 1831 West Grace Street in Richmond,
had the maiden name of Minnie Wilson Duane. She was married February 24, 1891, to William Scott Young, who died in
1901. By her first marriage she had two daughters. Miss
Thelma Duane Young, of Philadelphia and Richmond, is secretary of the Commonwealth of Virginia. The deceased daughter
was Elsie Scott Young, who married T. O. Day, of Philadelphia,
and they had three children, named Thurman Oscar, Louise
Duane and William Curran Day.

Mrs. Webb by her marriage to Mr. Clinton Webb is the
mother of two children, Dorothy Webb, at present connected
with a real estate firm and makes her home with her mother,
and Clinton Webb V, the latter now a student in Richmond
University.

CARROLL W. CHEWNING, Doctor of Dental Surgery, is a resident of Orange, and in his profession and as a private citizen
represents one of the prominent families in this section of
Virginia.

The Chewnings came from England, there being three
brothers who settled in this country in 1760. Doctor Chewning's
grandfather, William H. Chewning, was a native of Spotsylvania County, Virginia, and during the Civil war served with
the Thirteenth Virginia Regiment. He was born August 12,
1837, and died April 5, 1915. He was twice married, his first
wife being Camilla L. Fleming, and after her death he married
her sister Fannie. Camilla Fleming Chewning died December
24, 1898. She was the mother of the following children: Alice
K., Oscar F. (who died in 1894), Lula, William O. (who died
in 1927), Zed W., Carlyle M., John C., Camilla, and Aubrey.

The parents of Doctor Chewning are Z. W. and Eula I.
(Pruett) Chewning. His father was born in Caroline County,
Virginia, August 11, 1868, and lives at Orange, where for many
years he has been a leading merchant. He is a deacon in the
local Baptist Church, has been Sunday school teacher and super-

Lucian H. Leacke.

intendent, and is a member of the local Chamber of Commerce. Z. W. Chewning and Eula I. Pruett were married December 27, 1899, and their children are: Inez P., Carroll W., Mabel C., Alice C., Camilla L., Zed W., Jr., and William Henry, twins.

Carroll W. Chewning graduated from the dental department of the University of Maryland in 1925 and has enjoyed a very successful career in his profession at Orange, which is his native city. He was born at Orange, September 6, 1902. Doctor Chewning's father graduated from the B. A. Davis School of Richmond in 1897. Doctor Chewning is a Democrat, member of the Baptist Church, and secretary of the Orange Rotary Club.

He married, October 29, 1927, Vivienne Akers. Her father, Robert R. Akers, for many years has been in the lumber business at Baltimore, Maryland. Mrs. Chewning was a small girl when her mother died. She was the second of three daughters, Catherine, Vivienne and Agatha.

LUCIAN H. COCKE, JR., general attorney of the Norfolk & Western Railway Company at Roanoke, inherits a splendid tradition of perhaps the most distinguished family group in Virginia's educational history, and is a member of the family that has been identified with Hollins College since its founding.

His grandfather, Charles Lewis Cocke, was founder of that institution, one of the oldest and best schools for the higher education of women in the South. Lucian H. Cocke, Jr., represents the tenth generation of the Cocke family in America. Its founder was Richard Cocke, Sr., who came from England prior to 1636 and patented 3,000 acres on the James River in Henrico County, Virginia. Through subsequent generations the family were known as extensive land owners and planters, and many of them filled honorable places of responsibility, officials of the county, members of the House of Burgesses, and responsive to the call of patriotism and duty on the battlefield.

Charles Lewis Cocke was born at Edgehill in King William County, February 21, 1820, and was educated at Richmond College, at what is now George Washington University at Washington, D. C., was professor of mathematics at Richmond College for five years, following which he became superintendent of the Valley Union Seminary of Roanoke County. In 1846 this institution was reorganized as Hollins Institute, and from that time until his death in 1901 the story of his life was the story of the institution. Charles Lewis Cocke married Susanna Virginia Pleasants. Of their family of children the daughter Matty L. succeeded her father as president of Hollins College.

Lucian Howard Cocke, Sr., who like some of his brothers and sisters was connected for a time with the faculty of instruction of Hollins College, was born at that institution March 27, 1858, and acquired his early educational training there. For three years he was a student in Richmond College, and after two years at Washington and Lee University graduated with the A. B. degree. He taught English and English literature at Hollins College during the year of 1878-79 and part of 1880. He was graduated with his law degree from the University of Virginia in 1881, and from that date had an honored membership at the Roanoke bar. From 1884 to 1895 he was a member of the law firm of Penn & Cocke, and until 1904 was senior member of the firm Cocke & Glasgow. In 1904 he became consulting attorney for the Norfolk & Western and subsequently was made its general attorney. He was also vice president of Hollins College and a trustee and rector of Washington and Lee University. In 1882 he was elected mayor of the Town of Roanoke and in 1884 became the first mayor of the City of Roanoke. He was a member and was president in 1919-20 of the Virginia State Bar Association, a member of the American Bar Association, the University Club of Washington, and was a Phi Beta Kappa and Beta Theta Pi.

Lucian H. Cocke, Sr., married, in 1885, Lelia M. Smith, who died in 1899. Her father, Francis H. Smith, was a member of the faculty of the University of Virginia many years. To this marriage were born four children, Charles Francis, Lucian H., Mary Stuart and Jane Harwood. Both sons were with the colors during the World war. Lucian H. Cocke, Sr., in 1903 married Mrs. Sarah (Johnson) Hagan, who at one time was vice president general of the Daughters of the American Revolution, and for a number of years has been a contributor to southern literature. Mr. Cocke died at Roanoke, Virginia, November 14, 1927.

Lucian H. Cocke, Jr., was born at Roanoke, May 24, 1889, and attended private schools in that city, the high school, and graduated from the University of Virginia with the Bachelor of Arts degree in 1910, Master of Arts in 1911, and Bachelor of Laws in 1913. He was admitted to practice in New York State and was in New York for a year. For twelve months he was in the general offices of the Norfolk & Western Railway Company at Philadelphia, and in the summer of 1915, returning to Roanoke, became assistant attorney to his father and was later made assistant general attorney of the Norfolk & Western Railway. On February 1, 1928, he succeeded his father in the position of general attorney of the Norfolk & Western Railway Company.

He enlisted in 1916, assisting in raising and organizing the Roanoke Coast Artillery. He was in training at Fortress Monroe, and Fort Myer, and in December, 1917, sailed for France, where he became a member of a French flying squadron, on duty as an observer. He was awarded the Croix de Guerre with Palm and Gold Star by the French government. Mr. Cocke returned home in June, 1919. He is a member of the Sigma Chi college fraternity, is a Presbyterian, member of the Roanoke Country Club, and Shenandoah Club, the Roanoke and Virginia Bar Associations, also the Westmoreland Club of Richmond, Virginia.

He married in 1923 Dorothy Latshaw, of Pittsburgh, Pennsylvania. She attended public schools in her native city and graduated with the A. B. degree from Hollins College in 1922. They have two children, Lucian H. III, and Mary Stuart.

ABNER TERRY SHIELDS is a citizen of Rockbridge County distinguished by the length and quiet efficiency of his public service, having given thirty-five years to the duties of clerk of Rockbridge County.

He was born at Lynchburg, Virginia, October 29, 1852, son of Col. John C. and Martha M. (Hardy) Shields, his father a native of Rockbridge County and his mother of Lynchburg. His paternal grandfather, Joseph Shields, was born in Rockbridge County, followed farming, and the Shields family have been property owners in that county since 1778. The maternal grandfather, Chesley Hardy, was in the furniture business at Lynchburg before the Civil war. Col. John C. Shields served with the rank of colonel of artillery in the Confederate army, entering the army as a lieutenant, being promoted to captain and

finally to colonel. Toward the close of the war he was assigned
duty as instructor at Camp Lee. Colonel Shields for many years
was a prominent newspaper man and writer. He was connected with the *Lynchburg Virginian,* later went with the *Richmond Whig,* and after locating on his farm in Rockbridge
County continued writing regularly for newspapers at Staunton
and the *Lynchburg Virginian.* He died at the home farm in
Rockbridge County in 1904. Colonel Shields was a member of
the Methodist Protestant Church, later becoming a Presbyterian, and was a member of the Masonic fraternity. Of his
fourteen children six are living.

Abner T. Shields attended school at Richmond and the Norwood School in Nelson County, and after leaving school he followed farming and also clerked in stores for several years. In
1885 he was appointed deputy clerk of court of Rockbridge
County, and has been identified with that office ever since, being
master of its routine and detail. He was elected for his first
term as clerk of court in 1893, and recently was reelected for
another eight-year term.

Mr. Shields has never married. He is a member of the
Presbyterian Church and Sunday School, having served as deacon of the church, and is affiliated with the Lodge, Royal Arch
Chapter, Commandery and Shrine of Masonry. He has been
secretary of his lodge for many years, and for over thirty years
has been master of exchequer, and is a former chancellor commander of the Knights of Pythias. Mr. Shields owns an interest
in his father's old homestead.

WALTER F. CRAWFORD, general manager of the Central Manufacturing Company, is one of the very substantial business men
of Roanoke, who has gained a position of influence in his special
line which is not always the lot for even a veteran to attain.
He has always been devoted to his business interests, but never
to the uttter exclusion of civic affairs, for he believes that they
broaden the man and enlarge his sphere of usefulness. Therefore he has taken a public spirited interest in the welfare of his
city and county, and though never an office seeker, he has supported every movement which in his opinion would promote the
advancement of the community or benefit the citizens of Roanoke
in general. Mr. Crawford came into the world in Rockbridge
County, Virginia, in 1870, and he is a son of John Franklin
and Mary (Quisenbury) Crawford, natives of Rockbridge
County, both of whom are deceased. The father was a carpenter and contractor, and did a large amount of building in his day
and neighborhood. Of the nine children born to the parents
five survive, and of them all Walter F. Crawford is the sixth
child. They were Baptists, and she was very active in church
work. From the time the Republican party was organized until
his death he voted its ticket.

Growing up in his native county, Walter F. Crawford
attended its public schools, and, learning the trade of a carpenter, worked at it in Rockbridge County for three years after he
completed his apprenticeship, and then, in 1887, came to Roanoke and continued work at his trade until 1890, when he
entered the employ of the Central Manufacturing Company as
a carpenter and bench hand, and has steadily risen until today
he is general manager. This company is a large concern manufacturing building material, and has a large trade connection
over all of this part of the state.

In 1896 Mr. Crawford married Miss Elizabeth Steele, who
was born in Rockbridge County, at Collierstown. Two children
have been born to Mr. and Mrs. Crawford: Emory Steele Crawford, who is in the employ of the Norfolk & Western Railroad
Company's car shops; and Evelyn, who is at home. Mr. Crawford is a Baptist, and his wife is a Presbyterian. He is a Scottish Rite and Shriner Mason, and is also a member of the Junior
Order United American Mechanics, and he is deeply interested
in the Commercial Club. Like his father before him he is an
active Republican.

Both he and his wife have interesting family histories. His
grandfather was George Washington Crawford, who was born
in Virginia in 1799, and he became a large planter and slaveowner. His wife, whose first name was Martha, was also born
in 1799. The maternal grandfather, E. A. Quisenbury, was also
a Virginian, and a miller. Mrs. Crawford's people, the Steeles,
settled in the Shenandoah Valley, and an old tavern, established
by a member of her family in 1776, is still standing. The Steeles
are connected with the Morrises, and both families are numbered among the old and honored ones of the Old Dominion.
Mrs. Crawford is also connected with the McCorkle family, and
is closely related to Governor McCorkle of West Virginia. Her
mother's maiden name was Wilson, and her cousins, Henry and
Walter McCorkle, are very prominent lawyers of New York
City.

HON. HIRAM WILBERT BERTRAM, circuit judge of Rockingham and Page counties, is one of the ablest attorneys and jurists
of Harrisonburg or the county, and a man who is accepted as
being an exponent of the best element in his profession and
community. He was born in Rockingham County, November 8,
1868, a son of P. A. and Amelia (Bowman) Bertram, both of
whom were also born in Rockingham County. Both are deceased, he dying September 30, 1895, and she on November 28,
1927, when she was eighty-seven years old. He was a merchant
and farmer, and one of the well known men of his day, and
active in the Democratic party. They had three children, two
of whom survive: Andrew D., who is a merchant of Keezel-
town, Virginia, and Judge Bertram. The paternal grandfather,
Andrew Bertram, was born in Rockingham County, Virginia, a
son of Julius Bertram, a native of Germany, who secured a grant
of land from the Government. The family had been established,
however, in Virginia, about 1762. The maternal grandfather,
Daniel Bowman, was a native and farmer of Rockingham
County, so that on both sides of the family Judge Bertram can
trace back several generations in the history of this county.

Following his graduation from high school Judge Bertram
entered Roanoke College, from which he obtained his degree of
Master of Arts in 1890, and he was a student of the law school
of the University of Virginia during 1891 and 1892, and in
October of the latter year was admitted to the bar. Entering
at once upon a general practice in Harrisonburg, he continued in
it until he was appointed to the bench by the governor, and later
by the Legislature.

In December, 1895, Judge Bertram married Miss Alice Lee
Gaither, born in Rockingham County, and educated in the
county schools and Bridgewater College. She is a daughter of
John W. and Lila (Lee) Gaither, the former a merchant during
the greater part of his life, and a Confederate veteran. Judge

S. S. Gole

and Mrs. Bertram have one son, Liston C. Bertram, who was educated in the University of Virginia and the law school of Yale University, and is engaged in the practice of his profession in New York City. Judge Bertram is an honored member of the Methodist Episcopal Church, South, to which his wife also belongs, and he is a trustee of it. In Masonry he has been advanced through the different bodies of the York Rite, and he also belongs to the Mystic Shrine. Long a member of the Knights of Pythias, he is a past chancellor commander of his local lodge and he is a trustee of the order. Professionally he maintains membership with the Virginia Bar Association and the American Bar Association. While he devotes all of his time to his office, he owns considerable town property and stock in the local newspaper. Although active in professional and fraternal life, Judge Bertram's strongest interests have always been centered in his home. The originality and profound grasp of his intellect have commanded respect from the beginning of his career, and yet these are not all of the man. In every relation of life is shown the light that comes from justness, generosity, truth, high sense of honor, proper respect for self, and a sensitive thoughfulness for others.

SPARRELL SIMMONS GALE, who died August 19, 1927, was one of the most accomplished surgeons of Virginia, one of the founders and until his death, the active head of the Lewis-Gale Hospital at Roanoke.

He was born July 20, 1876, on a farm owned by his maternal grandfather, Capt. Sparrell Simmons, near Salem in Roanoke County. His father, Dr. Joseph A. Gale, was for nearly half a century chief surgeon for the Norfolk & Western Railway and one of the pioneer members of his profession in Southwestern Virginia. The late Sparrell Gale continued to exemplify the professional spirit and energy of his honored father, with added accomplishments of skill. Mrs. Joseph A. (Simmons) Gale is still living, a resident of Roanoke.

Sparrell Simmons Gale attended the Salem High School, the Episcopal High School at Alexander, Virginia, Roanoke College and later gradated from Columbia University in the School of Physicians and Surgeons, and while there was a member of the Phi Delta Theta. He had hospital training in New York City, and before returning to Roanoke had charge of the Miners' Hospital at Welch, West Virginia. In 1909 he and Dr. J. N. Lewis founded the Lewis-Gale Hospital of Roanoke. Doctor Lewis was killed in an automobile accident a year or so later, and from that time Doctor Gale was the active head and manager of the institution, which is used for all cases from the Norfolk & Western Railway. Doctor Gale also succeeded his father as chief surgeon for the Norfolk & Western. The wizardry of skilled fingers, combined with highly developed mental training and sound judgment, imparted to Doctor Gale all that was required to become a surgeon of considerable note. He was credited with the performance of some of the most difficult operations known in the modern technique of surgery, and the success that attended his work brought him a high degree of fame among his professional brethren not only in Virginia but elsewhere. In his home community of Roanoke he was known as something more than a successful surgeon, being active in business, a director in the State and City Bank, a director of the Roanoke Chamber of Commerce, a steward in the Greene

Memorial Methodist Church, a worker for civic welfare, and a man who had a host of friends and admirers. He was a member of the Roanoke Country Club, Shenandoah Club and one of its directors, was a Scottish Rite Mason, member of the building committee of Kazim Temple of the Mystic Shrine and was vice president of the Kiwanis Club. He belonged to all the important medical organizations, and for years had kept in touch with surgery by attending clinics, resorting frequently to the great clinics of Mayo Brothers at Rochester, Minnesota. He was a fellow of the American College of Surgeons. He had also been elected to active membership in the American Society for Thoracic Surgery. He was eleceted in June, 1927, President of the Roanoke College Alumni Association.

On October 18, 1911, Doctor Gale married Miss Margaretta (Gretchen) Harding, of Canon City, Colorado, where she was born and reared. Mrs. Gale's parents were Theodore Marsh and Margaretta (Minnie) (Lahm) Harding. Her father was born in Cincinnati, Ohio, October 6, 1855, was educated at Cincinnati, and was descended from an old English family that settled in Massachusetts about 1623. Theodore M. Harding at the age of fifteen began employment with a hardware concern, and in 1878, when a young man of twenty-three, he located at Canon City, Colorado, established himself in the hardware business, and from that time until his death in June, 1913, was first and foremost in everything representing the progressive development of that western community. His business brought him a large measure of material success, and his store is still operated by a son at Canon City. At the time of his death he was president of the Chamber of Commerce, was a Royal Arch and Knight Templar Mason, and in 1911 was elected president of the Colorado Implement and Hardware Dealers' Association. He left nothing undone that would contribute to the making of Canon City an orderly and prosperous center of business, homes and institutions. He helped secure the establishment of the Odd Fellows Home there and was also active in the good roads movement, insuring water works for the city, and in building forty miles of sidewalks. He was also head of the Fair Association, was a vestryman in the Episcopal Church.

Theodore M. Harding married, December 4, 1882, Miss Margaretta Lahm, who was born in Canton, Ohio, June 13, 1855, daughter of Samuel Lahm, a prominent and eloquent lawyer of Ohio, and a congressman from that state before the Civil war. One of his speeches on slavery was quoted in the famous debate between Lincoln and Douglas in 1858. Samuel Lahm married Henrietta Faber, who was born at Chambersburg, Pennsylvania, in 1818, and died in 1915. Her grandfather came from Germany to America in 1776 and was one of the pioneer ministers of the German Reformed Church in Pennsylvania. Mrs. Lahm at the age of six years removed from Pennsylvania to Ohio, traveling in a carriage. Mrs. Gale's mother was educated at Canton, Ohio, and for many years has been a prominent social and club leader in Canon City, being a regent of the University of Colorado, and head of the Scholarship Club of the Federation of Women's Clubs of Colorado, an organization which has loaned many thousands of dollars to girls to complete their education. Mrs. Gale was educated in New Milford, Connecticut, in an exclusive girls' school there. She is prominent at Roanoke in the Parent-Teachers movement, being vice president of the local body and vice president of the Central Council. Mrs. Gale has one brother,

T. M. Harding, Jr., who is now the active head of his father's hardware business at Canon City.

Doctor and Mrs. Gale had four children, Margaretta, born November 19, 1912, and died July 14, 1914; Theodore, born December 6, 1913; Josephine, born July 22, 1915; and Sparrell S., Jr., born June 9, 1919. Doctor Gale's hobby was golf, and he was a member of the "Hole in One Club." During the World war he was a member of the Roanoke Medical Advisory Board.

ELMORE S. DEANE, physician and surgeon, has had an exceedingly busy practice in Greene County, starting his professional work there immediately after graduating from medical college in 1914.

Doctor Deane was born in Madison County, Virginia, July 12, 1878, son of George Weeden and Martha (Anderson) Deane. His father, George Deane, was a Confederate soldier in the Seventh Virginia Infantry and for several months was a prisoner at Point Lookout, Maryland. The maternal grandfather, Obediah Anderson, was also a soldier in the Confederate army, and died in a hospital at Richmond during the war. George Weeden Deane was born in Greene County, devoted his active life to his farm and was little concerned with politics beyond voting as a Democrat. Both he and his wife were active members of the Church of the Disciples. He died in 1899, and his wife, who was born in Madison County, died in 1910.

Dr. Elmore S. Deane graduated in 1910 from the Shenandoah Collegiate Institute and School of Music. He had grown up on a farm, and since early manhood has been making his own way. He took his medical degree at the Medical College of Virginia at Richmond in 1914, and at once located at Standardsville. He has kept close to his professional duties, and being a man of unusual ability has built up a splendid practice. He answers calls to all parts of Greene County.

Doctor Deane, who is unmarried, is a member of the Piedmont Medical Association. He is affiliated with the Royal Arch Chapter of Masonry at Charlottesville and has membership in the Presbyterian Church at Lexington, the church of which Gen. Stonewall Jackson was a member.

JAMES E. PARROTT is a commonwealth attorney of Greene County, with home at Standardsville.

He was born near Standardsville, May 10, 1894, son of George B. and Sallie E. (Catterton) Parrott, and grandson of Bazeleel Parrott and Finks Catterton. All were natives of Green County. His grandfather Catterton was a physician and planter. Bazeleel Parrott, a farmer of Greene County, died at the advanced age of ninety-eight years. George B. Parrott, in addition to managing his farm, has for several years been with the Virginia State Department of Agriculture as inspector of seeds and fertilizer. He is a Democrat, member of the Independent Order of Odd Fellows and the Methodist Episcopal Church, South.

James E. Parrott was the fourth in a family of nine children, seven of whom are living. He was educated in the McGaheysville High School in Rockingham County, attended Randolph-Macon College at Ashland in 1915, continuing in the academic department of the University of Virginia, following which he took up the study of law and received his diploma from the law school of the University of Virginia in 1920. He was licensed to practice before he graduated, and in November, 1919, was elected commonwealth attorney of Greene County. He is now serving his second term and divides his time between his official duties and his general law practice. Mr. Parrott, who is unmarried, is a Democrat and a member of the Methodist Episcopal Church, South.

SAMUEL PAGE DUKE, president of the State Teachers College at Harrisonburg, is a native son of Virginia, and has had a prominent part in the state's educational interests for twenty years.

He was born at Ferrum, Virginia, September 5, 1885, son of Thomas Page and Jennie Gray (Ward) Duke. He received his preparatory education in Randolph-Macon Academy at Bedford, took his A. B. degree at Randolph-Macon College at Ashland in 1906, and for post-graduate study was awarded the Master of Arts degree by Columbia University in 1913. After graduating from Randolph-Macon Mr. Duke went West, and from 1906 to 1908 was an instructor in the Willie Hallsell College at Vinita, Oklahoma. Since then he has been a Virginia school man. He was principal of the high school at Chase City, 1908-10, principal of city schools at Richmond, 1910-14, and for five years was director of County Teachers Institute, director of the Department of Education in the State Teachers College for Women at Farmville, and state supervisor of Secondary Schools of Virginia. Since 1919 he has presided over the State Teachers College at Harrisonburg.

Mr. Duke is a life member of the National Education Association, is a Phi Delta Kappa and Kappa Alpha, and a director in the Rockingham Memorial Hospital. He is a Democrat and a member of the Methodist Episcopal Church, South. He married, August 26, 1908, Miss Lucille Campbell, of Georgetown, Texas. They have four children, Samuel Page, Julia Lois, Robert Campbell and Marshall Ward.

J. ROBERT SWITZER. One of the outstanding figures in the political life of Harrisonburg and Rockingham County, as well as a lawyer of proven ability, J. Robert Switzer is rendering a much appreciated service as county clerk after having already held the office of deputy county clerk. He was born on a farm in Rockingham County, December 25, 1883, a son of John A. and Carrie S. (Roller) Switzer, the latter of whom was born in Rockingham County, but the former was born in Hardy County, Virginia, now in West Virginia. Both are deceased, passing away after years of usefulness, he having served for twelve years as sheriff of Rockingham County, and without doubt could have been reelected had he cared to come before the public a fourth time. For a long period he was engaged in farming, and he was a man very well liked and highly respected. Of the four children born to him and his wife two survive, namely: Mrs. N. Wilson Davis, who resides in Harrisonburg, where her husband is engaged in the practice of civil engineering; and J. Robert Switzer. The parents were consistent members of the Reformed Church, and he was one of its elders. The Democratic party had in him a strong supporter. During the war between the states he served under General Mosby, and was a gallant soldier. The paternal grandfather of J. Robert Switzer was Valentine Switzer, a native of Hardy County, and a miller of that region. The maternal grandfather was Col. Peter Roller,

Henry H. Puttrough

of Mount Crawford, Virginia, who received the title of colonel during the war between the states for his services in training soldiers for the Confederacy. By occupation he was a farmer.

J. Robert Switzer attended the public schools of Mount Crawford and Harrisonburg, and then had two years of work in Randolph-Macon Academy at Front Royal. His degree of Bachelor of Laws was taken from Washington and Lee University in 1906, and that same year he entered upon the practice of his profession in Harrisonburg, in which he continued with gratifying success until he was appointed deputy county clerk in 1920. In November, 1927, he was elected county clerk, which office he is still filling with dignified capability.

In December, 1911, Mr. Switzer married Miss Virginia Armentrout, born in Middletown, Virginia, a daughter of G. W. and Cora (Willey) Armentrout. Mr. and Mrs. Switzer have two children: John Robert and Virginia Anne. Reared in the faith of the Reformed Church, Mr. Switzer has made it his own, and he is an elder of the local church, to which his wife also belongs. He is a York Rite and Shriner Mason, and is a past high priest of the Chapter and a past eminent commander of the Commandery. For sixteen years he has been secretary of the local order of the Benevolent and Protective Order of Elks, and he is also a member of the Knights of Pythias and the Independent Order of Odd Fellows, and is a past chancellor commander of the former. For years he has been very active in the local Democratic party, has served as chairman of the county committee and been a delegate to various state conventions. In his duties, to which he now gives all of his attention, Mr. Switzer finds his knowledge of the law a very valuable asset, and the people of Rockingham County may rest assured that while he is in office everything under his jurisdiction will be done in accordance with the strict letter as well as the spirit of the law.

HENRY H. RUTROUGH became identified with the automobile business before the war, and has shown almost a genius in achieving a volume record of sales of one of the finest cars manufactured, and at Roanoke has developed an establishment for sales and service almost unequaled in the state.

Mr. Rutrough was born on a farm three miles from Roanoke, January 2, 1892, son of Franklin P. and Eva A. (Huff) Rutrough and grandson of Solomon Rutrough and I. H. Huff, both of whom were Floyd County farmers. Franklin P. Rutrough was born in Floyd County and his wife in Roanoke County, and they still live in the latter county. Franklin Rutrough is a farmer and dairyman, is a Democrat in politics and an active member of the Presbyterian Church. Of their five children four are living: Florence, wife of J. T. Metcalf, an attorney at Winchester, Kentucky; Henry; Pauline, wife of O. B. Watson, an attorney at Richmond; and Eva, wife of R. A. Bagley, a physician practicing at Richmond.

Henry H. Rutrough attended public school at Roanoke and was a student of agriculture and related sciences at the Virginia Polytechnic Institute at Blacksburg, following which he had three years of training and experience as a practical farmer.

On leaving the farm Mr. Rutrough was in the seed and grain business at Roanoke two years and in 1916 acquired the local agency for the Cadillac car, conducting a sales and service station in Bristol, Virginia. He had developed a very promising business during the eighteen months from when he started, but left it to answer the call to the colors in 1917.

Mr. Rutrough was in the artillery branch of the army, his first training being given at Fortress Monroe, after which he was at Curtis Bay, Maryland, and Newport News, and received his honorable discharge at Camp Meade, Maryland, in 1918, after the armistice. After his return to Roanoke from the army camp Mr. Rutrough resumed automobile salesmanship, handling the Hudson and Essex cars for Doctor Cooper for four years. In September, 1923, he established the Rutrough-Gilbert Motor Company, Incorporated, of which he is president and active manager, with Dr. John E. Topping, vice president and W. P. Gilbert, secretary and treasurer. They handle and distribute the Packard cars, and more than half of the total sales of Packards credited to Virginia were made through the Roanoke agency, which establishes a rather remarkable record in the automobile business. In connection with the sales department Mr. Rutrough has developed a service based on the most skillful mechanics he can secure and other facilities that have caused his service department to be highly commented by many buyers throughout the country. As a result of this department and a fine reputation of the cars handled Mr. Rutrough has one of the leading automobile agencies in the state.

He is a member of the B. P. O. Elks, the Shenandoah Club, the Roanoke, German Club, Roanoke Country Club and Kiwanis Club.

IRBY HUDSON, president of the Hudson-Morgan Electric Company, is one of the leading business men of Lynchburg, who is not only achieving a material success, but is also doing a citizen's duty by his home city. He was born in Prince Edward County, Virginia, in 1874, a son of Littleton M. and Mary Elizabeth (Hardaway) Hudson, both of whom were born in Lundenburg County, Virginia, and are now deceased. Throughout his life the father was a farmer with the exception of the last two years of the war between the states, when he served in the Confederate army, and, although captured, escaped and joined his regiment. Eleven children were born to him and his wife, of whom two are living: Irby and Ethel Ward Hudson, the latter now the wife of Thomas Smith, Newport News, Virginia, with the Newport News Shipbuilding Company as engineer. The parents belonged to the Methodist Episcopal Church, South, and she was very active in its good work. The paternal grandfather, Irby Hudson, was also an agriculturist. The maternal grandfather, Edward Hardaway, was also a farmer.

After he had completed the high school course in Lynchburg Mr. Hudson, of this review, learned the electrical trade in the employ of the Second Electric Company of Virginia, beginning, while still a boy, to read meters, and being promoted to an office position. After he had learned his trade and gained a thorough knowledge of the business from the office end, he went into business for himself in 1890, under the name of Irby Hudson, electrical contractor. In 1910 he incorporated his present company, and is now carrying on a general electric business, contracting and selling, and handling everything electrical. The excellence of the work and the quality of the stock, combined with the service have brought the company a large volume of trade, and this is one of the leading concerns of its kind in a wide territory adjacent to Lynchburg.

In 1894 Mr. Hudson married Kate V. Frye, a native of Virginia, educated in the local schools and institute. Mr. and Mrs. Hudson have three children: Cecil Irby, who was educated in the Lynchburg High School, is with his father; Randolph Ward, who is attending the Virginia Polytechnic Institute; and Elizabeth Brown, who is attending the Lynchburg High School. Mrs. Hudson's father, Col. Philip Brown, served with the rank of colonel in the war between the states, and later was elected to the United States Senate, being one of Virginia's distinguished statesmen. He married a Miss Adams. Mr. and Mrs. Hudson belong to Saint John's Episcopal Church of Lynchburg, and to the local country club. Beginning life with nothing, Mr. Hudson's progress has been somewhat remarkable and he has every reason to be proud of what he has accomplished. While his family suffered reverses during the war period of the '60s, it is an old and aristocratic one of the Old Dominion. He has in his possession the deed to a grant of land in Prince Edward County, Virginia, from King George III of England, which he greatly prizes, although the property, given to the family 174 years ago, has now passed from their possession.

NICHOLAS W. PUGH. The record of the accomplishments of some men in the brief span of their life's period reads like a romance. Without knowledge of all conditions, it seems almost impossible that one man could be so successful or find the time to superintend the details of so many interests, and yet there are numerous business men who are of inestimable value to their communities because of the interest they excite in financial circles, which is a healthy stimulus to trade. One of these men who is connected with many enterprises at Roanoke, and is one of its most influential citizens, is Nicholas W. Pugh, one of the leading merchants, not only of Roanoke but of his part of the state.

Nicholas W. Pugh was born in Virginia, May 27, 1889, a son of Charles B. and Laura Frances (Baber) Pugh, he born in Nelson County, Virginia, and she in Albemarle County, Virginia, but both are now deceased. For about forty years the father was a merchant and postmaster at Avon, Nelson County. Of the five children born to the parents four survive: Effa Laura, who married Dr. Mack Berryhill, a dentist of Charlotte, North Caroline; Nicholas W., who is the second child; Virgie Homer, who is engaged in the automobile business at Afton, Virginia; Charles Basil, who resides at Afton, Virginia, but is not in business; and one who is deceased. Both of the parents were active members of the Rhodes Methodist Episcopal Church, South. His fraternal connections were those which he maintained with the Independent Order of Odd Fellows. A man of strong convictions, he never tied himself down to any one party, but voted independently. He was a son of Nicholas W. Pugh, also a native of Virginia, and a planter upon an extensive scale, who served in the Confederate army during the latter part of the war between the states. The maternal grandfather was William Baber, also a Virginian, who died during the war between the states.

Mr. Pugh of this review attended an excellent private school, and went into his father's store at an early age and remained there until he was eighteen years old. He then went with B. F. Dickerson, of Charlottesville, Virginia, as a clerk, and continued in his employ for six years, learning the business in every detail. Going then to Bristol, Tennessee, he was buyer and manager of several departments of the H. P. King Company store

for two years. His next broadening experience was obtained as
buyer and manager for the M. M. Newcomer Company stores of
Knoxville, Tennessee, but after three years he left that concern
as an employe and bought the interest of Mr. Newcomer, and
for three years more conducted the business. In 1920 he sold his
interest and came to Roanoke, where he bought the store of
Rosenbaum Brothers and formed a new company. Still later he
bought the interests of the Hancock Dry Goods Company and
combined the two concerns, the business now being conducted as
both a wholesale and retail one. In the wholesale branch he has
men traveling in five states. The company operates under the
name of the Pugh Dry Goods Company, wholesale, and that of
N. W. Pugh Company, retail. The company also owns the Pugh,
Blackmore, Stricklen Company of Staunton, Virginia, the largest
department store in Virginia outside of the large cities. Mr.
Pugh is president of the Pugh-Bane Company of Pulaski, Virginia, and has other interests in several department stores in the
state. Starting in commerce with nothing but his knowledge of
the business and a natural talent for trading, he has built up a
wonderful business, and is a man of large affairs. His first commercial interest was secured with borrowed money; today he is
a very wealthy man, and a director in the American National
Bank.

In September, 1912, Mr. Pugh married Miss Mary Naomi
Payne, who was born in Charlottesville, Virginia, a daughter of
John Payne. They have three children: Nicholas W., Junior,
who is attending the Roanoke High School; Robert B., who is
attending the grade schools; and Mary Jean, who is the little
one at home. Mr. and Mrs. Pugh are valued members of the
Greene Memorial Methodist Episcopal Church, South, of Roanoke, and he is one of its stewards. He belongs to the Kiwanis
Club, but otherwise has no outside distractions, all of his time
and attention being given to his business affairs. Widely known,
conceded to be a man of ripened judgment, refined tastes and
sagacious counsel, Mr. Pugh is sought by many and his friendship is prized beyond that of most men.

JOHN W. MORRISON is a citizen of one of the most progressive communities of Virginia, Harrisonburg, where he has practiced law, given time and leadership to public enterprises and
helped to realize some of the most important projects for the
city's development and betterment.

He was born at Linville, Rockingham County, December 9,
1876, son of John and Mary (Wagner) Morrison. His father,
who died in 1894, came from Ireland, served with a Louisiana
regiment in the Confederate army and at the close of the war
remained in Virginia. His wife was a native Virginian and
died in 1883.

John W. Morrison was reared at Linville, Virginia, was educated locally, clerked in a store and later was a clerk in the
Interior Department at Washington, where he attended the law
department of Georgetown University. After graduating he returned to Rockingham County and has since engaged in a successful law practice at Harrisonburg. His offices are in the
First National Bank Building. Mr. Morrison has been president of the Harrisonburg Chamber of Commerce, and in 1920
was elected mayor and reelected mayor in 1928, his administrations coinciding with a period of constructive progress when
Harrisonburg was enlarging its schools, improving its public

utilities and laying the foundation for a greater and better city. Mr. Morrison during the World war was chairman of several of the drives for Red Cross and other purposes. He is a past exalted ruler of the B. P. O. Elks and has served as district deputy grand exalted ruler for Virginia-West.

C. C. DURHAM. The average man is seldom brought face to face with the stern realities of life until he has reached years of near maturity. He is generally given the opportunity to make a choice of occupations—allowed to follow his inclination in as far as circumstances do not prevent. Showing an early predilection for one of the learned professions, for one of the fields open in the marts of trade and commerce, or for the hazardous activities of public life, he may be given the chance to develop his talents in his chosen line, and his success or failure rests upon the manner upon which he exercises his inherent gifts. It is not the average man, however, who reaches the highest place. History and biography definitely prove that the man who achieves distinction, who grasps the great things of life—the man to whom men look—has had his start in obscurity. It would seem that the mere necessity of self support and self protection, which really mean self reliance, develop indwelling power that would, in other circumstances, have lain dormant. The one who takes upon himself the responsibilities of manhood when still in the days of his youth, who puts aside personal ambitions to assume duties thrust upon him by the will of fate, who unselfishly bends his every energy toward the accomplishment of those things which chance has placed upon him, and who finally triumphs over all and tastes the sweet fruits of victory is far above the average individual.

C. C. Durham, whose Mick or Mack stores are known over a wide territory, is a man who has earned every dollar he has today, and they are many, and has worked his way up from his original somewhat lowly position to his present one of wealth and prominence, and yet is still a man barely over the line of thirty, in the very prime of active achievement and vigor of life, for he was born November 13, 1897, in Burlington, North Carolina, a son of J. C. and Eliza E. (Ripply) Durham, both of whom were born in Alamance County, North Carolina. For the past twenty years the father has been with the Burlington Coffin Company. He is an active member of the Baptist Church, and belongs to the Knights of Pythias, the Junior Order United American Mechanics, and is a Democrat in political faith. Of the seven children born to him and his wife, C. C. Durham is the eldest. The paternal grandfather, Thomas Durham, was also born in Alamance County, North Carolina, and he was a farmer by occupation. The maternal grandfather was a native of Alamance County, these two families, Durham and Ripply, being old ones of the county.

After he left high school C. C. Durham entered a preparatory school at Boiling Springs, North Carolina, and then had a year in the North Carolina State College, Raleigh. His first connection with the world's workers came during a six-months period in the railroad shops of Salisbury, North Carolina, and later he was a clerk in a store at Salisbury, North Carolina, for a few months. Going to Baltimore, Maryland, he was in the paymaster's department of the Henry Sonneborne Company for nine months. With this country's entry into the World war he entered the army, and was trained in the camp at Ral-

eigh, North Carolina, but was not sent overseas. After his
honorable discharge he returned to Baltimore, and for four
years was in the employ of the McCormick Company, during
three years of that time being on the road, covering practically
the entire State of Virginia and portions of eighteen other
states, at different times, visiting only the large cities. He
opened a Piggly Wiggly store at Staunton, Virginia, in 1922, and
did splendidly with it, and later opened a store of his own in
Harrisonburg, later adding a second one, two at Staunton, and
a wholesale grocery establishment in the last named city. In
1927 he sold all of his stores, moved to Roanoke, bringing his
wholesale business with him, and began opening his chain of
stores which he operates, as before stated, under the name of
Mick or Mack. In 1928 he has four of these stores in successful
operation in Roanoke, one in Covington, Virginia, one in Harrisonburg, Virginia, and one in Princeton, West Virginia, and
proposes to open others in the near future at the rate of two
a month. The business is incorporated under the name of
Durham Brothers & Company, Incorporated, of which C. C.
Durham is president; N. R. McVeigh is vice president, and there
is no outside capital interested. The firm is now operating
thirty-five stores in four states. The First Baptist Church of
Roanoke holds his membership, and while he was in Staunton
he was chairman of the finance committee of the Baptist Church
of that city. He is a member of the Masonic fraternity, of the
Roanoke Kiwanis Club, the Roanoke Country Club and other
organizations, and is deservedly popular in all of them. Mr.
Durham is unmarried. In the above brief record is clearly
proven that Mr. Durham is not an average man, for such a man
could not have attained to Mr. Durham's present standing
through his own efforts, as he has done, and the people of
Roanoke realize this fact and are proud of him and what he has
accomplished.

HON. WARD SWANK. During all of the period of his professional career Hon. Ward Swank has steadily maintained a
high position at the bar, and at the same time has attained to
political eminence as well, now representing his district in the
State Senate of Virginia. In Harrisonburg, throughout Rockingham County and the entire state he is recognized as a very
able lawyer and a statesman of more than ordinary attainments.
At an early period in his professional life he was fortunate in
securing the confidence and esteem of those engaged in large
affairs; and this he has always retained. No interests are so
important that those concerned in their management hesitate
to commit them to him when the occasion arises, either for counsel or the assertion or defense of their rights in the courts. His
methods are honorable, open and fair. No suspicion of sinister
or devious efforts to secure secret or undue advantage has ever
been harbored by his opponents. Indeed it may be truly said
that he is ever animated by a fixed and stern integrity which is
one of the admirable, as it is the most commanding, trait in his
character.

Senator Swank was born in Edom, Rockingham County, November 10, 1885, a son of Perry J. and Mary E. (Horn) Swank,
both of whom were born in Rockingham County. He was a
farmer and stockdealer, and prominent citizen. Both he and
his wife were devout members of the Lutheran Church, and they
died firm in its faith. For many years he served as a member

of the Board of Supervisors of Rockingham County. Of the ten children born to him and his wife six survive, and of them all Senator Swank is the youngest. The paternal grandfather, John Swank, was born in Augusta County, Virginia, and he was a life long farmer, but the family came from Pennsylvania, the great-grandfather being its founder in Virginia. The maternal grandfather, Jackson Horn, was born in Rockingham County, and here he was a farmer and a justice of the peace for many years.

Growing to manhood in his native county, Senator Swank attended the local schools and the high school of Harrisonburg, and was graduated from the latter in 1908. In 1908 he attended the University of Virginia, and was graduated therefrom with the degree of Bachelor of Arts in 1911, and with that of Bachelor of Laws in 1913. Immediately thereafter he entered upon the practice of law in Harrisonburg, where he has since remained, building up a wide and valuable connection, as already indicated, and handling cases in all branches of his profession. He has been clerk of the City Council of Harrisonburg since 1916; in 1923 he was elected state senator at a special election, and reelected at the regular elections of 1923, 1924 and 1928, having had no opposition the last two times. While in the Senate he has served on the committees of public institutions and education, moral and social welfare, and agriculture and courts of justice, and is ranking member on the last named committee. For years he has been a delegate to the conventions of his party, local, county and state, and is accepted as one of the leaders of his party.

On June 19, 1918, Senator Swank married Miss Elsie Miller, who was born in Stephens City, Frederick County, Virginia, a daughter of Samuel A. Miller, a woolen-mill inspector, who died in 1917. Senator and Mrs. Swank have one child, Carolyn Miller. Mrs. Swank is a member of the Methodist Episcopal Church, South. He belongs to the Ancient Free and Accepted Masons, the Benevolent and Protective Order of Elks and Phi Kappa Psi. Senator Swank is a man of singular independence of mind and entirely fearless in the assertion of his convictions. When it becomes his duty to criticize judicial decisions he does not in the least abate these qualities. He vigorously and courageously attacks ignorance, sophistry and error, whether promulgated from the bench or from some quarter less calculated to secure tacit assent, if not to command respect, so that in every way he is an outstanding figure in the history of his times and locality.

SAMUEL L. FERGUSON, Appomattox attorney, has enjoyed many important relationships with his community in a professional, business and political capacity.

Mr. Ferguson, who is now serving his third term in the Virginia State Senate, was born in Appomattox County, October 18, 1869, and represents a family that have lived in this section of Virginia for a number of generations, and his parents were George Lafayette and Martha Victoria (Lewis) Ferguson, both natives of Appomattox County. His paternal grandfather, Thomas Ferguson, was born in the same county, where he followed farming. The maternal grandfather, Daniel Lewis, was descended from the historic Lewis family of Old Virginia. George L. Ferguson volunteered in the Confederate army in Company H of the Second Virginia Cavalry and saw active service until April 6, 1865, when, at the battle of Sailors Creek, shortly before the surrender at Appomattox, he was wounded and captured and was held a prisoner of war until July, 1865. He returned home barefoot, began the industrious task of rebuilding his own fortune as a farmer on a place owned by Major Flood, and lived there forty consecutive years, until a few years before his death. At that time he lived on the farm of his son, Samuel L. Ferguson. He was a Democrat and a member of the Baptist Church. Of his nine children four are living.

Samuel L. Ferguson was a boy on the farm and attended an old field school, and later went to a private school five miles away, walking the distance. In September, 1893, he entered the University of Virginia, taking the academic and law courses, graduating in law in 1895, when he was admitted to the bar, and in the same year began practice at Appomattox. The first motion he made before a court was to secure a pension for the Confederate soldier. His experience has brought him a very satisfactory practice, not only in Appomattox, but in adjoining counties.

Mr. Ferguson married, February 12, 1896, Adelia Celestia Mann, who was born in Appomattox County and was educated in schools there and in a private school at Petersburg, Virginia. She is a daughter of Charles R. Mann, of Appomattox, and granddaughter of Joel Mann, originally of Henrico County, Virginia, and a cousin of R. H. Mann, a prominent attorney of Petersburg. The Mann family has been a prominent one in Virginia, represented by men high in official life. Mrs. Ferguson's mother was a Penick, a relative of Bishop Penick. Six children were born to the marriage, five of whom are living: Virginia, wife of Daniel B. Henderson, an insurance man in Appomattox County and a nephew of Professor Henderson, one of the prominent members of the faculty of the University; Russell May, wife of Ned A. Wagers, a traveling salesman living at Appomattox; S. L. Ferguson, Junior, who attended the Richmond Law School and is now practicing law at Appomattox; Rachel Adelia, wife of J. R. Lawson, interested in the Chevrolet car agency at Brookneal; and Joseph D., a business man at Appomattox.

Both Senator and Mrs. Ferguson are prominent members of the Methodist Episcopal Church, South. He is a steward and she is chairman of the Social Service Committee. Mr. Ferguson is a member of the Masonic fraternity. Besides his law practice he owns approximately seven thousand acres of Virginia land. He is the largest farmer and tax payer in his county. He is director and attorney for the Bank of Appomattox.

He was elected a member of the Virginia Senate from the Eleventh Senatorial District, composed of the counties of Appomattox, Buckingham, Charlotte and Cumberland, in 1918, for the unexpired term of the late Senator Gayle, and the same year for the regular term, and was reelected in 1922 and 1926, without opposition, for the Democratic nomination, opposition in general election only once in 1922, when he was triumphantly elected. He has been one of the most useful members of the Senate's organization, and its recognized leader, being chairman of the Senate Caucus, chairman of the committee on banks and insurance, member of finance, roads, and privileges and elections committees, and was chairman of the committee on executive expenditures until he resigned. Senator Ferguson is chairman of State Democratic Central Committee of the Tenth Virginia Congressional District, and served as chairman of the Democratic party in Appomattox County for many years, and was a delegate to the National Conventions of New York in 1924, and Houston in 1928. He is president of the Appomattox Tobacco Warehouse Company and president of J. E. Sears and Company, tobacco manufacturers, and is recognized as one of the foremost business men of his county.

JOHN WALTER WAYLAND, Ph. D., teacher and writer, is distinguished by his appreciation of his native country, the rich and picturesque Shenandoah Valley, by his devotion to its highest interests and his remarkable skill in popularizing its history and stories, and as a writer and teacher of history he ranks with the ablest men of his generation in Virginia.

Doctor Wayland was born at Mount Jackson, Shenandoah County, December 8, 1872, son of John Wesley and Anna M. Kagey Wayland, and on both sides is descended from some of the old established families of the Shenandoah Valley. He represents a typical element in the population of the Valley, the German migrations from Pennsylvania and also the strain of English and related elements in the early settlement of the Valley. His great-grandfather Wayland came from England, the first home in Virginia being Madison County. Doctor Wayland's grandfather, John Wesley Wayland, was born in Madison County and died there at an early age. Doctor Wayland's father, also named John Wesley, was born in Shenandoah County and was a man of remarkable talents and individual skill. He was a teacher, both before the Civil war and afterwards, and was a mechanic, skilled in the use of tools, being a cabinet maker and a clock and watch maker. During most of his life his home was a small farm at Wood Lawn, three miles north of Mount Jackson. He was not in sympathy with slavery or secession, but served during the first two years of the war in Stonewall Jackson's command. He was a lifelong member of the German Reformed Church and for a number of years was affiliated with the Republican party. He died April 23, 1899, at Bridgewater, Virginia. His wife, Anna Kagey, was born in Shenandoah County in 1831 and died April 5, 1901, in Missouri. Her people were of German Swiss lineage, the Kageys and Neffs having been identified with the Valley of Virginia from an early period, and from that section having spread to many other states. Her parents were Jacob and Barbara (Neff) Kagey.

John Walter Wayland, the fourth and youngest child of his parents, grew up at the old homestead in Shenandoah County, and the groundwork of his mental training was given him by his parents. He attended a local school from the age of eleven and in 1890, at the age of eighteen, began teaching in his native county. In 1893 he enrolled in Bridgewater College, spending two years in the preparatory department and four years in the collegiate department. He was graduated with the A. B. degree in 1899, being class poet, and during the last three years had been instructor in history. On graduating he was chosen professor of history in Bridgewater College and in the intervals of teaching there spent several years in residence in the University of Virginia, where he was awarded the Doctor of Philosophy degree in 1907. He was instructor in history at the University of Virginia from 1906 to 1909, and since September, 1909, has been professor of history and social science at the State Teachers College at Harrisonburg. In that post of duty for twenty years he has afforded inspiration, zeal of scholarship, as well as technical training to thousands of men and women who have gone forth from the college to teach in Virginia and other states. He has taught in summer schools in the University of Virginia and in other universities and colleges.

Doctor Wayland is a member of the Virginia Historical Society, Virginia State Teachers Association, the Raven Society of the University of Virginia, is a Phi Beta Kappa, Delta Sigma Rho, a Democrat, Baptist and Mason, and a member of the Colonnade Club at the University. On October 16, 1928, he was elected an honorary life member of the Kansas State Historical Society.

Through all the years of his teaching Doctor Wayland has been a constant contributor to local and national literature. He has written poetry, history, educational works, was author of the words of "Old Virginia," set to music by Professor Will Ruebush, and won in 1909 the *Baltimore Sun* prize offered for the best definition of "Gentleman." Chief among his published writings are: *Paul, the Herald of the Cross*, published in 1901; *The Twelve Apostles*, published in 1905; *The German Element of the Shenandoah Valley of Virginia*, 1907; *The Political Opinions of Thomas Jefferson*, 1907; *Sidney Lanier at Rockingham Springs*, 1912; *History of Rockingham County*, 1912; *How to Teach American History*, 1914; *History Stories for Primary Grades*, 1919; *Christ as a Teacher*, 1919; *A History of Virginia for Boys and Girls*, 1920; *History Helps*, 1921; *Guide to the Shenandoah Valley*, 1923; *Ethics and Citizenship*, 1923; *Art Folio of the Shenandoah Valley*, 1924; *Historic Landmarks of the Shenandoah Valley*, 1924; *The Fairfax Line*, 1925; *History of Shenandoah County*, 1927; *Rambles in Europe*, 1927; *Whispers of the Hills*, 1928.

Doctor Wayland married at Bridgewater, June 8, 1898, Miss Mattie V. Fry, who was born at Bridgewater and was educated in Bridgewater College. Her parents were James A. and Annie (Wine) Fry. Doctor and Mrs. Wayland have two sons: Francis Fry, born May 27, 1907; and John Walter, Jr., born April 15, 1909. The elder son is a member of the class of 1930 in Bridgewater College; the younger is a student (1928) in the National Business College, Roanoke, Virginia.

LAIRD L. CONRAD. Genius may be the motive power of success, but many who take the trouble to study the lives and leading characteristics of the man who have accomplished something are led to believe that experience and sound judgment must be combined with natural inclination to produce the best results. In the majority of cases where a man has risen above his fellows it will be found that his rise has come gradually through persistent and conscientious efforts. There are many qualities which help to form the character, such as self-reliance, conscientiousness, energy and honesty, and they all work together to produce the highest standing and most satisfactory rewards. The above is certainly true of Laird L. Conrad, one of the leading attorneys practicing at the bar of Harrisonburg. He is honored and respected not only by his professional colleagues, but by the public as well.

Laird L. Conrad was born in Harrisonburg, June 16, 1884, a son of Edward S. and Jennie S. (Irick) Conrad, both of whom were born in Rockingham County, Virginia. His father died in 1916, but his mother survives and is living in Harrisonburg. His father was an able lawyer, and studied law at the University of Virginia; he was engaged in the practice of his profession in Harrisonburg until his death. There were four children, two dying in infancy. The elder son, Dr. Charles E. Conrad, is a physician of Harrisonburg, specializing in diseases of children. Both as a member and steward of the Methodist Episcopal Church, South, of Harrisonburg, the father was active in religious affairs; he was frequently a delegate to the annual conference of his church and at one time a delegate to its General Conference. The mother is also active in the same church. One of the outstanding figures in Masonry, he was advanced through all of the bodies of the York Rite, was a past master of his local lodge, a past high priest of the local chapter, a past commander of the local commandery, and was also a Past Grand High Priest of the State of Virginia. He assisted in organizing a Masonic School of Instruction. In political faith he was a Democrat. The paternal grandfather, George O. Conrad, was a native of Rockingham County. During the war between the states he served in the Confederate army, was wounded, and also taken a prisoner. The maternal grandfather, Andrew B. Irick, was the first president of the First National Bank of Harrisonburg.

Laird L. Conrad was graduated from the Harrisonburg High School, from Randolph-Macon College, Ashland, Virginia, taking the degree of Master of Arts, and from the University of Virginia in 1907, with the degree of Bachelor of Laws. Immediately thereafter he established himself in a general practice in Harrisonburg, where he has since remained, building up wide and valuable connections. He is attorney and a director of the Rockingham National Bank and is attorney and vice president of the Harrisonburg Loan and Thrift Corporation, and he is a trustee of the Rockingham Memorial Hospital. He is also the General Receiver and Commissioner in Chancery of the Circuit Court of Rockingham County, Virginia, and a director in numerous business corporations.

In 1927 Mr. Conrad married Miss Margaret B. Davis, who was born in Virginia, a daughter of Richard Sale and Ida Melville (Biscoe) Davis, of Richmond County, Virginia. She is an Episcopalian and he is a Methodist. He belongs to the Masonic Order, and to Phi Kappa Sigma, Phi Delta Phi legal fraternity, the Kiwanis Club, of which he is an ex-president, and the Spottswood Country Club. A man of broad information and of intelligent investigation along many lines, he ever lives up to his opportunities and gives something of himself to help others to do the same.

ERNEST HAROLD STRICKLER. It is well for a community when its industries continue to be operated by the same interests that have made a success, for such a condition serves to stabilize business and protect all classes. The Strickler interests in the milling industry of Harrisonburg and the county are large, and although J. M. Strickler, for years the outstanding figure in their management, has passed away he has left behind him in the person of his son, Ernest H. Strickler, a worthy successor, and the progressive policies he inaugurated are still governing the management of the mills.

Ernest H. Strickler, manager of the J. M. Strickler Mills, and a sound and efficient business man of Harrisonburg, was born in Page County, Virginia, October 5, 1883. His father was also born in Page County, but his mother, Mrs. Virginia

(Moyers) Strickler, was born in Luray, Virginia, and she died when she was sixty-two years old, while he died when he was sixty-nine, in November, 1923. She was a daughter of John Moyers, a native of Page County. The paternal grandfather of Ernest H. Strickler was Abraham Strickler, an extensive planter and slaveowner and a veteran of the war between the states, whose life was spent in Page County.

J. M. Strickler remained on his father's plantation until he was sixteen years old, at which time he went to Luray to learn the milling business under John B. Groves. In 1870 he secured a farm from his parents and began operating it, but a disastrous flood washed away all the buildings on his property as well as those on the homestead, and for a year thereafter, in order to get a start, he conducted the local ferry. Once more he went to Luray, and eventually bought the Robert Mauck Mill in Page County, but, after running it for six or seven years, he sold it to Philip M. Kauffman, who still owns and operates it. Mr. Strickler then went to Newmarket, Virginia, and bought the old Moore Mill, continuing to operate it for eighteen years, and then selling it. Going then to Mount Jackson, he leased a mill and conducted it for three years. His next step was to buy the mill owned by the Berryville Milling Company at Berryville, Virginia, in 1912, taking charge of it in 1913. This he operated for six years, and then in 1919 he bought property in Harrisonburg and was out of the business for several years. However, in 1922, he bought the plant of the Harrisonburg Milling Company, the owners of which were C. F. Cauffman, William M. Joseph and G. C. Dovel, of Harrisonburg, and D. H. Dixon, of North Carolina. With characteristic energy he began operating this mill, and was actively engaged in this work until his death. Three children were born to him and his wife: Virgie, who married Charles G. Sanger, an orchardman residing near Harrisonburg; Ernest H., whose name heads this review; and Reba, who married Frank O. Liskey, assistant manager of the mills, and lives on the home place in Harrisonburg. J. M. Strickler and his wife were Presbyterians and both active in church work. He was a Democrat in political faith.

Ernest H. Strickler was educated in the high school of Rockingham County and Bridgewater College. When he completed his studies he started in the milling business with his father, and is now manager of the mills for the estate which owns a mill at Pleasant Valley, which is a feed and grain mill, and also an elevator. The estate recently bought, in January, 1927, a mill at Newmarket, known as the Plains Mill. The Harrisonburg plant has a daily capacity of 300 barrels; that of Newmarket has a capacity of seventy-five barrels; and that of the Pleasant Valley is about the same. The storage capacity is 50,000 bushels at Harrisonburg, 40,000 bushels at Newmarket and 10,000 bushels at Pleasant Valley, and in 1927 this storage capacity was taxed to the utmost.

In October, 1927, Mr. Strickler married Miss Ruby Maiden, who was born in McGaheysville, Rockingham County, Virginia. There are no children. They are members of the Presbyterian Church. Mr. Strickler devotes his entire time to his business and has but little interest for outside matters and therefore has not formed connections with fraternities or clubs. However he does want good men elected to office and a fair administration of his community's affairs.

Moss Abram Plunkett. The law is known as a stern mistress, demanding of her devotees constant and unremitting attention and leading her followers through many mazes and intricacies before she grants them success at her hands. This conception precludes the idea of the successful lawyer indulging in activities outside of the straight path of his profession, but there are men who find time and inclination to develop their tastes and expand their circle of usefulness, and when they do they are able to go far, for their intensive studies have made it possible for them to grasp other matters both rapidly and thoroughly. Moss A. Plunkett, of Roanoke, is known not only as a devotee of the law but as a close student of business administration, a man of intellect and masterly attainments.

Moss A. Plunkett was born in Franklin County, Virginia, March 2, 1888, a son of Algernon Wade and Emma Judith (Bell) Plunkett, natives of Virginia, the father born in Franklin County and the mother in Henry County. After many years spent as a contractor and builder the father is now living in comfortable retirement in Roanoke. Of the six children born to the parents Moss A. Plunkett is the second in order of birth. In religious faith the parents are Baptists, and they are earnest church workers.

Having been a resident of Roanoke City since 1890, Moss A. Plunkett received his early instruction in the public schools of Roanoke, graduating from the Roanoke High School in 1904. Immediately thereafter he became connected with the law firm of Robertson, Hall & Woods of Roanoke, where he served as stenographer and bookkeeper and later as court reporter, during which time he became interested in and began the study of law. In 1909 he entered the University of Virginia, was admitted to the bar in 1910 and completed his law course in 1911. Returning to Roanoke, he became a member of the firm of Hall & Woods. In 1916 he and his brother, Walter C. Plunkett, formed the firm of Plunkett & Plunkett, for the general practice of law.

Upon the entry of the United States in the World war both members of the law firm gave up their practice to serve their country. The war record of Moss A. Plunkett discloses that he entered the Second Training Camp, Fort Myer, Virginia, on August 23, 1917, was commissioned first lieutenant, infantry, November 27, 1917, and ordered to report at Camp Meade, Maryland, December 16, 1917, where he was assigned to Company K, Three Hundred and Fourteenth Infantry; that he sailed from Hoboken, New Jersey, June 30, 1918, on transport *Duca Degli Abruzzi*, as member of the Advance School Detachment of the Seventy-ninth Division, landed at Brest, France, July 13, 1918, attended Infantry School, First Corps, American Expeditionary Forces, at Gondrecourt, as student from July 22 to August 18, 1918, was assigned to Training Area at Genevrieres, Haute Marne, with Company K, Three Hundred and Fourteenth Infantry, from August 9 to September 7, 1918; that he participated in the following engagements: Sector 304, defensive, September 13 to September 25, 1918; Meuse-Argonne offensive from September 26 to October 1, 1918; Troyon Sector, defensive, from October 8 to October 20, 1918; that he served as instructor, Army Candidates School at La Valbonne, Ain, October 20 to December 14, 1918; rejoined Company K, Three Hundred and Fourteenth Infantry, at Lamorteau, Belgium, and served with the Army of Occupation from December 30, 1918, to January

20, 1919; and that he sailed from St. Nazaire, France, May 16, 1919, on transport *Princess Matoika,* arrived at Hoboken, New Jersey, May 26, 1919, and was honorably discharged from service on June 2, 1919, at Camp Dix, New Jersey.

Moss A. Plunkett married on October 22, 1919, Miss Billie Puett, born in Temple, Texas, and educated in the public schools of Temple, Baylor College, University of Texas, Randolph-Macon Woman's College, University of Virginia, Goucher College and Columbia University. They are members of the First Baptist Church of Roanoke and are engaged in mission Sunday School work near Roanoke. Since 1913 Mr. Plunkett has been a member of the American Bar Association, the Virginia State Bar Association, and the Roanoke Bar Association. He is also a member of the Rotary Club of Roanoke, a director of the local Y. M. C. A. and takes an active part in the civic and welfare work of Roanoke. Mr. and Mrs. Plunkett have two children: Moss Abram, Jr., born March 24, 1922, and June, born July 23, 1924. Mr. Plunkett's labors have not only been an element in promoting his own success, but have also constituted a potent factor in maintaining the high standard of the bar of Roanoke City and in elevating the general business practices of his community.

WILLIAM FRANK SHAVER. Efficiency is the keynote of success, without this characteristic man can make but little permanent progress, nor can he win standing or confidence among his associates. No matter in what line his efforts may be directed, without the ability to make every action count for something definite his accomplishments will fall below the average, and he will find himself at a standstill, if he does not go backward. When he is efficient he accomplishes something worth while and whenever a position ahead is open he is very liable to be advanced, for those in authority soon come to recognize that he will effectively discharge new responsibilities just as he has done in the past. Such has been the happy experience of William F. Shaver, superintendent of the Buckeye Incubator Company of Harrisonburg, Virginia.

William F. Shaver was born in Fauquier County, Virginia, in 1891, a son of George S. and Minnie B. (Rhodes) Shaver, the latter of whom was born in Rockingham County, Virginia, and is still living, making her home in Harrisonburg, but the former is deceased. All his life he was a farmer, and a Republican. The United Brethren Church held his membership, and he was active in its work. Five children were born to him and his wife, namely: William F., who is the eldest; Perry E., who is connected with the Sun Shipbuilding and Dry Dock Company of Philadelphia, Pennsylvania; Other F., who is a farmer of Pleasant Valley; Nina C., who married Ernest Neff, is a widow residing with her mother; and Paul O., who resides in Harrisonburg, is in the employ of the Staley Silks Corporation. The paternal grandfather, George F. Shaver, was a native of Virginia and a farmer all his life. The maternal grandfather, John F. Rhodes, was also a farmer.

Growing up on a farm in Pleasant Valley, Virginia, William F. Shaver attended the local schools, and his first outside work was done in connection with the West Virginia Pulp & Paper Company of Covington, Virginia, where he was a millwright. Subsequently he went with the New Town Incubator Corporation of Harrisonburg, until that concern was bought out by the Buckeye Incubator Company, and he was made superintendent of the plant in 1918, which important position he still holds. Mr. Shaver has 130 persons under his supervision, and is working the plant at capacity. The company sells its product all over the United States and to foreign countries, and the incubators put forth by it are recognized to be among the most satisfactory on the market.

Mr. Shaver married Miss Elizabeth S. Whissen, who was born in Augusta County, Virginia, and educated in Pleasant Valley. Mr. and Mrs. Shaver had one child, William Frank, Jr., but he is now deceased. They are consistent members of the United Brethren Church, and he belongs to the Benevolent and Protective Order of Elks and the Harrisonburg Rotary Club. His interests centered in Harrisonburg and Rockingham County, Mr. Shaver is deeply interested in the continued prosperity of this region, and willing to do everything in his power to advance the welfare of the people.

JOHN PAUL. Among the more notable attorneys practicing at the bar of Harrisonburg who have established a reputation for ability and integrity none are more worthy of mention in a history of Virginia than John Paul of Harrisonburg. He has not only won distinction in his profession, but has made his influence felt in other lines, and is an excellent representative of the best element in his calling. He was born in Harrisonburg, December 9, 1883, a son of John and Katherine (Green) Paul, both natives of Virginia, he born in Rockingham County and she in Warren County. He died in 1901, but she survived until 1927. They had seven children born to them, of whom six are living, and of them all John Paul was the fourth in order of birth. The father was raised in the Presbyterian Church, but the children became members of the Episcopal Church, of which their mother was a member. The father was also a lawyer, educated in Roanoke College and the University of Virginia, and he began the practice of his profession in Harrisonburg. Enlisting early in the war between the states, he rose to a captaincy, but was captured in 1864 and confined in a Federal prison until the close of hostilities, when he was released. Returning to Harrisonburg, he resumed his practice and in 1883 was appointed a Federal judge, in which capacity he continued to serve with great ability until his demise. Judge Paul also served in the Virginia State Senate and in the Lower House of the National Congress, and was one of the most distinguished men of the state. His father, Peter Paul, was born in Rockingham County, and here was engaged in farming all his life. The Paul family was established in Virginia 200 years ago, and during all of that period has given to the Old Dominion many men of high ability and stainless reputation. The maternal grandfather, Charles Green, was born in Warren County, Virginia.

Given exceptionally good educational advantages, John Paul was graduated from the Virginia Military Institute in 1903 and from the University of Virginia in 1906, receiving his degree of Bachelor of Laws from the latter institution. Then, being admitted to the bar, he settled in Harrisonburg in 1906, and has since been engaged in the practice of law. In 1912 he was elected to the Virginia State Senate, and continued to serve in that body until 1916. In 1917 he entered the army for the World war, and was trained at Fort Myer, Virginia, where he was commissioned a captain of field artillery. In 1918 he was sent overseas, where he remained until 1919, and saw some heavy service at the front. Returned to the United States, he was honorably discharged in May, 1919, and coming back to Harrisonburg, resumed his practice. Almost immediately thereafter he was again elected to the Senate, and in 1920 was elected to Congress, and was candidate for reelection in 1922, but was defeated. From then on to the present he has continued his practice.

In 1914 Mr. Paul married Miss Frances Danenhower, of Alexandria. She died in 1919, while Mr. Paul was in France. Mr. Paul is an Episcopalian. He belongs to Kappa Alpha and Phi Delta Phi, the law fraternity. Like his father before him he is a stalwart Republican and a leader in his party, which he has represented in four national conventions, those of 1912, 1916, 1920 and 1924. Both thorough and practical, Mr. Paul is admirably equipped to take a leading part in all matters in which he is interested, and as a man of marked intellectual activity his labors have been of great importance to Harrisonburg, his district and Virginia.

ASHBY C. BYERS, M. D. The study of the life and accomplishments of a successful man is full of educational value, especially when such a man has achieved tangible and practical results, has raised the standards of business and professional life and sets an example which goes to form a real bulwark of Americanism. A comprehensive knowledge of such a man brings an appreciation of him and of his motives; and, when he is one who is devoting himself to the medical profession, that most exacting and self-sacrificing of callings, then are these above facts emphasized. A record of the accomplishments of some men in the brief span of their life period already passed reads like a fictional account. Without knowledge of attending conditions, it seems impossible that one man could win so much, but in the case of Dr. Ashby C. Byers of Harrisonburg this is true, and he is not only one of the very capable and widely esteemed physicians of Rockingham County, but he and his brother, Sam Byers, under the firm name of Byers Brothers, have been for the past fifteen years the leading breeders of pure-bred Hereford cattle in Virginia.

Doctor Byers was born in Staunton, Virginia, June 17, 1875, a son of Sam and Catherine (Cline) Byers, both of whom were born in Augusta County, and are now deceased. During his lifetime he was a farmer and stockraiser, breeding and importing thoroughbred horses. During the war between the states he served in the Confederate army under General Ashby. Five children were born to the parents, two of whom survive, Doctor Byers' partner being the other child, and he, Sam Byers, is a resident of Burketown, Augusta County, Virginia. The parents belonged to the Presbyterian Church, and were active workers in it. In politics he was a Democrat, and for four years he served as sheriff of Augusta County. His father, Sam Byers, grandfather of Doctor Byers, was born in Pennsylvania, and came to Virginia about 1800, secured land from the Government and lived upon it until his death, and this farm is owned by Doctor Byers and his brother. The maternal grandfather, Sam Cline, was born in Augusta County, Virginia, at Cline Mill. He was a miller and heavy landowner.

After completing his preliminary studies Doctor Byers entered the University of Maryland, from which he was graduated in 1897 with the degree Bachelor of Arts, and he took his medical training in the same institution, from which he took his degree of Doctor of Medicine in 1901. After a year of in-

terneship he entered upon a general practice at Lacy Springs, Virginia, and continued there for nine years, going from there to Harrisonburg, where he still continues in a general practice with remarkable success.

In 1902 Doctor Byers married Miss Daisy Sherman, who was born in Mount Crawford, Virginia, a daughter of John W. Sherman, a miller. Doctor and Mrs. Byers have had the following children born to them: Catherine, who was graduated from Randolph-Macon College, married David B. Horner, Junior, with the Loan & Trust Bank of Lynchburg, Virginia; F. L,. who is a senior in the medical department of the University of Virginia; Charlotte, who is attending a woman's college; A. C., who is a junior in the Augusta Military Academy; Carl, who is in his third year of high school; Nancy, who is in her second year in high school; and Dorothy, who is of the eighth grade. The family all belong to the Methodist Episcopal Church, South, of which he is a steward. He belongs to the Ancient, Free and Accepted Masons, the Benevolent and Protective Order of Elks, the Rockingham County Medical Society, the Virginia State Medical Society, the Shenandoah Valley Medical Society and the American Medical Association, and is very popular in all of these organizations. He is also a charter member of the Rotary Club.

WALKER PETTYJOHN, who served two terms as mayor of the City of Lynchburg, is a contractor, a business and profession he has followed since early manhood, and is the active head of the firm of J. P. Pettyjohn & Company, the nominal head and founder of the business being his venerable father, John P. Pettyjohn, still living in Lynchburg past the age of four score.

Walker Pettyjohn was born in Amherst County, Virginia, November 2, 1870, son of John P. and Nannie R. (Old) Pettyjohn. The record of his father is given on other pages. Walker Pettyjohn was educated in public schools and Randolph-Macon College at Ashland, and at the age of nineteen went to work in his father's sash and door factory at Lynchburg. He has been associated with the business of J. P. Pettyjohn & Company ever since, a period of over thirty-five years, during which time the operations of the firm have been widely extended over Virginia and adjacent states. They have handled an immense amount of construction work for railroad companies, particularly the Norfolk and Western, building stations, shops and other buildings. The firm has also erected many cotton mills and tobacco factories, business structures of different kinds, and some of the buildings on the campus of the Randolph-Macon Woman's College at Lynchburg. Mr. Pettyjohn is also vice president of the Peoples National Bank of Lynchburg and has been a director in a number of other corporations. He was president of the Glamorgan Pipe & Foundry Company of Lynchburg for several years.

Mr. Pettyjohn served two terms as a member of the Lynchburg City Council and in September, 1924, was elected mayor of the city, being reelected in 1926. During his administration Lynchburg accomplished an immense amount of constructive progress, involving the service of some of the best engineering talent, and a great deal was done in the way of planning as well as actual construction to make the city adequate for its future destiny as a commercial and industrial metropolis of Southwest Virginia. Mr. Pettyjohn is a Knight Templar Mason and

Shriner, member of the Oakwood Country Club, and since boyhood has been active in the Court Street Methodist Episcopal
Church, South, serving on its Board of Stewards. For thirty
years he was also musical director for the Sunday School. Mrs.
Pettyjohn is a Presbyterian.

He married, October 30, 1895, Miss Mary Raine, of Danville,
who was educated in public schools there and in the Randolph-
Macon Woman's College. She is a daughter of the late Charles
A. Raine, a tobacconist. Mr. and Mrs. Pettyjohn have six
children. The son Charles Raine Pettyjohn, born November 11,
1896, was educated in public schools, graduated in 1918, with
the degree Mechanical Engineer, from Cornell University, was
an ensign in the navy during the World war and later in the
aviation department, and since the war has been associated with
his father's contracting firm. He is a member of the Phi Delta
Theta college fraternity. Charles R. Pettyjohn married Mildred
B. Hudson and has two children, Mary Jane and Charles Raine,
Jr. The second child of Mr. and Mrs. Walker Pettyjohn is
Nannie Old, wife of E. L. Carrington, one of the executive heads
of the Lynchburg Shoe Company. Michaux M. Pettyjohn was
educated in the Lynchburg schools and the Virginia Military
Institute. Mary M. Pettyjohn is the wife of Wilbur Winfree,
with the Lynchburg Foundry Company. Walker Pettyjohn, Jr.,
is a student in the Virginia Military Institute, and Clunett H.
Pettyjohn is in the Lynchburg Junior High School.

THE WINCHESTER PUBLIC SCHOOLS have a place of unique
prominence and influence in the history of education in Virginia,
and their present high standing reflects in large measure the
progressive policies and effective executive and scholastic administration of the present superintendent, Hugh S. Duffey.

As touching the development and admirable service of the
public schools of the City of Winchester, the beautiful and historic old metropolis and judicial center of Frederick County, the
following narrative, previously published in magazine mediums,
is worthy of perpetuation in this connection, with minor changes
in the reproduction:

"Volumes have been written on the history centering in this
locality and the magnificence of the surrounding country, but not
one of them bears a legend more fascinating than the historical
background of the John Handley Foundation, probably the only
endowed public school system in the country. Judge John Handley, the benefactor, was born in Ireland, of poor parents, in 1835.
He came to America at the age of fifteen and located in Washington, D. C. Working as a carpenter, he studied law in his
leisure hours, and thereafter practiced in turn at Rochester and
Scranton, Pennsylvania, in which state he passed the later years
of his life, his death having occurred in 1895.

"Judge Handley became much interested in Winchester on
account of its historical surroundings, and this led to his leaving the residue of his large estate to the City of Winchester for
the erection of school houses. It was felt by the citizens that
the sum ($2,000,000) was too great to be devoted entirely to
building purposes, and a construction by a court in law was obtained permitting the setting aside of $1,200,000 as an endow-
ment fund, while the remainder of the benefaction ($800,000)
was made applicable to building. The endowment fund is not
entrusted to the school board but to the Handley Board of Trustees, a fiduciary board. The Handley school building in Win-

chester is of one-story type, Colonial brick, 535 feet long by 180 feet deep. It is distinctly of the Colonial type, the architect having followed as a motif the buildings of the University of Virginia. The auditorium of this splendid building has a seating capacity of 1,600. Another feature is the regulation indoor tennis court. Besides the many class rooms the building provides: Superintendent's private office, meeting room for the school board, educational research room, men's rest room, high-school principal's private office, a similar provision for the principal of the elementary school, a school store, ladies' rest room, clinic and dispensary, ample storerooms, art gallery and museum (20 by 150 feet), and twenty-four class rooms for elementary grades. The junior and senior high school section provides twenty-six class rooms, all equipped in the most modern way. The special departments provided are business department, science laboratories, science lecture room, sewing and cooking laboratories, art studio, music studio and industrial shops. The gymnasium is 56 by 78 feet in the clear, with a gallery at each end, seating 400 persons.

"This plant is but the setting for an effort upon the part of the Winchester Board of Education and the school administration to build up in their city a superior system of schools. Great progress has been made in reaching the standards of accomplishment since the reorganization that took place about the year 1921, and the methods now used are those in vogue in the better school organizations of the country. Colored children are provided for in a separate building in another part of the city.

"Columbia University used the Winchester schools as an observation school and sent numbers of its students to Winchester for two or three weeks of observation and investigation."

Hugh S. Duffey, the present superintendent of the Winchester public schools, was born at Falls Church, Fairfax County, Virginia, August 25, 1887, and is a son of Rev. Jefferson Waite Duffey and Nannie Troutwine (Hyler) Duffey, both likewise natives of Virginia, though the former was born at Moorefield, present judicial center of Hardy County, West Virginia, his father, John Duffey, of Irish lineage, having come to Virginia from Frederick County, Maryland, and having become a pioneer in what is now West Virginia. Rev. Jefferson Waite Duffey gave many years of able and consecrated service as a clergyman of the Methodist Episcopal Church, South, and he is now living retired in the City of Washington, D. C., he being eighty-one years of age at the time of this writing, in 1928, and his wife being eighty years of age. Mrs. Duffey's ancestors were numbered among the early Colonial settlers in Virginia, and the original spelling of the family name was Heiter.

Hugh S. Duffey is one of a family of four children, all of whom are living, and his earlier education was obtained in the public schools of Washington, D. C., and Harrisburg, Pennsylvania. In 1909 he was graduated from Randolph-Macon College, with the degree Bachelor of Arts, and he soon afterward became teacher of English and mathematics in Frederick College, Maryland, where he remained two years. In the autumn of 1911 he came to Winchester and assumed the position of teacher of English and mathematics in the Handley High School, he having given major attention to English while attending college. In 1918 he was advanced to the office of principal of this high school, and of this position he continued the incumbent until the autumn of 1923, since which years he has been giving a signally resourceful and progressive administration as superintendent of the Winchester public schools, he having achieved a splendid work in advancing the standards of these schools and having received the loyal and valued cooperation of the Board of Education and of the Handley Board of Trustees, which administers the Handley Fund, as previously noted in this context. The Winchester schools now have an enrollment of 2,100 students, and there is retained a corps of seventy efficient teachers. Mr. Duffey did post-graduate work in Harvard University, and from this historic institution he received the degree of Master of Education. Mr. Duffey takes loyal interest in all that concerns the civic and material welfare of his home city and native state, and his political allegiance is given to the Democratic party. He is affiliated with the Masonic fraternity, and is a valued member of the local Rotary Club, of which he has served as president.

At Winchester was solemnized the marriage of Mr. Duffey and Miss Vera Lynch, whose father, Morris M. Lynch, is a representative member of the bar of this city. The two children of this union, two sons, are Maurice Jefferson and Richard.

JAMES MAGRUDER WARREN, M. D. While the career of Dr. James Magruder Warren belongs to the past rather than to the present of Virginia history, his death having occurred thirty years ago, he is still remembered by many of the older residents of Bridgewater as a skilled physician and surgeon whose practice covered an area of many miles and who was well known not only for his professional talents, but for his humanitarianism and public spirit. Although his death occurred when he was only forty years of age, he had already accomplished as much as many men would deem sufficient after a full lifetime of earnest effort.

Doctor Warren was born in Orange County, Virginia, May 3, 1858, and was a son of Edward Tiffin and Virginia (Watson) (Magruder) Warren. The Magruder family were early settlers of Orange County, and were prominent in various activities of life. Col. James Magruder, the maternal grandfather of Doctor Warren, was the owner of a very large estate in Orange County, and four of his sons were killed during the war between the states while serving in the Confederate army. Edward Tiffin Warren was born in Virginia and was educated for the law, which he practiced at Harrisonburg until the conflict between the North and the South. He enlisted in the Confederate army and rose to the rank of colonel, meeting a soldier's death while leading his men in the bloody engagement of the Wilderness.

James Magruder Warren attended the Rome (Georgia) Military Academy and received his degree from the Medical University of Maryland. For two years thereafter he was engaged in practice at New Hope, Virginia, and then moved to Bridgewater, Rockingham County, where he was engaged continuously in practice until his death July 13, 1898. Doctor Warren carried on a country practice for the most part, and during his career always kept three fine horses ready so that he might answer instantly any call for his services, no matter how far distantly located. He was one of the physicians of the old school, who placed their profession above all thought of personal profit, and although he was successful in his financial affairs, he was always ready to give the same attention to the poverty stricken as he did to his most affluent patient. Although his practice was necessarily general in character, he preferred surgery, and performed numerous successful operations, both minor and major, all over the county. His death was universally accounted a severe loss and was mourned by hundreds. Doctor Warren was a member of the Episcopal Church and of the Masonic fraternity, and in politics he was an adherent of the Democratic party.

Doctor Warren married Miss Williette Sprinkel, who was born at Harrisonburg, and is a graduate of a female institute of Winchester, Virginia. She is a daughter of Capt. Charles Alexander and Sara Eliza (Carter) Sprinkel, her father having gained his title as an officer of the Confederacy during the war between the states, following which he was engaged in the hardware business at Harrisonburg for many years. Mrs. Sprinkel was born in Nelson County, Virginia, her father being one of the Carters of the James River community, and a direct descendant of King Carter. Doctor and Mrs. Warren became the parents of two children. The elder, Carter Magruder, married Wade Cothran, a leading cotton dealer of Greenville, South Carolina, and has one child, Wade Cothran. The younger, James Magruder, who is identified with the big real estate firm of Deckert & Company of Harrisonburg, married Frances Lackland Sublett and has three children: James Magruder III and Frank and Wade, twins. Mrs. Warren, who survives her husband, now resides at 409 South Main Street, Harrisonburg, where she is active in the work and charities of the Episcopal Church.

FRANK STACEY TAVENNER as lawyer, public official, orchardist and business man has been a commanding figure in the affairs of the Shenandoah Valley for many years. His home is at Woodstock, where he has practiced law since 1892.

Judge Tavenner was born in Frederick County, Virginia, April 25, 1866, son of Jonah and Mary Jane (Keckley) Tavenner. He is a descendant of George Tavenner, of English ancestry, who settled in Loudoun County about 1760 and whose son, Jonah Tavenner, was the father of Stacey J. Tavenner, grandfather of Judge Tavenner. Stacey J. Tavenner was a teacher as well as a farmer and lived for many years near Opequon in Frederick County. Members of the Tavenner family have moved out of Virginia and gained distinction in other states.

Judge Tavenner's father was born in Loudoun County, Virginia, in February, 1832, was reared in Frederick County, and spent the greater part of his life as a farmer and stock man at Gainesboro, where he died in 1912. He was county chairman of the Democratic party. He married in 1865 Mary Jane Keckley, who was born in 1832, daughter of Benjamin Keckley.

Frank S. Tavenner, only son of his parents, was educated in local schools, spent one year in Winchester Academy, and taught while attending college. He graduated with honors from Roanoke College at the age of twenty-one, following which for two years he was principal of the high school at Strasburg and one year at Woodstock. He left school work to complete his law course at the University of Virginia, and in the fall of 1892 began practice at Woodstock.

Since 1900 Judge Tavenner has been interested in the wonderful horticultural possibilities of the Shenandoah Valley, and his personal initiative and enterprise have contributed to the development of that industry around Woodstock and other localities. He owns extensive orchard holdings at Mount Jackson,

and is a member of the firm Tavenner & Zea at Woodstock and
Tavenner & Eastman at Gainesboro. Mr. Tavenner is an
officer in and manager of other extensive orchards, growing
peaches and apples. From these holdings the fruit is picked and
packed and sold on board cars or consigned for sale. Judge
Tavenner is also attorney for two banks in Shenandoah County
and has been admitted to practice in the State Supreme Court
and the United States Supreme Court.

By appointment of the Legislature he was judge of the
County Court until the reorganization of the judiciary system
under the new constitution of 1902. He was a member of the
State Senate from 1904 to 1908, and again from 1912 to 1916,
and in both terms had important committee assignments. He
was a member of the Shenandoah County Draft Board during
the World war. Judge Tavenner is a member of the Sigma Chi
fraternity, the Masonic fraternity, and the Methodist Episcopal
Church, South.

He married in December, 1892, Miss Lou L. Stephenson, who
was born at Parkersburg, West Virginia, in 1861, daughter of
Kenner B. and Bettie G. (Bird) Stephenson. Her father was
educated at the University of Virginia, was a Confederate soldier and member of the Virginia Legislature during the war,
and for many years practiced law at Parkersburg, where he
died. His wife, Bettie Bird, was a daughter of Judge Mark and
Sarah C. M. (Hite) Bird, Sarah Hite being a descendant of the
famous Hite family that acquired a large part of the land in the
Shenandoah Valley and led the way for the emigration into
that region from the German settlers of Pennsylvania. Judge
and Mrs. Tavenner had two children, the only one now living
being Frank S. Tavenner, Jr.

Frank Stacey Tavenner, Jr., graduated from the Woodstock
High School, from Roanoke College with the A. B. degree, took
his Master's degree at Princeton University, and during the
World war attended the Officers' Training Camp at Fort Myer,
Virginia, being commissioned a first lieutenant. In June, 1918,
he went overseas, and was a participant in the two most conspicuous campaigns of the American Expeditionary Forces, St.
Mihiel and the Argonne. He was with the Army of Occupation
in Germany, and returning home after attending the A. E. F.
School at Baune and the Horticultural School at Versailles he
received his honorable discharge in July, 1919. He graduated
in law from the University of Virginia in 1922, and has since
practiced at Woodstock. Frank S. Tavenner, Jr., married Sarah
Zea, of Strasburg, Virginia. They have two children, Harriett
Stephenson and Frank Stacy III.

CHARLES GRATTAN PRICE, of Burke & Price, general insurance, one of the largest insurance agencies in Virginia, is one
of the best known men in his part of the state, and one upon
whom many honors have been heaped, for he is one who wins
and holds the confidence of all with whom he comes in contact.
Whatever he undertakes he carries through to a successful completion, whether it be something connected with his private
affairs or those of a more public nature. He was born four
miles north of Harrisonburg, September 6, 1883, a son of James
R. and Mary (Marshall) Price, he born in Monroe County, now
in West Virginia, but then still a part of Virginia, and she born
in Augusta County. He was a farmer in early life, but later
became a merchant at Dayton, Virginia, where he remained for

nearly fifteen years, and then went to Salem, Virginia, returning to Harrisonburg in 1911, where he died in April, 1925. The mother died in Harrisonburg in 1928, in her eighty-third year. Of the six children born to the parents five are living, and of them all Mr. Price of this review is the fifth in order of birth. The parents were active members of the Presbyterian Church, and he was an elder for a number of years. His fraternal connections were those which he maintained with the Independent Order of Odd Fellows. During the latter part of the war between the states he served in Company I, Fiftieth Virginia Infantry. All his life he was a staunch supporter of the Democratic ticket. The paternal grandfather, Rev. Addison H. Price, was a Presbyterian minister and evangelist, and traveled throughout the South on his Master's business. The maternal grandfather, Mansfield Marshall, was a kinsman of Chief Justice Marshall, and was born in Rockingham County, where his father, William A. Marshall, a schoolteacher and a native of Fauquier County, had settled at an early day.

Charles Grattan Price attended the public schools of Dayton, Virginia, and took a business course in Shenandoah College. His first work was done in a law office as a stenographer, after which he was remittance clerk in the Rockingham National Bank, being promoted to assistant cashier, and continuing with the bank ten years in all, leaving it to become deputy county treasurer under George B. Keezel. A year later, however, in 1912, he went into the insurance business, which, as before stated, has become a very well known agency and operates under the name of Burke & Price. He is a director of the Harrisonburg Building & Loan Association; is president of the Shenandoah Apartments, Incorporated; is secretary and treasurer of the Harrisonburg Realty Corporation; secretary of the Harrisonburg Baking Company, Incorporated; is a past president of the Virginia Association Fire Insurance Agents, having served the latter as president in 1918. Since 1916 he has been fire insurance representative of the Board of Virginia State Teachers Colleges, operating at Harrisonburg, Radford, Farmville and Fredericksburg. Recently he was elected treasurer of the Harrisonburg Library Association, a new feature in this community. For four years he was a member of the Democratic State Committee, serving with Governor Byrd.

On June 10, 1917, Mr. Price married Miss Julia Page Pleasants, born in Fort Worth, Texas, a daughter of Howard Peterkin Pleasants, who was born in Richmond, Virginia, but was in business in Fort Worth at the time of his death, when only twenty-eight years old. Mr. and Mrs. Price have two children: Charles Grattan, Junior; and Page Pleasants. Both Mr. Price and his wife are members of the Presbyterian Church, of which he is an elder. High in Masonry, he has been advanced through all of the bodies of the York Rite, and is a past master of Rockingham Lodge No. 27, A. F. and A. M.; a past high priest of Rockingham Chapter No. 6, R. A. M.; a past eminent commander of Rockingham Commandery No. 10, K. T. For twenty-five years he has been a representative of Acca Temple, A. A. O. N. M. S., of Richmond, and for one year he was district deputy grand master of District No. 6. He is a past president of the Harrisonburg Rotary Club and belongs to the Spottswood Country Club and the Westmoreland Club of Richmond. For many years he has taken an active part in civic affairs, and in 1927 was president of the Harrisonburg Chamber of Commerce. During the World war he was secretary of the First, Second, Third and Fourth Liberty Loan drives and was treasurer of the United War Workers campaign. He is secretary and treasurer of the Rockingham Memorial Hospital, and in every way within his power renders effective assistance to all projects having for their object the furtherance of the best interests of the people of Harrisonburg, Rockingham County and the Shenandoah Valley.

GEORGE BERNARD KEEZELL, of Keezletown, Rockingham County, as a farmer, newspaper publisher, legislator, has for a half century been one of the most influential and useful men in the citizenship of his home county.

Mr. Keezell owns and occupies a farm of 500 acres, a place that is frequently referred to as one of the model farms in the Valley of Virginia. It was on this farm that he was born in 1854. The village of Keezletown, which is his post office, was named for his grandfather, George Keezell. The Keezell family have been in this locality since Colonial time. The Keezells came from Germany and first settled in Pennsylvania, and like many other Pennsylvania Germans moved down into the Valley of Virginia. The Keezells furnished soldiers to the War of the Revolution and the War of 1812, and Mr. Keezell's ancestors were represented in both those wars. Mr. Keezell now occupies the home which he built in 1892, replacing the original home built by his grandfather on the farm in 1794. Mr. Keezell is a son of George and Amanda Fitzallen (Peale) Keezell.

George Bernard Keezell finished his early education in Stuart Hall at Baltimore, Maryland, attending that school two years. When he left school in 1871 he returned to the family estate, and that has been the home and the scene of his career as an agriculturist for more than half a century.

Mr. Keezell married, November 10, 1886, Miss M. Kate Hannah. She died in October, 1902, and in 1903 he married her sister, Belle C. Hannah, who died May 1, 1924. Mr. Keezell's children, all by his first marriage, were: Walter B., born September 7, 1888, and is married and has three children, named George Berry, David Berry and Walter B. Junior; Katherine, born August 2, 1890, is the wife of Claude V. Smith and has four children, George B., Martha, Claude V. Junior, and Edward; Rembrant, born April 10, 1892, served as a captain overseas with the Eightieth Division during the World war, is married and has two children, Rennie and Narice Travis; Florence, born September 10, 1894, is the wife of J. F. Simms and has a daughter, Cornelia Katherine; George Orvil, born July 20, 1896, died at the age of eight years; and Nathaniel H., the youngest, born June 25, 1898, is a graduate of the Virginia Military Institute.

George Bernard Keezell was elected a member of the Virginia State Senate in 1883 and later served from 1895 to 1899 and from 1903 to 1907. He was a member of the Senate in 1904 and also served as chairman of the finance committee. He sat as a delegate in the Constitutional Convention in 1901-02. For twenty years he was a member of the Commission of Fisheries of Virginia and served as treasurer of Rockingham County in 1911. In addition to other public duties and the management of his farming interest Mr. Keezell was a newspaper publisher, the largest stockholder of the *Harrisonburg Daily News Record* from 1911 to 1914. He sold out the newspaper to Governor Byrd

and associates. In 1922 Mr. Keezell was elected a member of the House of Delegates, and is still serving in that body. In the House of Delegates he has served on the finance, Federal relations, privileges and election committees. When he was elected to the State Senate in 1883 he was its youngest member and is now the oldest member of the House of Delegates. Mr. Keezell was on the building committee which contracted for and supervised the rebuilding of the State Capitol at Richmond. He has been instrumental in the passage of much valuable legislation, being author of the bill to establish the Harrisonburg State Teachers College. In the fight for the present highway law of Virginia he was largely instrumental in securing the defeat of the plan to bond the state for building highways and in securing a modification of the measure to provide for paying for all roads as built.

LLOYD A. MYERS is one of the popular business men of Lynchburg, proprietor of the L. A. Myers Company, and has been dealing in motor cars in Central Virginia for the past thirteen years, being one of the older men in that line of business.

He was born in Hickory Forest, Pittsylvania County, Virginia, November 3, 1886, son of Robert Lee and Ida Baines (Rice) Myers. Both his grandfathers, John Myers and Capt. Ibsen Rice, were Confederate soldiers, Captain Rice commanding a company. Captain Rice was a native of North Carolina and spent his life as a farmer in that state, while John Myers was born in Pittsylvania County, Virginia. Robert Lee Myers until he retired in 1917 gave his life to his farm, and is now living with his wife at Lynchburg. He is a Democrat and a Methodist. He was born in 1863 and his wife, in 1865, in North Carolina.

Lloyd A. Myers is the oldest in a family of five sons and four daughters. He was educated in public schools and found occupation for his energies on a farm until he was twenty. At Lynchburg he had several years of experience in a retail hardware concern and then went on the road as traveling representative for the Simmons Hardware Company of Saint Louis. He sold the Simmons line for six years and in 1915 left the road to engage in the automobile business at Lynchburg. At first he handled the Reo car, and later the company took on the Packard car and Republic truck. During 1928 he has taken on the Packard car exclusively in a large territory.

Mr. Myers as a successful business man has found the capital to indulge his interest in agriculture, and owns a beautiful country property in Campbell County, where he engages in farming on a large scale, and is also developing a fine herd of cattle.

Mr. Myers married in 1906 Miss Mary Anderson, of Lynchburg. She died in 1924, leaving two children: Lloyd A., Jr., born in 1911, a student in Washington and Lee University, taking the law course; and Billy, a pupil in the Lynchburg public schools. Mr. Myers in 1925 married Lillian S. Stevens, daughter of Judge Stevens, of Nelson County. At the time of her marriage she was the widow of Russell Thurman. Mr. and Mrs. Myers are members of the Rivermont Methodist Episcopal Church, South. He is a York and Scottish Rite Mason and Shriner, a charter member and former director of the Kiwanis Club, and is also affiliated with the B. P. O. Elks.

WILLIAM JACOB STIREWALT has added to his role of service as a school man the unusual distinction of being also a banker. Mr. Stirewalt is president of a bank at New Market and for eight years has been principal of the New Market High School.

He was born in that community of Shenandoah County August 5, 1879, son of J. Paul and Amelia (Coffman) Stirewalt, both of whom reside at New Market. Mr. Stirewalt is a great-great-grandson of Johan Steygerwalt, who was born in Hanover, Germany, July 9, 1732, and on September 26, 1749, left Germany and by way of England came to America, landing at Philadelphia. He died November 21, 1796. His wife, Mary, was born December 27, 1737, and died April 2, 1823. Their grandson, Jacob Stirewalt, was born in 1805 and died in August, 1869. He married Henrietta Henkel. J. Paul Stirewalt was born in 1850, and gave half a century to the ministry of the Lutheran Church. He is a graduate of the New Market Polytechnic Institute. He served a number of churches in Rockingham and Shenandoah counties as pastor, his longest term of service with any one church being thirty years at the Raders Church. Though retired from the active ministry he continues active in the councils of his denomination and in organizing the synods of the State of Virginia. He and his wife had two children: William J. and Martin L. Martin L. was born July 24, 1882, is a minister of the English Lutheran Church, and is now a professor in the Lutheran Theological Seminary at Maywood, Illinois.

William J. Stirewalt attended local schools in the Shenandoah Valley, graduated from Lenoir College at Hickory, North Carolina, in 1900, and during 1903-05 continued his advanced work at the University of Virginia, which subsequently gave him the Master of Arts degree. Between his graduation from Lenoir and the time he entered the University of Virginia he taught a term in the New Market High School and then taught at Hickory, North Carolina. From the University of Virginia he returned to Hickory as an instructor in Lenoir College, where he remained from 1905 to 1913. During that time he also acted as college treasurer. Mr. Stirewalt in 1913 took up his duties as principal of the New Market High School, and has not only found a very congenial work there in his old home community, but has had the satisfaction of seeing the school steadily improve in standards and equipment.

Mr. Stirewalt has been president of the Citizens National Bank of New Market since February 1, 1927, at which time he was elected to succeed C. N. Hoover. He also carries on a real estate business, and is individually owner of much desirable property in this rich and attractive section of Virginia, including a home at New Market and farm land in the county.

He is a director of the Rotary Club and the Chamber of Commerce at New Market, a deacon in the English Lutheran Church, and for ten years has been church treasurer and assistant superintendent of the Sunday School. During the World war he was active in committee work for the sale of Liberty Bonds and War Savings Stamps.

Mr. Stirewalt married, December 21, 1907, Miss Mabel Rosealia Rhodes, daughter of John M. and Margaret Susan (Aderholt) Rhodes, of Lincolnton, North Carolina. Her father was a cotton manufacturer and banker in that milling center of North Carolina. He was a Republican in politics and for several terms was registrar of deeds of the county. He died May 6, 1921, and his wife, October 19, 1917. The children in the Rhodes family were: Ada, wife of George Huss, of Florida; D. Polycarp, of Lincolnton; Lillian, wife of J. L. Cromer; Violet, wife of Dr. John B. Wright, of Raleigh; C. Junius, of Bessemer, North Carolina; Mrs. Stirewalt; and Georgie, wife of M. C. Quickle, of Lincolnton. To the marriage of Mr. and Mrs. Stirewalt were born four children: Margaret Amelia, born January 18, 1911, now a student at the Randolph-Macon Woman's College, Lynchburg, class of 1931; William Jacob, Jr., born November 26, 1918, and died March 18, 1921; Mabel Susan, born December 4, 1924; and John Miles, born June 8, 1927.

WILLIAM CRANK FORD, physician and surgeon, has been a prominent member of his profession in Shenandoah County for over thirty years. His home is at Woodstock.

Doctor Ford is a native Virginian, born at Luray in Page County November 8, 1866, son of Frederick M. and Margaret (Tyler) Ford, and grandson of Charles Fleming Ford and George Tyler, the former a native of England and the latter of Prince William County, Virginia. Frederick M. Ford was born in Fairfax County, Virginia, in 1810, and in 1863 moved to Page County, where he managed his agricultural holdings until his death in 1897. He was too old for service in the war between the states, but two of his sons by his first marriage were in the Confederate army, one of them being killed just before the surrender at Appomattox. Margaret Tyler, the second wife of Frederick M. Ford, was born in Prince William County and died in 1871, at the age of forty-five. Of her six children Dr. William C. was the youngest. The only other one now living is Vernon H., a business man at Luray, Virginia.

William C. Ford was reared on a farm in Page County, attended the Luray High School, and was a student in Georgetown University at Washington, D. C., where his father was in business for several years. Doctor Ford had some years of business experience and later entered the College of Physicians and Surgeons at Baltimore, graduating in 1896. He was an interne in the City Hospital of Baltimore and for a time served on the staff of the Emergency Hospital at Washington. After a brief period of practice at Harrisonburg he located at Woodstock in 1898 and has been most faithful in his devotion to the work of his profession for thirty years. He has served as city and county health officer, local surgeon to the Southern Railway Company, has been president of the Shenandoah County Medical Society, member of the Shenandoah Valley and Virginia State Medical Associations, and during the World war was county medical examiner for the draft board, and was active in behalf of the Red Cross and other campaigns. Doctor Ford is a past master of the Masonic fraternity and belongs to the Royal Arch Chapter and Knights Templar Commandery. He has served on the Town Council at Woodstock, as a trustee of the schools, and is a director of the Shenandoah National Bank, Shenandoah Farmers Union and Shenandoah County Fair Association.

He married at Baltimore January 10, 1900, Miss Elizabeth Miller Heller, who was born at Woodstock in 1873, and was educated at Miss Winston's School near Staunton and completed her musical training in the Peabody Institute at Baltimore. She is a daughter of Adolph and Ella (Lichleiter) Heller. Her father was a native of Austria and became a merchant at Woodstock. Doctor and Mrs. Ford have one daughter, Eleanor Randolph Ford, who is an A. B. graduate of William and Mary College. Mrs. Ford and her daughter are members of the Presbyterian Church.

THE HANDLEY LIBRARY is one of the splendid institutions lending to the material attractiveness and advanced cultural facilities of Winchester, the historic old city that is the capital of Frederick County. On other pages of this publication, in an article entitled Winchester Public Schools, is given record of the princely contribution made by the late Judge John Handley of Scranton, Pennsylvania, for the advancement and maintenance of the public schools of Winchester, and this city further profited by his benefaction and his generosity through his endowment of the free public library that perpetuates and honors his name. C. Vernon Eddy, the loyal and efficient librarian of the splendid institution, has provided the data from which this brief review is prepared.

The Handley Library was bequeathed to the City of Winchester by Judge John Handley, whose incidental endowment makes enduring provision for its maintenance, expansion and service. The library building, monumental and ornate in design, is constructed of Indiana limestone and was erected in 1907, at an expenditure of $150,000, aside from its equipment. This imposing structure is situated at the corner of Braddock and Piccadilly streets and on a choice lot that is 180 by 250 feet in dimensions, the surrounding lawns being enhanced in beauty by well selected trees and shrubbery. The cornerstone of the library was laid May 26, 1908, with Masonic ceremonies, and with an address delivered by Major Holmes Conrad, who was then president of the Board of Trustees of the library. The new building, duly equipped, was opened formally for the free use of the people of Winchester on the 21st of August, 1913.

In addition to its reading and reference rooms the building provides a lecture hall, conference rooms and smaller rooms for special study work. The lecture hall has a seating capacity of 300, and among its provisions are modern projection apparatus.

The Handley Library now has more than 18,000 volumes, effectively covering a wide range of literature in all lines, and each successive year records an average increase of approximately 1,000 volumes, while the circulation of books in 1928, at the time of the preparation of this review, is over 60,000. Twenty daily newspapers from ten principal cities of the United States are on file in the reading room, as well as more than seventy-five magazines, including England publications.

The collection of reference books is especially complete and comprehensive, and proves one of the most valuable in the various departments of cultural and informative service given by this fine communal institution. The general service of the Handley Library has been extended outside the borders of Frederick County, and it is to be noted that circulating books are thence sent regularly to Clarke, Warren, Shenandoah, Fairfax and Alexandria counties in Virginia, and to Jefferson, Berkeley and Hampshire counties, West Virginia. The school children of the community make almost daily use of the advantages of the library in connection with their studies and routine school work, and this service may well be held as one of the most important rendered by the library. In October, 1921, was established in the Douglass school building a branch library for the colored people of the community, and the service of this branch has not lacked

for appreciation and use by this element in the population of Winchester, while it has proved specially valuable to the colored pupils of the local public schools.

C. Vernon Eddy, the popular librarian of the Handley Library, is an enthusiast in his work, is a man of broad culture and distinctive civic loyalty, and his administration has been intent in making the Handley Library a medium for maximum efficiency of service in all departments. The Handley Library is justly a source of pride and satisfaction to the people of the beautiful and historic Virginia city in which it is established. Mr. Eddy has been for a number of years secretary of the Handley Board of Trustees, which administers the endowment fund of both the Handley School and the Handley Library.

FRED W. McWANE, a dealer in investments and securities at Lynchburg, represents a family that for generation after generation has been identified with the iron and steel industry, both in America and in Scotland. At Lynchburg the McWanes were the men chiefly responsible for founding and creating the Lynchburg Foundry Company and the Glamorgan Pipe and Foundry Company, two of the largest of the local industrial plants of that city.

Mr. McWane was born at Lynchburg, March 23, 1889, son of Henry Edward and Blanche (Roberts) McWane. His maternal grandfather, John G. Roberts, was born in Richmond and was one of the founders of the Christian Church at Lynchburg. Mr. McWane's grandfather, Charles P. McWane, established an early foundry at Wytheville and later established the Lynchburg Plow Company, erecting a plant primarily for the manufacture of a plow of which he was the inventor and which was made and widely distributed over the Virginias and Carolinas and was a highly regarded agricultural implement. Charles P. McWane lived to be nearly ninety-two years of age. He was deeply religious and a man of splendid character. His father, Charles McWane, assisted Cyrus McCormick in making his first reaper.

Henry Edward McWane was born at Wytheville, Virginia, and died in 1914. He spent practically all his life in the cast iron pipe business. He built the plant of the Glamorgan Pipe & Foundry Company in 1888, serving as its president and general manager and in 1902 erected the plant of the present Lynchburg Foundry Company, remaining at the head of that industry until his death. He was succeeded as president by his son Lawrence H. McWane, who died in 1925, while Fred W. McWane became general manager. Henry E. McWane was a member of the Christian Church at Lynchburg and was chairman of its Board of Deacons for many years. He was also at one time president of the Anti-Saloon League and in politics was a Republican. His wife, Blanche Roberts, was born at Richmond and died in 1925. They had a family of six daughters and four sons, seven of whom are living: Fred W.; Mrs. P. B. Harrah, of Wilmington, North Carolina; Mrs. E. A. Watson, wife of an automobile dealer at Roanoke; Henry E., Jr., vice president of the Lynchburg Foundry Company; Mrs. Elisha Barksdale, whose husband is a surgeon at Lynchburg; Lena C.; and Edith L.

Fred W. McWane was educated in the Lynchburg grammar and high schools, spent one year in Roanoke College and in 1913 took the A. B. degree from Washington and Lee University.

While at the university, he was president of the Athletic Association and was also president of his class and manager of the football team. After his college career Mr. McWane turned to the foundry business and was soon assigned the duty of supervising the construction of a cast iron pipe plant at Anniston, Alabama, as a branch of the Lynchburg Foundry Company. He remained in Alabama for two and one-half years and then returned to Lynchburg, and in 1915 was made general manager of the Lynchburg Foundry Company. During his active connection with the business he increased the production of the plant by 340 per cent. He was general manager for eleven years, finally resigning in 1926. After taking a well earned six months vacation Mr. McWane in 1927 engaged in the investment and security business, with offices in the Peoples National Bank Building, and his extensive business experience and his work as a manufacturer have enabled him to afford a splendid service to individuals and firms seeking investments in the industrial security field.

Mr. McWane married, September 24, 1913, Ida Lynham, of Richmond, where she was reared and educated. Her father, W. J. Lynham, is a retired business man of that city. Mr. and Mrs. McWane have two sons, Fred W., Junior, born in 1914, and Lawrence H., born in 1915. The family are members of the Christian Church. Mr. McWane has served as a member of the board of his church, is a York and Scottish Rite Mason and Shriner, member of the B. P. O. Elks, is a past president of the Rotary Club, member of the Sigma Nu college fraternity and the Phi Beta Kappa honorary scholastic fraternity. He is a member of the Board of Trustees of the Lynchburg College, and is chairman of the Court of Honor and vice president of the Lynchburg Council of Boy Scouts. He is also a member of the Lynchburg City School Board. In 1924 he was the Republican candidate for Congress from the Sixth District and also a delegate to the Republican National Convention at Cleveland, Ohio. In 1928 he was one of the two Republican electors at Large for Virginia. Mrs. McWane is a member of the United Daughters of the Confederacy and twice was chosen president of the Fort Hill Club.

JOHN GRAY BEVERLEY, corporation clerk of the City of Winchester, the beautiful and historic judicial center of Frederick County, assumed this municipal office March 15, 1925, when he succeeded his honored father in the position, the latter having died the preceding month.

Mr. Beverley was born in Loudoun County, Virginia, January 19, 1886, and is a scion of one of the old and honored families of that county, the original English representatives of the name in America having settled in Virginia in the Colonial period of our national history. William Avenel Beverley, grandfather of the subject of this review, passed his entire life in Loudoun County and was long one of its influential citizens. J. Gray Beverley is a son of James Bradshaw Beverley and Anne Douglas (Gray) Beverley, the latter of whom was a resident of Leesburg, Loudoun County, at the time of their marriage, she having been born and reared in that county and having been likewise a member of one of its prominent families. James Bradshaw Beverley was reared in his native county and established his residence in Winchester nearly forty years ago, in connection with his contract operation in railroad construction. He became president of the Beverley Granite Company, which had its headquarters in Winchester and represented one of the important industrial enterprises of this part of the state. January 1, 1915, he assumed the office of corporation clerk of Winchester, and of the same he continued the valued incumbent until his death, February 23, 1925, at the age of seventy-four years, his widow being still a resident of Winchester and having long been a popular figure in its representative social life.

J. Gray Beverley supplemented the discipline of the Winchester public schools by attending Shenandoah Academy and thereafter by continuing his studies in the Virginia Military Institute. As a youth he found employment with the United States Steel Corporation in the City of Pittsburgh, Pennsylvania, and five years later the corporation transferred him to its headquarters at Birmingham, Alabama. He represented the United States Rubber Company as a traveling Salesman ten years, and then returned to Winchester, where, as previously noted, he succeeded his father in the office of corporation clerk of the city in the spring of 1925. In his civic loyalty and official administration he is well upholding the honors and prestige attaching to the family name in its association with this community.

In Winchester was solemnized the marriage of Mr. Beverley and Miss Susan Baker Faulkner, daughter of Isaac Hamilton Faulkner, of this city, and here her death occurred June 23, 1927. Mrs. Beverley had been a popular factor in the social and cultural affairs of her home city and was affiliated with the local organizations of the Daughters of the Revolution and the Colonial Dames.

DAVID MOSES KIPPS, physician and surgeon, has been the trusted professional advisor, friend and counselor of hundreds of families in Warren County for thirty-five years.

He was born in Shenandoah County, Virginia, December 10, 1865, son of Nickolas and Mary Catherine (May) Kipps. Both parents were born in Virginia. His grandfather, George Kipps, was born in Germany, settled in Virginia in early manhood and lived to be ninety-two years of age. Nickolas Kipps spent his active life as a Shenandoah County farmer. During the Civil war he was employed by the Confederate government in the saltpeter works in connection with the manufacture of powder. For a number of years he was a Democrat but in later life voted as a Republican. Both parents were members of the Lutheran Church. Of their eleven children Doctor Kipps was the youngest. Five of them are still living.

Doctor Kipps was educated in public schools and the New Market Polytechnic Institute. He attended the College of Physicians and Surgeons at Baltimore, graduating in 1888, and afterwards did post-graduate work in 1891-92. Doctor Kipps first practiced two years at Wardensville and eighteen months at Burlington, West Virginia. In the spring of 1892 he established his home at Front Royal, and in the large and steady volume of practice the community has expressed its appreciation of his fine services.

Doctor Kipps has also been a leader in the organized work of his profession. The Tri-County Medical Society was organized in his office fifteen years ago, and he has served several times as its president. He is also a former president of the Valley Medical Association, member of the Medical Society of Virginia, the Southern and American Medical Associations. He has attended a number of conventions of the American Medical Association, having been at Atlantic City, Boston, New Orleans, New York, Detroit, Chicago and Washington. Doctor Kipps is a member of the Lutheran Church. He owns a large farm in Warren County and for fifteen years was a breeder of Shorthorn cattle.

He married, April 29, 1891, Miss Susan Jane Trout, who was born at Ridgeville, West Virginia, daughter of Isaac Trout, a merchant and farmer. They have two children: Edwin Trout Kipps and Susan Catherine Kipps. The daughter was educated at Fort Louden Seminary at Winchester.

PHILIP CADY MILLS, optometrist, is practicing his profession at Mineral in Louisa County. He is a native Virginian, and has had a very successful professional career.

He was born in Surry County, September 5, 1874, son of Alexander P. and Annie (Doughty) Mills. His father was a native of Massachusetts, moved to Virginia at an early age, and acquired and operated six hundred acres of land in Surry County. On that land he made a specialty of growing peanuts, being one of the pioneers in this important Virginia industry. He became the largest grower in Surry County, raising the Spanish, Virginia and Jumbo varieties.

Philip Cady Mills attended public schools, grew up on his father's plantation, and took his A. B. degree at a college in Philadelphia. In 1894 he was graduated from Allegheny College of Meadville, Pennsylvania. He was graduated from the Philadelphia Optical College and has since practiced as a specialist in Optometry. For a number of years he made his office headquarters at Emporia, Virginia, then at Danville and since 1923 at Mineral. He is also a registered pharmacist, and is interested in a Mineral drug store. He is a Knight Templar Mason, being a past master of his lodge, belongs to the Independent Order of Odd Fellows and is a lay-minister and vestryman of the Episcopal Church and he teaches a class in Sunday School.

Mr. Mills' father died in 1914. Mr. Mills married, January 17, 1896, Miss Mamie J. Jones, daughter of Dr. John R. and Mary W. (Taylor) Jones. Her father was a physician who died in 1906 and her mother passed away in 1927. Mr. and Mrs. Mills have seven children: Irene, born May 10, 1897, is the wife of Rev. J. H. Cudlipp, of Baltimore; Randolph, born March 5, 1899, is in the banking business in New York City; Petros, born in 1903; Pearl, a school teacher at Mineral; Virginia E., born in 1909, a student in college; Philip C., Jr., born 1911; and Williamina T., born in 1913.

WILLIAM H. COCKE, an alumnus of the Virginia Military Institute, after many years successfully spent in business life and the practice of law returned to Lexington to become superintendent of the great school, which has been called the West Point of the South.

General Cocke was born at City Point, Virginia, September 12, 1874, son of Henry Teller and Elizabeth Welsh (Horner) Cocke. He was graduated in 1894 from the Virginia Military Institute with the degree Civil Engineer. During the next three years he was commandant of cadets and professor of mathematics in the Kemper Military Academy at Boonville, Missouri. In 1898 he graduated from the law department of Washington University at Saint Louis, and practiced law in that city from 1899 to 1907. In 1907 he founded and became president of the

Bernard H. Kyle, M.D.

Southern Acid & Sulphur Company of Saint Louis, and gave close attention to this large and important commercial organization until he retired and became superintendent of the Virginia Military Institute October 1, 1924. He is a director of the American Trust Company and the Southern Coal, Coke & Mining Company of Saint Louis.

General Cocke was a first lieutenant in the Fourth Missouri Infantry during the Spanish-American war, served with the rank of major of infantry in the United States Army during 1917-18, and during a part of 1918 was a member of the Army General Staff College at Langres, France. He was a brigadier-general of the Virginia National Guard in 1924.

He is a member of the American Bar Association, American Mathematical Society, National Economic League, is a Phi Beta Kappa and Kappa Alpha, a Democrat, and member of the Episcopal Church. He belongs to the Noonday, Racquet and Saint Louis Country Clubs of Saint Louis, and the Army and Navy Club of Washington. December 20, 1905, he married Anne Jaenatte Owen, of Saint Joseph, Missouri.

BERNARD H. KYLE, orthopedic surgeon, the only specialist in that line in Lynchburg, had the experience of a general practice for some years, but after the war, in which he played a notable part as a medical officer, he prepared himself for the specialization which he now follows.

Doctor Kyle was born at Buffalo Ridge Springs, Nelson County, Virginia, April 17, 1887, son of Joshua Warner and Ella Catherine (Agee) Kyle. His grandfathers, Joseph Kyle and Benjamin Agee, were farmers, and both of them served the Confederacy as loyal soldiers. Joseph Kyle lived in Amherst County and Benjamin Agee in Goochland County. Joshua Warner Kyle was born in Amherst County, his wife in Goochland County, and he died in 1910, the widowed mother now residing at Lynchburg. Joshua W. Kyle was in the shoe business and for twenty-seven years was traveling salesman for wholesale shoe houses. He was a member of the Episcopal Church, a Mason and a Democrat. There were two children, Doctor Kyle, and Ella, who is the wife of William S. Mundy, a merchant at Lynchburg.

Doctor Kyle had his early education under a private governess, and from 1902 to 1906 was a student in the Virginia Polytechnic Institute at Blacksburg. He graduated Bachelor of Science, then spent three years in the study of medicine at the University of Virginia, and in 1911 graduated from the Medical College of Virginia at Richmond. Doctor Kyle practiced one year at Magnolia, North Carolina, engaged in general practice.

He was the first Lynchburg doctor to leave for active service in the war, being assigned to the Twelfth Field Artillery of the Second Division. He was in every fight of that famous division during 1918, being on the front lines at Verdun, Chateau Thierry, Soissons, St. Mihiel, in the Champaigne and the Argonne, and afterwards with the Army of Occupation in Germany. On December 5, 1918, he was assigned to duty in Base Hospital No. 41 of the University of Virginia, and in April, 1919, came home with the rank of major. Doctor Kyle received several citations during the war, three from the French government and one from the American, this being a division citation from Maj. Gen. John A. Lejeune, the commander of the Marine Corps. His division was for some time supporting the

Marines in their tremendous drives. Doctor Kyle has a Croix de Guerre with Palm and Star.

After leaving the army he spent a number of months at Boston studying orthopedic surgery, and was on house duty in the Children's Hospital of that city. On returning to Lynchburg and opening his office he limited his practice to orthopedic surgery. Doctor Kyle while attending the University of Virginia was instructor in chemistry during 1907-08, having classes in both organic and inorganic chemistry. He is a fellow of the American College of Surgeons, the Southern and American Medical Associations, South Piedmont Medical Society, Medical Society of Virginia, and the Lynchburg and Campbell County Medical Society. He belongs to the Pi Mu medical fraternity, the Phi Kappa Sigma social fraternity, and is an active member of St. Paul's Episcopal Church, in which he has been a vestryman.

Doctor Kyle married in 1920 George Putnam Watkins, who was born at Lynchburg, daughter of George P. and Jennie Lee (Watts) Watkins. Her father was a pioneer in the shoe business at Lynchburg, member of the well known firm of Witt & Watkins. Doctor and Mrs. Kyle have one child, Jimmie Watkins Kyle, born July 27, 1921.

WILLIAM CLEMINSON ARMSTRONG, for many years clerk of court of Rappahannock County, since retiring from office has been practicing law at Front Royal, where he is member of the prominent law firm of Weaver & Armstrong.

He was born in Rappahannock County January 8, 1879, son of Samuel Ringgold and Ella (Miller) Armstrong, both natives of that county and now deceased. His grandfather, William C. Armstrong, was also born in Virginia, where the family settled on coming from England subsequent to the War of 1812. William C. Armstrong married a Miss Slaughter, of a family which had seven representatives in the Continental Army in the War of the Revolution. Mr. Armstrong's maternal grandfather was Benjamin Franklin Miller, a farmer of Rappahannock County and descended from the Miller family that came from Germany and settled in Berks County, Pennsylvania. Samuel Ringgold Armstrong spent his life as a farmer in Rappahannock County. In 1864, at the age of sixteen, he enlisted in the Confederate army and served under General Mosby. He and his wife were active members of the Baptist Church, and he was a Democrat and a Mason. Of their four children three are living: William C.; Sadie, wife of George Tate Greer, of Roanoke; and Rena, wife of J. Hill O'Bannon, of Woodville, Virginia.

William C. Armstrong attended the Little Red School on the Hill in Rappahannock County, and in June, 1897, was graduated from the College of William and Mary with the degree Licentiate of Instruction. Then followed two years of teaching, and he became clerk of court of Rappahannock County and filled that office twenty years. Mr. Armstrong studied law, took the examination before the Supreme Court and was admitted to the bar in 1909. However, he made no effort to engage in practice until 1922, when he formed a partnership with Aubry G. Weaver at Front Royal. They handle an extensive general practice in all the courts of this district.

Mr. Armstrong married, November 26, 1902, Miss Mary Moffett, a native of Rappahannock County, daughter of Horatio Gates Moffett, a lawyer by profession, who served as commonwealth attorney twenty-six years. Mr. and Mrs. Armstrong have two children: William C., Jr., born in 1904, who was educated in William and Mary College and the University of Virginia; and Mary Moffett, who attended the State Teachers College at Farmville and is a teacher in the schools of Arlington County, Virginia. Mrs. Armstrong and children are members of the Episcopal Church. He is a York Rite Mason and Shriner, is a past grand of the Independent Order of Odd Fellows and organized the first lodge of that order in Rappahannock County.

ALEXANDER THOMAS BROWNING, judge of the Ninth Judicial Circuit of Virginia, composed of the counties of Orange, Culpeper, Louisa and Goochland, was born in Orange County, Virginia, September 10, 1873. His paternal ancestors have belonged to Virginia since the days of its early Colonial settlement, he being in the ninth generation of descent from Capt. John Browning, who, born in England in 1588, immigrated to Virginia, sailing on the *Abigail* from Gravesend, England, and landing at Jamestown in 1622, and who was a member of the House of Burgesses of Virginia from 1629 to 1635.

Judge Browning is the son of G. Judson Browning and Sarah (Thomas) Browning and grandson of John Dabney Browning and of Dr. Robert Thomas.

John Dabney Browning was the son of John Browning, who was a soldier in the Continental army throughout the Revolutionary war, enduring the hardships of the winter of 1777-78 at Valley Forge and being at the surrender of Cornwallis at Yorktown.

His (John Browning's) grandfather, Francis Browning, Sr., who was the great-great-grandson of Capt. John Browning, the immigrant, moved his residence to Spotsylvania (now Rappahannock) County about 1730, where he was granted by King George the Second the lands on which G. Judson Browning, the father of the subject of this sketch, was born.

G. Judson Browning was a captain in the Sixth Virginia Cavalry during the Civil war, in which he was wounded, and after leaving the hospital he was transferred to the fortifications around Richmond, continuing in the service until the end of the war. After the war he was elected a member of the House of Delegates from the district comprising the counties of Orange and Culpeper, serving in the session of 1866-67. Captain Browning resided at "Oakley," an estate of 500 acres near the Town of Orange, where he engaged in farming and stock raising until his death on April 9, 1885, and where his wife died June 10, 1910. They were members of the Protestant Episcopal Church. Their children were four in number: Robert Dabney, a farmer; G. Judson, Jr., a merchant at Orange; Alexander T.; and John William, who is clerk of the Circuit Court of the County of Orange.

Alexander T. Browning grew up at "Oakley" and attended the public schools of Orange County until 1885 and thereafter attended private schools in Orange and Madison counties and the University of Virginia until he was admitted to the bar in 1895, and practiced law at Orange from that time until his election as judge of the Ninth Circuit in January, 1922. He was elected commonwealth attorney of Orange County in 1908 and was reelected for successive terms in 1912, 1916 and 1920, resigning in 1922 to qualify as judge. From 1913 to 1922 he was associated in practise with Hon. George L. Browning, a cousin, under the firm name of Browning and Browning. He is a Mason, being a past master of Orange Lodge No. 138, A. F. and A. M., and also a member of the local chapter of Royal Arch Masons, and of the lodge of Independent Order of Odd Fellows.

He and his wife are communicants of the Protestant Episcopal Church, holding their memberships in St. Thomas' Church at Orange. He married, October 17, 1906, Adra, daughter of William L. and Mary Beverly (Shaw) Bradbury, and granddaughter of William B. Bradbury, widely known composer of sacred music. Judge and Mrs. Browning have four children: Alexander T., Jr., born September 11, 1907; William Beverly, born September 15, 1909; John Judson, born April 10, 1914; and Adra B., born July 22, 1918.

WALLACE B. MCFARLAND, county treasurer of Augusta County, continues a succession in that office beginning with his father, and between them the duties of handling and conserving the funds of the county have comprised a service of fidelity and exacting care for upwards of half a century.

Mr. McFarland was born in Augusta County, September 22, 1878, son of James Nathaniel and Mary Elizabeth (Wallace) McFarland, both natives of the same county. His grandfather, Rev. Francis McFarland, was born in Ireland, came to this country when a young man, first locating in Pennsylvania, and he was educated for the Presbyterian ministry at the Princeton Theological Seminary. He did his first preaching in Pennsylvania, then was located for a time at Bethel, Virginia, was called back to Philadelphia on church matters, remaining there four or five years, after which he returned to Virginia and was pastor of a church in Augusta County for over forty years. Mr. McFarland's maternal grandfather, William Wallace, was born in Virginia and was a Virginia farmer and planter.

James Nathaniel McFarland, who died in September, 1927, was reared and educated in Augusta County, served with the rank of first lieutenant in the Confederate army, and was several times wounded and for eight months a prisoner. After the war he was on his father's farm, was elected once or twice as commissioner of revenue, and was then chosen to the office of county treasurer and gave a consecutive administration of the office for over forty years, retiring some years before his death. He was an active member of the Presbyterian Church, belonged to the Masonic fraternity, Independent Order of Odd Fellows and Knights of Pythias, and was always extremely loyal to his old comrades of the Confederacy, helping many of them secure pensions. For many years he was a member of the Board of Trustees of the Mary Baldwin Seminary at Staunton.

Wallace B. McFarland is the only one now living of two children. He attended private schools, being a student in the Bethel Military Academy and Hampden-Sidney College. He had some experience in newspaper work, and for two years was connected with the Virginia Portland Cement Company. In 1903 he became an assistant in the office of his father, county treasurer, and for a quarter of a century has given almost his undivided attention to the important duties of this office. He was elected county treasurer in 1923 and reelected in 1927.

Mr. McFarland married in December, 1911, Miss Lutie Luckett Moore. She was born in Texas and finished her education in the Mary Baldwin Seminary at Staunton, and also

attended school in New York. Her parents were William Worth
and Lou Sue Moore. Her father was a wholesale grocery man
of Texas for many years. Mrs. McFarland is a member of
Trinity Episcopal Church, while he belongs to the First Presbyterian Church of Staunton.

DWIGHT G. RIVERS, pediatrist at Lynchburg, was born September 26, 1885, at Taylorsville, North Carolina, son of Dr. James
J. Rivers, who married Eola J. Hill, daughter of Andrew Adams
and Nannie M. Hill. A. A. Hill was a North Carolina farmer
who entered the Confederate army and was twice wounded, the
second time at the battle of Gettysburg. Dr. Dwight Rivers
comes of a family of physicians and surgeons—his paternal
grandfather (an Englishman) graduated from an English medical college. His father, Dr. James J. Rivers, born in North Carolina, was educated at the College of Physicians and Surgeons in
Baltimore, and practiced medicine in his native state until his
death at the age of thirty-three. Dr. James J. Rivers and his
wife Eola had two children, Dr. Dwight Gray and Miss Jamie,
a resident of Charlotte, North Carolina.

Dwight Gray Rivers was a small boy when his father died,
and his advancement to the goal of his professional ambitions
was the result of his own earnings and efforts. He attended
school in North Carolina and graduated M. D. from the University of Maryland, in Baltimore, in 1910. For one year he was an
interne in the University of Maryland, was assistant superintendent one year of Bay View Hospital at Baltimore. He is a
member of the Nu Sigma Nu medical fraternity. He practiced
medicine in Lake City, Florida, from 1910 to 1917.

Though past draft age he volunteered for service in the
World war in 1917, having two months of training at Fort Oglethorpe, Georgia, as first lieutenant, and then assigned to the
Three Hundred and Seventeenth Infantry, Eightieth Division,
Medical Corps, at Camp Lee. He sailed overseas on the *Nanse-
mond*, May 26, 1918. He was promoted to captain in reward of
an act of bravery and awarded the Victory medal April 9, 1919.
He was in service with the American Expeditionary Forces from
May 26, 1918, to June 1, 1919. He received two citations from
his commanding officer, Col. Charles Keller, of the Three Hun-
dred and Seventeenth Infantry. The first reads as follows:
"Captain Dwight Rivers' service with the 317th Infantry, since
October, 1917, has been of the highest order. He participated
in all the engagements of the regiment. In the active sector
(British) in August, 1918, and the Meuse-Argonne (American)
September 26th-November 11th, 1918. During the latter campaign I had frequent occasion to observe his unfailing devotion
to duty and courageous and meritorious performance thereof.
His promotion to captaincy was the result of his splendid work
in combat." From February 28, 1919, he served as regimental
surgeon and was honorably discharged September 5, 1919.

For one year after the war he did special work in children's
diseases at Johns Hopkins University, Baltimore, and in 1920
located in Lynchburg, where he has limited his professional work
to pediatrics. He is a member of the Virginia Pediatric Society,
the Lynchburg and Campbell County Medical Society, the Piedmont Medical Society, Southern Medical Association, the Medical Society of Virginia, and the American Medical Association.
He is a member of the visiting staff of the Marshall Lodge Me-

morial Hospital and the Virginia Baptist Hospital, and member of the active staff of the Lynchburg Hospital.

Doctor Rivers married at "Scott-Greene" near Farmville, Prince Edward County, October 19, 1911, Martha Venable Edmunds, who was born March 17, 1886, daughter of Henry Watkins Edmunds, of "Rotherwood," near Farmville, a Confederate veteran, and his wife, Harriet Anne Venable of "Scott-Greene," Prince Edward County. Mrs. Rivers is a member of the Daughters of the Revolution, the United Daughters of the Confederacy, the American Legion Auxiliary, and the Woman's Club of Lynchburg.

The two children of Doctor and Mrs. Rivers are Dwight Gray Rivers, born August 18, 1912, and Betty Venable Rivers, born December 3, 1915.

Mrs. Rivers is descended from some of the oldest and most distinguished families of Virginia; one line of descent is from Abraham Michaux and Susanne Rochet, Huguenot refugees, as follows: Susanne Rochet, wife of Abraham Michaux; Anne Madeline (Michaux) Woodson; Elizabeth (Woodson) Venable; Samuel Woodson Venable, a graduate of Princeton University, who was a soldier in the Revolutionary war; Nathaniel E. Venable, who served in the War of 1812; Mary Priscilla (Venable) Venable; Harriet Anne (Venable) Edmunds; and Martha Venable (Edmunds) Rivers. Another line that should be noted is that of descent from Col. George Carrington, Burgess from Goochland, 1747, 1749. This line is: Col. George Carrington; Judge Paul Carrington, Sr.; Mary Scott (Carrington) Venable, wife of Samuel Woodson Venable, where it joins the preceding line. Mrs. Rivers' father, Henry Watkins Edmunds, was a son of Edwin Edmunds, Jr., whose mother was Mildred Stuart (Morton) Edmunds, the latter being a daughter of Col. William Morton, an officer of the American Revolution. Virginia history makes frequent reference to the individuals and families included in these lines of genealogy, and the records of all those mentioned and many other ancestors can be found in such genealogical works as *Venables of Virginia, Cabells and Their Kin, Bishop Meade's Old Churches* and *Families of Virginia*, etc.

Mrs. Rivers' father, Henry Watkins Edmunds, was a private in the Twenty-third Virginia Cavalry, Fitzhugh Lee's Brigade, J. E. B. Stuart's Division, and was desperately wounded at Kelly's Ford, Culpeper, Virginia. Mrs. Rivers was married in one of the notable old homes of Virginia, "Scott-Greene," where she was reared and remained with her parents until her marriage. Scott-Greene from 1834 to 1860 was the most beautiful place in Prince Edward County. It came into the Venable family as a wedding gift to Mary Priscilla Venable from her father when she was married to her second cousin, Thomas Frederick Venable, in 1834. The wonderful trees, among the largest oaks in all Virginia, bounded the approach to the house from the main road, boxwood of rare beauty adorned the lawn and garden, and in the open space around the mansion were many buildings usually found on the large Virginia plantations, including the "office," sometimes also used as a school room, ice house, carriage house and stables, greenhouse, and the quarters or cabins for the domestic servants. The mansion itself was a frame structure which "grew"—a room here and there as the demands of the family increased. Tiny windows with numerous panes of glass, the front porch with its plain Doric columns, the five tall chimneys and the jutting side porches lent a distinct charm to the outline. All the adjuncts of an ante-bellum home were there: the commodious wine cellars, the storerooms and kitchen in the ample basement. There were spacious rooms with waxed floors, claw-footed mahogany furniture, a library with books and musical instruments, drawing room—often used for dancing, with its spinnet and engravings and portraits. People of distinction and fine social quality were frequent guests of "Scott-Greene," students and professors from Hampton-Sidney College, and members of the families of neighboring planters.

The peaceful life of the home was ended by the war between the states. "Scott-Greene" was situated not many miles from Appomattox Court House and lay just in the path of the opposing armies. Occasionally Union commanders placed guards to protect house and property. Once General Grant sent his army band to serenade the ladies of the family. But with starvation and want generally prevalent throughout the district, the mansion and the plantation shared the neglect and some part of the devastation meted out to so many of the fine old southern homes, and since the surrender of Lee time has completed the disintegration begun during the four years of war. The porches were blown away in a storm, the gardens were plowed up for a tobacco field, nearly every one of the stately trees has gone one way or another, and from the present view it is difficult to reconstruct even in imagination the "Scott-Greene" of 1860.

GILES POLLARD BURKE, a veteran in the railway service of the Chesapeake & Ohio System, lives in one of the attractive rural communities around Charlottesville in Albemarle County.

Mr. Burke was born in Prince Edward County, Virginia, June 12, 1871, son of John and Kate (Fowlkes) Burke, also natives of Prince Edward County. His grandfather, George Burke, married a member of the Minor family, which was of Persian descent. The Burkes come from England and Ireland to America in Colonial time. John Burke was a farmer, grist miller and merchant, and during the Civil war served in the Confederate army under General Bowling. He was slightly wounded and captured and for eighteen months was held in a northern prison. He was a man of leadership in his community, a member of the local school board, a good Democrat but seldom accepted political honors. After selling his property in Prince Edward County he moved to Lunenburg County, where he was a tobacco grower. He took some prizes for the quality of his tobacco. Some of the plants weighed a pound a piece. He was a member of the Campbellite Christian Church. John Burke was born in 1837 and lived to be eighty-nine years of age. His wife died in 1882, at the age of forty. There were eight children; and seven are now living, Giles P. being the third.

Mr. Burke attended home schools and has been earning his own way in the world since boyhood. He helped his father in the grist mill and began learning the trade of milling at Richmond. While there he accepted an offer to take charge of a farm, and this work he continued until about the time he reached his maturity, in 1892.

Mr. Burke has been continuously in the service of the Chesapeake & Ohio Railway Company since 1892. He started as a fireman and has been one of the tried and trusted engineers of the company since 1900. He is still in active service. Mr. Burke is an able business man and has acquired some valuable property near Charlottesville. He handles real estate as a business, and besides his property in Albemarle County has some land in Central Florida, where he raises oranges and other tropical fruit. Some years ago Mr. Burke came into possession of a fine sideboard which was made and owned by Thomas Jefferson and had been part of the dining room furniture at the famous Jefferson home at Monticello. Many offers have been made Mr. Burke for this wonderful piece of furniture, but he declined to sell it except to the Jefferson Home Committee, when they made desire to secure it to aid in the restoration of the old Jefferson Home. Mr. Burke is a Democrat, a member of the Masonic fraternity and the First Baptist Church of Charlottesville.

He married, May 22, 1899, Miss Clara E. Perkins, of Washington, D. C., daughter of Nelson and Alice (Speiden) Perkins. She was the third in a family of seven children. Mrs. Burke died August 5, 1926. One daughter was born to this union, a very talented young woman, Alice Rebecca, born May 10, 1901. She was educated in William and Mary College and graduated from the law department of the University of Virginia in 1925. She has made a very interesting record as a practicing attorney of San Antonio, Texas.

WILLIAM N. KEY, mayor of Buena Vista, has given many years to the flour milling industry, and since 1906 has been the active head of the Buena Visto Flour Mills.

He was born in Augusta County, Virginia, November 21, 1867, son of James P. and Jane A. (Baskin) Key. His great-great-grandfather, Capt. William A. Baskin, was a soldier in the Revolutionary war. The Key family came from Scotland, and in Colonial time settled in Nelson County. James P. Key during the Civil war served in the quartermaster's department of the Confederate army and spent his active life as a farmer. He was a Democrat and died in 1900. His widow now lives in Ohio. Of their five children Margaret A., James B. and Charles P. are deceased. William N. is the oldest and his sister Nannie is the wife of W. A. Dellinger, of Urbana, Ohio.

William N. Key attended public schools in Augusta County, Virginia, and a Lutheran school at Bethany near Waynesboro, Virginia, conducted by Professor Bowles of the University of Virginia. Up to the age of twenty-four his life was spent on his father's farm and he was thoroughly grounded in practical methods of farming. In his later years among other properties he has accumulated considerable farm lands and is a grower of beef cattle and fruit. Also owns a large orange and grapefruit grove in Polk County, Florida. Mr. Key engaged in farming on his own account near Hermitage, Virginia, in 1891. After seven years on this farm he bought a general store near Waynesboro, conducting it two years and in 1901 located at Lexington. There he entered the flour milling business in association with his brother-in-law, D. D. Furr. In 1904 they bought the Glass Brothers Milling Company at Buena Vista. In 1906 they effected an interchange of their mutual holdings, Mr. Key concentrating his capital in the Buena Vista Mill while Mr. Furr acquired the Lexington Mill. Mr. Key subsequently bought out the other stockholders in the Buena Vista Mill and for a number of years has owned and conducted one of the chief plants of the kind in this vicinity.

While living at Lexington Mr. Key served as a member of the City Council, and subsequently was elected to the Council of

Buena Vista and was chosen mayor in 1924. As mayor he is ex-officio police judge. He has also served on the school board. Mr. Key in every respect represents the solid and substantial interest of his community. He is chairman of the Board of Deacons of the Baptist Church, for a number of years was superintendent of the Sunday School and now teaches a class of young ladies, and was chairman of the building committee when the new church was erected in 1927. He is a past master of Buena Vista Lodge of Masons, No. 186, a thirty-second degree Scottish Rite Mason, member of the Improved Order of Redmen and Junior Order United American Mechanics.

He married in 1889 Miss Augusta A. Furr, of Augusta County, daughter of Edward and Sarah (Wine) Furr. Her father, who was a farmer, died in 1920, and her mother is still living. Mr. Key some years ago acquired the old Furr homestead and that is part of his landholdings. Mrs. Key was the second in a family of eleven children, the others being Charles C., Dorsey D., Minnie M. (deceased), Addie A., Floyd F., Ernest E., Burnett B., Arthur C. and Ruth, twins, and Laura. Mr. and Mrs. Key have given their children a liberal education, the son J. Frank having graduated in 1912 from Washington and Lee University and married Eva Bromley, of Buena Vista. The second son, James Edward, graduated from Washington and Lee in 1919, and married Clara Jeffries, of Buena Vista. Hugh N., who married Ruth Thacker, is in the aviation service of the Government, stationed at Bolling Field, Washington. The daughter, Ruth F., is a graduate of Randolph-Macon Woman's College at Lynchburg, class of 1928, and the youngest son, Charles W., is attending Virginia Polytechnic Institute at Blacksburg, Virginia.

ROGER S. CREEL, one of the outstanding and popular hotel executives of the United States, is retained as manager of the fine George Mason Hotel in the historic old City of Alexandria, and his able administration of the various departments of this modern hotel has tended to gain it rank as one of the best in Virginia and in the regional area of the national capital. The success and the popular prestige of Mr. Creel are the more interesting to note in this connection by reason of his being a native son of Virginia.

Roger S. Creel was born at The Plains, Fauquier County, Virginia, July 19, 1900, and is a son of Randolph T. and Margaret L. (Stickley) Creel, the former of whom likewise was born at The Plains and the latter of whom was born at Front Royal, judicial center of Warren County. In his native county Randolph T. Creel was reared to manhood and there he continued his activities as a farmer until 1916, when he moved to Fairfax County, where he and his wife have since maintained their home and where he is a substantial and representative agriculturist and stock-grower, with special attention given to the raising of pure-bred Holstein cattle.

Roger S. Creel attended the schools of his native county, thereafter continued his studies at Randolph-Macon Academy in Front Royal, and finally was graduated from the Lewis Hotel School in the City of Washington, D. C., where he thus made preliminary preparation for the vocation in which he has since gained marked success and precedence in his native state. After leaving this school Mr. Creel served as chief file clerk in the offices of the national civil service commission in Washington

until 1920, when he left there and became front clerk in the
Wardman Park Hotel. Thence he was transferred to the position of chief room clerk of the Washington Hotel, and upon the
opening of the celebrated Mayflower Hotel in Washington, in
1924, he was obtained as its assistant manager. In this capacity
he continued his effective administration until September 21,
1926, when the American Hotels Corporation assigned him to
Alexandria as manager of the new and modern George Mason
Hotel, in which connection he has gained rank as one of the nation's youngest and most popular hotel managers. About the
opening of the year 1928 the American Hotels Corporation, appreciative of his ability and loyalty, decided to transfer Mr.
Creel to a larger field of service, but at the urgent importunities
of the local Board of Directors of the George Mason Hotel he
was permitted to remain as the manager of this hostelry, which
under his direction had been brought to the highest of standards
in all departments of its service. Mr. Creel has inviolable place
in the confidence and esteem of the people of this community
and also of the traveling public that gives its support to the
hotel of which he is the popular manager. He is supervising
manager of the Virginia zone for the American Hotels Corporation, which operates twenty-eight high-grade hotels, and in this
capacity he has supervision of the George Washington Hotel at
Winchester, Virginia, and the Hotel Shenandoah at Martinsburg, West Virginia. Mr. Creel is a member of the Hotel Men's
Mutual Benefit Association, a national organization, and has
served as an official of the Hotel Greeters of America, which has
a larger membership than any other hotel association in the
world. He is now a member of the Board of Governors of the
latter organization, and he is a valued member also of the Southern Hotel Association. In his present home community Mr.
Creel is a member of the Kiwanis Club, the Belle Haven Country
Club and the Belle Haven Gun Club.

The political allegiance of Mr. Creel is given to the Democratic party and he and his wife have memberships in the Methodist Episcopal Church, South. He takes much satisfaction in
his affiliation with Washington Lodge No. 22, A. F. and A. M.,
at Alexandria, of which Gen. George Washington was the first
master. His Masonic affiliations are extended to Mount Vernon Chapter, R. A. M.; Old Dominion Commandery No. 22,
Knights Templar; and Acca Temple of the Mystic Shrine in the
City of Richmond, besides which he is a member of the Shrine
Club of Alexandria.

June 2, 1926, recorded the marriage of Mr. Creel and Miss
Dorothy Stoddard, daughter of John G. and Janie L. (Hudson)
Stoddard, who were born in Washington, D. C., Mr. Stoddard
having been a skilled stone mason and having served as foreman
in the eerction of the Washington Monument in the national
capital, his death having occurred in 1923 and his widow being
still a resident of Washington. Mrs. Creel has become a prime
favorite in the social life of Alexandria and vies with her husband in popularity.

From a local newspaper article that appeared at the time
when there had been a proposal to transfer Mr. Creel from Alexandria are taken the following quotations: "The decision to
permit Mr. Creel to remain in Alexandria is viewed with great
satisfaction by a host of personal friends who appreciate the
importance to the city of having at the head of its leading hotel
a man of Mr. Creel's character and ability. Under his able man-

George MacBain.

agement the George Mason Hotel, with its metropolitan service, has become nationally popular, with resultant credit to Alexandria."

GEORGE MACBAIN. A notable business grew up under the guiding hand and mind of the late George MacBain, Sr., who at his death on May 20, 1927, left as a monument to his commercial enterprise the MacBain Department Store, one of the largest and most complete mercantile enterprises in the entire State of Virginia.

Mr. MacBain was born in Scotland, in 1861, was reared in that country and had the thorough training accorded to mercantile clerks, a training entering into the fundamental processes of manufacture as well as accounting and management. Mr. MacBain came to America in 1882, and shortly afterwards located at Roanoke, which was just beginning to bid for recognition as one of the coming towns of Southwest Virginia. At Roanoke in 1890 he established a dry goods store, and for thirty-seven years he watched the business grow and develop, adding new facilities from time to time, until years before his death the MacBain Department Store was a household word in all the trade territory of Roanoke, and provided all the standard facilities of high grade merchandise to be found in the larger cities of the country.

Mr. MacBain was not only a successful merchant but a leader in everything opening new lines of progress for his home city. He was a director of the Chamber of Commerce, and through that organization he worked for a number of years to give Roanoke new industries and special privileges. One achievement especially credited to his initiative was the organization and erection of the plant of the Carolina Cotton Mills. He served as food administrator during the World war, was a member of the Second Presbyterian Church, a regular contributor to charitable organizations, and was a member of the Knights of Pythias.

He married, November 18, 1891, Miss Nellie Louise Lively, of Lancaster, Pennsylvania. Mrs. MacBain died in 1924. They are survived by one son, George MacBain, Jr., who was reared and educated at Roanoke, was associated with his father, and after his father's death took over the active management of the MacBain Department Store.

HENRY DONALD CAMPBELL, A. B., Ph. D., Sc. D., dean of Washington and Lee University, is one of the very distinguished men of Virginia, and a recognized authority upon many subjects, especially geology and the allied sciences. His appointment as dean of historic Washington and Lee is, in itself, proof positive of his erudition and experience. This great educational institution of Lexington, chartered in 1782 as Liberty Hall Academy, and presided over for a brief period of five years by General Robert E. Lee as president, holds a place second to none in the hearts of Virginians. Like many movements the one which resulted in the present Washington and Lee University began very humbly when Augusta Academy was founded in Augusta County in 1749 by Robert Alexander, to provide instruction for the eager pupils of that neighborhood. This little nucleus grew into Washington College, widely known all over the South, and named for George Washington, Virginia's great son. After the close of the war between the states the leader of the forces of the Confederacy, and the idol of the

Southern people, was proffered the presidency of the college, and after his death, his name was added to that of Washington, and from then the university has been known as Washington and Lee. The great heart of Robert E. Lee did not long continue to beat after Appomattox, and he died while president of the college, October 12, 1870, five years and ten days after he was installed in the office. He is buried in the college chapel, where a noble recumbent statue in marble marks his resting place.

Doctor Campbell was born on the campus of Washington College, now Washington and Lee University, July 29, 1862. His family has been connected with this institution since 1782, in which year his great-grandfather, Alexander Campbell, became a trustee. Doctor Campbell is a son of John Lyle and Harriet (Bailey) Campbell, he born in Rockbridge County, Virginia, and she in Pittsfield, Massachusetts. John Lyle Campbell was graduated from Washington College in 1843, and from 1851 to 1886 he was professor of chemistry, dying while holding that chair. He also held the office of superintendent of schools of Rockbridge County for seven years, being the first one the county had, and he was also a noted geologist. Of the ten children born to him and his wife five are living, namely: Mrs. William A. Dabney, a widow living in New Orleans, Louisiana; Rev. R. F. Campbell, D. D., who is a minister of the Presbyterian faith now stationed in Asheville, North Carolina; Mrs. James M. Townsend, who died December 10, 1928; Dr. H. D. Campbell, whose name heads this review; and Virginia W. Campbell, who resides in Greenwich, Connecticut. All of the family are Presbyterians, and the father was long an elder in the Presbyterian Church of Lexington. The paternal grandfather was Robert S. Campbell, born in Rockbridge County, Virginia, where he was a farmer and assessor of taxes for the county. It was his father, Alexander Campbell, farmer and county surveyor, who began the long connection of the Campbell family with Washington and Lee. Alexander Campbell came from Berkeley County to Rockbridge County in young manhood. The maternal grandfather was R. W. Bailey, who was a native of Maine, and a graduate of Dartmouth College. A Presbyterian minister, he went to South Carolina prior to the war between the states, and later came to Staunton, Virginia, where he established Augusta Female Seminary that subsequently developed into Mary Baldwin Seminary, now Mary Baldwin College. Both parents of Doctor Campbell taught in Staunton, the mother in Augusta Female Seminary, and he in Augusta Academy. Rev. R. W. Bailey was later president of Austin College, Sherman, Texas, taking that office after leaving Augusta Female Seminary. From the above record it is not difficult to understand Doctor Campbell's entry into educational work, for he is a teacher by inheritance as well as inclination.

His early training secured in an excellent private classical school, Doctor Campbell took his degrees of Master of Arts and Doctor of Philosophy from Washington and Lee University, and then, going abroad, had a year of work in Berlin, Germany, and one year in Heidelberg, Germany, and then, in 1888, returned to Washington and Lee to assume the duties of professor of geology and biology to which chair he had been elected while in Germany. Prior to that he had been elected, in 1887, to the chair of chemistry in Central University, Kentucky, but did not accept, preferring to complete his studies abroad as he had

4

planned. He is still professor of geology and dean of the university. In former years he did work during the summers for the United States Geological Survey and for the Geological Survey of Virginia.

On July 18, 1888, Doctor Campbell married Miss Martha Miller of Georgetown, District of Columbia, a daughter of Benjamin Miller, who was a native of Virginia. Mrs. Campbell was educated in private schools. Two children survive of those born to Doctor and Mrs. Campbell. The eldest was Henry Donald Campbell, whose death occurred in childhood; Edmund D. Campbell took his degree of Bachelor of Arts from Washington and Lee, that of Master of Arts from Harvard, and was graduated in law with the degree of Bachelor of Laws from Washington and Lee; Ben M. Campbell was a graduate of West Point Military Academy, a first lieutenant in the Eighty-second Field Artillery, and was killed by a falling horse in Texas; and Robert Bailey Campbell, who took his degree of Bachelor of Arts from Washington and Lee University, studied law for one year, and has been teaching for several years. Doctor Campbell and his family are all members of the Presbyterian Church, of which he is a deacon. He belongs to Alpha Tau Omega, Phi Beta Kappa, is a fellow of the Geological Society of America and of the American Association for the Advancement of Science. Formerly he was a member of the Board of Health of Lexington for a number of years, and one of the first to so serve, and while on the board recommended the water supply now drawn upon by the Lexington people. During a long period he has been a member of the Lexington school board and chairman for several years; is a member of the executive committee of the Association of Colleges and Secondary Schools of the Southern States; and was chairman and is still a member of the commission on Institutions of Higher Education in the Southern Educational Association; and is a trustee of Mary Baldwin College.

In addition to his scholarly attainments, his executive ability and public-spirit, Dean Campbell has the warm sympathy and thorough understanding that enables him to get in close touch with the students and influence them by his life and example, as well as his words. Dean Campbell is worthy to be numbered among the great men of Washington and Lee, and the institution has gained much from his long connection with it.

ALFRED R. HARWOOD, cashier and manager of the Farmers National Bank of Appomattox, has had a very successful business career. He was born in Appomattox County, grew up on a farm, but since early manhood has been either a merchant or a banker.

He was born in Appomattox County, November 21, 1880, son of John William and Alice M. (Drinkard) Harwood. His father was born in England, married in that country, came to America for the purpose of recouping himself financially and his first wife died soon after he located in Virginia. He then married Alice M. Drinkard, a native of Appomattox County, daughter of John Drinkard, a Virginia farmer and planter who entered the Confederate army and died a prisoner of war at Norfolk. John William Harwood became one of the well-to-do farmers of Appomattox County, and the old homestead is still occupied by his widow. He died in 1909. Both parents were active members of the Baptist Church. John W. Harwood became a Democrat, and was chosen to represent this county in the

Legislature in 1891-92. He was a man of good education and always enjoyed the confidence and esteem of his fellow citizens. By his second marriage there were eight children, seven of whom are living.

Alfred R. Harwood, the oldest of the children, was educated in the district and high schools of Appomattox County, and had a place on the home farm until 1923. He entered commercial life as an employe of the Bluefield Hardware Company, a large and important wholesale organization at Bluefield, West Virginia. After eight years of experience with that organization he returned to Appomattox and established a hardware business which was incorporated in 1910 and of which he is secretary and treasurer. However, during the past ten years most of his time has been devoted to the Farmers National Bank, which he organized in 1918 and of which he has been cashier ever since. The president of the bank is C. W. Hancock, long a resident of Appomattox but best known as one of the leading contractors of Virginia, his business headquarters being at Lynchburg.

Mr. Harwood married, in 1905, Bessie Sears, daughter of Samuel and Collie A. (Gilliam) Sears, of Appomattox County. She was born and reared in that county. Mr. and Mrs. Harwood have four children: Bessie Virginia, a teacher at Richmond; Alice Sears, attending William and Mary College; Eleanor Austin, a student in high school; and Alfred Rice, in the grade schools. Mr. Harwood is a deacon in the Baptist Church.

CARROLL EDWARD FOLEY, eye, ear, nose and throat specialist, is practicing at Front Royal. Doctor Foley represents an old and prominent family of Northern Virginia.

He was born in Clarke County in 1886, son of Benjamin Franklin and Sallie Jane (Rust) Foley. His parents were born in Loudoun County, Virginia. In that county the Foley family made their first settlement in Virginia, taking up land granted them by Lord Fairfax. This land was in the continuous possession of the family until Doctor Foley's father sold it. In the maternal line Doctor Foley is a grandson of James Rust, who was descended from one of three brothers who came from England, one locating in Warren County, Virginia, and the other two in Loudoun County. Doctor Foley's father served three years in the Civil war. He was wounded and captured and held as a hostage for Dalgreen's men, who made the raid on Richmond. For many years he was in business as a farmer and stock dealer, and was serving as postmaster of Berryville when he died in 1915. The mother now lives at Winchester, Virginia. Doctor Foley was next to the youngest in a family of ten children, eight of whom are living. His father was a Baptist and his mother a Lutheran.

Doctor Foley grew up in Clarke County, attended the Berryville High School, and then went to Richmond, where he continued his education in the Virginia Mechanics Institute and in the Massey Business College. He clerked in a bank and for a time was assistant to the actuary of the Atlantic Life Insurance Company at Richmond. Mr. Foley was graduated from the University College of Medicine at Richmond in 1913. For one year he was an interne in the Sheltering Arms Hospital at Richmond. Doctor Foley as a specialist has the training and experience of a general practitioner. He practiced medicine in Lovettsville, Loudoun County, until the fall of 1921. In the meantime he had been commissioned in August, 1917, and answered the call to

A. W. Terrell, M. D.

the colors in October of that year. He gave his service at Camp Lee and at the Walter Reed Hospital at Washington.

He received his honorable discharge in January, 1919. Doctor Foley in September, 1921, closed his practice in Loudoun County and during the next two years was in hospitals in New Orleans and New York studying and preparing for practice as a specialist in eye, ear, nose and throat. For eighteen months he was located at Washington, for two years was at Raleigh, North Carolina, and in 1927 established himself at Front Royal, where he has built up a reputation all over this section of Virginia in his special field. Doctor Foley is a member of the Medical Society of Virginia, the Warren County and American Medical Associations, and also has membership in the medical fraternity.

He married in December, 1914, Miss Charlotte Christian Woody, of Lynchburg, where she was reared and educated. She is a member of the Methodist Episcopal Church. Doctor Foley is a member of the Masonic fraternity.

ALEXANDER W. TERRELL, physician and surgeon at Lynchburg, continues the honorable tradition of the Terrell family in the profession of medicine in Virginia, a tradition closely associated with vital service to community and state for more than a century. While this branch of the family has been closely identified with the profession of medicine, the Terrells of Virginia, including the many branches and divisions of the family since Colonial times, have furnished eminent names in all the professions, in military and civic affairs, and to be a Virginia Terrell is almost a patent right to social prominence and the possession of the most enviable qualities of character.

Doctor Terrell's grandfather was Dr. Christopher J. Terrell, who was born in Campbell County, Virginia, and married Susan Kennerly. Christopher Terrell moved out to Missouri in pioneer times, locating at Boonville, where he died in 1833 during an epidemic of cholera.

His son, John J. Terrell, was born in Patrick County, Virginia, August 8, 1829, and was only four years of age when his father died. He was sent back to Virginia, grew up in Campbell County, and was closely associated with the Society of Friends who founded the Quaker Memorial Church, of which both his grandfather and aunt were members. He was educated in Campbell County, at Floyd Court House, at Emory and Henry College, and Richmond College. At the age of seventeen he enlisted and for four months was in training as a soldier during the war with Mexico. He began reading medicine under a physician in Bedford County, and in 1853 was graduated M. D. from the Jefferson Medical College of Philadelphia. Doctor Terrell then located near Lynchburg, and for fully half a century was one of the most popular and busy physicians in Campbell County, in the early days his practice extending even beyond the borders of the county. During the Civil war he volunteered as a surgeon, and at Lynchburg was assigned duty as assistant to the chief of staff and was put in charge of Burton's Hospital at Fourth and Harrison streets. This hospital for several years was always filled with patients and Doctor Terrell had little time to attend to his private practice during the four years of the war. Atfer the war he established his home at the old Terrell homestead in Campbell County, going back and forth between his home and his office at Lynchburg. His last years were spent

at the homestead and he died there November 7, 1922, at the age
of ninety-three years, three months. Dr. John Terrell, almost
from the time it was organized, was a member of the Campbell
County Board of Health. He was regarded as one of the most
progressive men in his profession, being the first doctor at
Lynchburg to use the clinical thermometer, and one of the first
to employ the hypodermic needle. He was devoted to his old
comrades of the Confederacy, and for many years acted as chief
surgeon to Garland-Rodes Camp, United Confederate Veterans,
and was also chief surgeon of the state organization. He represented Campbell County in the House of Delegates from 1885
to 1889.

Dr. John J. Terrell married, March 17, 1857, Miss Sue Wade,
of Franklin County, Virginia. They celebrated their sixty-second wedding anniversary March 17, 1919, and she passed away
in October of the same year. They had a family of nine children, and two of them became doctors, Thomas K. and Alexander W.

A brother of Dr. John J. Terrell was Alexander W. Terrell,
who served as a general in the Confederacy, and for many years
was one of the most distinguished citizens and lawyers of Texas,
serving as minister to Turkey under President Cleveland.

Dr. Alexander W. Terrell of Lynchburg was named for this
distinguished Texas uncle. He was born July 11, 1861, was educated at Randolph-Macon College, where he spent three years,
attended the Medical School of the University of Virginia one
year, and in 1886 was graduated from the Louisville Hospital
College of Medicine. He did post-graduate work in New York
City in 1887-88, practiced three years with his father at Lynchburg, and for twenty years was associated with Dr. Samuel Lile.
Doctor Terrell has been one of the outstanding representatives
of his profession in Campbell County for over forty years. Since
1893, the year of its organization, Doctor Terrell has served as
physician at the Randolph-Macon College for Women, and was
also surgeon for the Southern Railway at Lynchburg. He was
a member of the Medical Advisory Board during the World war.
His Masonic Lodge membership is in Marshall Lodge, of which
his father at the time of his death was the oldest member. Doctor Terrell is a Master Mason, member of the B. P. O. Elks,
Rotary Club, and has been a steward in the Court Street Methodist Episcopal Church, South.

He married, November 6, 1889, Miss Lily King, daughter of
Judge Thomas F. King of Florida. The children born to their
marriage are King, Helen and Virginia John. The son King
attended the Virginia Military Institute and Randolph-Macon
College, was in training with the Marine Corps at Paris Island
four months during the World war, and subsequently took up a
career in banking.

REV. ELLIOTT BENGER MEREDITH is rector of one of the old
Episcopal churches of Albemarle County, the parish at Scottsville, which was established more than a hundred years ago by
Reverend Doctor Redout, who was not only a minister but also
a greatly beloved physician in that early community. During
the Civil war the church with all its records was burned, and the
edifice now used is one of comparatively recent construction.

Rev. Elliott Benger Meredith was born in Stafford County,
Virginia, May 17, 1873, son of Rev. Jacklin and Ellen (Bankhead) Meredith. His father gave more than fifty years of his

life to the Episcopal ministry in Rappahannock Parish. He
served as captain of a company under General Jackson during
the Civil war. The Meredith family came from Wales and were
Colonial settlers in Virginia. Ellen Bankhead in one line of
descent had as an ancestor Elliott Benger, from Scotland, who
was private secretary to Col. Alexander Spotswood. He married
Helen Brain, whose sister, Dorothy, was the wife of Colonel
Spotswood. Rev. Jacklin Meredith and wife had a family of
eleven children, five sons and six daughters. Two of the sons,
John Scott and Reuben, in addition to Elliott B., entered the
Episcopal ministry, the former being located at Greenwood, Virginia, and the latter at Oxford, North Carolina, and one of the
daughters married John Robison, an Episcopal minister of Redout, Virginia. Rev. Jacklin Meredith died in 1923 and his
wife, in 1921.

Elliott Benger Meredith attended Roanoke College four years
and graduated in a special course at the Virginia Episcopal
Seminary at Alexandria in 1901. He was ordained a deacon and
his first charge, for one year, was in Middlesex County, Virginia.
For three years Mr. Meredith was in the far West, locating at
Elko, Nevada. On returning to Virginia he was for some time
in Bedford County, then at Christianburg, and since 1910 has
had the duties of the parish at Scottsville. Rev. Mr. Meredith
is a member of the Masonic Order and an independent voter.

He married in June, 1901, Miss Esther Montague, of Fred-
ericksburg, Virginia, daughter of Doctor Thaddeus and Belle
(Roamey) Montague. Her father was a physician, a Confed-
erate soldier, and died in 1911, while her mother is still living.
Mr. and Mrs. Meredith have five children: Belle, wife of L. A.
Burgess, of Birmingham, Alabama; Elliott B., Jr., now in the
United States Aviation Corps; Bessie M., of Baltimore; Jacklayn
M. and John Claybrook, both attending school.

WILLIAM H. EAST, of Churchville, member of the Virginia
State Senate, is well fitted to represent the essential interests
of his locality in the State Legislature. Senator East for many
years has been a practical farmer and horticulturist, and owns
one of the best fruit and stock farms in Augusta County.

He was born on the old East homestead near Spring Hill, Augusta County, August 26, 1868, son of Samuel A. and Lucy
(Howell) East. His family has been in America since the seventeenth century, coming from England and settling in Pittsylvania and Campbell counties. His grandfather, David C. East,
was a farmer near Lynchburg. Col. Samuel A. East, a native
of Rockbridge County, was a farmer in Augusta County and for
many years was a member of the county school board and held
other offices in the county and district. He served with the rank
of colonel of militia during the Civil war. He died February 3,
1893, and his wife, who was born in Augusta County, died January 23, 1912. Senator East had two brothers and one sister.
His brother John P. is an attorney in New York City. Mary E.,
a graduate of the Mary Baldwin Seminary of Staunton and of
the New York Museum of Art, has taught art for many years
and is now art instructor in the Federal Rehabilitation Camp
near Poughkeepsie, New York. The other son, Charles M. East,
was an attorney and banker, and died in 1927.

William H. East attended the Fishburne Military School at
Waynesboro, and attended in 1887 Staunton Military Academy.
After his marriage he took charge of the 135-acre farm com-

prising a part of his wife's estate. Since then he has greatly
added to the property, now owning 500 acres. It is a general
purpose farm, with fifty acres planted to apples of different
varieties, and he keeps a herd of from 135 to 150 Hereford and
Holstein cattle, besides hogs and sheep. His business is one of
the factors contributing to Virginia's steady climb to agricultural
supremacy.

Senator East has always been interested in politics. He
served on both the county and district school boards, resigning
in 1923 when elected a member of the State Senate. He has
been a member of the Democratic County Executive Committee
and is now a member of the State Democratic Committee. Senator East has affiliation with the Independent Order of Odd
Fellows at Churchville and is an elder in the Hock Willow
Presbyterian Church.

He married, December 4, 1890, Miss Irene Dudley, daughter
of Washington M. and Martha (Hanger) Dudley, of Augusta
County. Her father was a farmer and stock man and died in
1885, and her mother passed away in 1886. She was one of a
family of ten children, three of whom are now living. Mrs.
East died July 20, 1922. She was the mother of two children.
The daughter, Virginia D., is the wife of R. E. Layman, who
graduated from Vanderbilt University at Nashville, and is a
teacher and farmer. They have two children, Denton and Douglas Howell,. John H. East, the only son of Senator East, is a
graduate of the Virginia Polytechnic Institute, was a first lieutenant in the Aviation Corps during the World war, being
trained at Fort Myers, Camp Lee, Fort Sill and Dallas, and
went to France as an observer. He was shot down by German
flyers, was captured and was in prison a short time before the
armistice. He is now associated with his father on the farm
and is a member of the American Legion Post. John H. East
married Evelyn Witt, of Charlottesville, and their three children are John William, Irene Witt and Evelyn Virginia.

HARRY ALBERT SAGER. Had it not been for the events that
culminated in the Spanish-American war, Harry Albert Sager,
of Herndon, probably would today be a member of the medical
profession, for he had already commenced his medical studies
when the call came for volunteers for that struggle. Answering
the call and seeing active service, the whole trend of his life was
changed. However, the profession's loss has been Herndon's
gain, as for many years Mr. Sager has rendered splendid public
service in the capacity of postmaster, a position which he has
held since 1902 with the exception of the two Democratic administrations that have intervened since that year.

Mr. Sager was born at North Bristol, Ohio, June 29, 1876,
and is a son of Jacob A. and Mollie (Thompson) Sager, natives
of the Buckeye State, but his earlier ancestors were all natives
of Virginia. His father was born and reared on an Ohio farm
and brought up to agricultural pursuits, which he followed until
the start of hostilities between the South and the North in 1861,
when he enlisted in the Sixth Ohio Volunteer Cavalry. He
served with this regiment until the close of the war, when he
engaged in the nursery business and carried on that vocation
during the active years of his life. Mr. Sager is now retired
at the age of eighty-eight years and resides at Bristolville, Ohio,
where his wife passed away in 1889. He is a man who is held in

high esteem in his community, and for six years served capably as treasurer of Trumbull County, Ohio.

Harry Albert Sager was reared at Bristol, where he attended public school, and then entered Hiram College at Hiram, Ohio, from which he was graduated as a member of the class of 1898. As noted before, it had been his intention to follow the profession of medicine, and he had started his studies for the practice of that science when, in 1898, his youthful patriotism caused him to respond to the call of President McKinley for volunteers for the Spanish-American war. Subsequently he was appointed to the post non-commissioned staff and remained in the Philippine Islands for four years, then returning to the United States, where he received his honorable discharge in 1902. In that year he took up his residence at Herndon and was appointed postmaster by President Roosevelt and subsequently by President Taft. He was out of office during the two Wilson administrations, but with the return of the Republican party to power was reappointed by Presidents Harding and Coolidge and is still the incumbent of the office. Mr. Sager has an excellent record as an official and has the confidence of the people of the community whom he has served in an expeditious and conscientious manner. In 1917 Mr. Sager went to the Officers' Training Camp and offered his services for the World war, but was refused because of disability. He has also served as a member of the Town Council of Herndon and as chairman of the School League. He is a past master of Herndon Lodge No. 264, A. F. and A. M.; a member of Loudoun Chapter No. 55, R. A. M., at Leesburg; The Plains Commandery, K. T., at The Plains, and Acca Temple, A. A. O. N. M. S., at Richmond, and Great Sachem for the State of Virginia of the Improved Order of Red Men. He belongs also to the Spanish-American War Veterans, and his religious faith is that of the Christian Church. He has always been active in Republican politics and wields a strong influence in the ranks of his party.

On June 19, 1902, Mr. Sager married Miss Theresa M. Porter, daughter of Charles Porter, of Pricetown, Ohio, who later moved to Herndon, where he died February 21, 1920. Mrs. Sager was born at London, England, and came to America at the age of five years. Four children have been born to Mr. and Mrs. Sager: Geraldine Martha, the wife of Gerald Fitz-Gerald, topographic engineer with the United States Geological Survey of the Department of the Interior; Charles Jacob, assistant postmaster of Herndon, Virginia; Margaret Ann, the wife of J. B. McDaniels, cashier of the Vienna (Virginia) National Bank; and Harry Albert, Jr., born in 1919, who is attending school.

JOHN SHIPMAN WITT was a progressive business man of Lynchburg, who gave to that city an important business, the Lynchburg Shoe Company, and whose spirit and activities were always disposed to cooperation with the community's inmost welfare and advancement.

He was born on a farm in Nelson County, Virginia, September 22, 1864, and was a comparatively young man, just at the high tide of his successful career, when death called him October 25, 1919. His parents were David and Elizabeth (Jones) Witt, both representing old Virginia families. Three brothers named Witt came from France in Colonial times, one settling in Kentucky, one in Virginia and one in Texas. The Virginia brother was the great-great-grandfather of John S. Witt. He was a French Huguenot who immigrated to this country due to religious persecution in France during the sixteenth and seventeenth centuries. David Witt owned and conducted a large farm he had inherited from his father. His wife was a daughter of George Jones, of English descent, who was prominent in the tobacco industry of Virginia in the early part of the last century, and was one of the Virginia tobacco men who made extensive shipments to Europe, and he made many trips abroad.

John S. Witt was educated in a small academy in Amherst, and at the early age of eighteen became identified with the shoe business, which was his chief commercial activity until his death. He started in a small way and later organized and incorporated the Lynchburg Shoe Company, a wholesale business which during his lifetime extended its trade over Virginia and surrounding states. He was vice president of the company until his death.

The late Mr. Witt was a member of Hill City Lodge of Masons, member of the Oakwood Country Club, the Piedmont Club, and was vestryman in St. Paul's Episcopal Church. He served as an alderman, and through the Chamber of Commerce directed his influence steadily for movements that meant a larger and better Lynchburg. He was liberal in behalf of charities, and in personal character his qualities won him a host of loyal friends, to whom his early death seemed an unmitigable calamity. He had lived well up to the essence of the motto "Do all the good possible and no harm."

Mr. Witt married, in 1892, Miss Annie Clarkson Langley, who was born in Gallipolis, Ohio, and was graduated with high honor from Stuart Hall of Staunton, Virginia. Her parents were Augustus and Mary (Clarkson) Langley. Her father was born in Ohio, was educated at Marietta College in that state, and her mother was born at Charleston, West Virginia, where she now resides, having been educated in Richmond. She is now eighty-one years of age. She is a member of the Colonial Dames and recently was invited to join the "Daughters of the Crown," an English society of which there are only about thirty-five families eligible to join in the United States. Mrs. Witt's father was in the wholesale commission business at Charleston for many years, continuing active there until his death. His mother was a member of the prominent Shenandoah Valley family of Millers. Other ancestors were the Clendenens, a very prominent family, several of whom, George, Charles and William Clendenen, were among the most prominent early settlers of Charleston, West Virginia, naming that city for Charles Clendenen. William Clendenen was a soldier in the War of the Revolution and also fought in the battle of Point Pleasant. Mr. Langley died in 1902, leaving two children, Mrs. Witt and Clark Langley, the latter of whom is a business man in Omaha, Nebraska.

Mrs. Witt, who continues to reside at Lynchburg, has been a very active member of the Episcopal Church, and has been identified with several woman's organizations. She is the mother of one son, John Augustus Witt, who was born at Lynchburg April 9, 1897. He is unmarried and resides with his mother. He was educated at Washington and Lee University, and while in the university enlisted for service in the navy and was trained at Norfolk. The signing of the armistice came shortly before he was ready for a commission as ensign. He then returned to Lynchburg, joined his father in the Lynchburg Shoe Company, was trained in the business in the home office, and after leaving

J. M. Kerr, D.D.S.

the company engaged in a general insurance business, of which he has made a more than ordinary success. He is a member of the Sigma Alpha Epsilon fraternity, B. P. O. Elks, Lions Club, Oakwood Country Club, and is a vestryman in St. Paul Episcopal Church.

JOHN M. HERR, Charlottesville dentist, one of the most skillful representatives of the modern profession of dental surgery, finished his education at Baltimore, but in early life lived in Pennsylvania.

He was born on a farm near Carlisle, Pennsylvania, August 27, 1882, son of Jacob M. and Anna (Hertzler) Herr, and grandson of Christian Herr and Abraham Hertzler, all of whom were Pennsylvanians, of German ancestry, and prosperous agriculturists of that state. His father served three years in the Union Army with a Pennsylvania regiment and was slightly wounded in one battle. He spent his active life as a farmer and was also a minister or elder in the Mennonite Church. He belonged to the Masonic fraternity. Mrs. Jacob Herr now resides at Mechanicsburg. There were ten children, Doctor Herr being the sixth in age.

John M. Herr attended public schools in Pennsylvania, also had a private tutor, and after some varied experiences in other lines of business he entered upon the study of dentistry. He graduated from the dental department of the University of Maryland in 1909, and since 1910 has practiced at Charlottesville. He is a member and president of the Charlottesville Dental Society, member of the Shenandoah Valley, Virginia State and National Dental Societies. Doctor Herr is a member of the Chamber of Commerce, the Kiwanis Club, is a Royal Arch Mason, and he and his wife are active members of the Baptist Church. For several years he has been on the Board of Deacons, is associate superintendent of the Sunday School, and his wife is superintendent of the Junior Department in Sunday School and treasurer of the Woman's Missionary Society.

Doctor Herr married, in 1911, Miss Belva Byrd. She was born in Accomac County, on the eastern shore of Virginia, and finished her education in Baltimore. They have four children, Margaret Byrd, Grace Elizabeth, Nancy Mason and Mary Belva.

ROBERT EDWARD AYLOR, principal of the high school at Stephens City, Frederick County, is one of the efficient and popular figures in the educational service in this part of his native state and is a representative of an old and honored family of Virginia. He was born at Chatham, Pittsylvania County, this state, August 14, 1903, and is a son of Robert E. L. Aylor, a prominent clergyman of the Baptist Church, and Ella (Vaden) Aylor, the former of whom was born in Rappahannock County, Virginia, and the latter in Pittsylvania County, Virginia. Stanton Aylor, grandfather of the subject of this review, was born in Culpeper County, where the family was established in an early period of Virginia history, three uncles of Robert E. Aylor having worn the Confederate uniform in the Civil war.

Robert E. Aylor attended the public schools of Scottsburg, Halifax County, and completed his high school studies at Red Hill, Albemarle County. His higher education was acquired in the historic old University of Virginia, in which he was graduated as a member of the class of 1925, and from which he received the degree of Bachelor of Science. In the pedagogic profession he is making a constructive and successful record as principal of the Stephens City High School, which maintains a corps of ten teachers working under the direction of the principal and which has an enrollment of 241 students at the time of this writing, early in 1928. As principal of the well ordered and distinctly modern high school department of the Stephens City public school system Mr. Aylor is not only a resourceful and progressive executive but is also teacher of mathematics and civics. He is a liberal and broad minded young man who takes lively interest in communal and governmental affairs and his political allegiance is given to the Democratic party, the while his religious faith is that of the Baptist Church, he being an active member of the church of this denomination in his present home community.

CHARLES C. CARLIN, JR., is an attorney, a member of the law firm of Carlin, Carlin & Hall, and enjoys a place of most interesting prominence by reason of his being president and editor of the *Alexandria Gazette,* the oldest daily newspaper in Virginia, established in 1784.

Mr. Carlin was born at Alexandria in December, 1900. His father, Charles C. Carlin, Sr., was an Alexandria attorney, who also was active in his profession at Washington and a former member of Congress from the Eighth Congressional District for sixteen years. Charles C. Carlin, Jr., was educated in the Alexandria High School and the Episcopal High School of that city, and took his law degree at the University of Virginia in 1923. He had been admitted to the bar in 1922, and for the past six years has enjoyed a large law practice.

He has been president and editor of the *Alexandria Gazette* since 1925. He is a member of the Bar Association, a Democrat, a member of the Methodist Episcopal Church, South. On October 9, 1926, he was united in marriage with Miss Sara Perine Bayol, of Alabama. They have one daughter, Sara Perine, born October 22, 1928.

JAMES MONROE ELLISON, one of the surviving veterans of the Armies of the Confederacy, is a resident of Crozet in Albemarle County, and for many years has been a successful horticulturist, engaging in the production of that famous crop of the Piedmont, the Albemarle pippin.

Mr. Ellison was born in Person County, North Carolina, June 25, 1846, son of J. Johnson and Martha (Persons) Ellison. His father was a native of Scotland, came to America when young and followed farming in Person County, North Carolina, until his death at the age of seventy-seven. His wife, who died at the age of eighty-four, was born in North Carolina, daughter of a Baptist minister. Of the ten children of these parents, five sons and five daughters, James Monroe is the only one now living.

He grew up and received his early schooling in Person County, and was seventeen years old when, in 1863, he joined the Confederate army, acting as a courier. He was captured by the enemy at Five Forks, Virginia, and toward the end of the war spent two months as a prisoner at Point Lookout, Maryland. After being released he returned home to North Carolina, but soon went to Augusta, Virginia, for a short time was a merchant there, and then became associated with a brother

Jay C Coulter M D

in merchandising at Waynesboro, Virginia. Seven years later he sold out, and ever since has made his home at Crozet.

Mr. Ellison has been a farmer and cattle raiser, but the industry that has brought him the largest amount of regular profits has been the growing of apples and peaches. He owns over 700 acres near Crozet, and of this land 340 acres are planted in orchards, practically all his apples being the Albemarle Pippin. His orchards give an average yearly crop of 2,000 barrels of apples and 500 crates of peaches. Much of his fruit is sent to Richmond and Baltimore, but the greater part helps supply the European demand for one of Virginia's finest product.

Mr. Ellison is a Democrat, and has interested himself in party affairs without ever accepting or desiring an office. He is a member of Lee Lodge No. 195 of the Masonic fraternity at Yancey Mills, Virginia, and belongs to the Baptist Church. He married, November 3, 1875, Miss Willie B. Woods, daughter of William P. and Ellen S. (Woods) Woods. Mrs. Ellison died in November, 1916. There are five living children: William Woods, of Amarillo, Texas; James A., of Los Angeles; John Grady, of Crozet; Elizabeth P., at home, and Julia, wife of Mc. C. Goodhall, of Staunton, Virginia. Mrs. Goodhall is the only child married. Her five children are Julia, Mrs. Eugenia Ivey, of Lynchburg, William W., McChesney and Ellen Park.

JAY C. COULTER, M. D., is a graduate of the University of Virginia, and after some years of professional experience elsewhere returned to Charlottesville, where he has practiced since 1913.

Doctor Coulter was born in Pennsylvania, October 4, 1881, son of Bernard L. and Emma E. (Campbell) Coulter, and grandson of Rev. James Coulter and Thomas B. Campbell. All of these forefathers were born in Pennsylvania. His maternal grandfather was a farmer, while Rev. James Coulter gave his active life to the ministry of the Presbyterian Church. Bernard L. Coulter was an oil operator, doing work as a driller and contractor in the development of some of the pioneer oil fields in the vicinity of Titusville, Pennsylvania. He was a Presbyterian and a member of the Masonic Order, Independent Order of Odd Fellows and Knights of Pythias, a Republican in politics. He and his wife had two sons, J. C. and L. D. Coulter. The latter was an oil well superintendent for the British American Oil Company in the British West Indies, but is now plant foreman for the Chance Manufacturing Company at Centralia, Missouri.

Dr. J. C. Coulter acquired his early education at West Sunbury, Pennsylvania and in the Grove City College at Grove City, Pennsylvania. As a youth he was thrown upon his own resources, and any advancement had to be secured at a cost of his own earnings and efforts. For three years he worked for the Standard Oil Company in West Virginia, using his savings to enroll him in the University of Virginia School of Medicine. While at the university he waited on table, delivered college papers, and accepted other opportunities presented in the university service to pay his expenses. He was regarded in university circles as a young man of great determination and capable talents, and eventually gained a well earned diploma as Doctor of Medicine. He began his studies at Charlottesville in 1902 and was graduated in 1907. Doctor Coulter was an interne in the South Side Hospital at Pittsburgh and then practiced at Cochran-

ton, Pennsylvania, until March 1, 1913. Since returning to
Charlottesville he has engaged in general practice as a physician
and surgeon, does a large business and has a great following of
loyal friends. He is a member of the Albemarle County and
Piedmont Medical Societies, Medical Society of Virginia and
American Medical Association.

Doctor Coulter married, in 1909, Miss Carrie Clark, a native
of Albemarle County, Virginia, and reared and educated at
Charlottesville. She attended Rawlins Institute. Her father,
R. W. Clark, was a car inspector for the Southern Railway. Doctor and Mrs. Coulter have one daughter, Martha Campbell Coulter, now attending school. The family are members of the Christian Church and Doctor Coulter is affiliated with the Independent
Order of Odd Fellows, Benevolent and Protective Order of Elks,
and is a past chancellor of the Knights of Pythias and a member of its social adjunct, the Dramatic Order Knights of Koras-
san.

MRS. ALEXANDER W. L. TROTTER, whose home is in Charlottesville, was before her marriage Miss Cameron Browning and
she represents the prominent Browning and Hoag families of
Virginia.

She was born at Richmond and when she was a small child
her parents moved to Bluefield, West Virginia, where her father,
Col. James S. Browning, was a coal operator, continuing active
in that industry until his death on February 26, 1928. Colonel
Browning was a Republican and one of the prominent leaders
of his party in the Ninth Congressional District, serving for a
time on the National Committee and was a particular friend of
President William McKinley. However, he never sought any
public honors for himself. He owned a farm which has long
been known as the Browning Homestead, located on the Virginia
and West Virginia line south of Bluefield.

Colonel Browning married Miss Olivia Hoag, of the well
known family of that name at Richmond. She is still living.
Through her Mrs. Trotter is connected with the distinguished
Howe family of English origin which settled in Pennsylvania
and was related to General Howe, the English general of the
Revolution. Colonel and Mrs. Browning had four children.
Reba is the wife of G. E. Countz, of Salem, Virginia, and has
two children, Edward and Virginia. Jane Browning, now living
at Elizabeth Town, Tennessee, was twice married, her three
children by her first marriage being Elizabeth McConnell, Olivia
Huff and Clifton Huff. James Browning, Junior, a coal man
at Bluefield, West Virginia, is married and has one daughter,
Betty.

Miss Cameron Browning was educated in the Mary Baldwin
Seminary at Staunton, Virginia, also attended the Bell Buckle
Preparatory School in Tennessee, and in 1904 she became the
bride of Maj. Alexander William Lewis Trotter. Major Trotter,
whose home was in Scurry, England, of an old and substantial
English family, served with the rank of major in the English
army, in the Yorkshire Regiment, but was put on the retired
list before the beginning of the World war. He came to America
and for some years practiced his profession as a civil and construction engineer, doing a great deal of railway building in
Southwestern Virginia and Tennessee. When the World war
broke out in 1914 he returned to England, enlisted as a private
and subsequently was promoted to major. During the battle of

Somme he was killed in July, 1916. Mrs. Trotter has two children, James S. Trotter, born in 1908, and William Cameron Trotter, born in 1912.

Mrs. Trotter is a member of the Daughters of the American Revolution and the United Daughters of the Confederacy, and is a member of the Episcopal Church.

CHARLES CLAYTON DONALDSON is a resident of Arlington County, is in the real estate business at Cherrydale, but for thirty-seven years of his life most of his work has been with the Federal and District Government in Washington.

He was born in Georgetown, District of Columbia, November 5, 1869, son of William A. and Mary A. Frances (Jenkins) Donaldson. Both parents were natives of Virginia, and his father was a mess sergeant during the Civil war. He spent many years in the service of the District Government and died in 1911, his wife passing away in 1873.

Charles C. Donaldson was reared and educated at Georgetown and at the age of nineteen went to work under his father, and has now given thirty-seven consecutive years to Government work in the District of Columbia. He now holds the office his father formerly held, that of chief inspector of construction material for sewers and streets in Washington. In addition to his Government work he has for the past seven years operated a real estate office at Cherrydale in Arlington County.

Mr. Donaldson married, October 18, 1893, Bertha Gingells, a daughter of James Oliver and Catherine (Ward) Gingells. Her parents were born in Maryland. Her father was a merchant and died in 1906, her mother passing away in 1907. Mr. and Mrs. Donaldson have had four children: Ethel Leora, who died at the age of four years, eight months; Bessie Estelle, born in 1896, wife of Robert L. Newton, of Cherrydale; Kathryn Havner, born in 1905, the wife of Ervin Van Horn, of Miami, Florida; and Elbert Oliver, born in 1911.

Mr. Donaldson has had a prominent part in the civic affairs of Arlington County. He has served as a member of the Cherrydale Fire Department since it was organized, and to him belongs the credit of bringing the first fire protection to Arlington County and the first fire engine, and he erected the first fire engine house. He is the founder and treasurer of the Arlington & Fairfax Firemen's Association. Mr. Donaldson is a member of the Junior Order United American Mechanics, Independent Order of Odd Fellows, is a life member of George C. Whiting Lodge No. 22, A. F. and A. M., at Georgetown, member of Potomac Chapter No. 5, Royal Arch Masons at Georgetown. He is a Republican and a member of the Methodist Protestant Church.

HENRY AMISS HORNTHAL, physician and surgeon, has a busy professional practice on both sides of the Potomac, in his home community in Arlington County and in the City of Washington.

He was born at Norfolk, Virginia, July 25, 1901, son of Henry Ward and Irma Christian (Amiss) Hornthal. His mother was born in the historic locality of Edenton, North Carolina, while his father was a native of Plymouth, North Carolina, and spent his active business life in the brokerage business in Norfolk. Doctor Hornthal is a direct descendant on his mother's side of Elizabeth Hathaway, of the famous Edenton Tea Party. He died in 1915, and the widowed mother now resides at Washington. His grandfather, Rev. Joseph Henry Amiss, was presiding elder of the Methodist Episcopal Church, South, for twenty-five years and was one of the state's best known ministers.

Henry Amiss Hornthal was reared and educated in Norfolk, attended high school there, and had a very liberal education preparatory to taking up his professional work. He attended St. John's College at Annapolis, Maryland, Georgetown University in the District of Columbia, also George Washington University, and in 1920 he entered the Medical College of Virginia at Richmond, graduating with the class of 1924. After graduating Doctor Hornthal was house surgeon in the McGuire Clinic and St. Luke's Hospital in Richmond. On beginning private practice he opened offices at Potomac, Virginia, and in Washington, and has enjoyed an unusually successful practice. His address on the Virginia side is 800 Mount Vernon Avenue, in Potomac, and in Washington he has his offices in the Fairfax Hotel at 2100 Massachusetts Avenue, N. W. Doctor Hornthal is unmarried.

He is president of the Arlington County Medical Society, also a member of the Fairfax County Society, the Medical Society of Virginia, District of Columbia Medical Society, and is a fellow of the American Medical Association. Doctor Hornthal in connection with his private practice is on the faculty of instruction in the Medical School of George Washington University. He is a member of Cathedral Lodge No. 40, A. F. and A. M., the Eastern Star Chapter, the Congressional Country Club, Sons of the American Revolution, and belongs to the Phi Chi national medical fraternity. He is a Democrat and a member of the Methodist Episcopal Church, South.

JOSEPH PERCIVAL BLAIR has spent practically all his life at Scottsville in Albemarle County, and has added to some of the honorable distinctions associated with the Blair and relative names of that section of the state.

He was born at Scottsville, October 9, 1869, son of John Thomas and Martha (Mathews) Blair. His grandfather, John Blair, was a physician. The Blairs came from Scotland and the family were represented by soldiers in the Revolutionary war. Mr. Blair's maternal grandfather was Richard Mathews, a native of Rockingham County, Virginia, who for many years conducted a jewelry business at Charlottesville.

John T. Blair was born at Richmond and his wife at Charlottesville. He was in the commission business and for many years a merchant at Scottsville. During the Civil war he was captain in the Nineteenth Virginia Regiment, and after being captured was held in a Northern prison six months before being exchanged. He died in 1895, at the age of forty-six. His widow survived until December 18, 1925, passing away at the age of ninety-two. There were three children: Joseph Percival; Amelia, of Richmond; and Theodora, wife of J. R. Guthrie. Amelia and Theodora were twins.

Joseph Percival Blair was reared in Scottsville, and for many years has practiced in the profession of dentistry there. He is a director of the Scottsville National Bank, has served as clerk of Scottsville and for thirty years as a member of the County School Board. He takes a keen interest in local affairs and the success of the Democratic party. Doctor Blair is an elder in the Presbyterian Church, while his wife and daughter are Baptists.

J.J. Brochtrup

He married, in 1895, Susie Nicholas Powers, of Scottsville, daughter of David Pinkney and Sarah (Staples) Powers, of Albemarle County, and granddaughter of John and Alice (Saunders) Powers. Her maternal grandmother was Ann Tompkins Staples. David P. Powers served as superintendent of schools in Albemarle County from the time free schools were started until his death. He was college educated and a man of fine gifts and abilities. David P. Powers and wife had ten children, five of whom are now living: Anna P., who married A. G. Bell, in the treasurer's office at Charlottesville; P. S. Powers, in the insurance business at Richmond; Mrs. Blair; Mary Etta, secretary of the city school board; and Lucy H., a teacher in the public schools at Richmond.

Doctor and Mrs. Blair have one daughter, Susie Nicholas. She graduated A. B. from Hollins College, took the Master of Arts degree at the University of Richmond, also attended the University of Virginia, and has been a successful teacher.

REV. JOHN JOSEPH BROCHTRUP, B. A., is pastor of the Church of the Holy Comforter in Charlottesville, and has been a hard working successful priest in this section of Virginia for the past six years.

Father Brochtrup was born at Little Rock, Arkansas, December 20, 1890, son of Bernard and Katherine (Pinter) Brochtrup. His paternal grandfather, a native of Westphalia, Germany, came as a young man to America and was a pioneer of Washington County, Wisconsin. His maternal grandfather, a native of the Rhine Province of Germany, came early in life to America and was a pioneer settler of Conway County, Arkansas. Mrs. Katherine (Pinter) Brochtrup died in 1927. Bernard Brochtrup, now living at Columbus, Ohio, had a family of four children, three of whom are living: Mary Ann, wife of John F. Ryan, of Columbus; John Joseph; and Nicholas Joseph, also of Columbus.

John Joseph Brochtrup, B. A., acquired his early education at Columbus and then spent twelve years in the Pontifical College Josephinum, being ordained a priest in 1917, and also acquiring his B. A. degree. He was immediately sent as assistant to St. Paul's Church at Portsmouth, Virginia, where he remained five and a half years. Some of his first and most cherished priestly work was done at the Navy Hospital at Portsmouth among the sailors and marines under the Rev. F. Joseph Magri, M. A. D. D. Thus all of his active work as a Catholic priest has been done in Virginia. He came to his parish at Charlottesville December 30, 1922. He has made himself very much loved in this locality, and has distinguished his pastorate by a great deal of constructive work. The cornerstone of the new Church of the Holy Comforter was laid in May, 1925, and the church was dedicated in December of the same year. The church occupied by the congregation when Father Brochtrup arrived was erected in 1880, and the pastor who built it was present at the ceremonies of the laying of the cornerstone in 1925. This pastor was Father John McVerry, who is now chaplain of the Sacred Heart Novitiate at Fortress Monroe. Father McVerry was not a resident priest at Charlottesville, attending this congregation as a mission from Staunton. The first resident priest was Father J. J. Massey, who in 1899 was succeeded by Rev. E. H. Walsh, of Norfolk, then in 1902 Rev. T. J. Crow, now at Staunton, took charge, and in December, 1913, Father Thomas A. Rankin became pastor. It was during Father Rankin's pastorate that Mr. and Mrs. Thomas F. Ryan contributed

$30,000 to the building fund which aided materially the erection of the present handsome church. At the suggestion of a kind friend and generous benefactor Mr. Ryan during the pastorate of Father Brochtrup added $2,500, making his total contribution $32,500, the balance of the building fund being contributed by friends and members of the church. Father Rankin was succeeded in 1921 by Rev. J. J. DeGryse, and a little more than a year later Father Brochtrup became pastor. The parish now has a membership of 300 souls. In 1930 will be celebrated the fiftieth anniversary of the establishment of the first Catholic church at Charlottesville. Father Brochtrup also acts as chaplain to approximately one hundred members of the Catholic Church attending the University of Virginia. In addition Father Brochtrup attends various missions around Charlottesville, including Gordonsville, where there is a chapel, and he also ministers to the spiritual needs of part of the Catholics of the adjoining counties of Orange, Fluvana, Greene and Louisa.

Father Brochtrup is a fourth degree Knight of Columbus, having membership in St. Paul's Council No. 418 at Portsmouth, Virginia, and he was chaplain of that council for three years. He is a member of the Charlottesville Young Men's Business Club.

DR. CHARLES FENTON RUSSELL, of Herndon, who at the age of eighty-nine years, with the vigorous step and active mind of a man of sixty, still attends to the details of a large medical and surgical practice, and keeps himself in knowledge and sympathy abreast of the new generation amongst whom he survives, like a monarch of the forest among the younger growths that surround it, is one of the oldest members of his profession in Virginia. What a transformation to be wrought under the eye and within the mature life of a single man! If the span of human life is measured by ideas, by new sensations, the life of this man is longer than those of the patriarchs who drew out centuries amid the monotony of the deserts in the dull round of pastoral pursuits.

Doctor Russell was born at Harpers Ferry, Jefferson County, West Virginia (then Virginia), August 13, 1839, and is a son of Israel and Maria (Littlejohn) Russell. He comes of splendid American stock, his great-grandfather being Col. W. M. Russell, an officer of the Revolutionary war, in which two of his grandfathers also fought as soldiers. His maternal grandfather served in the War of 1812 and remained in the army until 1831, when he resigned his commission to take up railroad construction. Israel Russell, the father of Doctor Russell, was born in Virginia and passed his entire life as a merchant at Harpers Ferry, where his death occurred August 13, 1886, Mrs. Russell having passed away in June, 1896.

Charles Fenton Russell was reared at Harpers Ferry, and after his graduation from the Episcopal High School spent two years in the West. He began the study of medicine in 1859, but like thousands of other youths of his day his career was interrupted by the outbreak of the war between the states, and April 14, 1861, he enlisted in the Confederate army and became a noncommissioned officer. His service lasted four years and twenty-seven days, and that it was an active and strenuous one is shown in the fact that he was wounded four times. After Appomattox he returned home and resumed his medical studies at the University of Maryland School of Medicine, from which institution he was graduated in 1867 with the degree of Doctor of Medicine, and in the same year commenced practice at Waterford, Loudoun County, Virginia. After four years Doctor Russell moved to Sharpsburg, Maryland, where he remained in practice for eighteen years, then accepting a call to the West Indies, where he practiced surgery and held an official position for two years. Returning then to Virginia, he settled permanently at Herndon, where he has continued uninterruptedly in the successful practice of his calling to the present. He is a member of the Fairfax County Medical Society, Virginia State Medical Society and the Medical Society of Virginia, District of Columbia and Maryland. As a fraternalist he belongs to the Masons and Knights of Pythias, and his religious faith is that of the Episcopal Church, while in his political convictions he is a Democrat. He is commander of Hatcher Camp of Confederate Veterans at Leesburg, and adjutant of Marr Camp of Fairfax. Doctor Russell is a careful and methodical business man, a kind and generous neighbor, a lover of books, and a great reader of current literature, history, professional subjects and passing events. He is a man of the present, despite his ripeness of years, alike careless of the dogmas of the dead past and the unsolvable problems of the future.

On May 10, 1870, Doctor Russell was united in marriage with Miss Margaret A. Grimes, daughter of George and Eliza (Buffington) Grimes, natives of Maryland. Mrs. Russell died in December, 1907, having been the mother of four children: Charles G., a civil engineer by profession, who is carrying on agricultural interests in Oregon; Margaret B., who is identified with the American Express Fruit Growers Company; Helen, who died in 1890; and Eliza G., the wife of William T. Pollard, an official of the Southern Railway, residing at Chevy Chase, D. C.

CHARLES PICKETT. If it be true, as it should be, the most fitting memorial that can be written of a lawyer is a simple and truthful record of hard work that has brought with it honor in an honored profession, then, indeed, it is an easy task to present such a memorial to Charles Pickett, although he belongs to the younger element in his calling. He is connected with the prominent firm of Barbour, Keith, McCandlish & Garnett, of Fairfax and Washington, which in itself is proof of his ability, and is with Thomas R. Keith and F. Sheild McCandlish in the Fairfax office. He is a grandson of Charles Pickett, who served with the rank of major and assistant adjutant general in the division commanded by his brother, Gen. George Edward Pickett, C. S. A., whose name will always be connected with "Pickett's charge" at the battle of Gettysburg. The Pickett family is one of the First Families of Virginia, having been established here as early as 1640. On his maternal side Charles Pickett traces back to Gabriel Maupin, who settled in Yorktown, Virginia, in 1701, and was a prominent citizen of Williamsburg. Through his forebears on both sides Charles Pickett is eligible to membership in the Sons of the American Revolution.

Charles Pickett was born in Norfolk, Virginia, September 13, 1894, a son of Henry Clay and Anne Eliza Maupin (Watts) Pickett, natives of Virginia. For many years the father was a merchant of Norfolk and Portsmouth, Virginia, and he died November 17, 1924, highly respected by all who knew him. The mother survives him and is still residing in Portsmouth.

Charles Pickett attended the public schools of Portsmouth, and was graduated from high school in 1913, after which he worked in the office of the president of the Seaboard Airline Railroad from 1913 to 1916, leaving that position to go to the Mexican border with the Norfolk Blues of the National Guard. Following his being mustered out of the service in 1917 he entered the Officers Training Camp, Fort Myer, Virginia, and was commissioned a second lieutenant and sent overseas, where he remained for fifteen months, and was promoted to a first lieutenancy. In July, 1919, he was returned to the United States and honorably discharged. Returning home, he began the study of law in George Washington University, from which he was graduated in 1924, with the degree of Bachelor of Laws. In 1923 he was admitted to the bar and entered upon the practice of his profession with his present firm, and has been deservedly successful.

On December 29, 1917, Mr. Pickett married Miss Katherine Ancrum Cobb, a daughter of Beverly Cameron and Mary (Wright) Cobb, natives of North Carolina. Mr. Cobb was an attorney engaged in the practice of his profession in Lincolnton, North Carolina, until his death, which occurred in 1901. Mr. and Mrs. Pickett have a son, Charles, Junior, who was born May 21, 1920. Mr. Pickett is a member of the Fairfax County Bar Association, and served as its secretary for two years and he also belongs to the Virginia Bar Association and the American Bar Association. He is a member of the Masonic order, the Elks, Phi Alpha Delta, the Greek letter legal fraternity, the American Legion, and the Fairfax Golf and Country Club. In religious faith he is an Episcopalian, and in political belief he is a Democrat.

SAMUEL NELSON GRAY, D. D. S., has his office in the City of Alexandria, and he brings to bear in his practice the best of training in a profession that represents both a science and a mechanic art. As one of the prominent young dental practitioners in Alexandria he is developing a substantial practice of representative order, and his office is a model in the facilities of both its operative and laboratory departments.

Doctor Gray was born in Gloucester County, Virginia, May 14, 1899, and is a son of Zachary T. and Matilda (Roane) Gray, who likewise were born in that county, where the father became an influential banker and merchant at Gloucester Court House, judicial center of the county, and was a leader in community affairs, he having represented his native county in the Virginia Legislature and having at all times taken deep and helpful interest in its welfare and advancement. His death occurred July 3, 1925, and his widow retains her home at Gloucester Court House.

The public schools of his native county afforded Doctor Gray his preliminary education and he was graduated from the high school at the county seat as a member of the class of 1917. In the autumn of that same year he matriculated in Randolph-Macon College, in which he continued his studies until 1920. He then entered the Medical College of Virginia, at Richmond, and in the dental department thereof he was graduated in 1924. In the autumn of the year that thus marked his reception of the degree of Doctor of Dental Surgery he engaged in the practice of his profession in Alexandria, and the intervening years have recorded his development here of a distinctly large and representative practice. He has membership in the Northern Virginia Dental Society, the Virginia State Dental Society and the

American Dental Association. He is affiliated with the Masonic fraternity, is vice president of the Alexandria Rotary Club at the time of this writing, in the summer of 1928, and has membership in the Belle Haven Country Club. His political convictions are indicated in his loyal allegiance to the cause of the Democratic party, and his religious faith is that of the Methodist Episcopal Church, South. The name of Doctor Gray remains on the roster of popular young bachelors in Alexandria, Virginia.

WALTER WILLIAM KING is a contractor and a lumber dealer who has done business in more than thirty different states, putting up many churches, Government and college buildings.

Mr. King was born at Wildwood, Virginia, August 6, 1869, son of James Franklin and Willie (McLane) King. His father is of English and his mother of Scotch ancestry, the McLanes having belonged to a Scotch Clan. Members of the McLane family have been in America for many generations and the Virginia branch furnished five soldiers to the Revolutionary army. Mr. King is a descendant of John King, who patented a large tract of land in Hanover County in 1648. The first member of the King family in Virginia was Henry King, who arrived on the ship *Jonathan* in 1620, at the age of twenty-two, settling in Elizabeth City County, where he died in 1669, leaving a large estate. There were fifty soldiers from the King family in the Revolutionary war, ranging from private to major. One famous descendant of the Kings of Virginia was Rufus King, vice president of the United States. The Kings of Fluvanna County settled there in Colonial time.

Walter William King was reared on a farm and attended country schools in Fluvanna County. He started life with only the knowledge of a good mechanical trade, that of carpenter, and later engaged in the retail lumber business. The King Lumber Company now represents a complete organization for contracting and the furnishing of all material and supplies needed in construction work. Mr. King as a contractor has specialized in Government postoffices and county and municipal buildings. His contracts have been carried out in many states, as far west as Washington and as far east as Connecticut. Their work has covered federal buildings and county courthouses, and his firm has erected a number of university buildings, some of them being on the campus of the University of Virginia.

Mr. King, whose business headquarters have been in Charlottesville for many years, is a member of a number of fraternal and social organizations in that city, including the Masons, Independent Order of Odd Fellows, B. P. O. Elks. He is a Republican in politics. He married at Charlottesville, June 10, 1891, Leatha Morris, who was born in Fluvanna County, August 21, 1869, daughter of Frank and Lillian Morris. They have three children: The oldest, Claude C. King, born September 10, 1892, at Charlottesville, was educated in public schools, in Randolph-Macon Academy, the University of Virginia and the Rose Polytechnic Institute at Terre Haute, Indiana, where he received a technical training that has made him a valuable aid and assistant to his father in the contracting business. He married in January, 1918, Bettie A. Minnick, who was born and educated at Toledo, Ohio. Subsequently attending the Southern Seminary at Buena Vista, Virginia. They have two children: Claude C., Junior, born October 22, 1919, and Donald A., born June 15, 1921. Mr. and Mrs. Claude King are active members of the First Baptist

Church of Charlottesville and he is a York and Scottish Rite Mason and Shriner, member of the B. P. O. Elks and Young Men's Business Club. He served six months in the Army during the World war, and is a member of the American Legion. The second son is Harry H. King, who is associated with his father's business as building superintendent. He was born at Charlottesville, August 1, 1894, was educated in public schools and Randolph-Macon Academy, finishing with a course in the Carnegie Institute of Technology at Pittsburgh. He married Nila Ketcham, of Wayne, West Virginia, and has a daughter, Maxine, born in 1927. Harry King served during the World war, being overseas in France two years, and is a member of the American Legion. The only daughter, Gladys King, was educated at Charlottesville and in the Southern Seminary at Buena Vista, and is now the wife of W. R. Ellington. They have three children, Delores, Maxine and Phyllis.

THOMAS RANDOLPH KEITH is the second member of the firm Barbour, Keith, McCandlish & Garnett, attorneys and counsellors at law, which is regarded as one of the leading law firms in the state, handling an immense volume of business in State and federal courts. Besides their offices at Fairfax, where Mr. Keith and F. Sheild McCandlish have charge, the firm occupies a suite of offices across from the Department of Justice at 1000 Vermont Avenue, in Washington.

Thomas Randolph Keith is of Scotch ancestry and was born in Fauquier County, Virginia, September 19, 1872, a descendant of Rev. James Keith, who came to Virginia from Scotland some time after the Stuart uprising in 1715. He was rector of Henrico Parish from 1730 to 1733, and for many years had charge of Hamilton Parish in what is now Fauquier County. He was at one time rector of St. John's Church where Patrick Henry delivered his famous "Liberty or death" speech. He married Mary Isham Randolph, daughter of Thomas Randolph, of Tuckahoe. Three of his sons served as soldiers in the American Revolution. One of them, Capt. Thomas Keith, who served first as a captain in the Continental line and afterwards as a commissary, married Judith Blackwell. Their son, Isham Keith, married Juliette Chilton, whose grandfather, Capt. John Chilton, was killed at the battle of Brandywine. They had two sons, both of whom were men of distinction, Isham and James. James after his service as a private in the Black Horse Cavalry and as adjutant of the Fourth Virginia Regiment became judge of the Eleventh Judicial Circuit and from 1895 to 1916 president of the Supreme Court of Appeals of Virginia.

Isham Keith, the other son, was born in Fauquier County in September, 1833, and died September 19, 1902. He was educated at the University of Virginia, served in the Black Horse Cavalry and under Mosby, and for many years was a Fauquier County planter. He married Sarah Agnes Blackwell, whose great-grandfather, Joseph Blackwell, was the first sheriff of Fauquier County after it was taken from Prince William County in 1759, her grandfather, Joseph Blackwell, was a soldier in the Revolution, and her father was William Blackwell. Sarah Agnes Blackwell was born February 14, 1837, and died November 3, 1912. She was the mother of a large family of ten children, the youngest being Thomas Randolph Keith. Two others, Lucien and John A. C., became lawyers, and James became a banker and was honored with the office of president of the Alabama Bankers Association.

Thomas Randolph Keith graduated from the law department of the University of Virginia in 1894, and compiled a quiz-book for the use of law students that year. He has practiced thirty-four years at Fairfax Court House, with offices in the National Bank Building, and his success as a lawyer has been accompanied by a public spirited participation in public affairs. He was made a member of the Virginia State Board of Law Examiners in 1910. In 1914 he was nominated by the Supreme Court of Appeals for appointment as a code reviser. He has served as first vice president of the National Bank of Fairfax, president of the Warrenton-Fairfax Turnpike Company, president of the Fairfax and Loudoun Light & Power Company, member of the Board of Visitors of the Virginia Military Institute, member of the Southern Society of Washington, University Club of Washington, Chi Phi college fraternity, vestryman and senior warden of the Zion Episcopal Church of Fairfax. He served on the local draft board, chairman of the finance committee of the Red Cross Chapter, and on Liberty Bond and other committees during the World war.

He married, November 16, 1899, Miss Edith Moore, who was born in Fairfax County, daughter of Thomas and Hannah (Morris) Moore, her mother being a member of the Gouverneur Morris family of New York. They had three daughters, Ann Gordon, Hannah Morris and Margaret Randolph. Ann Gordon married Carlos C. Drake and Hannah Morris married Dr. Charles P. Howze.

FAIRFAX SHEILD McCANDLISH, member of the strong legal firm of Barbour, Keith, McCandlish & Garnett, attorneys and counsellors at law of Fairfax, Virginia, and Washington, District of Columbia, is one of the most forceful members of the bar in Virginia, and for years has been credited with standing in the front rank of jury lawyers. The elasticity of his mind, his keen faculties of perception and analysis, and his mastery of the principles of the common law have made him a remarkably striking and successful advocate. If there is a close legal point involved in any issue his examination of authorities bearing upon it is exhaustive. With a thorough knowledge of the case in all its bearings and unerring and ready application of the principles of the law, his addresses before court and jury are necessarily models of clearness and convincing logic. Quick to perceive and guard the weak phases of his own case, he never fails to assault his adversary at the point where his armor is defective. In a word, Mr. McCandlish has developed to quite a remarkable degree the necessary talent of the modern court lawyer, to think and act both quickly and powerfully, on his feet.

Born in Saluda, Virginia, August 10, 1881, Mr. McCandlish is a son of Robert and Nannie E. (Montague) McCandlish, natives of Williamsburg, Virginia, and King and Queen County, Virginia, respectively. The father was an eminent lawyer, and was engaged in the practice of his profession in Southern Virginia, but maintained his office and residence in Saluda. He was a Confederate veteran, having entered the army at the age of sixteen years, and was seriously wounded in action. His death occurred December 19, 1900, but the mother survives and is still living in Saluda.

Growing to useful manhood in his native town, Attorney McCandlish of this review attended both its private and public schools, and later spent four years in William and Mary College, being graduated from the latter institution in June, 1901, with the degree of Bachelor of Laws. In June, 1907, he was graduated in law from Georgetown University, with the degree of Bachelor of Laws, and June 1, 1908, he began the practice of his profession in Fairfax, where he has since continued, having from the beginning been a member of his present firm. The Fairfax offices of the firm are in the Fairfax National Bank Building, while those in Washington are at 1000 Vermont Avenue, opposite the Department of Justice. Associated with Mr. McCandlish are Thomas R. Keith and Charles Pickett in the Fairfax offices, while the Washington office is in charge of John S. Barbour and Christopher B. Garnett. These gentlemen form one of the strongest law firms in this part of the country, and handle a vast amount of vitally important litigation with masterly ability.

In November, 1911, Mr. McCandlish married Miss Mary Le-Grand Donohoe, a daughter of Capt. S. R. and Susie (Moore) Donohoe, natives of Virginia. He held a commission as captain during the Spanish-American war, and was serving as prohibition commissioner of the State of Virginia at the time of his death, and he was also operating the *Fairfax Herald,* so that he was one of the outstanding figures in the life of the city and state in which his useful career was passed. The death of this prominent citizen occurred in 1924, and the wife and mother is also deceased. Mr. and Mrs. McCandlish have three children: Mary Walton, who was born November 21, 1914, a student of the National Cathedral School for Girls, Washington, D. C.; Nancy Montague, who was born November 11, 1916; and Fairfax Sheild, Junior, who was born October 28, 1918. Mr. McCandlish belongs to the Fairfax County Bar Association, the Virginia State Bar Association and the American Bar Association. He belongs to the Masonic order, and Phi Beta Kappa fraternity. Politically he is a Democrat, while in religious faith he is an Episcopalian, and is serving his church as a vestryman and is a teacher of the Men's Bible Class in the Sunday School. The McCandlish residence in Fairfax is one of the beautiful homes of the town, and here a most gracious hospitality is dispensed that has all of the flavor of the oldtime Southern spirit that made this section famous in the ante-bellum period, and which is still preserved by those of the old families of Virginia, than whom there are few better. Both Mr. and Mrs. McCandlish are very active socially, as he is professionally, and their friends are legion.

ERNEST WELDON JENKINS. The American Agricultural Chemical Company is an important industrial corporation that operates thirty-two factories, and of the branch of the business that the company maintains in the City of Alexandria, Virginia, Ernest W. Jenkins is the resourceful and popular manager.

Mr. Jenkins was born at Oak Park, Madison County, Virginia, May 24, 1886, and is a son of William H. and Julia (Shotwell) Jenkins, who passed virtually their entire lives in Madison County, where both were born and reared and both representatives of sterling old families of Virginia. William H. Jenkins went forth as a loyal young soldier of the Confederacy in the Civil war, served during the entire course of that conflict, and thereafter continued to be substantial exponent of farm industry in Madison County until his death, which occurred in February, 1908, his widow having passed away in December, 1925.

Ernest W. Jenkins passed his childhood and early youth in his native county, received the advantages of the public schools of Oak Park and thereafter was a student in turn in Locust Dale Military Academy, a preparatory school at Locust Dale, and in the Piedmont Business College at Lynchburg. He next gave two years of service as bookkeeper for the Keystone Coal & Coke Company at Keystone, West Virginia, and he then went to Washington, D. C., where he gave a short period of service in the auditor of passenger accounts office of the Southern Railway. His next business alliance was with the old Alexandria Fertilizer & Chemical Company, in his present home city. He was factory foreman one year, then timekeeper two years, and during the ensuing fifteen years he was a successful traveling salesman for this company. In 1926 Mr. Jenkins was advanced to the position of active manager of the plant and business, and in December of the following year was made manager of the Alexandria branch of the American Agricultural Chemical Company, which had become the owner of the Alexandria plant and the headquarters of which are maintained in New York City, with branch plants in strategic points throughout the United States. The Alexandria branch gives employment to 200 persons and operates one sales office, all departments of the business in and from this city being under the direct supervision of Mr. Jenkins, who is local manager.

Mr. Jenkins maintains an independent political attitude and as a citizen he is emphatically loyal and progressive. He is a valued member of the Alexandria Chamber of Commerce and of the local Kiwanis Club, besides having membership in the Virginia State Chamber of Commerce. He is affiliated with the York Rite bodies of the Masonic fraternity, as well as the Mystic Shrine and the Order of the Eastern Star, and he is a member of the Benevolent and Protective Order of Elks and of the Travelers Protective Association. He is a member of the Methodist Episcopal Church, South, and Mrs. Jenkins is a member of the Episcopal Church and is affiliated with the Order of the Eastern Star. The marriage of Mr. Jenkins and Miss Anna Magruder occurred July 2, 1927, and they are popular figures in the representative social activities of their home city.

SAMUEL FULTON COOPER. Because of the scope and importance of his business and financial interests and the leading part that he takes in all civic enterprises, Samuel Fulton Cooper is justly accounted one of the most valued and valuable citizens of Arlington County. He is another of the substantial men of this county who has traveled the difficult road of self-made success, having started his career at the key of a telegraph instrument about thirty-five years ago. During this period he has developed his abilities with the appearance of opportunities, and is now manager of the Rosslyn Loan Company of Rosslyn, and president of the Peoples State Bank of Cherrydale.

Mr. Cooper was born at Richview, Washington County, Illinois, October 27, 1874, and is a son of William P. and Mary (Hoke) Cooper. He traces his ancestry back in this country to the year 1660, and one of his ancestors was the first town clerk of Boston, Massachusetts. Several members of the family fought in the Patriot Army during the War of the Revolution, and gradually various branches of the family moved toward the West, the grandfather of Mr. Cooper having been the founder of the first newspaper published at Alton, Illinois. William P. Cooper, the father of Samuel Fulton Cooper, was born near Carlisle, Clinton County, Illinois, in 1842, and during the war between the states served in the Union army as a member of the Sixty-second Illinois Infantry, rising to the rank of sergeant. At the conclusion of his military service he returned to his native state and engaged in the mercantile business at Richview, which continued to be his home until 1908. He then retired from business activities, and at the present time is a resident of Cherrydale, Virginia. Mrs. Cooper, who was born at Richview, Illinois, died in March, 1927, aged seventy-eight years.

Samuel Fulton Cooper was reared at Richview, Illinois, where he attended public schools, and worked in his father's store until reaching the age of twenty years, when he learned telegraphy and was employed as an operator in his native state for about one year. In 1896 he moved to Washington, D. C., where he entered the employ of H. K. Fulton, who was engaged in the loan business, and continued with him until 1914, when he embarked in a jewelry business on his own account. During that time, in 1923, he had been one of the chief factors in the organization of the Peoples State Bank of Cherrydale, Virginia, and became its first president, a position which he still retains. Under his management this has become one of the sound and substantial institutions of Arlington County, and has the confidence of the people, being known as "The Friendly Bank." It has a paid in capital of $70,000, surplus of $28,000 and undivided profits of $2,000, and at the close of business in 1927 had deposits of $426,674.03. In 1924 the bank built its present handsome banking house at Cherrydale, in addition to which the institution maintains branches at Ballston and Arlington, this state. Mr. Cooper's associates in this financial enterprise are A. L. Kelley and Glegge Thomas, vice presidents; A. B. Honts, cashier; W. E. Robey, assistant cashier and manager of the branch at Ballston; J. H. White, Jr., assistant cashier and manager of the branch at Arlington; Cameron Dye and Jesse Stein, bookkeepers; and C. R. Ahalt, S. F. Cooper, A. B. Honts, T. H. Jones, A. L. Kelley, Fletcher Kemp, J. R. McCormick, J. L. May, Ruby Lee Minar, E. E. Naylor, E. W. Rauth, Hugh Reid, W. R. Rose, J. L. Saegmuller, E. M. Shreve, B. A. Thissell, Glegge Thomas and Frank Upman, directors. In September, 1924, Mr. Cooper moved to Rosslyn, where he organized the Rosslyn Loan Company, Inc., of which he has since been the manager and which is now one of the most successful enterprises of its kind in the county. In addition to furnishing loans, this concern deals in diamonds, watches, jewelry, etc., and has a large and important patronage at its new building, which was completed early in 1928. Mr. Cooper takes a helpful interest in all civic affairs, and after settling at Cherrydale served two terms as a member of the school board of Arlington County. He is a Blue Lodge and Royal Arch Mason and a Presbyterian, and in politics votes the Democratic ticket.

On September 21, 1898, Mr. Cooper married Miss Harriet Sprecher, a daughter of David and Henrietta (Fox) Sprecher, the former of whom was a native of Wytheville, Wythe County, Virginia, and the latter of Lancaster, Pennsylvania. Reverend Sprecher was a minister of the Lutheran faith and spent many years of his life in preaching in Iowa and Illinois. Mrs. Sprecher

Dan O. Via D.D.S.

survived her husband some years and passed away in 1920. Three children have been born to Mr. and Mrs. Cooper: Theodora, the wife of R. M. Baker, an income tax expert of Portland, Maine; Dan, who has won considerable reputation as an interior decorator and has offices at New York City; and Mary Frances, who is attending public school at Fairfax. For twenty years Mr. and Mrs. Cooper made their home at Cherrydale, but at present are residents of Fairfax.

DAN O. VIA, Doctor of Dental Surgery at Charlottesville, is a native of that community, and his people have lived in Albemarle County for a number of generations.

Doctor Via was born in Charlottesville May 9, 1896, son of Anderson W. and Lena (Harris) Via, natives of Albemarle County. Both his grandfathers, Charles H. Via and H. F. Harris, were Confederate soldiers in the Civil war, and were substantial farmers of Albemarle County. Anderson W. Via has for many years followed the business of contracting. He and his wife live at Charlottesville. He is a deacon in the Baptist Church and two of his sons, Guy F. and Dan O., likewise performed the duties of that office in the church. He is a member of the Independent Order of Odd Fellows and a Republican.

Dr. Dan O. Via was the third in a family of eight children, seven of whom are living. He was reared at Charlottesville, attended high school there and entered the Dental College of the University of Maryland at Baltimore, where he was graduated in 1918. While in college he was called to the colors, was in training three months at Camp Lee, then finished his dental course and was sent to Fort Oglethorpe, Georgia, and assigned to duty with Dental Company No. 1 until discharged. Doctor Via took the board examinations on Friday and started practice the following Monday, and for the past ten years has enjoyed a steadily increasing practice and reputation as an able representative of his profession. He is a member of the Charlottesville, Shenandoah Valley, Virginia State and American Dental Societies. Doctor Via is a Royal Arch Mason and member of the Kiwanis Club.

He married, July 10, 1918, Miss Josephine Carter, who was born at Charlottesville and was reared and educated in the schools of that city. Her father is A. G. Carter, a well known merchant.

SAMUEL PETTIT VANDERSLICE, JR., M. S. With the exception of a short period during the World war when he was engaged in military duties, the entire career of Samuel Pettit Vanderslice, Jr., M. S., has been devoted to educational work, in which he has made rapid advancement through the possession of a splendid intellect, finished scholarship and the qualities that make for executive equipment. His preparation for his profession was thorough and comprehensive, and in his present office as principal of the Washington-Lee High School at Clarendon he has accomplished commendable work for the school, the cause of education and the community in general.

Professor Vanderslice was born at Suffolk, Virginia, July 25, 1896, and is a son of Samuel Pettit and Susan (Baker) Vanderslice, the latter also a native of Suffolk. His father, who was born at Rose Mills, Nelson County, Virginia, went to Suffolk in young manhood and engaged in the practice of law, but subsequently took up his residence at Memphis, Tennessee, where he practiced his profession with great success for fifteen or twenty years. He is now retired and a resident of Norfolk, this state.

The boyhood of Samuel P. Vanderslice, Jr., was passed at Suffolk, where he graduated from high school in 1914, and then entered the University of Virginia. During 1917 and 1918 he taught school at Suffolk, but in the latter year resigned and enlisted in the United States Marine Corps, and during his term of service was stationed at Paris Island as drill instructor. On receiving his honorable discharge, January 31, 1919, he returned to the University of Virginia, from which institution he received the degree of Bachelor of Science in 1921, and later, in 1924, was the recipient of a Master's degree from the same university. In the meantime, in 1921-1922, he had served as principal of the Arlington County High School, and in the latter year went to Norfolk as assistant principal of the Blair County High School, remaining until 1923. In that year he returned to Arlington County to take his present position as principal of the Washington-Lee High School, which is a large, modern and splendidly equipped institution, located between Cherrydale and Ballston.

Professor Vanderslice is a member of the Virginia Education Association and the National Education Association, and has a high standing in his profession, both as an instructor and an executive. He has won and held the confidence and esteem of the people of the community and the friendship of teachers, parents and students. He is a member of the American Legion, the National Monarch Club, and the Phi Delta Kappa fraternity. Politically he is a Democrat, with no desire for political preferment. A constant student, he has taken post-graduate work at George Washington University and the American University, Washington, D. C. Professor Vanderslice is a member of the Clarendon Methodist Episcopal Church and teacher of the Berea Class in the Sunday School, composed of young married men.

On November 23, 1921, Professor Vanderslice married Miss Dorothea Wilkins, daughter of Joseph H. and Lou India (Little) Wilkins, the former a native of Nansemond County, Virginia, and the latter of the State of Georgia. Mr. Wilkins, who was a merchant of Jessup, Georgia, for a quarter of a century, died in 1923, and Mrs. Wilkins survives him as a resident of that place. Two children have been born to Professor and Mrs. Vanderslice: Samuel Pettit III, born February 26, 1924; and Dorothea Little, born October 31, 1925. The family home is located at 525 Pershing Drive.

ANDERSON BRUGH HONTS, cashier of the Peoples State Bank of Cherrydale, has had eight years' experience with the uncompromising and accuracy-compelling methods of monetary science as revealed behind the counters of Virginia financial institutions. As are all successful and reliable cashiers, he is methodical in his habits and practical in his ambitions. Steadiness of life's aim has been imparted to him by progenitors who came to the Old Dominion at an early day, and he has not only established himself firmly in public confidence as a banker, but also has taken part in civic activities and in the social life of his adopted community.

Mr. Honts was born at Eagle Rock, Botetourt County, Virginia, December 31, 1898, and is a son of George E. and Maude (Brugh) Honts, natives of the same county. His father learned the blacksmith trade in his youth and for twenty years conducted a shop in Botetourt County, which was patronized by all of the people of that section who appreciated reliable and expert work in his line. During the administration of President Wilson he was appointed postmaster at Eagle Rock. He is now treasurer's deputy of Botetourt County. He has large farming interests and is one of the influential and highly esteemed men of his locality.

Anderson B. Honts was reared at Eagle Rock, where he attended public schools, and after graduating from high school in 1916 entered the University of Richmond, where he received the degree of Bachelor of Arts in 1920. He started his career as an educator, but after one year as an instructor at Randolph-Macon Academy embarked in banking as an employe of the Eagle Rock Bank. Mr. Honts started in at the bottom of the ladder, learning the business in all of its details through contact and practical experience, and by reason of his natural ability and fidelity rose, within four years, to the position of assistant cashier. In 1926 Mr. Honts joined the Peoples State Bank of Cherrydale as assistant cashier, and one year later was promoted to the position of cashier, which he now holds. He is also a stockholder in the bank and a member of the Board of Directors, and as an energetic and reliable banker has done much to promote the interests of this institution. The condensed financial statement of this bank at the close of business December 31, 1927, was as follows: Resources—Loans and discounts, $324,530.08; overdrafts, $297.16; bonds guaranteed, $39,750; stocks and bonds, $89,528; building and lot, $35,224.94; furniture and fixtures, $13,248.14; cash and due from banks, $91,-995.89; all other assets, $362.52. Liabilities—capital stock paid in $70,000; surplus, $28,000; undivided profits, $2,000; bills payable, $25,000; bonds guaranteed, $39,750; reserve for taxes, $25.34; reserve for interest, $2,065.36; dividends unpaid, $1,422; deposits, $426,674.03. The officers of this institution are: President, S. F. Cooper; vice presidents, A. L. Kelley and Glegge Thomas; cashier, Anderson B. Honts; assistant cashiers and branch managers, W. E. Robey and J. H. White, Jr.; bookkeepers, Cameron Dye and Jesse Stein; and directors, C. R. Ahalt, S. F. Cooper, A. B. Honts, T. H. Jones, A. L. Kelley, Fletcher Kemp, J. R. McCormick, J. L. May, Ruby Lee Minar, E. W. Rauth, Hugh Reid, W. R. Rose, J. L. Saegmuller, E. M. Shreve, B. A. Thissell, Glegge Thomas and Frank Upman. The bank was organized in 1923 and in the following year erected its handsome modern banking building at Cherrydale, in addition to which it now operates branches at Ballston and Arlington. Mr. Honts is a promoter of stable and conservative interests, and as a citizen and banker maintains standards in keeping with the best welfare of the community. In October, 1918, he was called into the United States Army, but remained in the service only sixty-five days, being stationed at Richmond, where he received his honorable discharge December 12, 1918. He is a member of the Blue Lodge, Royal Arch Chapter and Commandery of Masonry and is a Shriner, and also belongs to the Modern Woodmen of America, the Monarch Club and the American Legion. In his political allegiance he is a Democrat, while his religious affiliation is with the Baptist Church, in which he is a member of the Board of Deacons and president of the Men's Bible Class.

On October 16, 1923, Mr. Honts was united in marriage with Miss Mattie Weaver, a daughter of Mark L. and Roberta G.

(Fishback) Weaver, natives of Rappahannock County, Virginia, where Mr. Weaver was engaged in agricultural operations until his death in 1920. Mr. and Mrs. Honts have one child, Anderson B., Jr., who was born March 21, 1925. The family residence is at 83 Fairfield Street, Cherrydale.

O. ROBERT HOWELL. The business career of O. Robert Howell at Clarendon dates only from 1926, but within the short space of three years he has achieved a success such as many men would regard a triumph if accomplished through a decade of patient effort. Coming here in the early manhood and at a time when the keenness of business competition, particularly in the matter of real estate transactions, rendered success impossible unless through the exercise of sound judgment, allied to a certain degree of venturesome determination, he has achieved a reputation and standing through his operations, largely at Glebewood, one of Clarendon's most delightful suburbs.

Mr. Howell was born August 17, 1892, in Augusta County, Virginia, and is a son of John H. and Susan Elizabeth (Reed) Howell. His father, a native of the same county, has passed his entire life there as an agriculturist and is known as one of his community's substantial men and progressive and public- spirited citizens. During a long and honorable career he has established a reputation for straightforward dealing and personal probity, and at all times has been an active and generous supporter of worthwhile civic movements. Mrs. Howell, also a native of Augusta County, passed away in November, 1921.

O. Robert Howell passed his boyhood on the home farm, where he assisted his father when not attending the country schools, and subsequently was sent to the Augusta Military Academy, which he attended in 1909, 1910 and 1911. He then returned to the home farm and again began assisting his father, but had no intention of spending his life as an agriculturist, and, accordingly, when he reached his majority, left the parental roof and went to Washington, D. C., where he accepted a position with the Washington Electric Company. After three years with that company he resigned and entered the general offices of the Wilson Packing Company, but in 1917 his career was temporarily interrupted by the entrance of the United States in the World war, and he secured a commission as sergeant. For the greater part of his term of service he was stationed at the Army Medical College, Washington, D. C., and received his honorable discharge January 3, 1919, at which time he resumed his civilian duties. For a time he was employed in an automobile garage at Washington, later was in the Bureau of Engraving of the United States Government, and subsequently for a time was connected with the Virginia Shipbuilding Company at Alexandria. In 1920 Mr. Howell established an automobile bus line at Fort Myer, and this he operated with some degree of success until April 1, 1926, when he sold out to engage in the real estate business at Clarendon, with which he has been identified to the present. He maintains offices at Clarendon, Virginia, and has a large and important clientele, buying, selling and carrying on a rental and general brokerage business. Mr. Howell is energetic and enterprising, has a broad knowledge of realty values, and has already made a success of several large projects. His home is at Glebe Road and Pershing Drive, and he is particularly active in the civic affairs of Glebewood, being secretary of the Glebewood Citizens Association. He fraternizes with

J. Fulton Williams, M. D.

the Masons and the Junior Order United American Mechanics, and belongs also to the American Legion and the Clarendon Chamber of Commerce. In his political views Mr. Howell maintains an independent stand, voting rather for the man than the party, and his religious faith is that of the Lutheran Church.

Mr. Howell was united in marriage with Miss Onie A. Riley, a daughter of James Riley, of Kentucky, who is deceased. To this union there have come two children: O. Robert, Jr., born May 15, 1922, and Richard Elmer, born April 29, 1926.

J. FULTON WILLIAMS, physician and surgeon at Charlottesville, represented the third generation of the Williams family in the medical profession in Virginia.

His grandfather, Dr. Edward Williams, was a native of Wales, was educated for medicine in England, and came to America in company with his brother-in-law, Dr. James Fulton, for whom the late J. Fulton Williams was named. Dr. Edward Williams practiced for many years at Greenfield, Nelson County, Virginia. He had two sons who followed his example in the choice of a profession, Dr. William Lewis Williams and Dr. Edward Williams, who went out to Missouri.

Dr. William Lewis Williams was born at Greenfield, Nelson County, April 18, 1818, and lived a remarkably long life, one filled with devoted service in his profession. He began the study of medicine under his father, graduated in 1841 from the medical department of Hampden-Sidney College and later attended the Jefferson Medical College, and for half a century was engaged in practice in Nelson County, his final illness having been due to exposure while making a call on a patient. He was just eighty-four years old when he died April 18, 1902. He had a prominent part in the reconstruction period, and in 1869, when all party lines were broken down, he was elected by a margin of forty-six votes to represent Nelson County in the State Legislature. The vote was a remarkable testimony to his personal leadership and popularity. Many negroes as well as whites supported him in the election, showing thereby not only their confidence in his political character but also a loyalty inspired by his unselfish service. In 1885 he was again elected to the House of Delegates. Three of his sons became doctors, John William Williams, of Albemarle County, Forest Ashton Williams, who lived in Nelson County, and James Fulton Williams.

James Fulton Williams was born at Avon, Nelson County, Virginia, January 19, 1872, son of Dr. William L. and Susan H. (Patrick) Williams. He attended school at Waynesboro, read medicine in his father's office, and in 1899 was graduated from the medical department of the University of Maryland at Baltimore, and remained there two years as an interne in the Baltimore Hospital. From 1902 to 1908 he practiced at Moormans River in Albemarle County, and from March, 1908, made his home at Charlottesville. He was a member of the Albemarle County Medical Society, the Medical Society of Virginia and the American Medical Association. He was a Presbyterian, a Mason and Elk.

Doctor Williams married, in 1900, Miss Kate Coleman, daughter of Dr. Hawes N. and Nannie E. (Watson) Coleman, her father a native of Nelson County and her mother of Albemarle County. Doctor Coleman was educated in the University of Virginia and Jefferson Medical College at Philadelphia, and for many years was one of the able physicians of Albemarle County.

During the Civil war he was assigned duty in looking after the families of the soldiers. Mrs. Williams' mother died in 1898. She was one of seven children, three of whom are now living. Her brother, Aylett B. Coleman, is a Roanoke attorney, and her other brother, Charles O. Coleman, is a railroad official in New York City.

Mrs. Williams, who makes her home at Charlottesville, is the mother of three children: Elizabeth Coleman, Rosalind Patricia and Louise Stuart Williams. The two younger daughters are at home with their mother. Elizabeth is the wife of Dr. Edward Halsell Fite, a physician at Muskogee, Oklahoma. Doctor and Mrs. Fite have two sons, Edward H. Fite, Jr., and Fulton Williams Fite.

HENRY JETER PHILLIPS. In considering the career and character of H. Jeter Phillips, of Clarendon, the impartial observer will be disposed to rank him among the leading members of the Arlington County bar. Whether one considers the obstacles which modest circumstances and obscurity opposed to his entrance upon a learned profession, his patience and persistence in overcoming them, the worthy motives which have impelled him through a long and busy life, the skill which he has brought to a difficult vocation, his resource of invention, or the profundity of his knowledge and aptness, one will be impressed that all these qualities, and others less marked, entitle him to be classed among the leading lawyers of his section.

Mr. Phillips was born at Pleasant View, Amherst County, Virginia, May 31, 1881, and is a son of Henry C. and Mary F. (Faris) Phillips, natives of the same county. Henry C. Phillips came of a family of planters and agriculturists, and as a young man took up farming as his life work and followed it throughout his life in Amherst and Albemarle counties. He was a man of industry and good judgment and eventually, after a hard struggle, won his way to success, being at the time of his death, October 23, 1918, accounted one of the substantial men of his community, where a large part of his seventy-six years had been passed. He was a volunteer infantryman in the Confederate army during the war between the states and fought valiantly until about six months before the close of the struggle, at which time he was taken prisoner by the enemy and confined in the Federal prison at Camp Chase, Ohio, until the close of the conflict. Mrs. Phillips survives her husband at an advanced age and is now a resident of Crozet, Albemarle County.

H. Jeter Phillips was a boy when taken by his parents from Amherst County to Albemarle County, and there passed his youth, securing his early education in the public schools and assisting his father in the work of the home farm. Subsequently he attended Fork Union Academy for three years, and then enrolled as a student at the Richmond College Law School, which is now known as the University of Richmond. On leaving this institution he began teaching school, a vocation in which he was engaged for a number of years, and in the meanwhile, from 1907 until 1923, continued to reside on the home farm and to carry on the tilling of the soil. Although successful as a husbandman, he had never lost his love of the law nor his ambition to engage in its practice, and this was realized in 1923 when he took the examination, was admitted to the bar and commenced practice at the little Town of Crozet. He soon found that he needed a broader field for the display of his legal abilities, and in the same year took up his residence at Clarendon, where he has since been engaged in the successful practice of his calling, with offices at Arlington Court House. During the comparatively short period of his career at Clarendon Mr. Phillips has succeeded in building up a good clientage in the general practice of his vocation and in establishing himself firmly in the confidence of the people of his adopted community. He is a member of the Arlington County Bar Association, and politically is a Democrat. An Episcopalian in religion, he was a choir singer in the church for many years, and while residing at Washington, D. C., was a teacher in the Sunday School. Mr. Phillips is eligible to membership in the Sons of the American Revolution, and his maternal grandfather, James Faris, served as a soldier during the War of 1812, his widow drawing a pension because of his service until she was claimed by death in 1896, at the age of ninety-two years.

On July 14, 1917, Mr. Phillips was united in marriage with Evelyn A. (Land) Mauro, who is of Revolutionary ancestry and eligible to membership in the Daughters of the American Revolution and the Society of Colonial Dames. Mr. and Mrs. Phillips reside at 4127 Harrison Street Northwest, Washington, D. C.

HORACE WOODVILLE DUDLEY. One of the leading attorneys and counselors at law of Arlington County, Horace W. Dudley, of Clarendon, in clearness, force and logical arrangements prepares briefs that rarely are surpassed. To untiring industry he joins a thorough knowledge of the law and an unsurpassed familiarity with authorities, and his citations are made with unerring judgment. In general argument upon the law and the facts of any given case, independent of authorities, he is equally effective. Wasting little time upon minor points or on technicalities, he devotes his energies to the main issues involved, bringing conviction by the logical sequence of his argument no less than by his force. His management of a case from the moment when he assumes charge of it until the close of the final hearing before the court of last review is planned with the same degree of careful thought that a general bestows upon a plan of campaign, and to this fact, in no small degree, may be attributed his extraordinary success.

Mr. Dudley was born in Princess Anne County, Virginia, July 19, 1878, and is a son of W. W. and Janie (Fisher) Dudley, natives of the same county. His father, an agriculturist by vocation, has farmed in that county throughout his life, and is accounted one of the successful men of his community. He is also a prominent and influential factor in public affairs, and has served for about ten years in the capacity of justice of the peace.

The boyhood and youth of Horace W. Dudley were passed in Princess Anne County, where he divided his time between assisting his father in the cultivation of the home farm and attending the public schools. Subsequently he was sent to Norfolk Academy, and later to Richmond College, where he pursued a full course in law and was graduated with the degree of Bachelor of Law as a member of the class of 1910. He did not, however, devote himself immediately to the practice of his profession, but returned to the home farm, where he continued to be associated with his father in the tilling of the soil during the six years that followed. In 1916 he commenced the practice of his calling at Norfolk, where he remained until April, 1925, and at that time removed to Arlington County Court House, where he has since remained in the general practice of his profession. Mr. Dudley has built up a large and prominent clientele, and has been identified successfully with a number of the important cases that have come before the courts in recent years. In addition to carrying on his large and constantly growing practice he is serving very capable in the capacity of commissioner of chancery. He is a valued and active member of the Arlington County Bar Association, and his political convictions make him a stanch and unwavering Democrat. He belongs to the Baptist Church, and while a resident of Norfolk taught the Men's Class in the Sunday School for twelve years. He is a helpful and constructive friend of all enterprises which are promoted for the public welfare and is accounted a citizen of judgment and farsightedness and of modern tendencies.

On August 4, 1900, Mr. Dudley was united in marriage with Miss Nettie G. Morrissette, daughter of Capt. Tully and Helen (Gibbs) Morrissette, natives of North Carolina, where her father resided for a number of years, and now residents of Norfolk, Virginia, where Captain Morrissette is owner and master of a ferry boat. Four children have been born to Mr. and Mrs. Dudley: Earle, born June 1, 1901, who holds a position with the United States Government at the Naval Base at Norfolk; Rosa May, born in April, 1904, who is now the wife of Robert Bell and resides at Norfolk; Janie Helen, born in January, 1908, and now the wife of Charles Crocker, of Norfolk; and Horace Wesley, born in February, 1910, who died in April, 1910. The pleasant family home of Mr. and Mrs. Dudley is located on McKinley Avenue, Ballston, Virginia.

THOMAS EDMUND DYSON. The great Metropolitan Life Insurance Company of New York has given to Thomas E. Dyson the executive position of manager of its business in the Alexadria district of Virginia, with headquarters in the City of Alexandria, the fine old metropolis of Arlington County. Mr. Dyson has been associated with this insurance corporation more than a quarter of a century and his advancement has been the result of his loyal and constructive service. He maintains his office headquarters at 427 King Street, and they are well equipped for the effective handling of the substantial business here controlled by the company.

Mr. Dyson was born in Charles County, Maryland, October 23, 1876, and is a son of James B. and Marth A. (Turner) Dyson, both of whom were born and reared in that county. James B. Dyson long figured as a substantial farmer and merchant in his native state, and his death occurred in October, 1920, his widow being now a resident of Washington, D. C.

The public schools of his native county were the medium through which Thomas E. Dyson acquired his earlier education, and in 1894 he was graduated from Charlotte Hall Military Academy in St. Mary's County, Maryland. During the ensuing period of about four years he was a successful teacher in the public schools of his old home county, where he continued his pedagogic service until December, 1898. In February, 1899, he entered the employ of the Metropolitan Life Insurance Company by connecting himself with its offices in Washington, D. C., and that he made his value evident was soon shown by his advancement, in 1901, to the position of assistant manager of the company's office in Alexandria, Virginia. Since November, 1916, he has been manager of the company business in the Alexandria district, and under his productive administration the business in this field has been notably expanded within the intervening years.

Mr. Dyson maintains an independent attitude in politics and gives his support to men and measures meeting the approval of his judgment, without reference to strict partisan lines. He has had no desire for public office, but his civic loyalty was distinctly shown in his service as a member of the Alexandria Board of Education. He is a valued member of the local Chamber of Commerce and the Kiwanis Club, and he and his wife are earnest communicants of the Catholic parish of St. Mary's Church. He is affiliated with the Knights of Columbus and the Holy Name Society. He is a past grand treasurer of the Virginia Grand Council of the Knights of Columbus, as well as a past grand knight of this fraternity. He is president of the Holy Name Society of his home parish and is treasurer of the general organization of this society in the diocese of Richmond.

In December, 1898, was solemnized the marriage of Mr. Dyson and Miss Ailean Chappelear, who likewise was born and reared in Charles County, Maryland, and who is a daughter of the late George I. and Mary (Montgomery) Chappelear, both of whom were born in Charles County. Mr. Chappelear was a representative merchant in his native county, served the county as sheriff, county commissioner and tax collector, and for some time he held the position of official tobacco inspector in the City of Baltimore. He served as a gallant soldier of the Confederacy in the Civil war. Mr. and Mrs. Dyson have six children: Thomas Reginald Chappelear, James Vernon, Clarence Frederick, Ailean Teresa, Martha Rita and Eleanor Veronica. Thomas R. C. is now engaged in the practice of law in Alexandria as one of the representative younger members of the bar of Arlington County.

HUGH THOMPSON CLARKSON is manager of the Chesapeake & Potomac Telephone Company of Virginia, with executive headquarters at 105 North Alfred Street in the City of Alexandria, Virginia.

Mr. Clarkson was born at Haymarket, Prince William County, Virginia, July 7, 1880, and is a son of Dr. Henry Mazyck and Jennie (Sayrs) Clarkson, the former of whom was born at Columbia, South Carolina, in 1835, and the latter of whom was born in Alexandria, Virginia, in 1840. Dr. Henry M. Clarkson, a physician and surgeon of marked ability, served as a surgeon in the Confederate army in the Civil war, and thereafter he was engaged in the active practice of his profession at Haymarket, Virginia, during a period of about forty years. In his Civil war service he was twice wounded, and in all other relations of his long and worthy life he manifested the same fine loyalty that marked his service to the Confederacy in the dark period of the war between the states of the North and the South. His death occurred in June, 1915, and his widow passed away in 1920.

John Roberts, great-grandfather of the subject of this review on the maternal side, was born in Cecil County, Maryland, of Welsh descent, and he was a young man when he came to Alexandria, Virginia, where he continued to maintain his home during the long period of fifty years and where he was a citizen of prominence and influence in both civic and business affairs.

He twice served as mayor of Alexandria, and it was within his period of administration that the so-called Holland Loan was negotiated and the construction of the Alexandria canal was thus initiated, Mayor Roberts having lifted the first spade of earth for the new canal. He was mayor of Alexandria at the time the public reception was here tendered to the Marquis de LaFayette, the American Revolutionary hero, and in this connection it was his privilege to receive and welcome LaFayette and the other honored guests on that occasion, October 16, 1824. In 1800 Mr. Roberts became a member of Washington Lodge, Ancient Free and Accepted Masons, and he was present at the Masonic banquet tendered to LaFayette at the Claggett Hotel, February 21, 1825. This sterling pioneer was known and honored as "Honest John Roberts," and his death occurred December 31, 1852, his funeral having been conducted under Masonic auspices. Of his children it may be recorded that Eliza became the wife of Dr. Edmond Fitz-Hugh; Matilda married Dr. John J. Sayrs and they became the maternal grandparents of Hugh T. Clarkson of this review; Sophia became the wife of Richard Washington; Henrietta married Francis Rozier; and Rebecca became the wife of Capt. James M. Gilliss, United States navy, who served as chief of the National Naval Observatory in Washington, D. C.

It should be noted that the late and revered Dr. Henry M. Clarkson gained high reputation not only in his profession but also as a man of exceptional literary talent. His admirable poetical productions gained to him the title of Poet Laureate of the South, and his second edition of poems was published in 1910. He wrote also many interesting articles pertaining to his experiences during the Civil war. After his retirement from the active practice of his profession Doctor Clarkson served more than a decade as county superintendent of schools in Prince William County. He was a graduate of the medical department of the University of Pennsylvania, and to his profession he gave many years of earnest and able service, as noted in an earlier paragraph of this sketch. He was an honored and veteran member of the Virginia State Medical Society and the Prince William County Medical Society at the time of his death, which occurred when he was eighty years of age.

Hugh T. Clarkson was reared and educated in his native Town of Haymarket, and he was a youth when he entered the service of the Chesapeake & Potomac Telephone company, the headquarters of which are in the City of Washington, D. C. He has continued his association with this corporation during the long intervening period of nearly a quarter of a century, and since January, 1919, has been manager of the Chesapeake & Potomac Telephone Company of Virginia for the Alexandria district, his assigned district having fourteen exchanges in Northern Virginia.

Mr. Clarkson has entered fully and loyally into the communal life of Alexandria, where he is president of the Civic Bureau in 1928, at the time of this writing, and a director of the Kiwanis Club and a valued member of the local Chamber of Commerce, besides which he has membership in the Arlington County Chamber of Commerce, the Warrenton Chamber of Commerce, the Fairfax County Chamber of Commerce, as well as the Clarendon Citizens Association, his home being maintained at Clarendon, which is a virtual suburb of both Alexandria and Washington, D. C. Mr. Clarkson is a stalwart in the ranks of the Democratic party, he and his wife are communicants of the Protestant Episcopal Church, and he is affiliated with the Sons of Confederate Veterans. His sons are members of the Children of the American Revolution, and his wife is president (1928) of George Johnston Chapter of the Daughters of the American Revolution. The attractive family home in Clarendon is at 69 Columbus Street, and is a center of gracious hospitality, with Mrs. Clarkson as its popular chatelaine.

On the 19th of October, 1909, was solemnized the marriage of Mr. Clarkson and Miss Mary Jolliffe, daughter of William H. and Mary (Scott) Jolliffe, who were born in Virginia and who long maintained their home in Baltimore, Maryland, where they passed the closing years of their lives. Mr. and Mrs. Clarkson have two children: Benjamin Jolliffe, who was born February 2, 1914, is now (1928) a student in Washington-Lee High School of Arlington County. William Hopkins, the younger son, was born January 26, 1918, and is a student in the public schools.

DAVID H. PITTS. The application of steam and electricity to transportation made a greater change in human environment than has occurred since the earliest period of recorded history, and opened up countless fields of industry in which the capabilities of men found expression. One of these was that of railroad construction, in which vast undertakings were carried to successful completion by men of brains the country over. Skill, experience, foresight and good management were and are required in operations of this kind, and one of the men of Virginia, now retired, who made a name for himself in former years as a railroad contractor is David H. Pitts, of Scottsville, Albemarle County, still owner of large farming interests, and formerly president of the Scottsville National Bank, of which he was an organizer.

David H. Pitts was born on Allen's Creek, Amherst County, Virginia, September 24, 1852, a son of Jonathan and Agnes (Snead) Pitts, both Virginians, he born in Richmond and she in Appomattox County. For many years he was a merchant and furniture dealer, but during the latter part of his life lived retired, and died when he was over ninety-nine years old. She died at the age of seventy years. They had thirteen children, seven of whom survive, and of them all David H. Pitts was the first born. Both were active church workers, he being a Methodist and she a Baptist, and he was a Mason and Odd Fellow. During the war between the states the father left his mercantile business at Scottsville and enlisted in the Confederate army, with which he served for about eighteen months, and was then honorably discharged for disability. Recovering, he reenlisted and served under General Pickett in the Fifty-ninth Virginia Infantry. The paternal grandfather of David H. Pitts was Henry Pitts, a native of Germany, who settled in Richmond upon coming to the United States, and there he married a Miss Cullingworth, an English lady.

Growing up in Scottsville, David H. Pitts attended the Powers private school, and began his contact with the world in railroad construction, and continued in it, rising to be a contractor and executing some very important contracts. About four years ago, in 1924, he retired.

In 1878 Mr. Pitts married Miss Cora Staples, of Albemarle County, who died in 1885, leaving no children. In 1904 Mr. Pitts married Miss Stella Crisp, of Baltimore, Maryland, and they

have two children: Stella Crisp Pitts, who is a teacher of Buena
Vista, Virginia, was graduated from the Harrisonburg Normal
School; and David Henry, Jr., who is attending the Scottsville
High School. From his youth up Mr. Pitts has been an earnest
member of the Baptist Church. Always active in politics, he has
worked in conjunction with the Democratic party, and for eight
terms he served in the Virginia State Legislature, and during
that period also served in three extra sessions. In the session in
which the vote to move the medical department of the University of Virginia to Richmond, Mr. Pitts was active in the opposition which finally won out, and consequently the medical department was saved for the University. For ten years he served as
a member of the commission that settled the state debt of Virginia and West Virginia, and he has held other offices, in all of
them showing a warm interest in the rights of the people and the
determination to see justice done. Having spent practically his
entire life in and about Scottsville, his interests are centered in
this region, in whose continued prosperity he has great faith.
In everything he has undertaken he has proven himself able,
conscientious and honorable, and the esteem in which he is held
by all classes has been fairly won.

CARL TECK DREIFUS, D. D. S., is engaged in the practice of
his profession in his native City of Alexandria, where he maintains office headquarters at 906 King Street, and has provided
the best modern equipment and accessories in both operative
and laboratory departments. His technical skill and his success
mark him as one of the representative dental surgeons of the
younger generation in Alexandria, where his personal popularity
is contributing its significant share to his professional advancement and prestige.

Doctor Dreifus was born in Alexandria on the 27th of February, 1902, and is a son of Albert and Pauline (Lowenberg)
Dreifus, the former of whom likewise was born in Alexandria
and the latter of whom was born in Germany. It was fully
seventy-five years ago that the paternal grandfather of Doctor
Dreifus established himself in the junk business of major order
in Alexandria, and in this line of enterprise Albert Dreifus became the associate and eventual successor of his father, the while
he extended the business to large proportions, his operations
having included the buying of Government ships that had been
retired from active commission, and he having long held rank
as one of the substantial and influential business men of the fair
old city in which he was born.

In the Alexandria public schools Dr. Carl T. Dreifus continued his studies until his graduation from the high school as
a member of the class of 1918, and thereafter he was a student
in Virginia Military Institute until he began preparation for
his chosen profession by going to the District of Columbia and
entering Georgetown University, where he was a student three
years and completed a partial course in the dental department.
He transferred to the department of dentistry at Tulane University, New Orleans, and in this celebrated institution he was
graduated in 1922, with the well earned degree of Doctor of
Dental Surgery. In 1926 he fortified himself further by taking
post-graduate work in the dental school of the Medical College
of Virginia, in the City of Richmond, as he had previously been
deflected from the work of his profession by his active service in
connection with the great national game, baseball. As a mem-

ber of various clubs Doctor Dreifus played as a professional baseball representative from 1920 until 1926, in which latter year he established himself as a dental practitioner in Alexandria, where he has since developed a practice that shows a constantly cumulative tendency and that marks him as one of the successful exponents of modern dental surgery in this part of his native state. The Doctor is a member of the Northern Virginia Dental Society, is independent in politics, holds the rank of lieutenant in the Officers' Reserve Corps of the United States Army, and is affiliated with the Benevolent and Protective Order of Elks and the Phi Epsilon Pi college fraternity.

December 14, 1926, marked the marriage of Doctor Dreifus and Miss Katherine Ulis, daughter of Jacob and Esther (Ornstein) Ulis, who came from their native Russia to the United States in 1905 and who are now residents of Brooklyn, New York. Jordan Albert, only child of Doctor and Mrs. Dreifus, was born January 5, 1928.

HENRY TREVILIAN MONCURE, principal of the high school in the City of Alexandria, was born at Williamsburg, judicial center of James City County, Virginia, November 4, 1894, and is a son of Dr. James D. and Blanche (Trevilian) Moncure, the former of whom was born at Fredericksburg, Spotsylvania County, and the latter in New Kent County, both families having been early founded in Virginia and the names of both having been prominently and worthily linked with the history of this venerable commonwealth of the Union. Dr. James D. Moncure attended the University of Virginia, including its medical school, and thereafter continued his professional studies in leading medical colleges and clinics in Germany. For a long period of years he owned and conducted a well ordered private hospital in the City of Richmond, and thereafter he held the office of superintendent of the Virginia Insane Hospital at Williamsburg during a period of eighteen years, he having been the incumbent of this position at the time of his death in October, 1898. His widow still maintains her home at Williamsburg. Doctor Moncure served as a surgeon in the Confederate army in the Civil war, and this experience further fortified him for the surgical branch of his profession. He long held prestige as one of the leading physicians and surgeons of his native state and became an authority in the treatment of mental diseases.

The public schools of Williamsburg afforded Henry T. Moncure his earlier education, and he was about four years of age at the time of his father's death. In 1913 he was graduated from William and Mary Academy, and thereafter he continued his studies in historic old William and Mary College, in which he eventually was graduated with the degree of Bachelor of Arts. He gave four years of intervening service with the DuPont Engineering Company in Virginia, Iowa and Minnesota, and he then returned to William and Mary College, where he continued his studies two years. After leaving college he was successfully engaged in teaching in the public schools of West Virginia, whence he came to Alexandria, Virginia, in 1924, to assume the position of principal of the Jefferson School. One year later he was advanced to his present executive and pedagogic office, that of principal of the high school of this city, and here he is continuing his efficient and loyal service as one of the influential factors in educational work in Arlington County. Mr. Moncure has membership in the National Education Association, the Virginia State Educational Association and the Alexandria Educational Association.

The political convictions of Mr. Moncure place him in the ranks of the Democratic party, he and his wife are communicants of the Protestant Episcopal Church, he is affiliated with the Kappa Sigma college fraternity, and in his present home community is a member of the Belle Haven Country Club.

November 30, 1927, recorded the marriage of Mr. Moncure and Miss Mary Boothe, who is now the popular chatelaine of their pleasant home, 117 West Maple Street, Rosemont.

CLARENCE HAVEN STRADER. In all departments of equipment and service the public schools of the City of Alexandria are maintained at a high standard, and here the efficient and popular principal of the Jefferson School is Clarence H. Strader.

Mr. Strader was born at Bane, Giles County, Virginia, April 20, 1894, and is a son of Sylvester J. and Lou (Bane) Strader, the former of whom likewise was born in Giles County, and the latter of whom was born in Tazewell County, their home being still maintained in the former county, where Sylvester J. Strader is a substantial representative of farm industry and is one of the honored and influential citizens of his native county.

In the public schools of his native county Clarence H. Strader continued his studies until he was graduated from the high school at Pearisburg, the county seat, as a member of the class of 1914. He then taught school one year, and he was a second-year student in Emory and Henry College at the time the nation became involved in the World war, in the spring of 1917. In December of that year Mr. Strader enlisted for service in the United States Army, and with his command he was on active overseas duty one year. The remainder of his two years' service was in the Aviation Signal Corps in the United States. He received his honorable discharge in July, 1919, having made a record that contributed its quota to the honors won by Virginia in connection with the great world conflict. While in France Mr. Strader availed himself of the privilege of attending the American University at Beaume, where he was a student three months.

After the close of his military career Mr. Strader returned to his native county, and after there teaching three years in the public schools he entered the University of Virginia, from which he received in 1924 the degree of Bachelor of Science and in the following year the supplemental degree of Master of Science. Since September, 1925, he has been principal of the Jefferson School of Alexandria, and his effective work in this connection is marked by characteristic professional loyalty and enthusiasm. While a student in the historic old University of Virginia Mr. Strader there served as assistant in the department of sociology and did special work in psychology. He has membership in the Alexandria Educational Association, the Virginia State Educational Association and the National Education Association.

To the Democratic party Mr. Strader accords loyal allegiance, and in their home city he and his wife are zealous members of the Methodist Episcopal Church, South, in the Sunday School of which he is teacher of the Boys' Class. In the Masonic fraternity the year 1928 finds him affiliated with Pearisburg Lodge No. 106, A. F. and A. M., and Pearisburg Chapter No. 29, R. A. M. He is affiliated also with the Phi Delta Kappa college fraternity and with the local post of the American Legion. His

mother has membership in the Daughters of the American Revolution and also in the United Daughters of the Confederacy, and his wife is eligible for affiliation with the Daughters of the American Revolution and the United Daughters of the Confederacy.

On the 22d of October, 1919, Mr. Strader was united in marriage with Miss Lillian R. Rankin, daughter of J. Edward and Nellie (Landis) Rankin, who were born in Augusta County, where the father is now a prosperous farmer, his wife having died in 1918. Mr. and Mrs. Strader became the parents of two children, of whom the younger is living. Sue Bane, the first born, died shortly after her birth, in March, 1922, and Betty Bane was born April 20, 1927.

R. HARRY HADEN, of Charlottesville, attorney-at-law began his professional career at Palmyra with his father, the late Linwood Overton Haden, who was not only an able lawyer but a man of the finest character, and had made his career one of substantial achievement in spite of lack of opportunities.

Linwood Overton Haden was born in Fluvanna County, January 18, 1867, son of John R. and Lou Haden. As a boy he attended public and private schools, but had to supplement by private study for the advantages of a college education. After leaving school he clerked in country stores and at the age of twenty-one was proprietor of a small store near Palmyra. At that time he married Miss Vara V. Haden, his third cousin. Gradually his little store enlarged its trade and became a fairly prosperous institution. During the boom in Southwest Virginia he lost nearly all he had accumulated, and soon after returning to Palmyra his store building and contents were destroyed by fire. At this crisis in his affairs he was twenty-five years of age. He made a deed of assignment of what property was left, and having the credit of good character and ability he was able to start over as a merchant, and gave his best energies to his business for several succeeding years, until he had paid all the debts growing out of his assignment.

When about thirty years of age he took up the study of law in the office of A. A. Gray at Palmyra. He was admitted to the bar in 1896, and for thirty years engaged in practice, getting a large volume of business and handling cases with a skill and resourcefulness that made him a reputation as one of the leading attorneys of the Fluvanna County bar. In 1898 he was appointed referee in bankruptcy by United States District Judge John Paul, then judge of the Western District of Virginia. Each two years he was reappointed, and after the death of Judge Paul, Judge Henry C. McDowell, the present judge, kept him in the office until his death at the age of sixty years, on May 23, 1927.

Judge Haden was a member of the Methodist Episcopal Church, South, was a member of the Independent Order of Odd Fellows, and enjoyed distinctive leadership in the Republican party of the state, serving as county chairman of Fluvanna County for fifteen years. Judge and Mrs. Haden had four sons and one daughter: Paul E., postmaster at Palmyra; R. Harry; Mrs. C. C. Conrad, of Palmyra; Fred L., state manager of the Investors Syndicate; and Louis L., a student in the University of Virginia.

R. Harry Haden grew up at Palmyra, graduated from high school there in 1912 and took his law work in Washington and Lee University, graduating in 1916. During the World war

period he was employed in the great Hopewell plant of the Dupont Company, and in 1919 engaged in law practice with his father at Palmyra.   He remained at Palmyra five years and in
1924 located at Charlottesville, where he has succeeded in establishing himself as one of the successful members of the Albemarle County bar, and has all the practice that he can attend to.
Like his father he is active in Republican politics and was defeated for the State Legislature in one campaign by only seventeen votes.   He is chairman of the Republican Executive
Committee of Fluvanna County and was a delegate to the State
Convention at Roanoke March 17, 1928.   He married, in 1917,
Lorain Jones, who was born at Norfolk. Her grandfather Jones
was one of the leading Baptist ministers of his day and was pas-
vor of one church at Churchland for over half a century.   Mrs.
Haden attended high school at Portsmouth.   Both are active
members of the Methodist Episcopal Church, and he is serving
as trustee of his home church.   Mr. Haden is a member of the
Loyal Order of Moose and Modern Woodmen of America.

JOHN DAVID NORMOYLE.   In his native City of Alexandria
Mr. Normoyle is successfully established in the real estate, loan
and insurance business, with office headquarters in the Alexandria National Bank Building.   He was born in this city on the
17th of June, 1872, and is a son of Michael A. and Margaret E.
(Keating) Normoyle. the former of whom was born in Ireland
and the latter in Virginia.   As a young man Michael A. Normoyle represented Virginia as a loyal soldier of the Confederacy,
and thereafter he was for many years engaged in the retail
grocery business in Alexandria, where his death occurred November 27, 1884, his widow having long survived him and having
here passed the remainder of her life.
The early education of John D. Normoyle was gained in the
schools of Alexandria and was advanced by his taking a course
in the Spencerian Business College in the City of Washington,
D. C.   In the District of Columbia he completed a course in the
law department of Georgetown University, in which he was
graduated as a member of the class of 1891, when he received the
degree of Bachelor of Laws, his alma mater having conferred
upon him in 1893 the supplemental degree of Master of Laws.
After completing his studies in the law school Mr. Normoyle
gave eleven years of service as deputy city treasurer of Alexandria, and he has never found it expedient to engage exclusively
in the practice of the profession for which he had fitted himself.
After retiring from his service in the office of the city treasurer
he gained fortifying preliminary experience in the real estate
and insurance business through alliance with the M. B. Harlow
Company.   Since March 1, 1904, he has been independently
established in the real estate, loan and fire insurance business
in Alexandria, where he now controls a large and representative
business of this order and incidentally has contributed his quota
to the civic and material advancement of his native city.   Mr.
Normoyle has been a director of the Alexandria National Bank
since September 1, 1917, and is likewise a director of the Alexandria United Charities.   His is an unqualified loyalty to and
appreciation of the fair old city in which he was born and reared,
and he served as a member of the City Council in the period
of 1901-03, besides having been for some time a valued member
of the local Board of Education.   He is a progressive member
of the Alexandria Chamber of Commerce, in which he has as-

signment to the civic committee. Since January, 1894, Mr. Normoyle has served continuously as a trustee of the German Building Association of Alexandria.

The political alignment of Mr. Normoyle is in the ranks of the Democratic party, and he and his wife are communicants of the Catholic Church. He is affiliated with the local organizations of the Knights of Columbus, the St. Vincent de Paul Society, the Benevolent and Protective Order of Elks and the Fraternal Order of Eagles. Mr. Normoyle is a past president of the Alexandria-Arlington-Fairfax Real Estate Board and is now chairman of the Appraisal Committee of the Real Estate Board and an active member of the board.

On the 2d of November, 1923, was solemnized the marriage of Mr. Normoyle and Miss Dorothy Lannon, who likewise was born and reared in Alexandria and who is a daughter of Thomas and Katherine (Dugan) Lannon, her father having been engaged in the grocery business in Alexandria from 1862 until his death, which occurred July 10, 1900, and her widowed mother, now (1928) eighty years of age, being still a resident of this city. Mr. and Mrs. Normoyle maintain their home at 201 North Pitt Street.

CHARLES HENRY SMITH, attorney at law, 123 South Royal Street, Alexandria, was born in Westmoreland County, Virginia, January 31, 1893, son of James Absolom Waller and Elena (Anderson) Smith. His father was born in Westmoreland County, while his mother was a native of New York State. His father spent his active career in the lumber industry, both as a manufacturer and dealer, with home at Oldhams in Westmoreland County, where he died December 18, 1920, at the age of fifty-eight. His widow still resides at Oldhams.

Charles Henry Smith married, June 24, 1919, Fanny Ellen Wellford Jones, of Gloucester, Virginia, youngest daughter of Dr. William Francis and Katherine (Hooe) Jones. Her father was born at Petersburg, Virginia, and her mother in Fauquier County. Doctor Jones, for half a century practiced medicine in Gloucester County, where he died in January, 1916, and where Mrs. Smith's mother continues to reside. Mr. and Mrs. Smith have three children: Charles Henry, Jr., born June 29, 1921; William Francis, born October 25, 1924; and Katherine Hooe, born July 31, 1926.

Mr. Smith is a Democrat and a member of the Virginia Bar Association and American Bar Association. His home is at 2109 King Street Road, Alexandria.

Mr. Smith spent his early years in Westmoreland County, attending public school. He completed his literary education in William and Mary College, and for two years was in school work as principal of the Achilles High School in Gloucester County. Mr. Smith took his law course at the T. C. Williams Law School in Richmond, was admitted to practice and had his first office in Gloucester County. He began practice in January, 1915, but after two years abandoned it on account of poor health. When he resumed his professional career in March, 1919, he located at Alexandria, where he has enjoyed the success and honors of a capable attorney. In 1921 he was elected to the Virginia House of Delegates, representing Alexandria City and Arlington County, and served in the regular and special sessions from 1922 to 1926, being majority floor leader in the House in 1926. His first political office was as examiner of records for the Thirteenth Judicial Circuit, and at Alexandria he has been referee in bankruptcy and is now commissioner in chancery. Mr. Smith since its organization in 1921 has been president of the Northern Virginia Investment Corporation. He is one of the directors of the Southern Oxygen Company of South Washington, Virginia, the main offices being in Washington, D. C.

CLARENCE A. KIBLER is a native of Shenandoah County, has been well known in the business life of that community and is now serving as commissioner of revenue.

Mr. Kibler, whose home is at Woodstock, was born January 6, 1887, son of James and Mary C. (Hisey) Kibler, both natives of Shenandoah County, where they still reside. His grandfather, Noah Kibler, was also a native of Virginia, served about two years in the Confederate army and had a brother, James Kibler, who was all through the war, was wounded, and is still living at the age of ninety-two. The maternal grandfather, Samuel Hisey, was a native of Virginia and a blacksmith by trade. James Kibler, father of Clarence A., has followed mechanical pursuits. He is a Republican in politics and a member of the Lutheran Church.

Clarence A. Kibler was the oldest in a family of twelve children, ten of whom are living. He was educated in country schools and learned the trade of blacksmith. For fourteen years he assisted in the operation of sawmills and threshing machines. In 1919 he was elected county commissioner from the Stonewall district, filling that office four years. In 1923 he was elected commissioner of revenue for the county and was reelected in 1927. Mr. Kibler is a Republican in politics and a member of the Lutheran Church.

He married, in 1907, Clara Sheetz, who was born in Shenandoah County and died in 1910, leaving one child, Audrey, now attending a business college at Washington, D. C. Mr. Kibler in 1917 married Bessie Finks, also a native of Shenandoah County. They have one child, Gyneth, now in the fourth grade of the public schools.

NEVELLE JOSEPH ROBERTS, D. D. S., whose well appointed office headquarters in the City of Alexandria are established at 113 North Columbus Street, controls a practice whose scope and importance clearly mark him as one of the representative younger members of his profession in his native city and county.

Doctor Roberts was born in Alexandria November 13, 1900, and is a son of Erven J. and Mary (Brown) Roberts, the former of whom likewise was born in Alexandria and the latter of whom was born in North Carolina. Erven J. Roberts became a skilled machinist, and as such he devoted the major part of his active career to service in the United States Navy Yards, principally those at Washington, D. C., he having died in January, 1928, at the age of fifty-one years, and his widow being still a resident of Alexandria.

In the Alexandria High School Dr. Nevelle J. Roberts was graduated as a member of the class of 1918, and in preparation for his chosen profession he entered the department of dentistry of Georgetown University, District of Columbia, where he completed the prescribed curriculum and where he was graduated in 1923, with the degree of Doctor of Dental Surgery. He forthwith established himself in Alexandria, where the effective coördination of his technical skill and his personal popularity in his

E. S. A. McGee Sr., and Family

native city and county has resulted in his building up a successful and representative professional business. His offices are of
the best modern equipment in both operative and laboratory
departments, and the service there given has proven the most
effective of professional and business assets. Doctor Roberts
is secretary of the Northern Virginia Dental Society at the time
of this writing, in 1928, and has membership also in the Virginia
State Dental Society and the American Dental Association. He
is a popular factor in the civic and social activities of his home
community, where he is a member of the Old Dominion Boat
Club and the Belle Haven Country Club, besides being affiliated
with the Benevolent and Protective Order of Elks. His political
allegiance is given to the Democratic party and he and his wife
are communicants of the Protestant Episcopal Church.

On the 15th of March, 1922, was solemnized the marriage
of Doctor Roberts and Miss Dorothy Dean, whose parents died
when she was still a little child. Doctor and Mrs. Roberts have
a winsome daughter, Nancy Dean Roberts, who was born September 13, 1925.

EDWARD OVERTON McCUE has been a member of the Charlottesville bar for thirty years, and has kept strictly within the
routine of a hard working attorney, earning professional honors
and success without seeking any of the special responsibilities
and honors of politics.

He was born in Albemarle County April 8, 1876. The McCues
came from Ireland and were early settlers in Virginia. The
McCue ancestry runs back to the time of King Heremon, who
was the first Monarch of Ireland, and according to the traditional
records reigned many years before the birth of Christ. Edward
O. McCue's grandfather, James C. McCue, was born in Virginia.
James Cyrus McCue, father of Edward O. McCue, was born near
Afton in Albemarle County, was well educated for his time, spent
his life as a farmer, and owned 1,900 acres near Afton, devoting
this large estate to the raising of thoroughbred cattle and hogs.
For years he shipped regularly cattle and hogs to the Baltimore
and Richmond markets. As a very young man he volunteered
and served as a captain in the Confederate army during the Civil
war. His wife, Sarah Jane Moon, was born at Batesville, Virginia. Their ancestors established a Presbyterian church in
Albemarle County. Both were active members of the Presbyterian Church. Of their eleven children, one daughter and ten
sons, five are now living: Will, who lives on the old homestead at
Afton; Leslie, of Charlottesville; Edward, of Charlottesville;
Frank C., of Charlottesville; and Harry, on the old home place.
The maternal grandfather of Edward O. McCue was Samuel
O. Moon, an Englishman, who achieved a great deal of wealth as
a tobacco merchant and left each of his five children property to
the value of $100,000.

Edward O. McCue was educated in the Greenwood School and
the University High School at Charlottesville, and attended the
Law School of the University of Virginia in 1897. The following year he established his office and began a general law practice, which has continued without interruption to the present
time. He is a member of the Virginia Bar Association, is a Democratic voter and a member of St. Paul's Episcopal Church.

He married, in 1900, Mary Pamela Michie, member of the
old and prominent Michie family of Albemarle County. Her
parents were John C. Chapman and Arabelle Michie. Mr. and

Mrs. McCue have had three children. The son Edward Overton McCue, Jr., graduated from the law department of the University of Virginia in 1926 and is now sharing some of the responsibilities in the conduct of his father's large practice. He married Isabel Chamberlin Cochran, and they are the parents of one son, Edward Overton McCue III. Mr. McCue's daughter, Mary Martha, is the wife of W. B. Merritt, a lieutenant in the United States Army, and they have a daughter, Mary Martha Merritt. Sarah Belle McCue, the other daughter, who died October 31, 1927, was the wife of A. D. Hosterman, Jr., of Springfield, Ohio, and left a daughter, Betty Poyntz Hosterman.

HUGH MCGUIRE, specialist in internal medicine, practicing at Alexandria, has a son who graduated from medical college in 1924, and thus is assured the succession of the famous name of McGuire in the medical profession of Virginia. It is a remarkable succession, continuing through four generations and over a period of more than a century.

The history of American surgery will probably have a lasting place of honor for the name of Hunter McGuire, who in his rare skill and attainments had few peers in his generation. Hunter McGuire was the father of Hugh McGuire of Alexandria.

Dr. Hugh McGuire was born at Richmond May 26, 1871, son of Dr. Hunter Holmes McGuire, and grandson of Dr. Hugh Holmes McGuire. Dr. Hugh Holmes McGuire, whose grandfather, Edward McGuire, established his home at Winchester, Virginia, in 1753, was born November 6, 1801, and died August 9, 1875. He began the practice of medicine after graduating from the University of Pennsylvania in 1822, and lived throughout his life at Winchester. He was an eminent surgeon and was founder of Winchester Medical College, and served as a surgeon in the Confederate army. Two of his sons became members of the medical profession.

Of these Hunter Holmes McGuire was born at Winchester October 11, 1835, and died September 19, 1900. He was educated at Winchester Academy and in the Winchester Medical College, graduating in 1854, and held the chair of anatomy in that college until 1858, when he became a quiz master in Philadelphia. Soon after enlisting in the Confederate service he was made medical director of the army in the Shenandoah Valley under Stonewall Jackson. After the death of his great leader at Chancellorsville he served with distinction as medical director of the Second Army Corps until the close of the war. While surgeon-general he inaugurated the custom of exchanging medical officers. In 1865 he was elected to the chair of surgery in the Medical College of Virginia and served in that capacity until 1878. He founded St. Luke's Home for the Sick in 1883, and in 1893 was one of the founders of the University College of Medicine and its adjunct, the Virginia Hospital. He was president of both the college and hospital. He was one of the founders of the Medical Society of Virginia in 1870, and in 1880 was elected its president. He was chosen president of the Richmond Academy of Medicine in 1869, in 1875 president of the Association of Medical Officers of the Army and Navy of Confederate States; president of the Southern Surgical and Gynecological Association in 1889; vice president in 1893 and president in 1896 of the American Medical Association, he being one of the first in Virginia to receive this great distinction. He was a contributor to some of the standard works on surgery and medicine. A vivid account of his career is detailed in the oration delivered by Maj. Holmes Conrad upon the occasion of the presentation to the Commonwealth of Virginia at Richmond, January 7, 1904, by the Hunter McGuire Memorial Association of a bronze statue of Mr. McGuire, which stands in the capitol grounds not far from the statue of Stonewall Jackson.

Dr. Hunter McGuire married, December 9, 1866, Mary Stuart, daughter of Alexander H. H. Stuart, of Staunton, who was the first secretary of the interior during the administration of President Fillmore. Of their nine children two sons, Stuart and Hugh Holmes, became physicians.

Dr. Hugh McGuire was educated at Richmond, graduated from the Virginia Military Institute in 1891, was a student in the University of Virginia in 1892-93, and in 1894 took his M. D. degree at the University College of Medicine at Richmond. He has practiced at Alexandria since 1895, and for many years has been regarded as an authority in internal medicine. During the World war he was medical member of the Alexandria Advisory Board. He is a member and an ex-president of the Medical Society of Northern Virginia, Maryland and the District of Columbia; chairman of the staff of Alexandria Hospital, member and a past president of the Alexandria Medical Society, member of the Medical Society of Virginia, and of the Southern and American Medical Associations. Doctor McGuire is a Phi Kappa Sigma and Pi Mu, member of the Belle Haven Country Club, Old Dominion Boat Club, Chamber of Commerce, a Democrat and member of the Episcopal Church.

He married, November 2, 1898, Sara E. Johnson, daughter of E. K. and Elizabeth (Winsatt) Johnson. Doctor and Mrs. McGuire have one child, Dr. Johnson McGuire, who graduated in medicine from the Johns Hopkins University at Baltimore in 1924, and is now an attache of Johns Hopkins Hospital.

JAMES MORTON DUNCAN, JR., is not only the efficient and popular chief of the fire department of his native City of Alexandria, but is also one of the active and successful young business men of the community through his association with the Snyder-Kane-Boothe Corporation, which is here a leading concern in the real estate and insurance business.

Mr. Duncan was born in Alexandria on the 4th of July, 1897, and is a son of James Morton Duncan and Mary Virginia (Cornwell) Duncan, both likewise natives of this city and both representatives of old and honored families of this part of the Old Dominion State. James M. Duncan, Sr., is now successfully engaged in the automobile business in Alexandria, where he has the agency for the Hupmobile.

The present chief of the Alexandria fire department gained his early education by attending the public schools of his native city and also Potomac Academy. He was graduated from the Alexandria High School as a member of the class of 1916, and thereafter he pursued in the University of Virginia a course in civil engineering. After leaving the university he continued to be associated with his father in the automobile business until June 1, 1924, when he was made chief of the fire department, of which office he has since continued the efficient and progressive incumbent, his vigorous executive policies having been potent in advancing the standards of service on the part of this important division of the municipal government. Since June 1, 1926, Mr. Duncan has been associated with the Snyder-Kane-

Boothe Corporation and has made a record of success in connection with the substantial real estate and insurance business controlled by this representative concern.

The year 1928-1929 finds Mr. Duncan in service as president of the Virginia State Firemen's Association. He maintains an independent attitude in politics, and he and his wife are zealous communicants of Grace Church, Protestant Episcopal, he being a member of the vestry of this parish. The basic Masonic affiliation of Mr. Duncan is with Alexandria Lodge, A. F. and A. M., and in the Scottish Rite of this fraternity he has received the thirty-second degree. He is affiliated also with the Phi Gamma Delta and the Lambda Pi college fraternities. He is a valued member of the local Kiwanis Club and has membership in Belle Haven Country Club, while he and his wife are popular factors in the representative social activities of their home city.

On the 25th of April, 1923, was solemnized the marriage of Mr. Duncan and Miss Ruth Birch Deahl, daughter of Charles J. and Jennie (Stoutenbergh) Deahl, the former of whom was born in Virginia and the latter in the State of New York, their home being now in Alexandria, Virginia. Mr. Deahl is engaged in the paper brokerage business in Washington, D. C. Mr. and Mrs. Duncan have one son, James Morton Duncan III, born November 25, 1928.

FREDERICK GARNER DUVALL has secure standing as one of the representative members of the bar of Alexandria, where he is engaged in the successful general practice of his profession, besides which he now holds the office of referee in bankruptcy for this district.

Mr. Duvall was born in the City of Dayton, Ohio, June 22, 1885, and is a son of Richard L. and Caroline (Minor) Duvall, both likewise natives of the old Buckeye State. Richard L. Duvall was engaged in the stock brokerage business in the City of Philadelphia during the greater part of his active career, his death having occurred May 25, 1912, and his widow having passed away December 9, 1924.

Frederick G. Duvall was reared in the State of Maryland and there profited duly by the advantages of the public schools, his high-school course having been completed in the Tome School, in which he was graduated in 1905. In preparation for his chosen profession he completed the curriculum of the law department of the University of Virginia, in which he was graduated as a member of the class of 1909. After thus receiving his degree of Bachelor of Laws he was for a time employed in the office of the clerk of the courts for Norfolk County, Virginia, in the City of Norfolk, and thereafter he passed a year of service in the law office of Hagan, Goodrich & Coughlan, 9 Wall Street, New York City. He then returned to Virginia, was admitted to the bar of this historic old commonwealth and engaged in the practice of law at Louisa, judicial center of the count of that name. In 1917, in connection with Governmental activities pertaining to the World war, Mr. Duvall went to Washington, D. C., and gave one year of service in the office of the Government custodian of alien property. Under the administration of the war President, Woodrow Wilson, Mr. Duvall was appointed special assistant United States attorney and given executive assignment at Alexandria, Virginia. Here he continued to retain this office until the election of President Harding, in 1920, since which year he has here continued in the independent practice of his

John S. Chapman

profession, his law business being now of substantial and representative order.

In 1922 Mr. Duvall was elected the first civil police justice of Alexandria, and his adminstration in this judicial office continued until 1926, since which year he has here held the office of referee in bankruptcy. He is a member of the Alexandria Bar Association, and the Virginia State Bar Association, his political allegiance is given unequivocally to the Democratic party, he and his wife are communicants of the parish of Christ Church, Protestant Episcopal, in their home city, he is a member of the Belle Haven Country Club, and he is affiliated with the Benevolent and Protective Order of Elks, and Mrs. Duvall maintains affiliation with the Colonial Dames.

In April, 1917, was solemnized the marriage of Mr. Duvall and Miss Gertrude Gordon Flournoy, daughter of Nicholas and Katherine (Wood) Flournoy, both natives of Virginia. Nicholas Flournoy was a loyal soldier of the Confederacy in the Civil war, and was long engaged in the drug business at Amelia, Virginia, where his death occurred in 1907, his widow being now a resident of the City of Richmond, this state. Mr. and Mrs. Duvall have three children, the names and respective birth-dates of whom are here recorded: Ann Flournoy, December 28, 1919; Katherine Reed, August 5, 1921; and Caroline Love, October 7, 1923.

JOHN S. CHAPMAN. The history of Virginia is written on the pages of the record of the world by those men who, rising above their surroundings and constituents, took the management of affairs into their capable hands and guided safely and well the ship of state. Through their efforts and intelligence the great commonwealth has been built up until it ranks among the foremost in the Union. Such men live forever, although all that is mortal, in the course of time, goes back to the dust from whence it sprung, for a forceful personality never dies, but continues to influence the actions of others until the end of time. The work of those gone before the present century is being continued by those still active in the various occupations and professions in which men find expression for their talents, and one of them who is living up to the high standards raised for him and his associates is John S. Chapman, attorney and banker of Standardsville, Greene County.

The birth of John S. Chapman occurred in Greene County, Virginia, September 24, 1861, and he is a son of N. B. and Fannie (Shearman) Chapman, both of whom were born in Greene County, and are now deceased. Throughout his life the father was a farmer, and he was a Confederate veteran having served throughout the war between the states. Both he and the mother were consistent members of the Methodist Episcopal Church, South. An active Democrat, he was supervisor of Greene County for several terms. Three children were born to him and his wife, namely: John S., whose name heads this review; Thomas, who is a farmer of Greene County; and Elizabeth, who married George T. Lancaster, of West Virginia, superintendent of the Electro Metallurgical Corporation. The paternal grandfather, William T. Chapman, was born in Madison County, Virginia, and the family is of English origin and was established in Virginia at a very early day. The maternal grandfather, George W. Shearman, was born in Virginia, and he lived to be ninety-five years old, and he too was of English descent, his family having been established in Lancaster County early in the country's history.

John S. Chapman was reared in his native county and attended its schools and Randolph-Macon College, after which he entered the University of Virginia and was graduated from its law school in 1888 with the degree Bachelor of Laws. In July, 1888, he began the practice of his profession in Standardsville, and here he has since continued carrying along a very large practice in all of the courts. For twelve years he served as commonwealth's attorney of Greene County, being elected each time on the regular Democratic ticket, and from 1902 to 1908 represented the Senatorial District of Greene and Abemarle counties in the State Senate. He is president of the Bank of Greene County, is a director of the National Bank of Charlottesville, and owns a valuable farm and a very desirable residence, all having been acquired through his own, unaided efforts, for he had to depend upon his own energy and resourcefulness from the start.

On August 20, 1896, Mr. Chapman married Miss Sallie H. Davis, who was born in Greene County, on the farm of her father, a farmer of Greene County and a Confederate veteran. Mr. and Mrs. Chapman have four children, namely: Nathaniel D., who took the degree of Chemical Engineer in the University of Virginia, is with the General Petroleum Company, Los Angeles, California, and married Barbara Burns, and they have one son, John S. Chapman III; John S., Junior, who was educated in the University of Virginia, is a practicing lawyer and a member of the firm of Boyd, Adams, Chapman & Vreeland, 57 William Street, New York City, and he married Frances E. Storms; Fannie Carr, married Henry Hunt, of the Bird Company of Baltimore, Maryland, and they have one son, Henry, Jr., and George W., who is at home. Mrs. Chapman is president of the Blue Ridge Grays Chapter of the United Daughters of the Confederacy. Mr. Chapman and his family all belong to the Methodist Episcopal Church, South. He is a member of the Benevolent and Protective Order of Elks and the Independent Order of Odd Fellows, and has passed all of the chairs. A man whose destiny has led him into important work, he has never lost his humanity or sympathy with others, and in giving much he has reaped abundantly in return and holds the full confidence and respect of his associates as well as the plaudits of the public. In casting his fortunes with those of Standardsville he acted wisely.

JAMES FRANKLIN MYERS is manager of the investment department of the Virginia Public Service Company and is also executive assistant to Martin J. O'Connell, who is vice president and general manager of the Northern Division of this important public utility corporation and who is individually represented on other pages of this publication, his personal sketch giving a general outline of the inception and the service of the company of which he is vice president and the headquarters of which are maintained in the City of Alexandria, with offices at 524 King Street.

Mr. Myers was born at Dranesville, Fairfax County, Virginia, March 17, 1872, and is a son of Charles William and Sally Ann (Virts) Myers, both of whom were born in Loudoun County, this state. Charles W. Myers gave the major part of his active life to farm industry, in Loudoun and Fairfax counties, and gave loyal service to the Confederacy in the Civil war, he having had charge of a wagon train with the army commanded by Gen. Jubal A. Early. He was born May 27, 1833, and his death occurred May 29, 1905, his widow, who was born in 1837, having attained to the age of eighty-seven years and her death having occurred in January, 1924.

James Franklin Myers was a lad of six years at the time his parents returned to Loudoun County from Fairfax County, and after duly profiting by the advantages of the public schools of the former county the subject of this review took a course in the commercial department of the University of Kentucky. After leaving this institution he was employed three years as a stenographer and bookkeeper in the City of Wasington, D. C., and he then established his residence in his present home City of Alexandria, where he became associated with his brother, Robert L., in the automobile business during the ensuing eight years. He then assumed charge of credits and collection with the firm of W. A. Smoot & Company of this city, and three years later, on the 1st of January, 1918, he was retained as auditor of the Alexandria County Lighting Company and the Arlington Electric Company. When these two corporations were merged into the Alexandria Light & Power Company Mr. Myers was • made manager of the investment department and assistant to the general manager, which dual office he has retained since the business and material properties of this company became, in 1926, an integral part of the important public utility system now controlled by the Virginia Public Service Company, in which corporation he is a stockholder.

Mr. Myers gives his allegiance to the Democratic party and is known and valued as one of the loyal and progressive citizens of Alexandria, where he gave three years of constructive service as a member of the city Board of Education. He is an active member of the Alexandria Chamber of Commerce, as well as of the Chambers of Commerce of Arlington and Fairfax counties. He and his wife are zealous members of the Methodist Episcopal Church, South, and he has served as a steward of the church at Alexandria during the past twenty-six years, besides which he was superintendent of its Sunday School during a period of twenty years, his retirement from his position, in which he had given earnest and constructive service, having occurred in October, 1927. In his home city he was a member of Andrew Jackson Lodge, Ancient Free and Accepted Masons, and the Royal Arch Chapter No. 14.

March 11, 1902, marked the marriage of Mr. Myers and Miss Bettie Sampson, daughter of Henry and Sarah (Francis) Sampson, the former of whom was born in England and the latter in Alexandria, Virginia, where their marriage was solemnized. Henry Sampson was reared and educated in his native land and was nineteen years of age when he came to the United States. As a skilled workman at the trade of moulder he was employed many years in the United States Navy Yard at Washington, D. C., and he was a resident of Alexandria at the time of his death in 1918, his wife having passed away in 1905. In conclusion of this review is entered brief record concerning the children of Mr. and Mrs. Myers: Lester Franklin, born February 1, 1903, is employed as a motion-picture operator. Wilmer Louis, born December 11, 1904, was for a time a student in the University of Virginia and in 1928 he is a student in the Virginia Polytechnic Institute at Blacksburg, where he is taking a course in commercial engineering. Helen Marguerite, born

September 7, 1909, was graduated from Strayer's Business College in Washington, D. C., and is now employed as a stenographer in that city. Earle Russell, born January 2, 1914, is (1929) a student in the Alexandria High School. Eleanor Louise was born January 12, 1918, and died November 18, 1920.

PETER BOOTHE PULMAN, M. D., is proving in his successful achievement the consistency of his choice of vocation and is one of the representative physicians and surgeons of the younger generation in his native city. He is engaged in the practice of his profession in the City of Alexandria and maintains his office headquarters at 108 North Washington Street.

Doctor Pulman was born in Alexandria on the 20th of March, 1899, and is a son of Charles O. and Irene (Carter) Pulman, the former of whom was born in Fairfax County, Virginia, and the latter in the City of Baltimore, Maryland. Charles O. Pulman was engaged in the retail grocery business in Alexandria for a term of years and thereafter gave his attention principally to the supervision of his valuable farm interests in Fairfax County. He was an influential and honored citizen of Fairfax County, and at Alexandria he served as a member of the Board of Aldermen, besides having been given a loyal and effective administration as superintendent of the public schools of the Eighth District of Fairfax County. He was an active member of the Alexandria Chamber of Commerce, was a Democrat in politics, and was an earnest communicant of the Protestant Episcopal Church, as is also his widow, who still maintains her home in Alexandria.

Doctor Pulman profited by the advantages of the public schools of Alexandria, where he was graduated from the high school as a member of the class of 1916. In 1917, soon after the nation became involved in the World war, Doctor Pulman enlisted for service in the United States Navy, in which he was given assignment to the medical department and in which he served until the close of the war, his entire period of service having covered twenty-eight months, and twenty-one months of this interval having been marked by his participation in overseas service. He received his honorable discharge August 1, 1919, and during the ensuing year he was a student in George Washington University, Washington, D. C. The next year he continued his studies by attending the University of Virginia, and he then returned to George Washington University, in the medical department of which he was graduated as a member of the class of 1926. After thus receiving his degree of Doctor of Medicine he further fortified himself by the valuable clinical experience he gained in his service as an interne in Garfield Hospital, Washington, D. C., and since August 15, 1927, he has been established in the general practice of his profession in his native city, where his professional ability and personal popularity assure him of cumulative success in his exacting and responsible vocation. The Doctor is serving in 1928 and 1929 as secretary-treasurer of the Alexandria Medical Society, and he has membership also in the Virginia State Medical Society, the Northern Virginia, Maryland and District of Columbia Medical Society and the American Medical Association.

Doctor Pulman shows his abiding interest in his former World war comrades by maintaining affiliation with the American Legion and the famous Forty and Eight organization of overseas veterans, besides which he holds the rank of first lieutenant in the Medical Reserve Corps of the United States Navy. His political alignment is in the ranks of the Democratic party, he is affiliated with the Theta Delta Chi and the Phi Chi (medical) college fraternities, and in his home community he is a popular member of the Belle Haven Country Club. On June 23, 1928, he was united in marriage with Miss Carolyn Burgess, of Culpeper County, Virginia. He retains the religious faith in which he was reared, that of the Protestant Episcopal Church, and is a member of St. Paul's Protestant Episcopal Church of Alexandria, Virginia.

HON. WILLIAM STUART SNOW. The lawyer is conservative, for the law represents stability and protective forces. In this country there is no established religion; no established school of medicine, but there is, however, an established law court, with its vast body of ministrants. In a country until recently jealous of governmental action, and where all possible things were left to private initiative, the people wisely refrained from intrusting to personal enterprise the organization and support of the courts. Thus in the case of the law there is an establishment; and, further, an establishment without rival. Therefore, it is but natural that the lawyer, and still more so the jurist, should be governed by precedent rather than impulse, and that he should seek to draw upon the wisdom of those who have gone before him instead of acting entirely upon his own initiative. Perhaps one of the best examples afforded by the bar and bench of Alexandria is Hon. William Stuart Snow, brilliant lawyer and judge of the Civil and Police Court of Alexandria, with offices in the Alexandria National Bank Building.

Judge Snow was born at Heathsville, Virginia, in April, 1894, a son of William Conway and Ella L. (De Shields) Snow, natives of Virginia. The father is a retired banker and manufacturer, who after years of successful operations in different lines is now retired and living in Alexandria in the midst of luxurious surroundings his own ability and hard work have provided for him. Not only was he a successful business man and financier, but he was a legislator of note, and while he served in the House of Delegates he made an admirable record.

Judge Snow was reared in Heathsville, and there he obtained the beginnings of his education, supplementing the instruction there obtained by a course in Randolph-Macon Academy, and Washington and Lee University, and in the latter he studied law, but completed his legal studies in Georgetown University, Washington City, from which he was graduated in 1921, with the degrees of Bachelor of Laws and Master of Laws. However, he had been previously admitted to the bar, in 1920, and was carrying on a general practice in Alexandria while pursuing his studies as above stated. In 1920 he was appointed judge of the Civil and Police Court of Alexandria to fill out an unexpired term, and held that office for eight months. In January, 1926, he was elected to the same office for a term of four years, and is still on the bench.

In January, 1913, Judge Snow married Miss Rosa Lee Jackson, a daughter of John A. Jackson, a native of Virginia, and long a resident of Lexington. His wife was also a Virginian, and both are now deceased. Judge and Mrs. Snow have one child, Barbara Stuart Snow, who was born October 15, 1914.

In addition to the office he is holding with the city Judge Snow is a member of the Game and Inland Fisheries Commis-

sion. He is a director in the Alexandria National Bank, and
belongs to the Alexandria Bar Association and the Virginia
State Bar Association. At the university he made Phi Kappa
Sigma and Sigma Nu Phi, the latter the legal Greek letter fraternity. In his membership with the Belle Haven Country Club
he finds congenial companionship and social diversion, and he
is one of the governors of that body. His political sentiments
make him a Democrat, and in religious faith he is an Episcopalian. His daughter, through Revolutionary forebears, is a
member of Children of the Revolution, and both of his grandfathers served in the war between the states, so that the family
has a distinguished military history.

Since he has been on the bench Judge Snow has presided
with ability, firmness and fairness. At the bar, while insisting
on his own rights, he respected those of others, in pleading his
cases depending on clearness of statement and force of argument
rather than an appeal to the sentimental tendencies of the jury.

NELSON TAYLOR SNYDER, JUNIOR. Varied interests directed
with dignified capability, coupled with a keen sense of duty in
either war or peace, are characteristics wihch make not only
for good citizenship, but also for successful and progressive
advancement. Alexandria because of its own advantages and
its close proximity to Washington affords any ambitious man an
excellent field for his operations, and in no line are there more
openings than those connected with realty transactions. One of
these typical Virginians of high character and recognized worth
is Nelson T. Snyder, Junior, president of the Snyder-Kane-
Boothe Corporation, realtors and insurers.

Nelson T. Snyder, Junior, was born in Jefferson County,
West Virginia, December 19, 1892, a son of Nelson T. and Emma
(McGary) Snyder, also natives of West Virginia, farmers and
apple growers during the earlier part of their lives, but now
retired and honored residents of Jefferson County, their estate
being near Shepherdstown.

Educated in the public schools of Shepherdstown and its
normal school, Nelson T. Snyder, Junior, taught school for several years, but later took a business course, in 1911, at Eastman's Business College, Poughkeepsie, New York, and a second
course at Strayer's Business College, Washington. In 1913 he
began to put to practical use the commercial training he had
obtained and entered the employ of the Southern Railroad Company, with which organization he continued until 1917, when
he went into the army for the World war. Commissioned a
second lieutenant, he was made an instructor at Camp Custer,
and remained there until he was honorably discharged in December, 1918, after which he returned to Washington and spent
one year more with the Southern Railroad as statistician, but
left in 1919 to organize N. T. Snyder & Company, real estate
and insurance, at Alexandria. In 1922 he was joined by Robert L. Kane, the two operating under the name of Snyder &
Kane, which firm in 1925, with the addition of Gardner L.
Boothe, became Snyder-Kane-Boothe Corporation. At present
this organization is doing some very important building and
development, and sells homes on the installment plan, financing
its projects through its own finance corporation. Perhaps the
most important of the development projects is Belle Haven, the
beautiful residential district in the neighborhood of the Belle
Haven Country Club, although the two Glendale Park develop-

ments and Rosemont Park are worthy of consideration. Mr. Snyder is president of the Del Ray Bank in the Town of Potomac, and he was one of the organizers of the Kiwanis Club and during 1927 served as its president. He belongs to all of the bodies in Masonry at Alexandria, including the Shrine, and he also belongs to the Shriner Club, the Independent Order of Odd Fellows, and the Belle Haven Country Club, of which he is a director. He is president of the Belle Haven Realty Corporation and is a director of the Northern Virginia Investment Corporation. Since its organization the American Legion has in him a zealous member. He is a Democrat in political faith. The Presbyterian Church is his religious home.

In July, 1917, Mr. Snyder married Miss Lydia Hammond, a daughter of Harry and Etta (Catts) Hammond, natives of Alexandria, where the father is in business as manager of the Mutual Ice Company. Mr. and Mrs. Snyder have two children: Harry Hammond, who was born December 30, 1920; and Nelson Taylor III, who was born September 17, 1924. The Snyder residence is in Belle Haven and is a beautiful home. Mr. Snyder's list of acquaintances is necessarily a long one and he comes into contact with men of note from all over the country, and the majority of them become his warm personal friends. His spirit of good fellowship leads him to exert himself to render the lives of others brighter and easier, and he is always ready to lend his efficient assistance to those measures which he believes will work out for the betterment of the majority.

WILLIAM MARVIN BASS, JR., bears a name that has been an honored one in Virginia educational history, and in the few years since his admission to the bar he has given the name some additional distinction in connection with the practice of the law at Staunton.

Mr. Bass was born in Campbell County, Virginia, August 20, 1901, son of William M. and Bernice (Hughes) Bass, and grandson of William Bass and Charles Hughes. William Bass was born in Chesterfield County, Virginia, and for about forty years practiced medicine at Lynchburg. Charles Hughes served as a Confederate soldier under Lee during the Civil war and was twice wounded.

William M. Bass, Sr., was born in Chesterfield County, was educated in the New London Academy at Forest and the University of Virginia, and since early manhood his career has been marked out along educational lines. He has been a teacher for over thirty years, and is still active in the work as principal of the Fairview Heights School at Lynchburg. He is a member of the Methodist Episcopal Church, a Democrat, and belongs to the Independent Order of Odd Fellows. His wife was born near Alta Vista, Campbell County, and they have three children: William M., Jr., Charles Edward, a graduate of the University of Virginia, who is now an instructor in geology at the university; and J. Wilford, a second year man at the Virginia Polytechnic Institute.

William M. Bass, Jr., was educated in the New London Academy at Forest, and is an alumnus of the University of Virginia, where he paid his expenses by work in the Bursar's office, as cashier of the university cafeteria, and though supporting himself he was one of the very popular members of the student body and also stood high in scholarship. He went to the university with a scholarship from Campbell County. Mr. Bass graduated in 1923, and in 1922 had been licensed to practice law. He has been practicing as an attorney at Staunton for five years, and has an office in the Barristers Row. He is a member of the Kiwanis Club, Knights of Pythias, is a Royal Arch Mason, and member of the Central Methodist Episcopal Church, South.

He married in June, 1927, Miss Jennie Hicks, of Campbell County, who was educated in the New London Academy and the Virginia Intermont College at Bristol. Her father, Ed Hicks, is a well known Campbell County farmer. They have one son, William Marvin Bass III, born August 30, 1928.

ROBERT LOUIS KANE. Without the efforts of the realtors of any community it would be almost impossible for it to attain to any permanent importance, and if this is true of the insignificant localities, it is all the more so regarding such a center of importance as Alexandria, whose proximity to the national capital alone makes it one of the most desirable residential sections of the country. During the past decade its growth has been remarkable, and its progress has been marked by a series of brilliant efforts on the part of the men who have devoted themselves to exploiting its advantages in every respect. Among those who have achieved more than passing prominence as a handler of realty is Robert L. Kane, secretary-treasurer of Snyder-Kane-Boothe Corporation, with headquarters at 614 King Street, Alexandria, a man whose record as an alert and reliable operator in this field is stainless and enviable. That he stands well with his business associates is further proof of his ability and integrity, and he is proud of the friendship of many of the leading men of the country.

Robert L. Kane was born in Warrenton, Fauquier County, Virginia, April 3, 1893, a son of Andrew D. and Margaret S. (Hefflin) Kane, also natives of Fauquier County, where the father was profitably engaged in farming until his death, February 10, 1921. The mother survives him and resides with her son.

Growing to manhood in his native county, Robert L. Kane attended the local school, and was graduated from the high school of Morrisville, Virginia, in 1909. Later he took a business course at Remington, Virginia, and upon leaving that institution of learning entered the employ of the Southern Railroad Company, and for five years worked in its transportation department. During this time he became interested in real estate, and upon leaving the railroad became a salesman for A. H. Agnew, of Alexandria. Still later he had charge of the Washington office of the F. C. Goodnow Company, realtors, and continued to hold that position until October, 1922, when he resigned as he had formed a partnership with Nelson Snyder, under the name of Snyder & Kane, realtors. The partners opened an office in Alexandria and entered upon a prosperous career that resulted in 1925 in their taking Gardner L. Boothe into the business, and incorporating under the present name. The corporation has branched out and does building and developing, selling homes on the installment plan through their own finance corporation. Among other developments is their beautiful Belle Haven near the golf and country club of the same name, of which they are justly proud; Glendale Temple Park 1 and 2; and Rosemont Park.

On September 22, 1925, Mr. Kane married Katherine S. Snyder, daughter of Nelson T. and Emma (McGary) Snyder, natives of West Virginia, where he has been engaged in farming for many years, but is now retired. Mrs. Kane is a sister of Nelson T. Snyder, of Snyder-Kane-Boothe Corporation. Mr. and Mrs. Kane have two children, Katherine Ann, who was born December 24, 1926, and Bettie Low, born December 1, 1928. Mr. Kane is a past president of the Alexandria, Fairfax and Arlington Company, real estate and bonds, and served as its secretary and treasurer for three years; is secretary of the Northern Virginia Investment Corporation, and is one of the outstanding figures in real estate developments in this part of the state. A high Mason, he has been advanced in the Scottish Rite to the thirty-second degree, and he belongs to the Shrine and the Shriner Club. Another fraternity in which he is interested is the Independent Order of Odd Fellows. He is a member of the Kiwanis Club and the Belle Haven Country Club. In political faith he is a Democrat, although he has never cared to enter public life. A Baptist, he is active in church matters, having been chairman of the Finance Committee for several years and teacher of the Baracca class in the Sunday School for one year. The Kane residence in Braddock Heights is one of the most desirable homes in this section, and is a center of social activities.

WILLIAM HENRY SWEENEY, city auditor of Alexandria, is a man who has been successful in several lines of endeavor, but is now rendering his most effective service, and has every reason to be proud of what he is accomplishing for his fellow citizens. A careful, conservative man, with a thorough knowledge of his work, he is the right man in the right place.

A Virginian by birth, Mr. Sweeney claims Loudoun County as the place of his nativity. He is a son of Timothy and Margaret (Moriarty) Sweeney, natives of Ireland, who came to the United States when young people, he arriving here prior to the war between the states. With the declaration of war he enlisted, but was honorably discharged before the close of hostilities on account of disability resulting from his being wounded in action. For many years thereafter he was engaged in farming in Fauquier and Loudoun counties, Virginia, and he died in April, 1909, highly respected by all who knew him. The mother passed away some years before him, dying in 1899.

Growing to manhood in Fauquier County, William H. Sweeney attended its public schools, and early displaying an aptitude for his studies, continued them in Saint John's Academy of Alexandria, and was also a student of the School of Languages of the same city. Entering the educational field, he was one of the leading teachers of his locality from 1886 to 1908, and in the latter year became superintendent of the schools of Alexandria, which position he continued to hold until 1923, when he resigned to accept the office of city auditor. During his long connection with the Alexandria schools he became a well known figure and the people came to have confidence in him, and this feeling has been augmented since he assumed charge of his present responsibilities.

On December 27, 1892, Mr. Sweeney married Miss Annie Keegan, a daughter of Capt. Patrick and Annie (Murtaugh) Keegan, natives of Virginia. For many years Mr. Keegan was a valued employe of the Pennsylvania System, which he served as railroad conductor, and he died in the service in 1887. The mother died in 1883. Mr. and Mrs. Sweeney have no children.

In addition to his political office Mr. Sweeney has farming interests in the neighborhood of Alexandria, and a very desirable residence at 801 South Patrick Street, where he and his wife maintain a pleasant home and welcome their many friends upon frequent occasions. He belongs to the Knights of Columbus, the Benevolent and Protective Order of Elks and the Lodge of Saint Vincent de Paul, a charitable organization connected with the church. A Roman Catholic, he belongs to Saint Mary's Church, and is examiner of accounts for it. In political faith he is a Democrat. In private life he is genial, whole-souled, a delightful host and always a welcome guest, and under all circumstances he measures up to the highest standards which mark the man as a serviceable factor in effecting the world's work for progress and advancement. Few men are more liberally endowed by nature with all that goes to constitute the perfectly rounded character than Mr. Sweeney, and in every relation of life he displays these high characteristics such as a keen sense of justice, generosity, truth, a high sense of honor, proper respect for himself and a sensitive thoughtfulness for others. More enduring than the granite hills as an enduring monument to his memory is a record like the one he is making, and his example is one all will do well to emulate.

GARDNER LLOYD BOOTHE II. That all men do not find the niche for which they consider themselves especially fitted is largely due to their inability to fit themselves for those niches which they could occupy with profit and honor. They do not concentrate upon that which they understand and for which nature and training have made them ready, but diffuse themselves over too wide a territory, and in the end accomplish little or nothing. The successful man in any line is he who develops his latent strength by the use of vigorous fitness, innate powers and expert knowledge, gradually attaining to an efficiency not possible in the beginning. Each line of endeavor demands certain special qualifications. Some men are born executives, being able to direct others to carry out plans which are formulated in the active brains of the leader; while others can only follow. However, whatever the work may be he who puts his whole heart into it is the one to whom ultimate success is sure to come. Such has been the experience of Gardner L. Boothe II, vice president of Snyder-Kane-Boothe Corporation, realtors and insurers, a man who is making his influence felt in the business life of Alexandria and vicinity.

Gardner L. Boothe was born in Alexandria, February 2, 1898, a son of William J. and Lucy (Lee) Boothe, natives of Alexandria. The father is a member of the Crane-Parris & Company, investment bankers of Washington City, one of the very solid financial institutions of the national capital.

Growing to manhood in Alexandria, Gardner L. Boothe was given exceptional educational advantages, first in the local schools and the Episcopal High School, from which latter he was graduated in 1916, following which he entered the University of Virginia, but left it to enter the army for the World war. He was commissioned a second lieutenant in the heavy artillery, and was stationed at Fortress Monroe until he was honorably discharged December 10, 1918.

With his return to civilian life Mr. Boothe entered the First National Bank of Alexandria, continuing with it until 1925, when he entered the business that now bears his name, joining

at that time Messrs Snyder and Kane. With his partners he has been instrumental in carrying out some very important development projects, notably Belle Haven, the 1 and 2 Glendale Parks and Rosemont Park. In his present work Mr. Boothe has found his niche and is making remarkable progress not only with reference to his individual interests, but also in gaining and holding the confidence and respect of his fellow citizens.

On June 16, 1923, Mr. Boothe married Miss Margaret Moncure, a daughter of William A. and Caroline (Pemberton) Moncure. Mr. Moncure was an official of the Pennsylvania Railroad, whose death occurred in 1920. Mr. and Mrs. Boothe have one child, William Moncure Boothe, who was born October 16, 1924. Mr. Boothe is secretary and treasurer and a member of the Board of Directors of the Belle Haven Country Club. He belongs to Washington Lodge, A. F. and A. M., of Alexandria, and he has been advanced in the Scottish Rite of that order to the thirty-second degree. Other organizations with which he is connected are the Chi Phi Greek letter fraternity, Washington Chapter, Sons of the American Revolution, the Kiwanis Club, the Washington Golf and Country Club, the American Legion, the Military Order of the World war, and he is a member of the executive committee of the Alumni Association of the Episcopal High School of Virginia. Mrs. Boothe belongs to the Daughters of the American Revolution and Colonial Dames. The political sentiments of Mr. Boothe are of such a character that he could not conscientiously support any but the Democratic party. An Episcopalian, he belongs to Christ Church of Alexandria. His beautiful residence is in Belle Haven.

ISAAC HENRY TRIMBLE, M. D., is a veteran physician who took his diploma in medicine more than half a century ago, and for a third of a century was working almost night and day in attending his extensive country practice in Highland County. During the past twenty years Doctor Trimble has made his home at Staunton, and still keeps up his professional activities in that city.

He was born in Highland County, Virginia, March 16, 1849, son of John and Hannah Hinkle (Harper) Trimble. The Trimble family has been in Virginia for several generations. His great-grandfather, James Trimble, was from Edinburgh, Scotland, joined the English army and came to America to fight against the American colonists. After the surrender at Yorktown he remained in this country and was the founder of a family which has been widely scattered over the state and has produced many men of importance and distinction. Doctor Trimble's grandfather, James Trimble, was born in Augusta County, Virginia, owned a large farm and was very successful. He married Mary Seybert, whose father, Nicholas Seybert, lived out on the frontier and saw eight of his own family tomahawked by the Indians.

John Trimble was born in 1822, was a merchant, farm owner, and a business man who made a success of everything he undertook. He lived to be ninety-four years of age. For many years he served as a justice of the peace, and in the Confederate army was in service in the commissary department. He had brothers who were soldiers in the war, William, James, John, Harvey, and another brother, George Washington Trimble, was killed in the battle of Port Republic while serving as a lieutenant. John Trimble was an active member of the Presbyterian Church. His wife, Hannah Hinkle (Harper) Trimble, who lived to be eighty-three years of age, was a daughter of Leonard Harper and a granddaughter of Moses Harper. These were members of the family which gave the geographical name of Harpers Ferry. John Trimble and wife had three children: Dr. Isaac Henry; Mrs. M. K. Fleisher, of Monterey; and Mrs. G. W. Hevner, of Charlottesville.

Isaac Henry Trimble was educated in public schools in Monterey, and was associated with his father in business until 1883. He was graduated from the University of Virginia in 1874 and took his medical diploma at the Bellevue Hospital Medical College of New York in 1875. In June of the same year he started practice at Monterey, and remained in that community for thirty-three years. In 1909 he removed to Staunton and is a member of the Augusta County Medical Society and the Medical Society of Virginia. Doctor Trimble owns two large farms, and prepares for the market from 100 to 125 head of cattle each year. He is a director of the First National Bank of Highland.

He married, February 28, 1879, Martha Cline Zirkle, daughter of John D. Zirkle, a merchant. They have one daughter, Miss Maude Trimble. She was educated at Monterey. Doctor Trimble and family are members of the Second Presbyterian Church at Staunton. He is a York Rite Mason and Shriner and served as master of his lodge for eight years.

HON. SAMUEL G. BRENT. The banks of a community are naturally accounted as being among the greatest assets it can have, and the men associated with them have to be proven capable and efficient repositories of great trusts, men of unusual business capacities and managers of vast interests, who can devise and carry out plans that require remarkable poise, judgment and self control. Such men have to assume responsibilities that would weigh down to an immeasurable degree those of lesser caliber, control policies, augment the usefulness of their institutions, popularize its coffers, and divert the investment of the revenues, all the while proving themselves to be full of wisdom and of great advantage to their people. Perhaps no man of his locality more fully measures up to the above standards than does Hon. Samuel G. Brent, president of the Alexandria National Bank and judge of the Circuit Court.

Judge Brent was born at Hot Springs, Virginia, June 28, 1855, a son of George William and Lucy (Goode) Brent, natives of Virginia. George William Brent served with the rank of major of the Seventeenth Virginia Cavalry during the war between the states, and surrendered with General Johnston's army. By profession a lawyer, he was engaged in practice in Alexandria the greater part of his life, and he died in that city in 1872, but the mother survived him until 1881, when she, too, passed away.

Reared in Alexandria, Judge Brent there secured his preliminary educational training in its public schools and Saint John's Academy. Going into business life, he worked for A. H. Nott & Company, wholesale wood and tableware dealers, and later for Warren & Moore, wholesale grocers. However, his tastes led him to begin the study of law in the office of Kent & Neal, and subsequently he entered George Washington University and was graduated therefrom in 1877, and later did post-graduate work in Columbia University. In June, 1877, he began the practice of law in Alexandria, and has been very successful. In 1878 he was elected commonwealth attorney, and held that office until 1882, and for ten years he was corporation attorney. Still later he was again elected commonwealth attorney and served until 1918, when he was appointed judge of the Sixteenth Judicial District, and has remained on the bench ever since, discharging his duties with dignified capability.

For two years Judge Brent has been president of the Alexandria National Bank, an institution that is under Government supervision and a member of the Federal Reserve System, with resources of $1,000,000; a capital of $100,000; surplus and undivided profits of over $45,000, and deposits of nearly $1,000,000. The officers of the bank are: Judge Samuel G. Brent, president; Luther H. Dudley, vice president and cashier, and these two, with William P. Woolls, commonwealth attorney, City of Alexandria, John D. Normoyle, prominent realtor and insurance man, William S. Snow, attorney-at-law, and Henry P. Thomas form the Board of Directors, a very strong organization and representative of powerful professional and business talent and capability.

On December 6, 1882, Judge Brent married Miss Louise Saunders, a daughter of Doctor Saunders, of Memphis, Tennessee, and they had one child, Samuel G., Junior, who is engaged in the cotton industry in Memphis, Tennessee. Mrs. Brent died in 1885. On November 23, 1887, Judge Brent married Miss Rebecca Lloyd Tabb, a daughter of Dr. J. Prosser and Rebecca Tabb, both of whom are deceased. Judge and Mrs. Brent had two children, namely: Jean, who married D. Milton French, and is now a widow residing with her father; and George William, who served with the rank of lieutenant in the United States army during the World war, and was stationed in San Francisco, California. The second Mrs. Brent died February 20, 1917. Judge Brent belongs to the Alexandria Bar Association and the American Bar Association, but has no lodge or club connections. All his life he has been a strong supporter of the principles of the Democratic party and is regarded as one of the strongest men locally. Dignified, learned, and yet strongly human, Judge Brent is a man who holds the warm affection of a host of friends, and the respect, amounting almost to veneration, of all who know him.

HON. HOWARD WORTH SMITH, judge of the Corporation Court of Alexandria, has earned a distinguished place at the bar and on the bench of the State of Virginia. It is forcibly indicative of his legal solidity and versatility that he should have made a high record as a private practitioner, a commonwealth's attorney and a learned, impartial jurist. A brief analysis of his most marked traits of character is explanatory of his unusual measure of success. While keen and logical, earnest and eloquent, he is also careful in the development of his legal plans, and has the faculty, strongly natural and persistently trained, of piercing to the foundation principles of any contention. Being thus firmly grounded, the details naturally arrange themselves, and the mind is left clear and positive to work along definite lines of thought. Thus it is that Judge Smith, whether as private practitioner, prosecutor or judge, always has had his case firmly in hand, and has never been diverted to side issues, which has been the prime secret of his great legal strength and success.

Judge Smith was born on a farm in Fauquier County, Virginia, February 2, 1883, and is a son of William Worth and

Lucinda (Lewis) Smith. His father was born in Fauquier County, where he spent the greater part of his life in agricultural pursuits, and was accounted a capable and progressive farmer. This reputation grew until he was appointed superintendent of the Arlington Experimental Farm, a position which he retained for ten years and in which he rendered valuable service. He was a man who was held in the highest esteem in his community and a public spirited citizen who supported generously all civic movements and enterprises. His death occurred at Arlington March 6, 1924, when he was seventy-two years of age. His worthy widow survives him and makes her home with her son, Judge Howard W. Another son, William Worth Smith, Jr., is a member of the Virginia State Senate from the Twenty-sixth Senatorial District, and divides his time between Richmond and his home City of Louisa.

The public schools of Faquier County furnished Howard W. Smith with his early educational training, and he grew up in an agricultural atmosphere and in his boyhood assisted his father in the operation of the home farm. Subsequently he was sent to Bethel Military Academy, and when he left that institution began the study of law at the University of Virginia, from which he was graduated with the degree of Bachelor of Laws as a member of the class of 1903, when he was only twenty years of age. As soon as he attained his majority and was admitted to the bar, in 1904, he opened an office at Alexandria, where he has since been successful in building up a large and prominent clientage. By 1916 his splendid abilities had become recognized and he was elected commonwealth's attorney for Alexandria, a position which he was holding at the time of his appointment, in October, 1922, to the bench of the Corporation Court. This was a gubernatorial appointment to fill a vacancy, and subsequently Judge Smith was retained on the bench by a vote of the Legislature and has occupied it to the present. Judge Smith has won the full confidence and respect of the people and the firm friendship and coöperation of the members of the bench and bar. He has long been in the public eye, having formerly served as president of the Common Council of Alexandria, and during the World war was assistant general counsel to the alien property custodian. His offices are situated at 109 North Fairfax Street. Judge Smith is a member of the Virginia State Bar Association and the Alexandria Bar Association, and as a fraternalist is affiliated with the Masons, the Benevolent and Protective Order of Elks and the Independent Order of Odd Fellows. In his political allegiance he is a supporter of the candidates and principles of the Democratic party, and is an Episcopalian in his religious faith. He resides in a pleasant home at 120 Walnut Street.

On November 3, 1913, Judge Smith was united in marriage with Miss Violet A. Proctor, and to this union there were born two children: Howard Worth, Jr., and Violet Adelaide. Mrs. Smith died January 16, 1919, and on June 22, 1922, Judge Smith took for his second wife Miss Ann Corcoran. During his work as a private practitioner Judge Smith, although absolutely devoted to the cause of his client in whatever field he worked, never forgot the ethics of his profession or stooped to unworthy means to gain an advantage. By close study and through his familiarity with a wide range of legal lore he usually fortified his positions with so many facts and precedents that only the leading practitioners could cope with him, and he won more than a majority of the cases that he tried. As a judge he has upheld the dignity of the court and has proven himself fair and impartial and careful in his decisions in complicated cases.

WILLIAM E. CRANK. Now serving in his second term as commonwealth's attorney of Louisa County, Hon. William E. Crank, of Louisa, is recognized as the highest type of loyal citizen and honorable manhood. Actuated by high ideals, his life is spent in close conformity therewith; his teachings and example are an inspiring force in the world, and his human sympathy and charities have brought men to him in the ties of close friendship. Endowed by nature with love of principle and strength of character, his career is free from defilement and one that redounds to his credit and places his name high in the estimation of his fellowmen. In his professional work he exemplifies truth, honor and justice, and is unfaltering in his adherence to the course which he believes to be best and invincible in his prosecution of offenders against the law. His ability to grasp a multitude of details and to show their general bearing on the points at issue, and a patient and courteous attitude toward all his confreres, with a broad knowledge of the law and promptness of decision, are traits of character that have made him an able lawyer and an ideal commonwealth's attorney.

William E. Crank was born in Louisa, Virginia, September 29, 1891, a son of William J. and Virginia E. (Miller) Crank. The parents were natives of Virginia, he born in Louisa County and she in Cumberland County, and she is still living, making her home in Louisa, but he died May 24, 1922. A man of many interests, he was successfully engaged in lumbering, merchandising and farming, and for sixteen years he was deputy treasurer of Louisa County. He was a consistent member of the Methodist Episcopal Church, South, to which his widow still belongs, and he was active in fraternal matters in conjunction with the Masonic order, to which he long belonged. The Democratic party had in him a strong supporter. His success in life was all the more commendable in that he made his own way. His father was John R. Crank, also a native of Louisa County, one of the first lumbermen of the county, and a farmer. During the war between the states he served in the Confederate army. The maternal grandfather was a native of Cumberland County, where his life was spent and where he was long engaged in farming.

The third child born to his parents, William E. Crank was carefully reared and sent to both private and public schools, and after he completed his high-school work he had two years in Washington and Lee University, and was graduated in law in 1915, with the degree of Bachelor of Laws. Entering into a partnership with Judge F. W. Simms, Mr. Crank began the practice of his profession in Louisa, and when that connection was severed was in practice alone until he entered the army for the World war. After being trained at Camp Lee, Virginia, he went overseas with the Thirty-seventh Division, and was in France for ten months, participating in the Meuse-Argonne offensive and the Alsace sector defensive as a private. During his period of service at the front he was slightly wounded, but recovered, and was honorably discharged in April, 1919.

Returning to Louisa, Mr. Crank resumed his practice in partnership with Lindsey Gordon, which association is still maintained, although in 1923 he was elected commonwealth's attorney and reelected in 1927 for another four-year period. In addition to the duties and responsibilities of his office and the cares of his private practice Mr. Crank is a director of the First National Bank of Louisa. He is a member of and deacon in the Christian Church of Louisa, and is zealous in church work. Fraternally his connections are with the Masons and the college fraternity Alpha Chi Rho. Like his father he is a strong Democrat. Professionally he belongs to the local, state and American Bar Associations.

On September 25, 1926, Mr. Crank married Phyllis C. Collins, who was born in Orange County, Virginia, a daughter of Lewis R. and Nannie (Mickie) Collins. Mrs. Crank was educated in the common and high schools of Orange County, and also attended several summer sessions of the University of Virginia, thus preparing herself for the profession of teaching, which she was following at the time of her marriage. Mr. and Mrs. Crank have one daughter, Fontaine Crank. In every relation of life Mr. Crank shows the light that comes from justness, generosity, truth, high sense of honor, proper respect for self, and a sensitive thoughtfulness for others. The Crank home in Louisa is a hospitable one where good cheer abounds and where Mr. and Mrs. Crank take great pleasure in entertaining their numerous friends.

JOHN BARTON PHILLIPS. Among the younger generation of lawyers practicing at the bar of Arlington County, one who has made rapid progress and become known as one of the prominent figures in his profession at Alexandria is John Barton Phillips. His career has been an active one in which he has made the most of his opportunities, and the position that he now holds has been gained solely through individual merit and not through any chance or adventitious circumstances.

Mr. Phillips was born in Alexandria, August 11, 1896, and is a son of Oscar W. and Mary E. (Dyer) Phillips, natives of the same place. For many years Oscar W. Phillips was engaged in mercantile pursuits at Alexandria, where he died July 29, 1928. Mrs. Phillips passed away April 11, 1921.

John Barton Phillips received his early education in the public schools of Alexandria, where he was graduated from high school in 1914. He then entered the University of Virginia, where he took the law course, and completed his legal education at' George Washington University, Washington, D. C., from which he was graduated as a member of the class of 1921, receiving the degree of Bachelor of Laws with distinction. By virtue of his class standing he was elected a member of the honorary legal fraternity, the Order of the Coif. He immediately entered upon the practice of his profession at Alexandria, where he has met with constantly increasing success, and is now accounted one of the leaders of the younger members of the bar. He has a thoroughly comprehensive knowledge of principles and precedents, and in their application is ready, forceful and accurate. His offices are situated at 105 South Royal Street. For five years Mr. Phillips served capably in the office of United States commissioner, and for a like period had been deputy clerk of the United States District Court. He is a member of the American Bar Association, the Virginia State Bar Association and the Alexandria Bar Association, among whose members he is highly esteemed for his adherence to the highest ethics of his profession.

W. Terrell Sheehan

Mr. Phillips gives his chief attention to his calling, but has many outside interests of much importance. He is secretary-treasurer of the Northern Virginia Hotel Corporation, which owns the George Mason Hotel of Alexandria; a member of the Board of Directors of the Northern Virginia Investment Corporation; a past master of Andrew Jackson Lodge, A. F. and A. M.; a past secretary-treasurer of the Kiwanis Club of Alexandria; and a member of the Alexandria Chamber of Cemmerce, the Belle Haven Country Club and others. Politically he is a stanch Republican, and at present is chairman of the City Republican Committee. His religious faith is that of the Episcopal Church. On February 25, 1928, he was united in marriage with Miss Anna M. Richards, of Washington, D. C. They reside at Jefferson Park, Alaxandria, Virginia.

Mr. Phillips had two brothers and one sister: Charles C., who saw service in France during the World war and later went to Germany with the Army of Occupation and now resides at 216 South Fairfax Street, Alexandria; Elizabeth H., who is unmarried and makes her home with her brother; and William L., who served on the U. S. battleship *Missouri* during the World war, and died October 2, 1918.

W. TERRELL SHEEHAN is one of the promising young attorneys of the Staunton bar, and in the brief time since he was admitted to practice he has shown the possession of those qualifications which are fundamental for a successful record in the legal profession.

Mr. Sheehan was born at Lynchburg, December 5, 1902, son of John and Ardehna (Hamilton) Sheehan, both natives of Amherst County, Virginia. His grandfather, John Sheehan, was a native of Ireland, and on coming to Virginia followed farming. The maternal family of Hamiltons were early settled in Virginia. Mr. Sheehan's parents spent many years at Lynchburg, where his father followed the contracting business. They were devout Catholics. Of the three children the oldest is John T., district manager for the Life Insurance Company of Virginia at Norfolk. M. A. Sheehan is secretary of the Lynchburg Finance Corporation, and W. Terrell is the third of the family.

W. Terrell Sheehan attended school at Lynchburg, and attended the law department of the University of Virginia in 1926. In the same year he was given a license and has since practiced at Staunton, his offices being in the Law Building in that city. He is a member of the Phi Alpha Delta law fraternity, the Knights of Columbus, and is a Catholic. On June 31, 1928, he was united in marriage with Miss Alma Elizabeth Kuykendall, of Romney, West Virginia.

MORGAN LAUCK WALTON is a resident of Woodstock. He has practiced law in the Valley of Virginia for more than half a century. Over the state at large he is known for a number of distinctive services. Mr. Walton was author of what is known as the Walton Election Law, the law passed in 1892 and adapting the Australian system of elections to Virginia. He is also a former grand chancellor of the Knights of Pythias of Virginia.

Mr. Walton was born at Woodstock October 13, 1853, son of Moses and Emily (Lauck) Walton, grandson of Reuben Walton and great-grandson of Moses Walton. The Walton family has been in the Shenandoah Valley since Colonial times. His great-

grandfather was born in Shenandoah County, served as sheriff
of the county and was a member of the State Senate. Reuben
Walton was a merchant at Woodstock and served as county
surveyor.

Moses Walton, father of Morgan L., was one of the eminent
lawyers of his generation. He was born in Shenandoah County
in 1826, graduated from Dickinson College at Carlisle, Pennsylvania, was in the Virginia Senate during the Civil war and
after the war attended the "Black and Tan" Constitutional Convention. He served as commonwealth attorney of Shenandoah
County, and for many years had a practice which brought him
regularly before the Supreme Court of Appeals and other higher
courts. He was a member of the Methodist Episcopal Church.
Moses Walton died in June, 1883. His wife, Emily M. Lauck,
was born in Page County, Virginia, and died in 1907. Her
father, Morgan A. Lauck, was a prominent member of the Masonic fraternity and died while assisting in establishing a Masonic Lodge.

Morgan Lauck Walton was the second in a family of seven
children, five of whom are living. He was educated at Woodstock, in Randolph-Macon College at Ashland, from which he
was graduated in 1872, and in 1875 completed his law course at
the University of Virginia. He was admitted to the bar in
July, 1875, and from that date forward has been engaged in
law practice at Woodstock. He was associated with his father
in the firm Walton & Walton until the latter's death in 1883.
Later he was with his brother-in-law, Judge E. D. Newman,
and in recent years with his son, Morgan L., Jr.

Mr. Walton was a member of the Virginia Senate from 1891
to 1894, and while there was author of the Walton Election Law.
He was a delegate to the National Democratic Convention of
1888 when Cleveland was nominated for a second term. During
the World war he was chairman of the Shenandoah County
Draft Board. Mr. Walton in addition to his law practice has
been interested in farming and has about a hundred acres in
orchard. He is a prominent layman of the Methodist Episcopal
Church in Virginia, having been chairman of the board of the
Woodstock Church, was chairman of the Sunday School Board
of the Baltimore Conference, and for a number of years served
as a member of the commission to bring about a consolidation
of the northern and southern branches of the church. He has
been a lay delegate to general conferences. Both he and his
son have filled the office of grand chancellor of the Knights of
Pythias for the State of Virginia.

Mr. Walton married, January 26, 1876, Miss Mary A. March,
who died March 12, 1928, more than two years after they had
celebrated their golden wedding anniversary. Mrs. Walton was
born at Churchville, Augusta County, Virginia. Her father,
James H. March, was a Methodist minister. Mr. and Mrs. Walton had seven children. Moses, the oldest child, is a resident
of Hamilton, Ontario, in the collection department of the International Harvester Company. Laura Walton, now residing at
White Sulphur Springs, West Virginia, is the widow of John H.
Dulin, who was a graduate of Randolph-Macon College and
Washington and Lee University, practiced law for many years,
and Mrs. Dulin has a daughter, Elizabeth, a successful teacher,
located at Meadville, Pennsylvania. Clyde E. V. Walton, the
third child, graduated in pharmacy at Richmond and died October 8, 1926. Miss Mabel Walton resides at Woodstock, is active

in church work and is general president of the Sigma Sigma sorority of the United States. She was educated in Randolph-Macon Woman's College at Lynchburg. Miss Mary Belle Walton, also living at Woodstock, was educated in Randolph-Macon Woman's College. Emily A. Walton, who attended the Woman's College at Lynchburg, is the wife of Chester C. Holloway, an educator and fruit grower living at Clearmont, Florida. Morgan Lauck, Jr., was educated in Randolph-Macon Academy at Front Royal, in Randolph-Macon College at Ashland, took his law degree at the University of Virginia, and during the World war was in training at Fort Myer, was commissioned a second lieutenant, promoted to first lieutenant, and was on duty in the Judge Advocate's Department at Camp Lee. He is now judge of the Juvenile Court of Shenandoah County.

WILLIAM THOMAS ROBEY is one of the veteran business men of Buena Vista, having been identified with this community for over thirty-five years, and his business activities have constituted an indispensable service and at the same time he always has been a loyal and public spirited citizen.

He was born in Loudoun County, Virginia, July 28, 1866, son of Frank E. and Martha E. (Gaines) Robey. The Robey family came to America from England before the Revolutionary war. His great-grandfather, Elijah Robey, was killed while a soldier in the War of 1812. Frank E. Robey was born in Loudoun County, and at the age of sixteen enlisted in the Confederate army under General Mosby. He was captured at Front Royal but soon escaped. He spent his active life as a farmer and merchant at Philomont, Virginia, for twenty years was superintendent of the Loudoun County Farm and for five years deputy sheriff. He was a very active and influential Democrat. Frank E. Robey died in 1923 and his wife, in 1921, and of their eight children six are living: William T.; Ernest F., of Charlottesville, Virginia; Edgar L., a farmer of Loudoun County; James E., a broker at Lynchburg; Clarence E., president of the First National Bank of Purcellville, Virginia; and Earle, wife of W. O. Whitman, of Philomont, Virginia.

William Thomas Robey grew up in Loudoun County, and after the local schools worked on his father's farm until he reached his maturity. On leaving the farm he became clerk in the store of J. B. Vansickler. Shortly afterwards his father bought that store and William was associated with him in its operation for three years. This was the training and business experience that Mr. Robey brought with him when he located at Buena Vista in 1890. He started a trucking and transfer business and gradually developing a livery and at one time had sixty horses for hire. With the advent of the automobile he gradually converted his livery into a garage business and in addition to his garage service has had the authorized Ford agency since 1917.

Mr. Robey is an active Democrat and for twelve years was a member of the City Council of Buena Vista. He served as registrar for five years and is a member of the Democratic County Committee. Fraternally he is affiliated with the Independent Order of Odd Fellows, Knights of Pythias and Junior Order United American Mechanics. He has been an usher in the Presbyterian Church for twenty years.

Mr. Robey in 1891 married Susan Connor, daughter of John T. and Helen (Brown) Connor, of Loudoun County. Her father was a shoe manufacturer and farmer, a Republican in politics and a member of the Methodist Episcopal Church. He died in 1918 and his widow resides at Philomont. Mrs. Robey was the second in a family of seven children. She died in 1902, leaving three children: Audry M., wife of T. B. Dillard, of Roanoke, Virginia; Marie, wife of Louis Musgrove, of Charlotte, North Carolina; and Russell.

Mr. Robey in 1902 married Corine Henkle, of Buena Vista, who died in 1904. Her son, William T., Junior, graduated from the University of Virginia in 1927 and is now associated with his father in the garage business. Mr. Robey in 1913 married Mrs. Myrtle B. Wright, daughter of Spotswood P. Nuckles, of Buena Vista. By her previous marriage she has a daughter, Mildred V. Wright, now the wife of Albert Griffith, a Buena Vista attorney.

Mr. Robey has seven grandchildren, six of them the children of his daughter, Mrs. Audry Dillard: Margaret, Charlotte, Jane, Blair, Doris and Martha Ann, and another, Marie Musgrove, daughter of Marie Musgrove.

JOHN S. MCDONALD. One of the leading men of Roanoke County, vice president of the First National Bank of Narrows, clerk of the Roanoke School Board, and interested in everything pertaining to the further advancement of his city and county, John S. McDonald is a well known figure in this part of Virginia. He was born in Giles County, Virginia, November 28, 1888, a son of Arthur B. and Margaret E. (Foster) McDonald, the latter of whom was born at New Hope, West Virginia, and died April 15, 1925, and the former of whom was born in Giles County, and survives, being a resident of Roanoke, to which city he retired after he stopped farming, although he still owns his farm in Giles County. The following children were born to the parents: John S., who is the eldest; Mary, who is a teacher in the public schools of Roanoke; William Lewis, who was a teacher in the public schools, is now a dairyman in the vicinity of Baltimore, Maryland; George Blake, who is operating his father's farm in Giles County; and a daughter who is deceased. Both the father and mother early united with the Methodist Episcopal Church, South, to which he still belongs. He is a Democrat, but not much of an office seeker. The paternal grandfather of John S. McDonald was Lewis McDonald, a native of Virginia, and a Confederate veteran. The McDonald family originated in Scotland, and the American founder secured a grant of land in Botetourt County, Virginia, from the English Crown, and on it he settled upon coming to this country, so that the McDonalds are among the First Families of Virginia. The maternal grandfather was William K. Foster, a Methodist minister, and a native of what is now West Virginia.

John S. McDonald attended Emory and Henry College, from which he was graduated in 1913, with the degree of Bachelor of Arts, after which he entered Johns Hopkins University, where he took post-graduate work. In 1913 he entered upon a long and useful career as an educator, his first work being done as principal of the Buchanan High School. After three years there he held a similar position with the Rocky Mountain High School for two years, and at the expiration of that period he came to Roanoke as a teacher in the science department of the Senior High School, and continued head of this department until August 1, 1927, when he was made clerk of the city school board, and is now devoting all of his attention to his onerous duties.

Aaron Grobaw

In 1915 Mr. McDonald married Miss Bessie Irene Phlegar, who was born in Giles County, Virginia. She attended its schools and the Harrisonburg State Normal School, and was a school teacher prior to her marriage. Mr. and Mrs. McDonald have one daughter, Margaret Elizabeth. Mrs. McDonald is a daughter of Mr. and Mrs. H. L. Phlegar, who reside at Bane, Giles County, where he is engaged in farming and stockraising upon an extensive scale. Raleigh Court Methodist Episcopal Church, South, holds the membership of Mr. and Mrs. McDonald, and he is one of its trustees, and at one time was superintendent of its Sunday School, but is now teacher of a class of boys. Fraternally he belongs to Virginia Heights Lodge No. 324, A. F. and A. M. Socially his connections are with the Lions Club, the University Club and the Giles County Fish Protective Association in all of which bodies he is deservedly popular.

AARON GRAHAM, of Christiansburg, has probably had as wide and varied a connection with the commercial life of this section of the state as any other citizen. For many years he was in business as a retail and wholesale merchant, and is also well known for his extensive lumbering operations and other enterprises.

He was born in Patrick County, Virginia, March 13, 1854, son of James and Rebecca (DeHart) Graham. His grandfather Graham was an early settler in Floyd County, Virginia. James Graham was born and reared in Floyd County, had a private school education and served in the ranks in the Confederate army in Captain Burrell Akers' company. After the war he was a carpenter and mechanic, and during the later years of his life lived with his son at Christiansburg, where he died October 24, 1908, at the age of eighty-five. He was born November 25, 1823. His wife, Rebecca DeHart, was born in Patrick County, attended private schools, and died about 1869. She was a daughter of Aaron and Tamer (Alexander) DeHart, of Patrick County. Her father was a large land owner and slave owner there. He went into the Confederate army, and finally was reported missing, and filled an unknown soldier's grave. Aaron Graham was one of two children. His sister, Melinda, now deceased, was the wife of Jefferson DeHart.

Aaron Graham acquired his education in several private and special schools, and had some very fine teachers during his youth. He was only about fifteen when he left school, and at once took employment as clerk in stores. When he was twenty years old he engaged in merchandising for himself at Shawsville, remaining there twelve years. On March 21, 1881, he became a clerk for his brother-in-law, J. H. Johnston, and fifteen months later they joined forces in the firm of Johnston & Graham. They were together until 1898 as retail merchants. In the meantime they started a wholesale grocery department, and after the death of Mr. Johnston, Mr. Graham continued the business as sole owner until about 1902, when he sold out. Many years ago he established at Christiansburg a foundry and machine shop, operating it for about five years, for the manufacture of building material and saw mill machinery. The plant was burned in 1906, at a heavy loss of about thirty thousand dollars. Prior to that time Mr. Graham's store at Shawsville had been burned, and also his house, and few business men have had heavier losses as a result of fires. After the burning of his factory in 1906 he resumed his connection with the wholesale grocery business as a member of the firm Graham Grocery Company. Later he affiliated this with the Surface Wholesale Grocery Company, of Cambria, Virginia, Mr. Graham having the management of both plants for one year. He then bought out the Surface Company and moved the business to Christiansburg, where it was conducted as the Aaron Graham Wholesale Grocery Company until 1920.

Mr. Graham about 1904 bought "The Old Fields of Toe" at Montezuma, North Carolina, from John A. Yoder, and also acquired other timber property. When Newland, North Carolina, was founded as the county seat of Avery County the town was built on the Graham lands, and Mr. Graham made a great success of the sale of town lots. He laid out the town and sold the lots on August 5, 1905. He had been for a number of years engaged in the lumber business at Christiansburg. He operated mills and had crews at work in the wood cutting staves for the Standard Oil Company, having mills in both Virginia and West Virginia. He also extended his lumber interests to North Carolina. At Christiansburg, Mr. Graham established the local telephone company, later selling to a concern in Pulaski, and the property was subsequently acquired by the Bell interests. Mr. Graham has put up a great many houses in Christiansburg and still owns considerable property there.

In recent years he has given his chief attention to the Christiansburg distributing agency for the Standard Oil Company, handling the oil and gas products of this corporation for Montgomery and Floyd counties. Mr. Graham is a member of the Chamber of Commerce. In 1900 he was a candidate for Congress against the famous Virginia statesman, Carter Glass, and carried his home town by several hundred votes. For ten years he was town treasurer of Christiansburg. It was largely through the influence of Mr. Graham that saloons were driven out of the county many years ago. He is an independent Democrat in politics, and for thirty-four years held the office of treasurer of the Presbyterian Church, and was treasurer of the church at Shawsville for eight years.

Mr. Graham married at Christiansburg, November 12, 1878, Miss Lucy T. Price, daughter of George and Harriet Price. Her father for many years conducted a tannery, and died about 1889, while her mother passed away about 1890, and both are buried at Christiansburg. Mrs. Graham attended the Christiansburg Female College and is a very devout church woman. She has read her Bible through over twenty-four times. For many years she taught a class in the Presbyterian Sunday School. Mr. and Mrs. Graham have three children, George E., Nellie C. and Mary J. George, now with the Barrow & Penn wholesale grocery house at Roanoke, is a resident of Christiansburg, married Sue Ireson, of Williamson, West Virginia, and four children were born to them, Malcom, Harold, Edith and George, Jr., the last child dying July 29, 1923. Miss Nellie C. Graham attended public schools, Mrs. Spindle's School for Girls, Baird's Private School and Sullins College at Bristol, Virginia, and is now secretary and bookkeeper for her father's business. She is active in the Presbyterian Church, is pianist for the Christian Endeavor, and is a member of the auxiliary Business Woman's League, the United Daughters of the Confederacy, and is eligible to membership in the Daughters of the American Revolution. The young-

est daughter, Mary, is the widow of Harry Schaeffer, who died at Christiansburg, Va., December 14, 1923, and she now resides at Roanoke, and she is a composer and publisher of music. She has four children, Catherine Augusta, Mary Eleanor, Charles H., Jr., and Burns Allen Shafer.

HAROLD M. RATCLIFFE is a young Virginian who has accumulated a number of the honors and distinctions of professional and public service in a comparatively brief period of years. He is the present commonwealth's attorney of Henrico County.

He was born in that county May 13, 1896, son of H. F. and Alice F. (Garthright) Ratcliffe, his father a native of Henrico County and his mother of Hanover County. His father lives on a farm in Henrico County, and is retired, after having given many years to farming. Harold M. Ratcliffe grew up on the old farm, attended the district schools and from them entered Richmond College, now the University of Richmond. He left his studies in 1917 to enlist in the Naval Aviation Corps for the period of the World war, and was on duty at Pensacola, Florida, and off the coast of New Jersey until honorably discharged December 9, 1918.

After the war he resumed his law course at the University of Richmond, and in August, 1919, passed the state board examination. He has been in practice since January, 1920, and has law offices in the Travelers Building at Richmond. In November, 1927, he was elected commonwealth's attorney for Henrico County for a term of four years.

Mr. Ratcliffe, who is unmarried, is a member of the Richmond and Virginia Bar Associations. He organized Post No. 45 of the American Legion and was elected the first commander. He is a member of the Cosmopolitan Club of Richmond, is a Democrat and a member of the Methodist Episcopal Church, South.

JOHN EVAN HARVELL. A self-made man in every sense implied by the term, few men made better use of their time and talent than the late John E. Harvell, of Petersburg, who by his own efforts rose to a position of eminence in the electrical world, by study and experiment acquiring an expert knowledge of that baffling science, electricity. A son of John Quincy Harvell, he was born November 4, 1867, in Petersburg, Virginia, where his entire life was spent.

Born in Southampton County, Virginia, John Quincy Harvell located in Petersburg when a youth of twenty years. He subsequently established himself in the commission business as head of the firm of Harvell & Hubbard. Meeting with good success in his venture, he carried it on until his death, at the age of thirty-three years. His wife, whose name before marriage was Mary Elizabeth Williams, was born in Petersburg, a daughter of William and Edith (Sturdivant) Williams.

But a young lad when his father died, John E. Harvell had very limited educational advantages. Forced by circumstances to hustle for a living, he found employment as a messenger boy, delivering cotton reports for one dollar a week. His promptness and fidelity to his duties attracted the attention of the telegraph company for which he was working, and subsequently that of the telephone company also. While thus employed Mr. Harvell became especially interested in the science of electricity, which Benjamin Franklin, with his metal-tipped kite and a conducting string, discovered early in the eighteenth century to be identical with lightning. He made a close study of the science, obtaining knowledge of value to him in his future work. In 1887 Mr. Harvell, as lineman for the Upper Appomattox Electric Company, set the first poles for electric wires erected in Petersburg. His ability as an electrician being recognized and appreciated, he was promoted to the position of operator in the Power House, later becoming its superintendent.

When this company sold out to the South Side Railway & Development Company he continued with that organization until 1909, when the Virginia Railway & Power Company came into existence, with which he became identified. Subsequently Mr. Harvell was given full charge of the operations of the Petersburg interurban lines; of the City Railway and Light and Power System of Petersburg; and in addition was given the entire supervision of the company's light and power system, including Richmond, Petersburg, Hopewell, Norfolk, Portsmouth, Suffolk, and Weldon, North Carolina, with the title of general manager.

During the period of the World war Mr. Harvell was assigned by the Board of Directors to superintend the construction of the 110,000 volt transmission line between Richmond and Norfolk. Under his wise management the work was completed promptly, and in a highly efficient manner.

On the bronze door of the power house the following tribute to Mr. Harvell is inscribed: "This entrance was erected and dedicated by the employes of the Virginia Railway and Power Company as a symbol of respect and esteem for their general manager, John E. Harvell." This paragraph is also found: "It was in a primitive electric plant located upon this site that he, as an unskilled youth, began his career in the electrical field on September 13, 1887. By study and experiment he mastered as far as one can the science of electricity, and his ability as an electrician was appreciated by his employers, who soon after his death sold their plant."

Enthusiastic and ambitious in his work, using brain as well as muscle, Mr. Harvell's health became impaired, and after an illness of six months, during which time everything possible was done toward alleviating his sufferings, he passed to the life beyond, his death occurring on May 18, 1924. On May 20, 1897, he was united in marriage with Miss Blanche Belsches Southall, of Petersburg, daughter of Henry Clay and Lucy (Belsches) Southall. He was survived by three daughters, namely: Elizabeth; Blanche, wife of Clarence A. Bentz, and they have a daughter, Betty Jane, born May 5, 1929; and Margaret.

Ever interested in public matters, Mr. Harvell served eight years as an alderman, during four years of the time serving as president of the board. Upon his retirement therefrom the members of the board presented him with a handsome gold cane, beautifully inscribed. Fraternally Mr. Harvell was a Mason, and Mrs. Harvell and two of their daughters belong to the Eastern Star Order. He was also a Knight of Pythias and an Elk. He was a trustee of the Washington Street Methodist Episcopal Church, of which he and all his family were members.

HENRY CLAY SOUTHALL. Acquiring his education mainly in the school of experience, Henry Clay Southall, late of Petersburg, became familiar with all branches of farm work while young, laboring day in and day out under his father's instructions. He was born in Amelia County, Virginia, where his father, William Daniel Southall, was, it is supposed, a life long resident. He there married a Miss Clay, a native of the same county.

In the eighteenth year of his age, inspired by patriotic ardor, Henry Clay Southall enlisted in the Confederate service as a member of the Richmond Light Infantry Blues, which formed a part of the Army of Virginia. With his command he took part in many important battles. In the engagement at Hatcher's Run he fought bravely all day, but at night, when he was busily engaged in throwing up breastworks, a sharp shooter in a near by tree sent a bullet through the left side of his neck into his body. It entered one of his lungs, stopping near his shoulder-blade. Mr. Southall was taken to the nearest hospital, and being there captured, was taken to Fort McHenry in Maryland, where he was discharged. He was meagerly clothed and without money.

A stranger, evidently a Southern sympathizer, seeing his condition, gave him a sufficient sum to pay his transportation expenses to City Point, and thence to Petersburg. Resuming work as soon as able, Mr. Southall was engaged in various industrial positions, the last few years of his active life having been in the lumber business. Having suffered a stroke of paralysis, he was forced to sit in a wheel chair the last twenty-five years of his life. Although physically injured, his mental faculties were unimpaired, his mind being keen and alert until his death, which occurred very suddenly in 1914, at the age of seventy years and six months.

Mr. Southall married Miss Lucy Belsches, who was born in Prince George County, a daughter of James H. and Therina (Gee) Belsches, and died in 1926, twelve years after the death of her husband. Four children were born into their household, namely: William, who died at the age of twenty-two years; Blanche B., wife of John E. Harvell, of whom a brief sketch appears preceding in this volume; Nettie L., wife of Ira B. White; and Henry Clay.

THOMAS CHARLES LEE was a manufacturer and business man who spent his active life in Norfolk County, and was a figure in the affairs and citizenship of that community, and whose memory is held in esteem by a great many people.

He was born December 9, 1859, and died at Norfolk April 2, 1925. His father, Thomas J. Lee, was a Confederate soldier, who lost an arm in one of the battles of the war. Thomas Charles Lee was educated in the old Norfolk Academy, and from early manhood was engaged in some line of commercial enterprise. For several years he was a road builder for the county, and later established a plant for the manufacture of packages for truck growers. This factory was located on the Cottage Toll Road. He was the owner of the business until 1908, when he sold his plant and business to the Farmers Manufacturing Company, exchanging some of his interest for stock in the company, and was retained by the new organization as manager of the business, and so continued until his death. He was a Democrat in politics and a member of the Presbyterian Church.

Mr. Lee first married Grace Bradbrook, who died leaving one child, Charles Lee, who is also deceased. His second wife was Savanah Hodges, and she died leaving two daughters, Vera,

wife of William Edward New, and Lettie, wife of John Purnell.
Mr. Lee in February, 1909, in Norfolk County, married Laura
Myra Wright, daughter of David and Rebecca Wright. The
Wrights were very early settlers in Norfolk County, locating
there in Colonial times, and they were represented in the Revolutionary war. Mrs. Lee's father was a farmer and county supervisor. Mrs. Lee survives her husband, residing at 2701 Cottage
Road. She has one daughter, Eunice Wright Lee, and both are
members of the Methodist Episcopal Church, South.

GEORGE W. REYNOLDS was one of the outstanding contractors
at Norfolk, and many buildings still stand in the city testifying
to the substantial character of his work.

Mr. Reynolds was born in Brooklyn, New York, in September, 1841, and died at Camden, New Jersey, in 1917. He was a
descendant of the Reynolds family that settled in New York
in Colonial times and have given a long line of business and
professional men, with an occasional educator among them. His
great-grandfather was a soldier in the Revolutionary war.

George W. Reynolds was eleven years of age when his parents, Mr. and Mrs. Peter Reynolds, moved to Portsmouth, Virginia. Peter Reynolds conducted an extensive contracting business with headquarters in Portsmouth and Norfolk before the
Civil war. George W. Reynolds served as a soldier in the Civil
war. He finished his education at Portsmouth, took up the trade
of carpenter and later entered contracting and was in touch
with the building interests of the Norfolk section during the
greater part of his active life. He finally removed to Philadelphia, where he made his business headquarters until his death.
He was a Republican in politics and a member of the Baptist
Church.

Mr. Reynolds married, August 16, 1911, at Norfolk, Annie
Daniels, who survives him and resides at 1711 Fountainbleau
Avenue in Norfolk. She is a daughter of Lafayette and Amelia
(Archer) Daniels. Her father was also a builder and contractor.
Mrs. Reynolds was one of a family of five children. She is a
member of St. Luke's Episcopal Church.

GEORGE EASTWOOD BUNTING, clerk of the Circuit Court of
Nansemond County, was born in Nansemond County, July 17,
1872, son of John J. and Elizabeth (Eastwood) Bunting, and a
grandson of George W. Bunting, who served with the Signal
Corps of the Confederate army in the war between the states,
and was a leader in the county, engaging extensively in agriculture and the mercantile business. Mr. Bunting's great-grandfather, Bennett Horatio Clarvoe, was an officer in the War of
1812. John J. Bunting (his father) was born in Nansemond
County and gave his active life to farming and the lumber
industry. After the Civil war he was justice of the peace and
acted as the first judge of the County Court of Nansemond
County. He died in June, 1890. His wife, who was born in
Yorkshire, England, died in September, 1872, a few weeks after
the birth of her son, George E.

George E. Bunting grew up in his native county, and was
educated in public and private schools in Nansemond County,
Suffolk Collegiate Institute and Randolph Macon College, Ashland, Virginia. After finishing his education he engaged in
farming and owned and operated 350 acres of land near Suffolk.

This land is a part of a tract owned by his grandfather, and on this land was located the Indian village from which Nansemond County received its name.

For over thirty years George E. Bunting was one of the most influential leaders in the educational and political development of Nansemond County and the Suffolk district. He was not a politician, but his influence was the direct result of his honesty, loyalty, integrity, faith in his fellowman, and unreserved charity towards all. His exceptionally strong personality drew his fellowmen to him and he had the capacity for holding their friendship.

In November, 1911, he was elected clerk of the Circuit Court of Nansemond County and performed the duties of the office from January, 1912, until his untimely death October 5, 1928.

Besides filling the office of clerk of the Circuit Court with unusual distinction, he served as clerk of the county school board, justice of the peace, secretary of the Democratic Executive Committee of Nansemond County, and he was said to have been one of the few clerks of the state who served on the draft board during the World war without making a single enemy. He was a Royal Arch Mason, member of the B. P. O. Elks, charter member of the Suffolk Lions Club, and was christened in the Episcopal Church, but later became a member of the Methodist Episcopal Church, South, and served as a member of the official board of Oxford M. E. Church, Suffolk.

Mr. Bunting's favorite recreation was fishing, and he was a charter member of the exclusive Nix Club on the Nansemond River.

He married, February 21, 1894, Adona Blanche Baker, daughter of Robert W. and Ida (Smith) Baker, her father a native of Gates County, North Carolina, and her mother of Nansemond County, Virginia. When her father died, June 3, 1928, at the age of seventy-nine, he was one of the oldest, most prominent and influential business men of Suffolk, having operated a furniture store and undertaking establishment there for more than forty years. Her mother is now eighty-one and a resident of Suffolk. Mr. Bunting as survived by his wife and one daughter, Susie Clarvoe, wife of Dr. William T. Gay, who served as a commissioned officer in the Medical Corps of the American Expeditionary Forces in France during the World war, and is now a surgeon in Lakeview Hospital, Suffolk. Mrs. Gay was born December 8, 1894. She is a member of the Oxford Methodist Church, the Davis Circle of King's Daughters, the Social Club, the Woman's Club, Tuesday Afternoon Book Club, Association for the Preservation of Virginia Antiquities and American Legion Auxiliary of Suffolk, Virginia. Mr. Bunting was also secretary of the Bell Hosiery Mills of Suffolk and member of the Chamber of Commerce.

At the time of Mr. Bunting's death the following editorial appeared in the Suffolk *News-Herald*:

"PRINCELY MAN PASSES"

"Suffolk and Nansemond will today follow to its last resting place the body of George E. Bunting, princely man, exemplary citizen and faithful servant of his people. Grief over his death is as general as it is genuine, for all who knew him feel that they have lost a personal friend. That in itself is a tribute to the memory of this man who for so long has stood in the white light of public life where every action and turn are under the critical gaze and scrutiny of those all too ready and willing to find fault. He stood the test—every test—of good citizenship and so in his passing a community mourns its everlasting loss.

"George Bunting was universally beloved for himself. He was in every sense a 'man's man' and he drew them to him and held them by the force of his magnetic personality. He was as true to his friendships as he was to his every obligation as a citizen, considering loyalty one of the highest traits of character. Out in the broad stretches of the county that honored him so long and signally the ties of that friendship he builded reach like silken cords to be long remembered and treasured in the recesses of the hearts of those who loved him. And not even death will sever the ties that bound his life with those who are following him home today.

"There was something infinitely fine and noble in the life of this Virginian that raised him above the average of men. Perhaps it was his gentleness or friendly interest in all with whom he came in contact; perhaps it was his charity toward all who needed a friend; or was it his simple faith in mankind? Whatever may have been the reason, George Bunting lived and moved through the grooves of his life making the world better and people happier as he passed. He loved the people of his county where his forbears helped carve a state out of the savage-infested wilderness. His sterling qualities of manhood and citizenship were probably the inheritance that came to him through the blood of his ancestors making it impossible otherwise than to be the clean, upright, honorable, Christian gentleman he was. It is unfortunate that with him passes the last of his line of that name.

"The community pauses today to pay its tribute to his memory and through tear-dimmed eyes watch the dust cover all that is mortal of the friend they have 'long loved and lost a while.' But for him death is only transition into the life fashioned for him since the beginning of time. It will comfort those of his grief-torn home to know that he whom they loved and idolized played his part in life so acceptably that all the community which knew him from boyhood shares their grief and mingled their tears with theirs. We mortals cannot understand why he should have been called in the prime of life and in the years of his greatest usefulness to his family and his state, but the Father of us all moves in mysterious ways. Although he has gone hence he has left behind much that will live and move and have its being—the good that he has done, the happiness he has radiated into the lives of others, and his upright walk through his little span."—Editorial from *Suffolk News-Herald*.

RICHMOND TERRELL LACY. Included on that roll of honor that is illustrated by the undying names of Virginia's illustrious sons are those of eminence in the professions. She is the "Mother of Presidents," and side by side with her chief magistrates, her soldiers and patriots have been inscribed names representing high merit, beneficent purpose and signal distinction in scientific discovery, medicine and the law.

An old and honorable professional name belonging for many years to New Kent County, Virginia, is that of Lacy, a prominent member of which was the late Hon. Richard Terrell Lacy, formerly and for many years commonwealth's attorney, and later an honored member of the Richmond bar.

Richmond Terrell Lacy was born in New Kent County, Virginia, in February, 1842, one of his parents' family of seven children, son of Richmond Terrell and Ellen (Lane) Lacy, the latter of whom belonged to a prominent old Southern family of Amelia County, Virginia. Richmond Terrell Lacy was liberally educated and creditably won his degree, but he was endowed with versatile talents and later became equally proficient in the law. He subsequently embarked in law practice in New Kent County, became interested in politics, and in 1838 was elected a member of the Virginia State Legislature, in which he served several terms, his broad vision and sound judgment is legislation benefiting both his state and community. Richmond Terrell Lacy, the second, grew up in a desirable social environment and with liberal educational advantages. His early training was provided by tutors, as was a usual custom at that time, then he attended private schools of which his father approved, and when the war between the states came on he was completing his course in Washington College at Lexington, Virginia, now Washington and Lee University. He entered the Confederate army and served with recognized valor until the end of the conflict, then applied himself to the study of law and was admitted to the bar. He then went to Arkansas, where he taught school most acceptably for several years, after which he returned to New Kent County, Virginia, and began the practice of law, but shortly after was called into public life as commonwealth's attorney, in which responsible office he served continuously for eleven years. After retiring from office Mr. Lacy continued to practice his profession there until 1897, when he came to Richmond, where he maintained his office and carried on his professional duties until his death in 1903.

Mr. Lacy married on October 4, 1876, Miss Elizabeth Winston, a member of one of the old Colonial families of the state, and for many years her father was one of the leading merchants of Richmond. She is a daughter of John R. and Elizabeth P. T. (Fauntleroy) Winston, and was educated at Stuart Hall, Staunton Virginia, now the Virginia Female Institute. Five of their family of children survive: Richmond Terrell, who bears the honored name of both father and grandfather, has been a student of law in Richmond College, and is now assistant to the city attorney of Richmond and is a member of the Virginia State and the American Bar Associations. Samuel Winston, who attended Richmond College and received his law degree from George Washington University, Washington, D. C., was officially connected with the Government Insurance Bureau during the World war, and is now attorney for the Veterans Bureau. He married Miss Mary Allen, of Washington. Lelia Lyle is the wife of Verner C. Aurell, who is established in business at Richmond, and they have one daughter, Elizabeth Winston. Virginia Payne and Alice May both reside with their mother, in the old home on Harvie Street, Richmond.

During the whole period of his professional life Mr. Lacy commanded respect and confidence and he was widely known, for he was connected with well known and important cases before the courts. Unwavering in his loyalty to the Democratic party all his life, he took an active part in both state and national campaigns at times and was able to number among his personal and grateful friends some of the best known public men of his day.   He belonged to the Virginia State and the American Bar Associations, in both bodies having a wide professional acquaintance, among whom he found a large degree of appreciation.   He belonged to the Masonic fraternity for many years and was a member of the R. E. Lee Camp, Confederate Veterans.   Mr. Lacy to a noticeable degree possessed the old-time courtesy and dignified bearing that marked an earlier day, and he was unpretentious in manner despite his deep legal learning and intellectual superiority.   Together with his entire family he belonged to St. John's Episcopal Church at Richmond.

PROF. HERBERT D. WOLFF. A man of wide education, having a mind well stored with knowledge gained mainly by study, observation and experience, Prof. Herbert D. Wolff, principal of the Petersburg High School, is numbered among the more energetic and successful educators of Dinwiddie County, the pupils under his charge bearing visible evidence of his excellent physical and mental training, and also of the moral lessons inculcated in the every-day affairs of the pupils of any well conducted school. A son of Rev. James H. Wolff, he was born and bred in Springfield, West Virginia, the descendant of an early family of that section of the state.

His paternal grandfather, John Wolff, was as far as known a life long resident of Berkeley County, Virginia, which is now included within the limits of West Virginia. He had a vigorous constitution, and lived to a venerable age, passing away at his Virginia home at the age of four score and ten years. Of his four sons two of them became ministers, preaching the Gospel in the Methodist Episcopal Church, South.

Rev. James H. Wolff was born in Martinsburg, Berkeley County, West Virginia, and as a young boy united with the Methodist Episcopal Church, in this manner making a public profession of his religious faith. Having acquired a good education in the common branches of learning, he studied theology. When thoroughly fitted for the ministry he was ordained as a preacher at a Baltimore Conference, and subsequently held pastorates in different places. On his retirement from the pulpit he located in CharlesTown, West Virginia, where he resided until his death. He married Miss Selma Hout, who was born in Shepherdstown, West Virginia, a daughter of David and Ann (Miller) Hout. Two children blessed their marriage, Eldridge E., a well known physician of Cambridge, Maryland, and Herbert D., of whom we write.

After laying a wise foundation for his future education under private tutors Herbert D. Wolff attended first the public schools of Winchester, Virginia, later becoming a student in the Shenandoah Valley Academy, from which he was graduated with an excellent record for his scholarship. Entering then the University of Virginia, he was graduated from that institution with the class of 1900 and with the degrees of B. A. and M. A. Beginning his career as a teacher, he taught for a year in Strasburg, Virginia, the ensuing year being similarly employed in York, South Carolina. Going north, he taught for a year in Milwaukee, Wisconsin, after which he located in Berryville, Virginia, where he taught school until 1907. He subsequently taught for two years in a private school in Petersburg, Vir-

Hugo Erfurth Jr

ginia, and later in the Petersburg High School until 1913. Being then appointed principal of the Petersburg High School, Professor Wolff has since performed the duties falling upon him in this capacity in a highly efficient and satisfactory manner, having won the love and respect of his pupils and the confidence of their parents.

On December 23, 1903, Professor Wolff was united in marriage with Harriet Louise Lowry, who was born in York, South Carolina, a daughter of Ernest and Julia (Bratton) Lowry, and into their home two children have made their appearance, Herbert D., Jr., a student in medicine of the University of Virginia, class of 1929, and Louise Lowry, a student at the Randolph-Macon Woman's College at Lynchburg, Virginia, class 1932. Mrs. Wolff was formerly an Episcopalian, but now both she and the Professor are members of the Washington Street Methodist Episcopal Church, South. The Professor is secretary of the Appeal Board of the church. He is a past treasurer of the Virginia State Education Association, and vice president of the R. E. Lee Council, Boy Scouts, a position of importance and influence.

HUGO FREDERICK HERFURTH, JR., has recognized precedence as one of the most progressive and successful contractors and builders in his native city of Alexandria, where he conducts his substantial and important business under the title of H. Herfurth, Jr., Incorporated, and maintains his headquarters in the District National Bank Building, Washington, D. C.

Mr. Herfurth was born in Alexandria on the 16th of May, 1885, and is a son of Hugo and Martha R. (Steurnagaul) Herfurth, the former of whom was born in Germany and the latter of whom was born in New York City, of German parentage. Hugo Herfurth, Sr., was a boy when he accompanied his parents from Germany to the United States, where he was reared to manhood, and for fully fifty years he has been engaged in business at Alexandria as a manufacturer of cigars, both he and his wife being venerable and honored citizens of this community and both being earnest communicants of the Lutheran Church.

In the Alexandria High School Hugo Herfurth, Jr., was graduated as a member of the class of 1906, and his higher education along academic and professional lines was acquired in Georgetown University, from which he was graduated as a member of the law class of 1925 and received the degree of Bachelor of Laws. From this university he attended the classes at the National University and after effective post-graduate courses, he received the degrees of Bachelor of Arts, Master of Laws, Master of Patent Law, and Doctor of Juridicial Science. He has never engaged actively in the practice of law, but has found his technical knowledge of great value in his wonderfully successful career as a contractor and builder.

After his graduation from high school Mr. Herfurth attended classes of the Y. M. C. A. night school, taking a course of architectural draughting, and he initiated his business career by entering upon an apprenticeship to the carpenter's trade in the shops of the Southern Railway. He thus served four years, and thereafter he was associated with Harry Wardman, a leading contractor and substantial capitalist in the City of Washington, D. C., until 1909, when he engaged independently in business as a contractor and builder. Though he has continuously maintained his headquarters in Alexandria his contracting operations have been largely centered in the national capital, while they have been extended also to virtually all sections of Virginia. His operations as a contractor are constantly expanding in scope and importance.

The political convictions of Mr. Herfurth place him loyally in the ranks of the Democratic party. He is affiliated with the Sigma Delta Kappa college fraternity, and he and his wife are communicants of the Lutheran Church, in the faith of which he was reared. The family home is a beautiful place in George Washington Park.

June 30, 1915, marked the marriage of Mr. Herfurth and Miss Minnie F. Stubener, daughter of August William and Mary (Miller) Stubener, the former of whom was born in Germany and the latter in Washington, D. C. Mr. Stubener was reared and educated in his native land, and there became a cigar manufacturer, but upon coming to the United States he engaged in the meat-market business in Washington, D. C., where he continued in this enterprise until his death, he having passed away July 1, 1909, at the age of sixty-two years, and his widow being still a resident of Washington, in which she was born January 17, 1854. The names and respective birth dates of the children of Mr. and Mrs. Herfurth are here recorded: Helen Margaret, February 26, 1918; Dorothy Louise Charlotte, June 23, 1920; Irene Frances, December 4, 1921; and Hugo Frederick II, May 16, 1924.

THOMAS NELSON CARTER, who was an active member of the Richmond bar more than thirty-five years, represented a family that has contributed many men of mark and distinction to Virginia from Colonial times down to the present.

The late Mr. Carter was born June 13, 1858, in King William County, on Pampatike Plantation. That old plantation has had important historical associations since Colonial times. It belonged to the father of Thomas Nelson Carter, Col. Thomas H. Carter. The latter was a soldier of the Confederacy, and for many years was head commissioner of the Southern Railway and Steamship Association, and after he retired from business he performed the duties of proctor of the University of Virginia until his death. Colonel Carter married Susan Roy, of Mathews County, Virginia, daughter of William H. Roy.

Thomas Nelson Carter was the oldest of four children and grew up in King William County, attending the Pampatike Plantation school. He graduated in law from the University of Virginia with the class of 1881, and at once located in Richmond, where his abilities brought him a successful position at the bar, and he gave his time to his clients and his increasing volume of general law practice until a short time before his death. He died at Powhatan in Clark County August 8, 1917, when in his sixtieth year. He was a member of the Richmond Chamber of Commerce, the Virginia State and American Bar Associations, and the Country Club. He at one time was president of the Metropolitan Bank of Richmond.

The late Mr. Carter had two sisters and one brother, Juliet Gaines Carter, Anne Willing Carter and Spencer L. Carter. Juliet Gaines married Capt. Robert E. Lee, a Virginia planter and youngest son of Gen. Robert E. Lee. Captain and Mrs. Lee have two daughters. The older, Anne Carter Lee, is the wife of E. Hanson Elly, Jr., a son of Major General E. Hanson

Elly, U. S. Army, one of the distinguished officers of the American Army in the World war. Mr. and Mrs. Elly have two children, E. Henson III, and Anne Carter. The second daughter of Captain and Mrs. Lee, Mary Custis, is the wife of William Hunter de Butts and mother of a son, Robert Edwin Lee de Butts.

Anne Willing Carter married H. Rozier Dulany, of Washington, D. C., and Fauquier County, Virginia. They have three children, H. Rozier, Jr., who married Tollie Weems and has two children, named Juliet and Benjamin; Anne, who became the wife of Capt. Frank Hayne, of the United States Army; and Tom Carter Dulany, deceased.

Spencer Carter, who is vice president of the Virginia & Carolina Chemical Company, married Roberta Atkinson, and they have two children, Eda Atkinson Carter and Susan Roy Carter.

Thomas Nelson Carter married, December 1, 1887, Miss Agnes Atkinson Mayo, who resides in Richmond, at 205 West Franklin Street, and also has a country home at Boyce, Virginia. Mrs. Carter is a member of the Mayo family, one of the first established in the Virginia colony. Her parents were Peter H. and Isabella (Burwell) Mayo. Mrs. Carter was educated at Richmond and in the Patapsco Girls School in Maryland. She is a member of the Richmond Woman's Club, Country Club of Virginia, Colonial Dames of America, United Daughters of the Confederacy, the Virginia Historical Society and the Sulgrave Institute. Mrs. Carter has one daughter, Isabelle Burwell, who attended school at Richmond, also St. Timothy School at Catonsville, Maryland, and is now the wife of Douglas Crocker, associated with the paper mill industry at Fitchburg, Massachusetts. Mr. and Mrs. Crocker have three daughters, Agnes Carter, Constance Bartow and Isabelle Carter

MOSES D. HOGE, JR., was a physician and surgeon, practiced medicine at Richmond over thirty years, and is held in special honor for the efforts he put forth to build up sound standards of public health in the schools of his home city and state.

He was the son of an eminent Virginia clergyman, Moses D. Hoge, Sr., who was born September 17, 1819, son of Samuel Davies Wood Hoge and Elizabeth Lacy Wood. Rev. Doctor Hoge graduated from Hampden-Sidney College in 1839, attended Union Theological Seminary, was licensed to preach in 1844, and became assistant pastor of the First Presbyterian Church of Richmond. In January, 1845, he organized the Second Presbyterian Church, and he remained its beloved pastor forty years. He ran the blockade to England during the Civil war in order to obtain Bibles and other religious works for the Confederate army. For several years he was an associate editor of the Central Presbyterian. He declined the presidency of Hampden-Sidney College. He was regarded as the most eloquent pulpit orator in the Southern Presbyterian Church. Rev. Doctor Hoge married in 1844 Susan Morton Wood, and of their four children Moses D., Jr., was the fourth.

Moses D. Hoge, Jr., was educated at Hampden-Sidney College, studied medicine in the University of Virginia, and continued his professional training abroad at Heidelberg and Berlin, Germany, from 1883 to 1887. He began private practice in Richmond in 1888, and remained constant in his devotion to his private practice and his public duties until his death thirty-two years later. He served on the Richmond City Board of Health, for many years was physician to the school board, and for twenty years he held the chair of medicine in the University College of Medicine of Virginia. During the World war he was chief surgeon of the Richmond Reserve Corps. He has been called the father of health development bills put forward in the interests of Richmond schools. He was not only interested in proper medical supervision and a health standard and programs for the schools, but for other matters affecting the efficiency of local school work. He was a Democrat in politics, a member of the Westmoreland Club, and belonged to the Academy of Medicine of Richmond, the Virginia State and American Medical Associations. Doctor Hoge was one of the founders and the first physician of the Sheltering Arms Hospital.

Mrs. Hoge, who resides at 1512 West Avenue in Richmond, is a member of the Colonial Dames and Richmond Woman's Club. Doctor and Mrs. Hoge were married June 18, 1895. Her maiden name was Alice Page Aylett, and she was reared in King William County, attending school at Richmond. She was the fourth of the seven children of William Roane and Alice (Brockenbrough) Aylett. Her father for twenty-five years held the office of commonwealths attorney in King William County.

The Aylett family runs back into early Virginia Colonial history. She is a descendant of John Aylett, who came from Essex, England, and settled in Virginia in 1648, acquiring an estate called Fairfield through a land grant given by the King of England. After eight generations Fairfield is still in the Aylett family. Mrs. Hoge is a great-great-granddaughter of Patrick Henry, and two other notable ancestors were John West, Lord of Delaware, and Robert Carter, a Virginia colonist and member of the House of Burgesses.

Doctor and Mrs. Hoge had four children: Alice, wife of Edward Waller, who is with the Federal Reserve Bank at Richmond, and has one son, Edward Waller, Jr., Bessie is the wife of Ellis Brown, of the University of Virginia; William Aylett is a business man at Richmond; and Miss Susan R. is attending school.

WILLIAM HENRY VENABLE, a prominent Norfolk attorney, was born in Prince Edward County, Virginia, September 2, 1870. He is a descendant of Abram Venable, Sr., a native of England, who came to America about 1685 and settled in Virginia, and it is traditional that he was one of the two sons of Admiral Venable, of the British Navy, who came to America with William Penn. Abram Venable, Sr., had a son, Abram Venable, Jr., born in 1700—died 1768, who served as a captain in the Colonial Militia and as county lieutenant of Louisa County, Virginia, and for twenty years was a burgess from that county. His wife, Martha Davis, was of the same family from which descended Jefferson Davis, and was a granddaughter of the famous Indian Princess Nicketti.

Nathaniel Venable, born in 1733—died in 1804, son of Abram and Martha (Davis) Venable, was a planter in Prince Edward County, was burgess from 1766 to 1769, captain in the Revolutionary war and a justice of the peace of his county, and was in the House of Delegates, also in the Virginia Senate from 1780 to 1782. He is credited with having been the real founder of

Wm Mahone

Hampden-Sydney College. He married Elizabeth Woodson, daughter of Richard and Anne Madelin Michaux Woodson, of Huguenot descent, and a descendant of Dr. John Woodson, who came to Virginia in 1619 and was a physician to the first company of soldiers sent to protect the settlers.

Richard N. Venable, son of Nathaniel, was born January 16, 1763, at "Slate Hill," Prince Edward County, Virginia. He was a planter, lawyer, for many years a member of the Virginia Legislature, and a member of the Convention of 1829-30. He died in 1838. His wife, Mary Morton (1779-1839), was a daughter of Colonel William Morton, a distinguished officer in the Revolutionary war, and granddaughter of Joseph Morton, a surveyor, who was one of the organizers of Prince Edward County and later of Charlotte County, and commanded a regiment in the Revolutionary army.

William Henry Venable, 1st, a son of Richard N., born in 1798—died in 1856, was a Virginia planter, also a tobacconist. His wife, Margaret McDowell Reid (1798-1870), was descended from Andrew Reid and Ephraim McDowell, early Scotch-Irish settlers of the Valley of Virginia and among the organizers of Rockbridge County, Virginia.

Andrew Reid Venable, the next in line of descent, was born in 1830, died in 1913. He was an officer in the Confederate army during the war between the states. Later he was a planter and merchant in Prince Edward County, Virginia. He married Louisa Cabell Carrington, who was born April 30, 1837, and died January 17, 1902. She was a granddaughter of Gov. William H. Cabell and also a descendant of the famous family of Carringtons of Virginia.

William Henry Venable, the Norfolk attorney, son of Andrew Reid, graduated from Hampden-Sydney College with the A. B. degree in 1892, and took his law degree at the University of Maryland in 1894. Since that date he has practiced law at Norfolk, and was commonwealth attorney in 1900-02. He was on the Executive Committee for Home Defense during the World war, and president of the Norfolk Defense Council. Mr. Venable, besides a general practice, has been counsel for the Traction, Gas and Electric Light Companies of Norfolk and the Virginia Electric and Power Company since 1902. He is a member of the Norfolk and Virginia State Bar Association and American Bar Association. He married, November 15, 1899, Elizabeth Berkley Wight, of Richmond, who was born September 2, 1870, and died February 17, 1909. Mr. Venable has two children. The daughter, Louisa Carrington, born August 11, 1903, was married in 1924 to William Emmett Kyle, a Norfolk attorney, and they have two daughters, Louisa Venable and Elizabeth Wight Kyle. The son of Mr. Venable is William Wight Venable, born September 9, 1905, a law student in Washington and Lee University, Virginia.

GEN. WILLIAM MAHONE by his fighting qualities rose to the distinction of a major-generalship in the Confederate States Army. In the years after the war he was a storm center in state politics, leader of the readjustment movement and for six years represented Virginia in the United States Senate.

He was born at Monroe in Southampton County, Virginia, on December 1, 1826, descended from Irish ancestors who settled in Virginia in Colonial times. His father, Col. Fielding Jordan Mahone, was a merchant in Southampton County and commanded the county militia during the Nat Turner insurrection. Gen. William Mahone derived many of his intellectual characteristics from his cultured mother, Martha Drew, who was born in North Carolina.

He attended rural schools, getting part of his education under his father, and then entered the Virginia Military Institute, from which he was graduated in 1847. After graduating he taught for two years in the Rappahannock Military Academy, following which he engaged in his profession as a civil engineer. He was engaged in the locating, surveying and construction of several new railroads in the state, including the Orange & Alexandria and the Norfolk & Petersburg. He displayed some of the highest qualities of an engineer in building the Norfolk & Petersburg, overcoming obstacles regarded up to that time as insuperable. When completed it was the straightest and firmest piece of railroad construction in the country. General Mahone was elected president of the company and soon began planning a consolidation of railroad lines that would give an efficient system of transportation between the mountain boundary at Bristol, Tennessee, and the seaport at Norfolk.

As soon as the war broke out he was made lieutenant colonel of the Sixth Virginia Regiment, taking part in the capture of the Norfolk Navy Yard in April, 1861. He had command of the defense of the James River, and from Seven Pines to Appomattox was one of Lee's most trusted generals. Lee appointed him to lead the successful flank movement at the battle of the Wilderness, and General Lee regarded him as second only to Stonewall Jackson as a fighting commander. He was promoted to brigadier-general, commanding what became famous as Mahone's brigade, and on account of his brilliant repulse of the Federals at Petersburg he was given the sobriquet "Hero of the Crater," and General Lee promoted him on the field, raising him to the rank of major-general. He and General Longstreet were the only general officers consulted by Lee at the council preceding the surrender at Appomattox. The following quotation may well serve as an index to the high place William Mahone held in the regard of General Lee:

"Hotel Chamberlin,
"McPherson Square.

"Washington, D. C., March 11th, 1889.

"My dear General:

"It gives me great pleasure to hand to you a written statement of a conversation at the table of Gen. R. E. Lee which years ago I stated to your wife, yourself and some twenty gentlemen at your table. The occasion was the first commencement of Washington and Lee University. Gen'l Wade Hampton delivered the address before the Literary Societies and I the address before the Alumni. Gen'l Lee gave a sort of state dinner, thirty gentlemen, I think I was the only officer at the table below the rank of colonel, and the honor was accorded to me because I was the orator of the day. After the cloth was drawn and the wine began to circulate, some gentleman, a Brigadier from Georgia, I think it was Gen'l Jackson, from the lower end of the table asked Gen'l Lee if he did not think that Gordon of Georgia had developed the highest qualities for command. Gen'l with his habitual quiet dignity replied, 'When all did so well certainly it would be invidious and improper for me to particularize. Gen'l Gordon was a brave and efficient soldier.' Then rising he said, 'Gentlemen, fill up your glasses, etiquette demanded that his official dinner should be made in accordance with rank, Gentlemen I propose a toast which all will drink with pleasure to the privates of the Army of Northern Virginia who I still sometime think came near winning immortal fame for us. The toast was drunk standing. After this the conversation became general and some one down the table seemed to be telling a good story. Gen'l Hampton sat on the right and I as an orator of day on left of Lee. Turning to Hampton Gen'l Lee said something in a low tone, I leaned back as I thought it was possible it might be something confidential. Laying his hand upon my knee he said lean over Major I only wish Hampton and yourself to hear. Then 'Gen'l Hampton in the dark days which preceded the fall of the Confederacy, for a good while I was almost hopeless, and you know I did not spare this poor life, for I thought it became me to fall on one of those fields of glory. My artillery was handled well, the cavalry was in the very hands, after the death of Stuart that I preferred to any other. But I often thought if a stray ball should carry me off who could best command the incomparable Infantry of the Army of Northern Virginia. Of course I could not nominate a successor that whole matter was in the hands of the President. But among the younger men I thought William Mahone had developed the highest quality for organization and command.

"The words were written down by me that evening and are in my desk at Ellwood. I write them now hastily in a public room. But I know they are accurate. We drifted so far apart politically and I so entirely condemned your policy and methods that I would not give them to the world. Now I cheerfully write them and as far as I am concerned this may be an open letter to the world.

"Very truly yours,
"I. HORACE LACY.

"To General William Mahone."

In the closing days of the war General Mahone had also been elected a member of the Virginia State Senate. After the war he gave his time to the rehabilitation of his railroads, becoming president of two companies and building up a transportation system from Petersburg to Bristol. He finally succeeded in having the Legislature confirm the consolidation of several lines into one as the Atlantic, Mississippi & Ohio Company. During the financial panic of 1873 this company was thrown into a receivership for the benefit of its outside creditors, chiefly English capitalists, and the property was eventually sold and reorganized as the Norfolk & Western Railroad Company. However, General Mahone managed to effect a contract with the purchasers whereby they were to pay the State of Virginia a half million dollars for her claims on the road, and also pay labor and supply claims and give the stockholders share for share in the new company. Out of the half million dollar fund thus provided the Legislature set aside a hundred thousand dollars for the building of the Colored Normal Institute at Petersburg, while the remainder was paid to the account of the free schools.

General Mahone had been drawn into state politics in 1869, engineering the organization of the "True Republican" ticket and the compromised platform of that party. The gravest question confronting the state government for years after the close of the formal reconstruction era was the settlement of the state debt. The funding bill passed in 1871 authorized the issue of bonds with tax-receivable interest coupons. General Mahone and his followers were bitterly opposed to this funding measure, obligating Virginia with a staggering debt, which among other results practically nullified the provisions for a free school system made by the same Legislature. This was the origin of the readjuster movement, as opposed to the party of funders, and by 1879 General Mahone and his followers inflicted a complete defeat on the regular Democratic party, known as funders. The Legislature had a readjuster majority in both branches and in 1880 General Mahone was elected to the United States Senate, taking his seat March 4, 1881. He was in the Senate until 1887. As one of the bravest soldiers of the Confederacy he had not been identified with the Northern Republican party in the reconstruction movement, but in 1881 his vote was the decisive ballot in saving the Senate to the Republican party and the administration, and thereafter his formal allegiance was with the National Republican party. Under General Mahone's leadership in 1881 a Republican governor, lieutenant governor and attorney general were elected in Virginia, and the Legislature was Republican in both branches. In 1883 the Republican regime in the state was overthrown. General Mahone was head of the delegation from Virginia at the National Republican Convention at Chicago in 1884, and was again the delegate of his party in the convention of 1888. He was nominated for the office of governor in 1889.

In his later years General Mahone concerned himself chiefly with business enterprises. He died at Washington City October 8, 1895.

He married Otelia Butler, who was born at Smithfield, Isle of Wight County, Virginia, daughter of Dr. Robert and Otelia (Voinard) Butler. Her father at one time was state treasurer of Virginia. Her mother was a daughter of Jacob Voinard, who came to America with General LaFayette and was a soldier on the Colonial side in the war for independence, subsequently settling at Petersburg, where he engaged in the tobacco business. General and Mrs. Mahone had three children: William, Otelia (who married W. L. McGill) and Henry Peabody Mahone.

WILLIAM L. McGILL is the active head of one of the oldest tobacco companies of Petersburg, a business that was established more than a century ago.

He was born at Petersburg, son of John McGill, Jr., and grandson of John McGill, Sr. His grandfather was a native of Ayr, Scotland, was reared and educated there and for several years was manager of a ship building plant on the River Clyde. On account of ill health he was obliged to resign his responsible work, and coming to America, located as a pioneer in Whitby Township, Whitby County, Ontario, Canada. He acquired a large tract of timbered land and for many years was busy with the task of superintending its clearing and improvement. He lived there as a farmer and stock raiser the rest of his life. His wife was Dorothy Leslie, who was born in Wigtonshire, Scotland. Both grandparents lived to be upwards of eighty years of age. They reared four children, Robert Leslie, John, William and Dorothy.

John McGill, Jr., was born in Whitby Township, Whitby County, Ontario, was well educated, and when sixteen years of age came to Petersburg, Virginia, to enter the employ of his uncle, who in 1818 had established a tobacco business which has enjoyed uninterrupted growth and service ever since, a period of 110 years. It is now the Maclin-Zimmer-McGill Tobacco Company. John McGill, Jr., acquired an interest in the firm and spent the rest of his life in Petersburg, one of the leading tobacco manufacturers of that city. He died at the age of eighty-eight. John McGill, Jr., married Helen Leavenworth, who was born at Charlotte, North Carolina, daughter of Abner J. and Elizabeth (Peabody) Leavenworth. Her father was born at Waterbury, Connecticut, of early Colonial ancestry, and was a Presbyterian minister. Her mother was born at Salem, Massachusetts, member of the well known Peabody family. Mrs. Helen McGill died at the age of seventy-eight.

William L. McGill was one of nine children and in early youth attended the McCabe School for Boys at Petersburg. He was sent abroad to Scotland, where he was a student in the Stanley House Academy at Bridge of Allen, and also studied in Hanover, Germany. In 1887 he returned home, spent two sessions in the University of Virginia, following which he became an active associate of his father in the tobacco business. He has been a figure in the tobacco industry of Petersburg nearly forty years and eventually became president of the Maclin-Zimmer-McGill Tobacco Company.

Mr. McGill married in 1895 Otelia Mahone, daughter of Gen. William and Otelia Butler Mahone. They reared three children: William Mahone McGill, Otelia Butler and Henry Peabody. The son Henry Peabody married Elizabeth Lester. Otelia married R. Mann Page. William married Mattie Strode Hover.

WILLIAM MAHONE III, division engineer of the Atlantic Coast Line Railway, with headquarters at Petersburg, is a grandson of the distinguished Virginia soldier and statesmen, Gen. William Mahone, whose record is published elsewhere.

William Mahone III was born at Petersburg, son of William Mahone, Jr., who was born at Petersburg in 1857. He was educated in the University of Virginia and for ten years was engaged in the tobacco business at Petersburg. He then removed to Norfolk to take a position with the Norfolk & Western Railway, and after resigning was appointed collector of customs at Lynchburg. Later he was appointed collector of customs at Petersburg by President McKinley and was reappointed by President Roosevelt. He served in that capacity until 1910, when he became deputy clerk of the Federal Court and United States commissioner at Norfolk, and was engaged in those official duties until his death on September 20, 1927. William Mahone II married Mary Tannor, who was born at Petersburg, daughter of John and Mary Ann (Rowlett) Tannor. Mrs. Mahone resides at Norfolk. She is the mother of three children: William; Marion, who married Rosalie Harrison and has two children, named Rosalie and Beverly Randolph Harrison; and Marie, wife of Harry Finch and mother of a daughter, Marie Elizabeth.

William Mahone III attended a private school at Lynchburg, prepared for college in the Petersburg Academy and was graduated in 1904 from the Virginia Military Institute. He has reached high positions as a railroad engineer. As a civil engineer he was with the Norfolk & Western Railroad for several years, later with the A., B. & A. Railroad Company and the Norfolk & Southern, and since 1927 has been a division engineer with the Atlantic Coast Line Railway. He is a member of the American Society of Civil Engineers, the Kappa Alpha college fraternity, and he and his wife are members of St. Paul's Episcopal Church. Mrs. Mahone is a member of the Daughters of the American Revolution.

He married, in 1916, Mary Isabelle Armistead, in Halifax County, at Dalkirk. Mrs. Mahone is a daughter of Edward Winston and Annie (Hobson) Armistead, and a granddaughter of William Harrison Armistead, who married Sarah Henry, a daughter of Winston Henry, who was the youngest son of Patrick Henry, Virginia's great orator, governor and statesman. Her father, Edward Winston Armistead, was an attorney and judge of the Circuit Court of Halifax County. Mr. and Mrs. Mahone have two children, Mary Armistead and William Mahone IV.

JAMES GORDON BOHANNAN, Petersburg attorney, former mayor of that city, who has served his community and state ably in various positions, was born in Surry County, Virginia, son of Aurelius P. Bohannan, a native of Portsmouth, grandson of George William Bohannan, a native of Matthews County. George William Bohannan was a son of John Gordon Bohannan, grandson of William Bohannan, and great-grandson of Ambrose Bohannan, all of whom were probably lifelong residents of Matthews County. George William Bohannan was a civil engineer and surveyor in Matthews County. He married Lucy Deal, daughter of Jarvis and Joicy (Hundley) Deal. Aurelius P. Bohannan left school to enter the Confederate army in Company D, Tenth Virginia Battalion, later was commissioned a lieutenant, and at the battle of Sailors Creek was captured and was a prisoner on Johnson's Island in Lake Erie until paroled after the final surrender. He was a merchant in Surry County and later elected county treasurer, an office he held until his death in 1905. He married Anna V. Deal, who was born in Isle of Wight County, daughter of James Hundley and Eliza Ann (Wilson) Deal, and granddaughter of Jarvis and Joicy (Hundley) Deal. Eliza Ann Wilson was a daughter of William and Sarah (Delk) Wilson, granddaughter of Willis and Sarah (Blunt) Wilson, Willis Wilson being a son of Sampson and Sarah Wilson. Mrs. Aurelius Bohannan died in 1908, mother of three children, Aurelius Wilson, James Gordon and Anna Eloise, who married Henry Galusha.

James Gordon Bohannan attended public schools in Surry County, graduated from William and Mary College with the degrees of Licentiate of Instruction and B. A., and after two years in the University of Virginia graduated with the degree Bachelor of Laws. He taught two years in Surry County, was instructor in the Model and Practice School Department of William and Mary College one year, and also taught a year in Smithfield. He was admitted to practice law in 1905 and began his professional career in Surry County, being elected and serving as commonwealth attorney until 1912. Since that year his home has been at Petersburg. He served as chairman of the Democratic County Committee of Surry County, has been a member of the Petersburg City Council, was elected mayor in 1926, and for several years was a member of the Hampton Roads Port

Commission and later chairman of the State Port Authority. He has also served as president of the Petersburg Chamber of Commerce and the Virginia State Chamber of Commerce, was one of the presidential electors of 1912, voting for Woodrow Wilson, is a member of the Pi Kappa Alpha, Phi Delta Phi, Phi Beta Kappa, and of the Masonic fraternity.

He married in 1909 Elizabeth Lamb, who was born in James City County, daughter of William Beverly and Katherine Stanard (Branch) Lamb. She died in 1924. Mr. Bohannan is a member of the vestry of St. Paul's Episcopal Church of Petersburg and is a director in the National Bank of Petersburg.

JAMES TASKER JONES, M. D. The career of Dr. James T. Jones, one of the capable and kindly physicians and surgeons of long standing at Herndon, has been filled with able achievements and faithful discharge of the responsibilities of his profession. From the time that he entered upon the practice of his chosen calling, in young manhood, he has been conscientious in the performance of what he has considered his duty to humanity, and his reward has not only been of a material character but of the kind embodied in the confidence and faith of those who have been the recipients of his ministrations.

Doctor Jones was born in Westmoreland County, Virginia, July 15, 1861, and is a son of Lindsay and Annie (Lewis) Jones, natives of the same county. His father, a sea captain, followed that calling throughout his life and died in February, 1875, when only forty-five years of age, while his mother survived until 1907 and was seventy years of age at the time of her demise.

James T. Jones received his early education in private schools and high schools in Maryland and the District of Columbia, following which he entered George Washington University and was graduated from that institution as a member of the class of 1893, receiving the degree of Doctor of Medicine. The next two years were spent in post-graduate work in New York, and in 1896 he commenced practice in Loudoun County, Virginia, where he remained until 1919. Since the latter year he has carried on his professional work at Herndon, where he has built up a large and representative practice. Doctor Jones is familiar with all branches of his vocation and therefore carries on a general practice in medicine and surgery without engaging in specialization. He is a constant student and keeps in touch with the discoveries and advancements made in his profession, both by reading and by membership in the Virginia State Medical Society, the Northern Virginia Medical Society, District of Columbia and Maryland Medical Society and Fairfax Medical Society. During the World war he was on the reserve list of the United States Medical Corps. He is a Presbyterian in his religious faith and while a resident of Loudoun served for twelve years as superintendent of the Sunday school. He takes a prominent part in all movements affecting the welfare and health of the community, and is an active supporter of worthy civic enterprises.

Doctor Jones was united in marriage with Miss Mary Towner, a daughter of C. J. Towner, a native of Loudoun County, Virginia. Mr. Towner, who was in the employ of the United States Government during the greater part of his life, died in 1925, Mrs. Towner having passed away in 1903. To Doctor and Mrs. Jones there were born two children, of whom one survives, Towner Francis, born February 13, 1897, who was a member of the Red Cross unit during the World war, and is now connected with the United States Emigration Service at New York City. Mrs. Jones died August 11, 1898, and June 13, 1901, Doctor Jones married Minnie Francis Johnston, a daughter of James and Minnie (Francis) Johnston, natives of Loudoun County. Mr. Johnston was a soldier of the Confederacy during the war between the states, following which he was engaged in farming for many years, and finally retired in 1902 and took up his residence at Washington, D. C., where his death occurred in 1926, when he had reached the advanced age of ninety-three years. Mrs. Johnston had passed away in 1915, when eighty years of age. Three children have been born to Doctor and Mrs. Jones: Irma Rowena, born June 25, 1902, who is secretary of the Public Service Company of St. Petersburg, Florida; Egbert Johnston, born February 16, 1904, who died August 4, 1913; and Mary Elaine, born August 12, 1908.

MORTON GRAHAM GOODE is senior member of the firm Goode & Barrow, attorneys and counsellors at law at Dinwiddie. Mr. Goode has practiced law with distinguished success and honor and has rendered practically a coincident service in public capacities, being former commonwealth's attorney and for several sessions a member of the Virginia State Senate.

He was born in Mecklenburg County, Virginia, June 29, 1886, son of Col. J. Thomas and Bessie (Morton) Goode, his father a native of Mecklenburg County and his mother of Charlotte County. Col. J. Thomas Goode entered the Confederate army with the Thirty-fourth Virginia Regiment, and had a distinguished military record. He was a cadet at the Virginia Military Institute when General Jackson was an instructor there. On graduating from the institute he was commissioned a lieutenant in the United States Regular Army and served several years, resigning his commission to join the Confederate forces, and in the last year of the war commanded a brigade, the famous organization known as Wise's Brigade. After the war he was a farmer and planter in Mecklenburg County, and he served two terms as a member of the General Assembly. Colonel Goode died April 3, 1916, at the age of eighty-one. He was born in 1835. His wife died in 1891.

Morton G. Goode was reared and educated in Mecklenburg County, attending public schools, the old Fredericksburg College, and graduated LL. B. from the University of Virginia in 1910. In the same year he began practice at Dinwiddie, and is one of the ablest lawyers of the county. In 1911 he was elected commonwealth's attorney, filling that office ten years. He resigned, having in the fall of 1920 been elected a member of the State Senate, and he served until the fall of 1927.

Mr. Goode married, April 23, 1912, Miss Lucy Barnes Homes, daughter of Judge William E. and Sarah Elizabeth Marshall (Puryear) Homes. Her parents were born in Mecklenburg County. Her father was a lawyer, was judge of the local court of Mecklenburg County, and died November 18, 1913, while her mother passed away January 6, 1928. Mr. and Mrs. Goode have four children: Lucy Marshall, born January 20, 1913; Bessie Morton, born January 11, 1915; Sarah Massie, born March 3, 1923; and Caroline Osborne, born August 15, 1925.

Mr. Goode was Democratic elector for the Fourth Congressional District in 1924. He owns farming interests, is a member of the Virginia Bar Association, is a past master of the Masonic Lodge, member of the Royal Arch Chapter at Petersburg, Appo-

mattox Commandery at Petersburg, and Acca Temple of the
Mystic Shrine at Richmond. He belongs to the Phi Gamma
Delta, the University Club at Richmond, and during the World
war was a member of the Legal Advisory Board at Petersburg
and chairman of the local Red Cross. He is a vestryman in the
Episcopal Church at Dinwiddie.

ROBERT MAYO ANDERSON, M. D. Prominent among the
earlier physicians of Dinwiddie County was Robert Mayo Anderson, M. D., who established a large practice, which he maintained until his death. A native of the county, he was born on
a large plantation, being a son of John W. Anderson.

A true Virginian gentleman of the old school, John W.
Anderson was a life long resident of Dinwiddie County, and one
of its extensive land owners. He married a Miss Harrison, and
managed the home estate, which is still in the possession of the
Anderson family, carrying on the farm with the aid of his slaves.

Robert Mayo Anderson, M. D., was prepared for college
under private tutorship, and later received the degree of M. D.
at Jefferson Medical College in Philadelphia. Immediately locating in Petersburg, he built up a good practice in that section
of the county. Like many another good citizen he met with
financial reverses, but he never lost his courage, and never made
complaint, bearing his many losses with heroic fortitude. He
bought and for several years occupied the estate at 109 South
Adams Street, where Mr. and Mrs. J. O. Barham are now living.

This mansion is very advantageously located, while its finish-
ings and furnishings are the pride not only of the family but of
the country roundabout. The two mantles in the house are hand
carved, and the stair railing, with its beautiful newel post, is of
solid mahogany. During the battle at the Crater fragments of
shell penetrated the house, and the scars are yet visible. The
house is beautifully furnished with heavy pieces of mahogany
and teakwood that add much to its value and interest. It was
in this celebrated house that the body of Henry Clay laid in
state while en route from Washington, D. C., to his home in
Lexington, Kentucky. Of the children born of the marriage of
Doctor and Mrs. Anderson, Mrs. J. O. Barham outlived all of
the others.

JOHN O. BARHAM. A lineal descendant, many generations
removed, four brothers who immigrated from England, one
dying on shipboard, to the United States in 1620, settling in
Virginia, John O. Barham, of Petersburg, is now living retired
from active pursuits, enjoying at his leisure the well deserved
fruits of his former years of labor and thrift. A son of Timothy
Barham, he was born on a Virginia plantation in Southampton
County, where he grew to manhood.

The Barham family have long held a place of prominence
in England, especially in social and naval circles. One Lord
Barham was an admiral in the Royal Navy, and from that day
to this there has always been a "Barham" in that branch of
the service and there has always been a gunboat named *Barham*
in the British navy. It is a matter of record that Sir Walter
Scott made a cruise on a gunboat named *Barham* in the Mediterranean Sea in search of health. One of the family, Sir Walter
Barham, having been taken seriously ill, was permitted to cruise
on the Mediterranean in a ship bearing the name *Barham*. Mr.
Barham's paternal grandfather, John Barham, was an extensive
landholder, operating his large plantation with slave labor.

Timothy Barham inherited a part of his father's estate, and subsequently, aided by his slaves, was for several years engaged in agricultural pursuits. Late in life he removed to Greensville County, where he lived retired until his death, at the age of sixty-two years. His wife, whose maiden name was Clarinda Lewton, belonged to one of the early families of Virginia. She died at the early age of thirty-five years. Of the children born of their union three grew to years of maturity, namely: Mollie, Fannie and John O., of whom we write.

Born on the home plantation in Southampton County, Virginia, John O. Barham acquired an excellent education in his youthful days, and at the age of sixteen years began his active career, for two years thereafter being bookkeeper in a local sawmill. The three ensuing years he was assistant revenue collector and deputy sheriff of Greensville County. Accepting then a position as clerk in the general store of J. F. Kull & Son, he remained with that firm three years. Entering then the employ of David Drake & Company, he became much interested in the business, and in three years became a member of the firm, and after another three years assumed the entire charge of the business, which he conducted most successfully until 1910, when he retired from work to enjoy a few years of freedom from business responsibilities.

Mr. Barham married, in 1896, Miss Lula B. Anderson, who was born in Petersburg, Virginia, a daughter of Dr. Robert Mayo Anderson, of whom a brief sketch may be found elsewhere in this volume. Mr. and Mrs. Barham occupy one of the most historic houses in Petersburg, a short account of which is also given in the sketch just alluded to. Mr. and Mrs. Barham are active members of Christ Episcopal Church, and are held in high esteem by their neighbors and friends.

CHARLES WOOLFOLK COLEMAN, of Portsmouth, has been a member of the Virginia bar since 1892, and for fifteen years has been on the bench as judge of the First Judicial Circuit.

The Coleman family have lived in Carolina County, Virginia, since Colonial times, and Judge Coleman's ancestors in the maternal line include prominent families of Southwestern Virginia, including the Edmondsons and Buchanans. Judge Coleman was born in Caroline County, son of Charles Woolfolk and Mary Graham (Gardner) Coleman. Judge Coleman was educated in the private classical school of E. G. Gwathway in Hanover County, graduated Master of Arts at Richmond College, also attended the University of Virginia and is one of many prominent lawyers who rejoice in the distinction of having been students of that master of the science of jurisprudence, John B. Minor, of the University of Virginia. Judge Coleman taught school for several years, being for a time head master of the Church and Academy of Norfolk County. He was admitted to the bar in 1892, and for twenty years gave his undivided attention to the demands of a large general law practice. He was elected judge of the First Judicial District in 1913, and has made a most enviable record in this court.

Judge Coleman in 1910 was president of the Norfolk and Portsmouth Bar Association. He is a member of the Virginia Bar Association. He married in 1891 Miss Virginia Griffin, daughter of John Thomas and Julia A. (Benn) Griffin. Her father graduated from George Washington University in 1859, taught in Columbia College in New York and received his Master of Arts degree there in 1860. He was an assistant engineer

H. Careton Hames.

in the Confederate army during the war between the states, and in 1866 was elected county surveyor of Nansemond County. In 1871 he became president of the Western Branch Bridge Company, president of the Norfolk Storage Company in 1884, and in 1885 president of the Merchants and Farmers Bank of Portsmouth, and was also president of the Southern Produce Company of Norfolk.

Judge and Mrs. Coleman have one daughter, Julia G., who married Edward T. White.

HON. H. EARLTON HANES. Many have passed of the old time lawyers who gave Herndon and Fairfax County a standing at the state bar. They were men of strong, sometimes stern, characters, and were not specialists even in the sense of confining themselvs to their profession, for, whatever their regular vocation, the greedy, growing community would have the services of its best men. As a municipality it had not been brought into any sort of a clear order, so that each capable citizen, who loved it and took a pride in its achievements, was ordered to report to various assigned duties connected with its public, social, educational, religious and other duties. H. Earlton Hanes is a soldier of the Old Guard and has never been a closet lawyer, for although his profession for twenty-three years has felt the beneficial interest of his acts and service, he has been liberal in the donations of his energy, ability and wise counsel to the uplifting forces of education and good citizenship. He is now serving his county in the House of Delegates, and has shown his faith both by the enthusiasm and firmness of his spirit and by the multitude of his good works.

Mr. Hanes was born at Ashburn, Loudoun County, Virginia, January 1, 1871, and is a son of George W. and Gertrude (Sheid) Hanes, natives of the same county. George W. Hanes was only fifteen years of age when he enlisted for service in the Confederate army during the war between the states, and was with Mosby's cavalry for six months and with the infantry division for two years. At the close of the war he completed learning the trade of blacksmith, and during the remainder of his life operated a shop at Ashburn, where his death occurred February 3, 1919. Mrs. Hanes still survives and is a resident of Ashburn.

The early education of H. Earlton Hanes was acquired in the public schools of Ashburn, following which he learned the trade of blacksmith under his father's guidance. This did not appeal to him as a life vocation, however, and after one year he applied himself to a mastery of the telegrapher's art, at which he worked during the summer months while teaching school in the winter terms. He continued to be thus engaged until 1898, and during the last five years was principal of the Herndon High School, where he taught English, mathematics, Latin, French and German, without ever having had a lesson in any of these subjects himself. He also taught Latin and mathematics at Eastern View Academy, Culpeper, Virginia, and in 1892 and 1893 conducted a business college at that place, teaching stenography, bookkeeping and other business branches. In 1898, during the Spanish-American war, Mr. Hanes enlisted for service in the United States Navy, and became a clerk at the Navy Yard at Norfolk. In the fall of the same year he was transferred to South Boston, Massachusetts, as stenographer for the naval constructor who was building two torpedo boats, Blakeley and DeLong, and after passing an examination in mechanical engineering and ship draftsmanship was sent to Boston as a mechanical enginer at the Navy Yard. At this examination there were fifteen in the class, many of them graduates of prominent colleges who had been mechanical engineers for several years, but the examination was so difficult that only two were able to pass. Mr. Hanes, in 1903, went to the Navy Department at Washington, D. C., where he drew the sail plans for several reproductions of old-time war vessels, being the only man able to accomplish this work. In the meantime he applied himself to the study of law at George Washington University, from which he was graduated in 1905 with the degree of Bachelor of Laws. In the following year he began the practice of law at Washington, where he has since carried on a large professional business, his present offices being at 246 Woodward Building, Washington, and at Herndon, Virginia.

In 1925 Mr. Hanes was sent by his county, Fairfax, as a representative to the General Assembly of Virginia, and was reelected in 1927 by an overwhelming vote of over two to one against well organized opposition. He is one of the representatives of Governor Byrd on the Virginia Park and Planning Commission, and a member of the State Audit Committee. In 1917 Mr. Hanes was the Democratic candidate for Congress of his district, but was defeated by C. C. Carlin, of Alexandria; in 1918 he again was a candidate and was defeated by R. Walton Moore, and in 1928 again made the race in the Democratic primary. Mr. Hanes is a member of the Virginia Bar Association. He is a thirty-second degree Mason and member of Acca Temple, A. A. O. N. M. S., and belongs to the Improved Order of Red Men, Knights of Pythias and Fraternal Americans, and is an honorary member of the auxiliary bodies, including the Pocahontas Auxiliary of the Red Men, the Order of the Eastern Star and the Daughters of the American Revolution. An active member of the Baptist Church, he is teacher of the Socii Class of boys and girls in the Sunday school, where he has taught for thirty years, and is vice president and former president of the Fairfax County Sunday School Association.

On October 5, 1892, Mr. Hanes married Miss Annie Blanche Fitz-Hugh, daughter of W. D. and Betty (Grayson) Fitz-Hugh, of Culpeper County, where Mr. Fitz-Hugh passed his entire life in agricultural pursuits. Three children have been born to Mr. and Mrs. Hanes: Harold F., born September 19, 1897, a graduate of George Washington University, who is engaged in the practice of law; Stanley Bartlett, born July 24, 1904, also a graduate of that institution and a practicing attorney; and Grayson Bland, born March 4, 1909, who is pursuing a course in civil engineering at George Washington University. Mrs. Hanes, who was born in Culpeper County, is active in club and social life at Washington and Herndon. She is a member of the Society of Colonial Dames and the Daughters of the American Revolution. She is a direct descendant of Richard Parks Bland, a first cousin of Admiral Grayson, U. S. N., and a descendant of George Mason.

CHARLES E. WHITLOCK, a native of Richmond, came to manhood after the war and reconstruction, and during the last quarter of the nineteenth century was a prominent figure in the lumber business of the Southeast.

He was born at Richmond in 1850 and died in that city in 1903. His father for many years was in the lumber industry in Virginia, and the son after attending a private school in

Richmond took up the same line of work, and in it found the business that satisfied his ambition for practical achievement and success. He extended his interests to other business organizations, and at one time was president of the Planters Bank of Richmond. He was a member of the American Bankers Association, the Westmoreland Club, was a Democrat and a member of the Episcopal Church.

Mr. Whitlock married in 1897 Miss Elizabeth B. Aiken, who survives him and resides in Richmond, at 820 West Franklin Avenue. She is a daughter of Albert N. and Elizabeth W. (Fraser) Aiken, both the Frasers and Aikens having been in Virginia since Colonial times. Her father was a Virginia planter. Mrs. Whitlock had three children, the only son, Charles E., being deceased. The daughter Elizabeth is the wife of Capt. F. G. Bird, of London, and had seven children, named Elizabeth, Charles, Fred G., Chase, Edward, Betty B. and Harold. Lulie W. Whitlock is the wife of Doctor G. Freeland, and they have one child.

WILLIAM BENJAMIN GATES, an educator of many years' experience, is president of one of the most distinctive schools for women in the state, Blackstone College for Girls.

Mr. Gates was born in Nelson County, Virginia, August 23, 1877. His father was Rev. James E. Gates, widely known throughout the Virginia Conference as a Methodist minister and educator. Rev. James E. Gates was born in Chesterfield County, Virginia, and married Pattie Prior Goodwin, a native of Nelson County. He was with the Confederate army during the Civil war as chaplain of a regiment. For thirteen years before he was ordained to the ministry he was principal of the Lancasterian Academy at Richmond. He had an important part in establishing one or two churches of his denomination at Richmond and was pastor of churches in many other localities. He died after a long life of labor and devotion in April, 1907, at the age of eighty-two, and his wife passed away in May, 1922.

William Benjamin Gates was educated in public schools, graduated in 1897 from Randolph-Macon Academy at Bedford, and spent the following four years in Randolph-Macon College at Ashland. He was awarded the A. B. degree in 1901 and the Master of Arts degree in 1902, and also did a year of postgraduate work in the University of Virginia. Mr. Gates for one year taught in the Millersburg Military Institute at Millersburg, Kentucky, and after returning to Virginia was principal of the Suffolk High School three years, principal of the high school at Martinsville eight years, and for nine years division superintendent at Martinsville, in Henry County.

Mr. Gates came to the Blackstone College for Girls in 1924, serving as dean and vice president two years, and since 1926 has been president of the institution. This college is conducted under the auspices of the Virginia Conference of its Methodist Episcopal Church, South. It was established in 1894, and has enrolled over seven thousand students, and its standards and facilities have steadily kept apace with the increasing efficiency of schools of this class in recent years.

Mr. Gates married in June, 1902, Miss Fannie Robbins Ladew, daughter of Harvey S. and Rebecca Henderson (Robbins) Ladew. Her father was born in New York and her mother in Maryland. Her father is a retired contractor now living at Ashland, Virginia. Mr. and Mrs. Gates have five children: Fannie Goodwin, who is the French instructor in the Blackstone

College for Girls; William Benjamin, Jr., member of the class of 1929 in Randolph-Macon College at Ashland; Anna Magruder, a student in the Blackstone College for Girls; Marjorie Nelson, attending public school; and Robbins Ladew, who was born in 1922.

During the years he lived at Martinsville, Mr. Gates was president of the Red Cross and chairman of the Safety Committee during the World war. He is president of the Park View Real Estate Company, Incorporated, of Martinsville. He is a member of the Masonic Lodge, Royal Arch Chapter, Pi Gamma Mu and Phi Kappa Sigma college fraternities, Rotary Club and the Blackstone Golf Club. He is a Democrat, and is an active Methodist, serving as superintendent in the college Sunday school

JAMES GRAY MCCANDLISH was a Petersburg business man, lived most of his life in that city, and his family have been well known in Dinwiddie County for a number of generations.

Mr. McCandlish was born in Richmond, Virginia, April 12, 1854, son of Robert McCandlish, a native of James City County, Virginia, and grandson of William and Polly (Taliaferro) McCandlish. Robert McCandlish was educated in William and Mary College, lived in Richmond several years, was a business man of Petersburg, but spent his last days at Williamsburg. He married Ella Gray, a native of Richmond, of Colonial ancestry. She died in 1876. They had a family of four children: James Gray, Robert, Ella E. and Stephen Taylor. Ella Gray was a daughter of James and Harriet (Wheary) Gray.

James Gray McCandlish attended McCabe's University School at Petersburg, and from the end of his schooling until his death on April 6, 1899, was in business at Petersburg, largely in connection with the commission trade.

He married, November 7, 1877, Miss Lelia J. Vaughan, who survives him and resides at 132 South Adams Street, in Petersburg. Mrs. McCandlish was born at Petersburg and is a descendant of Salathiel Vaughan, a native of England, who was the founder of this branch of the Vaughan family in Dinwiddie County. His son, Peter Vaughan, was born in that county, served as high sheriff for several years and owned and operated a large plantation. He married a Miss Boisseau. Their son, Lemuel Holt Vaughan, grandfather of Mrs. McCandlish, was born in Dinwiddie County, became a planter there, and married Thirza Boisseau, of French-Huguenot extraction. Benjamin Boisseau Vaughan, father of Mrs. McCandlish, was born on a plantation in Dinwiddie County and at the age of nineteen was graduated with the Master of Arts degree from Princeton College. Following that he attended Harvard University, taking the law course, and after completing it returned to Dinwiddie County and for several years practiced law. However, the greater part of his active career was spent as a tobacco inspector at the West Hill Warehouse, where he was on duty for twenty-five years. He died in 1881.

Benjamin Boisseau Vaughan married Sarah Ellen Vaughan, daughter of James and Jane Hatchett (Craddock) Vaughan, of Amelia County. The Amelia County Vaughans were not related so far as known to the Dinwiddie Vaughans. Mrs. McCandlish's mother died June 27, 1903. She was one of five children, Lemuel Holt, Benjamin Boisseau, Sarah Eugenia, Ada Virginia and Lelia Jane.

Hugh B. Marsh

Mrs. McCandlish's brother, Benjamin B., was a cadet at the Virginia Military Institute in 1862, when with other cadets, in May, he was called out for service by Gen. Stonewall Jackson. After McDowell's victory he returned to the institute, but soon resigned and enlisted in Amelia County in Company G of the First Virginia Cavalry, serving under Gen. Fitzhugh Lee. He was captured at the battle of Sailors Creek, April 6, 1865, and was a prisoner at Point Lookout, Maryland, until June, 1865, when he was paroled and returned home. He became a tobacco dealer at Petersburg, was president of the National Bank of that city, and served as lieutenant commander of A. P. Hill Camp of Confederate Veterans.

Mrs. McCandlish was educated in the Southern Woman's College at Petersburg. She is an active member of the Presbyterian Church. Her children were: Sarah Ellen, Elsie Gray, James Gray, Lelia Vaughan, Benjamin Vaughan, and Walter Taliaferro. Sarah married Frank Miller, of South Carolina, and died leaving three children, Lelia, Rachel and Elsie Gray. Her sister, Elsie Gray, is the second wife of Mr. Miller. James Gray McCandlish, Jr., died at the age of thirty-six. Miss Lelia V. McCandlish resides with her mother. The son Benjamin V. entered the United States Naval Academy at Annapolis, and during the World war was a lieutenant in command of a destroyer, and since the war has been promoted to the rank of commander. He married Margaret Wood, of New York. Mrs. McCandlish's younger son, Walter T., married Emily Lipscomb.

HUGH BROWNING MARSH. Although one of the younger attorneys practicing at the bar of Fairfax, Hugh B. Marsh evinces a broad knowledge of the law, a conscientious regard for all classes of litigants and fine executive ability in the dispatch of business, and during his career he has had the advantage of being associated in practice with Hon. Wilson M. Farr, one of the noted men of his profession, now commonwealth's attorney of Fairfax County.

Hugh B. Marsh was born in Charlottesville, Virginia, September 20, 1900, a son of John R. and Jennie B. (Yeatts) Marsh, natives of Albemarle County, Virginia, and Pittsylvania County, Virginia, respectively. John R. Marsh is connected with the Southern Railroad, his run being from Washington City to Salisbury, North Carolina, but he resides in Alexandria, Virginia.

It was in the latter city that Hugh B. Marsh was reared and was given his preliminary education, as his parents moved to Alexandria when he was two years old, and he was graduated from high school in June, 1919. Entering the University of Virginia, he took two years of academic work and three years in the law department, and was graduated in June, 1924, with the degree of Bachelor of Laws. For a few months thereafter he was connected with the Southern Railroad as a law assistant, and then, January 1, 1925, he came to Fairfax and entered upon his present association with Mr. Farr. In the years that have followed he has been very successful, and his name is becoming well known not only in his profession but to the public generally.

Mr. Marsh is unmarried. He belongs to the Fairfax County Bar Association and the Virginia State Bar Association. A Mason, he belongs to Andrew Jackson Lodge, A. F. and A. M., of Alexandria, and to Alexandria Chapter, R. A. M. Since coming to Fairfax he has become a member of its Chamber of Commerce, and he is eligible to membership in the Sons of the Confederacy. His political beliefs make him a Democrat, and he is interested in party affairs.

PRESTON COCKE was an eminent Richmond attorney, and in giving some account of his individual career and family appropriate occasion is afforded to review briefly the distinguished ancestry of the Cocke family and some of its relationships with Virginia history.

Richard Cocke, first of the name, came from England prior to 1632, and made his place of settlement twelve miles below Richmond. In 1632 he was a member of the House of Burgesses from Weyanoke, and in 1654 he represented Henrico County. From this founder of the family in Virginia the line was continued through his son Richard Cocke II and his grandson Richard Cocke III. Then came Bowler Cocke I, who was in the House of Burgesses from 1756 to 1761. It was Bowler Cocke I who by land patents secured through Gov. William Gooch in the name of King George II obtained the tract of 2,400 acres on the south side of the James River on Muddy Creek, comprising the plantation long known as the Oakland Estate. This plantation was inherited by Bowler Cocke II, who served in the House of Burgesses from 1767 to 1769. Its third owner was his son, William Cocke, who married Jane Armistead, of Hesse, Gloucester County.

The next possessor of Oakland Estate was William Armistead Cocke, son of William and Jane (Armistead) Cocke. William Armistead Cocke married Elizabeth Randolph Preston, daughter of Major Thomas Lewis and Edmonia Madison (Randolph) Preston, the latter a daughter of Edmond Randolph. After the close of the Civil war Gen. Robert E. Lee and family were offered the use of Oakland Estate as a residence by Elizabeth Randolph Preston Cocke, and while they did not accept the large house, they took the small house on the plantation called Derwent, a part of the Oakland Estate. This was the home of General Lee from June until September before he accepted the call to the presidency of Washington College, now Washington and Lee University.

William Armistead Cocke and wife, Elizabeth Randolph Preston, had four sons: William Fauntleroy Cocke, who was killed at the battle of Gettysburg; Thomas Lewis Preston Cocke, who by his marriage with a Miss Lewis had a daughter, Elizabeth Randolph Preston Cocke, and his second wife was Mary Curtis, who became the mother of six children, named William Fauntleroy, Harriet Throckmorton, Charles Curtis, Maria, Randolph Preston and Betty Meredith; Capt. Edmond Randolph Cocke, who first married Phoebe Preston, by whom he had a daughter, Sally Lyle, and his second wife was Lucia Harrison, by whom there were six children, Elizabeth Randolph, Edmund Randolph, William Armistead, Edmonia Madison, Nelson Page and Catherine McKim; and Preston Cocke.

Preston Cocke, the Richmond attorney, was born on Oakland Estate in Cumberland County November 8, 1845, and was in the seventy-second years of his life when death called him January 15, 1917. He acquired his early education in the Virginia Military Institute, where during his first year he fought in the battle of New Market and later entered the cavalry of the Confederate army and served until the end of the war. He was once wounded, but upon recovery, rejoined his command. After the war he attended Washington and Lee University, and in 1870 was graduated in law at the University of Virginia. He at once entered the law firm of Judge Meredith, and later became associated as a partner with Charles V. Meredith under the firm name of Meredith & Cocke. This firm was in existence for the notable period of forty-seven years, and during that time Preston Cocke was recognized as one of the outstanding members of the Virginia bar in learning, resourcefulness and the dignity and experience of a man of affairs as well as a man of the law. He was a member of the Virginia and American Bar Associations and had a life-long affiliation with the Episcopal Church.

Preston Cocke married in 1870 Eliza Bernard Meredith, daughter of John Alexander and Sarah Ann (Bernard) Meredith. Mrs. Cocke was reared and educated in Richmond. They had a family of three daughters. Miss Ella Meredith Cocke, who resides at 923 West Franklin Street in Richmond, is a member of St. James Episcopal Church, the Richmond Woman's Club, Country Club, Colonial Dames, A. P. N. A., Little Theater League, Belle Bryan Day Nursery and Memorial Home for Girls, through which organizations she finds a most interesting diversity of occupation for her talents and her culture. The second daughter, Sarah Bernard, who was also educated at Richmond, was married October 18, 1910, to Mr. Joseph Pope Nash, member of the firm Golsan & Nash Realtors, a firm that has been in business at Richmond fifteen years. They have three children, Preston, Joseph Pope, Jr., and Bernard Meredith Nash. Mrs. Nash is a member of St. Stephens Church and the Country Club. The youngest of the three daughters is Miss Elizabeth Preston Cocke, who finished her education in Sweet Briar College. She is a past president of the Junior League, member of the Little Theater League, A. P. N. A., Confederate Memorial, Sunnyside Day Nursery, Crippled Children Hospital, and St. James Episcopal Church. During the World war she was an occupational theropist at the U. S. Hospital No. 10 at Boston, Massachusetts.

CHARLES LUNSFORD, JR., of Petersburg, is the present secretary and treasurer of the American Bonded Warehouse Company of that city. A son of Charles Lunsford, Sr., he was born in Petersburg, of English ancestry.

William Lunsford, the founder of the Virginia family of Lunsfords, immigrated from Sussexshire in England to Northumberland County, Virginia, in 1649. His descendant, Swanson Lunsford, was born in Northumberland County, Virginia, in 1705. His son Isaac was born in Northumberland in 1734, and his son Leroy Lunsford, great-grandfather of the subject of this sketch, was born in the same county in 1767. In early life he moved to Dinwiddie County, Virginia, and having purchased land at Cherry Hill, improved a good plantation that he operated with slave labor until his death. He married Alice Shortt Abernathy, who was born in Dinwiddie County, a descendant of an old Virginia family.

Lewis Lunsford, through whom the line was continued, was born at Cherry Hill, Virginia, in 1799, and spent his entire life in Dinwiddie County, having for many years been actively engaged in the insurance business at Petersburg. He married Grace Stillman, who was born in New Haven, Connecticut, a daughter of John Pierson Stillman and Esther Johnson Stillman, his wife. He died at a comparatively early age.

Charles Lunsford, Sr., was born in Petersburg, Virginia, in 1846, and there acquired his preliminary education. In March, 1864, although a lad of seventeen years, he renounced his studies to enter the Confederate service as a member of Martin's Battery of Sturdivant's Battalion of Artillery. In his obituary notice, written by a friend, and printed in the *Index* on September 16, 1922, special mention was made of Martin's Battery, as follows: "This organization did much valiant service during the war between the states. It was near Appomattox at the time of the surrender, and rather than have the guns fall into the hands of the enemy, he, with others, buried them in Buckingham County. It fell to his lot to fire the last shot of the battery, and that was virtually the last shot of the four years' war."

Returning to his Virginia home, Charles Lunsford, Sr., embarked in the grain and feed business, which he carried on most successfully until his death, September 15, 1922.

His wife, whose name before marriage was Jean Rose Berry, was born at Amherst Court House, Virginia, a daughter of Capt. Taylor Berry, who married Martha Irving. From the beginning of the Civil war Captain Berry commanded a company attached to Armistead's Brigade, Pickett's Division, and took an active part in many important engagements, including the battle of Gettysburg. At the close of the conflict the Captain served as state senator and as circuit judge, filling both positions ably and satisfactorily. Mrs. Lunsford passed to the higher life in 1918, leaving to mourn her loss her husband and six children, namely: Mrs. J. W. Friend, Mrs. W. H. Wills, Helen S., Charles Jr., Irving C., and Lewis.

Securing his elementary education in private school, Charles Lunsford, Jr., subsequently continued his studies at the Petersburg Academy for a time, and then entered the Episcopal High School near Alexandria, where he received his diploma in 1914. In May, 1917, having previously spent two years in the academic course in the University of Virginia, Mr. Lunsford entered the United States service as a member of the "Richmond Blues," enlisting as a private and being first stationed at Camp McClellan. He was subsequently transferred to Camp Taylor and commissioned as second lieutenant of artillery. He was later sent to Camp Jackson, where he remained until after the signing of the armistice. Receiving his honorable discharge, he returned to Petersburg, and there engaged in the grain and feed business at the old stand, continuing it until 1927. Disposing of his interest in that business in that year, Mr. Lunsford accepted his present position as secretary and treasurer of the American Bonded Warehouse Company.

Mr. Lunsford married, in 1918, Miss Frances Virginia Thompson, who was born in Norfolk, Virginia, a daughter of John H. and Ida (Alley) Thompson, and into their home two children have made their appearance, Frances Thompson and Martha Irving. Mr. Lunsford is a member of the Delta Tau Delta fraternity. Both Mr. and Mrs. Lunsford belong to St. Paul's Episcopal Church.

LESTER BOYD DUTROW. Among the specially useful citizens
of Petersburg, Lester B. Dutrow occupies a place of prominence
as a civil engineer and an inspector of public buildings, detecting
any flaw in their erection that might eventually prove a menace
to life and property. A son of the late Jonathan M. Dutrow,
he was born at Harrisonburg, Rockingham County, Virginia, of
good old Holland stock.

David Dutrow, grandfather of Lester B. Dutrow, was born
near Frederick, Maryland, near the spot on which his immigrant
ancestor settled on coming from Holland to America in early
Colonial days, the surname then, it is said, having been spelled
"Duderer." David Dutrow was a lifelong resident of Maryland,
where he owned a large plantation that was operated with slave
labor.

Jonathan M. Dutrow was born in the vicinity of Frederick,
Maryland, and there reared and educated. He was in Baltimore,
Maryland, when, on April 19, 1861, a Massachusetts regiment
was mobbed when passing through that city, and the first soldier
of the Civil war was killed on the eighty-sixth anniversary of the
battle of Lexington and of Concord, Massachusetts. He volunteered for service in the Confederate army, and ere long was
delegated as courier for Gen. Robert E. Lee, often carrying
important messages for him, and on several occasions working
his way through the Union lines. He continued in active service
until the close of the war, doing his full duty in camp or on the
firing line. Subsequently, with his brothers Amos and John, he
was engaged in the commission business at Harrisonburg, which
he resigned to become deputy clerk of the court of Rockingham
County. Later he accepted a position as clerk in the office of a
tannery company at Harrisonburg, Virginia, with which he was
associated until his death, at the age of sixty-three years.

The maiden name of the wife of Jonathan M. Dutrow was
Sarah Clementine VanPelt. Coming from early Colonial Dutch
ancestry, she was born in Harrisonburg Virginia, a daughter of
Maj. Andrew Jackson and Lucinda (Wortman) VanPelt.
Although beyond military age at the outbreak of the Civil war,
Maj. A. J. VanPelt received his commission as major from
Governor Wise, and served for two years in the Confederate
army. Mrs. Jonathan M. Dutrow, mother of the subject of this
sketch, died in 1916. To her and her husband six children were
born, namely: Edna, William B., Margaret, J. Paul, David A.
and Lester B.

After his graduation from the Harrisonburg High School in
1905, Lester B. Dutrow continued his studies one term at Washington and Lee University. Securing then a position as clerk
in the office of the tannery in which his father was employed,
he labored energetically, and when, by means of thrift and wise
expenditure, he had accumulated a sufficient sum to warrant
him in so doing he returned to the university, and was there
graduated in 1910 with the degree of Bachelor of Science as a
civil engineer. Three years later Washington and Lee University conferred upon him the professional degree of civil
engineer.

From 1910 until 1917 Mr. Dutrow was in the employ of the
Southern Railroad Company, and the following year was en-
gaged in road construction as a civil engineer in North Carolina.
Locating then in Petersburg, he served as engineer for the
Atlantic Coast Realty Company from 1918 until 1920, during the
latter year being chief engineer. In 1920 he was appointed by

Governor Davis a member of the State Board of Engineers for the examination and certification of engineers, architects and land surveyors, serving on that board five years. From 1920 until 1924 he was in business on his own account as an engineer. In 1926 the offices of building inspector and director of public safety were combined, and Mr. Dutrow was appointed director of public safety and building inspector, and has continued these offices ever since, his work being highly approved by all concerned.

Mr. Dutrow married, in 1916, Miss Martha Wesley Canter, who was born in Elliston, Virginia, a daughter of John W. and Mattie (Mayes) Canter. Two children have blessed their union, Gladys VanPelt and Jane Canter. Fraternally Mr. Dutrow is a Scottish Rite Mason and Shriner, and a member of the local Kiwanis Club and Chamber of Commerce. True to the religious faith in which he was reared, he belongs to Trinity Methodist Episcopal Church, and is a member of its Board of Stewards.

JAMES T. D'ALTON. The business activities of Petersburg have been most intelligently advanced and maintained by men of unquestioned ability and worth, and prominent among the number that were largely instrumental in placing its mercantile interests on a substantial basis was the late James T. D'Alton, for many years an extensive and prosperous dealer in groceries. He was born in 1844 in Dublin, Ireland, which was likewise the birthplace of his father, Henry D'Alton. His paternal grandfather, James D'Alton, was born in France, but subsequently removed to Ireland, where his surname, originally spelled deAlton, was changed to its present form, D'Alton, and there spent his remaining years.

Henry D'Alton, a native of Ireland, was reared and educated in Dublin, where he lived until after his marriage with Julia Karney, also of Dublin. A few years later, accompanied by his wife and children, he came to the United States in search of remunerative employment, locating first in Norfolk, Virginia. Removing to Petersburg in 1855, he built up a large and successful grocery trade, which he carried on successfully until his death at the age of about seventy-two years.

While yet a youth James T. D'Alton came with his parents to Virginia, and as soon as old enough began clerking in his father's grocery. Becoming familiar with the details of the business, he subsequently embarked in the wholesale grocery business, which he managed with highly satisfactory results until his death when but fifty-two years of age. On January 14, 1875, he was united in marriage with Miss Ida Benedict, who was born in Easton, Pennsylvania, February 7, 1859, a daughter of Isben Benedict, Jr., and grand-daughter of Isben Benedict, Sr. Her immigrant ancestor, William Benedict, came from Nottingham-shire, England, to America in 1635, locating first at Southold, Long Island, from there going to Danbury, Connecticut, where he established one of the first hat factories in America, while his son James had the distinction of being the first white male child born in that state. Enlisting in the Continental Army, he served as lieutenant of a company commanded by Captain Watson. James Benedict, the next in line of descent of whom we have record, was a native of Danbury, Connecticut, and his son, Amos Benedict, was born at Fabius, New York, in 1736. Capt. Isben Benedict, Sr., Mrs. D'Alton's grandfather, was born at Fabius,

New York, in 1780, while her father, Isben Benedict, Jr., was born in 1818 in Richmond, Virginia.

Capt. Isben Benedict, Sr., was for many years engaged in trade with foreign countries, commanding his own vessels. He married Miss Fannie Weymouth, whose father, William Walker Weymouth, came to Virginia from England, his native country, settling in Richmond, where he met and married Miss Frances Age, whose father, John Age, immigrated from England to Richmond, Virginia, where he built the large stone house now known as the "Edgar Allen Poe Shrine."

Isben Benedict, Jr., was educated in Philadelphia, and when very young began a seafaring life on his father's vessels, and while yet in his teens was given command of one. At the age of twenty-one years he embarked in the spice and coffee trade in Richmond, being the first to engage in that line of business, and met with such success that he continued it until his death at the age of seventy-two years.

Isben Benedict, Jr., married Eliza Jane Cross, who was born in Delaware, a daughter of John Cross, of that state. She, too, attained the age of seventy-two years. They were the parents of eight children.

At the death of her husband Mrs. D'Alton was left with a family of nine children, the youngest being but four months old, as follows: Marion E., Henry B., James T., Isben B., William B., Frederick A., Clarence J., Walter E. and Aubrey V. Marion E. married, November 15, 1899, Irvin Willis Moon; Frederick A., married November 25, 1899, Susan May Sadler, of Norfolk, Virginia, and they have one son, James Frederick; Clarence J. married, July 7, 1917, Frances Nork, they have three children, Clarence J., Robert F. and William B.

WILLIAM HARRIS GAINES. Not only is William H. Gaines one of the ablest attorneys practicing at the bar of Fauquier County, but he is also commissioner-in-chancery, commissioner of inheritance and assistant commissioner of accounts, and both professionally and officially is taking a very important part in the life of Warrenton and the county, and is one of the outstanding figures of his time and neighborhood. He was born in Warrenton, Virginia, March 8, 1887, a son of Grenville and Lizzie (Harris) Gaines, natives of Warrenton and Norfolk, Virginia, respectively. The maternal grandfather, William Harris, was surgeon general in the United States Navy, and a man eminent in his profession. The paternal grandfather, W. H. Gaines, was also a man of note, and served for many years as county judge of Fauquier County, and died in 1885. Grenville Gaines served as a colonel of the Third Virginia Infantry, State Militia, for some years, and he was a distinguished lawyer and citizen. Graduated in law from the University of Virginia in 1876, he immediately established himself in practice in Warrenton, and continued his professional work the remainder of his life, dying May 2, 1922, aged sixty-six years. For several terms he was mayor of Warrenton, and during his administration placed the city on a solid basis. During the World war his standing as a lawyer and citizen received signal recognition at the hands of the Federal Government in his appointment as fuel administrator of Fauquier County. The mother died October 30, 1921.

Growing to useful manhood in his native place, William H. Gaines attended its schools, Bethel Military Academy of Warrenton, the Episcopal High School of Alexandria and the Uni-

versity of Virginia, and was graduated in law from the latter
in 1909, with the degree of Bachelor of Laws.   Locating in
Arlington County, he formed a partnership with R. C. L. Moncure and Judge Richard Tebbs, under the caption of Moncure,
Tebbs & Gaines, with offices in Arlington court house, but after
a year this connection was severed by mutual consent, and for
the following two years Mr. Gaines was editor of the Rosslyn
Commonwealth.   Returning then to Arlington Court House, he
began practicing law alone, and continued there until 1916, when
he came to Warrenton and was engaged in practice with his
father until the latter's death, since which time he has continued
alone, with great success, his practice being a large and very
important one.

On August 23, 1917, Mr. Gaines married Miss Margaretta
Wrigley, of Macon, Georgia, a daughter of William and Ida
(McPherson) Wrigley, natives of Georgia and Virginia, respect-
ively.   Mr. Wrigley was a Confederate veteran, and was engaged
in the banking business in Macon, Georgia, at the time of his
death.   Mrs. Wrigley is also deceased, having passed away in
April, 1923.   Mr. and Mrs. Gaines have three children: William
H., Junior, who was born June 6, 1918; McPherson Wrigley,
who was born August 2, 1920; and Margaretta, who was born
December 30, 1923.

Mr. Gaines has always been interested in politics as a strong
supporter of the Democratic party, and he has served as a member of the Town Council.   For several years he has been an
active figure in the Warrenton Chamber of Commerce.   He
belongs to the Warrenton Bar Association, Delta Tau Delta,
Phi Delta Phi the legal fraternity, and the American Legion, as
well as to the Fauquier Club.   In religious faith he is an Episcopalian.   On August 25, 1917, Mr. Gaines entered the Second
Officers Training Camp at Fort Myers, but was honorably discharged because of a broken bone in his foot.   While Mr. Gaines
is the only son in the family of his parents, he has two sisters,
both of whom are living, namely: Mary, who is the wife of
Joseph A. Bell, of Charleston, South Carolina; and Elizabeth,
who is the wife of George A. Dawson, a graduate of Cornell
University, now a resident of Pottstown, Pennsylvania.   The
Gaines residence in Warrenton is one of the most desirable in
the city, and here a delightful home life is enjoyed and a warm
hospitality is extended to the many family friends.

GEORGE NELSON JAMES.   A wide-awake, enterprising man of
business, far seeing and venturesome, George Nelson James, now
filling the mayor's chair at Colonial Heights, is eminently worthy
of representation in a work of this character.   A son of William
James, he was born at Ettricks, Chesterfield County, Virginia,
where his early life was pleasantly passed.

His paternal grandfather, Thomas James, was born in Amelia
County, Virginia, in 1792, being a lineal descendant of an old
and honored family.   Filled with patriotic ardor, he took an
active part in the War of 1812, gladly performing his duty on
the field of battle.   During his years of activity he operated his
plantation, but later in life he moved to Ettricks, where he spent
the closing years of his life.   He married Irene Waltrope, of
Amelia County, a lifelong resident of the Old Dominion, which
prides itself on its Revolutionary heroes.

William James was born in Amelia County, Virginia, in
1833, and was there educated.   At the very commencement of

the Civil war he offered his services to the Confederacy, but was rejected on account of physical disability. A few months later he joined the "Reserves," a company formed for the protection of Petersburg, and historical records show that these men did valiant service when called upon. At the close of the conflict he entered railroad service as an engineer, and operated on what is now a part of the Norfolk & Western Railway. He subsequently located in Petersburg, where his death occurred at the comparatively early age of sixty years. He was twice married, by his first union having nine children, George Nelson being next to the eldest. He married Pocahontas Arabella Stewart, who died at the age of forty-two years. Of the second marriage, to Elmira Chappell, there was one child, William James.

Having completed his studies in public and private schools of Ettricks and Petersburg, George Nelson James turned his attention to mechanical pursuits. Having completed an apprenticeship at the carpenter's trade, he first worked as a journeyman, but later, locating in Petersburg, became a contractor and builder. In 1920 he went to Colonial Heights, a very beautiful suburb of Petersburg, and there continued his chosen work. At the time of the incorporation of Colonial Heights, in September, 1926, Mr. James was elected mayor of the city, which is one of the most attractive municipalities of the county.

Mr. James married first Eliza Virginia Eanes, who was born at Ettricks, Virginia, a daughter of Henry Eanes. Three children were born of their union, namely: Daisy; Harry N., who married Mrs. Eloise (Jordan) Munford; and Kate, wife of H. B. Brockwell. Mr. James married for his second wife Mrs. Isabel (Booker) Morgan, a daughter of Thomas Tabb Booker, of whom a brief sketch may be found on another page of this volume. Mrs. James is a valued member of Saint Paul's Episcopal Church. She belongs to various organizations, including the Daughters of the Revolution, the U. D. C., the Virginia Historical Society, and is eligible to the order of Colonial Dames through nine or more lines.

THOMAS TABB BOOKER, father-in-law of George Nelson James, of whom a brief biography in given in the preceding sketch was born in Amelia County, Virginia, of distinguished ancestry, being a lineal descendant of Edward Booker, the founder of the American family of Bookers, the line being thus traced:

Edward Booker, Capt. Richard Booker, Richard Booker, John Booker Sr., John Booker Jr., William Marshall Booker, William Marshall Booker, and Thomas Tabb Booker.

Edward Booker was born in Gloucester, England, in 1590. In 1632 he immigrated to Virginia, where he had several grants of land in several counties. He served as a member of the Virginia Council, and was influential in public affairs until his death in 1648. Capt. Richard Booker was commander of a company in the Colonial Militia. He married first Rebecca Leake, daughter of John Leake, a prominent lawyer, and married for his second wife Mrs. Hannah (Hand) Marshall, widow of Capt. William Marshall.

Richard Booker had a grant of land in that part of Amelia County that now is a part of Prince George County. He married Margaret Lowery, a daughter of William and Frances (Purefay) Lowery. John Booker, Sr., who served as justice of

the peace and as sheriff of Amelia County, married Phoebe
Warsham. John Booker, Jr., who served as a delegate to the
House of Burgesses and as a soldier in the Revolutionary war,
married Elizabeth Giles. William Marshall Booker, a soldier in
the War of 1812, and a wealthy planter, married Sallie Blanken-
ship. His son was William Marshall Booker. Thomas Tabb
Booker, a native of Amelia County, Virginia, has been prominently associated with its development and advancement, ever
performing his full duty as a public citizen, and has reason to
be proud of his family. He was a farmer and merchant. He
enlisted in Company C, Twenty-third Regiment, Virginia Infantry, "Stonewall" Brigade, served throughout the entire conflict, and was wounded at the battle of Winchester, September
19, 1864. After leaving the hospital at Staunton he returned to
his home in Amelia County, where he married Mary Elizabeth
Vaughan, daughter of Samuel Daniel and Elizabeth Davis
(Allen) Vaughan. There were four children: Mary Elizabeth,
who married Peter Dabney Glinn; Isabel Frances, who married
first Dr. Daniel H. Morgan, of the United States Navy, and
second George Nelson James; John Thomas, who married
Blanche Quarles; and Roberta Grace, who married Bradley Tyler
Johnson.

GEORGE OTHO SLEDGE, JR. As superintendent of the Petersburg Hospital, George O. Sledge, Jr., is at the head of one of
the more important institutions of Dinwiddie County, a responsible position for which he is amply qualified, and which
he is filling with characteristic ability and fidelity. A direct
descendant of one of the older families of Virginia, he was born
in Southampton County, on the very farm on which the birth
of his father, George O. Sledge, Sr., occurred in 1850.

Many years ago Sterling Sledge, father of George O. Sledge,
Sr., purchased land in Southampton County, and on the farm
he improved both he and his wife spent their remaining years,
laboring with zeal to wrest from the soil somewhat more than a
mere living for himself and family.

Succeeding to the ownership of the old home estate, George
O. Sledge, Sr., has since been industriously engaged in general
farming, his efforts being well rewarded. His wife, whose
maiden name was Lucy Spiers, was a daughter of James and
Lucy (Sledge) Spiers. She died in middle life, her death having
occurred December 27, 1926. Seven children were born into
their home, namely: Lula J., wife of G. W. Orthey, of New
York; Nannie I., wife of Joseph B. Taylor, of North Emporia,
Virginia; Sterling Stanley, living on the home farm; George O.,
Jr., the subject of this brief sketch; Berta, wife of G. F. Williams, of North Emporia, Virginia; Joseph B., of Petersburg,
Virginia; and Jesse Herbert, of Ashland, Virginia.

Brought up in the parental household, George O. Sledge, Jr.,
was educated in the rural schools of his neighborhood, in the
meantime, under the tuition of his father, obtaining a practical
knowledge of the different branches of agriculture. On attaining his majority he began life for himself as clerk in a general
store of merchandise at Petersburg. He was subsequently employed as an insurance collector or as a bookkeeper until 1926,
when he accepted his present position as superintendent of the
Petersburg Hospital. In this capacity Mr. Sledge has displayed
rare good judgment, his knowledge of details and his skill as a

Geo. H. Davis M.D.

manager of affairs rendering him especially fitted for this high position.

Mr. Sledge married, December 15, 1925, Miss Bessie R. Young, who was born in Greensville County, Virginia, a daughter of William T. and Lucy Young. Mr. Sledge is an Odd Fellow. Both he and Mrs. Sledge are active and faithful members of the Second Baptist Church.

GEORGE HITER DAVIS, M. D., has shown in both his loyalty and his success the consistency of his choice of vocation, and he is established in the practice of his profession in the City of Warrenton, the county seat of old Fauquier County.

Doctor Davis was born in Spotsylvania County, Virginia, May 5, 1884, and is a son of Dr. John W. and Drusilla (Mason) Davis, both likewise natives of that county. Dr. John W. Davis served as a surgeon in the Confederate army in the Civil war, and thereafter he continued in the practice of his profession in his native county during the remainder of his active career, his home having been maintained at Partlow, where his widow still resides, she being eighty years of age at the time of this writing, in the summer of 1928. Dr. John W. Davis long held honorable prestige as one of the representative physicians and surgeons of Spotsylvania County, and was there the revered dean of his profession when his long and earnest life came to its close, he having been ninety-two years of age at the time of his death, in November, 1927. He was a stalwart in the ranks of the Democratic party, was affiliated with the United Confederate Veterans and with various medical societies, and was an earnest member of the Baptist Church, as is also his venerable widow.

After profiting by the advantages of the public schools of his old home town of Partlow Dr. George H. Davis entered the Fauquier Military Academy, and in this insitution he was graduated in 1903. In preparation for the profession signally honored by the character and services of his father he then entered the University College of Medicine in the City of Richmond, this being the medical department of the University of Virginia. In this institution he was graduated as a member of the class of 1907, and after thus receving his degree of Doctor of Medicine he had the fortifying privilege of being associated with his father in practice one year. During the ensuing seventeen years he was engaged in practice in the village of Bethel Academy, Fauquier County, and he then, in 1924, removed to the county seat, Warrenton, where he has continued his successful general practice, including ministration to many of the families that he had previously attended while residing at Bethel Academy, which is a virtual suburb of Warrenton. The Doctor is an active member of the Virginia State Medical Society, the Northern Virginia Medical Society, the District of Columbia Medical Society, the Fauquier County Medical Society and the American Medical Association. His political allegiance is given to the Democratic party, he and his wife are members of the Baptist Church, and he is affiliated with the United Sons of the Confederacy.

In October, 1908, was solemnized the marriage of Doctor Davis and Miss Norma Smith, daughter of Dr. Thomas W. and Mary (Blackwell) Smith, of Bethel Academy, Fauquier County, where Doctor Smith long maintained prestige as one of the able and honored physicians and surgeons of his native county, and where his death occurred in November, 1908, his widow

being now a loved member of the family circle of Doctor and
Mrs. Davis, and she, like her husband, having been born and
reared in Fauquier County. The names and respective birth
years of the children of Doctor and Mrs. Davis are here
recorded: Thomas W. S., born in 1910; Drusilla Norman, 1913;
George H., Jr., 1915; James Blackwell, 1917; and John Wilson, 1919.

In addition to meeting all demands placed upon him in his
professional capacity Doctor Davis finds diversion and much
satisfaction in giving a general supervision to his fine farm
estate in Fauquier County, this estate comprising 500 acres of
the valuable land of this section of the state.

BENJAMIN TEMPLE. The Temple family in Virginia has a
consecutive record running back prior to the War of the Revolution, and each generation has furnished strong and self-reliant
citizens, patriots, and in vocations their tendency has been
markedly for the lines of trade.

The founder of the family was Joseph Temple, who with his
wife, Anna Arnold, came from Germany. Their son, Benjamin
Temple, raised and equipped a regiment of horses for service in
the Revolutionary war. This Benjamin Temple became a large
importer and erected several warehouses on the York River for
handling goods used in trade. He was the father of three sons,
Robert, Benjamin, and Lester. Of these sons Benjamin went to
Kentucky and married a sister of the famous explorer Clark.

Another Benjamin Temple, grandson of the founder of the
family in America, was born in 1801 and died in 1871, spending
all his life in Virginia. He married Elizabeth Skyrin, daughter
of Parson Skyrin, whose wife was Miss Lucy Moore, a descendant of Governor Spottswood, and connected with the Lee family.
Benjamin Temple while educated for the law devoted his active
life to the management of his wife's estate.

Benjamin Temple married in 1825 Lucy Lilly Robinson, of
a family that settled in Virginia in Colonial times. The children
of their union were: Robert Henry, a civil engineer, who married Miss Crouch and had a son, Twohig; Charles Wilford, who
became an educator; Benjamin Brooke, a physician, who married Mary Glidden and had a son, George Temple; John Taylor;
William Skyrin, who became a merchant; Vernon Moore, who
was a civil engineer, one of the builders of the Gulf, Colorado &
Santa Fe Railroad in Texas, and had two children, Vernon and
Louise; Ludwell, who also followed a career as a civil engineer;
and Miss Lucy Lilly Temple, who resides in Richmond, at 1112
West Avenue.

REV. CHARLES BARTON RICHARDS, a minister of the Christian
Church, who has preached in numerous localities in Eastern and
Southeastern Virginia, is also a business man of Petersburg,
manager of the wholesale department of the Delta Oil Company.

He was born on a farm in Fauquier County, Virginia, son
of Samuel B. Richards, a native of Loudoun County, and grandson of Barton Richards, also of Loudoun County. The Richards
family was established in Virginia in Colonial times. Samuel
B. Richards grew up on a farm and at the age of nineteen entered
the Confederate army, serving in the cavalry under Gen. J. E. B.
Stuart. He was in many battles, including that of Spotsylvania
Court House, where he was severely wounded and was in a
hospital until the final surrender. He became a Loudoun County

farmer and later bought a farm near the courthouse in Fairfax County, where he lived until his death at the age of sixty-four. He married Katherine Elizabeth Hospital, who was born in Loudoun County, daughter of Josephus Hospital. She died at the age of seventy-eight. Their four children were Berkeley D., Edgar F., Charles Barton and May F.

Charles Barton Richards was reared on a Virginia farm, was educated in rural schools, and also had training in a business college at Washington, D. C. He later prepared for the ministry of the Christian Church at Hiram College, in Ohio, an institution of which President Garfield was at one time the head. He was ordained in the Seventh Street Christian Church at Richmond. Rev. Mr. Richards was pastor of the Christian Church at Petersburg from 1903 to 1909. He subsequently was pastor of churches at South Norfolk, Port View, Newport News and at Winston Salem, North Carolina, at Ashland and Covington, Virginia, and in later years has been attending churches in Warwick and Goochland counties.

Mr. Richards in 1920 returned to Petersburg to become manager of the wholesale department of the Delta Oil Company. He is a very busy man, carrying important business responsibilities and also a large amount of church work.

He married in 1903 Miss Ida M. Atwell, who was born at Washington, D. C. Her father was a lieutenant in the Union army in the Civil war. Mrs. Richards died in 1905, and in 1909 he married Mary Blanche DeShazor, a native of Petersburg, daughter of James M. and Emma (Snead) DeShazor. Rev. Mr. and Mrs. Richards have three children, Louise Taylor, Samuel Decatur, and Virginia Gray.

THOMAS FREEMAN EPES has been engaged in the routine of a practicing attorney at the Virginia bar for over thirty years. His home is at Blackstone, and he has been repeatedly honored with positions of trust in that community. He is at present commonwealth's attorney of Nottoway County.

He was born in Nottoway County November 9, 1874, son of John S. and Fannie W. (Epes) Epes. John S. Epes was the son of T. Freeman Epes I, and Jacquelin Segar Hardaway. Fannie W. Epes was the daughter of Francis Washington Epes and Susan Doswell. The parents were born in Nottoway County and the Epes family is one that was established in Virginia in the early Colonial period. John S. Epes was a private in the Confederate army, and after returning home from the war engaged in farming, an occupation he followed until his death on January 14, 1909. His widow survived him until April, 1921.

T. Freeman Epes grew up on the family farm in Nottoway County, attended public schools. pursued his law course in Washington and Lee University, and graduated LL. B. from George Washington University with the class of 1896. He began the practice of law at Blackstone in 1897, and there has been no interruption to his work as a lawyer except as from time to time the duties of public office have interfered. He was a member of the Virginia House of Delegates in 1916.

Mr. Epes married, September 5, 1900, Miss Agnes Sturgis, daughter of Rev. J. R. and Alice (Bradshaw) Sturgis. Her father was born in Maryland and her mother in Westmoreland County, Virginia. Rev. J. R. Sturgis was a minister of the Methodist Episcopal Church and died in May, 1921, while her mother resides at Blackstone. The only child of Mr. and Mrs. Epes is Susie Doswell, now the wife of Dr. B. S. Burks, a dentist practicing at Crewe, Virginia.

Mr. Epes was elected commonwealth's attorney of Nottoway County in 1923 and was reelected in 1927. He is a Democrat, a Presbyterian and is a member of the Masonic fraternity, the Kappa Sigma, the Kiwanis Club and the Blackstone Golf Club.

EDWIN FENTON CLEMENTS. Known in legal circles and in the business world as a man of ability and strict integrity, Edwin F. Clements, of Petersburg, has attained success as an attorney because he is in every way worthy of it. Born in Petersburg in 1892, he is a descendant in the fourth generation from Reuben Clements, the line being continued through Capt. Edwin R. Clements, Edwin M. Clements and Edwin F. Clements.

Reuben Clements was born in Dinwiddie County, Virginia, where his parents settled on coming from England to America in Colonial times, when the country roundabout was still in its pristine wildness. During the War of 1812 he offered his services to his country, and with a company of volunteers from Petersburg marched to Canada, where they took a brilliant part in many engagements. The gallantry of this special company attracted the attention of President Madison, who subsequently designated Petersburg as the "Cockade City." A history of Petersburg published in 1878 says that of the one hundred and three men that started, October 21, 1812, to march to Canada, Reuben Clements was the only one then living. On his return to Petersburg he engaged in the grocery business, which he carried on until his death.

Capt. Edwin R. Clements took an active part in the Civil war, serving at the head of a company belonging to the Confederate army and attached to Pegrim's Battery. He continued with his command until a few days before his death, which occurred in camp, where he was stricken with pneumonia. The maiden name of his wife was Mary Edwards.

Edwin M. Clements was born, reared and educated in Petersburg. A good student, interested in journalism from his school days, he began his active career as printer's devil in the office of the *Index Appeal*. Being industrious and observing, he obtained an excellent knowledge of journalism during his apprenticeship, and later established the *Daily Progress,* a clean, newsy paper, which he published most successfully until his selling out in 1915, thenceforward living retired until his death in 1920. His wife, whose name before marriage was Mary T. Tierney, was born in Petersburg, a daughter of Michael Tierney. Her father was born in County Limerick, Ireland, and as far as known was the only member of his family to cross the broad Atlantic. Engaging in the grocery business in Petersburg, Mr. Tierney built up a prosperous trade, which he continued during his remaining years.

Edwin Fenton Clements received his preparatory education in the Saint Joseph Parochial School, continuing it at Rock Hill College. Subsequently entering the law department of the University of Virginia, he was there graduated with the degree of LL. B. in 1913. Beginning the practice of his profession in Petersburg, he has since been actively employed in both private and public work, since 1915 having served both as civil and police judge and judge of the Juvenile and Domestic Relations Court.

J Harold Richards

Mr. Clements married, in 1913, Mary Coleman, who was born in Petersburg, a daughter of James T. and Mary (Hanrahan) Coleman. Three children have been born to the union of Mr. and Mrs. Clements, namely: Mary Louise, Mildred Fenton and Edwin Manie.

Since casting his first presidential ballot for Woodrow Wilson, Mr. Clements has been a firm adherent of the Democratic party. He is one of the directorate of the Petersburg Savings and American Trust Company, of the Petersburg Insurance Company and past president of the Petersburg Kiwanis Club.

JAMES DONALD RICHARDS has been one of the leaders of the Fauquier County bar for twenty years, and at the same time has exhibited the qualities of a very determined leader in public affairs. He was one of the early champions of the good roads movement in this section of Virginia.

Mr. Richards was born at Upperville, Fauquier County, December 30, 1880, son of Washington L. and Martha C. (Megeath) Richards. His father was born at Upperville, and spent his active life as a farmer, dying at the age of sixty-nine. The mother died January 16, 1926, at the age of eighty-four.

J. Donald Richards was one of five children. He grew up in a rural section in Fauquier County, attended local schools, the Randolph-Macon Academy, and Columbian University, now George Washington University, and was graduated in law at the University of Louisville, Louisville, Kentucky, June 9, 1903. Mr. Richards has practiced law at Warrenton since May, 1905, and is now senior member of the law firm Richards & Richards, his partner being his nephew, Paul C. Richards, Jr.

He is a Democrat in politics. He was chairman of the Warrenton Board of Trade and leader of the fight for the first road bond issue in Fauquier County. He and some other good roads enthusiasts organized a turnpike company and built twenty-two miles of road in Prince William and Fairfax counties, with a view to securing a highway outlet from Warrenton to Washington. Mr. Richards served as a member of the staff of Governors Stuart and Davis from 1914 to 1922.

For many years he has taken an active part in Masonry, being a past master of Mount Carmel Lodge No. 133, A. F. and A. M., member of Warren Chapter No. 5, Royal Arch Masons, Piedmont Commandery No. 26, Knights Templar, is a thirty-second degree Scottish Rite Mason and member of Acca Temple at Richmond and for five years was imperial representative to the Mystic Shrine.

He married, June 5, 1907, Miss Elizabeth Hinton Gridley. They have one son, Upton Hill, born October 7, 1914.

PAUL COCHRAN RICHARDS, JR., is a young attorney, now junior member of the firm Richards & Richards at Warrenton.

He was born at Delaplane, Fauquier County, August 6, 1903, son of Paul C. and Mary (Gridley) Richards. His father was born in Fauquier County July 4, 1871, while his mother is a native of Missouri. Paul C. Richards, Sr., is a civil and mining engineer by profession, and for a number of years has been also engaged in the automobile business at Warrenton.

Paul C. Richards, Jr., was reared and educated in Fauquier County, graduated from the Stuyvesant Preparatory School in 1919, and took his law degree at the University of Virginia in

June, 1927. On July 1, 1927, he became a law partner with his uncle, J. Donald Richards, at Warrenton.

Mr. Richards is a member of the Warrenton and Virginia Bar Associations, Warrenton Chamber of Commerce, is a Democrat, and was confirmed in the Episcopal Church in 1916.

BERNARD WOODARD MATTHEWS. Energetic and enterprising, and having in a large measure inherited the prudence and ability characteristic of his more immediate ancestors, Bernard W. Matthews, of Petersburg, has established a large and profitable mercantile business, which he is managing with highly satisfactory results. A son of Rev. Richard L. and Mattie E. (Lockett) Matthews, of whom further notice may be found elsewhere in this volume, he was born September 2, 1881, in Petersburg, which he has always claimed as his home.

Having acquired his preliminary education in the Sixth Ward School, Bernard W. Matthews subsequently continued his studies in the Petersburg High School, which was then located on North Union Street, occupying the present site of the Y. M. C. A. Building. On leaving school he embarked in business with his father, with whom he was associated for many years, gaining under his instructions such an intimate knowledge of the buying and selling of groceries that each year his assets far exceed his liabilities, a very satisfactory record, considering the fact that he is now sole proprietor and manager of the business.

Mr. Matthews has been twice married. He married first, June 25, 1901, Miss Essie Maude McCann, who died in early womanhood, leaving seven children, as follows: Ruth Lee, Kenneth Eugene, Audrey Geneva, Bernard W., Jr., Ethel McCann, Albert Leverett and Lois Welton. Mr. Matthews married for his second wife, September 6, 1925, Miss Sallie Ann Wells, who was born in Dinwiddie County, a daughter of George P. and Ella (Collier) Wells.

Ever interested in educational matters, Mr. Matthews served as an active member of the local school board for eight years. Both he and his wife belong to the Second Baptist Church, in which they are active workers. Fraternally Mr. Matthews is a Shriner Mason and an Odd Fellow, and a member of Council No. 17, Junior Order United American Mechanics. Both he and his wife are members of Alpha Chapter, Order of the Eastern Star, and Mrs. Matthews belongs to George Thompson Council, No. 13, Daughters of Liberty.

REV. RICHARD L. MATTHEWS. Endowed with abilities of a solid and influential character, Rev. Richard L. Matthews, pastor of the Woodlawn Baptist Church of Chesterfield County, has a deep and lasting love for his profession, and takes an active and intelligent interest in promoting all activities pertaining to the advancement of public affairs. A son of Albert L. Matthews, he was born November 19, 1859, on the Heath Plantation in Prince George County.

A native of Amelia County, Virginia, Albert L. Matthews was there brought up and educated. After his marriage with Minerva Heath, a daughter of Henry Heath, he settled on that part of the Heath Plantation that came into the possession of his wife through inheritance. At the outbreak of the Civil war he enlisted in the Confederate army, and as he never returned to his home it is supposed he was killed, and was buried with the unknown, heroic dead. Henry Heath, his father-in-law, was a life long resident of Prince George County, belonging to a family of much prominence. He owned a large plantation, which he operated with slave labor, his estate being well improved and quite productive. Of the union of Mr. and Mrs. Albert L. Matthews three children were born and reared, namely: Laura, Edmonie and Richard L.

A small child when the tocsin of war rang throughout the land, Richard L. Matthews began the battle of life on his own account when young. He first found employment on a farm, receiving his board and twenty-five dollars in money for a year's work. As his strength and knowledge increased his wages were advanced, having been forty dollars the second year, then sixty dollars a year, and finally eighty dollars a year. Wisely saving his money, and ambitious to acquire an education, he first attended a public school in Chesterfield, later continuing his studies in the Petersburg High School.

In 1876 Mr. Matthews engaged in the grocery business on a very small scale, investing the sum of $10.74 in the daring venture. The business increased with amazing rapidity, in 1927 four clerks being kept constantly busy, and two delivery teams being required to convey the purchases from the store to the homes of the many patrons.

Having been converted in his youthful days, Mr. Matthews united with the Baptist Church, and subsequently as a local minister preached throughout Dinwiddie, Prince George and Chesterfield counties, in the meantime for twenty years teaching a Bible class. In 1913 he was ordained and given charge of the Woodlawn Baptist Church in Chesterfield County, where he has since served steadily and faithfully, his patient labors being widely and sincerely appreciated.

Mr. Matthews married, in 1879, Miss Mattie Lockett, a daughter of Lawson Lockett, and into their pleasant home six children have been born, as follows: Bernard W., Albert L., Garland E., Bertie L., Grace L. and Mary E.

CHARLES EVANS WINGO earned as his first distinction a creditable record as a Confederate soldier, and after the war his name attained increasing prominence at Richmond in connection with one of the largest boot and shoe houses of the state, the firm of Wingo, Ellet & Crump representing not only a great business in physical plant and assets, but also in those intangible assets of good will and good name.

Charles Evans Wingo was born in Amelia County, Virginia, July 12, 1843, and died at Richmond March 30, 1911. He was a son of William A. and Sarah Jane (Johnson) Wingo.

Colonel Wingo was educated in schools in Amelia County and attended a private school. He was sixteen years old when in 1859 he entered the firm of Eggleston & Fitzgerald at Richmond, serving without remuneration. Later he was with Samuel N. Price & Company, and resigned his position at the outbreak of the war to enlist. On account of his youth he was not accepted, but on reaching the age of eighteen he joined the Richmond Howitzers and was with that famous organization until wounded at the battle of Sharpsburg. Afterwards he rejoined his command and was with Lee's forces at the concluding scene at Appomattox. For many years after the war he was an honorary member of the Richmond Howitzers and the Confederate Veterans. The war over, he returned to Richmond and became an employe of Steinback & Company, and then with Garden & Carleton, a wholesale shoe house. There he learned the boot and shoe business, and in later years he organized the Wingo, Ellet & Crump Company, manufacturers of boots and shoes, undoubtedly one of the outstanding firms of its kind in Virginia. He was president of this company until he retired from business in 1907.

Colonel Wingo at the time of his death was vice president of the American National Bank of Richmond and a director of the Commonwealth Bank. He was twice elected to the General Assembly and in 1886 was chairman of the City Democratic Convention. He served on the staff of Governor O'Ferrall with the rank of colonel. Colonel Wingo was a member of Robert E. Lee Camp No. 1, United Confederate Veterans, was a past master of the Masonic Lodge, member of the Country Club and Westmoreland Club, and served on the financial committee of the First Baptist Church.

At Richmond, in 1878, he married Miss Sally Belle Knight, daughter of Col. William Carter and Cleverine (Thomas) Knight, of Nottaway County. The Thomas family came from New England to Virginia in 1790. Col. William C. Knight was an attorney and planter, was a graduate of the University of Virginia, served at one time as president of the Virginia Agricultural Society, and in the early '50s he owned the Wilton estate on James River, selling this land in 1868. He then moved to Richmond and became editor of the *Southern Planter*. Col. William C. Knight had four children: William O., who is connected with the Southern Railway Company; Wray T., former postmaster of Richmond; Mrs. Sally Belle Wingo; and Creed Thomas, of Meridian, Idaho: Mrs. Wingo was educated in Richmond Female Institute.

Four children were born to the marriage of Mr. and Mrs. Wingo, all of whom were liberally educated, the sons attending the McGuire School for Boys. The oldest, Jane, is the wife of James Mullin, a Richmond attorney, whose father is a judge on the bench, and they have one son, James Whedbee Mullin. C. Wingo, Jr., graduated from the Virginia Military Institute in 1901 and finished his technical education at Cornell University, taking the degree of Mechanical Engineer in 1903. He is a member of the I. J. Smith & Company, contractors, this firm having had the contract for building the Mayo Bridge over the James River at Richmond, the first concrete bridge across that stream. William W. Wingo graduated from the Virginia Polytechnic Institute in 1904, and is an electrical engineer, now connected with the Caroline Chemical Company. He married Maria Vass Tuggle, of Blackstone, Virginia, daughter of Wilford and Clara (Vass) Tuggle, her father a prominent tobacconist of Blackstone.

John Trivilin Wingo graduated B. A. and A. M. from the University of Virginia in 1909, took the degree Bachelor of Law at that institution in 1909, and is a leading Richmond lawyer. He is a member of the Raven Society and Phi Beta Kappa. He married Miss Elizabeth Dallas Brown, a daughter of J. Thompson Brown and Cassie Tucker Brown, of Bedford County, Virginia, and they have three children, Charles Evans III, Peronneau Brown and Elizabeth Dallas. Mrs. John T. Wingo is a daughter of the late J. Thompson Brown, who died May 15, 1921, after a distinguished career. He was born at Petersburg, son of H. Peronneau and Frances (Coalter) Brown, and finished his education at the University of Virginia. Most of his life was

R.O.Fifield

spent at his farm, Ivy Clift, in Bedford County, and he represented that county several terms in the State Legislature and was a member of the Constitutional Convention of 1901-02. His public service was largely in behalf of the development of the state's rural and agricultural institutions. For twenty-seven years he was a member of the Board of Visitors of the Virginia Polytechnic Institute, and in 1900 he was appointed rector of the board, serving until 1908, and in 1912 was again appointed to that office and filled it until his death. He was also for several years chairman of the State Live Stock Sanitary Board and a member of the State Board of Crop Pest Commissioners, was a trustee of the New London Academy, member of the board of the Agricultural High School in Bedford County, and had been president of the State Agricultural Society during the '70s, being president at the time President Hayes attended the State Fair. He was founder of the Richmond Stove Works and a member of the George Wyatt Plow Company. He married Cassie Tucker, daughter of Dr. David Tucker, and Mrs. John T. Wingo was one of the six children who survived him.

Mrs. Wingo, who resides at 902 Park Avenue, in Richmond, is a member of the Society of Colonial Dames, Richmond Woman's Club, and her daughter, Mrs. Mullin, is a member of the Virginia Country Club and the Colonial Dames. Mrs. Maria Vass Tuggle is also a Colonial Dame.

REN A. FIFIELD thinks and works along progressive lines and is not only one of the representative members of the bar of Fauquier County, where he is engaged in the practice of his profession at Remington, but he is also editor and publisher of the *Remington Press,* a well ordered weekly newspaper that effectively represents the communal intersts of the little city in which it is publishd and also those of the district throughout which it is circulated.

Mr. Fifield has good reason to claim a goodly heritage of the vitality and progressiveness so significantly associated with the far northern part of our national domain, for he was born in Wabasha County, Minnesota, March 8, 1892, and is a scion of pioneer ancestry in that state, within whose borders were likewise born his parents, Seth E. and Helen V. (Pierce) Fifield, who came to Virginia in 1906 and established their home in Fauquier County, where they now reside on their well improved dairy farm, the same being operated in accord with modern scientific methods and with policies notable for progressiveness.

Ren A. Fifield acquired his early education by attending the public schools of Minnesota and was a lad of fourteen years when the family home was established in Fauquier County, Virginia. Here he attended the high school at Remington, and thereafter he prepared for his chosen profession by completing a course in the law department of Richmond College, now the University of Richmond. In this institution Mr. Fifield was graduated as a member of the class of 1913, and after thus receiving his degree of Bachelor of Laws and being admitted to the Virginia bar he initiated the practice of his profession at Remington. Here he continued his practice until he responded to the call of a higher duty, that of patriotism. In 1917, the year marking American entrance into the World war, Mr. Fifield enlisted in the United States Army, and thereafter he was with his command in fourteen months of active overseas service with the Twenty-sixth Division of the American Expeditionary

Forces. His entire period of service covered eighteen months, and he was in France at the time the now historic armistice was signed. After the war thus closed he returned with his command to his native land, and he received his honorable discharge on the 13th of May, 1919. He then resumed the practice of law at Remington, and here he now has a substantial and important general practice of representative order. He is also the progressive editor and publisher of the *Remington Press, as* previously noted, and is a director of the State Bank of Remington.

Mr. Fifield has membership in the American Bar Association, the Virginia State Bar Association and the Fauquier County Bar Association. He is affiliated with the Masonic fraternity, including Acca Temple of the Mystic Shrine, in the City of Richmond. At Warrenton, judicial center of his home county, he is a member of the Rotary Club, and he is there a past commander of John D. Sudduth Post of the American Legion. His political support and that of his newspaper are given unreservedly to the Democratic party, and in their attractive home community he and his wife have membership in the Methodist Episcopal Church, South.

September 14, 1921, recorded the marriage of Mr. Fifield and Miss Willa B. Oden, who was born and reared in Fauquier County and who is a daughter of William B. and Sadie (Wood) Oden, her father having been born in Rappahannock County, this state, and her mother in the City of Fredericksburg, Spotsylvania County. William B. Oden became a merchant at Warrenton and later established himself in the general merchandise business at Remington, where he continued to be thus engaged until his death, December 30, 1923, his widow being still a resident of this community. Mr. and Mrs. Fifield have a winsome daughter, Helen Wood, who was born November 8, 1926.

GEORGE LUDLOW WHITE, B. C. S. Beliving in education as the first stepping stone to success, George Ludlow White, B. C. S., established the White School of Business, an institution in which many of the young people of Petersburg and its suburbs are acquiring knowledge that will be of inestimable value to them in future years. A native of New Brunswick, he was born near Fredericton, which was likewise the birthplace of his father, Charles Whitfield White.

Mr. White's paternal grandfather, Michael White, was a son of William White, a life long resident of New Brunswick, and a grandson of Henry White, who during the Revolutionary war left his home on Long Island, New York, fleeing to New Brunswick with such of his neighbors as were loyal to the British Crown. William White married a Miss McNally, who was of Scotch ancestry. Michael White married a Miss Ruth Estabrook, who was born in Marysville, New Brunswick. He was engaged in agricultural pursuits during his entire life, his home having been at Nashwaak.

Charles Whitfield White attended first the rural schools of his native district, later completing his early studies in the Fredericton, New Brunswick, Seminary. As a civil engineer he was for many years employed in surveying land and lumber, but is now living retired from active work. He married Mrs. Henrietta (Kilburn) Miles, who was born at Macnaquac, New Brunswick, a daughter of John and Ann (Hammond) Kilburn. She died at the age of sixty-four years, leaving four children, namely: Vivian, Rilla and George L. and Sarah E., twins.

Brought up on his native soil, George L. White attended first the Durham Bridge School in York County, New Brunswick, and later the Fredericton High School. Leaving home at the age of sixteen years, he entered the Coleman National Business College at Newark, New Jersey, and on leaving that institution began his career as a teacher in Palmer College, Philadelphia, later accepting a similar position in the Braddock High School. Mr. White then entered the University of Pittsburgh at Pittsburgh, Pennsylvania, from which he was graduated with the degree of B. C. S. Going soon after to Marion, Ohio, he taught for a time in the local high school; going westward to Des Moines, Iowa, he had charge of the commercial department of the West High School for three years. Returning then to his home in New Brunswick, Mr. White served as principal of the Fredericton Business College until 1922. Coming then to Virginia, he purchased the Bowman Commercial College, and having changed its name to the White School of Business has since conducted it most successfully, his patronage being large and widely extended.

Mr. White married, in 1916, Theo Beatrice McLean, who was born at Hubbards, Halifax County, Nova Scotia, a daughter of Donald McLean. Mr. and Mrs. White have one child, George L. White, Jr. Mr. White is a Mason, and a member of the Petersburg Rotary Club.

ROBERT GREENE BASS. A self-made man in every sense implied by the term, Robert Greene Bass has steadily climbed the ladder of progress, working his way upward rung by rung, at the preesnt writing being clerk of the Hastings Court, Petersburg. He was born in Petersburg, Virginia, which was likewise the birthplace of his father, Robert Greene Bass, Sr.

Christopher Bass, his paternal grandfather, was born and reared on a plantation lying about three miles from the Dinwiddie courthouse. He was the owner of a large plantation, which he operated with slave labor. Brave and patriotic, he served in the War of 1812, taking an active part in several engagements. He married a Miss Greene, and both lived happily for many years thereafter. Seven children were born to their marriage, as follows: George Moody Troupe, who served a number of years as superintendent of the Petersburg schools; Jane, who taught school in Petersburg for forty years, became the wife of William E. Maddera; Joseph, who went to Texas in 1850, established a successful business and there spent his remaining years; Fannie married John H. Cooper; Minerva married John H. Brown; Rebecca married John H. Hargrove; and Robert Greene Bass, Sr.

The youngest child of his parents, Robert Greene Bass, Sr., acquired his early education in the Petersburg schools, subsequently continuing his studies at the Monson Academy in Monson, Massachusetts, where he took a course of four years. Returning home after his graduation, he entered the Confederate army, enlisting in Company B, which was commanded by Capt. William Fischer, and attached to the Twelfth Virginia Cavalry. He continued with his command until the close of the conflict, having participated in its various battles and campaigns, and at the final surrender having been near Appomattox Court House.

Making his way back to Petersburg as quickly as circumstances allowed, he found no one to greet him, his family having refugeed. With clothes tattered and torn, he was leaning against a lamp post when Major Comstock, a Federal officer, came along with a horse and buggy. Stopping his horse, he said, "What are you doing here?" "Nothing," he replied. "What have you been doing?" "Fighting the Yankees." The Major then said, "As you are through fighting, how would you like to work for a Yankee?" "All right," was the reply. "I like the looks of your face," said the Major, "and think I can make use of you." Being asked about his clothes, Mr. Bass said those he had on were all that he owned. Major Comstock took him to a clothing store and outfitted him with a full suit, including hat and shoes. His first work for the Major was the checking of barrels of flour as they were unloaded. When, two years later, the Major was transferred he recommended Mr. Bass to his successor, Colonel Fulsome, who subsequently recommended him to his successor, Major Johnson. He continued in the employ of the U. S. Government for eleven years, during the last five years superintending the laying out and improving of the National Cemeteries at City Point and Danville, Virginia. Resigning his position with the Government, he was engaged in the meat packing business at Petersburg until 1880, when he entered the employ of the Norfolk & Western Railway Company, with which he was associated until his death, at the age of sixty-nine years. His wife, whose maiden name was Arabella Lavinia Burcher, was born in Petersburg, a daughter of John and Winifred Burcher. She passed to the Great Beyond in 1911.

The only child of his parents, Robert Greene Bass was given excellent educational advantages, beginning his studies in the Anderson School and later attending the old high school then standing on North Union Street. He subsequently attended the University of Virginia, after which he read law in the office of Richard H. Mann. Being admitted to the bar in January, 1906, Mr. Bass was very successfuuly engaged in the practice of his profession in Petersburg until 1913, when he was elected to his present position as clerk of Hustings Court in Petersburg.
Mr. Bass was very successfully engaged in the practice of his Enniss, who was born in Petersburg, a daughter of Albert W. and Mattie P. (Smith) Enniss. Mr. Bass is a Mason. He is identified with the Second Presbyterian Church, while Mrs. Bass is a member of the Wesley Methodist Church, South.

JAMES MORTON TOWNSEND. Possessing a keen intellect, a well ordered mind, and the courage of his convictions, James Morton Townsend, of Petersburg, is eminently deserving of the high rank he holds among the better known attorneys of Petersburg. A son of William Fisk Townsend, he was born in Georgetown, Delaware, coming on the paternal side of English ancestry.

His grandfather Townsend, a life long resident of Maryland, owned at Royal Oak a large plantation, on which he kept a large number of slaves busily employed. He married a Miss Benson, who came from another Maryland family of prominence.

Laying a substantial foundation for his future education at Dickinson College in Carlisle, Pennsylvania, William Fisk Townsend began the study of law in the office of Judge Teakle Wallace, of Baltimore, Maryland, where he was admitted to the bar. Subsequently purchasing the *Sussex County Journal,* he devoted his time and talents to the publishing of that paper until his death, which occurred at the comparatively early age of forty-seven years. His wife, whose name before marriage was Mary Eleonore Orr, was born in Petersburg, Virginia, of Scotch and Quaker ancestry. Her father, James Orr, was born in Londonderry, Ireland, of thrifty Scotch forebears. Her grandfather, Hugh Orr, was for many years captain of a vessel engaged in the East Indies trade, and was lost at sea.

James Orr, Mr. Townsend's maternal grandfather, in early manhood came to Petersburg, Virginia, to join his two older sisters, Mrs. Hill and Mrs. Simmons. At the outbreak of the War of 1812 he had not become a citizen of the United States, and for a time he was in a concentration camp. He subsequently took the oath of allegiance to the United States, enlisted in the army, and continued in service until receiving his honorable discharge. Engaging in the manufacture of tobacco, he continued in active business until his death in 1875. His wife, whose name before marriage was Anna Eleonore Peters, was born in Petersburg, Virginia, a daughter of Frederick D. Peters, who was born in Germany, and educated at Heidelberg University. Soon after his graduation he located at Petersburg, Virginia, where he was prosperously engaged in the tobacco business until his untimely death, which was caused by a fall from a horse.

At the death of her husband Mrs. Eleonore (Orr) Townsend was left with two small children to care for. One of them, a daughter named Anna E. Townsend, died when but seven years old. Returning to Petersburg, she soon after accepted a position in the Department of Charities and Correction in New York City, where she remained many years. Subsequently retiring with a pension, she made her home in Petersburg, spending her winters, however, in Florida until her death at the age of eighty-three years.

After the death of his father James Morton Townsend lived with his maternal grandmother in Petersburg, where he obtained his early education. He attended McCabe's University School and later continued his studies for a year in Stuttgart, Germany, on his return entering the University of Virginia, which conferred upon him the degrees of B. A. in 1898 and of M. A. in 1899. He then taught for one year in St. Matthews Military School on the Hudson, and a year in Kenyon Military Academy at Gambier, Ohio. Entering then the law department of the University of Virginia, he made good use of his time, and in 1902 was admitted to the bar. Beginning the practice of his profession in Petersburg, he was associated with George S. Bernard until his partner's death in 1913. Since that time Mr. Townsend has been a member of the firm of Mann & Townsend, of which Bernard Mann is the senior member.

This firm has its full share of the legal business of this section of the state, being division counsel for the Atlantic Coast Line Railroad; local counsel for the Norfolk & Western Railroad; local counsel for the American Railway Express Company, and with these companies to care for, legally, and its other business this firm is kept busy.

On April 14, 1899, Mr. Townsend married Elizabeth Bryan, who was born in Clarke County, Virginia, a daughter of Corbin Braxton and Mary Sidney Caldwell (Scott) Bryan. Her father, Dr. C. B. Bryan, was an Episcopal clergyman, and for several years was rector of Grace Episcopal Church in Petersburg. Her grandfather, John Randolph Bryan, was a native of Georgia, as was his father, Joseph Bryan. Joseph Bryan was a classmate and an intimate friend of John Randolph of Roanoke, with whom he served in Congress. Upon the death of Joseph Bryan his son John, Mrs. Townsend's grandfather, was placed in the care of John Randolph, who brought him to Virginia. This John Randolph Bryan subsequently married John Randolph's favorite niece, Elizabeth Coulter, daughter of Judge Coulter, of the Supreme Court of Virginia, whose wife was Fannie Tucker, a daughter of Judge St. George Tucker, also of the Supreme Court of Appeals of Virginia.

Mr. and Mrs. Townsend have five children, namely: Eleanore Peters; Braxton Bryan, Morton, Walter Scott and Elizabeth Bryan. Mr. and Mrs. Townsend are active members of Christ Episcopal Church.

SIMON SEWARD. Naturally studious and industrious, and possessed of abilities that have made him a thorough scholar in many branches of the law, Simon Seward, of Petersburg, is well worthy of the high position he holds among the leading attorneys of Dinwiddie County. A son of Hatcher Seward, he was born in Petersburg in 1899, of early Colonial ancestry, being a descendant in the seventh generation of Carter Seward, an early settler of Virginia, the line of descent being traced as follows: Carter, Alberton, Carey, Joseph, Simon E. V., Hatcher S., and Simon.

Carter Seward served as a soldier in the Revolutionary war, having been a member of Captain Holcomb's company, Fourth Virginia Regiment, which was under the command of Col. Thomas Elliott. Joseph Seward located in Petersburg, Virginia, several years prior to the Civil war, and having established himself as a grocer there conducted a prosperous business until his death. He married Sarah Frances Bole, and into their household three sons and three daughters were born. Simon E. V. Seward, born in Petersburg in 1846, was there reared and educated. During the Civil war, as a lad of eighteen years, he enlisted for service in the Confederate army. On June 28, 1863, he was captured near Rockville, Maryland, and was first taken to the Capital Prison in Washington, D. C., but six weeks later was transferred to Point Lookout. A few weeks afterward he made his escape, but ere he left the prison grounds he was seen by the Union guards. The night was very dark, and the water not very far away. Although the bullets whizzed around him, he reached the water in safety and swam across the Chesapeake Bay, striking, fortunately, a sandbar, on which he rested for awhile, although he was in the line of shell fire until he reached the shore. As most of the residents of that locality were true Southerners, they gladly assisted him as best they could, giving him food and shelter when possible. Crossing the Rappahannock in a leaky boat, he reached Richmond, Virginia, where he called on General Wender, who gave him a pass to Petersburg.

After visiting friends and relatives a short time, Simon E. V. Seward joined his regiment, which was attached to Gen. J. E. B. Stuart's command, and continued in service until the close of the conflict. Returning then to Petersburg, he engaged in business as a miller, and likewise established the trunk and bag manufacturing business now being conducted by his sons.

On February 11, 1866, he married Sarah Nunnally, who was born in Petersburg, Virginia, of early English ancestry. Nine children were born to their union, namely: Joseph W., Lulu Frances, Lee, Percy, Harvey, Rosa May, Hatcher, Alice and

Laurence R. R. Curtis and Wife

Annie Belle. Both were members of the Baptist Church, and reared their children in the same religious faith.

Hatcher S. Seward is a prominent manufacturer of Petersburg. He is president of the Seward Trunk and Bag Company, and vice president of the Petersburg Dairy Company.

Simon Seward acquired his preliminary education in a private school, and prepared for college at the Episcopal High School. Entering the University of Virginia he was graduated from its law department in 1923, and has since been actively and successfully engaged in the practice of his profession in Petersburg. He married in 1924 Miss Frances C. Churchman, who was born in Staunton, Virginia, a daughter of John W. and Annie (Johnson) Churchman. Mr. and Mrs. Seward have one child, a daughter named Frances Churchman. Mr. Seward is a Mason, and a member of two college fraternities, the Phi Kappa Sigma and Phi Delta Phi. True to the religious faith in which he was reared, he is a member of the Baptist Church.

LAWRENCE ROBERT ROSE CURTIS is a native son of Stafford County, has been a farmer, civil engineer and lawyer, and is now performing the duties of commonwealth attorney of the county.

Mr. Curtis, who has his home and law offices at Falmouth, was born March 3, 1890, son of William H. and Susan E. (Bloxton) Curtis, natives of the same county. His father, who died in September, 1898, spent all his active life as a Stafford County farmer. His mother died in June, 1928.

L. R. R. Curtis was reared and educated in his native county, and while farming took up the study of law privately and was licensed to practice in 1913, at the age of twenty-three. For several years he continued the active work on his farm while attending court in behalf of his clients. He also studied and qualified himself for the profession of civil engineering, and from 1919 to 1924 made that his chief occupation, and is frequently employed in work of that nature. Mr. Curtis resumed the practice of law in 1924, with offices at Falmouth, and in November, 1927, was elected commonwealth attorney of Stafford County for a term of four years.

He married, October 8, 1918, Miss May Lunsford, daughter of Floyd and Sadie (Irvine) Lunsford. Her father has for many years been one of the well-to-do farmers of Stafford County.

In addition to his duties as commonwealth attorney, Mr. Curtis for the past fifteen years has been commissioner in chancery. He is a Republican, member of the Baptist Church, and teaches a men's Bible class in the Sunday school.

WILLIAM NEWTON GRUBB is a citizen of Norfolk distinguished by the quiet efficiency with which he has performed a varied routine of duties in business, social life and public affairs.

Mr. Grubb was born at Richmond in 1852, son of John Grubb and grandson of John Grubb. His great-grandfather, Andrew Grubb, was a resident of Pennsylvania. The grandfather, John Grubb, was a resident of York County, Pennsylvania, in 1776, and there is a record showing that he lived in Jefferson County, Virginia, in 1796. He married Elizabeth Kilton. Their son, John Grubb, was born at Alexandria, Virginia, later moved to Richmond, and became a daguerreotype artist, making many of the daguerreotype portraits which were famous and are prized relics of many old families today. He lived to be only thirty-two years of age. His wife, Emily Pratt, was born in Norwich, England, November 23, 1822. Her father, William Pratt, was born in Norwich January 18, 1790, and her mother, Elizabeth Stevens, was also a native of England, and they were married at St. Ives April 22, 1819. In 1831 the Pratt family came to America, living for a time in Washington, D. C., and then moving to Alexandria, Virginia. William Pratt was a highly educated and cultured gentleman, gifted in music, and he taught music in Washington and Alexandria. His widow survived him and went to the University of Virginia to live with her son William A., who for several years was supervising architect at the university. This son during the Civil war was in the Confederate service as a blockade runner and made many successful trips across the ocean, bringing in supplies needed by the Confederate government. Mrs. Emily (Pratt) Grubb acquired a good education, being gifted in art and music, and before her marriage she was for a time governess at Arlington, the home of Robert E. Lee, and taught some of the Lee children. Lee at that time was a major in the United States Army. After she was left a widow with one child she resumed teaching at Richmond, where she made her home during the war until February, 1865, when she went to Norfolk, being passenger on a boat carrying a flag of truce. William Newton Grubb still has the pass, signed Gen. B. F. Butler, allowing them to pass through the Union lines. In Norfolk after the war she opened a girls' school, which she conducted for several years, and she spent her last days in the home of her son. She died at the advanced age of eighty-nine.

William Newton Grubb received most of his early education from his mother. He attended public schools one year and at the age of fourteen began work in a photograph store. He remained only one year and then became office boy with the Norfolk Gas Company and eventually was promoted to secretary of the company, in whose service he remained twenty-eight years. Since 1895 Mr. Grubb has been in the accident insurance business, and has one of the large and prosperous agencies at Norfolk, located at 108 Charlotte Street.

He married, October 22, 1878, Miss Mary Griffith, who was born in Norfolk in 1854, daughter of Edward J. Griffith. Mrs. Grubb died February 2, 1923. They had a family of five children: Elizabeth Moss, William Abbott, Edward Stewart, Emily Louise and John Gilbert. The son William married Bertie Jeffress Nicholson. Edward S. married Kate Evans and has a son, named Edward Stewart. John G. married Mae Gertrude Sawyer, and their two children are Mary and John Gilbert. William A. is in the printing and rubber stamp business, and J. Gilbert is the president of the J. Gilbert Grubb Motor Company, Incorporated. Edward S. Grubb for the past twenty-five years has been an employe of the Newport News Ship Building & Dry Dock Company.

Mr. Grubb is a member of the Freemason Street Baptist Church and all his family belong to that church except Edward S., who is a Presbyterian and trustee of his church. Mr. Grubb has been a deacon of the Baptist Church. Another interest by which he is well known in Norfolk is his official connection with Ruth Lodge No. 85 of the Masonic fraternity. He was elected secretary of this lodge in 1879, and continuously by reelection has served, being now in the fiftieth year of his official connection with the lodge.

N. L. Willis

NORMAN LINDSEY WILLIS is junior member of the firm R. L. Willis & Son, general merchandise, at Remington in Fauquier County. Mr. Willis is a World war veteran, was overseas, and since the close of his military experience has been working steadily and effectively to build up the resources and extend the trade of the commercial organization founded by his father.

His father, Robert L. Willis, was born in Fauquier County, was educated in public schools there, and in early life had the experience of the home farm. During the past forty years he has given his energies exclusively to merchandising. He was a merchant at Bealeton until 1898, when he established his store at Remington and for thirty years has dealt with the people of a large community around Remington in general merchandise. He served fifteen years as a member of the Board of County Supervisors and for six years was mayor of Remington. He organized and is president of the State Bank of Remington and also supervises the operation of a farm of two hundred acres in Culpeper County. He is a Democrat in politics and a member of the Methodist Episcopal Church.

Robert L. Willis married in 1888 Miss Minnie Melvin, a native of Fauquier County. They had three children: Edith, who died in 1919, Marion, who died in 1917, and Norman Lindsey.

Norman Lindsey Willis was born at Bealeton, Fauquier County, July 3, 1895, and was reared and educated at Remington. As a boy he helped in his father's store, and thus gained a good knowledge of business before reaching his majority. He left the store in 1918 to join the colors and was with the Eightieth Division overseas. He was in action on the front lines in five major offensives, including the great battle of the Argonne Forest, where he had some narrow escapes. He was overseas about a year and received his honorable discharge June 6, 1919.

Mr. Willis after the war rejoined his father and since 1924 has been a member of the firm of R. L. Willis & Son. He married, December 27, 1920, Miss Florence Cowne, daughter of Thomas Whiting and Arabella Cowne, natives of Fauquier County, where her father is a farmer. Mr. and Mrs. Willis have one child, Jean Hope, born March 29, 1927. Mr. Willis is a member of the Masonic fraternity, is a Democrat, and member of the Episcopal Church. Mrs. Willis has membership in the Daughters of the American Revolution.

EDWIN ELLETT HUDSON has given all the active years of his manhood to the Newport News Shipbuilding & Dry Dock Company, being connected with the production manager's department of that industry.

He was born at Wytheville, Virginia, March 26, 1875, a son of Charles Edwin and Margaret (Giboney) Hudson. His father was born in Louisiana, was educated privately, and for many years lived at Wytheville, Virginia, where he was in the mercantile business. He died in 1885 and is buried at Wytheville. His wife, Margaret Giboney, was born in Wytheville, attended private schools there and the Wytheville Female Academy, and the old home where she grew up and in which she lived for many years occupied the site now covered by the convent. She is eighty-one years of age, very active mentally and physically, and has a host of friends in her former community of Wytheville and also at Newport News, where she lives with her son.

There were just two children, R. G. Hudson, of Plainfield, New Jersey, and Edwin Ellett.

Edwin Ellett Hudson attended the Campbell School at Wytheville, the Virginia Polytechnic Institute, and for about a year after leaving school was on the road as a traveling salesman. In 1903 he entered the service of the Newsport News Shipbuilding & Dry Dock Company, and has worked for that corporation ever since, giving more than a quarter of a century to its service. He started as a fitter's helper, but for a number of years has been with the production department. Mr. Hudson is a thirty-second degree Scottish Rite Mason, member of Khedive Temple of the Mystic Shrine, is a Democrat and a Presbyterian. For a number of years after going to work for the Newport News Company he kept his home at Wytheville, but later moved to Newport News, where he and his mother reside at 117 Fifty-fifth Street.

His older brother, R. G. Hudson, was born at Wytheville, attended the Campbell School, for several years was in the employ of the Bertha Mineral Company of Pulaski, later with the Pulaski National Bank as assistant cashier for about five years, and from there went to New York with the Clyde Steamship Company. He is now connected with the New Jersey Zinc Company, one of whose plants is at Austinville, Virginia, this being the oldest lead and zinc property in the state. He is assistant secretary of the company. R. G. Hudson married Margaret D. Scarburgh, of the Eastern Shore of Virginia, and they have two children, Margaret D. and Mary S. Hudson. Margaret resides with her father at Plainfield. Both are graduates of the high school there, and Mary, who also graduated from Holyoke College in Massachusetts, is married and lives at Plainfield.

MERRILL HEARN TILGHMAN, who died at Richmond in April, 1919, was for many years a prominent figure in the lumber industry of the southeastern states, his interests being widely dispersed over Virginia and the Carolinas. While his chief output was cooperage stock, he was identified with practically every phase of the industry, owning many tracts of pine and hardwood lands, and the milling and other facilities for working up the timber into finished material.

Mr. Tilghman was born at Salisbury, Maryland, August 16, 1846, and lived a long and useful life of more than three score and ten. His father, Littleton Tilghman, a Maryland planter and lumberman, married Mary Elliott, and of their eight children Merrill was the oldest.

The late Mr. Tilghman had his education in the public school at Maryland, and as a youth became associated with his father, who owned a large amount of land in Maryland and was in the lumber business. The son had a practical apprenticeship in every phase of the business, from cutting timber through the operation of mills and the selling of the product. Mr. Tilghman transferred his headquarters of operations to Virginia in 1890, building a plant at Norfolk for the manufacture of barrels, crates and similar products. He built up an enormous industry, utilizing the superior shipping facilities of Norfolk for the distribution of his output. His timber lands were acquired in large tracts over the Carolinas, and he had a factory for some years at Sellers, South Carolina, then established one at Dunn, North Carolina, and another at Marion, South Carolina. He was presi-

dent and treasurer of the corporation which owned and operated
these widely scattered properties over the Southeast, and in
later years his sons became associated with him, and at his
death the business was divided among his four sons, and the
separate plants are still in operation, a fact that is indicative
of the substantial conservative way in which he managed his
business affairs.

Mr. Tilghman was a member of the Lumber Men's Association, and the industry throughout the United States recorded
his death in a loss of one of the notable figures among the lumber
men of the past generation. He had many friendships and
associations that linked him with Virginia, and he was always
a staunch Democrat in politics.

He was twice married, his first wife being Oliva Holloway,
of Maryland, and his second wife Clara Bright, of Georgia. His
children were four sons and one daughter, all by his first marriage, the youngest child having been reared by Mrs. Tilghman,
who resides at Richmond at 1005 West Avenue. The oldest
child is Horace, a lumberman, owner of the Marion mill in
South Carolina; Granville is owner and manager of the mill at
Dunn, North Carolina; Charles, the third son, is deceased;
Harriett is the wife of William McCabe, Jr.; and Merrill Howard
lives at Wayne, Pennsylvania.

PATRICK HENRY DONAHOE was known in Richmond, his native city, a merchant, a man of uncompromising commercial
integrity, very popular, influential in politics, so that in a comparatively brief lifetime he left an impress for good.

He was born in Richmond December 13, 1862, and died in
that city January 11, 1917. His father, John Donahoe, a native
of County Tyrone, Ireland, was in business as a merchant at
Richmond for a number of years, locating there before the
war. John Donahoe married Martha Yates Binns, of Virginia.
They had three sons: John M., Rev. Charles E., a Catholic priest,
who was ordained in 1883, and who was a beloved pastor at
Portsmouth, Virginia, when he died November 27, 1916, and
Patrick Henry.

Patrick Henry Donahoe was educated in the school of St.
Patrick's parish at Richmond. His start in a business career
was made as an express messenger for the Adams Express Company. In 1886 he became a general merchant. From that time
until his death, thirty-one years later, he was in business at one
location, 910 North Seventeenth Street, and he made his store
a recognized institution of that locality.

Mr. Donahoe served sixteen years on the Board of Aldermen,
representing the Madison Ward. His unassuming character and
generosity won for him a multitude of friends both in his business relations and his associations with the city government.
He was exceedingly charitable. He belonged to Magill's Catholic Club, St. Vincent de Paul's Society and the Holy Name
Society, and he and his family were members of the Sacred
Heart Cathedral.

He married Miss Mary Ryan, who was born in Richmond and
educated at St. Patrick's School. Her parents were Martin and
Ann (Lillis) Ryan. Her father for many years was in business
as a merchant at Richmond. In the Ryan family were nine
children: Catherine, deceased; Mrs. Mary Donahoe; Annie B.;
John A., deceased; Lillis B.; Thomas M., deceased; Margaret,

who is the wife of J. S. Disney, of Richmond, and has three children, named John Lillis, Elizabeth and Ethel, Mr. Disney being connected with the Southern Railway; James I. Ryan, a Spanish-American war veteran, who was in Cuba during the war; and Teresa M. The father of these children came from Kilkenny, Ireland.

Mrs. Donahoe, who continues to occupy the old home at 1907 Grove Avenue, has three living children. Charles Joseph, the son, now living at Lee, Massachusetts, married Hazel Delarue, of Richmond, and has two children, Charles Joseph, Jr., and Henry. The two daughters of Mrs. Donahoe are Mary Agnes and Lillie Bernadette, the latter a dramatic artist.

ANDREW ESKRIDGE KENNEDY was born at Charlestown, West Virginia, March 9, 1873, son of Andrew E. and Maria Pendleton (Cooke) Kennedy, both natives of Virginia. Andrew E. Kennedy was an attorney by profession and for a number of years held judicial office in Charlestown.

His son, Andrew Eskridge Kennedy, attended school in Charlestown, learned the machinist's trade, and for several years was employed in the Miller Safe & Iron Works at Charlestown. He served in the Spanish-American war with the Signal Corps in Cuba, and subsequently entered the employ of the United States Navy Yard at Washington, and held an official position there. He died at Hyattsville, Maryland, in March, 1905. He was a member of the Episcopal Church.

Mrs. Kennedy, whose home is at 1617 Grove Avenue in Richmond, is a member of a prominent Virginia family. Her maiden name was Blanche Breeden. She and Mr. Kennedy were married June 2, 1902. Mrs. Kennedy was born in Richmond. Her father, Powhatan Breeden, was for forty-seven consecutive years in business as a dry goods merchant at Richmond. In 1900 he took up the real estate business and continued it successfully until his death. He was a vestryman and treasurer of the Monumental Episcopal Church and was one of the prominent men of his generation in the capital city. Mrs. Kennedy's maternal grandfather was John Pigram, who served with the rank of major in the Confederate army, and he and two brothers were killed at the battle of Manassas. Through her mother Mrs. Kennedy is also a descendant of the distinguished Harrison family of Virginia, one of her ancestors being the Harrison who was one of the signers of the Declaration of Independence. Powhatan Breeden and wife had six children: Powhatan, Jr., married Emma Potter and had two children, Powhatan III and Mary; Mrs. Blanche Kennedy is next in age; William is deputy clerk of the Hustings Court at Richmond; Edward married Saddie Brackett, of Powhatan County, and has a son, Edward, Jr.; Maria May is the wife of N. B. Thayer, of Philadelphia, and has two children, Maria May and James Gardner; and the sixth of the family is Byrd Harrison.

Mrs. Kennedy has three daughters, Miss Maria May, Elizabeth Pendleton Norton and Miss Blanche. Maria May is now physical director of the North Carolina Orthopedic Hospital, an institution for crippled children. Elizabeth Pendleton Norton is the wife of William E. Norton, connected with a trust company in New York City.

C. O'Brien

CHARLES ORMOND WRENN. From the time he was fourteen years of age until his death in 1923 the late Charles Ormond Wrenn was identified with the vehicle industry of Norfolk, primarily as a manufacturer of wagons, carriages and buggies, and later as a dealer in automobiles. During a long period of years he was president of the firm of A. Wrenn & Sons, which was established prior to the war between the states, and at one period this concern was known throughout the country for the excellence of its products and for its own substantial position in the business world. Naturally the advent of the automobile and its subsequent development and adoption as the standard method of transportation drove many vehicle concerns from the field of operation, but until the end of his career Mr. Wrenn remained one of the leading business figures of Norfolk, where he was also greatly esteemed for his high character and constructive citizenship.

Mr. Wrenn was born at Norfolk, October 5, 1856, a son of Aurelius and Martha Virginia (Holmes) Wrenn. The Wrenn family was established in Virginia at an early period in Colonial times, and its members have always been leaders in business, professional, public and military life. The ancestors of Charles Ormond Wrenn settled at Norfolk from Mathews County, Virginia, prior to the Revolutionary war. Aurelius Wrenn was born at Norfolk, and as a youth was apprenticed to the trade of wagon maker, at which he was employed for a number of years. Eventually he embarked in business on his own account and founded the firm of A. Wrenn & Sons, admitting his sons to partnership as they came of age. It was the pioneer concern of its kind in the locality and soon gained a reputation that it never relinquished. Aurelius Wrenn married Martha Virginia Holmes, a descendant of the Holmes family which was prominent in the early history of Virginia.

Charles Ormond Wrenn received his education in the public schools of Norfolk and at Norfolk Academy, and at the age of fourteen years went to work in his father's store, which was connected with the manufacturing business. When he reached the age of twenty-one years he was taken into partnership by his father in the firm of A. Wrenn & Sons, and continued therein until his death August 21, 1923. At the time of his father's demise he became president of the concern, which then adopted the style of A. Wrenn & Sons, Incorporated, and which continued to manufacture various kinds of vehicles, which had a country-wide market. Mr. Wrenn's far sightedness enabled him to see that the automobile was to take the place of horse-drawn vehicles, and some time before his death the business was changed to an automobile concern, still carrying the name of A. Wrenn & Sons, Incorporated, and being carried on by his sons, with agencies at Norfolk and Portsmouth, as representatives of Cadillac motor cars. Mr. Wrenn was held in great esteem by his business associates, and once was president of the National Carriage Builders Association. Mr. Wrenn was a man of great public spirit, and in addition to subscribing to all worthy civic projects, was a generous contributor, in a very unostentatious way, to charitable and religious causes. He was a member of the Methodist Church, and belonged to the Old Virginia and Burr Clubs. Politically a Democrat, he took a keen interest in public affairs, and for a time served capably as a member of the City Council of Norfolk, in which body his work was of a constructive character.

On November 5, 1884, Mr. Wrenn was united in marriage with Miss Jessie Richards, a member of a family which came from London, England, at an early day and settled in Fauquier County, Virginia. Mrs. Wrenn was educated at Baltimore, Maryland, and Staunton, Virginia, and is a daughter of the late Burr Howard Richards, a native of Fauquier County, who for many years was a leading wholesale merchant of Baltimore and prominent in that city's public affairs. She survives her husband and is residing at 703 Colonial Avenue, where she is the center of a circle of sincere and appreciative friends. Five children were born to Mr. and Mrs. Wrenn: Charles Ormond, educated at Norfolk and now the proprietor of an automobile agency at Portsmouth, who married Blanche Dogan, daughter of Rev. Robert Dogan, D. D.; Howard Aurelius, who died when eleven and one-half months old; Miss Josephine, who was educated at Norfolk and at the Ogontz School, Philadelphia, a finishing school for young ladies; B. Richards, who was educated at Norfolk and Woodbury Forest, now proprietor of the Dodge Brothers automobile agency at Norfolk, married Cleone Stairley and has one child, Betty Stairley; Lawrence, educated at Norfolk and Woodbury Forest, who is now identified with the Dodge agency at Norfolk; and McDonald Edward, educated at Norfolk, Woodbury Forest and the University of Virginia, from which latter institution he was graduated with the degree of Bachelor of Laws as a member of the class of 1928, is now engaged in the practice of his profession at Baltimore.

TARLTON FLEMING HEATH had a long and successful career as a business man of Petersburg, a grain merchant, a banker, a citizen of high standing whose personal character accorded well with his distinguished Virginia ancestry.

He was born at Glen Heath in Goochland County, Virginia, November 30, 1860. There were two brothers, Robert and John Heath, who came from England, landed at Jamestown and settled in Surrey County. One of their descendants was William Heath, born June 17, 1731, who married Margaret Bonner, who was born in 1731 and died in 1804. William Heath died in 1771. His son, Jesse Heath, was born in Prince George County, Virginia, November 5, 1765, was a planter and slave owner and occupied the old Heath homestead in Prince George County, where he died September 4, 1850. He married Agnes Peebles, who was born March 15, 1772, daughter of Lemuel and Rebecca Peebles. She died January 17, 1816.

Their son, Hartwell Peebles Heath, grandfather of the late Tarlton F. Heath, was born in Prince George County March 21, 1794, and for many years was in business as a commission merchant at Petersburg, where he died January 31, 1837. He married Eliza Cureton Rives, of Sussex County, a sister of Francis E. Rives, a prominent Virginia statesman. Her parents were Briggs and Ann (Cureton) Rives, and she was a granddaughter of Timothy and Sally (Gee) Rives. Hartwell P. and Eliza (Rives) Heath had three sons and two daughters. The oldest son, John Francis, studied in German university after graduating from Harvard, and studied medicine at Philadelphia. Roscoe Briggs, the second son, graduated from the University of Virginia, married Bettie Mason, daughter of John Y. Mason, who was ambassador to France and later secretary of the navy, and they were the parents of four children.

Jesse Hartwell Heath, third son of Hartwell Peebles Heath, was born at Petersburg in 1832, and he spent many years of his life as a planter at Glen Heath in Goochland County. At the outbreak of the Civil war he joined the Goochland troops, each member furnishing his full equipment, including a horse. The troop was commanded by Col. Julian Harrison, of Elk Hill, and was attached to Stuart's Division. He was in the service until the end of the war, returning home in poor health and died in August, 1866, at the age of thirty-four. Jesse Hartwell Heath married Sarah Eleanor Fleming, who was born in 1832 at Mannsville, Goochland County, daughter of Tarlton and Rebecca (Coles) Fleming, and a lineal descendant of Sir Thomas Fleming, second son of the Earl of Wigdon, who came to America in 1666 and settled at Jamestown, later moving to New Kent County. Sir Thomas Fleming married a Miss Tarlton, and their descendants are found numerously in Virginia and other states. Mrs. Sarah Eleanor Heath died in February, 1916. She reared five children, Eliza F., Maunsell White, Jane Rives, Tarlton F. and Ellen Hartwell. Eliza F. died unmarried at the age of twenty-five. The daughter Miss Jane Rives Heath, now the only survivor of the children, was liberally educated, and later acquired an interest in St. Timothy's School at Catonsville, Maryland, and for many years was its associate principal. She now lives retired with her sister-in-law, Mrs. Tarlton Heath, at Petersburg. The daughter Ellen Hartwell married Thomas F. Parsons, and they had three sons, William F., Jesse Heath and Tarlton F. Jesse H. married Mary Maury Binford and has three children, Ellen, Mary G. and Jesse. Tarlton Parsons was commissioned a lieutenant during the World war, went overseas with his command in 1918, was promoted to captain, and married Elinor Flournoy and has a son, Tarlton F., Jr.

Tarlton Fleming Heath was reared in Petersburg, spending most of his early years in the home of his grandmother. He attended public schools and the McCabe School, and at the age of fourteen began working in commercial establishments, and from this humble employment eventually made himself one of the outstanding bankers of Southern Virginia. In 1887 he engaged in the grain business, at first as Cabaniss & Company and later T. F. Heath & Company, Incorporated. Mr. Heath was also a director and vice president of the Petersburg Telephone Company. He was made president of the National Bank of Petersburg in 1914, and subsequently was president of the Petersburg Savings and Trust Company. He was a Democrat in politics and a member of the Episcopal Church.

Mr. Heath continued active in his manifold business responsibilities until his death on July 25, 1924.

He married, January 12, 1887, Rosa Gilmour Arrington, who was born at Warrenton, North Carolina, daughter of Samuel P. and Hannah B. (White) Arrington. Samuel P. Arrington was a member of Company C, Twelfth North Carolina Regiment, and with his company participated in more than a hundred skirmishes and battles, being at the final surrender at Appomattox. His father, John Arrington, was a planter and slave owner in Nash County, North Carolina. Samuel Arrington for some years was in the commission business at Petersburg, but then returned to Warrenton, North Carolina, where he died. Samuel Arrington married Hannah Bolton White, who was born in Warrenton, daughter of John and Priscilla (Jones) White. She is still living at the age of eighty-eight. Her father, John White, was a native of Scotland, came to America at the age of sixteen and located at Warrenton. During the war between the states he was commissioned by Governor Vance to go to England to buy supplies for North Carolina soldiers. The vessel on which he sailed was named the *Lord Clyde*. He was very successful in running the blockade and securing the supplies, and afterwards the vessel became one of the most famous blockade runners of the war, its name being changed to *Ad-Vance*.

Mr. and Mrs. Heath had three children, Rosa Arrington, Jesse Hartwell and Tarlton F., Jr. Rosa Arrington is the wife of William Lunsford Long, and their children are Rosa Arrington, Ruth Mason and William Lunsford. Jesse Hartwell Heath, who became associated with his father in business, married Emily Gordon Gilliam, and their children are Emily Gordon, Jesse Hartwell, Sarah Fleming and Hannah White. Tarlton F. Heath, Jr., married Mary C. Riddle.

WILLIAM E. W. SMITH lived the greater part of his life in the City of Richmond, was a printer by trade and had a useful and honorable part in the printing and publishing industry of the capital city.

He was born at Danville, Virginia, in 1860, and died October 15, 1893. His father, William Smith, enlisted from Danville for service in the Confederate army, and when about thirty years of age was killed in the battle of Seven Pines, near Richmond. William Smith married Elizabeth Petigo, of Montgomery County, Virginia. There were two children, Lillian Adner and William E. W.

When William E. W. Smith was a very small child his mother moved from Danville to Richmond, and he grew up in the capital city, graduating from the public schools there. He served his apprenticeship as a printer, and after learning his trade was employed in the printing department of the *Religious Herald* for many years. The only interruption to his service with that paper was several years with the *Richmond Dispatch*. He was a Democrat in politics and belonged to the Richmond Blues military organization.

Mrs. Smith is a member of the First Baptist Church and is affiliated with the Maccabees. Mr. Smith married Miss Emma P. Tinsley, of Hanover, Virginia, November 6, 1886. Mrs. Smith was reared and educated at Hanover. Her father, William Joseph Tinsley, was a farmer in that county and also held office as a magistrate. Her grandfather, Capt. Corbin C. Tinsley, served in the War of 1812. The mother of Mrs. Smith was Susan George, a native of Goochland County, Virginia. Mrs. Smith was the oldest of six children, the others being Alma, Josephine, Charles, Lucian and Corbin.

Mrs. Smith resides at 2804 West Grace Street in Richmond. She has one daughter, Lessie Maude, who is now Mrs. S. W. Bowers, of Richmond. Mr. Bowers is a veteran railroad man of Richmond. They have one daughter, Eunice Arlett Bowers.

JAMES BURRELL CLOPTON. In a business career of more than forty years James Burrell Clopton, of Richmond, came to rank as a man of deep and penetrating knowledge and insight, of utmost commercial integrity, and in the hardware trade particularly was an outstanding figure along the South Atlantic Coast.

He was born at Richmond February 28, 1854, and died in that city as a result of an accident February 19, 1919, when sixty-five years of age. His parents were Ed and Ann (Latane)

A. B. Chandler Jr.

Clopton, the latter a native of Virginia and of the prominent French Huguenot family of that name. Ed Clopton was born in Vermont and served in the Civil war.

James Burrell Clopton had only such educational advantages as were possible during the troubled period of the Civil war, and he prepared himself for life largely by practical work and experience. One of the first places he was employed was a hardware store, and the hardware business became his life's vocation. When about twenty years old he engaged in the retail business for himself. After several years he became an official in the Watkins Cottrell Hardware Company, and resigned from that house to join A. B. Clark & Sons, and had a responsiblle place in that organization until the time of his death.

Mr. Clopton was a member of the Richmond Business Men's Association. He was a Democrat, and a vestryman of the Lee Memorial Episcopal Church.

On May 28, 1890, at Richmond, he married Miss Carrie Archer, member of the distinguished family of that name in old Virginia. Her father was Dr. Edgar Archer, a leading physician of Richmond and Chesterfield, who graduated in medicine from the University of Pennsylvania. Doctor Archer married Martha Archer, a native of Amelia County, Virginia. They had four children, John Harvie, Wister, Eveleen and Mrs. Carrie Clopton, who is now the only survivor of the family. Mrs. Clopton became the mother of two children, the only one now living being Harvie A. Clopton, who graduated from the John Marshall High School of Richmond and Richmond University, class of 1917.

A. B. CHANDLER, JR., president of the State Teachers College at Fredericksburg, Virginia, was born at Bowling Green, Virginia, May 12, 1870, son of Algernon Bertrand and Julia Yates (Callaghan) Chandler.

Mr. Chandler was educated for the law and practiced that profession until he accepted the natural bent of his gifts for education. He took his A. B. degree at the University of Virginia in 1893, after which he studied at Washington and Lee University and Cornell University, and was engaged in the practice of law at Atlanta, Georgia, from 1895 to 1897. He taught in the Miss Ellett's School for Girls and Nolley's School for Boys at Richmond, was principal of the high school at Clifton Forge, Virginia, and from 1903 to 1910 principal of elementary schools at Richmond. He was professor of English in the Virginia Mechanics' Institute at Richmond from 1907 to 1910.

Mr. Chandler has been identified with the State Teachers College at Fredericksburg since 1915, for four years as dean and since 1919 as president. He was a member of the State Board of School Examiners from 1910 to 1912. For a number of years he has been a writer and teacher on educational topics, and is author of the Virginia Supplement to Frye's Higher Geography. Mr. Chandler was vice president of the State Teachers Association in 1905-08, and again in 1915-19. He is a member of the Virginia Historical Society, the Sons of the American Revolution, Westmoreland Club of Richmond, Phi Beta Kappa at the University of Virginia, the National Geographical Society, and was president of the Fredericksburg Rotary Club in 1923-24. He is a member of the Christian Church. Mr. Chandler married, July 23, 1902, Blanche Montgomery, of Warsaw, Virginia.

JOSEPH WILLIAM STARRITT, who was a railroad man and later a general contractor, became well known in many localities of Virginia, which was his native state, and he was distinguished among his fellowmen as a man of action, of high integrity, and deserved the affection and admiration of his many friends.

He was born at Saltville, Virginia, September 7, 1860, and died at Marion in this state May 19, 1916. His parents were Andrew and Minerva (Brooks) Starritt, both natives of Virginia. His father was a farmer in later years, a Government employe. Their six children were Amanda, Preston, James, Joseph William, Margaret and Josephine.

Joseph William Starritt was educated in private school, and at the age of sixteen entered the service of the Norfolk & Western Railroad. After several years he located at Bristol, Tennessee, and for two years was associated with his brother-in-law, M. D. Andes, in the general mercantile business. He sold out to enter the service of the Chesapeake & Ohio Railroad, was put in charge of the station at Sabot, Virginia, later was transferred to the general offices at Richmond, and successive promotions eventually made him first chief clerk of the maintenance of way department. It was failing health that caused him to resign this post in 1908.

Subsequently he took up contracting, doing railroad work and other heavy construction. He constructed the Ashburton and Forest Park Lake at Baltimore and for fifteen and one-half months was employed in railway construction work in Kentucky. On his return he spent some time in recuperating at his farm at Albemarle, Virginia, and after selling that property located in Marion, where he acquired a controlling interest in the Marion Machine & Foundry Company, and continued its active head until his death. Mr. Starritt exemplified the enterprise that makes big opportunities of small ones, and there was hardly a time when his business career could not be considered successful. He was a Democrat, a member of the Methodist Church and the Woodmen of the World.

He married, June 21, 1882, Miss Katie C. Dunn, who was born in Washington County, Virginia, and finished her education at Sullins College, Bristol, Virginia. Her father, Col. Isaac Baker Dunn, at the age of sixteen was a clock salesman, educated himself, finally attending Abingdon Academy, and then took up the mercantile business. For six years, 1849-54, he was in the Virginia Legislature, was a presidential elector, and under the Confederate government was appointed commissary general. Colonel Dunn married Mary Lynch, of Abingdon, Virginia, and they had the following children: Annie, Alice, Sallie, John, all deceased; Alice, who married Geo. R. Cowan, was the mother of four sons and three daughters, one of whom died in infancy, the others being William R. Cowan, Mrs. Nannie Pile, I. B. Cowan, deceased, Dr. Connelly M. Cowan; J. Merchant Cowan and Mrs. Susie Jones, all of Bristol; Molly, wife of W. H. Connor, of Bristol, Tennessee, and the mother of two children, Mrs. Mary York and Mrs. Annie Buell; I. B. Dunn, also deceased; Mrs. Katie Starritt; and Susan Dunn, wife of Charles Worley, of Bristol, Tennessee, they had one daughter Mary; and I. B. Dunn, Jr., had two sons, Connelly and Worley; also four daughters, Nannie, Susie, Lillian and Kathleen.

Since the death of her husband Mrs. Starritt has removed to Richmond and resides at 2034 West Grace Street. She is a past president of the Junior League of the Methodist Church and was formerly in charge of publicity for the W. C. T. U. in Smith

County. Mrs. Starritt had a family of seven children: Mary M.; A. M., who married Louisa Payne, of Huntington, West Virginia, and has two children, Joseph and Helen; Leo B., who married Frances Smith, who died leaving two children, Virginia and Alice, and later he married Zelna Patten, of Toledo, Ohio, by whom he has two sons, William and Robert; Nancy is Mrs. R. C. Hayes, of Marion, Virginia, and has one daughter, Nickettii; Fred D. married Annie Jones of Scottville, Virginia, and has two sons, Frederick D. and Zack Benjamin, and one daughter, Katherine Virginia; Katherine is Mrs. J. E. Saunders of Roanoke; and J. William, an attorney, married Mary Sheahan, of Toledo, Ohio.

The son Fred D. Starritt volunteered and was assigned duty with the United States Marine Corps January 26, 1918. He was trained at Paris Island, and in April, 1918, went overseas to France. On June 25, 1918, at the battle of Belleau Wood, he was wounded three times in fifteen minutes and was sent to Vichy Hospital, returning to Brooklyn, New York, November 4, 1918. His company reecived two citations for bravery and service at Belleau Wood. His brother, J. William Starritt, was in the chemical warfare division at Willoughby, Ohio, up to the time of the armistice.

ANDREW NEWTON POLLARD was a native Virginian, and for forty-two years was engaged in the real estate business at Richmond, where he was accorded a distinctive place not only in business but as a citizen.

He was born in King William County, Virginia, in April, 1857, and was sixty-five years of age when he died November 9, 1922. His father, Elijah Pollard. was a native of King and Queen County, but spent most of his life in Hanover County. He was a minister of the Church of the Disciples. Elijah Pollard married Mary Elizabeth Morris, daughter of a land owner and planter of King William County and a veteran of the Confederate army.

Andrew Newton Pollard attended public schools and finished his education in the University of Virginia. When he was twenty-three years of age he took up real estate and loans as a business, and about that time established an office at 832 East Main Street in Richmond. He gave undeviating attention to this one line of business for two years, and in addition was a silent partner in Branch & Company, members of the Richmond Stock Exchange. He was a member of the Richmond Real Estate Board, and also belonged to the Country Club, was a Democrat and a Presbyterian. Mrs. Pollard is a member of the Daughters of the American Revolution, the United Daughters of the Confederacy, and is a member of the board of the Community Church.

Mr. and Mrs. Pollard were married December 6, 1880. Her maiden name was Dolly Elizabeth Broach. She was born in King and Queen County. Mr. and Mrs. Pollard bought a home at Studley, the birthplace of Patrick Henry. Augustus M. Broach, father of Mrs. Pollard, was born in King and Queen County and was an extensive planter and land owner. He married Indiana Jackson, whose mother was a member of the Carleton family, a wealthy and prominent connection in King and Queen County. Augustus M. Broach was a lawyer by profession, and was the father of six children: Cora Ann, Thomas N., Mary Lillian, James, now deceased. Indiana and Dolly Elizabeth.

Mrs. Pollard had three children. Her son Ernest Clifford, now deceased, was a Richmond business man and married Kate

Jones. The daughter, Lena Odessa, is the wife of George L. Lowman, a lawyer by profession, who has had a prominent career in Kingfisher County, Oklahoma, being a former judge of that county, and has also served on the staff of the governor of Oklahoma, and is a regent of the Normal School at Norman.

Claude Brocke Pollard, the other son of Mrs. Pollard, married Miss Eva Zimmerman, of Buena Vista, Virginia. He had been studying medicine two years when America joined the allies in the war, and he at once volunteered, training with the Engineer Corps. He went overseas to France in 1917 with some of the first American troops and was on duty seven months, until disabled by gas. He was decorated by the French government.

JOHN FRANKLIN GIBBONEY, who for many years was active in business at Richmond, a pharmacist by profession and later in the real estate field, represented an old and prominent family of Southwestern Virginia.

His birthplace was Wytheville, where he was born in August, 1872. His father, John H. Gibboney, fought in the war between the states under the great Stonewall Jackson, and owned a large farm in the vicinity of Wytheville and for some years conducted a livery stable in that city. John H. Gibboney was a son of Robert Gibboney, founder of a large and important family at Wytheville. The children of John H. Gibboney and wife were: Rush, an artist, Marie, Elizabeth, John F., Burnett, Willie, Warfield, who served in the Spanish-American war, and Louis.

John Franklin Gibboney was educated in the schools of Wytheville, attended the Virginia Polytechnic Institute, and graduated from the College of Pharmacy at Richmond in 1892. For some five or six years he was manager of the T. A. Miller Drug Company at Richmond, and on resigning he took up real estate as a business and built up a large clientage and conducted an important service in that line until his death, which occurred June 24, 1915. His real estate offices were at 1014 East Main Street. Mr. Gibboney was a Democrat and attended Grace Baptist Church. He was a member of the Richmond Real Estate Board and the Masonic fraternity.

He married, October 29, 1895, Miss Sallie Louise Harris, of Powhatan County, who was educated at Cumberland and by private tutors. Her father, Henry J. Harris, was a planter. Her mother, Amelia Jane Webster, was a daughter of John Webster, of Amelia County, who was a first cousin of Daniel Webster, the great orator and statesman. Mrs. Gibboney, who resides at 4914 Grove Avenue in Richmond, was the youngest of her parents' children. Her sister Ida was Mrs. N. D. Harris, of Richmond, and her sister Elizabeth is Mrs. E. D. Walton of the same city.

Mrs. Gibboney is the mother of three children. Her son, John Franklin Gibboney, Jr., was educated in the John Marshall High School at Richmond, was editor of the *Richmond Daily Record* when America entered the World war, and though rejected when he volunteered he was later, in 1918, accepted for service in the Engineering Corps as a private of the first class, was promoted to sergeant-major, and died of the influenza in May, 1919. The older daughter is Marie Amelia, who attended the John Marshall High School and the University of Virginia, for a time was a teacher of Spanish in public schools, and is now the wife of H. I. Thompson, a traveling salesman of Richmond, and they have a son, John H. Thompson. Louise Gib-

boney, who attended John Marshall High School, graduated from the Harrisonburg State Teachers College, and taught science in public schools, is now Mrs. C. D. Lewis, of Hartford, Connecticut, and has a son, C. D., Jr. Mr. C. D. Lewis was for three years county agricultural agent of Giles County, Virginia, and is now an Agricultural Club leader at Hartford, Connecticut.

DAVID TUCKER BROOKE, whose ancestry includes many distinguished names in Virginia history, used his inherited talents and training with brilliant success in the field of law, and for many years was an outstanding member of the Norfolk bar.

He was born at Richmond April 28, 1852, and died at Norfolk March 28, 1915, at the age of sixty-three. He was a son of Henry Laurens and Virginia Sarah (Tucker) Brooke. His first American ancestor, William Brooke, settled in Virginia in 1621, locating in the region of the Rappahannock River which soon afterwards became Essex County. His grandson, Robert Brooke, married Katharine Booth. Their son Robert was the father of Richard Brooke, who married Ann Hay Taliaferro, of another branch of distinguished Virginia ancestry. John Brooke, son of Richard and Ann Hay (Taliaferro) Brooke, married Ann Mason Mercer Selden. These were the grandparents of the late David Tucker Brooke. Richard Brooke, fourth of the name, was a Virginia planter, and his sons played a notable part in Revolutionary and early state history. One of them, John Taliaferro Brooke, became a governor of the state, while his brother, Francis Brooke, served as judge of the Supreme Court of Appeals. Dr. Laurens Brooke was surgeon on the *Bonhomme Richard* commanded by John Paul Jones.

David Tucker Brooke's maternal ancestry was the noted Tucker family, which included Judge St. George Tucker, poet and professor of law in William and Mary College. Henry Laurens Brooke, father of David T., was an able lawyer well known in the profession both at Richmond and Baltimore. He was an early captain of the Richmond Grays.

David Tucker Brooke attended private school at Richmond, and completed his education in the University of Virginia. For nine years he was a teacher in public and private schools, chiefly in Norfolk, and while teaching he studied law under Tazewell Taylor of Norfolk. He was admitted to the bar in 1874 and at once began practice, associated with George McIntosh in the firm of McIntosh and Brooke. They dissolved partnership in 1879, and from 1880 to 1884 he was a member of the firm Borland & Brooke, his law partner being Thomas Borland. Mr. Brooke in 1884 was elected by the Virginia Legislature to fill an unexpired term as judge of the Corporation Court, and in 1888 was again elected for a six-year term. He declined reelection. He was a member of the Virginia Constitutional Convention and chairman of the committee on counties, cities and towns, and member of the committee on corporations. In 1903 he formed a partnership with Milton C. Elliott, and the firm of Brooke & Elliott continued until 1907, at which time Mr. Brooke took in his son, Henry Lawrence, as a partner. The firm of Brooke & Brooke continued until the death of the senior member in 1915.

David Tucker Brooke was in every sense a fine lawyer, scholarly, careful, a man whose integrity made him a trusted advisor of rich and poor, individuals and great business corporations. He was a member of the Chesapeake Club, and throughout his life dispensed a generous charity in his community.

He married, April 7, 1880, Lucy Borland, daughter of Ignatius Higgins, a Norfolk banker. Her father's people came from

Ireland and Mrs. Brooke is also a descendant of the well known Newton, Hutchins and Drummond families of Virginia, being related to Lord Drummond of the Eastern Shore. Mrs. Brooke survives her honored husband and resides at 619 Boissevain Avenue in Norfolk. Mr. and Mrs. Brooke had six children. Lucy Drummond, who was educated at the Georgetown Convent, is the wife of William Hubert Witt, and they have three children, D. Tucker Brooke Witt, William Asa Witt and Robert Brooke Witt, all attending school. Eloise Minor Brooke was educated at Norfolk, and during the World war was employed in the supply office of the British Admiralty at Norfolk. The son H. Laurence Brooke was educated in the Norfolk Academy and the University of Virginia, and has had a successful career as a lawyer. May Walton Brooke was educated at Norfolk and is in the advertising business there. Lena Randolph Brooke studied art at New York and Philadelphia and is the wife of Al McNamara, well known in New York City advertising circles. Mr. and Mrs. McNamara have three children, David Brooke, Lucy Baker and Thomas Randolph. The youngest child of Mrs. Brooke is Marguerita Custis, who was educated at Norfolk and is the wife of Lee Douglas Williams, a Norfolk attorney.

CHARLES SMITH THURSTON was for many years closely identified with the business and civic affairs of the City of Richmond. His chief business was building contracting, and he also enjoyed much influence as a citizen, had a large following of loyal friends and made his name respected throughout the city, which was his birthplace and where he lived out his life of sixty-four years.

He was born in Richmond in 1857 and died October 9, 1921. His father, John C. Thurston, was also a native of Virginia, was a Confederate soldier in the war, and married Lucy Ford, of another old family of Virginia. They had four children, Jennie, Charles S., Lucy and Willie.

Charles S. Thurston was educated in both public and private schools, and also had technical training in architecture and the building trades to fit him for the business which he followed until he retired. He built up an organization that handled many notable building projects in Richmond and elsewhere over the state. Mr. Thurston was a Democrat in politics and a member of the Baptist Church, and was affiliated with the Masonic order and Improved Order of Red Men. Mrs. Thurston is a Baptist and a member of the Eastern Star.

Mr. Thurston married, August 10, 1893, Miss Elmira Bernice Mann, of Powhatan County, Virginia, where she was reared and educated. Her parents were Alexander and Edmania (Heath) Mann, her father a native of Powhatan County and her mother of Hanover, Virginia. Her father spent his active life as a farmer. Mrs. Thurston has a sister, Josephine, now Mrs. G. D. Powell, of Richmond, and the mother of six children, named Charles, George, Lottie, Josie, Alexander and Harrie, and she had a brother, Charles Mann, now deceased.

To the marriage of Mr. and Mrs. Thurston were born five children. The son John C. was a young Virginian who gave up his life during the World war. He enlisted with the Canadian Expeditionary Forces, joining in January, 1915, and in June of that year was sent overseas and participated in the first battle in July. In 1916 he was among the slain on a battlefield in Flanders Field near Ypres, Belgium. Mrs. Thurston had two other sons who were soldiers, Charles A. and Wilbur J., both of whom joined the colors with the United States forces, Charles becoming a lieutenant and Wilbur a sergeant. Charles A. Thurston married Effie Saterfield, of Virginia, and has one child, Audrey. Wilbur J. married Irene Schraf, of Richmond. The two youngest children of Mrs. Thurston are Bernard and Bernice E., twins. Bernard married Saddie Farmer, of Richmond, and has one child, Bernard Linwood. Mrs. Thurston's home in Richmond is at 3135 West Franklin Street.

JOHN JOSEPH TURNER was a Virginian who came to manhood about the close of the Civil war and for nearly half a century was identified with the growing business prestige of Richmond, where he was prominently connected with the shoe industry.

He was born at Columbia, Virginia, May 14, 1844, and died in Richmond December 10, 1916, at the age of seventy-two. His father, I. N. Turner, was a merchant at Columbia, Virginia. The mother was Rebecca Winston Argyle, whose father was a graduate in medicine at Edinburgh, Scotland, and on coming to the United States settled at Talllahassee, Florida, where he practiced until he fell a victim of the yellow fever. I. N. Turner and wife had three children: William Argyle, who was a shoe manufacturer at Wilmington, Delaware, Frank Daniel and John Joseph.

John Joseph Turner acquired his education at Columbia and Richmond, Virginia, finishing in a private school conducted by a Mr. Mason at Columbia. As a young man he worked for several years with the Richmond dry goods house of Christian Lathrop Company, there laying the foundation of the experience which he utilized throughout his subsequent career. Eventually he bought an interest in and became secretary of Stearns & Company, one of the outstanding wholesale manufacturers of shoes in the State of Virginia, and he was active in that business until his death. Mr. Turner and family were all members of the Episcopal Church.

He married Miss Ellen Kean, of Lynchburg, Virginia, a member of a prominent Virginia family. Her grandfather, Andrew Kean, was educated at the University of Dublin, Ireland, where he graduated in medicine, and on coming to America settled in Goochland County, Virginia, and for several years practiced at Charlottesville. He then returned to Goochland County, where he superintended his three plantations and gave his professional services to his tenants and neighbors. He married Kittie Vaughan, and their two children were Julian Kean, who also took up the profession of medicine, and John Vaughan Kean. John Vaughan Kean, father of Mrs. Turner, first married Mildred Hill, of Hanover County, and had two sons, Lancellot M. and Robert G. H. Robert G. H. Kean became a distinguished Virginia attorney. He took his Master of Arts degree at the University of Virginia and for twelve years was rector of the Board of Visitors of the university. During the first year of the war he was on the staff as an aide of Gen. George Randolph, and subsequently was chief of the Bureau of War at Richmond, and during the evacuation of the capital he and his chief clerk took Confederate papers from the archives and fled with them to South Carolina. The second wife of John Vaughan Kean was Martha Callis, whose father, Col. William Callis, was a Revolutionary war veteran. By this marriage there were ten children, one of whom is Mrs. Turner. Mrs. Turner's father, John

Vaughan Kean, was for a number of years a member of the
faculty of the college at Olney in Caroline County, and after
retiring he managed his plantations.

Mrs. Turner, whose home has been in Richmond since 1907,
residing at 1107 West Grace Street, is the mother of three children. Her son John Argyle, for a number of years connected
with the tobacco industry of Richmond, married Rachel Urquhart. William Trevilian Turner, who was educated at Richmond,
entered the service of the Southern Railway Company, and by
his marriage with Claire Adams, daughter of H. P. Adams, of
Lynchburg, had one son, W. T., Jr. Robert Kean Turner, the
youngest of the three sons, married Eunice Henderson, of Nelson
County, Virginia, and has a son, Robert Kean, Jr.

ROBERT EDEY STEED, who since 1891, thirty-eight years, has
been in the service of the City of Norfolk, is descended from
one of the charter founders of that city, and several lines of
his ancestry have been identified with Virginia since Colonial
times.

The Steed family, according to Hasted's *History of Kent,
England*, published in 1782, were in England before the Norman
invasion, and there is a consecutive record of them in County
Kent since about the middle of the fifteenth century. This history records that Edwin Steed came to Virginia in 1737, having
been granted a tract of land on the Roanoke River in Brunswick County. Edwin Steed was a son of Dutton Steed, and a
grandson of Sir Edwin Steed, a governor of Barbadoes.

The first American ancestor of Robert Edey Steed was Robert Steed, who went from England to Bermuda and then to
Norfolk. He was an educated gentleman of considerable means
and a loyal member of the Church of England. Robert Steed
married, March 27, 1768, Hannah Edey, who was born January
29, 1749, daughter of Solomon and Hannah Edey, granddaughter
of John Ivey, and great-granddaughter of Thomas Ivey, who
was born at Norfolk in 1645 and was church warden of Norfolk.

A son of Robert and Hannah Steed was Robert Edey Steed,
born October 5, 1773. He married, March 26, 1801, Frances
Ramsey, daughter of John and Mary (Hutchings) Ramsey.
Mary Hutchings was a daughter of John Hutchings, whose name
appears in the list of aldermen appointed in the original charter
of the Borough of Norfolk, granted September 15, 1736, and of
him Forrest's *History of Norfolk* states: "The next name is
John Hutchings, who also opposed the Stamp Act, and was one
of the committee appointed by the Sons of Liberty. His earthly
remains also lie in the yard of old St. Paul's, near the south
gate. A daughter of his married Dr. John Ramsey, a native of
Scotland, a warm and fearless patriot, and a Son of Liberty."

George Washington Steed, son of Robert E. and Frances
(Ramsey) Steed, was born November 19, 1813, was educated in
Norfolk College, served as commissioner of revenue of Norfolk,
and was a man possessed of a high degree of public spirit. He
was a Democrat and a member of St. Paul's Episcopal Church.
He married Josephine Brumley, who was born in King and
Queen County, Virginia, February 5, 1836, daughter of Robert
and Mildred Brumley.

They were the parents of Mr. Robert Edey Steed, who was
born in King William County, Virginia, at "Cherry Lane," July
13, 1856. He was educated by Rev. G. S. Carraway in the Epis-

copal High School at Alexandria, and at Norwood College, Nelson County, Virginia. From 1882 to 1891 he was a clerk and bookkeeper for Norfolk business firms. On June 1, 1891, he entered the city treasurer's office as assistant to the treasurer and as bookkeeper and clerk to the council. On September 1, 1906, he was appointed the first incumbent of the newly created office of city clerk, and by repeated elections has filled that office continuously to the present time. Mr. Steed is a trustee of the Norfolk Y. W. C. A., trustee of the United Charities, the Society for Prevention of Cruelty to Children, the Seaman's Friend Society, and the Howard Association. Since early manhood he has had a leading part in the Disciples or Christian Church at Norfolk and was chairman of the building committee when the handsome new church of his congregation was erected on Colonial Avenue.

Referring not only to the religious but the secular side of his character the *Christian Evangelist* a year or so ago stated that Mr. Steed had exemplified the spirit of the motto of "The Union of Those Who Love in the Service of Those Who Suffer." The article went on to say: "That good religion of kindly service R. E. Steed has practiced all his life. As a result it may be truly written of him that he has been a helper of many. If every kind deed he has done, every encouraging word he has spoken to men and women on the long trail were to return upon himself he would be overwhelmed by the wealth of beauty and joy he has put into the world. He is a Virginia gentleman of the old school, who has taken over all that is best in the new. The times cannot outrun him, but the old, fine things of the religion and culture of the past are reflected in his bearing and conduct. He has led a quiet, steady life, but his strong and genial influence has been felt in all works of public good in his city. His life is tied up to a great many things, so that he is always busy with the enterprises of making a better world." Any man would be proud to have these things said of him through such a source, and the quotations undoubtedly express a correct measure of Mr. Steed's place and part in the community of Norfolk.

Mr. Steed married at Lanesville, King William County, July 3, 1883, Miss Ellen Ida Johnson, daughter of John Pemberton and Ellen (Smith) Johnson. Her father was a veteran of the Confederate army from 1861 to 1865, and owner of the estate "Cedar Lane" in King William County. Mrs. Steed was educated in the Henley School for Girls. They have two children. The son, George Hubert Steed, born at Norfolk July 29, 1884, was educated in the Norfolk High School, took the B. A. and M. A. degrees at Bethany College, is a prominent minister of the Christian Church, with home at Saint Petersburg, Florida. He married Emily K. Pritts, of Somerset, Pennsylvania. The daughter of Mr. and Mrs. Steed is Ellen Carraway, born January 10, 1891, at Norfolk, now the wife of Harold E. Masengill, of Tennessee, a Norfolk banker. Mrs. Masengill is very active in the social, civic and religious activities of Norfolk.

CLYDE ROMULOUS TARKENTON. Engineering, that branch of science dealing with the design, construction and operation of various machines, structures and engines used in the arts, trades and everyday life, is divided into many branches, among the most important being electrical engineering, which includes the application of electricity to mechanical and industrial pursuits, as derived from other sources of energy. Among the men who are winning distinction in this highly specialized and intensely interesting profession is Clyde Romulous Tarkenton, of Norfolk, who is representative of the John A. Gurkin Company for the southern half of the State of Virginia, from Richmond south to the North Carolina state line.

Mr. Tarkenton was born in Tyrrell County, North Carolina, in October, 1880, and he is a son of John Tarkenton, who for many years was a noted contractor of Tyrrell County, and a Confederate veteran of the war between the states, in which he saw active service. Mr. Tarkenton's uncle, Col. John Brabell, was a colonel of North Carolina troops during the entire period of that struggle. Clyde Romulous Tarkenton attended the public schools of his native state, following which he pursued a course in electrical engineering at Columbia University, New York City, from which he was graduated with his degree. Having specialized in steam engineering, he was chief engineer for some years on steamboats plying the waters of the Atlantic coast, and when the World war broke out was appointed an ensign in the United States Navy, being assigned as an expert at the New York Navy Yards as inspector of steam and electrical equipment for the navy under the mine sweeper division. He also was railroad engineer on the train between Georgetown, South Carolina, in the building of the Georgetown Bar Jetty. He also acted as engineer on boats and in the shop at Perico, Cristobal and Balboa, Panama Canal Zone. When relieved of his duties at the close of the war he entered the business of building and ensembling and repairing the largest marine shops of New York, after which he was appointed shore engineer of New York Harbor. The U. S. Shipping Board engaged his services for a number of years. He engaged in the electrical business on his own account, but gave up this enterprise to accept the appointment of representative of the John A. Gurkin Company of Norfolk for the southern half of the State of Virginia, from Richmond to the North Carolina state line. This company deals in electrical machines, apparatus and appliances of all kinds, and Mr. Tarkenton is widely known to both the wholesale and retail trade of his territory. Being himself an expert in his line, his services are of incalculable value to his company, and he has the fullest confidence of his employers and the respect and admiration of his associates, both professionally and in a business way. He is a Democrat in his political allegiance, but has been too busily engaged with his work to take an interest in politics save as a public spirited citizen of enlightened and progressive views. He is a thirty-second degree Mason and Knight Templar, and a consistent member of the Methodist Church.

On April 22, 1922, Mr. Tarkenton was united in marriage with Miss Judith Mackey Vail, a member of the family which, originating in England, settled in North Carolina in the early Colonial period, since when it has contributed members who have helped to make business, professional and political history in that state. Mrs. Tarkenton was educated in the public school of Washington County, North Carolina, and is a daughter of Josephus and Mary Frances (Watson) Vail. Mr. Vail enlisted in the Confederate army when eighteen years of age and served until the close of the war between the states. Subsequently he became a prominent merchant and planter of Washington

WILLIAM P. HARNLY

County, where he was also active in civic life and for many years served as a member of the school board. Mrs. Tarkenton is an active member of the Episcopal Church and is also interested in club and social life at Norfolk, where the attractive family home is situated at 311 Westover Avenue.

WILLIAM PHILLIP HARNLY was an electrical, refrigeration and ventilating engineer who founded and built up an extensive business at Norfolk, and was one of the active figures in the commercial life of that city until his death at the comparatively early age of forty-five, on April 4, 1925.

He was born in Lancaster County, Pennsylvania, March 20, 1880. His father, John Phillip Harnly, came from Germany in 1840, settled in Pennsylvania and was prominent in the iron and steel industry, serving for many years as superintendent of the Glasgow Iron Works at Pottstown, Pennsylvania. He married Louise Reighter, and of their family of thirteen children, William Phillip was the seventh in age.

William Phillip Harnly attended school in Pennsylvania and as a boy began his apprenticeship in the Glasgow Iron Works under his father. He was something of a genius for industry and mechanics, and as a result of rapid promotions he was, at the age of nineteen, master mechanic of the Glasgow Iron Works. He worked during the day and utilized some of his night hours in the study of refrigeration and electrical engineering, later took a course in those subjects and a diploma, and was employed as boiler inspector on the steamer Sierra at the Cramps Shipyard. When that boat was completed he was made chief electrician and refrigeration engineer and served three years. After resigning he was for nine years with the Pennsylvania Bridge Company as mechanical draftsman.

Mr. Harnly in 1908 established himself in business in Norfolk as a heating and ventilating engineer. He conducted business under the firm name of Harnly Engineering Company. This organization for a number of years handled a great deal of important work. He was employed in equipping the Marine Barracks and the officers' quarters at Portsmouth, installing ice and other plants. During the World war the Government employed him to install heating, sewerage and water systems at the army and navy bases. He also did much work in equipping municipal buildings in Norfolk. Mr. Harnly was a member of the Norfolk Chamber of Commerce, was vice president of the Master Plumbers Association, a member of the National Union, the Lutheran Church, and a Democrat in politics.

Mr. Harnly married in November, 1907, Ruth May Foreman, of Norfolk County, where she was reared and educated. She is a descendant of Franklin Foreman, who served as a general in the Revolutionary war. The Foremans settled in Virginia, coming from England in Colonial times, and the family have lived for a number of generations in Norfolk County. Mrs. Harnly's father, James W. Foreman, was a farmer in Norfolk County. Her mother was Virginia Williams. Her father took a very active part in Democratic politics in his district. Mrs. Harnly is a member of the Free Mason Street Baptist Church at Norfolk. Her home is at 615 Boissevain Avenue. She is the mother of three children, William Phillip II, John Patrick and Ruth Irvin, all of whom have been given liberal educational advantages.

WILLIAM LEWIS COGBILL was for thirty years in the railroad service, with the Southern Railway, and became a highly respected citizen of Richmond, where he lived all his life. His wife, Mrs. Ada Elizabeth Cogbill, and their children still reside at Richmond, her home being at 2727 West Grace Street.

Mr. Cogbill was born at Richmond November 4, 1864, and died February 23, 1913. His father, William B. Cogbill, was a native of Chesterfield Courthouse, Virginia, where for many years he was engaged in business as a carriage manufacturer and finisher. William B. Cogbill married Mary Barbara Latimer, a native of Richmond and descended from an old family of the state.

William Lewis Cogbill was the oldest son in a family of six children and was reared and educated at Richmond. At the age of nineteen, after leaving school, he went to work for the Southern Railway Company as a fireman, and after nineteen months he was promoted to the post of engineer. He was an engineer on different divisions and remained with the company thirty years, being one of the most faithful and trusted engineers on the staff of the company. He met death in a railroad wreck near Jennings, Virginia. He was a Democrat and he and his family were members of the First Baptist Church of Richmond. Fraternally he was affiliated with the Masonic order and Improved Order of Red Men, and also the Brotherhood of Locomotive Engineers.

Mr. Cogbill married, March 31, 1886, Miss Ada E. Goulden, who was born in Caroline County, Virginia. Her father, Silas Goulden, a native of the same county, was a planter and land owner there, and her mother, Lucy L. Taylor, was born in the same locality. Silas Goulden and wife had the following children: Andrew Jackson, Samuel Patrick, Highter L., Virginia Lee, Georgia A., Dora N. and Ada E. Cogbill.

The children of Mr. and Mrs. Cogbill are Minnie M., William Lewis, Jr., and Elizabeth J. Minnie is a graduate of the Woman's College of Virginia and is a talented teacher of music.

William Lewis Cogbill, Jr., graduated as a mechancial engineer from the Virginia Polytechnic Institute. He volunteered at the time of the World war and was with the Three Hundred and Twenty-fourth Infantry, Eighty-first Division. For ten months he was on active duty in France and later was transferred to London, England, where he was an instructor of technical mechanics in a London university.

WILLIAM ROANE RUFFIN. Distinguished as an upright, honorable citizen, and an able representative of the agricultural interests of Dinwiddie County, the late William Roane Ruffin, of Petersburg, was born July 3, 1845, in Albemarle County, Virginia, a son of Col. Francis Gildart Ruffin. He was of early Colonial ancestry, his paternal grandfather, William Ruffin, having been a native of Dinwiddie County, where his parents settled in pioneer days.

When a young man William Ruffin moved to Brunswick County, Virginia, from there going to North Carolina, where his twin brother was then living. Subsequently removing to Mississippi, he remained there until his death, which occurred a few years later. His wife, whose maiden name was Frances Gildart, was of substantial Revolutionary stock, her father having had command of a company attached to Colonel Tarleton's Cavalry.

Francis Gildart Ruffin was but seven years of age when his parents died. His uncle, Albert Ruffin, his father's twin brother, went to Mississippi after him, and having brought him to Virginia legally adopted him. He received good educational advantages, and later acquired a plantation in Albemarle County and operated it with slave labor. During the Civil war he served in the commissary department, holding the rank of colonel. After selling his plantation in Albemarle County he bought one in Chesterfield County, about four miles from Richmond. At the close of the war he became second state auditor, and on his removal to Richmond occupied the house in which John Marshall, statesman, soldier and jurist, and one of Virginia's noblest sons, once lived. He continued his residence in Richmond during his remaining years.

Francis Gildart Ruffin was twice married. His first wife, the mother of his children, was Caryanne Nicholas Randolph. She was born at Edge Hill, Albemarle County, Virginia, a daughter of Col. Thomas Jefferson and Jane Hollins (Nicholas) Randolph. Colonel Randolph was born in Virginia, a son of Thomas Mann and Martha (Jefferson) Randolph. Martha Jefferson was born in Monticello, Virginia, a daughter of Hon. Thomas Jefferson, one of the most distinguished of Americans.

At the outbreak of the Civil war William Roane Ruffin was a cadet in the Virginia Military Institute, and in 1863 was called into active service in an artillery company. In the engagement at Salem Creek he was captured by the enemy, and was subsequently confined as a prisoner on Johnson's Island, Lake Erie, until the close of the conflict. Being then paroled, he returned home and managed his father's farm until his marriage, when he settled on that part of the Valley Farm that his wife inherited from her father's estate. There he continued as a successful planter until his death in 1889.

Mr. Ruffin married Miss Sally McIlwaine, who was born in Petersburg, Virginia, August 30, 1851. Her father, James McIlwaine, was born in Ireland, of Scotch ancestry. As a young man he came with his brothers Archibald, Joseph, John and Thomas, to the United States, settling in Virginia; Archibald and James were the only ones that reared families. James was educated in Ireland, and after coming to Virginia located in Petersburg, where he was engaged in mercantile pursuits until his death in 1856.

James McIlwaine, Mrs. Ruffin's father, married Fanny Dunn, who was born in Petersburg, Virginia, a daughter of Robert Dunn, of whom further notice may be found in connection with the sketch of Willis B. Smith. Mrs. Ruffin still maintains her pleasant home in Petersburg, where she has many sincere friends. She has reared seven children, namely: James McIlwaine, Francis Gildart, Caryanne Randolph, William Roane, John Francis Walthall, Mary McIlwaine and Sallie Wallthall.

PHILIP SEIBEL. Under all conditions the fire department of a large city is the most important in the protection of life and property. It may be argued that the police department occupies a similar position of importance, but the police, as a rule, are called upon to deal with individuals, whereas the fire-fighters must contend with a foe that is merciless and all-destroying, and the "smoke-eaters" must be men of the highest order of bravery. In these modern days, with the fire department fully motorized and with equipment at their command that has been fashioned by the last word in human ingenuity, a large part of the personal element of danger has been eliminated, but in the days of horse-drawn vehicles of several decades ago the equipment was more greatly human than mechanical, and the firemen then had to face conditions unheard of today, in addition to which there must be taken into consideration the fact that there was a much larger percentage of inflammable matter to contend with, this being before the passage of modern fire laws and precautionary measures.

Although twenty-two years have passed since his death, Philip Seibel is still remembered, not only in the Norfolk Fire Department, but by the public generally, as one of the bravest and most faithful men who ever donned a helmet. A member of the department for eighteen years, he set a splendid record for heroism and courage and left an example to be followed by those who were to come afterward and sustain the high standards and traditions of the organization.

Mr. Seibel was born at Norfolk, March 10, 1860, the eldest in the family of six children of Henry and Mary Seibel. His father was a resident of Norfolk all of his life and followed the trade of cabinet-maker, being known as a skilled craftsman and a reliable citizen. The youth acquired a public school education and learned the baker's trade, subsequently opening an establishment of his own on Church Street, of which he was the proprietor for six years. In 1888 Mr. Seibel qualified for membership in the Norfolk Fire Department, and from that time until his death was connected therewith, principally as driver of a chemical truck. Automobile fire apparatus then was unheard of, all of the vehicles being horse drawn, and Mr. Seibel's work was cut out for him from the sound of the alarm, for it was a serious and highly dangerous task to guide, at full speed, his truck to the scene of the conflagration. During the long period of his connection with the department Mr. Seibel was faithful and brave in the performance of duty, equal to any emergency that might arise, and on many occasions his heroism won him the praise of his department superiors and the plaudits and gratitude of the public. In his death, which occurred September 9, 1906, the department lost one of its most valuable men and the city one of its valuable citizens. Mr. Seibel was a member of the Firemen's Social Club and the Ancient Order of Hibernians. In politics he was a Democrat.

On February 28, 1883, Mr. Seibel was united in marriage with Miss Ellen McCauelly, of Long Island, New York, who was educated at Norfolk, and is a daughter of John and Bridget McCauelly. In the period of the war between the states John McCauelly was a soldier of the Confederacy and saw active service in the defense of Richmond. Later for many years prior to his death he was a Government employe at Norfolk. A brother of Mrs. Seibel, William McCauelly, has been an engineer in the Norfolk Fire Department for eighteen years, and has a splendid record. Of the children born to Mr. and Mrs. Seibel three survive: Henry, a plumber of Norfolk; Nellie, who is employed by the Watts Company of this city; and Mary, connected with the Smith & Weldon Company of Norfolk. Mrs. Ellen Seibel, who survives her husband, resides at Olney Road, West, in which community she is very highly esteemed and has a host of sincere friends.

MR. AND MRS. ROBERT W. WEBB

ROBERT WILLIAM WEBB was born at Portsmouth, judicial
center of Norfolk County, Virginia, August 10, 1863, and his
death occurred in the City of Norfolk, this county, on the 4th of
June, 1923. The span of his active career was marked by his
earnest service as a clergyman and evangelist of the Methodist
Episcopal Church, South, and also by large and effective achievement as a business man, he having been at the time of his death
one of the prominent exponents of the real estate business at
Norfolk. His character was the positive expression of a strong,
noble and loyal nature, and he made his life count for good in
all of its relations.

Mr. Webb was a son of Thomas Howard Webb and Mary E.
Webb, who continued their residence in Norfolk County until
their death, the father having given many years of administration as general manager of the Old Dominion Steamship Line.
The name of the Webb family has been worthily linked with the
history of Norfolk County and Virginia since the Colonial period,
and it is to be recorded that ancestors of the subject of this
memoir made settlement at Portsmouth in 1781, while four
successive generations of the Webb family have figured con-
structively in the civic and material advancement and communal
life of this favored section of the Old Dominion.

As a boy and youth Robert W. Webb attended both private
and public schools in his native county, and in 1882 he was graduated from the fine old Virginia Military Institute. He then took
a position of clerical order in the offices of the Old Dominion
Steamship Company, of which his father was general manager,
and after six years of service in this connection he assumed
a clerkship in the Norfolk offices of the Norfolk & Western Railroad. In his early youth Mr. Webb had become an earnest member of the Methodist Episcopal Church, South, and upon leaving
the railway service just mentioned he was ordained a clergyman
in the Virginia Conference of this religious body. His first pastoral charge was in Henry County, and later he was pastor of the
church in his native city of Portsmouth. His fervid zeal and
consecrated labors found further exemplification in his five
years of service as an evangelist, and in this service he conducted
revival meetings in various states of the Union, with marked
success.

After about ten years of active work in the ministry Mr.
Webb retired therefrom and engaged in the real estate business
at Norfolk as a member of the firm of Rippard, Hanberry &
Webb. After the passing of six years this partnership alliance
was dissolved, and from that time onward until his death
Mr. Webb continued independently in the same line of business.
As a realtor he did much to further the development and progress of the Norfolk area, and it is to be specially noted that he
was the exploiter and developer of the fine Little Bay district of
Ocean View, a suburb of Norfolk. He was ever alive to matters
of civic and material progress and was known and valued as one
of the public spirited citizens and business men of his home city
and native county. Through the entire course of his active and
exacting business career Mr. Webb continued with characteristic zeal and earnestness his labors in behalf of religious service,
and he frequently was called upon to officiate as a pulpit orator
and to appear in other church services long after he had retired
from the active work of the ministry, his widow likewise being
a zealous member of the Methodist Episcopal Church, South, in
her home city of Norfolk. The political allegiance of Mr. Webb

was given to the Democratic party, and while he took loyal interest in public affairs he had no ambition for political office.

On the 7th of May, 1885, was solemnized the marriage of Mr. Webb and Miss Florence E. Garden, who had received the advantage of private and public schools in Norfolk and who is a daughter of the late Doctor Pulaski and Elizabeth (Webster) Garden, the latter a direct descendant of the great American statesman, Daniel Webster. Both the Garden and Webster families have, in successive generations, produced many men of prominence in professional and business life, while many have figured prominently in public affairs. Mrs. Webb still maintains her home in Norfolk, at 622 Redgate Avenue, and she has been long a loved factor in church and social circles in this community.

Of the eight children of Mr. and Mrs. Webb the eldest is Thomas Howard, who is a successful business man in Norfolk and who is here serving as steward of the Methodist Episcopal Church, South. He married Elizabeth Akhurst, and their three children are Elizabeth, Thomas Howard, Jr., and Richard. Edward Hugh, the second son, is engaged in the real estate business in Norfolk, the maiden name of his wife having been Cleo Sowell. Robert William, who likewise is actively associated with business enterprise in Norfolk, married Miss Jack Guy. He holds the rank of captain in the fine old military organization known as the Norfolk Light Artillery Blues, and with this command he entered World war service, the Blues having been constituted as Company B, One Hundred and Eleventh Field Artillery in the United States Army, and having had eighteen months of overseas service. The battery was in France at the time the armistice brought the great world conflict to its close, and Captain Webb received his honorable discharge after returning home with his gallant command. He is now affiliated with the American Legion. Mary Arminger, eldest of the daughters, is the wife of L. M. Holmes, who is publicity man with the Virginia Pilot Publishing Company, Norfolk, and their two children are Leland L. and Helen Garden. Miss Dorothy Elizabeth, next younger of the daughters, remains with her widowed mother. Annie Garden is the wife of George Garey, a Norfolk business man, and their one child is a son, Robert Raynor. Morris Godwin, next younger of the children, has followed in the footsteps of his honored father and is engaged in the real estate business in Norfolk. Maxwell died at the age of eleven years.

JANE MAUD CAMPBELL, librarian of the Jones Memorial Library at Lynchburg, has been in library work for many years and in addition has had some very interesting experience in various forms of social service activity.

Miss Campbell was born at Liverpool, England, in 1869. Her father, George Campbell, was of an old Scotch family, the son of Benjamin and Anne (MacDonald) Campbell, of Caithness, Scotland. George Campbell came to America in 1855, and was in the hardware business at Petersburg, Virginia, until the outbreak of the Civil war. He then returned to Scotland, and after the war was in the tobacco business. For many years he held contracts with the British government for American tobacco. George Campbell married Jane Cameron, daughter of Alexander and Sarah Cameron, of Grantown, Inverness County, Scotland. She died in England in 1870, when her daughter Jane Maud

John Creston McConnell

was an infant. George Campbell's second wife was Rosalie Higginbotham, daughter of Dr. Edward G. and Julia (Thompson) Higginbotham, of Richmond, Virginia. George Campbell was the father of ten sons and two daughters. He was a member of the Presbyterian Church and the Masonic fraternity.

Jane Maud Campbell was reared at Edinburgh, Scotland, attended the Edinburgh Ladies College there, from which she graduated, and has the certificate from the University of Edinburgh. After coming to America she was employed for eighteen months in the public library at Newark, New Jersey, where she carried on her special studies in library technique. For seven years she was librarian for the public library at Passaic. Social work and sociological investigation also made a strong appeal to her, and she took charge of the educational work for the North American Civic League for immigrants in New York and was appointed a member of the New Jersey Immigration Commission by Governor Stokes, investigating immigrants' conditions in that state in 1907. Miss Campbell for a period of seven years lived in Boston, Massachusetts, where she was director of the library work with foreigners for the Massachusetts Public Library Commission. Miss Campbell has had charge of the Jones Memorial Library since 1922.

JOHN PRESTON MCCONNELL, president of the State Teachers College at East Radford, has been actively engaged, not only in educational work, but has participated in altruistic, humanitarian, and reformed movements as well as in various fields of business. He has been a leader in movements for better agriculture, improvement of rural life, health and sanitation, and the development of the industrial possibilities of Virginia.

Doctor McConnell was born in Scott County, Virginia, February 22, 1866, son of Hiram Kilgore and Ginsey Elizabeth (Brickey) McConnell. His paternal ancestor came from North Ireland to Pennsylvania, where he reared his family. His great-grandfather, George McConnell, and his wife, Susanna Snavely McConnell, migrated to Scott County, Virginia, about the beginning of the nineteenth century. He was an early settler and took part in the organization of Scott County in 1814 and served as member of the County Court and as sheriff. The grandfather of Doctor McConnell was Joab W. McConnell. Hiram Kilgore McConnell was born and reared in Scott County, attended private schools, served as a lieutenant in Company E, Sixty-second Virginia Infantry, in the Confederate army. After the war he was a farmer and stock raiser, a justice of the peace, clerk of the school board and road commissioner. He was in his ninetieth year when he died in 1927. His wife was reared at Fort Blackmore, Virginia, attended private schools there, and was a Primitive Baptist, while her husband was a Methodist, but later joined the Free Will Baptist Church. She died in 1920, in her eightieth year. Of their seven children one died in infancy. Besides Dr. John P. McConnell the other living children are: Dr. Robert W., a practicing physician at Fort Blackmore; Henry M., an attorney at Custer, Oklahoma; Victoria, wife of Nathan Carter, of Fort Blackmore; and Hiram Kilgore, a physician of Gate City, Virginia; a daughter, Rebecca, who died in 1925, was the wife of Otto Lubker, of Grand Junction, Colorado. Her first husband was Ballard Carter.

John Preston McConnell attended public schools in Scott County, graduated from Milligan College, Tennessee, with the Bachelor of Arts degree in 1890 and Master of Arts degree in 1896, and in 1904 was awarded the degree of Doctor of Philosophy by the University of Virginia. Doctor McConnell was professor of Greek and Latin at Milligan College from 1890 to 1896, and for almost two years acting president of the college, and then resumed his duties as professor of Latin and Greek. From 1900 to 1904 he was a graduate student and licentiate of instruction in the University of Virginia, where he became one of the charter members of the Raven Society. From 1904 to 1913 he was professor of history and dean of Emory and Henry College of Virginia. In 1911 he was unanimously elected the first president of the Radford State Teachers College, but for two years continued his service at Emory and Henry College. During this time he determined the location and type of all the buildings, planned the development of the grounds, organized the courses of study and in 1913, at the formal opening of the new college, he moved to Radford. The subsequent development of the school and all its policies are a reflection of the energy and wisdom of Doctor McConnell. At the opening the school had practically a high school curriculum with two years of training for teachers. The entrance requirements were steadily raised, courses of study strengthened, and a larger and better trained corps of teachers enlisted. After three years all high school work was eliminated, and later the curriculum was extended to four years of college work. The institution is now recognized as an A grade standard college and has membership in the Southern Association of Colleges, and is an an A grade teachers college accredited by the American Association of Teachers Colleges. It is also a member of the American Council of Education. The college has a campus of about twenty-five acres, with a group of modern fireproof buildings. The faculty comprises forty-eight teachers and the regular enrollment is about 1,400 during the year including the Summer Quarter, while about 750 students are enrolled for the correspondence and extension courses.

Doctor McConnell is president of the Farmers and Merchants National Bank of Radford, director and a member of the executive committee of the Radford Finance Corporation, director of the Radford Real Estate and Insurance Corporation, director of the Radford Hospital Corporation, director and member of the executive committee of the Baldwin Land Company.

Doctor McConnell is a Phi Beta Kappa, member of the Rotary Club, a Democrat, a life long prohibitionist, and for seven years president of the Anti-Saloon League of Virginia. He is an elder in the Christian Church, a member of the National Board of Education of that denomination, a member of the National Board of Recommendations of the Disciples or Christian Church, and was for many years on the board of managers of that church. He was vice president for twenty years of the Co-Operative Education Association of Virginia, and for four years its president. He was president of the State Teachers Association in 1911-12, chairman of the Virginia Educational Conference in 1912, president of the Southern Education Association in 1919-22, and was one of the organizers and since 1925 has been president of Southwestern Virginia, Incorporated. He was president of the Virginia Association of Colleges and Schools for Women in 1915-16, chairman of the executive committee of the State

Conference of Charities and Corrections for a number of years and president of the Conference in 1919-23. In 1922 he was president of the Southern Co-Operative League for Education and Social Service.

He has written many articles, and pamphlets on educational topics, and was a contributor to *The South in the Building of a Nation*, and to *The Library of Southern Literature*. He is author of a volume, *Negroes and Their Treatment in Virginia*, 1865-67. By appointment of the governor he has served as a member of the Virginia War History Commission, and is an advisory member of the State Conservation and Development Commission of Virginia.

He has been or now is actively associated as director or president with a large number of state-wide organizations. In addition to his educational and business interests and activities he has given much time and attention to the agricultural and industrial interests of the state. He has been particularly active in the development of agriculture, road development, dairying, horticulture and rural pursuits and interests.

Doctor McConnell married at Milligan College, Tennessee, May 21, 1891, Clara Louisa Lucas. They were married by Dr. Josephus Hopwood, president of Milligan College. Mrs. McConnell attended public schools in Montgomery County, holds the Bachelor's degree from Milligan College, taught school in Montgomery County, and since her marriage has been active in educational and church work, president of the Radford Woman's Christian Temperance Union, president of the Woman's Missionary Society, and president of the Community League. Since 1919 she has been a member of the State Board of Public Welfare, having been appointed by three successive governors. She was the first woman appointed or elected to an important state position in Virginia.

Mrs. McConnell is a daughter of Charles D. and Nancy (Charlton) Lucas. Her father, at an advanced age, served in the Home Guard during the war between the states. Eight of his sons were in the Confederate army. Two of them lost their lives. He died in 1885, aged eighty-five. Mrs. McConnell's mother died in 1919 at the age of eighty-six. Doctor and Mrs. McConnell have five children. June Evangeline, a graduate of Emory and Henry College, did post graduate work in Vanderbilt University and Cornell University, and is the wife of H. C. Graybeal, professor of Education in Emory and Henry College. They have five children named David McConnell, Henry Charlton, William Samuel, Lydia Claire, and Burke Douglas. Robert Lucas McConnell, the oldest son, educated at Emory and Henry College, the Richmond Dental College, and Atlanta Dental College, was a first lieutenant at Camp Lee during the World war, and now practices dentistry at Radford. He married Jeffie Louis Nidermaier, of Abingdon, who died in 1926, leaving three children, Nancy Elizabeth, Robert Lucas, and Leo Jefferson, the last child deceased. His second wife was Miss Martha Townsend of Lunenburg County. Carl Hiram McConnell took his Bachelor's degree at Lynchburg College, his Master's degree from the University of Virginia, was a volunteer during the World war and served in France, pursued his graduate studies in biology in British Guiana, and is now instructor in biology and candidate for the degree of Doctor of Philosophy at the University of Virginia. He married Rio Tucker, of Beckley, West Virginia. John

Paul McConnell, the youngest son, obtained his Bachelor's degree from Lynchburg College, Master of Arts from William and Mary College. He is a fellow in the Graduate School of the University of North Carolina, now on leave of absence from the faculty of the Radford State Teachers College. The youngest child, Annie Ginsey, received the Bachelor's degree from the Radford State Teachers College where she is now critic teacher and supervisor of instruction in the Training School system. She is the wife of Ernest C. Grigsby, a graduate of the Virginia Polytechnic Institute, and County Agricultural Demonstration Agent of Pulaski County.

LAWRENCE STAPLETON was one of the prominent men in the cotton business at Norfolk during his active years. Several of his children have made splendid records in their respective vocations, and a daughter of the late Mr. Stapleton, Miss Mary E. Stapleton, has achieved remarkable success in the real estate field at Norfolk.

Lawrence Stapleton was born at Newburgh, New York, in 1858, son of James Stapleton. He was reared and educated at Newburgh, and some years after the close of the Civil war came South and located at Norfolk, where he became a cotton buyer, and eventually had connections all along the Atlantic Seaboard, and his business activities contributed to the steadily rising prestige of Norfolk as a great shipping and commercial center. Mr. Stapleton was only thirty-nine years of age when he died, July 4, 1897. He was a Democrat and a member of the Catholic Church.

He married, June 17, 1883, Teresa Browne, who was educated at West Philadelphia. She was a member of the Presbyterian Church. There were four children. The son Thomas Lawrence was educated for the ministry and is now instructor in a theological school. James Edward, the second son, who married Marian Hamilton, was one of the early realtors in the Florida real estate boom and amassed a fortune by his operations in that state. The oldest of the children, Leonore, now deceased, was the wife of Hugh Slevin, Jr., of New York, an architect.

The daughter Miss Mary E. Stapleton was reared and educated in Norfolk and for several years has been in the real estate business. He has made a remarkable success in selling some of the newer additions, including Ocean View, a water front development adjacent to Norfolk. She resides in Norfolk, at 1446 Westover Avenue.

CHARLES HERBERT HARDY, manager and treasurer of the Town of Blackstone, has lived nearly all his life in that locality and has been well known for his business enterprise, as well as for his civic and public spirit.

He was born near Blackstone, Nottoway County, Virginia, August 14, 1880. His parents were Charles Betts and Jennie Clarkson (Barnes) Hardy, both born in Lunenburg County. His father was lieutenant of a company in the Confederate army and was severely wounded. For eighteen years after the war he was a farmer, in Mississippi, and after selling his interests returned to Virginia and lived on a farm in Nottoway County until he died in 1913, at the age of seventy-seven. The mother died December 9, 1928.

Charles Herbert Hardy attended public schools and the Hoge Military Academy at Blackstone, and at the age of seventeen engaged in the tobacco business. He became a dealer in tobacco and operated extensively over South Side Virginia until 1921, when the Farmers Tobacco Growers Association was formed, at which time he sold his interests. After that he took up the automobile business, having the local Ford agency from 1921 to August, 1928. Mr. Hardy became town manager and treasurer of the Town of Blackstone in October, 1925, and has charge of the administration of the town under the direction of the mayor and council.

He married, May 20, 1903, Miss Mary Hobson Robertson, daughter of W. A. and Bee (Southall) Robertson. Her mother was born in Amelia County and her father was born in Nottoway County and was for many years a merchant in Nottoway Court House. Mr. and Mrs. Hardy have one daughter, Virginia Southall, born August 18, 1905. She graduated from the Randolph-Macon Woman's College at Lynchburg in June, 1927, and is now a teacher at Burlington, North Carolina.

Mr. Hardy has for a number of years been a member of the Democratic County Committee. He is affiliated with Lodge No. 79, A. F. and A. M., for several years was high priest of the Royal Arch Chapter, is a member of the Independent Order of Odd Fellows, the Blackstone Golf Club, and is an elder in the Blackstone Presbyterian Church and for about fifteen years superintendent of its Sunday school.

WOODIE EMMETTE HERRING, cashier of the State Bank of Remington, Incorporated, is one of the popular young financial executives in Fauquier County and is a progressive citizen and business man of his attractive little home city of Remington.

Mr. Herring was born at Lignum, Culpeper County, Virginia, June 25, 1897, and is a son of George A. and Irene (Jones) Herring, who likewise were born in Culpeper County, and who now maintain their residence at Remington, where the father owns and operates a blacksmith shop.

Woodie E. Herring was reared and educated at Remington, and after completing his studies in the public schools he was employed in a drug store during a period of eighteen months. He thereafter had two years of active experience in farm work, and this discipline did much to fortify him in physical vigor. On the 15th of July, 1918, he became a bookkeeper in the State Bank of Remington, Incorporated, and with this well ordered institution he has since continued his executive connection, his advancement to his present office, that of cashier, having occurred March 5, 1926, and his effective administration since that time having amply justified his selection for the position. The State Bank of Remington, Incorporated, was organized February 7, 1913, is duly incorporated under the laws of Virginia and bases its operations on a capital stock of $15,500. The bank maintains a surplus fund of $6,000 and that its solidity and communal service are duly appreciated is manifest when it is noted that its deposits now aggregate fully $110,000. R. L. Willis is president of the bank, J. R. Day and C. B. Chilton are its vice presidents, and John W. Stone is assistant cashier. The popular and efficient cashier, Mr. Herring, is a stockholder not only of this bank but also has expanded his communal service by acting as agent in the issuing of life insurance policies. His political alignment is in the ranks of the Democratic party, his religious faith is that of the Baptist Church, and he is affiliated with the Masonic fraternity. At the time of preparing this sketch the name of Mr. Herring still remains on the roll of eligible young bachelors in Fauquier County.

JEFFERSON DAVIS SCHELL was for more than a quarter of a century a valued employe of the Newport News Shipbuilding & Dry Dock Company, which figures as one of the most important industrial concerns of its kind on the Atlantic seaboard of the United States, and in the large plant of this company he was assistant foreman of the ship fitting department at the time of his death, which occurred December 3, 1921. His executive duties in this connection were specially important during the period of the nation's participation in the World war.

Mr. Schell was born in James City County, Virginia, in March, 1864, about a year prior to the close of the Civil war, and the parental loyalty to the Confederate states was indicated in the giving to the son the name of Jefferson Davis in honor of the revered president of the Confederate government. Mr. Schell was the second in order of birth of the seven children of James and Henrietta Schell, who passed their entire lives in the Old Dominion State, the father having been a farmer by vocation during the major part of his active career.

The youthful education of Mr. Schell was acquired in the schools of his native county and those of York County, and from his boyhood until he was twenty-seven years of age he continued to be associated with farm enterprise. He then, in 1891, established his residence in the City of Newport News, and from that year until the close of his earnest and worthy life he here continued in the employ of the Newport News Shipbuilding & Dry Dock Company. He became a skilled workman as a ship fitter, and as such was eventually advanced to the position of assistant foreman of the ship-fitting department, in which capacity his loyal and efficient service was continued until the close of his life. He was thus in the employ of this corporation during the long period of twenty-seven years, and his sterling character and genial personality gained to him a secure place in the confidence and good will of those with whom he came in contact in his business affairs and in his social life.

Mr. Schell never permitted himself to deviate from the ancestral political faith, and was a loyal supporter of the cause of the Democratic party, though he had no ambition for public office. He was an active member of the Methodist Episcopal Church, South, as is also his widow, who still resides at Newport News, and he was affiliated with the Heptosoph fraternity.

In June, 1892, Mr. Schell was united in marriage to Miss Sadie Donegan, of Williamsburg, she being a daughter of the late Maurice and Endoxia (Blessingham) Donegan, of whose nine children she was the second in order of birth. By reason of the fact that her father was a loyal soldier of the Confederacy in the Civil war Mrs. Schell is eligible for and is actively affiliated with the United Daughters of the Confederacy. On the maternal side she is a representative of the Blessingham family, which has been one of prominence in Virginia annals since the Colonial days and which has given to the state many able professional and business men. Sadie S., eldest of the four children of Mr. and Mrs. Schell, is the wife of Harry Sutton, who is in the service of the Chesapeake & Ohio Railroad, and they reside in Newport News; Joseph Charles is in the employ of the Newport News Shipbuilding & Dry Dock Company; James is now a resident of New York City; and Miss Florence, who remains with her widowed mother, holds a position in the local offices of the Chesapeake & Ohio Railroad.

WILLIAM CONWAY WHITTLE, JR., a citizen of Norfolk and Virginia, was born June 27, 1881, and died August 2, 1927, at the comparatively early age of forty-six years. He first saw the light of day in Norfolk, at the old Page home on Freemason Street, where five generations of his mother's family have lived; and his last days were spent on a portion of the same ancestral land, but in a modern home of his own. He was given his early schooling in Norfolk, and graduated from the University of Virginia, after which he entered upon a business career in his native city. During the greater part of his business associations he was connected with one of the largest fertilizer manufacturing companies of the country, and was advanced to the responsible position of auditor on the staff of the organization; for the last several years of his life he represented the fiduciary department of one of the leading banking institutions of the state. He was a communicant of St. Luke's Episcopal Church and for a long time was a member of its vestry.

The father of William C. Whittle, Jr., was Capt. W. C. Whittle, who graduated from the Naval Academy at Annapolis, served in the United States Navy; and in the war between the states was an outstanding officer in the Confederate navy. In the latter service Captain Whittle was the executive officer of the cruiser *Shenandoah* when it made a name for itself in history by its extensive and successful raiding operations in the Arctic Ocean and other Northern seas. The mother of William Whittle, Jr., was Elizabeth Calvert Page, and her father was Gen. Richard Lucien Page, a nephew of "Lighthorse" Harry Lee and first cousin to Robert Edward Lee. Richard L. Page had his first military experience in the United States Navy and later served in the Army of the Confederacy. While under the flag of the United States he had an active part in the war with Mexico; and under the Confederate flag his distinguished service won for him the rank of brigadier-general.

William C. Whittle, Jr., had one brother, Richard Page Whittle, who died when twenty-one years old. His sisters are Alexina Page, Elizabeth Sinclair, Mary Beverley (Mrs. James Cabell Dabney) and Edmonia Lee. The subject of this sketch married Georgiana Randolph Charrington, of Warrenton, Virginia, who is a daughter of Percy W. Charrington, of Surrey, England, and Mary Harrison Randolph, of Millwood, Clarke County, Virginia, and a granddaughter of Maj. Beverley Randolph and Mary Conway Randolph, of "The Moorings" in the same county. The children of the marriage are William Conway III and Georgiana Charrington, twins, and Beverley Randolph. The older son is a graduate of Virginia Military Institute, class of 1929; the daughter completed her schooling at St. Michael's Hall, Sussex, England, and the younger son is now a student at old Norfolk Academy.

By both inheritance and association William Conway Whittle, Jr., was the possessor of an old and fine tradition, and he lived its code in every phase of his life. He was generous in his im-

pulses, loyal in his friendships, and quick to sympathy and helpfulness; he was careful in his judgments and of scrupulous integrity in his dealings. Courtly in bearing, he yet had a warm
and genial manner, full of simple, unconscious charm. He was
devoted to his family and they to him; and he lived a quiet but
unswerving, Christian life. William Conway Whittle, Jr., was
the very flowering of his fine forebears, and his example is a
priceless legacy and inspiration to his children.

> "His life was gentle, and the elements
> So mix'd in him, that Nature might stand up
> And say to all the world, 'This was a man!'"

HENRY EDWARD LEE came to the Virginia bar about a year
after the death of his father, and in his work has continued the
tradition and reputation of the Lee family in South Side Virginia, where for over half a century the name has been an outstanding one in the legal profession.

Henry E. Lee was born at Lee Hall, Lunenburg County, Virginia, July 10, 1871. His home and his office as a lawyer have
been for many years at Crewe, Nottoway County. His father
was the late Maj. Henderson Lee, a native of Lunenburg County,
and who held the rank of major in the Confederate army. He
was with Pickett and Armistead's brigade and was wounded at
Gettysburg, carrying the results of his injuries the rest of his
life. After the war he practiced law in Lunenburg County and
gained a reputation practically all over the state for his ability
and resourcefulness. He also operated a large plantation, owning five thousand acres. He died in March, 1894. Major Lee
married Lucy Scott, who died in March, 1888.

Their son, Henry E. Lee, was reared and educated in Lunenburg County, attended Bethel Academy in Fauquier County and
Montgomery Academy at Christiansburg. He studied law under
his father, and strove to emulate the distinctive abilities of the
older Lee as a lawyer. He was admitted to the bar in 1895,
and since 1897 has made his home at Crewe, enjoying a large
and successful practice. He was elected and served four years
as mayor of Crewe, resigning that office to become a member
of the House of Delegates as representative from Amelia and
Nottoway counties. He was in the Legislature one term, and in
May, 1904, was appointed commonwealth's attorney, and held
that office consecutively for nineteen years. For ten years he
was president of the National Bank of Crewe and is now legal
representative of the Morris Plan Bank.

Mr. Lee married, June 30, 1907, Miss Helen Epes Fitzgerald,
daughter of John and Caroline M. (Harris) Fitzgerald, both
natives of Nottoway County. Her father spent all his life as a
farmer in Nottoway County. Her mother, at the age of seventy-
six, lives at the home of Mr. and Mrs. Lee, who have no children.

Mr. Lee, like his father, has always been interested in planting and owns and operates 1,300 acres. He is a member of the
Virginia State Bar Association, is president of the Nottoway
County Bar Association, is a past master of the Lodge of Masons
at Crewe, member of the Knights of Pythias, is a Democrat and
a Presbyterian. He has given much time to the church, serving
as elder, and for a number of years taught a class in Sunday
School. Mrs. Lee is a member of the United Daughters of the
Confederacy.

S. Milnor Price

SAMUEL MILNOR PRICE. In the heyday of life, when a man is achieving beyond his fellows and winning favor and applause, public honors and private admiration, his compelling personality may have much influence, but after he has passed from the scene of his endeavors and his deeds, his triumphs, his failures and successes are visioned with the cold and unbiased criticism that posterity accords even its highest and greatest, his true character stands out and his measure of usefulness to mankind is fully revealed. The student of biography and history knows full well how often this acid test brings only disappointment. When, then, a community can point proudly to a man of true nobility from the ranks of his daily life, how valuable is the story and how far reaching may be its influence. To the memory of such a man too much special and deserved esteem very seldom can be shown. When the test above referred to is applied to the record of the late Samuel Milnor Price, one of the important factors in the business life of Norfolk, he is found to have measured up to the highest standards as a man and a citizen, and in his death his city sustained an immutable loss.

Samuel Milnor Price was born in Richmond, Virginia, November 14, 1868, and died in Norfolk, Virginia, December 18, 1920. He was a son of Samuel Mosby Price, long a merchant of Richmond. Being beyond the military age during the war between the states, he served with the rank of lieutenant in the Richmond Home Guards. All his life he was active in politics, working in connection with the Democratic party. He married Miss Sarah Milnor Armstrong, and they had twelve children, of whom Samuel Milnor Price was the eleventh in order of birth; William Armstrong Price and John Marshall Price, of Richmond; one son was a Presbyterian minister, Rev. Charles Dabney Price; a daughter, Elizabeth Averton Price, was graduated from a New York Hospital, and she was the first trained nurse to settle in Richmond; and another daughter, Charlotte Pleasants Price, the only survivor of these children, is living with Mrs. Price. The Price family is of Welsh origin, and was established in this country by John Price, who settled in Hanover County, Virginia, in 1620. Capt. Thomas Price was the great-grandfather of Samuel Milnor Price, and he served in the American Revolution. Throughout the history of the family in this country its members have been active in professional and business life.

The Norwood University School of Richmond educated Samuel Milnor Price, and when he left school he became a clerk in the machinery supply business of the Smith Courtney Company, in whose employ he rose through successive promotions until in 1898 he was made its vice president, and he served in that office until 1900, when he resigned to become president of the Henry Walke Company of Norfolk. In 1902 he resigned and organized the S. M. Price Machinery Company, of which he was president until 1918, when he reentered the machinery supply business, and was a manufacturers' representative until his death.

On November 17, 1897, Mr. Price married Miss Elizabeth Lines Cannon, of Richmond, a daughter of Henry Gibbon Cannon, an attorney of Richmond, and a member of the City Board of Aldermen, and a sister of former State Senator Cannon, now serving in his second term as city attorney of Richmond. Mrs. Price was educated in the Merrill School for Girls of Richmond. Her family is an old and aristocratic one, of Huguenot descent, the American founders having fled religious persecution in France and settled in New England, from whence migration was later made to Richmond, Virginia, long prior to the American Revolution. One of her distinguished ancestors, Parson Blair, a clergyman of the Presbyterian faith in the Colonial epoch, was her great-grandfather.

Mr. and Mrs. Price had four children born to their marriage, namely: Sarah Milnor, who married Robert Lee Nutt, Junior, a business man handling railroad supplies and a son of Robert Lee Nutt, chairman of the Board of Directors of the Seaboard Air Line Railroad, and they have two children, Robert Lee III, and Juliet McLure; Margaret Blair, who married William Garland Jones, a cotton factor of Norfolk, a veteran of the World war, in which he served as an instructor with the rank of lieutenant, and they have two children, William Garland, Junior, and Milnor Price; Elizabeth Milnor, who married David Graham Shelburne, a Government employe, manager of supplies at the naval base; and Charlotte Dabney, who is with her mother.

Among the public activities of Mr. Price may be mentioned his assistance in the organization of the Southern Supply Dealers Association, which he served as president in 1912; his membership with the Norfolk Chamber of Commerce, and his loyal service to the Democratic party. He belonged to the Virginia Club and the Country Club, and was very active in the First Presbyterian Church of Norfolk, to which his widow also belongs, and served it as deacon for a number of years. A man of unusual force of character, genial and wholesouled, he made and retained friends, and was generally liked wherever known. In his own field he had few competitors, and his worth was deeply appreciated by the various concerns with which he was associated.

LEE MICHAEL ELLIS was a merchant of Richmond, spending the greater part of his life in managing a business which represented one of the most important retail stores in a large shopping district in that city.

Mr. Ellis was born in Goochland County, Virginia, in November, 1861, and died at Richmond December 31, 1922, when sixty-one years of age. His father, Leroy D. Ellis, was a native Virginian, a farmer and planter by occupation, and was a soldier in the Civil war. He married Sue Puryear. In their family there were seven children: Lee, Willie, Dabney, Walter, Hattie, Annie and Bessie.

Lee Michael Ellis grew up on his father's farm, attended public schools in Goochland, and it was in 1883, when he was twenty-two years of age, that he located in Richmond and entered the grocery business. He was in the retail business there for thirty-nine years, a man noted for his constancy and integrity. He was a member of the Baptist Church.

Mr. Ellis was twice married. His first wife was Nannie Taylor Gilman, and by that union there were seven children: Winton; Virgil Lee, wife of Dr. James Shelbourne; Edith, wife of J. W. Jones; Richard; Dabney; Nannie Sue; and Reba, now Mrs. Ernest Butler. All these children reside in Virginia.

On August 30, 1916, Mr. Ellis married Miss Sallie Eliza Mitchell, who was born and educated in Greensville County, Virginia. Her father, William Robert Mitchell, was a native of the same county, a farmer and land owner, and was a soldier in the Confederacy, being under General Mahone in the Army of Virginia. William Robert Mitchell married Mary Luvinia, also of Greensville County. They were the parents of six children: Robert T.; Walter G., who married Harriet Meade Fuller, of Sussex County, Virginia; Sallie E., now Mrs. Ellis, with home at 2239 West Grace Street, Richmond; Lucy Cato, wife of Cary B. Hatch, of Richmond; Edgar Hartley, who married Edith Campbell; and Raymond E., who married Beulah Lynn, of Richmond.

Mrs. Ellis is the mother of two children, both attending school at Richmond, William Robert and Raymond Cato Ellis.

JOHN BROUGHTON, JR., representative of a family that in the different generations have been distinguished in several states of the South, made his home at Norfolk for many years, and was prominently connected in marine transportation circles.

He was born at Macon, Georgia, in April, 1862, and died at Norfolk in August, 1917. His grandfather, George Broughton, had for many years been editor of a newspaper at Norfolk. His father, Dr. John Broughton, was a druggist at Macon, Georgia, and married Martha Gorman, of that city.

John Broughton, Jr., was educated in the old Norfolk Academy and began his career as a purser with the old Bay Line of steamers. Later he went with the Old Dominion Steamship Company, and was connected with that organization in different capacities for a period of thirty years, until his death.

He married in December, 1896, in Princess Anne County, Katherine Willett. Mrs. Broughton, who survives her husband and resides at 733 Raleigh Avenue in Norfolk, is a member of the Willett family which has had prominent representatives in the wars of the nation, and of equal distinction in the affairs of peace. She was reared and educated at Norfolk. Her father, A. W. Willett, was a farmer and land owner in Princess Anne County, owning the noted Pembroke farm. A. W. Willett married Alice Davis, and Mrs. Broughton was one of seven children. One of Mrs. Broughton's ancestors was a colonel in the Revolutionary war and was sent by General Washington to the governor of Georgia to make a peace treaty with the Indians at Stone Mountain. There was another member of the family who was at Valley Forge with Washington, and in Colonial times there was a Willett among the early mayors of New York City. Mrs. Broughton has a daughter, Katherine, who is the wife of Charles F. Pelley, connected with the Craig Shipbuilding Company of Norfolk.

HERBERT MILTON NOBLE, representing a prominent family of that name in Amelia County, spent his life there, where he was a tobacco grower and planter. Since his death his widow, Mrs. Louise L. Noble, has located in Richmond.

The Noble family came from England and has been in Virginia since early Colonial times. Herbert Milton Noble was born in Amelia County May 20, 1845, and died February 28, 1900. He was a son of Milton Ford and Lucy (Povall) Noble, the former a native of Amelia County and the latter of Powhatan County and of French ancestry. His father was owner of several plantations and worked them with slave labor.

Herbert Milton Noble, one of seven children, was reared and educated in Amelia County and as a young man had several years of experience clerking in country stores. He took up the work of agriculture in the years of depression following the war, and his enterprise culminated in his becoming one of the large scale tobacco growers of the state. His home plantation was at Wyliesburg in Charlotte County. He was a Methodist in religion, while Mrs. Noble and her children are Baptists.

He married, September 13, 1893, Miss Louise Lewis. They were married near Laurel Grove in Pittsylvania County, Virginia, where she was reared and educated. Her grandfather was David Lewis, a brother of Abner of Virginia. Her father, Charles Lewis, was for four years in the Confederate army during the war between the states. Aside from his experience as a soldier he followed farming and planting all his active life. Mrs. Noble's mother was Sarah Elizabeth Chaney, daughter of Henry Clay Chaney, a planter of Pittsylvania County. The Chaney family was founded in Virginia by Henry (better known as Hickory) Chaney, who settled on land granted by the King of England in 1700. This land has remained in the family ever since. It is in Pittsylvania County. Charles Lewis and wife had two children. The daughter Alice, now deceased, married William Henderson, of South Boston, Virginia, and their five children were Edgar, Albert, Lillian, Irene and Carson. The second daughter is Mrs. Louise Noble.

To the marriage of Mr. and Mrs. Noble were born five children. Rosina is the wife of R. A. Dix, a traveling salesman with home in Richmond, and their three children are Lewis, Francis and Evelyn. Miss Merle Noble is secretary and treasurer of the Miller Manufacturing Company of Richmond. Herbert Carleton Noble married Gladys Goodjahn, of Chicago. Earle Lewis Noble, in the automobile business, married Blanche Lively and has three children, named Earle Lewis, Barbara Lively and Julia Louise. The youngest child of Mrs. Noble was Hazel Elizabeth and is now deceased.

JOHN COLLINS ARMISTEAD, who died at Portsmouth in May, 1915, was a cultured representative of families that have been in Virginia and adjacent states from the early Colonial period. This branch of the Armistead family moved to Virginia from Maryland. One member of the family was the Captain Armistead who was the gallant defender of Fort Henry at Baltimore in the War of 1812.

J. Collins Armistead was born in April, 1876, on the Armistead farm, called "Glensheallah," in Norfolk County. This farm was part of an original grant to the Herbert family. His father, Beverley A. Armistead, was a well-to-do farmer and a prominent financier, being the president of the Bank of Portsmouth and one of the men of leadership in all the public affairs of Norfolk County. Beverley A. Armistead married Laura Collins, a daughter of John W. Collins. Her father, John W. Collins, married Margaret Braidfoot, whose grandfather was an Episcopal minister, known as the "Fighting Parson." The Braidfoot family were connections of the Moseleys. William Moseley, of Rotterdam, came to Virginia with his family in 1649, and in the same year was appointed court commissioner at Jamestown. Rev. John Braidfoot married Blandinah Moseley on March 12, 1773. They left one son, William Braidfoot, who married Sophia Herbert on the 26th of March, 1800. Their daughter, Margaret Braidfoot, married John W. Collins.

J. Collins Armistead was educated in the McCabe's University School at Petersburg, in the Episcopal High School at Alexandria, and the Page School of Keswich. After leaving school he

WILLIAM R. JACKSON

entered the real estate and insurance business, becoming a member of the firm of Armistead & Myers Company at Portsmouth. Finally, on account of ill health, he retired from business, and during most of the remaining years of his life he engaged in farming.

Mr. Armistead married at Norfolk in April, 1904, Miss Louise Heath, of Norfolk, who survives him and resides at 113 Middle Street, Portsmouth. Her father, James E. Heath, was a native of Northampton County, Virginia, and served as county judge for many years and afterwards practiced law in Norfolk County. Her mother was Indiana Nottingham, of Northampton County. The Heath family came from England and settled on the eastern shore of Virginia in the latter part of the seventeenth century, while the Nottinghams had lived on the eastern shore since 1645. Mrs. Armistead was the fifth in a family of seven children. Mrs. Armistead has one child, Beverley Arthur, who was educated in Fishburne Academy and the University of Virginia, and is now connected with the Chesapeake & Potomac Telephone Company at Norfolk, Virginia.

WILLIAM ROWLIN JACKSON became an expert in his trade that of jeweler and watchmaker, and his active business career was largely marked by his association with the jewelry business. He was one of the sterling and highly esteemed citizens of Norfolk at the time of his death, February 5, 1905, and in this city his widow still maintains her home—at 1036 Redgate Avenue.

Mr. Jackson was born at Edenton, judicial center of Chowan County, North Carolina, on the 9th of May, 1856, and thus his death occurred a few months prior to the forty-ninth anniversary of his birth. He was the sixth in order of birth of the eight children of Samuel and Sarah (Sandsberry) Jackson, who continued their residence in North Carolina until their death, Samuel Jackson having served as a loyal soldier of the Confederacy in the Civil war and his vocation during the greater part of his life having been that of merchant tailor.

William R. Jackson gained his early education mainly through the medium of private schools in his native town, and as a young man he served about two years as overseer of a farm owned by Dr. W. R. Capehard in his old home county. In 1872 he initiated his apprenticeship to the jeweler's trade at Elizabeth City, North Carolina, where he completed his training and became a skilled workman and where he remained until 1881, when he came to Norfolk, Virginia, and took a position in the jewelry establishment of Weed & Company. Later he engaged in the same line of enterprise in an independent way, but within a short period he sold his store and business, on Bank street, opposite the courthouse, and went to Washington, D. C. He was employed in a jewelry establishment in the national capital about one year, and failing health then compelled his retirement. He returned with his family to Norfolk, and in this city he thereafter lived retired from active business until his death, as he never regained his health. Mr. Jackson never had inclination to enter the arena of practical politics but was a loyal supporter of the cause of the Democratic party, his religious faith having been that of the Methodist Episcopal Church, South, of which his widow likewise is an earnest member.

In August, 1881, Mr. Jackson was united in marriage with Miss Addie Capps, who survives him, as do three of their four children. Mrs. Jackson was born in her present home city of

Norfolk and her education was received principally at Elizabeth City, North Carolina. She is a daughter of Virginius M. and Rosa (Fox) Capps, of whose seven children she was the first born. Virginius M. Capps was long and successfully engaged in business as a contractor and builder, and in the Civil war he served as a gallant soldier of the Confederacy until he was captured by Union troops, his release having not been effected until the close of the war. His father, William Stewart Capps, was one of the substantial farmers and prominent citizens of Princess Anne County, Virginia. Of the three surviving children of Mr. and Mrs. Jackson the eldest is Julian S., who is now manager of the Norfolk office of the Virginia Electric & Power Company; Miss Elsie L. remains with her widowed mother and holds a position in the Norfolk office of Swift & Company, the great Chicago meat packing concern; and Alvin F. is serving as armorer of the Virginia National Guard Armory in Norfolk. Mrs. Jackson is consistently proud of the loyal and patriotic service given by her two sons in the World war period. The elder son, Julian S., gained the rank of captain, and his overseas service covered a period of eighteen months, he having been with the One Hundred Eighty-third Division of the American Expeditionary Forces, and having been a participant in much conflict at the front, the while his brave and gallant service gained to him from the French government the distinguished Cross de Guerre. Alvin F., the younger son, was but sixteen years of age when he enlisted for World war service, and he was stationed with his command at Camp Anderson, Alabama, at the time the signing of the now historic armistice brought the great war to a close. Both of the sons are actively and prominently affiliated with the local post of the American Legion and are popular young men who in Norfolk are well upholding the honors of the name which they bear.

WESLEY LYNN SNELSON was a Virginian whose years of service were identified with the business and profession of railroading. He was engineer of one of the finest passenger trains over the road between Richmond and Washington, and gave up his life while still on active duty.

He was born in Louisa County, Virginia, July 9, 1877, and died April 2, 1924. His father, Wesley Honeyman Snelson, was also a native of Louisa County, a highly respected and prosperous farmer there, and the Snelsons have lived in that section of Virginia from an early date. They are of Scandinavian origin. Wesley Honeyman Snelson married Ella Fielder, also a native of Virginia, her people having come to the state before the Revolution. In the family were ten children: Alma, Walter M., Wesley L., Ella Glyn, Mildred, John, Wilson J., Sherard H., Gilbert and Myrtle.

Wesley L. Snelson grew up on his father's farm in Louisa County, attended public schools there, and was nineteen years old when he entered the service of the Richmond, Fredericksburg & Potomac Railway. He went to work under the spell of a typical enthusiasm for railroading, and his promising abilities brought him steady promotion until he was made engineer on one of the finest trains over this important division in the long run from Florida to New York. He was in the service thirty years, and lost his life in the wreck of his train. He enjoyed the confidence and respect of his superiors and was an active member for many years of the Brotherhood of Locomotive

Engineers, serving as an officer for several terms. In politics he was a Democrat.

Mrs. Snelson, who survives him and resides at 2013 Floyd Avenue in Richmond, is a member of the Daughters of America, the Maccabees, and is vice president of the auxiliary branch of the Brotherhood of Locomotive Engineers. She and her family are members of the Baptist Church.

Mr. and Mrs. Snelson were married March 8, 1909. Her maiden name was Florence Franck, and she was born, reared and educated in Richmond. Her father, Charles A. Franck, was born in Virginia, son of Benjamin Franck, who saw four years of active service in the Confederate army in the war between the states. Charles A. Franck was well known in Masonry, being a past master of Metropolitan Lodge No. 11 at Richmond. The mother of Mrs. Snelson was Belle C. Franklin, also a native of Richmond. Mrs. Snelson is the mother of five children, named Wesley L., Jr., Eleanore, Franklin F., Catherine and Florence M., all of whom are attending schools at Richmond.

CHARLES PIERSON SHAW, lieutenant commander in the United States Navy, was retired with this rank in the year 1883, after a record of distinguished service, and thereafter he found opportunity for equally loyal and effective service in connection with the affairs of civic and private life. After a protracted illness this sterling naval officer and honored citizen died at his Willoughby Beach home, Norfolk, Virginia, on the 26th of April, 1922, and to him as a native son of the Historic Old Dominion State and as a man of noble character and worthy achievement this history of Virginia consistently pays memorial tribute. From an appreciative estimate that appeared in a Norfolk daily newspaper at the time of his death are taken the following significant extracts:

"In the death of Lieutenant Shaw the community loses a citizen whose earnest efforts were always put forth for what he believed to be the right. He was a man who was always on the highest plane and who gave liberally of his time, energy and money in behalf of the good of his city, state and nation. He was widely known and esteemed in this community. His tall, upright figure, clear-cut, striking features and dignified, courteous manners made him a man to be observed in any gathering.

"During a considerable portion of the time that he resided in this community Lieutenant Shaw devoted much time to work for the good of the public. For some seventeen years he was a member of the National Municipal League and was on its advisory committee. He was also a member of the council of the National Civil Service Reform League and of the advisory council of the Proportional Representation League. Lieutenant Shaw was president of the Norfolk Municipal League and a member of the executive committee of the Commission Government League of this city. He was a member of the committee of the League of Virginia Municipalities that drafted the city charter optional act. He drafted the amendment to the constitution of Virginia which enables cities to employ city managers and other technical experts without regard to their residence. He assisted in an unofficial capacity in the drafting of the present commission-manager charter of Norfolk, being present at nearly every sitting of the commission. * * *

"Lieutenant Shaw made his home for a number of years in Norfolk, but of late he has resided at Willoughby. Despite the handicap of partial blindness, he kept well abreast of the happenings of the day and managed to do considerable literary work. He was a well informed man on almost every topic, and was a delightful companion."

Lieutenant Shaw was a man of well fortified views touching economic and governmental matters, and he was a student of and worker in behalf of civic mediums of progress. Aside from his activities in the connections noted in the preceding quotations he was significantly and influentially prominent in the furtherance of the good-roads movement that has done much to advance national transportation facilities. Lieutenant Shaw had the distinction of establishing the first good-roads organization in the entire United States, and was issued the first certificate by the National League of Good Roads, under date of December 6, 1892. He was the instigator of the Monticello Good Roads Association, of which Gen. Fitzhugh Lee was made the president. At the time of the death of General Lee had been completed a large part of the Monticello highway, extending between Monticello, the historic old home estate of President Thomas Jefferson, and the University of Virginia, the work on this important thoroughfare having been interrupted by the death of General Lee. It is gratifying to note in this connection that the movement to purchase and maintain Monticello as a national shrine second only to Mount Vernon in importance is being carried successfully forward at the time of this writing.

Charles Pierson Shaw was born at Wytheville, judicial center of Wythe County, Virginia, on the 4th of May, 1849, and his death occurred a little more than a month prior to his seventy-third birthday anniversary. He was a son of Charles B. and Isabella (Watson) Shaw, his father having been born and reared in the State of New York and having thence come to Virginia, where he became a citizen of prominence and influence and where he served as state engineer.

The rudimentary education of Lieutenant Shaw was acquired in his native city and he was fourteen years of age when, in 1863, he was appointed a cadet in the United States Naval Academy, Annapolis. In that institution he was graduated as a member of the class of 1867, and from that time forward he was in active service in the United States Navy during the long period of twenty years, he having been retired in 1883, with the rank of lieutenant commander. His retirement, June 6, 1883, was mainly the result of the impairment of his vision. For a number of years thereafter he maintained his residence in Albemarle County, Virginia, and at the inception of the Spanish-American war he thence reentered active service in the United States Navy and was assigned to duty at the Washington Navy Yard. At the close of the Spanish-American war he was offered court martial duty in New York, Philadelphia and Norfolk, and choosing the latter, reported there for service, which continued until his retirement for age. When the United States entered the World war he volunteered for duty at the age of sixty-eight years and was again assigned to court martial duty at the Norfolk Navy Yard, where he remained until the end of the conflict, never missing a session of the court.

As a youth Lieutenant Shaw was a midshipman on the old Franklin when Admiral Farragut was in command of the European station, and thus he took part in the historic naval cruise of 1867-68. As flag lieutenant on the Hartford, with Admiral Trenchard and Captain Luce, the subject of this memoir was with his ship at Norfolk in the Centennial year, 1876, and was manager of the ball given in this city in honor of Grand Duke Alexis. In the last two years of the Civil war Lieutenant Shaw was detailed to a vessel that was assigned to the capturing of Confederate war ships, but no vessels were captured.

The domestic chapter in the life history of Lieutenant Shaw was one of ideal phases. In 1891 was solemnized his marriage to Mrs. Matthew Gault Emery, Jr., who was born at Hudson, New York, and whose maiden name was Helen Lawson Simpson, and who was a daughter of Joel Tucker and Sallie (Kershow) Simpson. Matthew G. Emery, first husband of Mrs. Shaw, was a lawyer by vocation, and his death occurred at Washington, D. C., in 1887, the one surviving child of this union being Ruth Emery, who is the wife of Lieutenant Horace C. Laird, of the United States Navy. Mrs. Shaw survives her honored husband and maintains her home at 1221 Graydon Avenue in the city of Norfolk.

Lieutenant Shaw was an earnest communicant of the Protestant Episcopal Church, he having been a member of St. Andrew's Church in Norfolk at the time of his death and his widow being still a zealous communicant of this parish, the rector of which, Rev. Myron B. Marshall, there conducted the funeral service of the honored citizen to whom this memoir is dedicated.

JOHN THOMAS SAWYER was for twenty years a prominent representative of the real estate business in the city of Norfolk, his retirement from active affairs having occurred in 1921 and he having thereafter continued his residence in Norfolk until his death in 1925.

Mr. Sawyer was born near Elizabeth City, North Carolina, April 12, 1869, the youngest of the three children of his parents, who passed their entire lives in North Carolina, where the Sawyer family was founded in an early day, the father of the subject of this memoir having represented his native state as a valiant soldier of the Confederacy in the Civil war and having thereafter been a prosperous farmer near Elizabeth City.

John T. Sawyer received the advantages of the schools of Elizabeth City, and at that place he gained his initial business experience as clerk in a mercantile establishment. He continued to be associated with business affairs at Elizabeth City, North Carolina, until about 1901, when he came to Norfolk, Virginia, and engaged independently in the real estate business, under the title of J. T. Sawyer & Company. He built up a substantial business and his activities marked him as one of the leaders in real estate enterprise in Norfolk County. From 1921 until his death he lived virtually retired, as previously noted.

Mr. Sawyer had no predilection for political activity but was loyal and progressive as a citizen and man of affairs and was a staunch supporter of the cause of the Democratic party. He was affiliated with the Independent Order of Odd Fellows and was a zealous member of the Cheat Methodist Church, in which his service was given as a steward and in earlier years as a teacher in the Sunday School. His widow was reared in the faith of this church, and in the same has continued an earnest member and active worker.

September 8, 1897, recorded the marriage of Mr. Sawyer and Miss Bettie Helen Lanier, who was born in Greensville County, Virginia, and whose early education was acquired principally in the city of Petersburg, this state. Mrs. Sawyer is a daughter of Wesley Richard Lanier and Sarah Elizabeth (Ridout) Lanier, of whose four children she was the second in order of birth, her father having been a prosperous farmer and merchant and having been a resident of Petersburg at the time of his death. The Lanier family was founded in Virginia in the Colonial period and was early established in Greensville County. Representatives of the Ridout family were patriot soldiers in the War of the Revolution, and in the War of 1812 the family found similar representation. The Ridout lineage is marked by immediate kinship with the distinguished old New England family that gave to the United States two presidents, John Adams and John Quincy Adams.

Both the widow and the one child of the subject of this memoir still reside in Norfolk, where their home is at 926 Moran Street. The son, Thomas Lanier Sawyer, received the advantages of the Virginia Military Institute and the Shenandoah Military Academy, and thereafter he was graduated in the law department of the University of Virginia, he being now one of the representative younger members of the bar of his native city of Norfolk, where he is established in the successful practice of his profession.

MICHAEL THOMAS FRIARY. It was only four days after the fiftieth anniversary of his birth that the subject of this memoir passed to the life eternal, his death having occurred at his home in the city of Norfolk February 13, 1919. He was sixteen years of age at the time he came to Norfolk, and it was about nine years later that he here initiated his notably successful career in the real estate business, of which he continued an able and honored representative until the time of his death, as one of the principals in the firm of C. H. Ferrell & Company.

Mr. Friary was born in the town of Granard, County Longford, Ireland, February 9, 1869, and the schools of the fair old Emerald Isle afforded him his early education, which was thereafter effectively supplemented by his well ordered reading and study and by his active association with the practical affairs of life. Mr. Friary was a lad of fourteen years when he severed the ties that bound him to his native land and came to the United States. He landed in the port of New York City, and after he had been in the national metropolis somewhat more than a year he heeded the advice of his physician and came to the South, as his health was somewhat impaired at the time. He was an ambitious youth of sixteen years when he arrived in Norfolk, Virginia, and here he found clerical employment. He was here a clerk in a furniture store for a few years, and when he was about twenty-five years of age he here formed a partnership with Charles H. Ferrell, who had here established himself in the real estate business about three years previously. The firm of C. H. Ferrell & Company soon gained status as one of the most progressive and successful exponents of real estate enterprise in this section of Virginia, and the effective partnership alliance was continued during the remainder of the life of the honored subject of this memoir. Mr. Friary, reliable, straightforward and progressive, made for himself an impregnable place as one of the substantial business men of his adopted city, and his sterling attributes of character won him the confidence and high regard of the community in which he long lived and wrought so worthily. He was a popular member of the local

Chamber of Commerce, the Board of Trade and the Real Estate Exchange. His political allegiance was given to the Democratic party and his religious faith was that of the Catholic Church, in the tenets of which he was reared by his parents, Patrick and Ellen (Kiernan) Friary, of whose children he was the second in order of birth of the four who attained to maturity.

In October, 1904, was solemnized the marriage of Mr. Friary and Miss Margaret Dunn, who was born and reared in the State of Massachusetts, a daughter of Daniel and Catharine (Mahanny) Dunn, the former a representative of a family early established in the western part of the old Bay State. Daniel Dunn was long a successful business man in the historic city of Chicopee Falls, Massachusetts. Since the death of her husband Mrs. Friary has continued to reside in Norfolk, where her attractive home is at 623 West Princess Anne Road. Mr. Friary is survived also by a son and a daughter, Daniel Dunn and Mary Ellen, who remain with their widowed mother and both of whom are still attending school at the time of this writing, in the summer of 1928.

ROBERT ROLEN MOORE II. From 1895 until his death, which occurred July 6, 1927, the late Robert Rolen Moore II was connected with a number of business enterprises, all identified with the growth and development of the thriving city of Pulaski. During this period of more than thirty years he established a reputation for sound business judgment and acumen, great industry and energy, and public spirit and civic pride that led him to participate in all movements for the general welfare of the state. At the time of his demise he was the manager of and largest stockholder in the R. R. Moore & Company Wholesale Grocers, one of the leading business institutions of Pulaski, and likewise had various other important connections.

Mr. Moore was born in Wythe County, Virginia, August 6, 1869, and was a son of Robert Rolen and Mary Margaret (Simmerman) Moore, and a member of an old and distinguished family of Virginia which has contributed men of prominence to every walk and activity of life. His father was born at Mount Sterling, Kentucky, where he received his education, and during the war between the states served as a member of the Home Guard. In addition to being a planter he was a stockman and on numerous occasions made many trips west and south to procure horses of fine breeding. By his first marriage he had no children, but by his marriage, with Mary Margaret Simmerman, he had six children: Mrs. Mary McBee; John, who died in South America; Mrs. Blanche Kabrich, of Wytheville; Robert Rolen II, of this review; Miss Emma, who resides at the old home place near Wytheville; and William B., who is deceased.

Robert Rolen Moore II attended the public schools of Wythe County and Judge Campbell's School, following which he pursued a course in the Virginia Polytechnic Institute. Upon leaving the latter he became identified with the Nelson Hardware Company of Roanoke, Virginia, with which he was identified for seven years, and in 1895 he took up his residence in Pulaski, where he established himself in the retail business as the Pulaski Grocery Company. He continued as the proprietor of that business until 1902, when he established the Pulaski Wholesale Grocery Company, of which he remained as manager until 1913. In that year he disposed of his interests and organized the firm of R. R. Moore & Company, Wholesale Grocers, of which he was the manager and largest stockholder until his death. In addition to being a business man of splendid abilities, Mr. Moore was widely known in public affairs and civic movements, and for years was a member of the City Council, in addition to being a member of the staff, with the rank of colonel, of ex-Gov. E. Lee Trinkle of Virginia. He was a thirty-second degree Mason and member of Kazim Temple, A. A. O. N. M. S., and belonged to the Rotary Club, the Pulaski Country Club and the Virginia Wholesale Grocers Association. In politics he was a Democrat, and his religious connection was with the Presbyterian Church, in which he was a member of the Board of Deacons.

At Bristol, Tennessee, March 15, 1897, Mr. Moore was united in marriage with Miss Ellen Jordan, who was born near Pulaski, and educated in the public schools and at Martha Washington College. She is one of the prominent women of Pulaski, of numerous accomplishments and graces, and is active in the work of the Presbyterian Church, the Woman's Club and the United Daughters of the Confederacy. Mrs. Moore is a daughter of Addison L. and Sarah (Caddall) Jordan, the Jordan family being noted for its large operations in live stock. During the war between the states Addison L. Jordan was a member of Company F, Fifty-fourth Regiment, Virginia Infantry, under the command of Gen. Joseph E. Johnston. He saw much active service, and during the latter part of the war was captured and held a prisoner at Camp Douglas, Chicago. After the close of the struggle he returned to Pulaski County, where he continued to be engaged in farming and stock raising during the remainder of his life, his death occurring May 6, 1926. His wife had passed away April 4 of the same year, and both are buried in the Thorn Spring Church Cemetery. Mrs. Jordan was a member of one of the prominent pioneer families of Virginia, and a part of the old Caddall property, which was a grant from King George of England, is still owned by Mrs. Moore. To Mr. and Mrs. Moore there were born three children: Mary Jordan, Sarah Elizabeth and Robert Rolen III.

Mary Jordan Moore was educated in the Pulaski County public schools and the State Teachers College at Farmville. She married Roger Jones Bear, of Washington, D. C., a civil engineer by profession, and a graduate of Washington and Lee University. They are the parents of one son: Roger Jones Bear, Jr. Sarah Elizabeth Moore attended the public schools of Pulaski County and the State Teachers College at Farmville, from which institution she was graduated as a member of the class of 1922. Robert Rolen Moore III, was educated in the public schools of Pulaski County, Greenbrier Military Academy at Lewisburg, West Virginia, and the Virginia Polytechnic Institute, and upon leaving the latter in 1925 entered the R. R. Moore & Company, Wholesale Grocers with his father, of which he became manager at the time of his father's death. He is accounted one of the capable young business men of his locality, where he is very popular and takes an active part in civic affairs. He is a member of the Rotary Club and a Democrat in his political allegiance. On May 17, 1928, at Dublin, Virginia, Mr. Moore was united in marriage with Miss Lula Vermillion, of that place, a daughter of G. A. and Claudia (Darst) Vermillion. Mr. Vermillion for years has been a prominent orchardist and agriculturist of Pulaski, and also has large and important realty interests at Dublin.

EMERY NIXON HOSMER. To the practice of his chosen profession of law, Emery N. Hosmer, one of the leading younger
lawyers of Clarendon, has brought the natural aptitude which is
inherent in a mind of rare logical and analytical power, as well
as the culture which is the product of a thorough education,
aided by intelligent and persistent study. Although he has been
engaged in practice for comparatively only a short time com-
pared with many of his contemporaries, interests of grave im--
portance not only to individuals but to the community have
been entrusted to his keeping. Intricate problems in constitutional law have been submitted to him for solution; the delicate
questions involved in the settlement of estates have been referred to his judgment and perceptive powers, and in no instance
has he proven inadequate to the task laid upon him or failed to
show that the confidence reposed in him was well placed.

Hr. Hosmer was born October 22, 1900, at Washington, D. C.,
and is a son of William H. and Rose K. (Hunsberger) Hosmer,
natives of Virginia, where William H. Hosmer has been in the
employ of the United States Government for a period of thirty
years. At the present time he resides at Arlington, where he is
held in high esteem as a reliable and substantial citizen, and
as a man of exemplary character.

Emery N. Hosmer attended the public schools of Arlington
County, following which he enrolled as a student in the Western
High School, Washington, D. C., where he returned to graduate
after the World war. He then pursued a course at Strayer's
Business College, and in 1921 entered the National University
from which he was graduated with the degree of Bachelor of
Laws in 1924. Following his graduation Mr. Hosmer settled
down to the practice of his profession, having passed the bar
examination in 1923 while he was still attending law school, and
now has a large and lucrative practice, with well appointed
offices at Arlington Court House at Clarendon. In addition to
caring for the interests of his large clientage Mr. Hosmer is serving in the dual capacity of commissioner in chancery and bail
commissioner. He is a member of the Arlington County Bar
Association and the Virginia State Bar Association, and has
attained and maintained a high position in the esteem and respect of his fellow practitioners. While he is a deep thinker and
profound student, he is genial and fond of social pleasures, and
belongs to the Independent Order of Odd Fellows, the Sigma
Delta Kappa law fraternity and the local Chamber of Commerce.
Politically he is a Democrat, and his religious faith is that of
the Episcopal Church. In 1916, when the unpleasantness occurred between the United States and Mexico on the Mexican
border, Mr. Hosmer, although a lad of only fifteen years, left the
parental roof and managed to get himself accepted in the army.
Subsequently he saw service on the border, and soon afterwards
answered the call to the colors to take part in the World war,
arriving in France at the age of sixteen years. He was probably
the youngest soldier in the army, and took part in all major engagements of the Second Division, A. E. F., until being seriously
wounded October 2, 1918. His wound was a desperate one, and
receiving a general citation he returned to the United States a
convalescent, and finally received his honorable discharge May
23, 1919. He is a member of the American Legion, the Second
Division Association and the Veterans of Foreign Wars.

On May 22, 1926, Mr. Hosmer was united in marriage with
Miss Gladys W. Moore, a daughter of Harry G. and Laura A.

Moore, natives respectively of Illinois and Indiana, the former of whom died in 1912, while the latter survives him and resides at Equality, Illinois. Mr. and Mrs. Hosmer reside at Virginia Avenue and Shelley Road, Arlington.

CHARLES LANDON SCOTT, director of public works for the City of Danville, has been engaged in engineering work since leaving the Virginia Polytechnic Institute. He was formerly connected with the State Highway Department and now has charge of all the public works and municipal facilities of one of the most progressive cities in Southern Virginia.

He was born at Rocky Mount, Virginia, March 22, 1883, son of Charles Landon and Louise (Everett) Scott. The Scott family is of Scotch-Irish ancestry and has been in Virginia since Colonial times. One of his ancestors, Alexander Scott, at one time owned a number of mills along the James River. This Alexander Scott was the father of Alexander Scott, who developed a farm and plantation and business enterprises in Albemarle County, the community taking the name of Scottsville in his honor. A son of this Alexander Scott was Dr. Samuel Scott, grandfather of Charles L. Scott. Dr. Samuel Scott was a highly educated physician and for many years practiced in Buckingham and Amherst counties. He died in Buckingham County at the age of eighty-four. Charles Landon Scott, Sr., was born and reared in Amherst County, attended public schools and the University of Virginia, trained for the law and practiced that profession for a number of years in Amherst County, and for twenty-four years was county superintendent of schools. He died in 1922, at the age of sixty-nine, and both he and his wife are buried at Amherst. He married Louise Montague Everett, who was born near Keswick, in Albemarle County, attended the private school at Edge Hill, and was reared in the faith of the Baptist Church, but after her marriage joined the Episcopal Church. She died December 27, 1927. The children of these parents were: Louise M., wife of C. A. Joubert, of Lynchburg; S. D. Scott, of Goldsboro, North Carolina; Charles L.; Mary E., wife of R. A. Meade, of Haymarket, Virginia; Ann Elizabeth, now Mrs. Victor Van Gemmingen, of Amherst; Lieut. Everett, who served with the Coast Artillery Corps in the World war and died January 4, 1919; Hester Harrison, now Mrs. I. P. Wailes, of Amherst; Clare Voorhees, who died at the age of sixteen; and Nell Thompson, who died when eight months old.

Charles L. Scott, Jr., attended public school in Amherst County, the Kenmore Preparatory School, and acquired his technical education in the Virginia Polytechnic Institute. He left school in 1903 and has had a wide experience in engineering work and practice during the past quarter of a century. For two years after leaving school he followed civil engineering, and then for two years taught in Amherst County. He was connected with the state highway department as an engineer until 1915, and during the following four years, including the World war period, was engaged in highway engineering work for Raleigh County, West Virginia. In 1919 he resumed his connections with the Virginia State Highway Department, and since 1925 has given his professional training and experience to the City of Danville, at first as city engineer and since 1926 as director of public works.

Mr. Scott is a director of the Danville Chamber of Commerce, is affiliated with Lodge No. 70, A. F. and A. M., is a member of the Lions Club and Wildwood Fishing Club, is a Democrat and a member of the Episcopal Church, and is on the vestry of the Epiphany Church at Danville.

He married at Amherst, Virginia, December 29, 1909, Miss Kate Whitcomb Randolph. She was educated in the Arlington Institute at Alexandria, Virginia, and the Randolph-Macon Woman's College at Lynchburg. She is a member of the Episcopal Church and was formerly very active in the United Daughters of the Confederacy, and one of her sisters is a member of the Daughters of the American Revolution and the Society of Colonial Dames. Mrs. Scott is a daughter of Major Peyton and Mary Elmslie (Fisher) Randolph. Her father was a prominent engineer and railway official, connected with the Richmond & Danville Railroad, and for a number of years general manager and later vice president of that road, an office he was filling at the time of his death. He served in the Confederate army. Major Randolph died in April, 1891, and his wife, on August 15, 1923. This branch of the Randolph family is descended from William Randolph of Turkey Island on the James River.

Mr. and Mrs. Scott have four children, Charles Landon III, Mary Elmslie, Clare Louise and Whitcomb Randolph. Charles and Mary E. are graduates of the Danville High School, and the daughter is now a student in Averett College at Danville, while the son is an employe of the state highway department. The two younger children are attending public school at Danville.

JAMES RICHARD TATE throughout his active career has been identified with the grocery business at Danville, first in retail, but for many years as a member of the firm of Tate & Thomas, now the corporation of Tate & Thomas Company, wholesale grocers.

Mr. Tate was born in Pittsylvania County, Virginia, September 30, 1875, son of William C. and Maria (Whitehead) Tate and a grandson of William Irvine Tate, a farmer and planter of Franklin County, who in the early days taught school for a number of years in Franklin and Halifax counties. He and his family are buried at the family cemetery near Rocky Mount, Virginia. William C. Tate was born in Franklin County, was educated in private schools, and during the war was purchasing agent for the commissary department of the Confederate army. After the war he followed farming and for a number of years was in the lumber business. He attained the good old age of ninety-four, passing away in 1921, and is buried in the family plot near Chalk Level. His wife, Maria Whitehead, was born and reared in Pittsylvania County, also attended private schools, and died in 1915, at the age of seventy-four. She and her husband were members of the Greenfield Baptist Church. Of their twelve children three died in infancy and Marshall and Nannie when children. Ida, now deceased, was the wife of E. R. Monroe; Carrie is Mrs. G. H. Vaden, of Chatham, Virginia; Blanche, deceased, was the wife of B. B. Hicks, of Richmond; Mary is Mrs. P. L. Booth, of Danville; James R. is the oldest surviving son; Carrington lives at Saxe, Virginia; and Emma is Mrs. L. F. Paulette, of Smithfield.

James R. Tate had good school advantages, attending public schools, graduated from the Lynchburg Business College and was also a student in the Davis Military School. In 1894 he came to Danville and for five years was with the Booth Retail

Grocery Company. He left that to become associated with Mr. J. M. Thomas in a retail grocery store under the name of Tate & Thomas, and these two merchants have been closely associated for nearly thirty years. Their business gradually developed on a wholesale basis, and since 1923 has been conducted as a corporation, Tate & Thomas Company, with several traveling salesmen in a territory comprising six or seven counties in Virginia and North Carolina. It is one of the very progressive concerns doing business in that section of Virginia.

Mr. Tate is a member of the Virginia State and American Wholesale Grocers Associations. He is active in the Kiwanis Club work, is a Democrat and for several years was a deacon in the First Baptist Church.

He married at Milton, North Carolina, November 22, 1899, Miss Annie Farley, of Milton, daughter of William P. and Elizabeth (Covington) Farley. Her father was a building and brick contractor. The Farleys and Covingtons are among the old families of Virginia and North Carolina, and Covington, Virginia, was named for one of the pioneers. Mrs. Tate attended private school at Milton and at Winston-Salem, North Carolina, and was a worker in the Baptist Church. She died December 5, 1917, and is buried in Green Hill Cemetery at Danville. Her five children were William Carrington, James Richard Jr., Louise Elizabeth, Thomas Bryan and Owen Farley. The son William C. attended public school at Danville, the Virginia Military Institute, and is now associated with the wholesale dry goods business of J. M. Thomas & Company of Danville. James R., Jr., after public schooling at Danville attended the Mercersburg Academy in Pennsylvania and is now at Newark, New Jersey. Miss Elizabeth graduated from Converse College of North Carolina in the class of 1929. Thomas Bryan is in the University of Virginia, and Owen is in public school at Danville.

Mr. Tate married at Danville, June 3, 1920, Miss Almeyda Coleman. Mrs. Tate for a number of years was prominent in educational work. She is a graduate of Averett College of Danville, also attended school at Louisville, Kentucky, and taught kindergarten at Randolph-Macon Institute, at Averett College, and was a teacher in the Institute for the Blind at Raleigh, North Carolina. She is a member of the First Baptist Church, is president of the Shakespeare Study Club and is a member of the Wednesday Club. Her father, George Coleman, was for many years a Pittsylvania planter and for forty years was in the tobacco warehouse business at Danville. He is now retired. Her mother died in 1915 and is buried in Greenville Cemetery.

EMERSON ROAKS PURKS has been a well known business man in King George County for a number of years. At the village of King George he is proprietor of the King George Motor Company, the authorized sales and service agency for the county for Ford cars.

Mr. Purks was born in King George County November 1, 1882, son of Charles T. and Matilda L. (Forloin) Purks. His father was born in Caroline County and his mother in Nelson County. His father served as a Confederate soldier and for a short time was a prisoner of war. He devoted his life after the war to farming and general merchandising, and is now living retired at King George.

Emerson R. Purks was reared and educated in his native county and as a boy worked in his father's store. For five years

he was in the general merchandise business for himself, and for seven years was a timber dealer.   Then for two years he resumed general merchandising at Charlottesville, and in December, 1923, returned to King George and took over the Ford agency under the name of the King George Motor Company.   Mr. Purks is also a director of the Bank of King George.

He married in September, 1909, Miss Alice D. Grigsby, daughter of John J. and Nimmie (Miffileton) Grigsby, who were born in King George County, where her father was a merchant. Mr. and Mrs. Purks have four children: Earle Roaks, born in 1910; Emerson Randolph, born in 1912; Marie, born in 1915; and Agnes, born in 1917.   The children were all given good educational advantages.   Mr. Purks as the father of four children has been a valuable member of the King George County Board of Education.   For two years he also served as constable and has been a member of the Board of Elections.   For twenty years he has been affiliated with the Order of Fraternal Americans, and is also a Mason and Odd Fellow, a Democrat in politics and a member of the Baptist Church.

GUY WEBB, of Norfolk, was one of the pioneer real estate operators in the Norfolk district, and has been responsible for a large measure of the great developments in the Virginia Beach section.

Mr. Webb has made a success of his business life without any special advantages or opportunities, relying solely on his concentrated purpose and industry.   He was born at Kinston, North Carolina, son of George Bell Webb, a native of the same place, grandson of James Barney Webb, who was born in Portland, Maine, and great-grandson of James Webb, who was descended from one of three brothers that came to America from England in the sixteen hundreds, two of these brothers settling at Boston, one at Braintree, Massachusetts, and another in Isle of Wight County, Virginia.   A complete history of the Webb family in America and also tracing back in England to the fourteenth century has been published by a Mr. James B. Webb of Illinois.   Mr. Webb's great-grandfather, James Webb, was a ship owner and a captain engaged in foreign trade, making his home at Portland, Maine.   His son, James Barney Webb, moved from Maine to Kinston, North Carolina, where he established a plant for the manufacture of wagons and carriages.   He married Margaret Laughinghouse, who was born in Perquimans County, North Carolina, member of a family of planters and slave owners.   George Bell Webb succeeded to the wagon manufacturing plant of his father and followed that business at Kinston throughout his active career.   He died in August, 1914.   His wife, Agnes Pittman, was born in Pitt County, North Carolina, daughter of Francis Marion Pittman.   She died in 1883, leaving three children.

Mr. Guy Webb had the advantage of public and private schools at Kinston, but on account of an injury to one eye left school and found employment as clerk in a drug store.   In 1898 he removed to Richmond, Virginia, sold typewriting machines for two years, in 1900 returned to North Carolina, was a hotel clerk at Wilson, and took up the life insurance business at Kinston.   It was soon evident that he had made choice of a proper field when he entered life insurance, and his success at the business brought him appointment as manager of the health and accident department of the Pacific Mutual Life Insurance Company at Kinston. Mr. Webb transferred his attention to the real estate field in 1904, spending two years at Goldsboro, North Carolina.

In 1906, seeking a larger and broader field, he recognized the great possibilities in the Norfolk territory, particularly the Virginia Beach section, and he secured large tracts of land which he has improved and sold. On account of its climate this section is rapidly becoming the most popular all-year-round residential area along the Atlantic Coast, and Mr. Webb has done a great deal to prepare local conditions and give proper publicity to the region.

He married, June 29, 1904, Miss Helen Gray, also a native of Kinston, North Carolina, daughter of Marshall E. and Mirtie N. Gray. They have a family of eight children: Jean, the wife of John Gordon Christian, Jr., of Houston, Texas, George Marshall, Guy, Jr., Helen, Margaret Gray, Anne Best, Agnes Pittman and Nell Doran. Mr. Webb is deeply interested in educational matters and has been a member of the Norfolk School Board. He has served as president of the Virginia Beach Real Estate Board, as president of the Board of Trade at Norfolk and as vice president of the Virginia Real Estate Association. He is affiliated with Owen Lodge No. 164, A. F. and A. M., and is a Knight Templar and Shriner Mason.

WALTER WOOD WADDILL, JR. The business of one of the oldest and largest insurance agencies in Southern Virginia constitutes the work that Walter W. Waddill, Jr., has followed since leaving college. The Waddill family has been long and prominently known at Danville, where Walter W., Jr., was born May 7, 1883.

The Waddills came to Virginia in early Colonial times and are of a commingling of Welsh and Scotch lineage. Mr. Waddill's grandfather, William H. Waddill, was a hat maker at Clarksville, Virginia. Walter W. Waddill, Sr., was born at Clarksville, was educated in private schools and for a number of years was in the book and printing business and later took up insurance. He was a member of the Baptist Church, served several terms in the Danville City Council and died in 1904, being buried in Green Hill Cemetery. His wife, Page Acree, was born in King and Queen County, Virginia, and was educated in the Roanoke Female College, now Averett College, at Danville. She is sixty-seven years of age and since girlhood has been a devout Baptist. There were seven children: Mary, who died at the age of sixteen; Walter W., Jr.; Llewellyn, who died when four years old; Nelson D., who died at the age of two years; Roland Acree, of Washington, D. C.; Edith Page, wife of Bernard R. Smith, of Asheville, North Carolina; and Rachel, who died in infancy.

Walter Wood Waddill, Jr., was educated at Danville, attending public school and the Danville Military Institute, and after completing his work there in the class of 1900 entered the Georgia School of Technology at Atlanta. After returning home he became associated with his father in the insurance business, and in 1904, after his father died, he formed a partnership with C. G. Holland, now known as the Waddill-Holland Company, Inc., with offices in the Burton Building. They handle every phase of insurance work, representing a number of old-line companies and also do a considerable volume of business as brokers. The present organization represents a consolidation of the Waddill Insurance Company and the C. G. Holland Insurance Company, and the business has been in existence now for over thirty-six years. Mr. Waddill is treasurer of the company.

His name is associated with a number of organizations expressive of the civic life of his home city. He is treasurer of the Danville Rotary Club, is secretary of the Danville Golf Club, a director of the Tuscarora Club, is a member of Roman Eagle Lodge No. 122, A. F. and A. M., a past high priest of Euclid Chapter, Royal Arch Masons, a past commander of Dove Commandery of the Knights Templar, and is also a Shriner. He is a Democrat in politics, and in the First Baptist Church teaches a class of boys in Sunday school. During the World war he was a member of various committees handling the local patriotic program, while Mrs. Waddill was captain of one of the canteen committees.

Mr. Waddill married at Danville, December 22, 1909, Miss Linda Hume Swain. She completed her education in Randolph-Macon Institute. She is a member of the Mount Vernon Methodist Episcopal Church, South, and the Music Study Club. Her parents were George W. and Mary (Ferguson) Swain, of Danville, where her father for many years carried on a business as a tobacconist. Mr. and Mrs. Waddill have two daughters, Mary Page and Linda Acree. Mary attended public school and Averett College at Danville and is now a student at Agnes Scott College of Atlanta, Georgia. Linda is a student in the Danville High School.

JAMES WILMER RAY was educated for the law, practiced the profession for a time, and then took up a business career. He is one of the prominent younger generation of business men in Danville, where he is manager of the Coca Cola Bottling Company.

Mr. Ray was born in Atlanta, Georgia, June 9, 1895, son of James A. and Ossie (Hardman) Ray and grandson of James A. Ray, a native of Monroe, Georgia, a farmer and a soldier of the Confederacy. The Ray family have lived for a number of generations in the two states of Georgia and North Carolina. James A. Ray, Jr., was born and reared in Walton County, Georgia, attended private schools and was a merchant at Monroe until his death in 1895, at the early age of thirty-nine. His wife, Ossie Hardman Ray, was born in Walton County, attended private schools and is still living at Monroe, the wife of John T. Robertson. She is a member of the Methodist Episcopal Church, South. Her father, Dr. William S. R. Hardman, was a surgeon in the Confederate army. Mrs. Ossie Hardman (Ray) Robertson has three children: Harry A. Ray, an insurance man at Monroe; Julia, wife of George W. Felker, Jr., of Monroe; and James W. Ray.

James W. Ray was educated in public schools and in 1917 took his law degree at the University of Georgia. Instead of going into law practice he joined the colors for service in the World war. He was sent overseas and spent twenty months in a varied routine of duty with the American Expeditionary Forces.

He received his honorable discharge at Hoboken, New Jersey, May 23, 1919, and then returned to Monroe, Georgia, and for a year and a half practiced law.

He left the law to join the Coca Cola Company at Atlanta, remaining there two and a half years and in 1923 came to Vir-

ginia as manager of the Coca Cola Bottling Company at Danville.
He has made himself a public spirited factor in the life of that
city. He is a member of the Kiwanis Club, Roman Eagle Lodge
No. 122, A. F. and A. M., the Scottish Rite bodies of Masonry,
Yaarab Temple of the Mystic Shrine at Atlanta, is a member
of the Danville Golf Club, and on the Board of Stewards of Mt.
Vernon Methodist Episcopal Church, South.

He married at Danville, April 7, 1923, Miss Genevieve Lupton Hazlewood, who was reared and educated in Danville and
attended Holland College and New England Conservatory of
Music at Boston. She is a prominent member of the Danville
Music Study Club and takes an active part in the musical work
of her church. Her parents are Newton H. and Ola (Lupton)
Hazlewood, of Danville, where her father for a number of years
has been connected with the Coca Cola Bottling Company. Mr.
and Mrs. Ray have two children, Genevieve Hazlewood, born
February 5, 1925, and James Wilmer, Jr., born January 22, 1929.

LEE BROCKENBROUGH FITZHUGH, Stafford County farmer
and attorney, with offices at Falmouth, is a descendant of the
distinguished Fitzhugh family of Virginia which was founded
by William Fitzhugh, who came to Virginia about 1670, settling
at Bedford, in what is now King George County. He was
appointed a crown counsel by the King of England, and in appreciation of his services he was granted 296,000 acres, extending
from the vicinity of what is now Washington to Chesapeake
Bay, and later he acquired as much more land. He and King
Carter were at one time the two largest land owners in Virginia
Colony. He married Mary Tucker, of the famous Tucker family
of Virginia, and to each of his five sons, William, Henry, John,
George and Thomas, he gave a large plantation and built a fine
home.

The grandfather of Lee B. Fitzhugh was George Fitzhugh,
who was born July 2, 1807, son of Dr. George and Lucy (Stuart)
Fitzhugh. George Fitzhugh largely through his own efforts
acquired a good education, studied law, and became a noted
criminal attorney at Port Royal. He became most widely known
as a lecturer on slavery. He claimed that slavery is the natural
and rightful condition of society, which when not founded on
human servitude tends to cannibalism. He wrote *Sociology for
the South of the Failure of Free Society*, published in 1854, and
Cannibals All, or Slaves Without Masters, published in 1856.
He died in Texas July 30, 1881. His son, Capt. Robert Hunter
Fitzhugh, was a member of the staff of Gen. Robert E. Lee.

Lee Brockenbrough Fitzhugh was born at Seaford, Delaware,
May 29, 1884, son of Rev. George Stuart and Angeline B. (Purnell) Fitzhugh. His father was born in Caroline County, Virginia, and his mother in Maryland. George Stuart Fitzhugh was
a Confederate soldier, and after the war entered the Episcopal
ministry. He died June 17, 1925, at the age of eighty-one. His
wife passed away October 20, 1905.

Lee Brockenbrough Fitzhugh was reared and educated in
many localities where his father was a minister—in Florida,
Kentucky, Maryland, Virginia. He spent two years as a law
student at the University of Maryland and one year in Richmond
College, and for two summer sessions was in the University of
Virginia. Mr. Fitzhugh was licensed to practice in Oklahoma in
1913, having for a number of years prior to that been connected
with the Fidelity Trust & Deposit Company of Baltimore. Mr.

David H Lindsay

Fitzhugh began the practice of law at Tulsa, Oklahoma, remaining there six years and for two years of that time served as assistant county attorney. He made his home at Sand Springs, a Tulsa suburb, and was the first postmaster of the town and the second city attorney. After leaving Oklahoma he practiced law at Newport News, Virginia, until 1922, and following that for five years was a lawyer in Northern Alabama, at Sheffield and Muscle Shoals. In August, 1927, he returned to Virginia and located in Stafford County, having his law office at Falmouth, and he resides on his farm, Poplar Grove Farm, ten miles northwest of Falmouth. This farm comprises 400 acres, and Mr. Fitzhugh is specializing in pure bred Jersey cattle.

He married, August 28, 1916, Sallie V. French, daughter of John I. and Lulu M. (Shelkett) French, natives of Stafford County. Her father spent his life as a farmer in that county and died in 1905, and her mother passed away in November, 1925. Mr. and Mrs. Fitzhugh have had three children: John French, born July 20, 1917; Virginia Lee, born December 30, 1918; and Lee B., Jr., born February 16, 1921, and died July 4, 1923.

Mr. Fitzhugh has membership in the State Bar Associations of Oklahoma, Alabama and Virginia, and the American Bar Association. He is a Democrat, member of the Episcopal Church, and the Sons of Confederate Veterans.

DAVID HAWKINS LINDSAY. A prominent member of the Gloucester County bar is David H. Lindsay, a leading citizen and commonwealth attorney of Gloucester County, Virginia. Bearing an old and honored family name, Mr. Lindsay through his enterprise and professional ability has preserved its high character and worthy aims, and today, although one of the younger members of the county bar, receives general recognition as a leader.

David H. Lindsay was born at Belroi, Gloucester County, Virginia, November 1, 1900, son of Benjamin F. and Emma J. (Williams) Lindsay, both natives of Virginia, the former born in New Kent County and the latter in Gloucester. For thirty years of his earlier life, before settling permanently in Gloucester County, the father of Mr. Lindsay was a sea captain, commanding a vessel running between New York City and South America. During the war between the states he suffered capture by the Union forces while driving a Confederate army wagon. After the war he returned to Gloucester County, where he continued to engage in farming and contracting until he retired, and still makes his home at Gloucester.

David H. Lindsay received his early educational training in the public schools of Gloucester County, and was graduated from the Gloucester High School in the class of 1919. Although very young to be given a position of so much authority, during the World war, while associated with the Dupont Company, he was placed in charge of the general stores and given an office force of sixty people. Later he was transferred to the Wilmington plant and, as manager of general stores, continued with the company during its erection of 750 houses at Pontiac, Michigan, for the Oakland Motor Car Company, and 1,000 houses at Flint, Michigan, for the Buick Company. He had shown such marked efficiency and dependable traits of character that when he retired from the Du Pont Company, in order to return to school, numerous other business connections were open to him.

Mr. Lindsay then entered the Detroit Institute of Technology for a course in civil engineering, but later, realizing that his natural urge was toward the law, became a student in the Detroit College of Law, and completed his law course at Washington and Lee University, Virginia, in the class of 1923, with his degree of LL. B. He immediately entered into practice and also taught commercial law at Fork Union Military Academy until 1925, when he came to Gloucester. He has built up a large private practice and since November, 1927, has filled the office of commonwealth attorney. He has additional interests as a realtor and handler of loans and insurance, and he also operates his 150-acre farm, situated on York River, Gloucester County, on which is his beautiful summer home.

Mr. Lindsay was married on January 20, 1926, at Scottsville, Virginia, to Miss Millicent Bledsoe Atkisson, whose young life closed June 28, 1926.

Active in the Masonic fraternity, Mr. Lindsay belongs also to the Odd Fellows and the Red Men, still keeps up his interest in his old Greek letter college fraternities the Phi Delta Epsilon and the Sigma Delta Kappa, belongs to the Virginia Bar Association, the Gloucester Bar Association, the Commercial Law League of America and the American Bar Association. He enjoys wholesome out-door exercise and is a member of the Gloucester Golf and Country Club, and to some extent is active in Democratic politics, loyally and proudly recalling the notable old leaders of a party that has always won his honored father's support. From early years a member of the Methodist Episcopal Church at Gloucester, he takes unmeasured interest in its work, and is the beloved teacher of the Young Men's Bible Class in the Sunday School.

JOSEPH BANISTER ANDERSON. The Anderson family of Virginia had its origin in Scotland and was found later in Northumberland County, England, where Sir Edward Anderson was chief justice in the fourteenth century. The first Virgina ancestor was Richard Anderson, a descendant of Sir Edward, who came over in the ship *Merchants Hope* in 1633, accompanied by his sons, Thomas and John, who settled at Gloucester Point, now Gloucester County, Virginia. They are forebears of the Andersons of Amelia, Cumberland, Hanover, New Kent, Louisa, Halifax and Pittsylvania Counties. Later on members of this family migrated to Kentucky, Tennessee and states south.

Richard Anderson, a descendant of Thomas, son of Richard, the first settler, came from New Kent to Amelia about 1760 and to Pittsylvania in 1784. A deed dated June 19th, 1784, recorded on page 372, deed book 7, in the office of the Clerk of Pittsylvania County, conveys to Richard Anderson, Sr., of Amelia County, three tracts of land lying on both sides of Banister River, containing in all 1,223 acres for 1,223 pounds.

Joseph Banister Anderson, a great-grandson of Richard Anderson, of Amelia-Pittsylvania, was born at Spring Garden, Pittsylvania County. He is a son of Joseph Eggleston Anderson and Minerva Caroline Terry, his wife. His maternal grandmother was Mary Clopton Terry, wife of Daniel Terry, a descendant of William Clopton, of New Kent County, whose ancestral home was Clopton Manor, Stratford-on-Avon, England.

Mr. Anderson received his preparatory educational training under Joseph J. Averett, A. E. Stebbins and A. B. Brown, D. D.

His collegiate education was in Emory and Henry College, from which he graduated in 1870, receiving the A. B. degree. In 1888 he was awarded the degree of A. M., honoris causa. His college mates were such men as James Atkins and E. Embree Hoss, Bishops of the Methodist Episcopal Church, South, Braxton B. Comer, Governor and United States Senator, Alabama; Samuel W. Small, evangelist and lecturer, Georgia; John A. Buchanan, Member of Congress and Judge of the Supreme Court of Virginia, and Henry C. Stuart, Governor of Virginia.

After leaving college Mr. Anderson was associated with his brother, Captain Abner Anderson, owner and editor of the *Danville Register*, in the editorial and reportorial work on that paper. This continued for about two years, and during the time that Captain Anderson, who was State Senator from Danville and Pittsylvania County, was in Richmond attending the sessions of the General Assembly, Mr. Anderson was in charge of the *Register*. He has often remarked that his connection with the *Register* gave him a most valuable literary and educational training.

For twenty-five years Mr. Anderson was Commissioner of the Revenue for the city of Danville. In 1921 he announced that he would not again be a candidate for that office. He was elected a member of the House of Delegates from Danville and Pittsylvania County in November, 1921, and served through the regular session of 1922 and the called session of 1923.

He was appointed a member of the Committee on Tax Revision in 1914 by Governor Henry C. Stuart. This committee was engaged for six months in studying the tax systems of the several states of our Union and comparing them with the antiquated Virginia tax laws and in holding sessions in various sections of the state to gather information on which to make recommendations to the Legislature. Mr. Anderson's experience as Commissioner of the Revenue, in administering the existing tax laws, made him a valuable member of this committee.

During the closing months of the Civil war—August, 1864, April, 1865. Mr. Anderson, a youth in his teens, was employed by his brother, Capt. Abner Anderson, who was owner and editor of the *Danville Register*, as proof reader and mailing clerk for the paper. The *Register* was issued daily during these closing months. Mr. Anderson relates some interesting personal experiences of this period.

When the battle lines before Richmond were evacuated by the Confederate troops on Sunday, April 2nd, 1865, President Davis, Mrs. Davis, the Cabinet, clerks and attaches entrained for Danville and arrived Monday afternoon of the 3rd. Major William T. Sutherlin met President Davis at the railway station and took him to his home on Main Street, where he remained a guest until after the surrender at Appomattox, when he left for the South. Secretary Judah P. Benjamin was the guest of Mr. John M. Johnston in his home on Main Street, now the remodeled Tuscarora Club; Secretary J. H. Reagan was the guest of Mr. W. S. Patton in his home on Main Street, on the lot on which the Elks Club House is now situated and the other members of the Cabinet were guests in other Danville homes.

The books, documents and archives of the secretarial department of the Confederate States Government were stored in the Bendick home on Wilson Street.

President Davis and his Cabinet assembled in the library of the Sutherlin Mansion on Wednesday morning, April 5th, and after discussing the situation, Mr. Davis wrote a proclamation to the people of the Confederate states. Mr. Anderson says that Judah P. Benjamin, Secretary of State, came into the Register office about midday and after greeting Captain Anderson, said: "President Davis has written a proclamation which he wishes you to publish in tomorrow's *Register*." Captain Anderson said that he would be glad to comply with the President's request. Mr. Benjamin said: "There are some interlineations and erasures in this," as he took the proclamation from his pocket. "Let me have some paper, and I will write a clear copy for your printer." Mr. Anderson says that he stood a few feet away and looked on with wide open eyes and open mouth, while Mr. Benjamin was writing and that he didn't miss a dip in the ink stand or a scratch of the pen. When completed Mr. Benjamin gave the written sheets to Captain Anderson who handed them to Lavalle, a typesetter, and said, "Put this in type." The manuscript of the editorials, local items, etc., after being put in type, were strung on a wire hook behind the press room door. The proclamation was published in the *Daily Register* of April 6th.

When information of the surrender of General Lee's army at Appomattox was received April 10th by President Davis and the Cabinet, they made hasty preparation and left for Greensboro. The *Register* ceased publication a few days thereafter when it was learned that General Wright's Sixth Army Corps was approaching Danville. When Captain Anderson went to the wire hook to get the manuscript of the proclamation it was missing. Lavalle had gone the day before, and it was supposed that he took the manuscript. No trace of it has been found.

A few days after the Federal troops came to Danville, several officers called on Captain Anderson and made a proposition to rent the office and equipment of the *Register*. They wished to issue a daily paper and offered Captain Anderson a salary to superintend the work. He consented to the proposition and *The Sixth Corps*, a four page daily paper, was published so long as the Federal troops remained in Danville.

Mr. Anderson married Miss Julia Millspaugh, daughter of Dr. Charles Millspaugh and his wife, Henrietta Talbott, of Richmond. Mrs. Anderson died in 1920. The children of this marriage were Maria Louise, Thomas Talbott, Henrietta Julia and Joseph Roscoe.

Thomas Talbott Anderson was first vice president and treasurer of Liggett & Myers Tobacco Company, St. Louis, Missouri. He died on July 19, 1929. Joseph Roscoe Anderson was manager of the Liggett & Myers manufacturing plant in Philadelphia until his death in 1924.

Mr. Anderson is a member of the First Baptist Church of Danville, and, for a number of years, was clerk of the Roanoke Baptist Association and moderator of that association for four years. He was a member of the Board of Trustees of Roanoke Female College, now Averett College, of Danville, for twenty-five years and president of the board for five years.

Mr. Anderson has not been engaged in business for several years. He says that he now has the hardest job of his life—"trying to learn how to loaf gracefully." He has an office, 724 Masonic Building, where he is always glad to welcome his friends.

JOHN CHILDS SIMPSON, A. B., A. M., has some important services to his credit, as an educator, business man and overseas soldier during the World war. He has for some years been connected with the Randolph-Macon system of schools and colleges and is now president of the Randolph-Macon Institute at Danville.

He was born at Lynchburg, Virginia, May 11, 1889, son of Rev. T. McNider and Jocasta Land (Gray) Simpson. One of three Simpson brothers who came from England in Colonial times settled in North Carolina and became the ancestor of a long family line. The grandfather, Thomas Simpson, for many years conducted a mercantile business at Hertford, North Carolina. Rev. T. McNider Simpson was born at Hertford, March 7, 1851, completed his education in Randolph-Macon College, and has given fifty-three years of his life to the ministry of the Methodist Episcopal Church, South, as a member of the Virginia Conference. He has held pastorates in a number of prominent churches, including the Lynn Street and the Main Street Churches of Danville, the Memorial Church of Lynchburg, the Monumental Church of Portsmouth, and Memorial Church of Norfolk. He was twice presiding elder of the Lynchburg District, once of the Richmond District, once of the Norfolk District and for a number of years was presiding elder of the Portsmouth and Newport News District. He is still active in the ministry, being pastor of the church at Smithfield, where he resides. His wife, Jocasta Land Gray, was born and reared at Windsor, North Carolina, attended public schools there and Murfreesboro College, and was a very important aid to and associate of her husband in their interests in the church. She died May 8, 1914, and is buried in the Hollywood Cemetery of Richmond. Seven children were born to the couple. T. McNider, Jr., is a graduate of the University of Virginia, took his Doctor of Philosophy degree at the University of Chicago, is professor of mathematics in Randolph-Macon College at Ashland, and also teaches in the summer school at the University of Virginia. Mary T. is the wife of Fred R. Chenault, pastor of the Broad Street Methodist Church at Richmond, where he has been located for thirteen years. George Gray Simpson is a merchandise broker in Norfolk. John Childs comes next in age. Janie is the wife of C. R. Wilcox, president of the Darlington School for Boys at Rome, Georgia. Miss Lellie Winfree lives with her father at Smithfield, and Miss Helen Land is dean of girls of a school in Norfolk.

John Childs Simpson acquired part of his public schooling in Danville, attended high school in Richmond, and was graduated from Randolph-Macon College in 1911, having completed five years work in four, receiving at the same time the degrees A. B. and A. M. He was president of his class and the student body, a member of the Phi Delta Theta (social) and Sigma Upsilon (literary) fraternities. Mr. Simpson had a part in Randolph-Macon which is pleasantly remembered by all the old alumni. He played on the football and basketball teams, was manager of the baseball team one year, and in 1910 was selected as all Eastern Virginia end in football. During his senior year he was an instructor in German.

After graduating he served two years with the McCallie School of Chattanooga, Tennessee, as profesor of French and German, and for three years was in the English department of the John Marshall High School of Richmond, and also taught in night high school there. He gave up school work to join Frederick E. Nolting & Company, security and investment bankers of Richmond, but resigned early in the spring of 1917 to enter the First Officers Training Camp at Fort Myer, Virginia. In November, 1917, he was commissioned a first lieutenant of field artillery, was married on December 1, and immediately went to Camp Meade, Maryland, where he was assigned to the Three Hundred and Eleventh Field Artillery, Seventy-ninth Division. In June, 1918, he was sent to France with a special detachment for special study. He crossed over on one of a group of transports and convoys, originally fifteen in number, but as a matter of fact thirteen boats comprised the fleet, and in defiance of superstitution they arrived in France in thirteen days on Friday the 13th of July. For two weeks he had special training at Le Valdehon near the Swiss border, then rejoined the Three Hundred and Eleventh Field Artillery and was in training at LaCourtine until November 13. His regiment had waited week after week for the call to the front, being in perfect readiness. After the armistice the regiment was moved to Audelot, a town about 20 kilometers from General Pershing's headquarters at Chaumont, and there he was made town major, in charge of billeting for officers and men in several villages. In May, 1919, he was promoted to the rank of captain, and towards the close of that month returned home and received his honorable discharge at Camp Dix, New Jersey, June 5, 1919.

After his release from military service Captain Simpson located at Norfolk and was a cotton and peanut broker there until 1921. Since 1921 he has been an administrative and teaching official of the Randolph-Macon system, at first as treasurer of the academy at Bedford and head of the English department, and since 1925 has been president of the Randolph-Macon School for Girls in Danville.

Captain Simpson is a member of Lodge No. 32, A. F. and A. M., was president in 1928 of the Danville Kiwanis Club and a delegate to the international convention at Seattle in June of that year. He is an independent Democrat in politics, is a lay leader of the Main Street Methodist Episcopal Church, South, and teaches a Bible class of men, about eighty in number, in the Mount Vernon Methodist Episcopal Church, South.

Captain Simpson married at Ashland, Virginia, December 1, 1917, Miss Anne Easter Marye, of Ashland, daughter of L. T. W. and Rosa (Bayard) Marye. She is a niece of Col. Morton Marye, former state auditor of Virginia. Her father was a prominent attorney, practicing in Richmond and Ashland, and served on the staff of Governor McKinney of Virginia. He died in 1927 and is buried at Ashland, and her mother now divides her time between the home of her daughter in Danville and the home of her son in Waycross, Georgia, Robert W. Marye, who is division engineer for the Atlantic Coast Line Railway. Mr. and Mrs. Simpson have four children: Anne Marye, John C., Jr., Littleton Waller and Rosa Gray. Anne and John are in the primary department of the Randolph-Macon School for Girls.

REV. JESSE R. HITE, pastor of the Keen Street Baptist Church at Danville, is a member of a Halifax County family, and is a lineal descendant of the pioneer leader of the Pennsylvania German settlements from Pennsylvania into the Valley of Virginia, Yost Hite, one of the most frequently recurring names in the early history of Western Virginia.

Yost Heydt, as he spelled the name before coming to America, was from Alsace-Lorraine, and it was largely as a seeker for religious freedom that he came to America about 1732. He married a French Huguenot girl in Holland. On coming to America he fitted out three ships and brought a large colony to this country. He made arrangements for the purchase of 40,000 acres in the Valley of Virginia, a part of the great Fairfax land grant, the arrangement being that he was to settle a hundred families on the land. It was matters growing out of this Yost Hite colony settlement in the Valley of Virginia that caused Lord Fairfax to send George Washington out to that wilderness region to survey these lands.

Rev. Jesse R. Hite was born at Virgilina, in Halifax County, October 1, 1890, son of R. S. and Mary (Tuck) Hite, and grandson of Spencer Hite. Spencer Hite was a Confederate soldier, and one of his sons, Howard, was killed in one of the battles of the war. The family have been planters in Halifax County for several generations. R. S. Hite grew up there, attended public schools, and has been a farmer all his life, being now retired and living in Virgilina at the age of seventy-seven. He is a member of the Baptist Church. His wife, Mary Tuck, was born and reared near Virgilina, and she died January 11, 1915. She was a very devout Baptist, and it was as a result of the interest of herself and her husband in education and religion that the building of a public school was erected on their farm. Mr. and Mrs. R. S. Hite had ten children, two of whom died in infancy, and those to grow up were John Spencer, Louis Cary, Caleb Green, Rev. Jesse R., Howard Wesley, Dr. Oscar Lee, Mary Ellen and Elizabeth.

Rev. Jesse R. Hite attended public school at Virgilina, was a student in the Oak Ridge Institute in North Carolina, and graduated A. B. from the University of Richmond in 1920. He took the degree Master of Theology from the Southern Baptist Seminary in 1923, and in the fall of the same year was ordained. He has been pastor of the Keen Street Baptist Church at Danville since 1923. This church has been in existence for twenty-five years. The congregation comprised less than 150 and they worshiped in a small frame building when Rev. Mr. Hite took charge. Under his energetic leadership during 1927-28 a beautiful new church was erected, of red brick and Colonial style of architecture. It provides facilities of a large auditorium, with departmental Sunday school rooms, kitchen and other equipment for carrying on the service of a metropolitan church. The cost of the new construction was about $40,000. At the present time the church has a membership of 500, and is one of the growing religious organizations of Danville.

Rev. Mr. Hite for several months taught in Averett College as a substitute to Dr. J. P. Craft, then president of the school. He is a member of the Southern Baptist Convention, the General Baptist Association of Virginia, is affiliated with Roman Eagle Lodge No. 122, A. F. and A. M., the Independent Order of Odd Fellows, is a member of the Rotary Club, Danville Music Club, and the "Pass It On Club." He is independent in his voting. Mr. Hite is unmarried.

His brother, Dr. Oscar Hite, of Richmond, was in the World war as a member of Company C, Three Hundred and Eighteenth

Infantry, Eightieth Division, and was wounded in action in the Argonne. He is now connected with the Tucker Sanitarium at Richmond. Two other brothers, Caleb and Howard, were with the colors during the World war, Caleb being in a training camp in South Carolina, and Howard at the Great Lakes Naval Training Station near Chicago.

THOMAS RANDOLPH PERKINSON, JR., a Danville tobacconist, did his bit as an American officer in the trenches overseas during the World war. Mr. Perkinson represents one of the very old and prominent families of South Side Virginia, Nottoway County, where he was born September 2, 1895.

His ancestor in the Perkinson line was Matthew Perkinson, who came from England in the early 1700s. Thomas, a son of Matthew, was the father of Thomas Jefferson Perkinson, and he in turn was the father of John Edward Perkinson, grandfather of the Danville business man. John Edward Perkinson served with the rank of captain in the Confederate army under General Lee. After the war he managed his large planting interests in Nottoway County. He is buried at Ward's Chapel in that county and his wife near Nottoway Falls, in Lunenburg County, at the old Williams estate. Her father, David G. Williams, at one time was one of the largest land owners in Lunenburg County. John Edward Perkinson and wife had three sons: Thomas Randolph Sr., John Edward II, a Danville tobacconist, and Bland, who died while a student at the Virginia Military Institute.

Thomas Randolph Perkinson, Sr., was born and reared in Amelia County, Virginia, was educated in private schools, and is now seventy years of age, a resident of Danville. During all the active years of his life he gave his time to farming his plantation in Nottoway County, the old Perkinson home there being known as "Linwood." His wife, Sallie F. Shore, was born and reared in Nottoway County, attended private schools and has always been a member of the Presbyterian Church. She and her husband had seven children: Edward Bland, in the automobile business at Washington, D. C.; Thomas Randolph, Jr.; Janie Elizabeth, wife of Paul Kneuer, of New York City; Louise Shore, wife of E. B. Hazelgrove, a civil engineer with the Portland Cement Company at Richmond; Markham Purnell, a tobacconist with the Imperial Tobacco Company at Danville; Poythress Doswell, a student in the Danville Military Institute; and Miss Virginia Frances, who graduated from Salem Academy in 1928 and is a student in the Danville School of Commerce.

Thomas Randolph Perkinson, Jr., was educated in public schools at Danville, attended the Cluster Springs Academy and was graduated in 1917 from the Virginia Military Institute. Having completed his education in the school that is regarded as the West Point of the South, he naturally joined the colors to render service commensurate with his training and abilities during the World war, and in June, 1917, entered Fort Myer, Virginia, where he spent two months in training, was commissioned a second lieutenant of infantry, following this training with two weeks more at Camp Lee and then at Camp Sevier, Greenville, South Carolina. He went overseas with the Thirtieth Infantry Division, and just before leaving was promoted to first lieutenant. While in France he was aide de camp to Brig.-Gen. S. L. Faison, being on staff duty until discharged. The first point of contact with the enemy came with the English troops on the Ypres front, where he followed trench warfare from July, 1918, to September of the same year. He was then transferred to the Somme and took part in the breaking of the Hindenburg line on September 29-30. During the last days of actual warfare he was again in the training area, and on April 2, 1919, he arrived back home, landing at Charleston, South Carolina, and received his honorable discharge at Columbia, that state, April 23, 1919.

Since the close of the war Mr. Perkinson has been associated in business with his uncle, John Edward Perkinson, and for a few months was located at Goldsboro, North Carolina, but since 1920 his home has been at Danville. He is a member of the J. E. Perkinson Company, real estate, and manager of the Danville Storage and Inspection Warehouse, one of the leading tobacco storage warehouse organizations in Danville.

Mr. Perkinson is a member of the Kappa Alpha fraternity, is a director of the Danville Rotary Club, a member of the Danville Golf Club, Y. M. C. A., Chamber of Commerce, Danville Post No. 10 of the American Legion. He is a Democrat, is an usher in the First Presbyterian Church and teacher of a boys' class in Sunday school.

Mr. Perkinson married at Washington, D. C., November 7, 1923, Miss Caroline Reid Boyd, of Sandy Spring, Maryland, formerly of Greensboro, North Carolina. She is a daughter of Samuel H. and Elizabeth (Settle) Boyd, formerly of Greensboro and Reidsville, North Carolina. Her father was in the lumber business at Reidsville, but for the past several years has been tax attorney at Washington, D. C., where he makes his home. Mrs. Perkinson's grandfather, Col. S. H. Boyd, was a prominent citizen of Reidsville, North Carolina. Mrs. Perkinson's mother was a daughter of Judge Thomas Settle, of the United States Supreme Court, and a sister of Thomas Settle, Jr., who several times represented his North Carolina district in Congress. Mrs. Perkinson thus comes of some of the oldest and most distinguished families of North Carolina. She was educated at Greensboro, at Washington and at Warrentown, Virginia, and is a prominent member of Danville social circles, being active in the Wednesday Afternoon Club and the Civic Music Club, and is a Presbyterian.

ARCHIBALD MURPHEY AIKEN, JR., has lived in Danville all his life, studied law at the University of Virginia, has had a very successful practice and for a time served with credit on the circuit bench.

Judge Aiken was born at Danville February 12, 1890, son of Archibald M. and Mary Ella (Yates) Aiken. The Aikens are a very old Virginia family, having come at the very founding of the colony on the banks of the James River. They held land by grant from the Crown and in after years extended their possessions into Tennessee. Members of this family served in the Indian, Colonial, Revolutionary, Mexican and Civil wars, and have always exemplified a high degree of patriotism.

Judge Aiken's father, who died in 1913, was also a lawyer by profession, and for many years served as judge of the Corporation Court of Danville. Most of his activities in politics were in behalf of his friends and various causes associated with good government. His wife died in 1911.

Archibald M. Aiken, Jr., only child of his parents, was graduated from the University of Virginia in 1913. He was admitted to the bar in 1912. His law offices are in the Masonic Temple Building at Danville. His term of service as judge of the Circuit Court of Pittsylvania County was during 1921-22. Judge Aiken is a Democrat, is a thirty-second degree Scottish Rite Mason, being a member of the lodge at Danville, and belongs to the Theta Delta Chi college fraternity. He married, December 13, 1922, Corinne Conway, daughter of Alexander and Corinne (Gray) Conway, who reside at Danville, where her father for many years has been in the real estate business. Judge and Mrs. Aiken have one son, Archibald M. III, born January 23, 1924. Mrs. Aiken was one of four children, Lillian, now Mrs. Lee A. Wilson, Mrs. Aiken, Mary and Alexander C.

WILLIAM SHANDS MEACHAM, editor of the *Danville Daily Register,* is one of the younger men in Virginia journalism. He was born at Petersburg, January 15, 1899.

The Meacham family came from England and first settled in Connecticut in the latter part of the seventeenth century, their home being at New London. Later a branch of the family moved to Virginia. Mr. Meacham's grandfather was Capt. Benjamin Thomas Meacham, who served all through the four years of the Civil war in Mahone's brigade, and was in battles and engagements all over Virginia, including the Siege of Petersburg. He and his wife are buried in the cemetery of old Blanford Church at Petersburg. His son, Benjamin Thomas Meacham, was born and reared in Petersburg, and has always called that city his home. In early life he was connected with the wholesale dry goods business, but is most widely known as an author and lecturer. He is a master of felicitous phrase, both written and spoken, and has employed his talents in writing poetry and in many years of work on the lecture platform. A book of his poems was published some years ago under the title *Rhymes of Cross Roads Man,* and the volume enjoyed considerable sale. He is still on the platform, and gives readings of his original poems and writings. He married Julia Amanda Webb, who was born and reared at Hickory Hill in Prince George County, Virginia, attending school there, and is active in St. Paul's Episcopal Church at Petersburg. She is a member of the Daughters of the American Revolution, United Daughters of the Confederacy and Daughters of 1812. She represents a line of Virginia lineage extending back, in the Shands line, to about 1630. The old Shands plantation was a grant of land bestowed by King Charles II. Her parents were Elijah Monroe and Sarah Cureton (Shands) Webb, the latter being a daughter of Gen. William Shands, a Confederate officer who for many years represented his district in the Virginia State Senate. Elijah Monroe Webb was also an officer in the Confederate army and afterwards lived on the farm and plantation known as Hickory Hill, the old Shands estate. A cemetery on the old plantation contains the bodies of many members of the family. Benjamin Thomas and Julia Amanda Meacham had a family of five children. Sallie Rives is the wife of William H. Evans, connected with the engineering department of the United States Government at Washington, and they have two children, Julia and Anne Meacham Evans. Frances Oliver Meacham married Roland C. Davis, an instructor in psychology at Columbia Uni-

B. J. Jenson.

versity. Harry Monroe Meacham, a commercial traveler living at Charlotte, North Carolina, married Lucy Christian Davies, of Petersburg, and has a daughter, Frances Christian. Mary Belle Meacham is Mrs. Robert B. Hall, wife of a peanut manufacturer at Petersburg, and has a daughter, Mary Webb Hall.

William Shands Meacham, the third youngest of the family, attended public school at Petersburg, and was about eighteen years of age when America entered the World war. He joined the United States Ambulance Corps and had training at Fort Thomas, Kentucky, Fort Benjamin Harrison in Indiana and Fort Riley, Kansas. After being released from the service he studied in the New York University School of Journalism, graduating in 1922. He was a reporter for the *Petersburg Progress-Index,* was promoted to editorial writer and then became literary editor of the *Norfolk Ledger-Dispatch.* During 1926 he took postgraduate work in the New York School of Journalism and then became editor of the *Danville Register.* Mr. Meacham is a member of the Public Health Committee of the Virginia State Chamber of Commerce, is a member of the Tuscarora Club, a Democrat and is an Episcopalian and a member of the American Legion.

BARTON IRVIN JENSON. Among the many able business men of James City County who have helped to build and establish its commercial prestige, there are few who have labored more earnestly or incessantly or who are held in such high esteem as is Barton I. Jenson, cashier of the Peninsula Bank & Trust Company, and deputy county treasurer of James City County, with headquarters at Toano. He was born at Ellsworth, Wisconsin, February 13, 1886, a son of J. B. and Anna M. (Johnson) Jenson, natives of Wisconsin.

After a service of twenty-eight consecutive years as clerk of the court of Pierce County, Wisconsin, J. B. Jenson found his health failing, and with the hope of bettering his condition he moved to James City County, Virginia, and began farming at Norge, where he resided until his death May 23, 1918. The wife and mother survives and still resides on the homestead.

Educated and self-supporting at the time of the family migration to James City County, Barton I. Jenson accompanied his parents and found employment in his new home as a clerk with the merchants of the vicinity. After several years of that employment he went into the hardware business at Norge, Virginia, and continued to operate his store until 1920. In the meanwhile, however, he enlisted in the Marine Corps for service in the World war, and was stationed on Paris Island and Quantico, Virginia. Commissioned a first lieutenant, he was honorably discharged with that rank in May, 1919. The following spring he went to Yorktown, Virginia, and took charge of the Peninsula Bank & Trust Company's branch, and remained there until February 22, 1922, when he was transferred to the branch of the same company at Toano. Associated with Mr. Jenson in this company are: W. A. Bozarth, president; F. R. Savage, vice president; and V. L. Nunn, assistant cashier.

On September 19, 1915, Mr. Jenson married Miss Clara Rustad, a daughter of L. A. and Amelia (Erickson) Rustad, natives of Minnesota. Mr. Rustad is a carpenter by trade, and is now residing at Norge, but Mrs. Rustad died in August, 1926. Mr.

and Mrs. Jenson have one child, John Henry Jenson, who was born January 8, 1917.

One of the active Democrats of James City County, Mr. Jenson, is favorably regarded by his fellow citizens, especially those of the same political faith, and in 1928 he was made deputy treasurer of James City County, an office he is fully qualified to fill. In addition to his banking connections he has farming interests in the county, and is a man of substance. Fraternally his affiliations are with the Masonic Order, the Junior Order United American Mechanics and the Woodmen of the World. He belongs to the American Legion and to the Rotary Club of Williamsburg. His religious home is the Lutheran Church. As the name indicates, the Jenson family originated in Norway, from which country Bardon Jenson, grandfather of Mr. Jenson of this review, came to the United States in 1842 and settled in Gettman Township, Pierce County, Wisconsin, and became one of the leading farmers of his township. When war was declared between the states he enlisted in the Union army and served until peace was declared. Mrs. Jenson's father is also a veteran of that same war, and the records of these two, combined with that of Mr. Jenson himself, give the Jenson children a fine background of military service on the part of their forebears.

FREDERICK HENRY DARLINGTON, who for a number of years has been associated with the management and ownership of a large commercial printing business at Danville, grew up in the atmosphere of a printing and newspaper office, his father having been a distinguished representative of the newspaper profession in Virginia and North Carolina.

Mr. Darlington was born in Henry County, Virginia, January 12, 1867, son of John T. and Armine (Bouldin) Darlington. His grandfather was Henry Darlington, and the Darlington family came from England in the early part of the eighteenth century, settling in South Carolina, where his home community took the name of Darlington, and Henry Darlington served as the first sheriff of the county organized there. He was a shoe manufacturer and spent his last years at Charleston, South Carolina. John T. Darlington was born at Darlington, South Carolina, was educated in private schools and in Erskine College, and during the war between the states was in the service of the Confederacy, at first with the navy and the last wto years with the infantry. He was wounded in the battle of Southern Pines. From the close of the war his interests and efforts were directed in the publishing and newspaper business. He was editor of the *Danbury Reporter*, editor of the *Henry News* at Martinsville, and for a number of years before his death was editor of the *Leakesville Gazette* at Leakesville, North Carolina, where he died in September, 1915, at the age of seventy-four. His wife, Armine Bouldin, was born and reared near Martinsville, Virginia, attended private schools in Henry County and died in April, 1912, being buried at Leakesville. She was a member of the Christian Church, while the Darlingtons were Methodists. Her five children were: Frederick H.; William M., who died at Wilkesboro, North Carolina, in 1915, at the age of forty-six; Joseph J., associated with his brother in the Danville Printing Company, married Anna May Cordes, of Wilmington, North Carolina, who died leaving four children, John, Thelma, Hannah and Elizabeth; Thomas Darlington was forty years of age when he died in Florida, in 1914; C. J. Darlington, the youngest of the family, is manager of the Acme Printing Company, a branch of the Marshall Field's industries at Leakesville, North Carolina.

Frederick Henry Darlington was educated in public schools at Leakesville, North Carolina, attended his father's old school, Erskine College in South Carolina, and from the time he left college his work was in the publishing industry, taking his place in a printing plant at Leakesville and becoming business manager and circulation manager of the *Leakesville Gazette*, of which his father was editor. When the latter died in 1915 Mr. Darlington disposed of his interests there and in 1917 moved to Danville, where he and his brother built up the Danville Printing Company as a business representing all the service that a modern commercial printing establishment can give.

Mr. Darlington is a member of the Rotary Club, is a Democrat in politics, and is a member of the Main Street Methodist Episcopal Church, South. He married at Leakesville, North Carolina, January 24, 1888, Miss Mollie E. Forbes, of Leakesville, North Carolina, formerly of Henry County, Virginia. She attended public school in Henry County. Mrs. Darlington also has a part as a working member of the Main Street Methodist Episcopal Church, South, is active in the Woman's Club of that society and is a member of the United Daughters of the Confederacy. Her parents were Capt. John C. and Betty (Wells) Forbes. Her father was a captain in the Confederate service and after the war was a planter and miller, owning and operating in Henry County a flour and corn mill. He died in 1878 and is buried in Center Church Cemetery in Henry County. After his death his family, in 1880, moved to Leakesville, where his widow lives at the age of eighty-three. Mr. and Mrs. Darlington have a family of seven children: Estelle, Mary, Henry, Thomas, Annie, James and Fred, Jr. Estelle is the wife of M. Escourido, of Danville, and has four children; Mary is the wife of Dr. Rowe, of Appalachia, Virginia; Henry married Miss Robertson and lives at Durham, North Carolina; Thomas married Miss Brown and is a resident of Winston-Salem, North Carolina; Annie is Mrs. Ben Sams, of Durham, North Carolina; James married Miss Wilson, of Leakesville, and is a resident of Winston-Salem; and Fred L., the youngest child, married Miss Collins of Burlington, North Carolina, and is a resident of Danville.

CHARLES E. STUART has several distinctions in the old county of Westmoreland. He is a progressive young attorney, is chairman of the Board of Supervisors, and is one of the extensive farmers and planters of that historic locality, his farm comprising a part of the historic Stratford estate, beloved by Virginians as being the birthplace of Robert E. Lee.

Mr. Stuart was born at Stratford April 24, 1892, son of Dr. Richard Henry and Lydia A. (Marmaduke) Stuart. His mother was born in Westmoreland County, while his father was a native of King George County, and spent his active life as a physician, practicing in Westmoreland County. Doctor Stuart was for twenty-four years county treasurer and chairman of the Board of Supervisors. He died August 19, 1924, and the widowed mother now makes her home with her son at Stratford.

Charles E. Stuart attended school in Westmoreland County, the Randolph-Macon Academy at Bedford, Randolph-Macon Col-

lege at Ashland, the Eastman's Business College at Poughkeepsie, New York, and the Virginia Military Institute. One year
of his law work was done in the University of Virginia. Mr.
Stuart was admitted to the bar in 1925, and has had a large
law practice in Westmoreland County.

Stratford, which he owns and to which he has given his personal management for a number of years, comprises over two
thousand acres. It is a scene of diversified agriculture, and Mr.
Stuart operates on his farm two canneries. He is also a director
of the Peoples Bank of Montross, which is the market town to
his country home. Mr. Stuart is a member of the Westmoreland
Club of Richmond, the Masonic fraternity and the Virginia Bar
Association.

He married, February 14, 1920, Miss Clara E. Delph. Her
parents were born in Grayson County, Virginia, and her father
was a farmer there. Her father died in 1913, and her mother,
Elizabeth C. (Phipps) Delph, died in 1927. Mr. and Mrs. Stuart
have one son, Charles Edward, Jr., born January 19, 1924. Mr.
Stuart is a Democrat, and now holds the place formerly occupied by his father as chairman of the County Board of Supervisors. During the World war he was a lieutenant. He is a
member of the Episcopal Church.

WILLIAM FAUNTLEROY GATLING, a retired resident of Petersburg, for many years was a Virginia farmer and planter, and is
a member of an old family of Prince George County.

Mr. Gatling was born in Raleigh, North Carolina, son of
George W. Gatling. His grandfather owned a large amount of
land in Gates County, North Carolina and had several hundred slaves. George W. Gatling, who was born in Gates County,
inherited some of this land and slaves, but before removing to
Virginia in 1859 he sold the slaves to themselves, taking their
notes in payment. The children all went with the parents, and
these slaves kept up the payment on their notes until 1876, when
George W. Gatling called them together and cancelled the balance due, though not without protest from some of the faithful
old negroes. George W. Gatling on removing to Virginia in
1859 settled in Prince George County and acquired the Spring
Hill farm property of three hundred acres and in addition
bought two thousand acres of low land, including numerous
streams and islands, filled with fish and game. George W.
Gatling lived at Spring Hill Farm until his death, in 1894. He
married Marceline Armetta Pescud, who was born at Petersburg, Virginia, daughter of Edward and Susan Brooke (Francisco) Pescud and granddaughter of Peter and Katherine
(Brooke) Francisco. Peter Francisco was a native of Europe
and was brought to America after being kidnapped. His wife,
Katherine Brooke, was a daughter of Governor Brooke of Virginia. Mrs. George W. Gatling lived to be eighty-two years of
age. Her children were: Edwin Brooke, William Fauntleroy,
George Pescud, Peter Francisco, Marie Marceline and Norman
Pescud.

William F. Gatling grew up on the home farm in Prince
George County, had a business education, and many years ago
acquired by purchase the interest of the other heirs in the estate.
This property gave him opportunities for many years of successful management of these farming interests. In 1917 the
United States Government bought the farm, including it in the
tract of land which became known as Camp Lee, where at times

Floyd Hollway

fifty thousand soldiers were encamped during the World war. Mr. Gatling after selling his farm moved to Petersburg and built a handsome residence on Walnut Hill, on Beckley Avenue, where he and his family have since resided.

Mr. Gatling married in 1888 Fannie Clarendon Hubert. She was born in South Carolina. Her father, Charles M. Hubert, was a native of London, England, was reared and educated there and when a young man came to the United States and located at Charleston as representative of William Rathbone of London, handling large exports of cotton to Europe and also becoming a coffee importer. The Hubert family during the summer months live in the Catskill Mountains of New York. Mr. and Mrs. Gatling reared two children, Annie Jayne, a teacher at Petersburg, and Hubert Rathbone. The Gatling family are members of Saint Paul's Episcopal Church in Petersburg.

FLOYD HOLLOWAY is a native son of York County and for the past eight years has been County and Circuit Court clerk of the county, with official headquarters at Yorktown.

He was born in York County May 18, 1894, son of John Franklin and Martha Susan (Carmines) Holloway, natives of the same county. His father devoted his active life to farming and to the operation of a boat on the Chesapeake Bay, and died December 21, 1908. The mother still occupies the old homestead.

Floyd Holloway grew up there, attended public schools in York County, and by working and earning his way acquired a liberal education. He attended the John Marshall High School, the high school of York County, the Smithdeal Business College at Richmond, and Richmond College, where he had an academic and law course. This is now the University of Richmond. Before he had finished his education he had acquired a wide range of business experience, being for five years employed by the Virginia Electric & Power Company, spent six months with the Atlantic Coast Line Railway Company, and was an employe of the Chesapeake Telephone Company. During the World war he was the first man in his home district to register for service.

Mr. Holloway in 1919 was elected clerk of the County Court and the Circuit Court in York County. This was a four-cornered race, and he was chosen for a term of eight years. In the primaries of 1927 he was elected for another term. He is also commissioner of accounts for York County.

Mr. Holloway married, June 1, 1921, Miss Jennie Holloway, daughter of R. T. and Jicie Ann (Forrest) Holloway, of York County. Her father spent his active life as an oyster planter and is now living retired at Denbigh. Mr. and Mrs. Holloway's children are: Hilda Forrest, born December 12, 1922; Martha Evelyn, born August 16, 1924, and Floyd Holloway II, born November 21, 1928.

Mr. Holloway owns his home and other rental property at Yorktown. He is a member of Williamsburg Lodge No. 6, A. F. and A. M., Yorktown Council No. 66, Junior Order United American Mechanics, and is a member of the Improved Order of Red Men. He is president of the Yorktown Chamber of Commerce, president of the Yorktown Epworth League, and has taught a class of boys in the Methodist Sunday School for a number of years. He is a member of the Yorktown Chapter of the Association for the Preservation of Virginia Antiquities, belongs also to Yorktown Lodge of Masons and is president of the York County Red Cross.

SAMUEL KING FUNKHOUSER, an ex-service man of the World war, is an attorney at law in Roanoke, Virginia, being the senior member of the firm of Funkhouser & Apperson. Mr. Funkhouser was born at Harrisonburg, Virginia, December 4, 1884, son of Abram Paul and Minnie S. (King) Funkhouser and a descendant from one of the oldest families of the Shenandoah Valley of Virginia, which has furnished many of its members to the professions and the important work of life. The Funkhousers are of distinguished Swiss lineage. They trace their ancestry to two brothers, John and Christopher Funkhouser, who left Berne, Switzerland, in 1692, and came to this country in 1700 and settled near Fredericksburg, Virginia. A son of John Funkhouser, Jacob by name, born in 1750, secured a large tract of land on Mill Creek, one and one-half miles west of Mount Jackson, Shenandoah County, Virginia, and there built his home in 1775, which home now remains and has remained since such date in the Funkhouser family. He fought as a soldier in the Colonial wars. His son, Abraham Funkhouser, born in 1789 and died in 1863, was a soldier in the War of 1812, and married Sarah Fisher, the daughter of John Fisher, a Revolutionary war veteran. Samuel Funkhouser, a son of Abraham and grandfather of the present Samuel King Funkhouser, was born September 25, 1823, and died October 31, 1864. In addition to being a large land owner he owned and operated one of the first woolen mills in the Valley of Virginia. His wife, Elizabeth Paul, was a daughter of Samuel Paul, whose family was among the first settlers in the Shenandoah Valley. Samuel Funkhouser was a soldier in the Mexican war and later a Confederate soldier. He died from wounds received in action. Abram Paul Funkhouser, a son of Samuel Funkhouser, was born December 10, 1853, and died July 6, 1917. He was graduated from Lebanon Valley College in Pennsylvania and Otterbein University in Ohio. Subsequently he studied at Columbia University and the Union Theological Seminary in New York. He was active in newspaper work as editor and owner from 1883-1898. He served as president of Western College, later Leander Clarke University in Iowa, and Lebanon Valley College in Pennsylvania and was founder of the Shenandoah Collegiate Institute at Dayton, Virginia. He married Minnie S. King, of Dayton, Ohio, whose forefathers for three generations were distinguished preachers and teachers. This is a very brief reference to the ancestry of Samuel King Funkhouser, whose people on both sides were strongly disposed toward intellectual, professional and religious activities.

Samuel King Funkhouser was graduated from the Virginia Military Institute in 1904, received his LL.B. degree from Ohio State University in 1910 and received the degree of Doctor of Jurisprudence at St. Lawrence University in 1916. He practiced law in New York City from 1910 to 1918 and for three years of that time was dean of the law department of Arbuckle Institute at Brooklyn, New York. On January 31, 1918, he was commissioned a captain of the 13th Company, Virginia Coast Artillery, National Guard, serving until December, 1918, when he was honorably discharged as captain of Battery C, Thirty-fifth Regiment, Coast Artillery Corps, United States Army. After the war he located at Roanoke, Virginia, and engaged in the general practice of law. In 1927 he was appointed valuation counsel of the Norfolk & Western Railway Company, having succeeded the late Judge Waller R. Staples, which position he

Richard F. Owens

now holds in addition to being engaged in the general practice of his profession.

He married, August 29, 1917, Jane Harwood Cocke, a daughter of the late Lucian H. and Lelia Maria (Smith) Cocke. His marriage also connects Mr. Funkhouser with a family of distinguished educational leadership. Mrs. Funkhouser is a graduate of Hollins College, Hollins, Virginia, which was founded by her grandfather, Charles Lewis Cocke, in 1847. Mrs. Funkhouser is a member of the Colonial Dames of America and the Daughters of the American Revolution. Captain and Mrs. Funkhouser have two children, a daughter, Jane King, and a son, Abram Paul.

REV. RICHARD S. OWENS, D. D.

Richard Spurgeon Owens, of King George County, Virginia,
1880—.
Son of William Windsor Owens, of King George County, and his
1835-1924
wife, Mary Susan Wilkenson,
Son of Austin Putnam S. Owens, of King George County, and
1840—
his wife, Jane Anmon Frank,
Son of Fielding Owens, of Westmoreland County, Virginia, and
1781-1827
his wife, Mary, widow of Benjamin P. Weeks.
Fielding Owens sold his land in Westmoreland County and settled in King George County.
Son of William Owens, of Westmoreland County, and his wife,
17—-1833
Anne Davis,
Son of William Owens and his wife, Rebecca Payne, daughter of William Payne, of Westmoreland County,
1720-1750
Son of John Owens and his wife, Dorothy Waters, both of Westmoreland County.
1712
(See Westmoreland Records.)
Grandson of Nicholas Owens, who came to Virginia and settled in Northumberland County in 1667.
Richard Spurgeon Owens, a great-great-great-grandson of William Davis, of King George County, Virginia,
A great-great-great-grandson of Ambrose Fielding, who settled in Northumberland County in 1667.

Rev. Richard Spurgeon Owens, D. D., pastor of the Calvary Baptist Church of Roanoke, Virginia, is one of the earnest, eloquent and useful ministers of the Gospel, and a man whose personal character exemplifies the faith he teaches. He was born in King George County, Virginia, October 28, 1880, a son of William Windsor and Mary Susan Wilkenson Owens. He, too, was a minister of the Baptist faith. They had seven children, namely, Mary Ausinetta Anmon, Otis Otho, Juanita Virginia, Luvenia and Richard Spurgeon. Of this number only three survive, namely, Mary Owens Price, Otis O., and Richard S., the latter of whom is the subject of this sketch. The father and his three brothers served in the war between the states; they being Richard H., James F., and Wesley W.

Doctor Owens was educated at Piedmont Academy, Fredericksburg College, University of Richmond and Colgate Uni-

versity. His first assignment was the Maryland Avenue Baptist
Church of Washington, D. C., where he remained for four years,
leaving it to go to Waynesboro, Virginia, in 1911, where for five
years he was pastor of the Baptist Church. He resigned there
and became engaged in teaching in Fishburn Military School,
acting as head master and instructor in English, continuing
this work four years.

In 1921 he assumed his present pastorate in Roanoke, Virginia, of Calvary Baptist Church, which has a membership of
over twenty-two hundred. Doctor Owens has two degrees,
that of Bachelor of Arts and Doctor of Divinity; the latter
degree having been conferred upon him in 1924 by the University of Richmond.

In 1905 Doctor Owens married Miss Anne Estelle Hall, who
was born in Poolesville, Maryland, and educated in Briarly Hall
and Fairview Seminary. She is a daughter of Thomas Randolph
Hall and Clarinda Beecher Hall, of Poolesville, Maryland. They
have one child, Richard Spurgeon Owens, Junior.

Mrs. Owens is directly related to Henry Ward Beecher, one
of the most distinguished divines this country has produced;
also, on the maternal side, to Lymon Lee Hall and Bishop Sat-
terlee. She is a member of the Daughters of the American Revolution, United Daughters of the Confederacy and Huguenot
Society.

Doctor Owens is a Scottish Rite Mason and Shriner and a
member of Sigma Phi Epsilon national fraternity. He is also
a member of the Knights of Pythias, Order of the Eastern Star,
the Lions Club, the Sons of the Confederacy and the Roanoke
Chamber of Commerce. He was president of the Roanoke Ministers Conference January, 1928-January, 1929; a trustee of the
University of Richmond and trustee of Bluefield College at
Bluefield, West Virginia.

HENRY WATKINS ELLERSON, president of the Albemarle
Paper Manufacturing Company, president of the Albemarle-
Chesapeake Corporation and vice president of the Chesapeake
Corporation, is one of the leading paper manufacturers of the
South, and a man whose business career has been marked from
the start by progressive accomplishments. In July, 1927, he was
honored by being appointed by Governor Byrd a member of the
Board of Visitors of the Medical College of Virginia, for which
he is particularly fitted, owing to his many activities connected
with the social welfare of Richmond and Virginia. It is said
that under his presidency the Crippled Children's Hospital,
which has just completed a new plant in North Richmond, has
succeeded in a striking way.

The birth of Mr. Ellerson occurred in Richmond in 1875,
and he is a son of John Hanckel and Ida (Watkins) Ellerson,
deceased. The Ellerson family was founded in America by
Andre Ellerson, a native of Norway, who established his home
in Philadelphia, Pennsylvania, before the Revolution, and became a surgeon and instructor in the University of Pennsylvania's medical school. His son, John Hanckel Ellerson, grandfather of Mr. Ellerson, married Laura Roy, of Mathews County,
Virginia, and their son, John Hanckel Ellerson, was the father
of Mr. Ellerson, and he was born in Mathews County. On his
father's side Mr. Ellerson is connected with the Roys of Virginia and the Boothe family of England. Through his mother
he is a descendant in the fifth generation from Obediance Jef-

ferson, a sister of Thomas Jefferson, twice president of the United States.

Mr. Ellerson began his business career as a youth in the offices of Kingan & Company, packing house products, of Richmond, and he became connected with the manufacture of paper in Richmond in 1907, as an official of the Albemarle Paper Manufacturing Company, of which he has been president for some years past. The Chesapeake Corporation, of which he is vice president, is a subsidiary concern which operates a large pulp plant at West Point, Virginia. The Albemarle Paper Manufacturing Company is one of the largest concerns of its kind in Virginia, being a three-plant organization. Blotting paper is made at the Hollywood plant, high-grade kraft paper at the Brown's Island plant, and cover and paper specialities at the new Riverside Mill. Together with its new subsidiary, which supplies Brown's Island plant with its pulp, the Albemarle Company's operations are carried on upon a very extensive scale. His company has grown amazingly in the little more than forty years that it has been in existence. The business originated as the Albemarle Paper Mill, which had an output of 10,000 pounds of blotting paper per day. Today three separate plants are conducted, and the company is recognized as one of the largest producers of blotting paper in the country, with an export trade that extends all over the world.

During the World war Mr. Ellerson took a very prominent part in war activities in Richmond. He was chairman of the Registration Board and of the Local Draft Board in Richmond. In addition, his entire plant, the Albemarle Paper Manufacturing Company, was turned over for war work without expense to the Government. This plant played a most important part in the development of smoke-filter for the gas mask and won highest commendation from the war department authorities, and for its war work generally the company received letters and certificates of unstinted appreciation from the Government. Mr. Ellerson was in the gas defense service during the World war as pulp and paper expert.

Mr. Ellerson married Miss Mary Patteson, and they have four children: Mary Patteson, Ida Roy, Henry Watkins, Junior, and Jean.

ARTHUR EGBERT CARVER was born in Missouri, was reared partly in California and partly in West Virginia, and for the past twenty years has been a resident of Montross, Westmoreland County, Virginia, engaged in a busy and important routine as a banker and business man.

Mr. Carver is a descendant of the famous Carver family of New England, the most distinguished member of which was John Carver, who came over on the Mayflower and was the first governor of Plymouth Colony. The direct ancestor of the Montross banker was Jonathan Carver, who married Ruth Bradford, daughter of Governor Bradford of Massachusetts.

Arthur Egbert Carver was born at De Soto, Missouri, July 30, 1884. His grandfather, Chester L. Carver, was a resident of Brattleboro, Vermont. He married Lucy M. Harlow. Egbert Martin Carver, father of Arthur S., was born at Brattleboro in 1838, was college trained in New York, became a banker in Saint Louis, Missouri, establishing his home at DeSoto in 1878, and in 1887 went to Monterey, California. He spent ten years on the Pacific Coast and then returned east, locating in Ritchie

County, West Virginia, and after retiring from business moved to Florida. He married Mary Emma Ashby, who was born at Saint Louis March 18, 1855, daughter of Elliott and Elizabeth Prescovia (Browning) Ashby.

Arthur Egbert Carver was three years of age when the family moved to California. He attended public schools in Pacific Grove, graduated from the high school of Harrisville, West Virginia, in 1900, and for two years attended Oberlin College in Ohio. After leaving college he was in the Ritchie County Bank at Harrisville, West Virginia, and until 1908 was connected with several banking institutions in that state.

Mr. Carver was the founder of the Bank of Montross, Incorporated, which opened November 5, 1908. He has been cashier and active manager of the bank for twenty years. The president is Dr. G. C. Mann and the vice president, B. L. Battaile. Mr. Carver has stock in other banks and in a number of business organizations, including the Carver Corporation, a general farming proposition, the Northern Neck Coca Cola Bottling Company, of which he is treasurer, and he has done much for the development of a sound program of agricultural production in this section of Virginia.

Mr. Carver is a Democrat, member of the Methodist Episcopal Church, South, the Masonic fraternity, B. P. O. Elks, Junior Order United American Mechanics, Patriotic Order Sons of America and Modern Woodmen of America. He married, August 25, 1909, Miss Alice Robertson, daughter of Joseph F. and Alice (Sutton) Robertson. Her people have lived in Westmoreland County for generations. Mr. and Mrs. Carver have two children: Arthur Egbert, Jr., born February 27, 1914, and Ashby Robertson, born December 8, 1920.

CLAUDE DAVIS CURTIS, B. S. In educational circles of Virginia a name that is becoming well and favorably known is that of Claude Davis Curtis, B. S., president of Martha Washington College at Abingdon. During the more than five years he has acted in this capacity Professor Curtis has demonstrated himself possessed of all the qualifications of a successful educator and able executive, and under his management and direction the college has developed materially in standards and membership.

Professor Curtis was born in Blount County, Tennessee, December 28, 1887, and is a son of M. B. and Eliza (Davis) Curtis, the latter of whom died in 1914. His father, who spent the active years of his life as an agriculturist, is now living in comfortable retirement in his pleasant home at Fountain City, Tennessee. He has important interests and is a very active member of the Methodist Episcopal Church, South.

Claude Davis Curtis attended Friendsville Academy, Friendsville, Tennessee, subsequently pursuing a course at the Blount County High School. Upon his graduation therefrom he entered Hiawatha College, at that time a four-year college of the first class, which since has been reduced to a junior college. He was graduated therefrom in 1908, with the degree of Bachelor of Science, and has since completed his post-graduate residence work at the University of Tennessee, but has not yet submitted his thesis for his degree. In 1908 Professor Curtis became principal of schools at Friendsville, Tennessee, a position which he retained one year, and then accepted the post of head of the department of science at the Maryville (Tennessee) Polytechnic

JOSHUA De KALB McCONNICO AND FAMILY

School, remaining in that capacity for six years. During the following year he was principal of the West Side School at Maryville, and then was made superintendent of city schools of Maryville and acted in that capacity for nine years. His splendid work in this position attracted decidedly favorable comment and attention, and in August, 1923, he was called to Abingdon to become president of Martha Washington College, a position which he has since filled. President Curtis, an educator by natural talent, training, experience and inclination, devotes his entire time to his college work and has accomplished much in building up and developing this excellent institution, a work in which he has been aided by a pleasing address and likable character. He is a member of the National Education Association and of various other leading educational bodies. He is an active member of the Civitan Club and of the Methodist Episcopal Church, South, and takes a keen interest in everything that pertains to the advancement and welfare of Abingdon.

In 1908 Professor Curtis was united in marriage with Miss Edna Cochran, of Maryville, Tennessee, daughter of Brice Cochran of that city, and a graduate of the Maryville Polytechnic School and the University of Tennessee. Mrs. Curtis was for four years principal of public schools in Knox and Blount counties, Tennessee, is a woman of splendid intellect and broad understanding, and at present is dean of women at Martha Washington College. She is active in the work of the Methodist Episcopal Church, South, and in all movements making for moral advancement and civic improvement. Three children have been born to Professor and Mrs. Curtis: Robert Cochran, aged eighteen years, a junior at Maryville College; Charles Robert, aged fifteen years, a senior at Kings High School; and Anna Louise, aged eleven years.

Martha Washington College has its own history, entitled "Three Quarters of a Century at Martha Washington College." Professor Curtis is governor of the Chesapeake District of the Civitan International Club, and a member of Pi Gamma Mu.

JOSHUA DE KALB McCONNICO. While the career of Joshua De Kalb McConnico belongs to the past rather than to the present, his death having occurred in 1909, and while he spent his life for the most part in North Carolina, it is fitting that a memorial be presented of a man who was upright and unswerving in integrity in all his business dealings, and who performed the duties and discharged the responsibilities of citizenship in a greatly commendable manner. A self-made man who started out in life with only ordinary opportunities, he won position and independence through his own efforts, and there are many who still remember his many sterling qualities of mind and heart.

Mr. McConnico came of an old and distinguished family which settled in this country prior to the Revolutionary war, and he was born in 1853 in Williamson County, Tennessee, a son of Washington Lafayette and Caroline Frances (Claud) McConnico. His father was named in honor of General Washington and Marquis Lafayette, both of whom had been visitors at the old McConnico home in Tennessee during their travels. It is interesting to note that Washington L. McConnico also was very prominent in Tennessee politics, an able lawyer and member of the State Senate, and became prominent in military affairs as an adjutant general in the Confederate army during the war between the states. He saw active service in the Vicksburg and Mississippi campaigns, dying during service at Union Spring, Alabama. He was a brave and efficient leader and was popular with his fellow officers and the enlisted men. One of his sons, Lemuel Burket McConnico, also served during this great conflict, and had the distinction of being the youngest commanding officer in the Western Army of the Confederacy, being but seventeen years of age.

Joshua De Kalb McConnico attended private schools in Tennessee until the Civil war broke out, and his father took the family in camp with him. They followed him to the South and it was in Atlanta Joshua De Kalb's only sister died and was buried. Conditions became so bad in camp that Major McConnico had his wife and son Joshua sent back to Southampton County, Virginia. It was from Southampton County that Joshua De Kalb McConnico, together with John Prince and Joe Gilliam, entered the Virginia Military Institute, which was then in Richmond, and they remained in school until General Grant took Richmond and the school was closed. Then they made their way back to Southampton County on foot, and had many adventures, among which was capture by the Yankees. Returning to Southampton County, Joshua De Kalb McConnico took up farming, but not being a farmer by nature he was not successful, and finally left Southampton County, going to Winton, North Carolina. There he went in business with Z. Early, the style of the firm being Z. Early & Company, dealers in family groceries, wines, liquors, cigars and tobacco. He remained in Winton for a number of years, finally going back to Southampton County after the death of his mother. Here he remained for a number of years looking after the family interest of his aunt (mother's sister), Mrs. Bettie Hardee, and it was here that he fell in love with and married on February 18, 1891, Priscilla Gregory Aumack. Having heired the property of his aunt, Mrs. Hardee, Mr. McConnico, not being a farmer, sold the farm and moved his family (who then numbered four) to Plymouth, North Carolina. Here he entered the grocery business and continued to live in Plymouth until the time of his death, April 11, 1909. For a number of years after retiring from the grocery business he was employed by the Washington & Plymouth Railway as captain on the passenger train running between those two points, and held this position until a short while before his death. He died at the age of fifty-six years. Mr. McConnico was a man of high character and business integrity, and had an established position in the confidence and esteem of those with whom he came in contact.

Of the children born to Mr. and Mrs. McConnico four survive: Caroline Frances, the wife of E. T. Henderson, of Washington, who has four children, Caroline Frances, John Thomas, and William Gregory and Robert Marion, twins; Zola Daniel, who is employed by the Seaboard Citizens National Bank of Norfolk, Virginia; Lessie Lee, the wife of M. C. Bayne, late of Macon, Georgia, and Norfolk, who has two children, Marmaduke Greshman and Alva McConnico; and Lemuel De Kalb, a business man of Charleston, West Virginia.

Following the death of her husband Mrs. McConnico removed to Norfolk, where she now resides at 627 West Olney Road.

MAJOR EDWARD BURSON is a member of an old Virginia family and on that in its backward tracings may lead to the Colonial period and early Virginia settlement, and from this old stock have come men of business achievement and men eminent in the church and in the law. A prominent citizen of Washington County worthily bearing this name is Major Edward Burson, a member of the bar at Bristol and formerly commonwealth attorney, who has large property interests in both city and county.

Major Edward Burson was born at Buffalo Pond, Washington County, Virginia, June 13, 1883, son of Major John E. and Martha J. (Phelps) Burson, grandson of Rev. Z. L. Burson, and great-grandson of Rev. Thomas Burson. The founder of the family in Bedford County, Virginia, was the great-great-grandfather, Nathaniel Burson, a native of North Virginia. His son, Thomas Burson, was reared in Bedford County and for many years was a Baptist minister there. His wife was a member of the old Colonial Lyle family of that county.

Major John E. Burson, father of Major Edward Burson, was born at Jonesboro, Tennessee, son of Rev. Z. L. and Susan (Hale) Burson, the former of whom was born in 1817 in Goose Creek District, Bedford County, and the latter in Tennessee. In his early manhood he removed to Bristol, where he followed the mercantile business for a number of years and with such success that he amassed a large fortune for that day. He was an honorable man and made good use of his wealth, educated his children, gave to the needy and furthered the work of the church and later in life entered the ministry, and, like his father, was a zealous and faithful pastor in both Virginia and Tennessee. While still in business at Bristol he served on the City Council. In early life he was trustee of Washington County, Tennessee.

The late Major John E. Burson was liberally educated and was a graduate of the University of Virginia. After completing his course in law he came to Bristol to practice his profession, where he subsequently gained eminence at the bar, and during his long period of practice, only terminated by his death on October 16, 1920, he commanded universal respect and confidence. During the Civil war he served as sergeant-major on the Fifth Tennessee Volunteer Infantry, and after the war, although he accepted no public office, was a good and earnest citizen. He belonged to the Masonic fraternity and was a member of the Presbyterian Church. He married Miss Martha J. Phelps, who was born in Russell County, Virginia. Her father, Martin Phelps, lost his life while serving as a soldier in the Confederate army during the Civil war.

Major Edward Burson attended the Virginia High School at Bristol, an institution of high scholarship, and then entered Roanoke College at Roanoke, Virginia, from which he was graduated in 1905 with his A. B. degree, and from the University of Virginia in 1907 with his degree of LL. B. After completing a post-graduate course at Harvard University in 1909 he located at Bristol for the practice of his profession, and has found satisfying conditions in his native county, which has been home to him during the greater part of his life. He has a large civil practice and many important clients. With the exception of two years as commonwealth attorney he has continued in private practice, but widely known.

Mr. Burson married on May 6, 1922, Miss Lourette Elizabeth Leonard, who was born and educated in Washington County,

Virginia, daughter of Solomon G. and Ora Esther Leonard, who
still reside on their farm. Her grandfather, William Anderson
Leonard, spent his life as a farmer in Washington County. In
1865 he was mustered into military service, but the Civil war
ended before he was called to serve. The military record in the
next older generation discloses that her great-grandfather, Stof-
fle Leonard, was a fifer in the Patriot Army in the Revolutionary
war. Mr. and Mrs. Burson have two daughters: Martha Elizabeth, born October 17, 1923; and Mettie Ethel, born May 21,
1927.

In political life Major Edward Burson has always been identified with the Democratic party, and takes a somewhat active
interest in local affairs. He owns a large farm and fine estate
situated four miles distant from Bristol, on which he maintains
his home amid beautiful surroundings, and he also has realty
holdings at Bristol. He and wife are members of the Presbyterian Church at Bristol, where they also have a pleasant social circle, and professionally he belongs to the Bristol and the Washington County Bar associations.

LYSANDER B. CONWAY, member of a prominent family of
Pittsylvania County, has individually been an important factor
in the commercial history of Danville. In early life he was a
banker, but for many years has given his best energies to the
Danville Knitting Mills, of which he is secretary and treasurer.

The Conway family came from England to Virginia in early
Colonial times. The history of the family in England has been
recorded through a number of generations and branches. The
Conway coat-of-arms was given to one of the ancestors for
valor when in the Moorish wars and he received knighthood
from the king. The Revolutionary ancestor of the Virginia
family was Lieut. James Conway, a lieutenant in the Sixth Virginia Regiment in the Continental army and who was killed
near Trenton, New Jersey, December 28, 1776. Lieutenant
Conway was the father of Christopher Conway, whose son,
James Washington Conway, lived in Pittsylvania County, was
a land owner, planter, slave owner and tobacco grower. James
Washington Conway was distinguished by a high type of citizenship. For many years he acted as a magistrate, and in that
office was a peacemaker out of court rather than helping to
foment litigation. He and his family are buried in the old Conway Cemetery in Pittsylvania County.

His son, Lysander B. Conway, Sr., was born and reared in
Pittsylvania County, attended private schools and was cashier
of a bank at Chatham when the Civil war broke out. He was
commissioned depositary for the Confederate government and
later went to the front as a soldier. After the war he spent a
number of years in the state treasurer's office at Richmond, later
was a tobacconist at Danville, connected with Star Warehouse,
and for a number of years served on the Danville School Board.
He died August 25, 1912, and both he and his wife are buried
in Green Hill Cemetery at Danville. Lysander B. Conway married Elizabeth Gouldin, who was born and reared in Caroline,
Virginia, and attended Rappahannock Academy. She and her
husband were members of the Baptist Church. She died August
23, 1917, and her eight children were: John, who died in infancy; Elizabeth, now Mrs. W. W. Holland; James W., deceased;
Coleman B., of Washington, D. C.; Powhatan Fitzhugh, of Dan-

ville; Lysander B., Jr., of Danville; Eustis R., of Henderson, Kentucky; and Brooke, who died in infancy.

Lysander B. Conway, Jr., was born at Danville, March 19, 1871, and attended public school in his native city. His business career began at the age of eighteen, and for some thirteen years he was connected with Patton's bank and for a time was assistant cashier of the Bank of Danville. Since about 1903 he has been associated with the Danville Knitting Mills, of which he is secretary and treasurer and manager. This is one of the largest knitting and spinning plants in Southwestern Virginia. It employs about 800 people, and manufacturers many grades of hosiery and cotton yarns, sold through the jobbing trade. Mr. Conway is also a director of the First National Bank of Danville, is a director of the Danville Traction and Power Company and of the Perpetual Building & Loan Association.

For two years he was president of the Danville Chamber of Commerce, and a number of responsibilities and honors of a public nature have been conferred upon him. He was for fourteen years in the City Council and during the World war served on several committees and was chairman of the war work drive. He is affiliated with Roman Eagle Lodge No. 122, A. F. and A. M., is a Knight Templar Mason, member of the Rotary Club, the Danville Golf Club and Tuscarora Club. He is a Democrat in politics and a member of the Baptist Church. Mr. Conway's chief pastime and hobby is his fine stock farm four miles from Danville, where he has specialized in pure bred Holstein cattle, Shropshire sheep and pure bred Tamworth hogs.

Mr. Conway married at Frankfort, Kentucky, January 9, 1899, Miss Mildred M. Hoge, of Frankfort, a member of a family that has been prominent in Virginia as well as in Kentucky. She is a daughter of Col. Charles and Ann (French) Hoge. Her father for many years was a leading banker, railroad contractor and builder in Kentucky. Mrs. Conway was educated by private tutors and in the Miller School at Cincinnati, Ohio. She is a member of the Baptist Church, the Society of Colonial Dames, the Wednesday Woman's Club. Mr. and Mrs. Conway had a family of seven children, two of whom died in infancy and the daughter, Mildred, at the age of twelve years. The living children are Charlotte E., Ann F., Lysander B. and French H. Charlotte and Ann attended preparatory school at Danville, Charlotte graduating from Sweetbriar College of West Virginia in 1928 and Ann in the class of 1929. Lysander is attending the Danville Military School, while French is in public school.

HUGH T. WILLIAMS, who was overseas during the World war and comes of a family that has been well represented in the military life of Virginia, is practicing law at Danville and has gained well deserved prominence in the professional and social life of that city.

Mr. Williams was born at Charlottesville, Virginia, September 1, 1887, son of Thomas David and Patty (Warren) Williams and grandson of Capt. Samuel C. Williams. Capt. Samuel C. Williams belonged to one of the prominent old families of Southern Virginia. During the Civil war he was captain of the Brooklyn Greys of Halifax County, and was killed in action in the skirmish at Mine Run, Virginia. He is buried at the old Williams homestead near Sutherlin. His brother, David T. Williams, furnished supplies to the Confederacy during the war, and for a number of years conducted the largest wholesale grocery business in Richmond. A sister of Samuel C. Williams became the wife of Attorney General Samuel W. Williams of Virginia.

Thomas David Williams was born and reared in Pittsylvania County, was educated in public schools and for over forty years was connected with the Dan River Cotton Mills. He is now living retired at Danville at the age of seventy-six. His wife, Patty Warren, was born and reared in Pittsylvania County, being a daughter of William and Lucy (Burnett) Warren and a sister of B. S. Warren, who represented his home county in the Lower House of the Virginia Legislature in 1922-23. Mrs. Patty Williams was educated in public schools in Pittsylvania County and also carried out a home program of education, and after her marriage had much to do with the practical education of her children. She was always a home maker and home lover, was a member of the Lee Street Baptist Church and died in 1917. Her family of four sons and four daughters are all living. The oldest, Wille E., is Mrs. Clay W. Daniel, of Danville. The second child, Samuel C. Williams, is purchasing agent for the Pacific Car and Foundry Company at Seattle, Washington. Hugh T. Williams was the third child. Marcus M. Williams, the fourth in age, is associated with his brother Edward, the seventh child in the *Lynchburg News*, published by Hon. Carter Glass. The other daughters of the family are: Virginia, Mrs. George M. Miller, of Danville; Maud, Mrs. J. Landon Robertson, of Danville; and Eldridge is now Mrs. Frank Spencer, of Lynchburg.

Hugh T. Williams grew up at Danville, attended public schools there and during 1914-15 was committee clerk of the Virginia State Senate. In 1915 he was appointed American vice-consul of Santiago, Cuba, but resigned in the spring of 1916, returning to Danville with the purpose of joining some local company for service in the World war, foreseeing the inevitability of America getting into the struggle. In the meanwhile he was in the law offices of J. O. Heflin at Hopewell, Virginia. He was the first man to enlist from Danville on the day that America declared war on Germany, April 6, 1917, and he became a member of Company C, One Hundred and Sixteenth Infantry, formerly Company M of the First Virginia Infantry. He was supply sergeant with his company overseas, and following the armistice he was appointed by General Pershing to the chair of Spanish in the A. E. F. University at Beaune, France.

Mr. Williams received his honorable discharge in May, 1919, at Camp Lee, Virginia, and resumed his law studies, with John W. Carter. He was admitted to the bar in June, 1920, and was associated with Mr. Carter as a law partner until January 1, 1927. Since that date he has practiced with offices of his own in the Masonic Temple Building at Danville. His abilities have brought him a fine clientage, and he is easily one of the leaders of his profession in Southern Virginia.

Mr. Williams has been much interested in American Legion work since the war and is district committeeman of the Fifth District, Department of Virginia. He also compiled in 1927 the History of the American Legion for the Department of Virginia, being official historian of the department and is a past commander of his local post. He is a member of the B. P. O. Elks, Improved Order of Red Men, Wildwood Fishing Club, is a Democrat and is affiliated with the Baptist Church.

C H Trumbleson

Mr. Williams married at Danville, June 11, 1923, Miss Mary Gibney Brockman, of Charlottesville, daughter of Clement and Ann Maria (Gibney) Brockman and granddaughter of Clement Brockman, who for a number of years conducted a noted tailoring house at Charlottesville, many of the oldest and most noted families of that distinguished town being his patrons. He and his family are buried at Charlottesville. Clement Brockman, father of Mrs. Williams, was for many years engaged in the printing business at Charlottesville and Danville. He died in 1917. Mrs. Mary Gibney Williams grew up and attended school at Charlottesville and Danville, is a member of the Episcopal Church and the Ladies Auxiliary of the American Legion. Mr. and Mrs. Williams have a very beautiful country home near Danville and are very popular in social circles there. His hobbies are fishing and boating and the raising of game chickens.

CHARLES HOWARD TUMBLESON, city sergeant of the city of Norfolk, has spent all his life in that community, a popular citizen whose services have brought him a high degree of esteem.

He was born on land now included in the city of Norfolk. His father, George W. Tumbleson, was born at Sewell's Point, near the present site of the Naval Base, in 1841. He served his apprenticeship as a blacksmith, and as soon as eligible joined the Norfolk Grays. He went with that organization into the Confederate army, and being a good mechanic, was soon transferred to duty at the Navy Yard at Richmond, where he remained until the end of the war. He then returned to Norfolk and followed the trade of blacksmith the rest of his active life. He died in 1913, at the age of seventy-two. His wife, Margaret A. Talbot, was born in Norfolk in 1846. Her father, George Talbot, was for some years keeper of the Indian Fall Bridge. George W. Tumbleson and wife had two sons, George T. and Charles H., both of whom are residents of Norfolk.

Charles H. Tumbleson was educated in public schools at Norfolk, and at the age of fifteen began an apprenticeship in his father's shop. He became a thoroughly skilled worker in the blacksmith trade, and that was his regular occupation and business in Norfolk for a period of a quarter of a century.

In the fall of 1921 he was elected city sergeant, having previously served as deputy sergeant, and was reelected to that office in the fall of 1925. Mr. Tumbleson is prominent in Masonry, being affiliated with Atlantic Lodge No. 2, A. F. and A. M., Norfolk Chapter No. 1, Royal Arch Masons, Grice Commandery of the Knights Templar, member of the Scottish Rite Bodies, thirty-second degree, Khedive Temple of the Mystic Shrine, also belongs to the B. P. O. Elks, and is a member of Elizabeth Camp No. 3, Woodmen of the World, and was first Past Head Consul of the jurisdiction of Virginia of the Woodmen of the World. He and his family are members of the Park Place Methodist Episcopal Church, South.

Sergeant Tumbleson married in 1895 Miss Bruce Austin. She was born on Roanoke Island, North Carolina, the birthplace of Virginia Dare, the first white child born in America. Her parents were Rev. Daniel B. and Sallie Austin, her father for many years a member of the Virginia Conference of the Methodist Episcopal Church, South. Mr. and Mrs. Tumbleson have a son, Talbot Austin Tumbleson. He was educated in the city schools of Norfolk, had his academic course at the University of Virginia, and was a student of medicine at Tulane University, New Orleans, when the World war came on. He enlisted and served in the Ambulance Corps, later was transferred to the Officers' Training Camp and was commissioned a lieutenant and was engaged in the training of recruits in different camps until the end of the war. He then resumed his studies at Tulane, graduated, and is now practicing medicine at New Orleans. Doctor Tumbleson married Miss Henrietta Pharr, of New Iberia, Louisiana, and they have one son, Charles A. Tumbleson.

CHARLES GRAHAM EVANS has for many years been one of Danville's most useful citizens. During his life there he has been an educator and business man, finding an outlet for his many interests and talents in welfare, civic and religious institutions.

He was born September 14, 1875, at Manteo, one of the most historic spots on the seacoast of North Carolina, a son of John W. and Rosa (Brinkley) Evans. The Evans family settled in North Carolina from Eastern Pennsylvania. The famous "Fighting Bob" Evans, of the United States Navy, was a cousin of John W. Evans. John W. Evans was also born and reared in Eastern North Carolina, attended a private school, served all through the four years of the Civil war except for the first six months, and after the war engaged in farming for a year or two, then clerked in a store at Plymouth, North Carolina, and started business for himself as a merchant with stores at Edenton, Manteo and Elizabeth City, and later also had an office at Norfolk, Virginia. He was a member of the Masonic fraternity and Independent Order of Odd Fellows, and was a Methodist. He died in 1926 and is buried at Manteo. His wife, Rosa Brinkley, was born and reared in Hertford County, North Carolina, attended private schools, graduated from Murfreesboro College and taught for several years. She died in 1897 and is also buried at Manteo. Of their six children two died in infancy and those living are Helen Lucile, Charles G., Eva Eola and Ruth Leland.

Charles Graham Evans grew up around Albemarle Sound, attended private schools and the Kinston Collegiate Institute, the Suffolk Military Academy, and was graduated A. M. in 1895 from Randolph-Macon College at Ashland. He remained at Ashland as instructor in English and for eleven years was with Randolph-Macon Academy at Bedford, being associate principal for nine years of the time. From Bedford Mr. Evans came to Danville as head of Randolph-Macon Institute, and served as president of this noted school for nineteen years, until 1925. Since giving up school work he has been connected with the Equitable Life Assurance Society as special agent, and since November, 1926, as field agent. He is also a member of the firm Evans & Boatwright, general insurance, representing fifteen insurance organizations, covering every phase of insurance. Mr. Evans and associates in 1926 organized the Atlantic Building and Loan Association, and he was vice president until November, 1928, when he resigned to become secretary and treasurer. He is also a director of the Frix Piano and Radio Company.

Such is a brief record of Mr. Evans as an educational executive and business man. Certain of his interests may be expressed through the mention of some of the many organizations of which he is a member. He is a director of the Wildwood Fishing Club. For the past four years he has been associate judge of the Juvenile and Domestic Relations Court at Danville. He is a thirty-second degree Scottish Rite and York Rite Mason, with affiliations with Roman Eagle Lodge, No. 122, A. F. and A. M. He has long been prominent in the work of the Kiwanis Club, being director and secretary of the local club, a past district trustee, lieutenant governor of the Second Division of the Capital District, embracing Delaware, Maryland, District of Columbia and Virginia. He was at one time tennis champion of Virginia and a member of the Danville Tennis Club. He is a Democrat, and both he and his wife have been prominently identified with the work of the Main Street Methodist Episcopal Church, South, for years. For fifteen years he was superintendent of the Sunday School, and is a member of the Board of Stewards and custodian of church property, and for the past seven years has taught the Men's Bible Class. He is also district lay leader of the Danville District Conference. Mr. Evans is president of the Hilltop Sanitarium, president of the Danville Y. M. C. A., president of the Virginia State Y. M. C. A., and for years has been a member of the State Executive Committee of the association. He is vice president of the Danville Community Chest, vice president of the Danville Community Welfare Association.

Mr. Evans married at Bedford, Virginia, June 16, 1904, Miss Jessie Marvin Quinby, of Bedford, formerly of Onancock, Virginia. Mrs. Evans is a graduate of Hollins College and of Randolph-Macon Woman's College of Lynchburg. She is a member of the Daughters of the American Revolution and the Wednesday Club. They have three children, Charles Graham, Jr., Upshur Quinby and Kerr Stewart Evans. Charles G., Jr., was educated in Randolph-Macon Academy at Front Royal, in Randolph-Macon College, graduated from the University of Virginia in 1928, and is now associated with his father in business. The two younger sons are students in the Danville Military Institute.

BLAKE TYLER NEWTON has been one of the most useful men in the citizenship of Westmoreland County. He is practicing law at Hague, is county superintendent of schools, owns and operates a large farm, is vice president of a bank and has accepted his full share of responsibilities in many movements and organizations.

He was born at Hague October 21, 1889, son of Edward Colston and Lucy Tyler (Yates) Newton. President John Tyler was a great-uncle of Lucy Yates.

Willoughby Newton, his grandfather, was born in 1800 and died in 1875. He owned and operated five thousand acres, employing the labor of 250 slaves, and was a Virginia planter who made his influence felt in the legislative affairs of both his state and nation. As a Whig he was a member of the House of Delegates five terms and represented the First Virginia District in Congress. He also served in the Legislature during the Confederacy. Willoughby Newton's wife was Mary Stevenson Brockenbrough, daughter of the distinguished Virginia jurist, William Brockenbrough.

Edward Colston Newton was born April 4, 1849, and died September 1, 1913, spending practically all his life at Linden Farm at Hague. He was well educated, and besides cultivating his farm he was in business as a traveling salesman, for eight years was deputy county treasurer and thirty years a justice of the peace. He was a Democrat, and a member of the Episcopal Church. His wife, Lucy Tyler Yates, was born November 8, 1856, and died June 19, 1919.

Blake Tyler Newton was one of a large family of children. He graduated in 1910 with the A. B. degree from the College of William and Mary, after which for two years he was principal of the Hamilton High School at Cartersville, was principal of the Blue Ridge Industrial School at Dyke in Greene County for one year, and on September 1, 1913, was elected county superintendent of schools for Westmoreland and Richmond counties. For over fifteen years he has had the responsibility of the administration of the general educational program for these two counties, and has brought to that work the experience of a successful teacher and an educator of fine vision, in close touch with modern ideas and ideals. He is a member of the National Education Association, Virginia State Teachers Association, and was a member of the Virginia Education Commission which made a survey of the state school system during 1919-20.

Mr. Newton read law at home, was admitted to the bar August 15, 1919, and during the past ten years has had a successful general law practice. He is also vice president of the Farmers Bank of Hague. He has both his office and residence on Linden Farm in the village of Hague, a property of 152 acres, which was inherited and developed by his grandfather, Willoughby Newton. Mr. Newton was chairman of the local Red Cross Chapter during the World war, and prominent in all the drives for funds and patriotic causes during the war. He is a Democrat and a member of the Democratic State Central Committee, has been vestryman and treasurer of the Episcopal Church, is affiliated with the Masonic fraternity and Junior Order United American Mechanics. He belongs to the Phi Kappa Alpha and the honorary scholarship fraternity Phi Beta Kappa.

Mr. Newton married, July 29, 1913, Miss Bertha Effingham Lawrence. They came to know each other while both were engaged in school work in the mountain district of Western Virginia. Mrs. Newton is a daughter in a prominent New York family, George Anderson and Charlotte Louise (Cooley) Lawrence, her father having been in the bonded warehouse business in New York for many years. Mrs. Newton graduated from the New York Training School for Church Women and for eight years before her marriage was a missionary of the Episcopal Church in the Blue Ridge Mountains. The children of Mr. and Mrs. Newton are: Edward Colston, born May 25, 1914; Blake Tyler, Jr., born October 17, 1915; and Bertha Lawrence, born July 16, 1917.

GEORGE EDWARD FRANKLIN is cashier of the Farmers Bank of Hague in Westmoreland County and is also one of the stockholders in that institution. The bank was organized in 1920, and has capital of $15,000, surplus and profits of $5,000, and deposits averaging $90,000. The bank occupies a modern banking home, which was erected in 1920. The president of the bank is Dr. W. N. Chinn, and the vice president, Blake T. Newton.

Mr. Franklin was born at Haynesville, Richmond County, Virginia, August 30, 1896, son of W. R. and Apphia J. (Sisson) Franklin, natives of the same county. His father, now living

Arthur Roberts

retired at Haynesville, has spent his active life in mechanical trades, as carpenter and machinist, and for some years also taught school.

George E. Franklin was reared and educated at Haynesville, graduating from the Emmerton High School in 1917. After a business course at Baltimore and at Washington he entered the service of the Treasury Department in Washington, where he was employed four years, getting valuable training for his career as a banker. He has been cashier of the Farmers Bank of Hague since 1924.

Mr. Franklin married, October 2, 1926, Miss Thelma Frances Barnes, daughter of J. Edward and Elizabeth Catherine (Allen) Barnes, both natives of Westmoreland County. Her parents reside at Coles Point, Virginia, and her father is captain of a freighter on the Potomac River and Chesapeake Bay. Mr. and Mrs. Franklin have one son, George Edward, Jr., born October 2, 1927. Mr. Franklin has farming interests in the vicinity of Hague. He is a Democrat, a Mason, active in the Baptist Church, and formerly secretary of the Sunday School.

ARTHUR ROBERTS, of East Radford, Virginia, is one of the veteran employes of the Norfolk & Western Railway Company, having been in the service forty-six consecutive years. In all that time he has drawn a full month's pay without interruption except for two weeks about thirty-five years ago when he was absent on sick leave. Few men in any line of service could equal such a record.

Mr. Roberts was born at Central Depot, now East Radford, Virginia, June 18, 1865, son of George E. and Julia A. (Cofer) Roberts. His father was born in the eastern part of the state, and when a young man moved from Petersburg to Central Depot, now East Radford, and during the Civil war worked in the shops at Central Depot as a mechanic for the Confederate government, after which he embarked in the mercantile business and continued in this up to the time of his death. He died June 7, 1887, and is buried at East Radford. His wife, Julia A. Cofer, was born in Pulaski County, Virginia, attended public and private schools there. She and her husband were active members of the Methodist Episcopal Church, South. She died February 24, 1895. There were six children: Walter R., who died July 6, 1914, aged fifty-four; Edwin G., who died November 7, 1906, age forty-two; Arthur; Frank E., who died September 25, 1918, age fifty-one; Virginia May, who died April 19, 1915, age forty, the wife of Dr. R. S. Carson, of Radford, now deceased; and Harry H., who died December 26, 1891, aged twenty-three.

Arthur Roberts attended public schools at Central Depot and for several years of his early manhood was associated with his father and brother Walter R. in the mercantile business. On November 26, 1883, before he was nineteen, he began his notable service with the Norfolk & Western Railway Company as shop clerk in the motive power department, under Foreman E. F. Gill. His services in this department covered a period of fifteen years. In January, 1898, he was made cashier and ticket agent and in November, 1899, was promoted to agent and yardmaster at East Radford, a post of duty in which he has officiated now for thirty-one years. In addition to his long and faithful record in railway service Mr. Roberts is a prominent participant in the business and civic affairs of his home community, being a di

rector and member of the loan committee in the Farmers &
Merchants National Bank, director in the Radford Sales Corporation and the Radford Finance Corporation, and is president
of Radford Park Corporation, also president and director of
the Radford Hospital Corporation. He is a past president of
the Radford Kiwanis Club, member of the Woodmen of the
World; for several terms was a city councilman and was also
clerk of the council and city auditor. He is a member of the
regular Democratic organization, and has been active in all
phases of the work of the Methodist Episcopal Church, South,
serving as delegate to district and annual conferences, and for
years as superintendent of the Sunday School; for about thirty
years as chairman of the Board of Stewards, and is now chairman of the Board of Trustees. He was chairman of the building committee when the handsome brick and stone church was
erected at East Radford, corner of Grove Avenue and Third
streets.

Mr. Roberts married at East Radford, May 24, 1888, Miss
Lucy J. Kuhn, who was educated in public schools at Radford
and the Marion Female College. She is a daughter of William
Henry and Victoria W. (Smith) Kuhn, her mother a native of
Prince Edward County and her father of Norfolk, Virginia.
W. H. Kuhn was a sailor for a number of years and served
during the war between the states in the Confederate Navy. He
was captain of the gun squad on the Merrimac during the en-
counter with the Monitor. After the war he went into the
service of the Virginia & Tennessee Railroad, now the Norfolk
& Western Railway Company, as wrecking master, and performed those duties until his death. Mr. and Mrs. Roberts had
a family of five children. Their daughter Ruby Clare Roberts
died at the age of twenty-two. She was educated in the public
schools at East Radford and at Sullins College, Bristol, Virginia.
She was the wife of A. F. Cannaday, special agent for the Richmond, Fredericksburg & Potomac Railway Company, at Richmond, Virginia. She left one son, A. F. Cannaday, Jr., now a
law student at the University of Virginia.

Lottie Jean Roberts was educated at the Radford High
School, Radford Normal, and Martha Washington College. She
is the wife of Rev. E. C. Jessee, of the Methodist Episcopal
Church, South. They live at Radford, Virginia, and have three
children, Arthur Clare, Betty Jane and Jeannette.

Essie Mae Roberts died at the age of sixteen, while a student in the Radford High School.

Annie Kuhn Roberts was educated in the Radford High
School (class of 1918), Radford State Teachers College (class of
1920) and Teachers College, Columbia University (class of
1922). Since graduation she has been a member of the Fine
Arts faculties of the following institutions: Horace Mann School,
New York City, State Teachers College at Radford, Virginia,
and Fredericksburg, Virginia, Florida State College for Women,
Tallahassee, Florida, and University of Virginia. She was president of her class while in college, and has served as president
of the Alumni Association of Radford State Teachers College.
She is a member of the Radford Branch of the American Association of University Women.

Arthur Roberts, Jr., was educated at Radford High School
(class of 1921) and Virginia Polytechnic Institute (class of
1925), and did post-graduate work in 1926, specializing in mechanical engineering. He was captain of Company H, battalian
commander of the Second Battalion. He was active in athletics

and made his letter in basketball, track and football. After leaving V. P. I. he was with the Standard Oil Company of New Jersey at Elizabeth, New Jersey, the Chesapeake & Potomac Telephone Company at Washington, and J. W. Branch, Inc., at Huntington, West Virginia. He is now mechanical engineer for the Lynchburg Foundry Company at Lynchburg, Virginia.

WILLIAM HENRY PARKER. During the past quarter of a century the name Parker has been prominently associated with the business district at Danville, where one of the largest stores carrying musical merchandise and books in South Virginia is conducted under the title of J. F. Parker & Son.

The founder of the business was the late James Franklin Parker, who was a musician and music teacher before he began selling musical merchandise. He was born in Rockingham County, Virginia, descended from an old family still numerously represented in that section of the state. He attended a private school and during the last year of the Civil war went into the Confederate army as member of a company of boys from Augusta County under Captain Marquis. He took part in the battle of Cross Keys. After the war he studied music in Dunkirk, New York, taught instrumental music and singing at Milan, Tennessee, and later at Jackson. His home was in Clarksville for twenty-five years, and he lived in Tennessee for over thirty years. In 1902 he moved to Danville, Virginia, and in association with his son, William Henry, started the book and music store which is still carried on under the old firm name. He died October 29, 1928, and is buried in Green Hill Cemetery at Danville. He was a member of the Baptist Church. James Franklin Parker married Charlotte Elizabeth Jesse in Clarksville, Tennessee, in 1880. His first wife was a Miss Hart, of Tuscaloosa, Alabama, who died in 1874, leaving one son, James F. Parker, now a resident of Dallas, Texas, and associated with the Clark & Courts Company, stationery manufacturers at Galveston, Texas. James F. Parker married Addie Adriance, of Galveston, and has two sons, J. F. Parker III and Jack Parker. Charlotte Elizabeth Jesse was a daughter of William Jesse, of Lancaster County, Virginia. Her birthplace was old "Epping Forest," which was a part of the estate of William Ball, father of Mary Ball, the mother of George Washington. Epping Forest has been appropriately marked by the Virginia Historical Society as one of the historic spots of old Virginia. Charlotte Elizabeth Jesse was educated in the Albemarle Female Institute and was a teacher in private schools at Milan, Tennessee, and at Clarksville Female Academy before her marriage. She was very active in the Baptist Church and a member of the Danville Wednesday Club, and served on the Board of Governors of the Danville General Hospital, now known as the Memorial Hospital. She died April 1, 1929, the mother of two sons, William H. and Richard Jesse. The latter died at the age of twenty-six years and is buried at Dallas, Texas.

William Henry Parker was born at Clarksville, Tennessee, September 6, 1882, and attended public schools at Clarksville, graduated from the Southwestern Presbyterian University of Clarksville in 1902 with the A. B. degree, and in the same year accompanied his parents to Danville, Virginia, and has been associated with the music and book and stationery business of J. F. Parker & Son continuously. This is one of the very popular stores of the kind and has in an important sense been the center of the cultural life of Danville.

Mr. Parker is a York and Scottish Rite Mason and Shriner, being a past master of Roman Eagle Lodge No. 122, A. F. and A. M., a member of Euclid Chapter, Royal Arch Masons, Dove Commandery of the Knights Templar and Acca Temple of the Mystic Shrine at Richmond. He was the presiding officer as worshipful master the first night the lodge was opened in the new Masonic Temple at Danville in 1924. He is also a past president of the Rotary Club, member of the Chamber of Commerce, a director of the Retail Merchants Association, and has had a helpful and sustaining part in the civic life of his community. He is a Democrat, and in the First Baptist Church is deacon and chorister.

Mr. Parker married at Clarksville, Tennessee, June 18, 1907, Miss Lillie Mae Cooksey of Clarksville. She attended public schools in Tennessee and the Clarksville Female Academy, and taught for a year before her marriage. She is a member of the Baptist Church. Her parents were E. N. and Mary (Dorrity) Cooksey, of Clarksville. Her father was a farmer and stock raiser in that section of Tennessee and died in 1927, while her mother passed away in 1916, both being buried in Greenwood Cemetery at Clarksville. Mr. and Mrs. Parker have two children, Mary Frances and William Henry, Jr. The daughter, Mary, is a graduate of Randolph-Macon Institute, attended Sweetbrier College of Virginia, and is now a student in the School of Journalism of the University of Missouri, member of the class of 1931. The son, William H., Jr., attended school at Danville, graduating from high school, and won a scholarship in William and Mary College, where he has completed two years of work.

HON. PRESTON WHITE CAMPBELL, judge of the Virginia Supreme Court of Appeals, distinguished alike as a legist and jurist, has occupied a pre-eminent place in the councils of the State of Virginia since his admission to the bar more than thirty-two years ago. Not alone by native talent and devoted service is he eminent, but also by inheritance of qualities from illustrious ancestors. As a judge it is stated of him that his opinions will live as long as the jurisprudence of the state shall endure. His qualities are not of the mere dazzling or brilliant kind which give ephemeral fame, but rather profound, practical and solid, entitling him to the real respect that men give to those whose achievements are of the lasting variety.

Judge Campbell was born at Abingdon, Virginia, January 24, 1874, and is a son of Dr. Edward McDonald and Ellen (White) Campbell, and was named for his uncle, Hon. John Preston White, who was chief justice of the Supreme Court of Texas for thirty years. He descends from Dugal Campbell, of Inverary, Argyllshire, Scotland, and belongs to that pioneer American stock which has rendered service to the state and nation from the birth of the Republic. His great-grandfather, Capt. John Campbell, commanded a company of Revolutionary troops under Gen. William Campbell at the battle of Kings Mountain, eighty miles northwest of Columbia, York County, South Carolina, October 7, 1780, when the Americans, under Campbell, Sevier and Shelby, won a decisive victory over the British under Ferguson. His grandfather, Edward Campbell, was born at Hall's Bottom, Washington County, and became one of the distinguished lawyers of his day and a leader of the Democratic party, as well as a prominent member of the Presbyterian Church. John Campbell, great-uncle of Judge Campbell, was a close friend of Andrew Jackson, and during that warrior and statesman's administration as president served as secretary of the treasury of the United States, and Hon. David Campbell, a great-uncle, also served as governor. Hon. William B. Campbell, a governor of Virginia, was a first cousin of Judge Campbell's grandfather. Still another uncle, John A. Campbell, held the rank of lieutenant-colonel in the Confederate army during the war between the states, and afterwards served as judge of the Circuit Court for many years. A first cousin, Hon. Edward K. Campbell, was appointed chief justice of the Court of Claims at Washington, D. C., by President Wilson, and another cousin, J. Garnett Campbell, has been a prominent judge in Oklahoma. Some member of the family has represented Washington County in every constitutional convention since 1781. The father of Judge Campbell, Dr. Edward McDonald Campbell, now deceased, was born at Hall's Bottom, Washington County, graduated from Jefferson Medical College, Philadelphia, and for more than thirty-five years practiced at Abingdon, becoming one of the most distinguished physicians and surgeons of the state. Originally a Whig, he later became a leader of the Democratic party in Washington County, and was a man of outstanding character, prominent in all affairs in his part of the state. He was a Mason and member of the Swedenborgian Church. During the war between the states he served as a surgeon in the Confederate army, being attached to the staff of Gen. J. E. B. Stuart. On the maternal side Judge Campbell is also descended from a family which has been prominent in making history in Virginia.

Preston White Campbell attended the public schools and Abingdon Male Academy, following which he entered the University of Virginia for the session of 1896-97. In the latter year he was admitted to the bar and began practice at Abingdon, which has been his home to the present. Judge Campbell in addition to his legal work immediately became immersed in public affairs, and in 1901-02 was elected a member of the Constitutional Convention, and although the youngest member of that body served with great ability. He was democratic elector in the Ninth District in the presidential race of 1912. When Hon. F. B. Hutton resigned as judge of the Circuit Court, in March, 1914, to become one of the code revisors, Governor Stuart immediately appointed Judge Campbell as his successor. Following his appointment he was twice elected by the Legislature without opposition. During his incumbency of that office he tried more than 1,000 criminal cases and was reversed but twice in such cases. He also tried more than 500 civil and chancery cases, in which he was reversed but thirteen times, and in six of these by a divided court. For eight years his circuit included Washington, Smyth and Scott counties and the city of Bristol. In 1922, because of the heavy work involved, Scott County was placed in another circuit. During his long service as commonwealth's attorney he became especially versed in criminal law. In 1924 Judge Campbell was elected judge of the Supreme Court of Appeals of Virginia, and was then elected by the Legislature for a twelve-year term, and during his incumbency there has established a splendid record for conscientious, dignified and able service. Judge Campbell is a member of the Bristol Bar Association, the Washington County Bar Association, the Virginia

Bar Association and the American Bar Association. He is a past grand of the Independent Order of Odd Fellows, and an elder in the Sinking Springs Presbyterian Church at Abingdon. (See sketch in "Who's Who in America.")

Judge Campbell married Miss Louise Elwood Howard, of Lynchburg, Virginia, daughter of Volney E. and Blanche (Carter) Howard, Mr. Howard being one of the most distinguished and accomplished members of the Virginia bar. Mrs. Campbell was educated at Stonewall Jackson College, Abingdon, and Randolph-Macon Woman's College, Lynchburg, and is a woman of many accomplishments and an active member of the Sinking Springs Presbyterian Church. Three children have been born to Judge and Mrs. Campbell: Preston White, Jr., aged thirteen years; Edward Malcolm, aged ten years; and Volney Howard, aged eight years.

LEONARD R. HALL. True success in the profession of law does not come to an individual possessed of perseverance and ability alone. Back of these necessary qualifications must be devotion to clients, and honesty of purpose which looks beyond the mere winning of one case to the client's future. Counsel and advice for which money cannot pay and which never appear in the attorney's bill for services must ever be present. The possession of these characteristics have been prominent factors in the success of Leonard R. Hall, one of the leading younger attorneys of Bristol, where he is well known for his important connection with large corporations. He has made this branch of the law a specialty, and his reputation extends far beyond the limits of his immediate field of practice.

Mr. Hall was born at Norton, Virginia, May 12, 1902, and is a son of Charles, Jr., and Rebekah (Fields) Hall, both now residents of Orlando, Orange County, Kentucky. His paternal grandfather was Henry Hall, who was born in Letcher County, Kentucky, where he became prominent in Republican politics and political affairs, and served some years as sheriff of his native county. Eventually he moved to Virginia, and is now living in retirement at Norton, after many years spent in successful agricultural operations.

Charles Hall, Jr., father of Leonard R. Hall, was born in Letcher County, Kentucky, and as a youth accompanied his parents to Virginia. A product of the public schools, when a young man he engaged in farming, but later was attracted to the real estate business, in which he was engaged for twenty-three years in Virginia, living for the most part at or in the vicinity of Norton. He was one of those to vision the opportunities that were to be found in his line of business in Florida, and accordingly moved to that state, both he and Mrs. Hall, also a native of Letcher County, Kentucky, residing at that fashionable and thriving community which bears the name of Orlando. Mr. Hall is primarily a business man and has shown little interest in politics save as a Republican voter. He and Mrs. Hall are consistent members of the Baptist Church. She is a daughter of Dan D. Fields, who was one of the most distinguished attorneys of the South, and who for many years prior to his death, April 6, 1926, resided in Letcher County, where he was chief counsel for the Louisville & Nashville Railroad.

Leonard R. Hall attended the public schools of Norton and after graduation from the high school at Norton and that at Fork Union, Fluvanna County, spent two years in the University

Waldeman Wallner

of Richmond, and pursued his law course in the Williams Law School at Richmond. Graduating in 1924 with the degree of Bachelor of Laws, he was admitted to the bar in the same year, and immediately commenced practice at Bristol, where he has since been located, his offices being in the Dominion National Bank Building. For a time he was associated with Hon. Frank DeFreise, but this connection was mutually severed, and Mr. Hall has since been engaged in general practice alone, handling only civil cases, and eschewing connection with cases of a criminal character. Much of his professional business comes from large corporations, and in this connection he is counsel for a large number of important interests. He enjoys an excellent reputation as a lawyer of ability and a young man of pleasing and attractive personality, and is a member of the Washington County Bar Association, the Virginia State Bar Association and the American Bar Association. Politically a Republican, he takes an active part in public affairs, and at present is secretary of the Republican Central Committee, being likewise secretary of the Bristol Bar Association. He belongs to the Kiwanis Club, the Sigma Phi Epsilon fraternity and the Sigma Nu Phi fraternity, and is a third degree Mason.

Mr. Hall married Miss Katherine Kipps, of Richmond, the daughter of L. Leonard and Katherine (Caulder) Kipps, residents of South America. Mr. Kipps has always been engaged in the tobacco business on an extensive scale, and spent some years in this business in China, in which country Mrs. Hall gained the major part of her education. She is a leader in club and social circles of Bristol and an active member of the Episcopal Church. Mr. and Mrs. Hall are the parents of one child, Leonard R., who was born at Bristol May 27, 1926.

WALDEMAR WALLNER is a prominent young representative of a comparatively few group of technical men in Virginia, the textile engineers, and is associated with the knitting mill industries in Southwestern Virginia, being general manager of the Paul Knitting Mills, Pulaski and Radford, Virginia, and the Inspiration Hosiery Mills, Wytheville, Virginia.

Mr. Wallner was born at Fall River, Massachusetts, August 20, 1902, son of Anton and Anna (Sirk) Wallner. His father was born in Austria, in 1859, was reared and educated there,, learning the trade of baker, and in 1885 came to America. He developed an extensive business as a baker in the New England mill communities of New Bedford and Fall River. He died March 6, 1923. His wife, Anna Sirk, was born in Austria in 1860. One of the sons has continued the baking business in New England, while two of them are knitting mill executives in Virginia, Thomas J. Wallner and Waldemar.

Waldemar Wallner was educated in public schools at New Bedford and graduated from the New Bedford School of Textile Engineering in 1923. He at once came to Virginia and became associated with his brother Thomas at Pulaski, where he was superintendent of the Paul Knitting Mills for about two years. In 1926 he was sent to Radford as manager of the Radford plant of the Paul Knitting Mills. The Inspiration Hosiery Mills at Wytheville, owned by the same group of interests as the Paul Knitting Mills, were established in 1927, and Mr. Wallner moved to Wytheville and has been manager of the plant. Mr. Wallner is a stockholder of the company and is associated with his

brother Thomas and others in the Cavalier Hosiery Mills at
Narrows, Virginia, also the Virginia Maid Hosiery Mills of
Pulaski.

Mr. Wallner is a member of the Masonic fraternity, the
Rotary Club of Wytheville, the Wytheville Country Club, and
is a Baptist and a Democrat.

ROBERT E. FORTUNE, M. D. Of the men devoted to the science
of healing at Damascus, none bring to bear upon their calling
larger gifts of scholarship and resource than Dr. Robert E. Fortune. Far from selecting his life work in the untried enthusiasm
of extreme youth, the choice of this genial practitioner was that
of a mature mind, trained to thoughtfulness by years of practical
experience in other fields of activity and to a full realization of
the possibilities and responsibilities which confronted him. The
result has been that he has won a high place in his profession,
not only at Damascus, where he has been engaged in the general
practice of medicine and surgery for more than thirty years, but
throughout Washington County.

Doctor Fortune was born November 29, 1870, at Asheville,
North Carolina, and is a son of W. P. and Nancy Eliza (Davidson Fortune. The Fortune family originated in Wales, whence
the original American progenitor immigrated to Caroline County
Virginia, where the paternal grandfather of Doctor Fortune was
born. About twenty years prior to the war between the states he
moved to North Carolina, and there was engaged in planting and
stock raising during the remainder of his life. The maternal
grandfather of Doctor Fortune was W. Davidson, of English-
Irish descent, who was born and reared in western North Carolina, and was a farmer and stockman by vocation, and a devout
member of the Presbyterian Church.

W. P. Fortune, the father of Doctor Fortune, was born in
North Carolina, where he received a public school education. As
a youth be became interested in railroad construction, and was
thus engaged at the outbreak of the war between the states,
when he enlisted for service in the Confederate army, and arose
to a captaincy in the Fourteenth Regiment, Company A, North
Carolina Volunteer Infantry. At the close of his military service
he resumed his activities as a railroad contractor, and as the
years passed became one of the best known men in his line of his
day. While he continued to make his home at Asheville, he constructed railroads over many states, and was accounted a positive
genius for resource in overcoming obstacles and putting through
his contracts on time. In the evening of life he retired from active pursuits and took up his residence at Abingdon, where he
passed away, his wife having passed away at Swananoa, North
Carolina. Mr. Fortune was an active Democrat, although not a
seeker after public office, and a consistent member of the Methodist Episcopal Church, South. He and his worthy wife were the
parents of the following children: Jennie, the widow of W. B.
Welch, of Lancaster, South Carolina; Rosa J., who is unmarried
and makes her home with Doctor Fortune at Damascus; Richard
Frank, who is engaged in the real estate business at Asheville,
North Carolina; Dr. Robert E., of this review; Walter H., who
is engaged in the feed and coal business at Damascus; and Katie,
the wife of Linn Stanton, formerly of Massachusetts, who is now
engaged in the automobile business at Swananoa, North Carolina.

Robert E. Fortune after attending the public schools of Asheville, North Carolina, was sent to the Shelby Military Academy at

Shelby, North Carolina, following which he pursued a course at old Trinity College, now Duke University. With this preparation for a career he became associated with his father and brother in railroad construction work, although his personal inclinations ran in a different direction. While engaged in this important field of enterprise he assisted in building the Carolina Central Railroad, the Cape Fear & Yadkin Valley Railroad, the Pametta Railroad, the Roanoke & Southern Railroad and the Virginia & Carolina Railroad. After the completion of the latter contract Doctor Fortune's father retired from active affairs, and the younger man, left to his own devices, entered the University College of Medicine at Richmond, Virginia, from which he was graduated with the degree of Doctor of Medicine as a member of the class of 1898. He immediately located at Damascus, where for more than thirty years he has ministered to the ills of his suffering fellow citizens, winning gratitude, confidence and universal respect. He maintains well appointed offices on Main Street, and in addition to his large personal practice is medical examiner for all the leading life insurance companies. He is a splendid physician and a man of great personal magnetism, and keeps fully abreast of the advancements made in his profession by taking special courses at the New York Polyclinic, subscriptions to the regular medical periodicals and membership in the Southwest Virginia Medical Society and the Virginia Medical Society. He is a Blue Lodge Mason and a member of the Methodist Episcopal Church, South.

In 1918 Doctor Fortune was united in marriage with Miss Sarah Poindexter, of Roanoke, Virginia, daughter of John D. Poindexter, of Bedford, this state. Mrs. Fortune, who was a woman of splendid accomplishments and a graduate of Lynchburg College and Randolph-Macon College, died June 18, 1926, without issue.

Roy B. Bowers, A. B., A. M. "The High School must be and remain the College of the People." This quotation from the writings of Prof. Roy B. Bowers, superintendent of the city schools of Bristol, Virginia, defines the attitude on a very important question of one of Virginia's most able and experienced educators, a man of broad intellectual training and vigorous thought. His entire life since boyhood has been devoted to educational work, and with so much success that his name is known and held in high esteem over a wide area.

Roy B. Bowers was born at Elizabethton, Tennessee, August 30, 1888, son of Rev. John L. and Martha (Slemp) Bowers, and grandson of John L. Bowers, who was originally of the Valley of Virginia but later removed to Tennessee. For many years Rev. John L. Bowers was one of the best known ministers of the Baptist Church, serving charges in Virginia, North Carolina, Tennessee and Kentucky, and on several occasions he was made church moderator and was tendered other positions of confidence. His worthy and beneficent life came to a close in 1902. His marriage was with Miss Martha Slemp, who was born in the home of her parents in Johnson County, Tennessee, and still resides at Elizabethton. She comes from a very old and prominent family of Southwest Virginia, members of which have served in public office in the national capital.

Roy B. Bowers received his early educational training in the schools at Carter County, Tennessee, then entered Wautaga Valley Academy in Carter County, and subsequently Carson and

Newman College at Jefferson City, Tennessee, from which he was graduated in 1910 with his degree of A. B. and in 1911 received his degree of A. M. from the same institution. Post-graduate work followed at Newton Institution, Boston, Massachusetts; University of Chicago, Illinois; and the University of Cincinnati, Ohio.

When Superintendent Bowers first taught school, in Carter County and at Fish Springs, Tennessee, he had but one room to overlook, primitive in appearance and lacking in equipments. His next was a four-room school at Hampton, Tennessee, and its successor was an eight-room school at Round Oak, Georgia. For the next three years he was occupied as supervising principal of the schools of Eustis, Florida, and for eighteen months afterward filled the office of elementary supervisor of the schools of Asheville, North Carolina. Then, during an important interlude, he served for eighteen months as field agents for the United States Bureau of Education, and upon retirement in 1919 he accepted election to the superintendency of the city schools of Bristol, Virginia. The high school building here is one of the finest and best equipped in Southwest Virginia, and the four other school buildings under his jurisdiction, the Thomas Jefferson, the Robert E. Lee, and the George Washington grade schools and the Douglas School for the colored pupils, all are good types of modern school structures. Superintendent Bowers has seventy-five teachers under his supervision, and the school population of the city of Bristol is 2,600.

From the very beginning of his work at Bristol Superintendent Bowers has sought to bring the benefits of the public schools more abundantly and still closer to those for whom they are designed. By tongue and pen, by personal example and winning influence, he has succeeded in bringing into his school rooms more purposeful ideas than of old, and believes that to the ordinary public school student the high school of the future will, in great measure, supply every intellectual necessity. Quoting again from Superintendent Bowers: "We must reach the point in our educational system where every American youth will be trained to do more perfectly what he will necessarily have to do to earn his living, and at the same time come into possession of those habits of skill, aptitude and perspective which will enable him to secure from life the most possible, in the way of happy and useful activities, of complete living."

Superintendent Bowers married, in 1907 Miss Myrtle Hathaway, of Hampton, Tennessee, daughter of John and Elizabeth (Ellis) Hathaway, the latter of whom survives. The father of Mrs. Bowers was formerly a merchant. He was of English extraction and it is not at all improbable that in days long back his people may have lived in the little town of Shottery, where Shakespeare found his wife, Anne Hathaway. Superintendant and Mrs. Bowers have four children: Roy, Jr., who was born in 1909, was graduated from the Virginia High School and is now a student in the University of Cincinnati; Martha Elizabeth, who completed her high school course when but fifteen years old, is a student in Sullins College; and Jane Austin, born in 1916, and Jerrie Hathaway, born in 1918, are both attending school at Bristol. Mrs. Bowers was educated at Hampton and at Jefferson City, Tennessee, and was a student in Carson and Newman College. She is a member of the Eastern Star and a past worthy matron, and, like the other members of the family, is active in the Methodist Episcopal Church, South.

Superintendent Bowers has been styled the best educated and most progressive educator of this part of the state, and the deep interest he takes in vocational public school training is the result of observation, close study and wide reading, accompanied, perhaps, by that inward demanding sense of justice that helplessness and disadvantage arouse when the weak have no safe foothold with the strong. He has spoken frequently on this and other subjects in commencement orations and before civic bodies. He is a member of the Virginia State and the National Educational Associations, is a Royal Arch Mason, a Knight of Pythias and a member of the Kiwanis Club.

CAPT. THOMAS S. USSERY, physician and surgeon, gained his military title as a result of more than two years of active service as a military officer at home and overseas during the World war. He is one of the ablest and most progressive doctors in Southwestern Virginia, having practiced since 1923 at Norton, Wise County.

He was born at Barnwell, South Carolina, October 5, 1890, but spent most of his early life in Georgia. He is a son of James P. and Crosia (Wooley) Ussery. His mother is still living. His father, who was in the insurance business for a number of years prior to his death, served eleven years as probate judge of DeKalb County, Georgia, and was an active member of the Baptist Church.

Captain Ussery is a graduate of the Decatur High School of Georgia, spent two years as a student of science in the University of Georgia at Athens, one year in the Philadelphia College of Pharmacy, and in 1915 graduated M. D. from Emory University at Atlanta. Doctor Ussery for one year was an interne in the Grady Memorial Hospital at Atlanta, and was engaged in private practice in that city from June 16 to August 1, 1917.

It was on August 1, 1917, that he answered the call to the colors, with a commission as first lieutenant in the Medical Corps. He was at Fort McPherson, Atlanta, then three months at Fort Joseph E. Johnston, four months at Kelly Field, San Antonio, Texas, and from Hoboken, New Jersey, sailed for France, landing at Southampton and proceeding at once to Brest. Doctor Ussery in home camps and while overseas had as his chief assignments of professional work duties in connection with the genito-urinary section of the Medical Corps. He was engaged in G. U. work at Brest six weeks, was then transferred for similar duty to the Emory University Base Hospital at St. Quentin, where he remained until December 8, 1918. He was then detached from his unit and put in the Thirtieth Detached Brigade of the Army of Occupation at Coblentz, Germany, doing G. U. work with the Army of Occupation until March 15, 1919. From Brest he sailed for Boston, landing April 16, 1919, and was returned to Fort McPherson, Georgia, employed in G. U. examination and inspection work until discharged November 13, 1919. He entered the army with the rank of first lieutenant and on September 15, 1918, was promoted to captain.

Captain Ussery after his honorable discharge was for twelve months connected with the United States Public Health Service at Atlanta. On December 1, 1920, he located at Dorchester, Virginia, was engaged in general practice there three years, and then moved to Norton. Doctor Ussery has taken post-graduate work in the New York Post Graduate School and Hospital, and has written a number of articles for medical journals. He is chief resident surgeon for the Metropolitan Casualty Insurance Company and is examiner for a number of life insurance companies. Doctor Ussery is a member of the Wise County Medical Society, Medical Society of Virginia, Southern and American Medical Associations.

He enjoys participation in social and civic affairs, and is one of the very popular representatives of his profession in Wise County. He is a thirty-second degree Scottish Rite Mason and Shriner, member of the Knights of Pythias, Kiwanis Club, is a Phi Kappa Psi and Sigma Alpha Epsilon, and member of the Methodist Episcopal Church, South. He married, November 13, 1920, Miss Lucille Roberts, of Rome, Georgia, daughter of William T. and Florence Roberts. Her parents now reside at Atlanta. Mrs. Ussery attended high school at Rome, Georgia. She is a member of the Civic Club of Norton, chairman of the Wise County Red Cross Association, and a member of the Methodist Episcopal Church, South. They have one son, Robert Douglas Ussery, born February 1, 1927.

GLENN TAYLOR FOUST, physician and surgeon at Norton, Wise County, represents a pioneer family of East Tennessee, where the Fousts have lived for three generations.

Doctor Foust was born at New Market, Tennessee, January 25, 1890, son of Milton L. and Mary Isabelle (Parrott) Foust. His grandfather, Wiley Foust, was descended from a family that came from Holland, first settling in Virginia and thence moving over the mountains into East Tennessee. Wiley Foust was captain of a company in the Union army with a Tennessee regiment, and died of smallpox during the war. He had been a merchant at Knoxville, Tennessee. Wiley Foust married a daughter of Col. John Sawyer, of an old Virginia family.

Milton L. Foust was born at Concord, Tennessee, April 18, 1846, and has spent his active life as a planter and farmer and as a veterinary surgeon, and is still living at New Market. He is a leading Republican in politics, an active member of the Presbyterian Church, and for a number of years was a member of the New Market School Board. His wife, Mary Isabelle Parrott, was born in Tazewell, Tennessee, in October, 1844. Her father, Prior Parrott, was a carpenter and contractor at Rutledge, Tennessee, and was a recruiting officer for the Confederate government during the Civil war. Prior Parrott married a Miss Jennings, whose father was one of the first settlers of East Tennessee, owning a large tract of land and had a tavern which is still known as Jennings Ford on the Clinch River.

Dr. Glenn T. Foust was the youngest of a family of children which have been represented in the educational and other professions as well as in business. Doctor Foust attended public schools in Tennessee, being valedictorian of his class in the high school at New Market. For one year he attended Maryville College at Maryville, Tennessee, and in 1911 was graduated valedictorian from Carson and Newman College with the A. B. degree. He then entered the University of Louisville, where he took his M. D. degree in 1915. He had a year of experience as an interne in the Lincoln Memorial Hospital at Knoxville, and for three years practiced at Dorchester, Virginia. He volunteered for service at the time of the World war, and in November, 1918, was commissioned a first lieutenant and was at Camp Greenleaf, Georgia, until honorably discharged on December 18, 1918. Since the war Doctor Foust has practiced at Norton. He has at-

R. S. Baughan

tended clinics at Louisville, Knoxville and elsewhere. Doctor Foust conducts a large general practice, and is known for his special skill and success in obstetrics, and has also employed the facilities of electro therapy in much of his professional work. Doctor Foust is a former president of the Wise County Medical Society, and is a member of the Clinch Valley, State of Virginia and American Medical Associations. He is physician for the Wise Coal & Coke Company, and does a great deal of examination work for life insurance companies.

He formerly held a commission as captain in the Virginia National Guard, attached to the One Hundred and Eighty-third Infantry. While in medical school at Louisville he organized a college Y. M. C. A. and was its president. He has organized classes for Bible study, and is a member of the Presbyterian Church. He is vice commander of the Norton Post of the American Legion, is a Knight Templar Mason and Shriner, member of the Junior Order United American Mechanics, Loyal Order of Moose, Knights of Pythias, Kiwanis Club, and is a member of the Norton School Board.

Doctor Foust married at Athens, Tennessee, June 8, 1916, Miss Irene Burke, daughter of Joseph and Mary (Walker) Burke. Her father was a prominent Republican in his section of Tennessee and for many years served as sheriff of McMinn County. Mrs. Foust finished her education in the Tennessee Wesleyan College at Athens. She is a member of the Daughters of the American Revolution and the Presbyterian Church. Doctor and Mrs. Foust have three children, Glenn Taylor, Jr., Burke and Irene.

RICHARD SPENCER BAUGHAN, chief of the fire department of the city of Norfolk, has risen to that position from the ranks. He has been in the fire fighting service for many years, and has distinguished himself both as an individual and in his capacity to command and direct others.

He was born in James City County, Virginia, January 24, 1884. His grandfather, Richard Baughan, was born in Caroline County, Virginia, and married Frances Demue. Their son, Sidney Lee Baughan, was also born in Caroline County, was educated in rural schools, and was in the service of the Chesapeake & Ohio Railway from early manhood until his death at the age of twenty-nine. He married Lelia Aragon Tyree, who was born in James City County, Virginia, daughter of Sidney Typree. She was left a widow with three children and after a few years married again. The three children were Richard S., Archibald Franklin and Ocie Sydney.

Richard S. Baughan from the age of nine to fourteen lived in a Baptist orphanage, where he was well cared for and given considerable school training. At the age of fourteen he began an apprenticeship at the carpenter's trade, and he is a skilled carpenter and followed the trade as a business until 1910. It was in that year that he joined the city fire department of Norfolk, beginning as a hose man, later was promoted to captain, then to deputy chief, and since November 12, 1927, has been chief of the fire department, at the fire headquarters at Plume and Talbot streets.

Mr. Baughan is a popular citizen of Norfolk, active in Masonry, being affiliated with Berkeley Lodge No. 167, A. F. and A. M., the various Scottish Rite bodies and Khedive Temple of the Mystic Shrine. He and his wife are Baptists. He mar-

ried in 1905 Mary Lavina Culpepper, member of the distinguished Culpepper family of Virginia. She was born at Norfolk,
daughter of Richard and Jennie Culpepper. The four children
of Mr. and Mrs. Baughan are Violette May, Richard Everett,
Virgie Lee and Robert Stanley.

RAYMOND DRAPER WILLIAMS is one of the brothers associated in the firm of Williams Brothers & Company at Pembroke,
a business that has been carried on for a great many years and
which has afforded the medium for the expression of the commercial activities and spirit of enterprise of various members
of this well known family.

Mr. Williams was born at Pembroke December 24, 1896. The
Williams family has been in Virginia since Colonial times. His
great-grandfather, Floyd Williams, was a pioneer farmer and
hunter in Giles County. Madison Williams, son of Floyd Williams, was born and reared in Giles County, and served all
through the four years of the Civil war as a soldier in the Army
of Northern Virginia under Lee. He was a carpenter and contractor, and an active member of the Methodist Episcopal
Church, South. He died in 1900 and is buried at Pembroke.

John Floyd Williams, father of Raymond D., was born at
Pembroke, attended private and public schools, and as a young
man had several years of experience clerking in stores. About
1888 he established a mercantile business of his own at Pembroke. The business for some years was conducted as J. F.
Williams & Company. He gave thirty-five years to this business, and continued active until his death on May 13, 1922. During his life time the business grew and constantly expanded,
taking on new departments of service. At the present time
there are two store buildings on opposite sides of the street, one
used for housing and displaying the great stock of hardware
and the other for undertaking parlors. J. F. Williams served as
postmaster of Pembroke during the McKinley and Roosevelt administrations. He owned a half interest in the Kirk & Williams
Roller Mills, was interested in farming, was twice director of
the First National Bank of Pearisburg and vice president and
director of the Bank of Pembroke.

John Floyd Williams married Anna Draper, who was born
and reared in Pembroke, attended public schools there, and has
always sustained a working part in the Methodist Episcopal
Church, South. She is a daughter of Jesse and Elizabeth
(Napier) Draper, and is a descendant of the famous family that
gave its name to Draper Valley in Pulaski County. Her parents
moved to Giles County from Henry County. John Floyd Williams and wife had a family of eight children: Lillian, wife of
Chapman Hoge, farmer and stock raiser at Pembroke, associated with his father, J. T. S. Hoge; Raymond D.; Mervin, member of the firm Williams Brothers & Company; Noel; Willard,
associated with the Community Loan Company at Bluefield,
West Virginia; Leon, a student of dentistry in the Medical College of Virginia; Doyle; and Mary, attending the Pembroke
High School.

Raymond D. Williams was educated in the grade and high
schools of Pembroke, graduating in 1914, following which he
took a business course in Massey Business College at Richmond.
From business college he returned to Pembroke, and from that
time has had an increasing share of responsibilities in the business founded by his father. After his father died he and his

two brothers, Doyle and Marvin, took over the business and retained the old name until 1929, when they assumed the title of Williams Brothers & Company. Mr. R. D. Williams is also a director in the First National Bank of Pearisburg and is vice president and director of the Bank of Pembroke. Since 1922 he has performed the duties of postmaster of Pembroke.

Mr. Williams is a Royal Arch Mason, being affiliated with Castle Rock No. 334, A. F. and A. M., and Royal Arch Chapter No. 34 of Pearisburg. He is a Republican, and is a member of the Board of Stewards of the Methodist Episcopal Church, South.

He married at Roanoke October 12, 1928, Miss Elizabeth Honaker, of Rocky Gap, Bland County, where she was reared and educated, attending high school and also the Roanoke High School and Marion College at Marion, Virginia. Before her marriage she spent two years teaching in the schools of Bland County. She is a member of the Methodist Episcopal Church, South, and is interested in Republican politics. Mrs. Williams is a daughter of James and Sallie (Jerrell) Honaker, a Bland County family noted elsewhere in this publication. Her father for many years has been a merchant there. Mr. and Mrs. Williams have no children.

Mr. Williams joined the colors as a volunteer in 1918, spending two months in training at Fort Thomas, Kentucky, five months at Fort Adams, Rhode Island, and went overseas in Company C of the Fifty-second Regiment, Coast Artillery Corps. He was located at Brest and St. Nazaire, France, and returned home with his regiment and received an honorable discharge at Camp Houston, Virginia, in May, 1919.

ADOLPHUS EMANUEL SEIBERT was one of the pioneer members of the profession of electrical engineering. It was a matter of pride with him that he had learned what then amounted to a trade in the handling of electrical apparatus under Thomas A. Edison, shortly after Edison came into fame with his early discoveries and inventions.

Mr. Seibert, whose home for many years was at Norfolk, and where he died September 26, 1915, was born in New York City, September 27, 1860. He was the oldest of the four children of Carl and Lillian (Noah) Seibert. His father was a native of Hamburg, Germany, and for many years followed the business of merchant tailoring in New York City.

Adolphus Emanuel Seibert was educated in schools in New York, and learned his trade with Mr. Edison in New Jersey. He gave up electrical work in 1879, and during the following ten years was engaged in the drug business. Mr. Seibert in 1889 located at Norfolk, and from that time until 1913 was associated with the Virginia Light & Power Company as electrical engineer. When he resigned his position with this comapny he became manager of the Jeff Hopheimer theatrical interests, and was thus engaged until his death. He was a very popular citizen, belonged to the Masonic fraternity, Independent Order of Odd Fellows, was a Democrat, and he and his wife were members of the Episcopal Church.

He married in New York City, in September, 1889, Miss Placitt Reed, of Norfolk, daughter of Joshua D. and Mary (Barr) Reed. Her grandfather, Joshua D. Reed, was a naval officer at the Navy Yard at Portsmouth for many years, and when he retired, just before the Civil war, he was presented with a silver serving set by the navy department. He became known as an authority on the construction of the type of warships used in the old navy. Mrs. Seibert's father was a hat manufacturer at Norfolk. Mrs. Seibert's six brothers, out of a family of eleven children, all became Norfolk business men. Mrs. Seibert resides in Norfolk, at 2605 Church Street.

WILMOT W. WALKER, who is county treasurer of Giles County, was born in that county and came to be known by his fellow citizens as a very capable and energetic business man and farmer, and has shown fine qualifications and efficiency in every public office to which he has been chosen.

He was born near Newport in Giles County, January 1, 1873, son of John F. and Maggie (Jones) Walker. His father was born in Botetourt County, Virginia, and as a youth entered the Confederate army, fighting in the battle of Manassas and many subsequent battles and campaigns until the end of the war four years later. During the war his father, George H. Walker, had moved to Giles County, and there John F. Walker rejoined his family and settled down to a life of farming and stock raising. He married after coming to Giles County. He was a merchant for a number of years, and was in business at Eggleston until his death in 1904. His wife, Maggie Jones, was born in Giles County, was educated in private schools and at Blacksburg. She died in April, 1928. Both parents were members of the Lutheran Church. There were eleven children: W. W. Walker, Luther V., J. Tracy, Georgie, W. Chapman, Mary Mae (now deceased), W. Austin, Lelia, Bessie, Annie Laurie, and Kyle, who is deceased.

Wilmot W. Walker was educated in public schools, in the Roanoke College at Salem, and after leaving college was employed for ten years by the Southern Express Company. He left the service of the express company to take up farming and stock raising, and he still owns and operates a fine blue grass farm at Eggleston. He represents that very prosperous agricultural class who are owners of some of the blue grass farms in this rich section of Southwest Virginia.

Mr. Walker in 1912 was elected commissioner of revenue, and served in that capacity eight years. Then, in 1920, he was elected county treasurer, and has been twice reelected to that office, being now in his third consecutive term. Mr. Walker is also a director of the First National Bank of Pearisburg and the First National Bank of Narrows.

Fraternally he is a member of the Masonic fraternity and Kazim Temple of the Mystic Shrine at Roanoke, the Independent Order of Odd Fellows, is a Democrat and a Lutheran.

He married at Rural Retreat, Virginia, October 31, 1905, Miss Rose Hankla, of Rural Retreat, where she was reared and educated. She taught school several years before her marriage and is deeply interested in her church. She is a daughter of Louis P. and Ella (Hawkins) Hankla, now deceased. Her father was a farmer and stock man at Rural Retreat, specializing in the growing of cabbages. Mr. and Mrs. Walker have five daughters: Anna Christine, Margaret Ellen, Mary Lewis, Aline Elizabeth and Martha Hankla. Anna Christine is a graduate of the Pearisburg High School and the Marion Junior College with the class of 1928. The daughters Margaret and Mary are in the Pearisburg High School, and the two youngest children are in grammar school.

Ethel Pilcher

MISS ETHEL PILCHER. Actively and successfully engaged in an occupation for which the country's future position among the nations of the world may largely depend, Miss Ethel Pilcher, of Petersburg, principal of the A. P. Hill School, is eminently qualified for the work in which she is engaged, her influence for the betterment of pupils, community and city being widely recognized and appreciated. A native of Petersburg, and a daughter of Rev. John Mason Pilcher, she is a descendant on the maternal side of one of the brave French Huguenots who, in 1685, after the revocation of the edict of Nantes, fled to England, where he spent his remaining years.

Miss Pilcher is a direct descendant of Richard Pilcher, who married Dorothea Watts, and a relative of Gen. William Stanton Pilcher, who was born in Virginia in 1802; went to Kentucky in 1830; volunteered for service in the Mexican war; and at the time of his death was serving as mayor of Louisville, Kentucky. Miss Pilcher's great-grandfather, Frederick Pilcher, was born in Stafford County, Virginia, in 1769, and in that same county the birth of her grandfather, John Alsop Pilcher, occurred in the year 1796. Frederick Pilcher married Margaret Alsop, a daughter of George and Mary (Wise) Alsop, and into the home they established several children were born.

A Virginian by birth and breeding, John Alsop Pilcher, Esq., followed the cooper's trade in Madison County, Virginia, for a time, subsequently locating on the James River, a few miles above Richmond. A good business man, he acquired much real estate in that vicinity and valuable residential property in Richmond. Active in public affairs, he served one or more terms as high sheriff of Henrico County. He married Elizabeth Ann Parsons, a daughter of Samuel Pleasants and Elizabeth Ann Parsons, and granddaughter of Amos and Sarah (Binford) Ladd. John Alsop Pilcher died January 28, 1852, aged fifty-six years. His widow survived him many years, passing away October 27, 1870.

One of a family of six children that grew to years of maturity, Rev. John Mason Pilcher prepared for college at the L. I. Squire Clerical School at Richmond, Virginia, and in 1861 was graduated from Richmond College with the degree of M. A. At the outbreak of the Civil war in 1861 he volunteered for service, but on account of weak eyes was not accepted. He subsequently taught school until July, 1862, when he became clerk in Military Hospital No. 10, in Richmond, Virginia. The following September he was transferred to the office of Medical Director E. S. Gaillard, of Richmond. In May, 1863, Mr. Pilcher enlisted in an artillery company that was a part of the Tredegar Battalion, and was attached to the Second Regiment of Local Defense Troops, continuing with his command until the close of the conflict. His parole, dated April 21, 1865, is carefully preserved by his son, Dr. William Pilcher.

In March, 1868, Rev. John M. Pilcher organized the Sydney, now the Grove, Avenue Baptist Church in Richmond, and in 1871 had charge of different pastorates in Alleghany and Bath counties. On February 27, 1870, he was ordained to the full work of the ministry, and in 1880 was elected general superintendent of the Sunday School Board of the Baptist General Association of Virginia, located in Petersburg, and retained the position until his resignation in 1908. He was the first chaplain of the A. P. Hill Camp of Confederate Veterans. In 1890 he had the distinction of having the degree of D. D. conferred upon him by Richmond College.

Rev. John Mason Pilcher, D. D., married, December 21, 1865, in Goochland County, Virginia, Mary Lucy DuVal, who was born April 20, 1845, in Chesterfield County, Virginia, a daughter of Edwin J. and Rhoda Thomas (Halsey) DuVal, and a direct descendant of Marion DuVal, a Huguenot who settled in Maryland in 1694. She passed to the life beyond October 23, 1904.

A close student from her girlhood days, Miss Ethel Pilcher attended first the Anderson School on West Washington Street, and after her graduation from Hollins College, class of 1905, began her career as a teacher. She taught first in the Anderson School, then in the R. E. Lee School, later in the high school, being very successful in her chosen occupation. Since 1918 Miss Pilcher has served as principal of the A. P. Hill School, which is located on Halifax Street, near the site of the battle in which the brave General lost his life. A fine statue of the General adorns the lobby of the building, a fitting memorial for the gallant soldier. Miss Pilcher is a member of the Virginia State and the National Education Associations, and is a Daughter of the Confederacy.

WILLIAM GRAY GWINN, whose home is at Rich Creek in Giles County, is a sterling representative of the younger generation of Southwest Virginians, a farmer, land owner, business man, a generous and public spirited citizen and one whose time and resources have been liberally given to the general welfare.

Mr. Gwinn was born at Rich Creek, August 7, 1894, son of T. M. and Lula (Shumate) Gwinn. The Gwinn family lived in Colonial times in old Augusta County, Virginia, and subsequently moved to Summers and Greenbrier counties in what is now West Virginia. T. M. Gwinn was born in Summers County, attended public schools there, and about 1890 moved to Rich Creek, Virginia. He was a teacher, farmer and cattle raiser, and died in 1918. His wife, Lula Shumate, was born on the site of the beautiful home of her son, William Gray Gwinn, at Rich Creek. The old Shumate house was a brick building which stood there during the Civil war, and the walls showed a number of shell holes made from the Yankee artillery fired from the other side of New River. Her father, Hardin Shumate, was a Confederate soldier, was wounded and died from the effects of the amputation of his leg. He is buried in Rich Creek Cemetery. The Shumates have been people of prominence in this section of Giles County for a great many years. Mrs. T. M. Gwinn lives at the home of her son at Rich Creek. She is a member of the Baptist Church and is eligible to membership in the Daughters of the American Revolution and the United Daughters of the Confederacy. She was the mother of two sons, Earl Gwinn, who died when two years old, and William G.

William Gray Gwinn attended public school in his home locality and the Concord State Normal School at Athens, West Virginia. He was in readiness for the call to the colors when America entered the World war, and in May, 1918, joined the United States Marine Corps and spent six months in training at Paris Island, South Carolina, and then for a few months was at Quantico, Virginia, until honorably discharged in January, 1919. During the past ten years Mr. Gwinn has given his attention to a diverse range of business interests, chiefly farming and cattle raising. He is a director of the First National

Bank of Narrows, director in the Virginia Wholesale Grocery Company, director in the Builders Supply Company, director in the Rich Creek Hardware Company.

He is active in the Masonic fraternity and is affiliated with Kazim Temple of the Mystic Shrine at Roanoke. He is a past commander of the American Legion Post at Narrows. He is a democrat, and a loyal member of the Baptist Church, having been superintendent of the Sunday School seven years and is now secretary.

Mr. Gwinn married at Narrows, Virginia, November 20, 1920, Miss Catherine Middleton, of Narrows, member of a prominent family of religious and social workers. She was educated in public schools at Lexington, Virginia, where she was born, and subsequently graduated from the high school at Limestone, Tennessee, and also attended Sullins College at Bristol, Virginia, and the State Teachers College at Radford, graduating in 1916. For two years she taught in Charlotte County, Virginia, and three years in Giles County. Mrs. Gwinn is a Methodist, member of the United Daughters of the Confederacy and Daughters of the American Revolution, and has filled all the offices in the Eastern Star. She is a daughter of John William and Sarah Virginia (Figgatt) Middleton. Her father was born in Rockingham County, Virginia, son of William and Ann Middleton, and was educated in Washington College in Tennessee. He served all through the war as a Confederate soldier in Company I of the Twenty-seventh Virginia Infantry. He was in Stonewall Jackson's Brigade and for some time was a Federal prisoner. After the war he followed civil engineering and farming, and died March 18, 1907. His wife passed away May 25, 1902, and both are buried at Limestone, Tennessee, where they lived for several years and where some of their children were educated. Mrs. Gwinn's brothers and sisters are: Ann, wife of J. M. Byer, of Lynchburg, Virginia; Nellie Dessler, a teacher at Benton, Tennessee; Ida, wife of Rev. C. H. Schad, both missionary workers living in Arkansas; Augusta, who is Mrs. Robert Fothergill, of Richmond, Virginia; John William, Jr., living at Portola, California; Sarah, Mrs. William Clipper, of Tampa, Florida; Rowena, the wife of J. B. Williams, of Fresno, California; Burgess Middleton, living at Fresno, California; Virginia, the wife of Rev. C. A. Hall, a minister of the Methodist Episcopal Church in the North Georgia Conference; Katherine, the wife of William G. Gwinn; and Florence, who is Mrs. Robert O. Crockett, of Tazewell, Virginia.

KYLE M. GEARHART, Doctor of Dental Surgery, is practicing at Pearisburg, with offices in the Law Building of that city. He is a member of a prominent family in this section of Virginia, and was born at Kimball, West Virginia, July 11, 1900.

His father, Andrew Jackson Gearhart, was born in Floyd County, Virginia, and for many years was connected with the coal business at Vivian, West Virginia. He died in 1905. He married Laura Betsy Lilly, who was born and reared in West Virginia, and is a member of the Methodist Church.

To their marriage the living children are: Corda Edna, Lora Bryant, Lota Sewell, Dr. Kyle Montague and Frank Harold. Mr. Gearhart's mother is now the wife of J. T. Coak, an engineer on the Pocahontas Division of the Norfolk and West Virginia Railway and live at Roanoke. To their marriage were born three children: Lenora Fay; Leolin Corinne and U. Louise.

Kyle M. Gearhart grew up at Roanoke, attending school there and also in West Virginia. He graduated from the Jefferson High School at Roanoke in 1922. During the World war he was enrolled in the Naval Reserve Corp. He had one year of preparatory work in George Washington University at Washington, and graduated from the dental department of Georgetown University at Washington in 1928. Doctor Gearhart after finishing his course succeeded to the practice of Dr. Frank B. Miller, deceased, at Pearisburg, purchasing his office and equipment in the Law Building, and his own thorough training and personality have insured his continued success in his profession. He is a member of the Xi Psi Phi fraternity, of the Virginia and Roanoke Dental Societies and the Southwest Virginia Study Club. He is a Mason, a Democrat and a member of the Methodist Church.

FREDERICK NICHOLAS BULL as a business man of Richmond devoted his entire active career to commercial lines, and the store he established and conducted for so many years has been continued since his death, a daughter being the active manager of the business.

He was born in Richmond, October 17, 1869, and died in that city March 27, 1924. His parents were Henry and Margaret (Victor) Bull. The Bull family came from Maryland and settled in Richmond immediately after the Civil war. There were three sons, George B., Charles Henry and Frederick Nicholas.

The late Mr. Bull was educated in Richmond, and as a young man worked two years in a chinaware store. His liking for outdoor occupations took him into the service of the Snyder Foundry Company of Richmond, and he was in every department of that industry, reaching the responsibilities of general foreman. Then, in 1917, he became a general merchant, and continued the active head of the business until his death. His store is widely known and patronized as "Bull Market," and is directed by his daughter Alice Virginia. The late Mr. Bull was a Republican and was affiliated with the B. P. O. Elks, Order of Owls, and the Lions Club. His daughter Margaret is an active worker in the Baptist Young People's Union, while Edna is a teacher in Sunday School, and all are members of the Baptist Church.

Frederick Nicholas Bull married Sallie Meredith Lipscomb, member of a prominent old family of Virginia. Mrs. Bull resides at 2228 Park Avenue, Richmond. She is a daughter of William Talleyrand and Agnes (Kinstrey) Lipscomb. Her grandfather, William B. Lipscomb, son of Pemberton and Lucy Lipscomb, of King William County, was born October 11, 1782, and died in 1850. He was twice married, and on December 30, 1820, married for his second wife Sallie Meredith, daughter of Samuel and Elizabeth Meredith, of King William County. She was born January 9, 1799. They had a family of eight children, the three sons surviving infancy being Capt. Martin Meredith, born March 5, 1823; William Talleyrand, born July 18, 1824; John B., born May 15, 1827.

William Talleyrand Lipscomb enlisted in the Confederate army, serving in Wise's Brigade, and was killed in action at Petersburg. Before the war he was a brick contractor in Richmond.

Mr. and Mrs. Bull had a family of four children: Grace Arants, who died at the age of twenty; Edna Irene, who was

educated in the Richmond Normal School and is a member of the Teachers Association; Alice Virginia, the wife of Everet Tillman, of Charlotte Court House; and Margaret Victor, wife of David Walter McGuire, a pharmacist, and they have a daughter, Sally Grace, born April 28, 1929.

WILLIAM PEDRO TAYLOR, who is manager of the Town of Crewe, had preparatory to taking that office a broad experience as a banker and in public office.

He is a native of Nottoway County, born in September, 1878, son of John K. and Mary L. (Morgan) Taylor, both natives of the same county. His father gave thirty-five years of his life to his farm and after that was in the employ of the Norfolk & Western Railway Company until his death in February, 1921. The mother died in August of the same year.

William P. Taylor was reared and educated in Nottoway County. His first experience off the farm was as a clerk in the local offices of the Norfolk & Western Railway Company. He was in the service of the railroad for over a quarter of a century, from 1895 to 1922. When he left the railroad service he was in the First National Bank of Crewe as assistant cashier until August, 1926, at which date he was chosen the first town manager of the Town of Crewe and was reelected to that office in September, 1927. His work has been a justification of the plan of local government whereby the executive and administrative duties are entrusted to Mr. Taylor through the cooperation and the supervision of the Town Council.

Mr. Taylor married December 10, 1910, Miss Esther Ellett, daughter of W. W. and Pattie (Emoughty) Ellett, natives of Nottoway County. Her father was yard master at Crewe for the Norfolk & Western Railway until his death.

Upon the organization of the Crewe Chamber of Commerce on March 29, 1928, Mr. Taylor was chosen its secretary. He has been active in town affairs for sixteen years and from 1912 to 1926 was commissioner of revenue. He has been secretary of the lodge of Independent Order of Odd Fellows since 1910, is a member of the Sons of Confederate Veterans and the Christian Church.

JOHN J. CARPER, the postmaster of Pearisburg, was born and reared in that locality, and has had a large amount of business experience. He has been a farmer, merchant and commercial salesman, and has handled the administration of the postoffice in a way to satisfy its patrons.

He was born near Pearisburg in Giles County November 16, 1878, son of John W. and Lula (Woods) Carper. His father was a native of Pulaski County and was ten years of age when the family moved to Giles County. He was educated in private schools, and was a soldier all through the four years of the Civil war in the Confederate army. He participated in some of the campaigns in the Valley of Virginia. After the war he was a farmer and stock man, and for several years was deputy treasurer under County Treasurer W. J. Woods. He died in 1917 and is buried in the family cemetery near Pearisburg. His wife, Lula Woods, was born and reared in Giles County, attended private schools and was a member of the Methodist Church. She died in 1885, the mother of eight children, seven of whom grew up: Nannie, Mirtie, William O., Edwin L. (a merchant at Pearisburg), John J., Sadie M. and Benjamin L. John W.

Carper after the death of his first wife married Miss Allie Wall, of Giles County, who died in 1905. Her five children were Emma E., Frank W., A. Eugene, Henry Clay (who died in infancy) and Fred.

John J. Carper grew up on his father's farm and was educated in public schools. He taught school two years, and followed farming and stock raising as his occupation until he entered merchandising at Pearisburg. He was in business there ten years and in 1918 became a traveling salesman, representing Leas & McVitty of Salem, Virginia, three years and was also located at Huntington, West Virginia, as representative for Anderson & Newcomb.

Mr. Carper was appointed postmaster of Pearisburg in 1923, being commissioned by President Coolidge. He is a Republican in politics and one of the leaders of his party in Giles County. Mr. Carper is a Knight Templar Mason, a member of Kazim Temple of the Mystic Shrine at Roanoke. He served two successive years as master of Giles Lodge No. 106, A. F. and A. M. He takes an active part in the Methodist Episcopal Church, South, and formerly taught a class in Sunday School. Mr. Carper is unmarried. During the World war he was enrolled for service with the Y. M. C. A., and had filled out his questionnaire for duty as an overseas secretary on the day the armistice was signed.

MRS. EVA D. BATTEN, widow of Edgar Batten, maintains her home in the city of Norfolk, her birth having occurred in this fine old maritime city in the year 1858, and her ancestral lines touching distinguished Colonial families of the South. Mrs. Batten, a gracious gentlewoman of culture, still continues her activities in church, and in her home community her circle of friends is limited only by that of her acquaintances.

Mrs. Eva Doretha (Fatherley) Batten received her youthful education principally in the city of Baltimore, Maryland, her father having there centered his business interests many years. Mrs. Batten is a daughter of the late William Joseph and Mary Susan (Lawrence) Fatherley, both of whom were born in Virginia. William Joseph Fatherley was a steamboat owner and operator both before and after the Civil war, with headquarters in Baltimore, Maryland, and he was long and prominently identified also with the lumber industry. He was a citizen of Baltimore at the time of his death, which occurred when he was sixty-nine years of age, and his wife passed away at the age of eighty-one years. Mrs. Mary Susan (Lawrence) Fatherley was a descendant of the Lawrence family that made settlement in Princess Anne County, Virginia, shortly before the inception of the Revolutionary war, in which conflict representatives of the family served as patriot soldiers of the Continental Line. Mrs. Fatherley was a daughter of William and Janet (Randolph) Lawrence, her father having been a soldier in Washington's army in the Revolution and having been with that army at Valley Force, the stage of one of the most noteworthy phases in the history of the great national struggle for independence. Mrs. Janet (Randolph) Lawrence was a descendant in the distinguished Randolph family, including William, Beverly, Edmund, early burgesses, and others, that has played so prominent a part in the history of the nation from the Colonial period onward, and that has been notable for leadership in connection with the history of Virginia. Mrs. Janet

Allan Epes

Lawrence (born October 2, 1810, and died February 22, 1862) was a granddaughter of Thomas Jefferson Randolph, who became the owner of a large and valuable plantation estate in Virginia and who was a grandson of President Thomas Jefferson, for whom he served as private messenger when that great American was president of the United States. Mrs. Batten of this review is likewise able to claim ancestral kinship with the Peyton family, likewise influential in the Colonial history of Virginia, in the Revolution and later in the Civil war. The Peytons intermarried with the Randolphs so that in later generations many Randolphs were Peytons and many Peytons were Randolphs.

Mrs. Batten is the elder of a family of two children, her sister, Ida Victoria, having become the wife of Harry Eugene Jenkins, a prominent hotel man in Baltimore, and having been a resident of the Maryland metropolis at the time of her death, her one surviving child having been her son Paul. In Norfolk County was solemnized the marriage of Eva Doretha Fatherley and Edgar Batten, who was a resident of Princess Anne and whose active career was marked principally by his association with agriculture. The one surviving child of this union is Gilmer Randolph Batten, who is associated with the Reynolds Tobacco Company of Winston-Salem, North Carolina. Gilmer Randolph Batten married Miss Flora Burch, of Atlanta, Georgia, and they have one child, June.

Mrs. Batten is a member of the Baptist Church, in which connection it may be recorded that one of her Colonial ancestors of the Lawrence line was a Baptist clergyman who preached the Gospel in Virginia wilderness districts prior to the War of the Revolution. Mrs. Batten, as may readily be inferred, is distinctly eligible for affiliation with the Daughters of the American Revolution, and to her remain many hallowed memories and associations that touch her ancestral history in both Virginia and Maryland.

ALLAN EPES is a member of the Nottoway County bar, practicing law at Blackstone. He has made his professional career in the community where he was born and reared and where his family has been known for generations. Many prominent men have borne the name Epes in Virginia since early Colonial times.

Mr. Epes was born in Nottoway County January 31, 1879, son of Freeman and Rebecca C. (Robinson) Epes. He traces his ancestry back to the year 1670, and his great-great-grandfather Epes settled in Amelia County, Virginia, about 1720. It was in 1793 that Nottoway County was formed from a portion of the older Amelia County. Mr. Epes' mother was a great-great-granddaughter of a captain in the Revolutionary army. Freeman Epes was born in Nottoway County, while his wife was a native of Amelia County. He was a private in the Confederate army, in Company E of the Third Virginia Cavalry, and following the war was a merchant at Nottoway Court House until 1880, when he removed to Blackstone and there conducted a dry goods and clothing business. During his later years he operated a fertilizer factory. He was successful in business and a man of more than ordinary influence in politics in his section of the state. He died April 15, 1916, and his widow now resides at Richmond.

Allan Epes was reared and educated at Blackstone, attending private and public schools, and was a student in Hoge Academy,

a very excellent preparatory school which had been founded
by his uncle at Blackstone. His professional education was acquired in Washington and Lee University, where he graduated
with the LL. B. degree in 1901. Mr. Epes began practice in
1902 at Newport News, and in 1905 returned to Blackstone,
where for over twenty years he has enjoyed a well deserved
leadership as a lawyer. Mr. Epes is a member of the County,
Virginia State, and American Bar Associations.

He married in December, 1920, Miss Inez Lambert, daughter
of J. P. Lambert, a native of Nottoway County. Her father
for many years lived and cultivated a large farm in Nottoway
County, but is now living retired at Blackstone. Her mother
died in 1893.

Mr. Epes is a man of more than one interest, and some of
these interests are invested with public importance. He has
always enjoyed the sport of hunting, has kept a pack of dogs,
and his recreation is fox hunting or bird hunting. At the present
time he is turning his interest as a sportsman to good account
by serving as commissioner of inland game and fisheries. He
also owns farming land. He is a member of the Phi Delta
Theta fraternity, is a Democrat and a Presbyterian, and a member of the Sons of the Confederacy.

JOHN T. BORUM is secretary and general manager of the
Eastern Shore Publishing Company of Onancock, publishers of
the *Eastern Shore News,* one of the most prosperous weekly
publications in Virginia and a newspaper that has no rival as
a news and advertising medium on the Eastern Shore.

Mr. Borum was born at Accomac Court House, Virginia,
His father was born in Mathews County, Virginia, and his
July 13, 1897, son of George B. and Blanche (Fogle) Borum.
mother at Baltimore. George B. Borum is a veteran old time
printer and newspaper man, and was one of the organizers of
the *Eastern Shore News,* which was established in 1897. He is
still a stockholder in the Eastern Shore Publishing Company,
the majority of the stock in which is owned by John T. Borum.

The later was reared and educated in Onancock, and since
the age of fourteen has known no other business and has given
practically uninterrupted service to the trade of printer and
the occupation of newspaper work. Since he was twenty years
of age he has been identified financially and in the management
of the Eastern Shore Publishing Company. In 1918 he acquired
a third interest in the business.

It was during the same year that he enlisted for service during the World war and went overseas, being with the Army of
Occupation. He received his honorable discharge in June, 1919,
and at once took over the active management and control of the
newspaper at Onancock. This paper was for a number of years
published as the *Accomac News.* In 1924 the company bought
the *Eastern Shore News* of Cape Charles, and the consolidation
has resulted in retaining the title of the latter journel, the
Eastern Shore News, now published by the Eastern Shore Publishing Company, Incorporated. The *Eastern Shore News* has
a circulation of 4,287 copies. It carries more advertising and
news than any other weekly paper published in Virginia. The
company has a thoroughly modern plant, equipped with presses
and linotypes and other machinery, and handles a large amount
of commercial printing. While Mr. Borum is the largest stockholder in the company, he has a group of associates and fellow

stockholders comprising some of the most prominent men on the Eastern Shore, his fellow directors being G. Walter Mapp, S. F. Rogers, Sr., J. N. Belote, E. V. Downes, J. H. Ayres, J. W. Topping, Roy D. White, J. S. Mills and J W. Wilson.

Mr. Borum is a member of the American Legion Post, the Rotary Club, Masonic fraternity, Junior Order United American Mechanics, is a Democrat in politics and a member of the Methodist Episcopal Church.

He married Miss Thelma Bradley, daughter of A. O. Bradley, a farmer at Riverton in Wicomico County, Maryland.

GEORGE A. VERMILLION, president of the Bank of Dublin, is one of the foremost men of Pulaski County, and formerly was deeply interested in agricultural pursuits. His advance has been steady and healthy, and what he has today he owes to his industry and sound business judgment. He and his family are very prominent in Dublin and Pulaski County, and are generous of their time and money in supporting all worthwhile civic movements.

The birth of George A. Vermillion occurred near Lynchburg, Virginia, May 9, 1864, and he is a son of C. E. and Martha (Morehead) Vermillion. C. E. Vermillion was born and reared in Campbell County, Virginia, and he attended several private schools, as at that time the public-school system was not what it is today. During the early part of the war he served in the Confederate army and participated in some of the engagements in the vicinity of Lynchburg, but was honorably discharged on account of disability and returned to his farm. In 1864 he came to Pulaski County, and continued his farming and stockraising until his death, which occurred in 1913, when he was seventy-five years old. His remains are interred in the Dublin Cemetery. The Vermillion family is of French extraction, and its members have long been prominent in Virginian affairs. Mrs. Martha (Morehead) Vermillion was born and reared in Pulaski County, and her education was secured in a girl's college at Wytheville. All her life she was active in the work of the Presbyterian Church, of which she was an earnest member. Her death occurred in 1915, when she was seventy-three years old, and she lies by the side of her husband in Dublin Cemetery. Seven children were born to her and her husband: George A., who is the eldest; Minnie R., who is the wife of I. H. Harry, of Falls Mills, Virginia; Sarah Frances, who is deceased, was the wife of J. T. Harper, formerly of Pulaski County, but now of Missouri; E. V., who resides at Clifton Forge, Virginia; A. B., who resides in Richmond, Virginia; C. E., who resides at Dublin; and Leona, who is the wife of T. P. Crockett, of Pulaski, Virginia.

George A. Vermillion attended public schools of Pulaski County, and when he left school he went to Lynchburg, where he entered the employ of R. E. Old, a merchant, and clerked for him and other merchants of Lynchburg for thirteen years. In 1894 he returned to Dublin, and bought the old Camp of Instruction farm near Dublin, where he continued to farm until 1925. While developing his estate, and becoming one of the orchardists of the county, he built up a large and very productive orchard, and carried on a store in Dublin. In 1925 he sold these interests. In the meanwhile, in 1901, he organized the Bank of Dublin, and has been its vice president or president ever since, his incumbency of the latter office covering a period of five years, or from 1923. He is also a director of the Pulaski Trust Company and of the Pulaski Veneer Company of Pulaski. An active Democrat, for a number of years he was a member of the City Council of Dublin, and while so serving was instrumental in securing some very constructive legislation in behalf of the city. During his earlier years he was an active member of the Odd Fellows and Knights of Pythias, and still belongs to these fraternities. A strong believer in co-operation, he is an aggressive member of the Business Men's Club. The Presbyterian Church holds his membership and receives his generous support.

On June 19, 1901, Mr. Vermillion married at Dublin Miss Claudia Darst, of Dublin. She was educated in the local schools and Martha Washington College, Abingdon, Virginia, and for a few years taught in the public schools of Pulaski County. Her intellectual attainments make her a valued member of the Dublin Woman's Club and other organizations, and she is a member of the Methodist Episcopal Church, South, and belongs to its Missionary Society. She is a daughter of Maj. James H. and Margaret (Tralkinger) Darst. Major Darst served most gallantly in the Confederate army during the war between the states, and after the close of the war he represented Pulaski County in the Virginia State Legislature for some years. By occupation he was a farmer, stockraiser and merchant, and a man of prominence in the business world, and when he died, in 1907, Dublin lost one of its most representative citizens. Mrs. Darst survives her husband, and, although eighty-seven years old, is still living in the old Darst home at Dublin.

Mr. and Mrs. Vermillion have had three children born to their marriage: Carl Wesley, who died at the age of four years; Lula Frances, who was educated in the Dublin High School and Elizabeth College, Salem, Virginia, and Martha Washington College, Abingdon, Virginia, married, May 17, 1928, Robert Rolin Moore, of Pulaski, manager of the R. R. Moore Wholesale Grocery Company; and Margaret, who is attending the Dublin public schools.

A man of unusual business capacity, Mr. Vermillion's years of abundant and orderly work have resulted in acquired wealth and the sane enjoyment of it, and he has at the same time maintained his interest in securing and preserving the welfare of his community. He has given strict attention to his business, conducting each line in which he has been engaged with a thoughtful and intelligent management which could not help but bring about satisfactory results. Mr. Vermillion keeps himself thoroughly posted on public events and matters of general interest, and is highly esteemed as a forceful, substantial man and excellent citizen.

GEORGE MASON, distinguished by many years of service as city attorney of Petersburg, was born at Hunting Quarter in Sussex County, Virginia, July 4, 1853. He was a descendant of Capt. John and Elizabeth Mason, of Surry County, one of whose sons, Col. David Mason, commanded the Fifteenth Virginia Regiment in the Revolutionary war. Isaac Mason, a son of Capt. John, was the father of John Mason, who married Elizabeth Peters, and their son, Anthony Mason, married Martha Lanier. Anthony Mason was the grandfather of the late George Mason.

John T. J. Mason, father of George Mason, was born April 10, 1813, in Sussex County, became a lawyer, served as clerk

Hugh R. Smith

of court, and died November 4, 1874. He married Susan Graves in 1846. She died in 1879 They reared four children, Mollie S., Martha Z., George and Lucy Frances.

George Mason was educated by a private tutor, attended the Brunswick Academy, and in 1871 entered the University of Virginia, pursuing the academic course for two years, and in 1874 graduated from the School of Law. He was a member of the Virginia bar nearly half a century, first practicing at Chesterfield Court House, and in 1880 locating at Petersburg. In 1893 he was elected city attorney and held that office consecutively thirty years, until his death on December 4, 1923.

Mr. Mason married, November 6, 1884, Ann Harrison Cocke, member of several distinguished families of old Virginia. She was born in Prince George County November 6, 1860. Her father, Commodore Harrison H. Cocke, was born in Surry County, son of Walter and Ann Carter (Harrison) Cocke, grandson of John and Rebecca (Starke) Cocke. Harrison H. Cocke married Emily Bannister, daughter of John Monroe and Mary B. A. (Volling) Bannister and granddaughter of John Banister, a Revolutionary soldier. The Harrison and Cocke families came from Yorkshire, England, three brothers, Walter, John and Thomas Cocke, settling in Surry County, Walter, the ancestor of Mrs. Mason, having his home at Montpelier in that county.

Mr. and Mrs. Mason reared three children, Emily Banister, John Blair and Ann Harrison Mason.

HUGH RITCHIE SMITH. Possessing the habits of thrift and industry characteristic of his Scotch ancestry, Hugh Ritchie Smith, of Petersburg, is favorably known as city commissioner of revenue, a position of trust and responsibility. A son of the late Hugh Ritchie Smith, Sr., Hugh Ritchie Smith has ever been a resident of his native city.

His paternal grandfather, James Smith, was born, reared and educated in Scotland, the famed City of Ayr having been his place of birth. Immigrating from there to the United States in early manhood, he came directly to Virginia, locating in Petersburg, where he subsequently began the manufacture of soap and candles, an occupation that proved so profitable he continued it for many years. His wife, whose maiden name was Ann Ritchie, came from Scotland to America in early womanhood, and soon after her arrival met the attractive young man, James Smith, who wooed and won her for his bride. Five sons were born to their union, William C., James, Hugh Ritchie, John Charles and Archibald. The four older sons served in the Confederate army during the Civil war, but Archibald was too young to leave home. Hugh Ritchie was the father of the subject of this sketch. James, who was in the employ of the Southern Railroad Company, resided in Columbus, Georgia, where he died. William C., of Nashville, Tennessee, was an architect and died in the Philippines. Archibald, living near Petersburg, is a florist, while John Charles was a farmer near Petersburg and died on his farm.

Hugh Ritchie Smith, Sr., was educated in the public schools of Petersburg, Virginia, and as a young man enlisted for service in the Confederate army, becoming a member of Company E, Twelfth Regiment, Virginia Volunteers, in General Mahone's Brigade. He was an active participant in many of the engagements in and around Richmond and Petersburg, and in the Gettysburg campaign. He was promoted to the rank of adjutant, and served until the close of the conflict. Then, until the death of his father, he was associated with him in the manufacture of soap, later succeeding to the business. After appointment as postmaster by President Cleveland he held the office four years. He was subsequently appointed city commissioner of revenue to fill out an unexpired term, and at its conclusion was continued in that capacity until his death in 1910. He married Mary Jane West, who was born in Petersburg, and here spent her life, passing away in 1912. Of their union four children were born, as follows: James R., who as a young man engaged in the insurance business, and died at the early age of twenty-eight years; Mamie, a resident of Petersburg; and Eugenia, who married James Clift, of Richmond, Virginia, and has one child, William Clift.

After his graduation from the Petersburg High School with the class of 1892 Hugh Ritchie Smith was first employed as assistant cashier of a building and loan association. He was later engaged for a time in mercantile pursuits, clerking for a while in a retail grocery, and subsequently occupying a similar position with a wholesale grocery company, and still later serving as clerk in a trunk factory. In 1910, on the death of his father, he was appointed city commissioner of revenue to fill out his father's unexpired term, and has since, by election and reelections continued in this position, his long retainment of it bearing visible evidence of his efficiency and ability.

Mr. Smith has been twice married. He married first, in 1907, Martha Elizabeth Brockwell, who was born in Petersburg, a daughter of James Brockwell. Her death, which occurred in January, 1919, was deeply deplored by a host of relatives and friends. Mr. Smith married, in May, 1921, Mabel W. Glinn, who was born in Richmond, Virginia, a daughter of Robert Glinn, a life long resident of the Old Dominion.

Mr. Smith cast his first presidential ballot for William Jennings Bryan. He is a Mason, and an active member of the Second Presbyterian Church, in which he is serving as elder.

GEORGE WALTER MAPP as attorney, member of the State Senate and as a citizen represents one of the very interesting sections of old Virginia, the Eastern Shore, Accomac County.

He was born in that county May 25, 1873, son of Dr. John E. and Margaret Benson (LeCato) Mapp, grandson of George Bowdoin and Ann Wharton (Edmonds) Mapp, great-grandson of George T. Mapp, and a descendant of John Mapp, who lived in Northampton County as early as 1634. The Mapp family is of English descent, while the LeCato family is French in origin. The Mapps have been planters and farmers on the Eastern Shore for a number of generations. Dr. John E. Mapp was a graduate of the College of Physicians and Surgeons at Baltimore, and for half a century he carried on the practice of medicine in Accomac County.

George Walter Mapp grew up in the home of his father, "Woodland," attended public schools, graduated with the degree of Licentiate of Instruction from the College of William and Mary in 1891, and while continuing his classical education there he served as assistant professor of English and history for two years under Dr. J. Leslie Hall. He graduated with the Bachelor of Arts degree in 1894, being president of his class. He was captain of the first football team of William and Mary, and active in other athletics. As a scholar he won membership in the distinguished fraternity Phi Beta Kappa. While teaching in Hagsett Military Academy at Danville, Kentucky, he studied law at Center College, the head of the law department being the famous Kentucky orator, the late J. Proctor Knott. He was graduated with his law degree in 1897, and in the same year was admitted to practice at both the Kentucky and Virginia bars. He has practiced thirty years in Accomac County, and has also been associated with law firms at Richmond and in other counties of the Eastern Shore.

He was elected chairman of the Democratic party of Accomac County in 1905. In 1911 he was elected a member of the State Senate, representing the Thirty-seventh District, comprising the counties of Accomac, Northampton and Princess Anne. He represented this important district in the Senate for twelve years. He was especially distinguished in the Legislature by his advocacy of temperance and welfare laws, the State Prohibition Law being known as the Mapp Act. He has also supported good roads legislation and all matters for the welfare of the schools. Senator Mapp is a farmer as well as a lawyer, owning and supervising several extensive farms in the Eastern Shore District. In 1918 he was defeated for the Democratic nomination for Congress by 148 votes, and in 1925 was likewise defeated for Democratic nomination for Governor of Virginia.

He has been president of the Accomac County Bar Association, is a member of the Virginia State Bar Association and is a member of the Board of Visitors of the College of William and Mary. During the World war he was a member of the Legal Advisory Board. In his law practice he has represented several of the prominent banking institutions of the Eastern Shore.

He married, November 27, 1900, Miss Georgia R. Quinby, daughter of Upshur B. and Georgia (Richardson) Quinby. Her father was a lawyer. Mrs. Mapp died July 31, 1901. Mr. Mapp married, November 10, 1910, Miss Mildred Townsend Aydelotte, daughter of Dr. John S. and Delia (Townsend) Aydelotte, of Snow Hill, Maryland. Senator Mapp has two children: John A. and George Walter, Jr.

FRANCIS BEATTIE HUTTON, of Abingdon, who died May 19, 1928, was for many years an outstanding representative of the Virginia bar. Outside of his own judicial district his most notable service to the state at large was as a member of the Virginia Code Commission.

Judge Hutton was born at Glade Spring, Virginia, January 28, 1858, son of Dr. Arthur Dixon and Sarah Buchanon (Ryburn) Hutton, both natives of Washington County, where their respective families were established at an early date. His father was a graduate of Jefferson Medical College of Philadelphia, served as a surgeon in a Virginia regiment in the Confederate army, and otherwise devoted his entire active career to the practice of medicine in his home county.

Francis B. Hutton took the A. B. and A. M. degrees at Emory and Henry College, attended the law department of the University of Virginia, and was a member of the bar of Washington County nearly half a century. In his later years a son joined him in sharing in the heavy practice of the law firm of Hutton & Hutton at Abingdon.

Judge Hutton served as commonwealth attorney of Washington County, and was United States district attorney in the first term of President Cleveland. He served twelve years as county judge and twelve years on the bench of the Twenty-third Judicial Circuit. He resigned from the circuit bench to become one of the three members of the Virginia Code Commission appointed by Governor Stuart. The commission was engaged in its important task of revising the Virginia code for four years, and to the accomplishment of this great task Judge Hutton gave the full benefit of his ripe scholarship, long and successful experience on the bench and in active practice.

Judge Hutton served as president of the Board of Trustees of Stonewall Jackson College of Abingdon. He was also president of the Board of Trustees of Hampden-Sidney College. He was an elder in the Presbyterian Church, member of the Masonic fraternity, the Virginia Bar Association and the American Bar Association. He was a Democrat.

Judge Hutton married Miss Jennie Orr Preston, who was born in Washington County in January, 1865, and died September 28, 1910. She was the mother of five children: Arthur Preston, lawyer, associated with his father until the latter's death at Abingdon; Edward John, who died May 26, 1917, a week after he had enlisted in the Richmond Blues during the World war; Dr. Francis B., Jr., a physician and surgeon at Abingdon, who had a distinguished record of service as a medical officer during the World war; Sarah Katherine, who graduated from Stonewall Jackson College and Hollins College, and has had a successful record of experience in educational work; and James William, who was in the Sixth Field Artillery, United States Army, during the World war.

Judge Hutton married, November 14, 1911, Sophia Ruby Clark, daughter of A. J. and Sophia (Baker) Clark. A. J. Clark was a native of Mississippi. Her mother was born in Virginia, daughter of the second comptroller of currency, under President Pierce, and appointed to a similar office in the Confederate government by President Davis. Mrs. Hutton has been president of the Chapter of the Daughters of the Confederacy. Judge and Mrs. Hutton had one daughter, Ruby Clark.

WALTER FRANCIS PAUL, manager of the George Wythe Hotel at Wytheville, is a native of the city of Washington, and had some of his first training in the hotel business in several of the hotels of the national capital.

He was born at Washington February 23, 1893, son of Nathaniel Safford and Mary E. (Dries) Paul. His father, who was born at Albany, New York, April 29, 1845, was member of a family that came from England and settled in New York City a number of generations ago. Members of the Paul family were in the wholesale drug business in the firm of Paul & Runkel.

Nathaniel S. Paul for a number of years lived in Washington, and he died at Washington, D. C., March 6, 1903. He is buried in Arlington National Cemetery. His wife, Mary E. Dries, was born in Washington and still resides in that city, where she attended school. She is a Catholic, while her husband was a Presbyterian.

Walter Francis Paul was the only child of his parents. He attended public schools in Washington, and his first employment after leaving school was as office boy in the Washington office of the Babcock & Wilcox Boiler Company. He remained four years, starting at a salary of ten dollars a month. In 1912 he

Walter S. Kelley

became an elevator boy for the Powhatan Hotel at Washington, at twenty-five dollars a month, and was with that one house five years, being finally promoted to superintendent of service. Since then he has enjoyed association with a number of prominent hotels, having been clerk in the old Chamberlain Hotel at Old Point Comfort, Virginia; for a year and a half was with The White, at White Sulphur Springs, West Virginia; for one year was clerk in the Grafton Hotel at Washington; and was assistant manager and later manager of the Arlington Hotel at Washington, having been with that one hotel for about six years. Upon the sale of the Arlington Hotel he went with the Annapolis Hotel at Washington for several years as chief clerk.

While in Washington he was secretary and later president of the Washington, D. C., Charter 31, Hotel Greeters of America, a national association of hotel managers and clerks, and at this time is president of the association for the State of Virginia.

Mr. Paul in October, 1927, became associated with the Grenoble Hotels, Incorporated, of Pittsburgh, operators of a chain of hotels, one of which is the George Wythe Hotel of Wytheville. Mr. Paul was sent to Wytheville to open and take charge as manager of this thoroughly modern hostelry. He is also supervising manager for the State of Virginia of the Grenoble Hotels, Incorporated, being a stockholder in the company and one of the directing committee.

Mr. Paul has interested himself in the community life of Wytheville since locating here. He is a member of the Rotary Club, is a Democrat and belongs to St. Mary's Catholic Church at Wytheville. He married at Washington, November 4, 1915, Miss Marion Alford Jones, of Remington, Virginia, where she was educated in public schools. She is a member of the Presbyterian Church. They have one daughter, Doris Mary, a kindergarten pupil.

WALTER SCOTT ALLEY, a resident of Petersburg, is widely known in insurance circles in Virginia and in other cities of the eastern states.

He was born at Petersburg, son of Henry Thomas Alley and grandson of Thomas Alley. The mother of Mr. Alley was Alexena Frances Kirkland, who was born in Dinwiddie County, Virginia, March 12, 1831, daughter of Benjamin and Lucy (Wynne) Kirkland. Her grandfather, Benjamin Kirkland, Sr., was born in 1756 and died in February, 1811. He was a private soldier in Capt. Robert Bolling's Company of cavalry in the Revolutionary war. His wife, Martha Jones, was born in 1770 and died in October, 1811.

Walter Scott Alley when only a boy had to become the head and main support of the family owing to the death of his father, who left his widow with a large family. Mr. Alley knows the meaning of hard work and privation and self sacrifice, and has done a great deal for others as well as for himself. He finished his education in the McCabe University School at Petersburg. He took up life insurance work, at first at Petersburg and then went with the company headquarters at Richmond, becoming assistant secretary. On returning to Petersburg he resumed agency work and later became special agent for the Lancashire Insurance Company of Liverpool, with headquarters at Richmond. Following that he was general agent for the Caledonian Insurance Company of Edinburg, with headquarters at Atlanta, Georgia, and subsequently became assistant United States manager for the Manchester Assurance Company of Manchester, England, and later assistant United States manager of the North British Mercantile Insurance Company of London and Edinburgh and vice president of its affiliated companies, including the Pennsylvania Fire Insurance Company of Philadelphia, the Mercantile Insurance Company of New York and the Commonwealth Insurance Company of New York. While representing these organizations he had his headquarters in New York, but in 1927 he resigned all active connections and returned to Petersburg, where he now enjoys well earned retirement.

WILLIAM RUSSELL ROGERS, M. D. A leading citizen and professionally prominent at Bristol, Virginia, where he has been established for over a quarter of a century, is Dr. William Russell Rogers, physician and surgeon, widely known and esteemed throughout Southwest Virginia, and formerly president of the Southwest Virginia Medical Society. He is a member of a representative old Washington County family, and the greater part of his life has been passed in this section.

Dr. William Russell Rogers was born at Fort Worth, Texas, August 9, 1875, son of John K. and Nancy A. (Thomas) Rogers, both now deceased, and both natives of Washington County, Virginia. The father of Doctor Rogers was a veteran of the war between the states, having served in the Confederate army, in the 48th Virginia Infantry, under command of that great soldier, Stonewall Jackson. Both before and after the war he was interested in farming and to some extent in local politics. He belonged to the Masonic fraternity, and both he and wife were active members of the Methodist Episcopal Church, South.

After his boyhood school period was over William Russell Rogers was afforded liberal higher educational advantages. After completing a course in King College at Bristol, Tennessee, he became a student in Emory and Henry College at Emory, Virginia, and then followed his medical course in the University of Maryland at Baltimore, and his graduation with his degree in 1901. A year or more passed while he was serving as an interne in the University and the Johns Hopkins Hospitals at Baltimore, and then Doctor Rogers entered into medical practice at Bristol, and this city has remained his chosen home ever since. Subsequently on many occasions he has attended clinics and taken advantage of special courses and demonstrations in large medical centers like Chicago and New York, in this way keeping in close touch with medical progress, and very often when he attends medical conventions has contributed scientific papers.

In the years that have passed Doctor Rogers has built up a large general practice that has reflected credit on the city as well as himself, and additionally has taken such deep concern as an earnest citizen in all her interests that more and more, as his professional responsibilities have increased, he has found himself called upon to assume at times a measure of leadership in relation to civic needs and social movements. This confidence of his fellow citizens has been appreciated, and his sound advice and practical ideas have been beneficial. In 1920 Doctor Rogers was elected one of the first members of the Bristol City Council under the commission form of government, then inaugurated, and he has continued to serve on this body ever since with the exception of three years. He is on the directing board of the Washington and Trust Bank.

In 1905 Dr. William Russell Rogers married at Bristol, Tennessee, Miss Nataline Haynes, daughter of Judge Hal H. Haynes, of the Tennessee Court of Appeals. Mrs. Rogers was educated in Salem Female Academy, Winston-Salem, North Carolina, and is an accomplished, cultivated lady, interested in social life and cultural clubs, and is a member of the Daughters of the American Revolution and of the United Daughters of the Confederacy. Doctor and Mrs. Rogers have four children: Nancy Katherine, who, although but twenty years old, is a graduate of Ward Belmont College at Nashville, Tennessee, and is proving an acceptable teacher at Silver Lake in that state; Margaret, aged twelve years, who is a student in the Virginia High School at Bristol; and Julia and John, who are aged respectively nine and six years.

Doctor Rogers is surgeon for the Southern Railroad and also for the Norfolk & Western Railroad, and is first vice-president of the Norfolk & Western Railway Surgeons Association. He is visiting surgeon to Kings Mountain Memorial Hospital at Bristol, and was one of the organizers of its predecessor, St. Luke's Hospital. He has a wide and honorable professional acquaintance and valued membership in the Bristol Medical Society, the Southwest Virginia, the Virginia State and the Southern Medical Societies and the American Medical Association. He is a thirty-second degree Mason and a Shriner, belongs also to the Order of Elks, Rotary International, and both he and Mrs. Rogers are active members of the Methodist Episcopal Church, South.

MARION LEE HARRISON, of Wytheville, is a banker and lumber man with business connections that permanently identify him with many localities in Southwest Virginia and adjacent states. Mr. Harrison is a member of one branch of the Harrison family of Virginia, and his ancestry includes a number of names in the Colonial history.

He was born in Cabell County, West Virginia, September 6, 1873, son of John Henry and Eliza (Chapman) Harrison. His mother died September 16, 1912, being a daughter of Henry M. and Polly Ann (Wooton) Chapman, the latter a daughter of Simon Wooton. Henry M. Chapman was a son of Jack Chapman, who married a Miss Menefee, of Buckingham County, Virginia. Jack Chapman was a son of John Chapman and grandson of John Chapman I, who was a soldier during the border Indian warfare of the Revolutionary period. John Chapman was a son of Isaac Chapman, of Culpeper County, Virginia. The Chapman family moved from Culpeper County to the Shenandoah Valley in 1768, and in 1771 to the New River Valley, where they were for years exposed to the dangers of Indian raids.

John Henry Harrison was born in Franklin County, Virginia, August 13, 1837, and died November 29, 1898. He and his wife were married December 27, 1870. He was educated in private schools, served as a private in the Confederate army during the Civil war for three years, and was three times wounded in action. After the war he settled in Cabell County, West Virginia, and was identified with the Chesapeake & Ohio Railroad during its construction. He lived on a farm for many years, and he and his wife are buried in the cemetery at Hurricane, West Virginia. They had a family of nine children: Emily F., born November 10, 1871, became the wife of George B. Soward, of Hurricane, West Virginia; Marion Lee; William H., born May 12, 1876, a resident of Huntington, West Virginia; Albertie, born July 11, 1878, married William Searles; Pearl S., born September 22, 1880, married Henry H. Soward, of Russell, Kentucky; Martha Virgie, born November 28, 1882, died at the age of thirteen; Lucy L., born in September, 1885, married Henry Howell, of Hurricane, West Virginia; Homer Harrison, born August 13, 1888, lives at Hurricane; and Charles, born November 27, 1892, is also a resident of Hurricane, West Virginia.

Marion Lee Harrison was educated in schools at Hurricane, West Virginia, until 1891, and during the following ten years was a telegraph operator and agent for the Chesapeake & Ohio on the Huntington Division. His railroad training was no doubt a valuable factor in his subsequent business career. He left the railroad service to take up the lumber business at Hurricane, West Virginia, where he remained until 1904, since which year his home and business headquarters have been at Wytheville. Mr. Harrison since 1902 has had a contract for furnishing cross ties and other timbers to the Norfolk & Western Railway Company. During 1919-20, under the United States Railway administration, he was supervisor of forest products for the railroads in the Pocahontas region.

The business organizations with which he is actively identified and which represent a large aggregate of industrial and financial power are the M. L. Harrison Tie & Lumber Company, of which he is president, the First National Bank of Pearisburg, Virginia, of which he is president and a director, the Farmers Bank of Southwest Virginia, at Wytheville, of which he is vice president and a director, the First National Bank of Bluefield, West Virginia, of which he is a director, the Harrison Hancock Wholesale Hardware Company, of which he is president, the T. & S. E. Railroad of North Carolina, of which he is vice president and a director, the Blackwood Lumber Company of North Carolina, in which he is a director, the Taylor Colquitt Creosoting Company of Spartanburg, South Carolina, of which he is vice president and a director, the Southwest Lumber Company of Alamogordo, New Mexico, of which he is a director, the Roanoke Tie & Lumber Company, of which he is vice president and a director, the Laval Sand Company of Hinton, West Virginia, of which he is president, the Kentucky Cardinal Coal Company of Cardinal, Kentucky, of which he is vice president and director, and the Wytheville Mink and Fur Farm, of which he is president.

Mr. Harrison is a Knight Templar Mason, member of Beni-Kedem Temple of the Mystic Shrine, B. P. O. Elks, Independent Order of Odd Fellows, Wytheville Rotary Club, Shenandoah Club. He is a Democrat, is a Baptist and for fifteen years has been superintendent of the Sunday School at Wytheville.

Mr. Harrison married, May 5, 1898, at Huntington, West Virginia, Miss Laura A. Swindler, who was reared and educated at Huntington, graduating from Marshall College in 1896, following which for two years she taught in public schools in Putnam County, West Virginia. She is a member of the Baptist Church, the Eastern Star and White Shrine of Jerusalem. Mrs. Harrison is a daughter of James L. and Evelyn Narcissus (Burgess) Swindler, of Putnam County. Her mother was born in 1854, daughter of Hiram A. and Amanda Melvine (Hutchinson) Burgess, and granddaughter of Hiram and Nancy (Bowling) Burgess. Members of the Burgess family have been in Maryland and Virginia from early Colonial times, and many of them were staunch Quakers. Nancy Bowling was a daughter of

PRESTON LeROY ROPER

Jesse Bowling, who served with the Maryland Continental troops in the Revolutionary war, and after the war settled in South-western Virginia. Mrs. Harrison's father was for many years connected with the Kanawha & Michigan Railroad in West Virginia. Mr. and Mrs. Harrison have two daughters, Evelyn Marion, born February 9, 1899, and Virginia Randolph, born July 30, 1914. Evelyn graduated from the music department of Hollins College and from the Peabody College of Music at Baltimore, spent some time abroad in study, subsequently taking two post-graduate courses in Peabody College, and is an accomplished leader in the musical life of Wytheville, being organist for the Baptist Church. The younger daughter, member of the class of 1930 in high school, has also exhibited much musical talent, being a violinist. Mr. Harrison has been much interested in educational movements, and was one of those responsible for the founding of the Bluefield College for Boys and is president of the Board of Trustees and a director of that school.

PRESTON LeROY ROPER, for many years active in the tobacco business at Petersburg, was born and reared there, being a son of LeRoy Roper, a native of the same city and a grandson of John Roper. John Roper was born in New Kent County, Virginia, where the Ropers established their home on coming from England in Colonial times. The family was founded by two brothers, John and William Roper, who came to Virginia to occupy a large block of ground granted them by the King.

John Roper was a millwright by trade and settled in Petersburg prior to the War of 1812. Several years later he exposed himself during a very destructive fire in the city and died of pneumonia when only forty years of age. LeRoy Roper, father of Preston L. Roper, acquired a fortune in the tobacco business at Petersburg, where he lived until his death. He married Emily Ann Bartlett. Her father, Josiah Bartlett, was a native of Massachusetts and a student and a distinguished figure in Colonial and Revolutionary times, being one of the signers of the Declaration of Independence, and a sketch of his biography is found in all the important collections of national biography.

Preston L. Roper was reared and educated at Petersburg and as a young man took up the tobacco business, which he followed with a large measure of success until he retired.

Mr. Roper married Helen Randolph Willson, who is connected by descent with many of the most illustrious old Virginia families. She was born in Richmond, Virginia, daughter of Nathaniel Friend and Mary (Donnan) Willson. Among many other ancestors was Col. Robert Bolling, who was born in England, December 26, 1646, came to America in 1660 and represented Prince George County in the House of Burgesses in 1702-03 and 1705-06. He married Ann Stith, daughter of Maj. John Stith, who settled in Virginia in 1650 and who was a lieutenant of the Charles City County Militia and had a prominent part on the Government side in Bacon's Rebellion. In 1680 he became major of the Charles City County Militia and later represented that county in the House of Burgesses. Mrs. Willson's great-grandfather, Thomas Friend Willson, was born May 23, 1775, son of Thomas Branch and Judith (Friend) Willson. Thomas Friend Willson married Maria R. Gilliam, who was born in Amelia County, Virginia, daughter of Samuel and Susanna (Bolling) Gilliam, Susanna Bolling being a daughter of Robert and Clara (Yates) Bolling and Clara Yates, a daughter of Rev.

William and Eliza (Randolph) Yates. This Eliza Randolph was a daughter of Edward Randolph, who was a son of William and Mary (Isham) Randolph, all of whom are names of fine social and civic distinction in Virginia. Mrs. Roper is a descendant of William Randolph, who was born in England in 1651, came to Virginia in 1670, was an officer in the Colonial Militia, a member of the House of Burgesses, being speaker of the House, clerk of the Assembly and attorney general of the colony.

Mrs. Roper's mother, Mary Donnan, was a daughter of John Donnan, who was born in Scotland, March 14, 1816, son of David Donnan, born in Galloway, Scotland, May 30, 1778. This family is said to be descended from Saint Donnan, an Irish convert who was put to death by a band of pirates in the year of 1607, A. D. David Donnan came to America in 1818, locating in Amelia County, Virginia. John Donnan was a cotton broker and merchant at Petersburg. John Donnan's mother was a Mc-Illwaine, one of whose brothers, it is said, went with the Prince of Orange to the conquest of Ireland in 1690.

Mr. and Mrs. Roper reared a family of three children: Mary Willson, Leonora Randolph and Willson Bartlett. Mary M. is the wife of Dr. Frederick Christian Schreiber and has a daughter, Mary Christian. Leonora R. is the wife of John Leonard McIllwaine, and their two children are Helen Randolph and Preston Roper. Willson Bartlett married Hontas Strachan Walke. Mrs. Roper is connected with many patriotic organizations, including the Daughters of the American Revolution, American Colonists, the United Daughters of the Confederacy, Descendants of the War of 1812 and other organizations. She is a member of Saint Paul's Episcopal Church at Petersburg.

SIMON KENTON GROSECLOSE, who was named for the famous Kentucky scout and explorer, has lived all his life in the Ceres community of Bland County, one of the localities of Southwestern Virginia with which this family has been identified from pioneer times. Mr. Groseclose is one of the leaders in agricultural enterprise and stock raising in that district.

He was born at Ceres, March 17, 1867, son of William Henry and Mary Jane (Wall) Groseclose, and grandson of one of the pioneer settlers of Bland County. William Henry Groseclose also spent his life at Ceres, was educated in private schools and was a farmer and stock raiser. He died about 1890. His wife, Mary Jane Wall, was a very active member of the Methodist Episcopal Church. She died in 1916 and is buried beside her husband in Sharon Cemetery. They had two children: Simon Kenton and Jennie, the latter of whom died at the age of thirty years, after her marriage to H. E. Peery, who is now a resident of Amarillo, Texas, and has a son, Frank Peery, and a daughter, Mary Ruth.

Simon Kenton Groseclose attended public schools in Ceres and the Wytheville Academy, and for over forty years has been diligent in looking after his business as a farmer and stock raiser. He owns three large farms, one in Smyth County and the other two in Bland County. He is also a stockholder in the Bank of Bland and for about twenty-five years served as a member of the school board. He is a Democrat and a trustee of the Lutheran Church. Mr. Groseclose married at Bland Court House in October, 1892, Miss Sarah Josephine Muncy, of Bland. She was educated in public schools and taught for several years before her marriage. She is a member of the Lutheran Church.

Her father was Andrew J. Muncy. Mr. and Mrs. Groseclose have four children, William Henry, Andrew Muncy, Samuel Kenton and James Benton.

The oldest son, William Henry, was educated in the grade and high schools at Ceres and in the Roanoke Business College. He is a farmer and stock raiser in Smyth County, and a member of Lodge No. 262 of the Masonic fraternity. He married Mary Belle Moss, of Burke's Gordon, Virginia, and has two daughters, Sarah Josephine and Ida Virginia.

Dr. Andrew Muncy Groseclose was educated in Roanoke College and graduated in medicine from Johns Hopkins University at Baltimore in 1922, and is now practicing as a physician and surgeon at Roanoke. He married Miss Catherine Camp, of Roanoke, and her only child died in infancy.

Samuel Kenton Groseclose attended the Ceres High School, graduated from the Annapolis Naval Academy and is now a lieutenant on the battleship *Wyoming*. He married Margaret George, of Iowa, who died in April, 1928.

James Benton Groseclose, the youngest of the four sons, attended school at Ceres and for two years was a student in Emory and Henry College. Since 1922 he has been associated with his father in farming and stock raising at Ceres, and is one of the splendid representatives of the younger generation of farm leaders in this section of the state. He is affiliated with Ceres Lodge No. 262, A. F. and A. M. James Benton Groseclose married Clara Crabtree, of Ceres, who attended high school there and also the high school at Rural Retreat. She is a member of the Lutheran Church and is a daughter of C. A. and Susan Alberta (Foglesang) Crabtree. Her father is a farmer and cattle raiser of Bland County, and for a number of years has served as supervisor of Sharon District. Mr. and Mrs. James Benton Groseclose have three sons, Joseph Byron, Donald Lee and Samuel Francis.

HENRY WALLACE CARNER. From the bench of a mechanic in a wagon factory to the position of representative of one of the largest piano manufacturing houses in the South was the advancement made by the late Henry Wallace Carner, of Richmond who retired from active business, due to illness, a short time before his death in May, 1925. He was a self-made man in all that the term implies, for he had only ordinary opportunities, educationally or otherwise, in his youth, and fought his own way through industry and perseverance. During his career he became well known in music circles in four states, and had the esteem and confidence of all with whom he came in contact.

Mr. Carner was born in Spotsylvania County, Virginia, April 23, 1873, and was a son of John and Annie A. (Jones) Carner. The family is of French origin, and the name was originally Carnot, being of the same line as Lazare Nicholas Marguerite Carnot, the famous French statesman, general and strategist, and of the latter's grandson, Marie Francois Sadi Carnot, president of the French Republic. On coming to America during the Colonial period the progenitor of the family in this country settled in Virginia, where the name became Carner. John Carner was born in Spotsylvania County, Virginia, and as a youth enlisted in the Confederate army and served during the four years of the war between the states. Following that struggle he returned to the peaceful pursuits of agriculture, in which he continued to be engaged during the remainder of his life. He married Annie A. Jones, and they became the parents of three sons and three daughters, of whom Emmett was a prominent attorney and for some years a member of the Virginia House of Delegates; and Carl was sheriff of Spotsylvania County for fifteen years.

The public schools of his native county furnished Henry Wallace Carner with his early education, and he was reared in the midst of rural surroundings, dividing his time between his studies and assisting his father in the work of the home farm. However, he had no intention of being an agriculturist, and as a youth applied himself to learning the trade of wagon-maker, after which he secured a position as a mechanic in a wagon factory at Fredericksburg. Through industry and fidelity he rose rapidly to a foremanship, but eventually gave this up to embark in the grocery business, in which he continued with some success for five years. When he disposed of his interests in this line he opened a music store at Fredericksburg, but eventually accepted an offer made by the Starr Piano Company to become their representative in the states of Virginia, West Virginia, North Carolina and South Carolina. In this capacity he traveled all over this part of the country, forming many friendly alliances and becoming known as a man of high integrity and character. In 1924, after a successful career, he retired from business cares, due to ill health and died at Richmond May 26, 1925. Mr. Carner was a member of the Masons, the Independent Order of Odd Fellows and the Benevolent and Protective Order of Elks, and with his family belonged to the Barton Heights Methodist Church.

On October 13, 1897, Mr. Carner was united in marriage with Miss Carrie L. Keene, who was educated in the schools of Fredericksburg and Staunton. The Keene family originated in Ireland, whence the American progenitor immigrated to Dorchester County, Maryland, shortly after the War of 1812. Mrs. Carner's parents were Samuel and Fannie Keene, of Fredericksburg, her father being a merchant. To Mr. and Mrs. Carner were born seven children, of whom five are living: Elsie, the wife of George Wood, a city officer of Richmond; Grace, the wife of Conway Levy, who is engaged in the automobile business at Richmond; Christine, the wife of Elmer Lightner, a railroad man of Fredericksburg, who has one child, June Virginia Lightner; Tacye Bryan, wife of Capt. John H. Parker, of the U. S. Marine Corp., whose son, Jackie Carner, died May 10, 1929; and Helen Wallace, who married Hugh Haskins, a merchant, and has one son, Hugh, Jr., and a daughter, Helen Wallace. Mrs. Carner survives her husband and resides at 2804 Griffin Avenue.

WILLIAM FRANCISCO SPOTSWOOD, city auditor and clerk of Council of Petersburg, is a lineal descendant of Gov. Alexander Spotswood, governor of the colony of Virginia in 1710.

Mr. Spotswood was born at Petersburg, son of Joseph Edwin Spotswood, a native of the same city, grandson of Dandridge Spotswood, who was born at Orange Grove in Orange County, great-grandson of John Spotswood, born at Sedley Lodge in Orange County, whose father, John Spotswood, born at Germania, Orange County, was a son of Gov. Alexander Spotswood.

Dandridge Spotswood was a wholesale druggist at Petersburg, and the drug business was also followed by his son, William Francisco Spotswood. Dandridge Spotswood married Katherine Brooke Francisco, who was born in Buckingham

County, Virginia, daughter of Peter and Katherine (Brooke) Francisco. Peter Francisco was a soldier in the Colonial army in the Revolution. His wife, Katherine Brooke, was a daughter of Gov. Robert Brooke.

Joseph Edwin Spotswood married Lucy Starke Cooper, daughter of Joseph and Rosina (Starke) Cooper, and they reared four children, William Francisco, Joseph, Edwin B. and John Brooke.

William Francisco Spotswood was educated in public schools at Petersburg and in Hampden-Sidney College. He has been auditor and Clerk of Council for the city of Petersburg since 1923. He is a member of the Presbyterian Church.

Mr. Spotswood married Rachel Custis Kinsey, daughter of Henry Clay and Lila (Meacham) Kinsey, granddaughter of Joseph and Rachel (Petit) Kinsey and Benjamin and Sally Ann (Whitehorn) Meacham.

Mr. and Mrs. Spotswood have two sons, William Francisco Spotswood, Jr., and Henry Kinsey.

CHARLES E. POLLARD. Well versed in legal lore, possessing a receptive mind and a retentive memory, and recognized as a forceful and effective public speaker, Charles E. Pollard, of Petersburg, has gained the confidence and esteem of his many clients and the respect of the entire community, his selection as commonwealth attorney for the city bearing evidence of his high standing as a man, a citizen and a lawyer. He was born in Petersburg, which was likewise the birthplace of his father, William E. Pollard.

James E. Pollard, Mr. Pollard's grandfather, was born and reared on a plantation located in Amelia County, Virginia. During the Civil war he enlisted for service in the Confederate army, in which he fought bravely for the Southern cause until the close of the conflict, returning then to Petersburg, where he lived until his death.

William E. Pollard has been a resident of Petersburg, Virginia, during his entire life, and has done his full share in advancing its interests. His wife, whose maiden name was Effie E. Brownley, was born in Wilson North Carolina, a daughter of Charles D. and Betty Brownley, who were born in Franklin County, Virginia, and Wilson, North Carolina, respectively. Loyal to his home and the South, he did brave service as a soldier of the Confederate army. Mr. and Mrs. William E. Pollard became the parents of six children, four sons and two daughters.

Having completed his elementary education in the schools at Petersburg, Charles E. Pollard obtained his first knowledge of law in the office of Lassiter & Drewry. Subsequently continuing his studies in the law department of the Washington and Lee University, he was admitted to the bar in 1915, and has since practiced his profession in Petersburg. Enlisting for service in the World war in 1918, Mr. Pollard was appointed personal secretary to Major-General Cronkhite, commanding the Eightieth Division, and served with the division headquarters of the Eightieth Division in all of its service in France. In May of 1918 he went overseas with his division, and served with it in its active part in many engagements, including service with the British; the St. Mihiel drive; and in the Argonne drive three times.

Returning to Petersburg in May, 1919, Mr. Pollard resumed the practice of law. In 1921 he had the distinction of being elected commonwealth attorney for the City of Petersburg, and in 1924 and 1929 was reelected without opposition for terms of four years each, now serving his third term. He is known as one of the ablest prosecutors in the state.

Mr. Pollard married, in 1922, Gladys (Durham) Duncan, who was born in Ripplemead, Giles County, Virginia, a daughter of W. T. and Anne (Durham) Duncan. Of their union one child has been born, Anne Durham Pollard. Fraternally Mr. Pollard is a Mason and Shriner. He is also identified by membership with several other organizations, including the Virginia and American Bar Associations; the Kiwanis Club; the Petersburg Post of the American Legion; and is a judge advocate of the Eightieth Division of the Veterans Association.

WILLIAM FORD GIBSON since early manhood has had almost a continuous experience in the lumber business. His associations have been with manufacturing and wholesale and retail lumber organizations in different sections of the country. In the course of his business experience his duties brought him to Virginia, and he is now a member of a firm at Wytheville doing a business as wholesalers and retailers all over the state.

Mr. Gibson was born at Washington, Pennsylvania, May 12, 1879, son of William B. and Sophia (Blayney) Gibson, and grandson of George Gibson. The Gibsons have lived in Pennsylvania since Colonial times. William B. Gibson was born and reared in Washington County, Pennsylvania, and specialized in fruit growing and nursery work. He died in 1918 and is buried at West Alexander, Pennsylvania. His wife, Sophia Blayney, was born and reared in Washington County, Pennsylvania, daughter of Joel P. and Johanna (Frazier) Blayney. Her great-great-grandmother was scalped in Southwestern Pennsylvania by the Indians in frontier days. Sophia Blayney was educated in the West Alexander Seminary for Girls and was a member of the Presbyterian Church. She died in 1927. There were six children: William Ford; Bruce Blayney, connected with the Oakland Pontiac Motor Car Company at Pontiac, Michigan; George Earl, who died at the age of four years; John C., with the W. A. Ring Advertising Agency at Chicago; Lloyd C., chief oil and gas engineer with the Treasury Department of the Federal Government at Washington; and Joel B., an architect and building contractor at Greensburg, Pennsylvania.

William Ford Gibson was educated in public schools in Ohio County, West Virginia, attended the West Virginia State Normal at West Liberty, and, entering the lumber business, has followed it successfully.

Mr. Gibson in 1918 located at Wytheville, Virginia, to become manager of the local interests of the W. A. Wilson Lumber Company. Five years later, in 1923, he bought the local interests of the Wilson Company, and has since been associated in partnership with W. C. Wilson under the firm name Gibson & Wilson, Limited. They have built up a steadily increasing business, handling all classes of lumber and building supplies, not only for the local market but for many miles around Wytheville and even outside the state. They operate a planing mill plant at Speedwell, Virginia, and have a large yard and general offices in Wytheville. Mr. Gibson is also a stockholder in the George Wythe Hotel.

He is a thirty-second degree Scottish Rite Mason, member of Wytheville Chapter, Royal Arch Masons, Osiris Temple of the Mystic Shrine at Wheeling, the Rotary Club, and is a Republican. He is a Presbyterian.

Mr. Gibson married at West Liberty, West Virginia, June 22, 1904, Miss Nellie Gardner, of West Liberty, daughter of John and Keziah (Cunningham) Gardner. Her father for over twenty years was a member of the State Board of Regents of West Virginia and was a leading Mason. He died in 1908 and his wife, in 1922. Mr. and Mrs. Gibson have had three children, one of them, Francis, dying at the age of two years. The son William Ford, Jr., was educated in the Wytheville High School, in Emory and Henry College, and is a member of the class of 1931 in the University of Virginia. Mr. and Mrs. Gibson have one daughter, Marjorie Nell, who graduated from the Wytheville High School in 1926 and from Virginia Intermont College in 1928. She is now associated with her father as secretary of Gibson & Wilson, Limited.

WILLIAM M. MARTIN has an interesting and important distinction as the result of forty years of undeviating loyalty and faithfulness as a worker and representative of the Norfolk & Western Railroad. Nearly all of that time has been spent at Wytheville as agent for this transportation company.

Mr. Martin was born in Albemarle County, Virginia, October 3, 1865, son of William L. and Elizabeth (Powell) Martin, and grandson of John S. Martin, an Albemarle County farmer, where he died and is buried. William L. Martin was born and reared in Albemarle County, attended private schools, and was a merchant until the Civil war. He entered as a private the medical department in General Stonewall Jackson's Brigade and was in the service from the beginning until the end. After the war he lived on a farm, and died in 1903. His wife, Elizabeth Powell, was reared in Albemarle County, attended a private school, and she and her husband were members of the Baptist Church. She died in 1877. The Powell family came to Albemarle County from New Jersey. William L. Martin and wife had two sons, John S. and William M. John S. Martin was an employe of the Chesapeake & Ohio Railroad Company when he died in 1879, when a young man. He married Susie Faulkner, of Gordonsville, Virginia, and left two children, Marvin and Edgar.

William M. Martin attended the Miller school in Albemarle County, and on leaving school went to work for the Norfolk & Western Railway Company, becoming a telegraph operator and agent. In all this long time he has had just three posts of duty. In 1886 he was stationed at Max Meadows and in 1888 at Crockett, and in 1891 was assigned to Wytheville, where he has served as agent ever since. Mr. Martin is also a vice president of the Wythe County National Bank. He is a Democrat in politics, and is one of the trustees of the Methodist Episcopal Church, South.

He married at Wytheville, October 10, 1889, Miss Carrie Stone Bourne. She was educated in a private school at Louisville, Kentucky, and at Wytheville, is a member of the Methodist Episcopal Church, South, and the United Daughters of the Confederacy. Her parents were Henry G. and Elizabeth (Simmerman) Bourne. Her father was a Wythe County farmer. Mr. and Mrs. Martin had four sons, William G., Harry Mansfield, Frank C. and John C. William G. was in France eighteen months during the World war, and died in 1921, at the age of thirty-one. The son Harry Mansfield died when twelve years old. Frank C. Martin, educated in the Wytheville High School, is claim adjuster for the Norfolk & Western Railway, with, headquarters at Pulaski, Virginia, and is a thirty-second degree Scottish Rite Mason and Shriner.

The youngest son, John C. Martin, attended high school at Wytheville, the Virginia Polytechnic Institute, and spent one year in Emory and Henry College. Since leaving college he has been associated with his father and has charge of the Wytheville office of the American Railway Express Company. He is a Mason and Shriner. In July, 1922, he married Alberta Raper, of Wytheville, where she was reared and educated. They have two daughters, Nancy Caroline and Billie Francis.

JACOB A. WAGNER, M. D., is a man who has lived a life of unusual service and activity in Bland County. He is, of course, best known as a capable doctor, but in early life he was a school teacher, and is now performing the duties of county superintendent of schools, elected to office for service beginning July 4, 1929, for four years. The people of the county associate many other facts with his name and his credit.

Doctor Wagner was born in Kimberling Valley, Bland County, March 10, 1861. His people were among the earliest settlers of Kimberling Valley, where his great-grandfather, George Wagner, and his grandfather, Adam Wagner, both lived as farmers. Not long after Doctor Wagner was born his father, James E. Wagner, entered the Southern army, was a brave and dutiful soldier for about a year, and died of typhoid fever in August, 1862. He was buried in Monroe County, West Virginia. He was born and reared in Bland County and had attended private schools. James E. Wagner married Elsie Muncey, who was born and reared in Giles County, Virginia, was educated in private schools and was a member of the Methodist Church. She survived her husband over fifty years, passing away in 1912, at the age of eighty-six, and is buried in the family cemetery. She was the mother of two sons and one daughter. The daughter died in infancy. The other son, David, volunteered for service during the Spanish-American war, and it is said that he was killed in action at the battle of Santiago, Cuba.

Dr. Jacob A. Wagner was educated in the grade and high schools of Bland County, and as a young man began teaching. Teaching was his chief profession for nineteen years. For about four years he was deputy clerk of courts of Bland County, and for four years was county surveyor. These offices indicate some of the versatility of his accomplishments. In the meantime he was studying medicine and was graduated M. D. from the Virginia Medical College of Richmond in 1901, and since that year has enjoyed a large practice. In 1920 he was elected county superintendent of schools, and is still serving in that capacity. Doctor Wagner is a charter director of the Bank of Bland County.

He is a member of the Bland County, Virginia State and American Medical Associations, is a Master Mason and member of the Eastern Star, and for years was active in the Independent Order of Odd Fellows and Junior Order United American Mechanics. He is a Democrat, and a member of the Methodist Episcopal Church, South, being a trustee of the church and parsonage, and teaches a class of men and women in Sunday School.

He married in Bland County, February 10, 1880, Miss Josephine Miller, a daughter of Dr. John L. and Martha (Bird)
Miller. Her father practiced medicine and surgery for many
years, being one of the doctors of Bland County during the Civil
war period. Mrs. Wagner was educated in Bland County, and
outside her home and family has found pleasant duties in the
Methodist Church, and has been an officer in the Eastern Star
since it was organized. She is the mother of two daughters,
Naomi J. and Effie B. Naomi J. Wagner is a highly educated
and competent leader in school work. She attended the Bland
public schools, Martha Washington College at Abingdon, Randolph-Macon Woman's College at Lynchburg and the University
of Virginia, and also the State Teachers College at Radford.
She is now teaching mathematics and English in the Bland
County High School. Her sister, Effie B. Wagner, was educated
in the Bland High School and Martha Washington College,
taught for several years, and is now the wife of John C. Mustard,
formerly of Mechanicsburg, now a farmer and stock dealer at
Hollybrook in Bland County. Mr. and Mrs. Mustard have eight
children, Marie, John C., Jr., Garland, Wayne, Josephine, Albert,
Andrew and Kermit. The two older children, Marie and John,
are students at Bland, while Garland, Wayne and Josephine are
in school at Hollybrook.   ,

HENRY C. JOYNER was an attorney-at-law and had offices
and his practice both at Powhatan Court House and Amelia. Mr.
Joyner was a teacher before he was licensed to practice law,
and was a native Virginian, member of some of the old families
of Southampton and adjoining counties.

He was born at Aydle in Southampton County, August 29,
1896, son of Alexander J. and Martha C. (Faircloth) Joyner,
both natives of the same county. Both of Mr. Joyner's grandfathers were Confederate soldiers. His father spent his life as
a farmer in Southampton County, and was deputy county treasurer and deputy sheriff and chairman of the Democratic Committee for a number of years. He died April 10, 1914, and his
widow resides at Sedley in Southampton County.

Henry C. Joyner was reared and educated in his native
county, graduating from high school in 1914, and also completed
a course in the Davis Waggoner Business College. He was a
student four years in the College of William and Mary. On
answering the call to the colors in 1917 he was made a sergeant
and was assigned duty as athletic director in the Students Army
Training Corps at the University of Virginia. He was granted
an honorable discharge September 21, 1918. The following two
years he continued his studies at the University of Virginia and
for six years was in school work as principal of high schools.
For one year he attended the T. C. Williams Law School at
Richmond. On June 1, 1925, he passed the bar examination and
in the same year began practice at Powhatan Court House. In
addition to his private practice he acted as commissioner in
chancery. Mr. Joyner was an enthusiastic student of Virginia
history. In addition to practicing law he owned farming interests and dealt in timber land and real estate, and acted as attorney for the North Carolina Joint Stock Land Bank and as attorney for the Peoples Bank of Giles, Virginia.

He married, December 23, 1923, Miss Mildred Bollinger, of
Amelia County, Virginia, daughter of Lester and Estelle
(Burch) Bollinger. Her parents were born in Catawba County,

North Carolina, both being members of prominent families of Virginia and North Carolina. Mr. Joyner was a Scottish Rite Mason, member of the Samis Grotto of Masons, Royal Arch Chapter of Richmond, the B. P. O. Elks, the American Legion, and was assistant county chairman of the Democratic party. He was a member of the old Friends Church in Southampton County, the church in which William Penn and George Fox preached.

Mr. Joyner died on April 8, 1929, at Stuart Circle Hospital, Richmond, Virginia, following a brief illness from an infection of the throat. He was buried in Rosemont Cemetery, Sedley, Virginia, on April 10, 1929.

JESSE ALFORD JOHNSTON is representative of a family that has lived for five generations in Giles County, and his own record, over a comparatively brief span of years, has been in line with the honorable reputation and accomplishment of his forefathers.

He was born at Trigg in Giles County October 16, 1892. His grandfather, Joseph E. Johnston, was a grandson of Hughey Johnston, who came from Ireland and joined the earliest settlers in what was then Montgomery County, from which has been taken Giles among other counties. Joseph E. Johnston was born and reared in Giles County, near the old Wabash camp ground, and served as a Confederate soldier, being all through the war, fighting in many battles before the end. One of the battles in which he participated was Cloyd's Mountain. After the war he resumed farming and cattle raising, and died in 1901, being buried in Wesley Chapel at Trigg.

Jesse Alford Johnston is a son of James Russell and Lizzie Jane (Stafford) Johnston. His father has spent all his active life in Giles County, and is a well-to-do farmer and cattle raiser on a farm near Trigg, and is a director in the Peoples Bank of Eggleston and a partner in the Eggleston Garage. His wife was born and reared at Trigg, and has always been active in the Methodist Episcopal Church, South. Her people, the Staffords, have been in Virginia for many generations. Jesse Alford Johnston is the oldest of five children. His sister, Roxie Ellen, is the wife of W. P. Stafford, of Pearisburg; Joseph Clarence lives at Trigg; Clyde Strowther lives at Eggleston; and James Russell, Jr., is in the class of 1930 in the Eggleston High School.

Jesse Alford Johnston attended public school at Trigg, graduated from the Pearisburg High School in 1912, was in the National Business College at Roanoke during 1913-14, and for about a year taught as principal of the school at Trigg. In 1916 he went to work in the First National Bank of Pearisburg.

Mr. Johnston on June 4, 1917, enlisted in the United States Coast Artillery, was in training at Fortress Monroe, Virginia, was promoted to line sergeant of Battery F, Seventy-fourth Railroad Artillery, and with that outfit went overseas in September, 1918, as supply sergeant. He was on duty at St. Nazairre, France, and at Mailly, France, until the armistice, and received his honorable discharge at Fort Totten, New York, January 4, 1919.

After his service overseas Mr. Johnston taught a year of school in Green Valley, Virginia, and also engaged in farming, and in 1921 again resumed his banking experience, with the Bank of Eggleston. Four years later, in 1924, the Bank of

Wirt Robertson

Eggleston was reorganized as the Peoples Bank of Giles, and he has since that time been cashier and one of the directors of this growing and prospering financial institution. He also owns farm lands in Giles County. Mr. Johnston is a Royal Arch Mason and formerly was active in the Independent Order of Odd Fellows, is a Democrat, member of the Methodist Episcopal Church, South, and for the past five years has been superintendent of the Sunday School.

He married at Poplar Hill, Virginia, June 4, 1919, Miss Annie Stewart King, of Poplar Hill, who attended public school there and Martha Washington College at Abingdon, and taught for three years in Giles County. She has made much success in work as a musical instructor, and is now teacher of music in the Eggleston High School and has also acted as assistant cashier of the Peoples Bank of Giles. Mrs. Johnston is a daughter of Thomas Biddle and Sallie Etta (Eaton) King, of a well known Poplar Hill family, referred to elsewhere in this publication. Mr. and Mrs. Johnston had three children, two of whom died in infancy. The surviving son is Ralph Emerson, now attending school at Eggleston.

WIRT ROBERTSON. Having, by governess and private tutors, been well drilled in both the common and higher branches of learning while young, Wirt Robertson acquired an excellent knowledge of books, and thereafter made a wise use of his educational privileges. A son of Dr. John Alex Robertson, he was born August 4, 1863, in Brunswick County, Virginia, where the earlier years of his life were spent.

Having received the degree of M. D., John Alex Robertson began the practice of his chosen profession in Brunswick County, Virginia, but subsequently removed to Amelia County, Virginia, where he built up an extensive and lucrative practice, which he maintained to some extent until his death at the age of eighty years. His wife, whose maiden name was Sue Orgain, survived him, passing away at the venerable age of four score and four years.

Wirt Robertson began life on his own account as an agriculturist, and having made use of his head as well as his hands, met with genuine success in his labors. Upon the completion of the railway through Amelia County he, foreseeing unlimited possibilities in its use, wisely invested his money in large tracts of timber land, and was very successfully engaged in the lumber business until 1914. Moving in that year to Colonial Heights, Mr. Robertson bought much real estate in that vicinity, and thereafter devoted his time and energies to its improvement and sale, his venture therein proving excedingly profitable. The house is beautifully located on a high bank, and not only overlooks all of Petersburg, but gives an extensive view of the surrounding country; and on this estate is a very tall, well-kept box hedge said to be more than a century old. In this beautiful, beloved home the death of Mr. Robertson occurred in 1916, his death being a loss not only to his family and especial friends and relatives, but to the entire community.

On June 3, 1891, Mr. Robertson was united in marriage with Miss Rosa Irby Bolling, a native of Lunenburg County, Virginia, being a daughter of John Edward Bolling, and granddaughter of John Stith and Elizabeth (Irby) Bolling. Her father had a valuable plantation bordering on the Appomattox River in Amelia County, and operated it with slave labor. He married

Mary Ann Thomas, who was born in Lunenburg County, Virginia, a daughter of Samuel and Ann (Williams) Thomas, and both he and his wife spent their last years on the home plantation.

Three children blessed the marriage of Mr. and Mrs. Robertson, namely: Ellen Nase, who married N. H. Williams and has three children, Rosa Harrison, Mary Ellen and Wirt Robertson; Mary Irby married James C. Heath and has three children, Virginia Irby, James Clyde and Ann Bolling; and John Bolling Robertson, the only son. Both Mr. and Mrs. Robertson united with the Presbyterian Church while living in Amelia County, but were subsequently transferred to the Tabb Street Presbyterian Church, which he served many years as deacon.

HON. WALTER CROCKETT, mayor of Dublin and owner of the Dublin Roller Mills, is a man who has advanced to a high position in business and civic life, and the esteem in which he is held is but the just reward of a life time of strenuous endeavor. Under his capable control the affairs of Dublin are in splendid condition, and he is planning further public improvements, for he is a progressive man, and very proud of his home city.

The birth of Mayor Crockett occurred near Graham's Forge, Wythe County, Virginia, June 23, 1875, and he is a son of John F. and Sarah Catherine (Dyer) Crockett. John F. Crockett was born and reared in Wythe County, and attended the private schools of his time and neighborhood. During the entire war period he served in the Confederate army as a member of the Forty-fifth Virginia Infantry, and participated in a number of the major engagements. After the close of the war he was engaged in farming and stockraising, and continued to operate along these lines until the time of his death, which took place June 25, 1896, at the age of sixty years. He is buried in the old Dyer Cemetery in Wythe County. His father was Drake Crockett, a descendant of Sir Francis Drake and a relative of Davy Crockett, whose name is connected with some of the most stirring events of the pioneer period in Kentucky and Missouri. The great-grandfather of Mayor Crockett was one of the pioneers of Wythe County. On his mother's side Mayor Crockett is a grandson of Nathan Dyer, of Carter County, Tennessee, where she was born. Mrs. Crockett attended several excellent private schools of Wythe County, to which she was brought by her parents when she was two years old. She survives her husband and is now residing at Wytheville, where she is active in the Presbyterian Church, of which she has long been a member. There were seven children born to the parents, namely: Miss Nannie B., who resides at Wytheville; a child who died in infancy; Pierce, who resides in Brandenton, Florida; Mayor Crockett, who is the fourth in order of birth; Bramlett, who died at the age of twenty-one years; John Dyer, who resides at Galax, Virginia; and W. D., who resides at Wytheville.

Mayor Crockett attended the public schools in Wythe County and the Virginia Polytechnic Institute. When he left school he began farming, and he was also engaged in merchandising for several years, but in 1904 he sold and, coming to Dublin, went into the milling business, in which he has since continued. Purchasing the Dublin Roller Mills, he has made his plant one of the most modern in this part of the state. His machinery is of modern design and manufacture, and is the best in the market for the production of flour, meal and feed. The specialty of the mills is the Crockett Cream of Wheat Flour, which brand meets with a ready sale wherever offered because of its superior quality. Mayor Crockett is a Knight Templar and Shriner Mason, and he belongs to Kazim Temple, to the United Commercial Travelers, the Dublin Business Men's Club and other organizations. A very active Democrat, he was appointed mayor of Dublin in 1922 to fill the unexpired term of George C. Mooman, who retired from the office. At the succeeding election Mr. Crockett was elected to succeed himself, and has been reelected every two years since, the last time in 1928. He has been a member of the Pulaski County School Board for the past eight years, and has accomplished much for the cause of education while on the board, for he realizes the necessity for the very best schools and teachers obtainable, and is willing to exert himself to the limit to obtain them. From his youth up a member of the Methodist Episcopal Church, South, he has been especially active in the Dublin Church, and is now a member of its Official Board and zealous in behalf of its different societies.

On October 26, 1898, Mayor Crockett married Miss Blanche Colfee, of Pine, Virginia. She was educated in the public schools of Pulaski and Martha Washington College, Abingdon, Virginia, and for a few years prior to her marriage she taught school in Pulaski. First as a member of the Christian Church and later as a Methodist, she was active in church work, and was beloved by a wide circle of warm personal friends, who with her family mourned her passing when she died December 13, 1927. She is buried in the Dublin Cemetery. Mrs. Crockett was a daughter of J. F. and Elizabeth (Sayers) Colfee, of Pulaski County. For many years Mr. Colfee was prominent not only as a farmer and stockraiser, but also as a hardware merchant, in the latter business operating under the name of the Pulaski Hardware Company, Pulaski, Virginia. Both Mr. and Mrs. Colfee are deceased, and they are buried in the family cemetery at Pine, Virginia.

Mayor and Mrs. Crockett had three children born to them: John Frank, Richard Nathaniel and Walter Pierce, and the latter died February 10, 1920, when he was seven years old. Of the other two, John Frank Crockett attended the common and high schools of Dublin and Virginia Military Institute, and was graduated from the latter in 1921, and he also took the degree of Bachelor of Science at Roanoke College in 1923. While at Roanoke he taught school during the summer session of the University of Virginia, and he had some work at Johns Hopkins University, Baltimore, Maryland. In the meanwhile he had been assistant principal of the high school of Appalachia, Virginia, in the intervals of obtaining his own education. In 1923 he went to Fort Defiance, Virginia, as instructor of science in the Augusta Military Academy. While there he was stricken with arthritis, and since then has been an invalid, and lives with his father in Dublin. The other son, Richard Nathaniel Crockett, known as Dick, also attended the common and high schools of Dublin and Roanoke College, and after two years in the latter institution, entered the University of Virginia, from which he was graduated in 1925, with the degree of Bachelor of Arts. For the succeeding year he was a student in the university law school, but during 1926 and 1927 was at home. He is now once more studying law, and will graduate in 1929. It would be difficult to find a man more universally liked or looked up to than Mayor Crockett, and Dublin is fortunate in having a man of his high character in charge of its municipal affairs.

ANDREW LEWIS FARRIER, cashier of the Sinking Creek Valley Bank at Newport, and a World war veteran, was born in Giles County, and his record causes him to share in the reputation his family has long enjoyed for useful and influential participation in the life of the locality.

Mr. Farrier was born at Newport, Virginia, September 27, 1895, son of Martin P. and Mamie (Foote) Farrier. He represents the fourth generation of the family in Giles County. His grandfather, Alpha Jacob Farrier, was a soldier of the Confederacy, and spent his active life as a farmer and merchant. He and his wife are buried in Clover Hollow Cemetery. Martin P. Farrier was born in Craig County, Virginia, attended public schools there and the University of Virginia, studied law, and since his admission to the Virginia bar has gained distinction as one of the very able and scholarly attorneys of the state. Before beginning the practice of law he was deputy county clerk. He was a student at the University of Virginia for two years. He practices with office at Pearisburg, but lives at Newport, where he owns a farm. For several years he was commonwealth's attorney of Giles County, and represented the county in the State Legislature in 1920-21. His wife, Mamie Foote, was born and reared at Pearisburg, attended public schools there, and finished her education in Martha Washington College at Abingdon. She is a member of the Daughters of the American Revolution and the United Daughters of the Confederacy, and is a Methodist. Martin P. Farrier and wife have four children: Andrew Lewis; Martin Pence, Jr., a farmer and county road engineer of Giles County, who married Frances Fisher, of Pearisburg, and has two children, named Harriet and Virginia; Frank Graham, head bookkeeper in the Hopewell Bank and Trust Company of Hopewell, Virginia; and John Jacob, a student in the Newport High School.

Andrew Lewis Farrier attended public schools at Newport, and was in Emory and Henry College until 1913. After he left the college he was on the farm, and also was employed in the Sinking Creek Valley Bank until America entered the World war.

Mr. Farrier was a volunteer and on June 24, 1917, joined the old Virginia Field Hospital Corps at East Radford. He was trained at Camp McClellan, Anniston, Alabama, and in July sailed from New York, landing at Liverpool, was sent to France and became part of the Twenty-ninth Division, Headquarters, with the One Hundred and Fourth Sanitary Train. He was on duty near the front lines in Alsace and in the final great drive of the Meuse-Argonne. Some months after the armistice he returned home and was honorably discharged at Camp Meade in June, 1919.

Mr. Farrier after the war resumed his connections with his old home community and since July, 1920, has been cashier of the Sinking Creek Valley Bank. He is also one of the directors of the bank. For four years he has performed the duties of justice of the peace. He is a Royal Arch Mason, a member of the Cohee Country Club of Blacksburg, Virginia, is a Democrat, a member of the Methodist Episcopal Church, South, and teaches a men's class in the Sunday School and is one of the stewards of the church.

Mr. Farrier married at Newport, October 6, 1920, Miss Marjorie Miller, who grew up at Newport, attending high school there and finishing her education in Sullins College. She takes

Susanna Poythress Bland Temple

an earnest part in the work of the Methodist Church and in the life of the community. Mrs. Farrier is a daughter of Mason J. and Sallie (Payne) Miller. Her father for many years has been a merchant and farmer at Newport, and a brief record of his life and family is published on other pages. Mr. Miller is vice president of the Sinking Creek Valley Bank. Mr. and Mrs. Farrier have a daughter, Jane Foote Farrier.

MRS. SUSANNA POYTHRESS (BLAND) TEMPLE. A true Virginian by birth, breeding and inheritance, Mrs. Susanna P. Temple, of Petersburg, is a distinguished representative of the Bland and Poythress families that have so long been prominent in the public and social affairs of the "Old Dominion," and is proud of the fact that her native state has produced five of the distinguished men that have ably served as Presidents of our glorious country. She was born in Prince George County, Virginia, a daughter of Dr. Theodoric Bland, and granddaughter of Col. Richard Bland.

Mrs. Temple's great-grandfather, Richard Bland, of Jordans Point, was made a delegate to the Second Continental Congress, which met in Philadelphia on May 10, 1776. Just before arriving there he was taken violently ill, and died on the steps of Independence Hall, his name therefore not appearing on that immortal document as one of its signers. His son, Richard Bland, Jr., said that the Declaration of Independence was one of the most intelligent documents ever written regarding the rights of the Colonists, and Mr. Jefferson subsequently referred to Mr. Bland as the smartest man ever reared on the south side of the James River. Richard Bland served as colonel of a regiment in the Revolutionary war. During the progress of the war his house was burned to the ground by the order of Benedict Arnold. Col. Richard Bland married Ann Poythress, who was one of the nine daughters of a prominent Virginia family.

Richard Bland, Jr., Mrs. Temple's grandfather, was a well-to-do planter, and a life long resident of Jordans Point, Prince George County, Virginia. He married Mary Bolling, who was born at Cobbs Island, Chesterfield County, Virginia, a daughter of Maj. John Bolling, a member of one of better known and more influential families of Virginia, and Elizabeth Blair, a niece of Dr. James Blair, the founder of William and Mary College.

As a young man Theodoric Bland turned his attention to the study of medicine, and was graduated from the University of Pennsylvania on April 27, 1827, with the degree of M. D. Locating in Prince George County, Virginia, he there continued in the successful practice of his chosen profession until after his marriage, when his wife induced him to retire from active labor. He subsequently lived on his plantation until his death, when but fifty-five years of age. Like many another Southern gentleman, he was fond of the chase, and while on a fox hunt took a severe cold that developed into pneumonia, which caused his death. He was greatly interested in public affairs, and for several years served as justice of the peace.

The maiden name of the wife of Theodoric Bland was Mary Harrison. She was born June 6, 1809, in Brunswick County, Virginia, a daughter of John and Polly (Cocke) Harrison, names that have long been prominent in the annals of Virginia. She passed to the higher life in 1860, at a comparatively early age. Of the children of the parental household five grew to years of maturity, namely: Sally Russell, Theodoric, Mary Susanna, Anna and Susanna Poythress. The parents were Episcopalians and reared their children in the same religious faith.

In early womanhood Susanna Poythress Bland became the wife of Edward Graves Temple, who was born at Jordans Point in Prince George County, Virginia, a son of James and Elmira (Graves) Temple, and grandson of Frederick and Betsy (Mallory) Temple. His brother, William D. Temple, served for three years in the Confederate army, and for thirty-nine years was clerk of Prince George County.

Born and brought up on the home plantation, Edward G. Temple was for a time engaged in agricultural pursuits. Subsequently becoming a dealer in real estate and lumber, he conducted a very successful business until failing health compelled him to retire from active work. Mr. and Mrs. Temple have four children, as follows: Elmira Graves, Mary Bolling Pocahontas, Sarah Randolph and Edward Graves. Elmira Graves Temple married Herbert Rogers, son of Capt. Asa and Alice (Broocks) Rogers, and they have four children, Susanna Poythress, Herbert, Theodoric and Magdaline Bland. Mary Bolling Temple married Charles F. Collier, son of Robert and Mary (Fisher) Collier, and has three children, Mary Fisher Collier, Susanna Poythress Bland Collier and Edward Temple Collier. Sarah R. Temple married Alfred Beverly Grant, of Richmond, and has one daughter, Mary Bolling Grant. Edward Graves Temple married Fannie Mason Harwood. The Bland and Temple families have always been prominently identified with the Episcopal Church. Mrs. Temple is a member of Frances Bland Randolph Chapter, D. A. R.; a charter member of the Pocahontas Association; a member of the Colonial Dames of America; and of Petersburg Chapter. U. D. C.

CLAUDE R. WOOD is a World war veteran, has practiced law with success and distinction in Buckingham County since shortly after his return from overseas, and is the commonwealth's attorney of that county.

Mr. Wood, whose home is at Dillwyn, was born in Buckingham County January 7, 1893, son of A. C. and Georgia A. (Harris) Wood, also natives of Buckingham County. His grandfather, Capt. A. C. Wood, was a Confederate soldier, and for many years after the war was a boat captain. He died in 1904, at the advanced age of eighty-five. A. C. Wood, the father of the commonwealth's attorney, is a well-to-do farmer in Buckingham County and for many years has been an influential factor in local politics, having served as chairman of the Board of Supervisors twenty-five years and has been a member of that board since 1899. He and his wife reared a family of thirteen children, all of whom are living, namely: Annie Cora; Sallie E., wife of Charles L. Marks; W. A., Jr., farmer and for two terms commissioner of revenue of Buckingham County; Charles H., merchant, farmer and postmaster in Nelson County; Claude R.; Albert J., a carpenter by trade, now living on a farm; Janie B., wife of J. C. Dunkum, of Dillwyn; Mildred C., wife of Juan R. Anderson; Roland C., a bookkeeper in Nelson County; John R., a farmer; George H., in the railroad service; Fred G., stenographer for his brother Claude; and Margaret L., in training as a nurse.

Claude R. Wood grew up on a farm in Buckingham County, attended local schools and the Chatham Training School, now known as the Hargrave Military Academy. From there he continued his education in the College of William and Mary and in Richmond College, now the University of Richmond, from which he received his degree in law with the class of June, 1920. Mr. Wood was admitted to the Virginia bar in 1919, and has had about ten years of experience with a growing practice at Dillwyn.

Before getting ready to practice law he had his military service during the World war. In 1917 he joined the colors with the Three Hundred and Eighteenth Infantry, Eightieth Division, and served twelve months overseas, part of the time as corporal and part of the time as acting color sergeant. He received his honorable discharge June 5, 1919. He was the first commander of Buckingham Post of the American Legion.

Mr. Wood is a Baptist, a Democrat and is a Royal Arch Mason and member of the Independent Order of Odd Fellows. He belongs to the Delta Theta Phi legal fraternity and is a member of the Virginia State Bar Association and American Bar Association.

He has been commonwealth's attorney of Buckingham County since January, 1928, having been chosen to that office without opposition. He was for a time mayor of Dillwyn, resigning to make the race for the Legislature, and represented Buckingham and Appomattox counties in the House of Delegates in the regular session of 1926 and the special session of 1927, but resigned his seat to become commonwealth's attorney.

Mr. Wood married, November 4, 1925, Miss Margaret Pierce, daughter of William F. Pierce. Her father was for many years foreman of a slate quarry in Buckingham County.

ANDERSON EVERETT SHUMATE, member of the Virginia State Senate, is a resident of Pearisburg, and has had many years of active association with the mercantile, banking and public affairs of Giles County.

He was born near Narrows in Giles County, December 24, 1879, son of Rufus Harrison and Celia Ann (Meador) Shumate, and a grandson of Anderson and Elizabeth (Robinson) Shumate, who lived for some years in Mercer County, West Virginia, and then located on a farm near Glenlyn in Giles County, a property that is still owned by this family. Elizabeth Robinson was a granddaughter of John Robinson, one of the prominent figures in the Colonial history of Virginia, who served both as president of the council and acting governor in the absence of the royal governor, William Gooch. He became acting governor in June, 1749, but served only a few months, dying September 3, 1749. Rufus Harrison Shumate was born in Mercer County, West Virginia, attended private schools there and Emory and Henry College. During the war between the states he was a teamster in the supply train with the Quartermaster's Department of the Confederate army, and later was sent to the salt works in Mercer County, West Virginia, where he helped make salt for the government. After the war he was a merchant, farmer and cattle raiser, and died in November, 1888, being buried at Bluff City. His first wife, Celia Ann Meador, was born and reared near Hinton, West Virginia, attended private schools, was a member of the Baptist Church, and died in 1885. Her first husband was Erastus Ferrell, and her two sons were William Ferrell, now deceased, and Erastus Ferrell, of Forest Hill, West Virginia. By her marriage to Rufus Harrison Shumate there were six children: Dr. C. R. Shumate, of Lynchburg, now deceased; Rosa Lee, wife of S. T. Pearis, of Lynchburg; Lula, wife of J. G. Alvis, of Los Angeles, California; Lennie, wife of James Adair, of Narrows; Anderson E.; and Bessie, wife of James E. Ford, of Hinton, West Virginia. Rufus Harrison Shumate after the death of his wife, Celia Ann, married Josie Hopkins Brown and had one son, Kelley R. Shumate, a resident of Narrows.

Anderson Everett Shumate was six years of age when his mother died. He was educated in the public schools, attended the Pearisburg Academy and the College of William and Mary, and taught for one year in Giles County. He clerked in the store of his brother, Charles R. Shumate, at Bluff City, for a few months, then bought the business, and, becoming proprietor at the age of twenty-one, continued as head of an expanding enterprise selling goods throughout the Bluff City territory. He remained a merchant there for twenty-seven years, disposing of the business in 1928. From time to time other business connections have been formed and for some years he has been president of the First National Bank of Narrows and a director in the First National Bank of Pearisburg since it was organized in 1904. He is president of the Giles County Motor Company and has holdings in coal and timber lands, in the lumber industry and the farming and cattle raising business. On his farm he specializes in the pure bred Hereford cattle. He is interested in the Giles County Insurance Company, and some of his business interests are in West Virginia.

Along with an active business career he has done his part as a public official. In 1907 he became a member of the Giles County Board of Supervisors and served eight years, two terms. While on that board he was elected to the House of Delegates from Giles and Bland counties, serving two terms, and in 1927 was elected without opposition to the State Senate, representing the district comprising the counties of Giles, Pulaski, Bland and Wythe. In his work in the Legislature he has the benefit of a long experience and unusual contact with the people of his section, and knows their needs and their wishes. Senator Shumate is a member of Pearisburg Lodge No. 106, A. F. and A. M., and belongs to Acca Temple of the Mystic Shrine at Richmond. He is a member of the Chamber of Commerce, the executive committee of the Virginia Bankers Association, and is one of the vice presidents of the National Banking Division of the American Bankers Association. In politics he is a Democrat, and he is a member of the Baptist Church.

He married at Bluff City, Virginia, February 29, 1904, Miss Lillian M. Hale, of Bluff City. Part of her education was acquired in private schools. She is a member of the Methodist Episcopal Church, South, the United Daughters of the Confederacy and the Daughters of the American Revolution. Her parents were Edward C. and Lucy (Guthrie) Hale, her father a farmer and stock raiser at Bluff City. The Hales are old Virginians of Colonial and Revolutionary stock. Her father died in 1910 and her mother is still active at the age of eighty-five and occupies the home farm. Senator and Mrs. Shumate have four children: Anderson Everett, Jr., Lillian Pauline, Rufus Hale and Celia Ann. The son, Anderson E., Jr., graduated from the Pearisburg High School, attended William and Mary College and Emory and Henry College, the Riddick Business College at Lynchburg, and in 1926 went with the First National Bank of

Pearisburg, and since June, 1928, has been bookkeeper for the First National Bank of Welch, West Virginia. He is unmarried and is a member of the Masonic fraternity. The daughter Lillian Pauline graduated from the Pearisburg High School in 1925 and from the Virginia Intermont College in 1928, where she was a member of the student council and was voted the most popular girl. During 1928-29 she was a junior in William and Mary College, and is specializing in home economics. The two youngest children of Senator and Mrs. Shumate are students in the public schools of Pearisburg.

WILMER GIBSON ROBERTSON has been a Petersburg business man for many years. He represents a family that for generation after generation has lived in Chesterfield County.

Mr. Robertson was born at Chestnut Ridge in Chesterfield County, son of George and Sarah Maria (Ivey) Robertson, grandson of James and Martha (Robertson) Robertson, great-grandson of James William and Fidelia (Archer) Robertson, great-great-grandson of James and Martha Field (Archer) Robertson, and great-great-great-grandson of Col. George Robertson. Col. George Robertson was a son of Rev. George Robertson, who was the founder of the Virginia branch of the family, and he was the ancestor of not only the paternal line above mentioned, but also of Martha Robertson, wife of James Robertson. Martha Robertson was a daughter of John Royal and Mary (Epps) Robertson. Rev. George Robertson came from Scotland, was a minister of the Episcopal Church, and said to have been a chaplain in the English navy. He came to America about 1693, and took charge of Bristol Parish, which had been formed in 1662, and extended on both sides of the James River to the falls of the Appomattox at Petersburg. He was the first settled rector of Blandford Church, which is located at the outskirts of the City of Petersburg. Later other churches were erected in the city and Blandford was abandoned, but in later years it has been restored and is now one of the most interesting historical landmarks of the city. Rev. George Robertson also attended the church at Bermuda Hundred and a chapel called Ferry Chapel at Petersburg. His salary was paid in tobacco, and one year the quality of the crop was so poor that his income amounted to only forty-five pounds sterling. He was active in his pastoral duties until his death in 1739.

His son, Col. George Robertson, located at Picketts in Chesterfield County, where he acquired a large tract of land. James Robertson, grandfather of Wilmer Gibson Robertson, was a planter and slave owner in Chesterfield County, where he spent practically all his life.

George Robertson, his son, attended a preparatory school at Grasslands in Chesterfield and a boys' school in Petersburg, of which Prof. William T. Davis was president. At the age of sixteen he entered William and Mary College, and won high honors as a Latin scholar. When the war broke out he and a majority of the students volunteered and on September 4, 1861, he was enrolled as a member of the Brunswick Guards. Later he was transferred to Company A, Fifth Virgina Battery, and after the battle of Sharpsburg this battery was consolidated with the Fifty-third Regiment, and he continued his service in Company H. At the battle of Gettysburg he participated in Pickett's charge and was then promoted to sergeant-major and acting drill master of the First Regiment of Engineers. When Lee surrendered at Appomattox he went through the lines and was one of the last soldiers of Virginia to surrender. He was given the standing of an honor graduate of William and Mary College.

After the war he engaged in teaching, and spent many years as an educator at Ettrick in Chesterfield County, being principal of the high school there. He lived to be seventy-three years of age. His wife, Sarah Maria Ivey, was a daughter of J. J. and Addie M. (Gresham) Ivey. They reared a family of eight children, Mary Adelaide, Wilmer Gibson, Nellie Wales, John Royal, George Walter (who died at the age of thirty-six), Robert Jeffries, Sarah Maria and Bessie Leigh. Mary Adelaide, the historian of the family, is the wife of Dr. Robert Thomas Webb, presiding elder of the Huntington District of the West Virginia Conference, Methodist Episcopal Church, South. Doctor Webb is a graduate of Randolph-Macon College, continued as a graduate student in Vanderbilt University, and has been a prominent educator and minister. He was associate president and later president of Morris Harvey College in West Virginia, and was pastor of many prominent churches in his conference. He has the degree of Doctor of Divinity bestowed by Randolph-Macon College. Doctor and Mrs. Webb have one son, James Vernon.

Wilmer Gibson Robertson attended a one-room schoolhouse in Chesterfield County, later the Ettrick High School, and since the end of his school days his career has been in Petersburg. He clerked in a grocery store for several years and in 1911 established a business which is widely known and patronized from many sections of Virginia and adjacent states, the Palms Restaurant at 108 North Sycamore Street, which has been under his able management for the past seventeen years.

Mr. Robertson married, in 1905, Eva Taylor Eanes, who was born at Ettrick, Virginia, daughter of Robert Edward and Sarah (Taylor) Eanes. They have four children, Wilmer Gibson, Jr., Mary Evelyn, Howard Clifton and Edgar Bolling. Mr. Robertson is a member of Petersburg Lodge No. 15, A. F. and A. M., and of Grace Episcopal Church.

PHILIP TAYLOR, M. D., practiced his profession at Richmond nearly forty years. He was thoroughly trained in schools at home and abroad, and had those personal gifts and the temperament for the ideal doctor.

He was born in New York City, April 9, 1850, and his death occurred in Richmond August 1, 1922, at the age of seventy-two. He was the only child of Philip and Louise Taylor, of New York. The late Dr. Philip Taylor was reared in New York, and after attending private schools entered the medical department of Columbia University, College of Physicians and Surgeons, from which he graduated in 1876. For two years he pursued work as an interne in the Royal Eye and Ear Hospital at Manchester, England, and with that training he located at Richmond in 1880, and gave his uninterrupted service to a widening circle of patients until he retired in 1918. He was a member of the Richmond Academy of Medicine and the American Medical Association, and was one of the first members of the Westmoreland Club of Richmond.

He married in December, 1891, Miss Sally Williams Lovell, of Front Royal, Virginia, who survives him and resides at 1030 West Franklin Street in Richmond. Mrs. Taylor's father was Judge John T. Lovell, of Front Royal, son of Charles Urquhart

and Mary (Long) Lovell. He was for many years a member of
the House of Delegates and later of the Virginia State Senate,
and was state chairman of the Democratic committee in 1876-
77. Judge Lovell married Lucy A. Williams, daughter of Samuel
C. Williams, of Woodstock, Virginia. Mrs. Taylor was one of
two daughters. Her sister, Mary Lovell, married Marshall
Jeffries, of Fauquier County, Virginia, and their children were
named Lucy, Susan Payne, Elizabeth L., Sallie, Marshall, Mary
Keith, Janet, and John L. Mrs. Taylor is a member of the
Country Club of Virginia and the Confederate Memorial Literary Society and Association for Preservation of Virginia Antiquities. She has one daughter, Phyllis Lovell Taylor, who is
the widow of Joseph M. Bauserman, Jr. Mr. Bauserman was
educated in Washington and Lee University, practiced law at
Woodstock, Virginia, and was a member of the Virginia State
and American Bar Associations, was a committee chairman in
the Sigma Alpha Epsilon national fraternity, and a member of
the American Legion.

WILLIAM R. TOONE was for many years a prominent leader
in the insurance business at Richmond, and like other successful
men in that field enjoyed a widely extended friendship and exercised much influence in the civic affairs of his home community.
He was born in Lunenburg County, Virginia, in September,
1858, and died at Catawba in the state in March, 1919. He
attended school in his native county, and had about ten years
of active experience as a farmer. On removing to Richmond
he took up insurance, and subsequently established a business
of his own and built up a successful organization with an extensive clientele. He continued active until retiring in 1914. He
was a Democrat and a member of the Baptist Church.
    Mr. Toone married in November, 1907, Miss Viola J. Cleaton,
who survives him and resides at 2801 Fourth Avenue in Richmond. She was reared and educated in Greensville County, Virginia, and is one of the five children of Mary W. and Francis H.
Cleaton. Her father served in the Confederate army, and spent
his active career as a farmer in Greensville County. Her mother
was Mary W. Dameron, daughter of W. H. Dameron, a Methodist minister, who had another daughter, Susan, who married
Lester Weaver, a minister of the same church. George and
Thomas Dameron, uncles of Mrs. Toone, were soldiers throughout the Civil war and died as a result of wounds or exposure.

EUGENE H. GRAYSON, commissioner of revenue of Radford,
is a resident of that city, where he was born and where he grew
up. His people have been in Southwest Virginia since early
times, and the family among other associations left the impress
of their name on one of the counties of Southwest Virginia.
    Mr. Grayson was born at Radford March 1, 1901, son of
Frank E. and Bessie M. (Howard) Grayson, and grandson of
Ephraim Grayson, who served four years in the Confederate
army under Colonel Radford. After the war he was a miller and
merchant at Radford, and died in 1918. His widow is still living at Radford, at the age of eighty-one. Frank E. Grayson
was born at Graysontown in Montgomery County, was reared
and educated there, and for a number of years was on the road
as a commercial traveler. He also carried on a real estate
business as member of the firm Grayson & Painter. At the
time of his death, which occurred May 21, 1925, he was com-

missioner of revenue of Radford City, an office he had held for eight years. His widow, Bessie (Howard) Grayson, was born at Childress, Virginia, attended school at Radford, and has always taken a part in the work of the Methodist Episcopal Church, and is a member of the United Daughters of the Confederacy. Her parents were Milton and Josephine Howard, her father having been a soldier of the Confederacy. Frank E. Grayson and wife had four children: Eugene Howard; Louise, who died in infancy; Frank, who graduated from the Radford High School in 1929; and Dorothy, who died in 1926, at the age of twelve years.

Eugene H. Grayson attended schools in Radford, graduating from high school in 1918, was a student for a time in Roanoke College, and completed a course in the National Business College at Roanoke. On leaving college in 1920 he was for two years connected with the Department of Public Utilities of the city of Radford, leaving that position to take charge of the supplies for the Virginia Iron, Coal & Coke Company. In 1924 he returned to the Department of Public Utilities, and in 1925, after the death of his father, he was appointed to fill out the unexpired term as commissioner of revenue, and in the fall of 1925 was elected to that office for a full term of four years, and gives his full time and energies to the administration of his office.

Mr. Grayson owns an interest in a farm near Radford. He is a member of Glencoe Lodge No. 148, A. F. and A. M., the Knights of the Mystic Chain and the Modern Woodmen of America, belongs to the Kiwanis Club, is a Democrat and a Methodist, being active in the church and a member of the choir. Mr. Grayson is unmarried.

ALBERT SIDNEY JOHNSON, JR., is a resident of East Radford, a practicing attorney with offices in the First National Bank Building, and has a very interesting record in his profession, as a former official in the postal service and as a World War veteran.

He was born at Roanoke, Virginia, March 15, 1893, one of the sons of Albert Sidney and Ila (Stone) Johnson. The complete record of his family is published on other pages of this publication. Mr. Johnson was educated in the grade and high schools of Radford, and graduated from the law department of Washington and Lee University with the class of 1915, having been admitted to the Virginia bar in June of that year. Mr. Johnson practiced law at Radford for about a year.

On August 3, 1915, he joined the Virginia Militia in the First Virginia Field Hospital, organized by Dr. J. C. Bowman, and in June, 1916, he was called to the colors and at Richmond was mustered into the Federal service. His outfit was sent to San Antonio, Texas, where it remained until March, 1917. In August, 1917, he again answered the call to the colors for duty during the World war, and was employed in recruiting until November, 1917, when he joined his company at Camp McClellan, Anniston, Alabama, as a member of the 115th Field Hospital, 104th Sanitary Train. In May, 1918, he entered the Officers Training Camp at Camp Taylor, Kentucky, and was detailed for duty as a riding instructor until December, 1918, when he received his honorable discharge.

After leaving the army Mr. Johnson resumed his law practice at Radford, and in September, 1919, was appointed contract officer for the Veterans Bureau. He resigned that to accept ap-

pointment as bond examiner in the postal savings department and was also examiner of claims for losses in the Postoffice Department. This was his work until January, 1923, when on account of failing health he resigned and spent several years recuperating. In January, 1928, he resumed the practice of law at Radford. While in Government service he was frequently entrusted with responsibilities in handling millions of dollars worth of Government securities, and at all times he enjoyed the full confidence of all officials. He has a host of friends, who admire and respect his integrity and have rejoiced that returning health enabled him once more to resume his professional career.

WILLIAM ASHTON REESE. Possessing an excellent knowledge of the many diseases to which mankind is heir, and the wisdom to cope with them, William A. Reese, M. D., of Petersburg, keeps well abreast of the progress of medical science, each day's experience broadening and enlightening his services as a physician in whom it is safe to place implicit trust and confidence. He was born on a farm in Prince George County, a son of Robert Thomas Reese, whose birth occurred in Southampton County, Virginia.

A small child when his father died, Robert Thomas Reese was brought up in the home of an aunt who lived in Sussex County. He became familiar with the three R's in the typical one-room schoolhouse with its primitive equipments, acquiring therein a good common school education. Locating as a young man in Petersburg, he secured work with the Norfolk & Western Railway Company, with whom he remained until the outbreak of the Civil war. His patriotic ardor then being aroused, he entered the Confederate army, enlisting in a company of heavy artillery that was under the command of Capt. Branch Eppes, and continued in the service until the close of the conflict. He was stationed first at Drewrys Bluffs, Virginia, later being at Harrison's Landing. With his regiment he followed General Lee to Appomattox, where he was paroled.

Returning to Petersburg, Robert Thomas Reese soon accepted a position as manager of a farm in Prince George County. Enjoying agricultural work, he purchased a farm on the Rives plank road, five miles from Petersburg, and there spent the remainder of his long life, passing away at the venerable age of eighty-nine years. His wife, whose maiden name was Jane Rives, was born in Prince George County, Virginia, a daughter of Thomas and Sarah (Heath) Rives. She died when but fifty-nine years old. Eight children were born to their marriage, namely: Robert Rives, who died at the age of eighteen years; Annie M.; Ida F.; Roberta Florence; Harriet M.; Sarah Jane; Alma B.; and William Ashton, with whom this sketch is chiefly concerned.

With the knowledge acquired in the rural schools of his district as a stepping stone for higher things, William Ashton Reese was subsequently graduated from the Petersburg High School with a good record for scholarship and attendance. His inclinations leading him to take up the study of medicine, he entered the Medical College of Virginia, from which he was graduated in 1915. The following years he spent as an interne at Grace Hospital in Richmond, where he subsequently engaged in the practice of his chosen profession for a year. Doctor Reese then entered the medical department of the United States

Navy with the rank of lieutenant, senior grade, with which he
was professionally connected for three years, in the meantime
being in active service. Receiving his honorable discharge in
1920, the Doctor began practicing medicine at Petersburg, and
met with such flattering success from the start that he has remained in the same location, his practice being extensive and
lucrative.

Dr. William A. Reese married, in 1918, Miss Helen Walker
Parrish, who was born in Fluvanna County, Virginia, a daughter
of Eugene M. and Elizabeth Parrish. The Doctor and Mrs. Reese
have two children, Jane Elizabeth and Helen Ann. Doctor Reese
is a member of the Petersburg Medical Faculty, South Side; of
the Virginia Medical Society; of the Virginia State Medical
Association; American Medical Association, and a member of the
Petersburg Hospital medical staff. Fraternally he is a Shriner
Mason and an Odd Fellow.

HAROLD W. RAMSEY is division superintendent of the Franklin County schools, with home at Rocky Mount.

He was born at Henry, Virginia, in 1902, son of Robert Lee
and Ida L. (Stone) Ramsey, grandson of Booker Ramsey and
great-grandson of Woodson Ramsey, all of Franklin County.
Booker Ramsey was a Confederate soldier, and died in 1898, at
the age of seventy-five. Robert Lee Ramsey was born in 1876,
and has given his active years to his farm in Franklin County.
His wife was born in Henry County, Virginia, in 1874, daughter
of Clayton Stone, who was also a Confederate soldier. Robert
Lee Ramsey and wife had two children, Edith and Harold W.
Edith was born October 12, 1906, attended the Ferrum School in
Franklin County and the State Teachers College at East Rad-
ford, and is now teaching in the public schools of Henry County.

Harold W. Ramsey graduated from the Hargrave Military
Academy at Chatham, Virginia, and in 1927 took his A. B. degree at the College of William and Mary. Soon after leaving
college he was appointed division superintendent of the schools
of Franklin County.

He is a member of Rocky Mount Lodge No. 201 of the Masonic fraternity and at William and Mary had fraternal affiliations with the Alpha Psi, Kappa Delta Pi, Phi Delta Gamma, and
the honorary scholastic fraternity Phi Beta Kappa. He is a
Democrat and an active worker in the Baptist Church.

EARL BURTON LANGE. The average man is seldom brought
face to face with the stern realities of life before he has reached
years of near maturity. He is generally given an opportunity to
make a choice of occupations—allowed to follow his inclinations
in so far as circumstances do not prevent. Showing an early
predilection for one of the learned professions, for one of the
various fields open in the marts of trade and commerce, or for
the hazardous activities of the public service, he may be given
the chance to develop his talents in his chosen line, and his
success or failure rests upon the manner in which he exercises
his inherent gifts. It is not the average man, however, who
generally reaches the highest goal. History and biography generally prove that the man who achieves distinction, who grasps
the great things of life—the man to whom men look—has had
his start in obscurity. It would seem that the mere necessity of
self support and self protection, which really mean self reliance,
develops indwelling power that would in any other circum-

stances have lain dormant. The man who takes upon himself the responsibilities of manhood in the days of his youth and bends his every energy toward the accomplishment of those things which chance has placed before him, and who finally triumphs over all and tastes the sweet fruits of victory is far above the ordinary individual.

The above applies to the career of Earl Burton Lange, vice president of the Pulaski Veneer Corporation, one of the outstanding industrial concerns of Pulaski County, and a citizen who is popular alike in business and social life, and active in all civic affairs.

Earl Burton Lange was born in Shelbyville, Indiana, March 27, 1885, a son of Samuel and Carrie (Swain) Lange, the former of whom was born, reared and educated in Shelbyville. His vocation was interior decorating, his avocation was water color painting, and he was a true artist, active until his death, which occurred April 1, 1920, in Shelbyville. His remains lie in the cemetery of his native place. The Lange family traces back to the famous Lange family of Ireland, of Scotch-Irish descent. Mrs. Carrie (Swain) Lange was born and reared in Manila, Indiana, and was educated in its public schools. All her life she was an earnest and zealous member of the Christian Church. She, surviving her husband, passed away in 1922, and is buried beside him. The Swain family traces back in an unbroken line to a passenger of the historic *Mayflower*, and claims close kinship with Gen. Winfield Scott, a member of the same family, and also to that sterling patriot Benjamin Franklin. Two children were born to Samuel and Carrie Lange, the younger one being Fred Lange, who is also connected with the Pulaski Veneer Corporation. He was educated in the Shelbyville High School.

Earl Burton Lange attended the common and high schools of Shelbyville, and took a business course with the La Salle Extension School of the University of Chicago. He then went with an uncle, B. F. Swain, in the lumber business in Indiana, and remained with him a few years, and accompanied him when the business was transferred to Indianapolis, Indiana, where it was operated as the National Veneer & Lumber Company, with which concern he remained for twenty-one years, and when he left, in 1926, he was holding the positions of treasurer and manager of that company. In 1926 he came to Pulaski, Virginia, to become vice president and manager of the Pulaski Veneer Corporation, and in this connection is accomplishing some very constructive results. His company gives employment to a large force of skilled workmen, and its payroll forms an important factor in the business life of Pulaski.

Mr. Lange is a thirty-second degree and Shriner Mason, holding membership in the latter with Murat Temple, A. A. O. N. M. S., in Indianapolis. He belongs to the Pulaski Rotary Club, the Pulaski Country Club and to other social and civic organizations, and is keen in his interest in all of them. For years he has been a member of the Methodist Episcopal Church, South, and he is steward of the body in Pulaski. While he has never been willing to accept public office, he is a staunch Republican, and always supports his party's candidates.

On June 14, 1923, Mr. Lange married Miss Marjorie Turner, of Indianapolis. She was educated in the public schools of Detroit, Michigan, and Wellesley College, Wellesley, Massachusetts, of which she is an honor graduate. For a few years prior to her marriage she taught in the Friends Central School, Philadelphia,

Pennsylvania, and also taught for two years in the Indianapolis Technical High School. She is active in the work of the Methodist Episcopal Church, South, of Pulaski, president of the Pulaski Music Club, and belongs to the Pulaski Woman's Club and the Pulaski Garden Club. Mr. and Mrs. Lange have two sons, Earl Burton Lange, Junior, and Samuel Lange.

Since the time Mr. Lange joined the world's workers he has continued to be energetic, forcible and industrious in whatever field he has found himself. It was not his to choose as a lad; he had his ambitions, and they have been gratified, but in his early years he had to wait upon opportunity, although aspirations were kept constantly existent. Mr. Lange is not an average men; his position as one of the high officials of a strong industrial corporation controlling the destinies of many workers and, through them, the prosperity of the houses with which they deal, could not have been attained by the ordinary man, and he has advanced through hard work and won his way to the forefront through that and the intelligent exercise of his natural abilities.

JOHN D. WYSOR, county agricultural agent of Montgomery County, a resident of Christiansburg, is one of the progressive younger group of men in Southwestern Virginia, was college-trained, was with the colors during the World war, and in his present official duties has the benefit of a successful experience as a farmer and stock man.

He was born at Dublin, Pulaski County, Virginia, August 27, 1893, son of R. E. and Margaret (Bimpson) Wysor, and a grandson of George Washington Wysor. The Wysors have been in Southwestern Virginia for generations. R. E. Wysor is a civil engineer by profession, a member of the engineering firm of Wysor & Trinkle of Dublin, and in connection with his profession has carried on farming and stock raising. His wife, Margaret Bimpson, was born at South Point, Ohio. She was a Presbyterian. She died in 1899 and is buried at Dublin. There were three children: R. E. Wysor, a captain in the Regular Army, who served in the Sixth Infantry with the American Expeditionary Forces and is now with the Fourteenth Infantry, stationed at Panama; John D. Wysor; and Julia Margaret, who died in 1922, the wife of John A. Blakemore, of Emory, Virginia, and left one daughter, Mary Blakemore.

John D. Wysor attended public schools in Ohio and Virginia, the Dublin Institute, for two years was in the Virginia Military Institute and had two years in the Pennsylvania State College, where he was graduated in 1915. With this technical training he returned home and took charge of his father's farm near Dublin, and remained there until he joined the colors on August 27, 1917.

He had his training at Fort Myer, Virginia, was commissioned a first lieutenant November 27, 1917, and was then sent to Camp Meade, Maryland, with the Sixth Training Battalion, 154th Depot Brigade. He received his honorable discharge, with the rank of captain of infantry, on April 30, 1919.

Captain Wysor immediately after the war resumed his place on his father's farm, and was there until 1923, when he was appointed county agricultural agent of Montgomery County, at which time he removed to Christiansburg.

Captain Wysor is affiliated with Henry Clay Lodge No. 280, A. F. and A. M., is a member of the Grange, the American Le-

W.H. Cuthbert

gion, is a Democrat and is active in the Presbyterian Church, having served as superintendent of the Sunday School for three years, until 1927. He is a deacon in the church. He and his wife are interested members of the Parent-Teachers Association.

Captain Wysor married at Dublin, September 5, 1918, Miss Cecil Moomaw, of Dublin. She attended public schools there and for three years was a student in Randolph-Macon Woman's College of Lynchburg, after which she taught at Forest and Ivor, Virginia. She is a daughter of George C. and Annie (Crownover) Moomaw, of Dublin. Her father has for many years been a banker and farmer, and was mayor of Dublin for some years. He specializes in fruit growing and the growing of watercress for the market. Captain and Mrs. Wysor have three children, Marguerite, George Moomaw and John Donald, Jr.

WILLIAM HARRISON CUTHBERT. The genial disposition, courteous bearing and high character of William Harrison Cuthbert, an insurance agent in Petersburg, have won him a position of note in business and social circles, and the respect and esteem of all with whom he is brought in contact. He was born November 14, 1851, in Petersburg, which was also the birthplace of his father, Charles H. Cuthbert.

William Cuthbert, grandfather of William Harrison Cuthbert, was born, reared and educated in Londonderry, Ireland. Coming in early manhood to the United States, he located in Petersburg, Virginia, where he worked at anything his hands could find to do. Having by means of industry and thrift accumulated some money, he engaged in the mercantile business. At that time there were no railways in the state, and his merchandise, which came mostly from New York, was brought in vessels via the James and Appomattox rivers, a slow mode of transportation. Being quite successful in his business, he spent the remainder of his years in Petersburg. His wife, whose maiden name was Eliza Raines, was a native of Sussex County, Virginia.

Charles H. Cuthbert was born, reared and educated in Petersburg. Possessing energy and good business ability and judgment, he was for a while engaged not only in mercantile pursuits, but in the manufacture of cotton cloth. He had two factories, one located on Canal Street, operated by water power, and the other on Bollingbrook Street, operated by steam. He was subsequently secretary for the Merchants' Insurance Company of Petersburg, and in 1856 founded the insurance business with which he was actively associated until his death. During the war between the states he was a member of the Home Guards, and was in active service when, in July, 1864, Petersburg was bombarded. He died July 12, 1895, aged sixty-eight years. He was twice married. His first wife, whose maiden name was Elvira M. R. Harrison, was a daughter of Jesse and Agnes (Heath) Harrison, and maternal granddaughter of Jesse and Agnes (Peebles) Heath. Her great-grandfather, William Heath, so tradition says, was a lineal descendant of one of two brothers, Robert and John, who settled in Jamestown in Colonial days. Further ancestral history may be found elsewhere in this volume, in connection with the sketch of Tarlton Heath, Mr. Cuthbert's cousin. Mrs. Charles H. Cuthbert died at the early age of twenty-seven years, leaving three children, William H., Charles H. and Elvira M. R. The father married for his second wife Isabelle H. Baskerville, who died in 1922, leaving four children, Annie H., Belle K., Blanche B. and James E.

During the war between the states William H. Cuthbert
spent the greater part of his time in Petersburg, being present
June 9, 1864, when the city was attacked. With some of his pals
he was in swimming when the firing began, and they all hurried
home. He saw the dead and wounded carried by the house, and
later went with his mother and the other children to Raleigh,
North Carolina. He was there when Johnston's army passed
through the city, and remained there until the conflict closed.
He and his brother sold papers, cigars and tobacco in the streets,
in this way earning enough to support the family and to pay
for transportation home, and also enough to buy a suit of clothes
for the other two children.

Mr. Cuthbert was a member of the first class organized at
McCabes Select School, and of the thirty boys in that class but
three were living in December, 1927. He subsequently attended
the Episcopal High School at Alexandria, and in 1870 entered
the academic department of the University of Virginia, where
the room assigned him was the one later occupied by Woodrow
Wilson.

Having completed his course in the University Mr. Cuthbert
became associated with the insurance business, with which he is
still actively connected. When it was incorporated he was
elected president of the company, a position he is filling effi-
ciently and satisfactorily. He is a faithful member of Saint
Paul's Episcopal Church, in which he is serving as warden and
vestryman.

GEORGE LOGAN MARTIN is one of the business men of the
college town of Blacksburg, where he formerly owned and conducted the Martin's Department Store. Mr. Martin was born
in Southwestern Virginia, and is of Holland-Dutch ancestry, his
great-grandfather having come from Holland and settled at a
very early date in Montgomery County, Virginia.

Mr. Martin was born at Newport in Giles County, June 10,
1870, son of John P. and Elizabeth (Kessler) Martin, and grandson of Andy Martin. John P. Martin was born in Montgomery
County, was privately schooled, and was in the Home Guards
during the Civil war. Following the war he was a farmer,
blacksmith and wagon maker, and died in 1912, being buried
at Blacksburg. His wife, Elizabeth Kessler, was born in Craig
County, Virginia, and died in 1916. Both parents were members of the Lutheran Church, of which the father was a deacon.
There were eight children in the family: J. A. Martin, who died
at the age of thirty-two; John, who died June 18, 1927; Willie
and Sallie, both of whom died in infancy, Annie, wife of D. H.
Kiester; Thomas C., of Radford; George Logan, a merchant at
Blacksburg, Virginia; Robert V., a leading merchant at Beckley,
West Virginia.

George Logan Martin attended public schools, Roanoke College at Salem, Virginia, and after leaving college spent about
three years with a mercantile business at Blacksburg. For
fifteen years he was a salesman for the National Cash Register
Company of Dayton, Ohio, with headquarters at Pittsburgh.
Mr. Martin in 1916 returned to Blacksburg and entered the
general mercantile business, and in 1923 put up the substantial
building which housed the Martin Department Store, carrying a
stock of general merchandise that afforded superior shopping
facilities for all this section of Montgomery County. Mr. Martin
in 1926 put up one of the beautiful homes in Blacksburg.

He is a member of the Independent Order of Odd Fellows, is a Democrat and a Methodist. At Salem, Virginia, June 6, 1898, he married Miss Emma Lewis Oakey, of Salem, where she attended public schools and the Girls' Seminary. She was a student and teacher in the Pittsburgh Bible Institute for several years, and is a deaconess of that institute. She belongs to the W. C. T. U. and Ladies Aid Society. Mrs. Martin is a daughter of John M. and Emma Lewis (Woolwine) Oakey. Her father for many years was proprietor of the John M. Oakey, Incorporated, funeral directors at Roanoke. He died in 1923 and is buried at Salem. Her mother, Emma Lewis Woolwine, died in 1889, and Mr. Oakey subsequently married Fanny Barnett, who resides at Salem.

Clarence Oakey Martin, only son of Mr. and Mrs. Martin, attended public schools at Blacksburg, continuing his education in Randolph-Macon College and William and Mary College, and did summer work in the Virginia Polytechnic Institute. He graduated from the School of Radio Engineering at Washington in 1925. For one year he was with the Westinghouse Electric Company at Springfield, Massachusetts, and was then transferred as a radio engineer to the Victor Talking Machine Company at Camden, New Jersey, spending two years in installing radio equipment. In 1927 he returned to Blacksburg and took charge of the music and radio departments in his father's department store. He handles radios, victrolas and other musical instruments. He is a member of the American Association of Engineers, the Rotary Club, is an independent voter and a Methodist.

Clarence O. Martin married at East Radford, February 27, 1929, Miss Helen R. Newell, of Reidsville, North Carolina. She attended school in North Carolina and Radford State Teachers College, graduating in 1929. For two years she was in the North Carolina State Teachers College, and is wonderfully gifted and trained in music, an art which she has taught successfully. Her father, J. R. Newell, is a business man of Reidsville, North Carolina.

DABNEY GREEN BARNITZ, Doctor of Dental Surgery, is a veteran representative of his profession in Southwest Virginia, and for many years has been the leading representative of dentistry at Christiansburg.

He is a son of the late Judge William M. Barnitz, one of the most distinguished members of the bar, a leader in public affairs, editor, judge and banker. Judge William M. Barnitz was born at Christiansburg, Virginia, September 29, 1827, a son of William and Mary (Travilo) Barnitz, both of whom were natives of Pennsylvania. Judge William M. Barnitz married, September 15, 1853, Elizabeth Frances Craddock, daughter of Edward and Jane Elizabeth Craddock, of Christiansburg.

Prior to the war Judge Barnitz read law under the late Judge W. R. Staples, one of the ablest lawyers and teachers of law in the South. Until the outbreak of hostilities between the North and the South he edited and published a newspaper in Montgomery County, the *Montgomery Messenger*. During the war he was with the commissary department of the Confederate army, stationed at Salem, and after the war was employed for a short time in the store of Major J. C. Green. In 1865 he was made commonwealth's attorney of Montgomery County, holding that office until 1868. In June, 1866, Charles M. Webber established at Salem the *Roanoke Times,* a weekly paper, of which Judge Barnitz became editor for a year. This was during the reconstruction period, and many of his editorials were splendid appeals to the people to accept the situation and by every honorable means restore peace and rebuild their ruined homes. In 1869 he was selected for the office of circuit judge, and in May, 1870, was succeeded on the bench by Alexander Mahood. He was then chosen commonwealth's attorney for the county of Roanoke, beginning his term on January 1, 1871, and served until July 1, 1879. When he left this office he also abandoned the law as a profession and entered banking. He was one of the organizers of the Farmers Savings Bank of Salem, and served as cashier while performing the duties of judge. He assisted in the organization of the Salem Loan & Trust Company, and for nearly two years was cashier of that institution. In many ways his name is closely associated with the financial and public history of Salem and the city of Roanoke. He and Henry S. Trout, J. B. Levy and others organized one of the first banking institutions at Roanoke, and he performed the duties of cashier until his successor could properly qualify.

Judge Barnitz in personal character was well fitted for the leadership he long enjoyed. He was a great advocate of the temperance cause, was a member of the Independent Order of Odd Fellows, being at one time grand master of the state, and was also prominent in Masonry. For over sixty years he was a Methodist. Judge Barnitz died in March, 1901, and is buried at Salem beside his wife, who passed away in April, 1893, on Easter Sunday. They were the parents of nine children: Jennie E., deceased; Blanche, deceased, who married Thomas R. Boone; Edward S., postmaster of Salem; Virginia, who died in infancy; William I., who died in infancy; Fannie, deceased wife of Davis Self; William F., deceased; Dabney Green; and Mary, wife of T. H. Cooper, of Salem.

Dabney Green Barnitz was born at Salem, September 17, 1869, and attended school there, continuing his education in Roanoke College, and graduated from the dental department of the University of Maryland at Baltimore in 1892. For eight years he practiced at Salem, and since 1889 has made his home at Christiansburg, where he is still active in his profession after forty years of continuous work in that community. He has always had a very large practice. Doctor Barnitz owns one of the most beautiful and spacious homes of the city. He is a member of the Virginia Dental Association, the South West Study Club, Independent Order of Odd Fellows, Knights of Pythias, Benevolent and Protective Order of Elks, Modern Woodmen of America, and was formerly active in the Junior Order United American Mechanics. He is a Republican in politics and is a trustee of the Methodist Episcopal Church, South.

Doctor Barnitz married at Lynchburg, January 11, 1899, Elizabeth Frances Williams, of that city. She attended public schools and the Lynchburg Woman's College. Her parents were Robert and Esther (Maze) Williams, of Lynchburg. Her father was a Confederate soldier and for years a leading railroad contractor and builder, who died in 1911. Doctor and Mrs. Barnitz had a family of five children, one dying in infancy. Elizabeth Frances is the wife of B. C. Cubbage, of Sewanee, Tennessee, and has a son, Benjamin C., Jr. William M. Barnitz, in the automobile and garage business at Shawsville, married Miss Lois

R. A. O'Brien

Mitchell, of Cambria, Virginia. Dabney Green Barnitz, Jr., is
a member of the senior class of the military institute at Sewanee,
Tennessee. Robert Maxwell Barnitz, the youngest, is attending
public school at Christiansburg.

ROBERT A. O'BRIEN. Although one of the younger members
of the bar of Roanoke, Robert A. O'Brien has won the appreciation and standing to which his natural and acquired talents
entitle him, and is enjoying a large practice. At the bar he is
always courteous, but forceful, logical, convincing and never a
quibbler over non-essential points. He prepares his cases with
patience, faithfulness and ability and seldom is involved by his
opponents in a phase of the litigation which he has not carefully
considered. As a counselor he is astute but conservative; that
he is a literary and cultured gentleman is evident not only from
his conversation and bearing, and his large and valuable library,
but by past achievements. While still in college he prepared
a paper on "Poor Relief in Colonial Virginia," of such unquestioned literary merit that he was awarded the J. Taylor Ellyson
Medal, and he has from time to time contributed articles of
interest to the local journals. These productions show that did
he care to give the time to literary work he could achieve by it
a permanent success.

Robert A. O'Brien was born in Appomattox, Virginia, March
10, 1899, a son of Frank A. and Mary (Torrence) O'Brien, both
of whom were born in Appomattox, and in its vicinity the father
has farmed all his life, and become one of the leading agriculturists of that region. The parents are very active members
of the Baptist Church, and in charitable work. He is a strong
Democrat, and is now serving as a member of the Board of
Supervisors of Appomattox County. Four children have been
born to the parents, namely: Mildred, who married R. E. Alvis,
of Lynchburg, Virginia, in the employ of the Norfolk & Western
Railroad; Robert A., whose name heads this review; Kate Elizabeth; and Lucile. The paternal grandfather, Robert A. O'Brien,
was also born in Virginia, and he served during the last two
years of the war in the Confederate army. The maternal grandfather, Alfred Torrence, was a farmer.

Reared in Appomattox, Robert A. O'Brien attended the Agricultural High School of that community, and was graduated
therefrom in June, 1916, following which he entered the University of Richmond, and was graduated from that institution
in 1919 with the degree of Bachelor of Arts. He took his degree
of Master of Arts in 1920, and that of Bachelor of Laws in
1923, all from the same university. He made Kappa Sigma and
the law fraternity Delta Theta Phi, as well as the honorary fraternity Omicron Delta Kappa.

Following his admission to the bar in 1923 Mr. O'Brien
established himself in a general practice in August of that year
in Roanoke, and he is widely and favorably known over a wide
territory. The First Baptist Church of Roanoke holds his membership. His fraternal connections are those which he maintains
with the Benevolent and Protective Order of Elks. Mr. O'Brien
is unmarried. His social connections are many and he is a great
favorite among the younger social set of Roanoke. He is a
member of the Roanoke Country Club, also a member of the
Roanoke, State and American Bar Associations, and of the
Roanoke Chamber of Commerce.

THOMAS JEFFERSON GARDNER was a well known farmer of Southampton County, living a life of commendable industry and of high ideals.

He was born in Southampton County in August, 1865, and died in that county in 1906. He was a son of Harmon and Elizabeth (Sherard) Gardner. He was very young when his father died, had a country school education, and from early youth until his death followed the industry of farming.

He married in December, 1890, in Southampton County, Miss Natalie Estelle Applewhite, daughter of Walter S. and Martha Applewhite. Mrs. Gardner's grandfather, Benjamin Applewhite, donated the land for the Applewhite Methodist Church in Southampton County. Mrs. Gardner, who now resides at 526 North Elm Avenue in Portsmouth, is an active worker in the Methodist Church. Mr. Gardner was a Methodist and a Democrat in politics. Mrs. Gardner's father was a farmer and business man of Southampton County.

Mrs. Gardner has six children. Walter Thomas, an employe of the Portsmouth Navy Yard, married Violet Hollis, and their three children are Frances A., Walter T. and Joella. William Richard Gardner is a newspaper man, and in 1917 enlisted in the One Hundred and Sixteenth Infantry, having previously been a member of Company F, Fourth Virginia Infantry National Guard at Suffolk. He spent eighteen months in France as an aerial photographer in the One Hundred Sixty-first Aero Squadron, and was given the grade of sergeant. Gladys Adair Gardner is the wife of C. D. Owens, an employe of the Seaboard Airline Railway, and has one daughter, Nancy May. Virginia Estelle is the wife of Guy Gerald, of the Navy Yard, and has two children, Guy Edward, Jr., and Elsie V. Martha Elizabeth Gardner married Walter Fletcher Taylor, of Winston-Salem, North Carolina and has one son, Gordon Bingham Taylor. Queenie May Gardner is the wife of Edward R. Burroughs, an artist, now one of the instructors in the Art Institute at Dayton, Ohio.

The Applewhites, who came from England, have been in Virginia since Colonial times, and the Colonial, Revolutionary and state records afford abundant evidence of their connection with the old land owning gentry, their professional, military and public services. Hotten in his "Early Emigrants to Virginia" infers that Henry Applewhite, the immigrant, came from the Barbadoes, as he speaks of the servants of Henry Applewhite in Barbadoes. In the various records the name was spelled Applewayte. In 1704 it is found spelled Applewhaite and since 1870 the spelling has been Applewhite. Mr. William G. Stannard, secretary of the Virginia Historical Society, has compiled from the state library archives a number of references to the family as found in the records of Isle of Wight County. A few of these notes follow: Henry Applewhite, living in Virginia in 1670. Henry Applewhite, burgess for Isle of Wight, 1726-1728. Henry Applewhite, vestryman, Newport Parish, Isle of Wight, 1724-1771. Henry Applewhite, sheriff, Isle of Wight, 1731. Henry Applewhite, burgess, Isle of Wight, 1685. Henry Applewhite, justice, Isle of Wight, 1702. Henry Applewhite, Jr., justice, Isle of Wight, 1712. Benjamin Applewhite, of Southampton County, living in 1836. Richard H. Applewhite and Mary Franklin Thrift, both of Norfolk, were married in 1847. Thomas H. Applewhite, of Southampton, living in 1785.

Thomas and John Applewhite, appointed justices of the peace, Isle of Wight, 1742.

From the record of wills in Isle of Wight County Mr. Stannard also compiled the following notes: Will of Henry Applewhite—(very sick)—sons Henry, Thomas, William and John; daughters, Anne Applewhite, dated August 26, 1703. Proved May 9, 1704.

Will of Thomas Applewhite—wife Martha, sons, *Thomas Henry* and John Applewhite: daughters, Hanel Copeland, Martha Weston, Mary Bern and Anne Applewhite, dated June 15, 1728, proved January 22, 1732.

Will of John Applewhite, wife Sarah. sister, Anne Applewhite, brother Thomas Applewhite, sister Martha Weston, dated December 20, 1735.

Will of Martha Applewhite—son, Thomas Applewhite, daughters, Helen Copeland, Martha Weston, Mary Bern and Anne Parker, granddaughter, Helen Applewhite, grandsons, James Bern and Henry Applewhite, son-in-law, William Parker. Dated January 30, 1739, proved February 25, 1739.

Will of Henry Applewhite—sons, John, Arthur and Thomas, Daughters, Sarah Applewhite, Anne Davis and Anne Gordon, granddaughter, Anne, daughter of son, Thomas. Wife, Anne (land where his mother, Mary Applewhite, lives, mentioned). Proved April 17, 1740.

Will of John Applewhite—sons Benjamin and John, wife, Mary, daughter, Mary Applewhite, brother, Arthur Applewhite, dated March 1, 1758, proved May 4, 1758.

(Southampton County.) Similar record from Southampton County notes the following:

Will of Henry Applewhite, wife, Anne, sons, Henry, Thomas, Hardy, John, Benjamin, William and Arthur. Daughters, Sally Applewhite, Priscilla Applewhite, Janey Applewhite, Rebecca Applewhite, Nancy Applewhite and Mary Barham. Dated May 11, 1738, proved July 10, 1783.

Will of Thomas Applewhite, dated June 26, 1787, legatees, Arthur, son of Arthe Applewhite, Henry Wills Applewhite, son of John Applewhite, Jean, daughter of Isham Carr, and George Thomas, son of Absolom Williams. Proved December 18, 1781.

Will of Anne Applewhite—sons William, Thomas, John and Hardy. Daughters Mary Barham, Sally Deshiel, Priscilla Jordan, Janey Applewhite, Rebecca Applewhite and Nancy Applewhite. Dated February, 1795, proved February, 1795.

Deed—April 8, 1756—from Henry Applewhite of Southampton County to Arthur Applewhite of Isle of Wight County.

Land granted to Henry Applewhite, grandfather of said Henry, party to his deed, on June 20, 1733, and for fifty acres the said Henry Applewhite, the grandfather, bought in 1710.

Deed—June 23, 1766, from Mills Applewhite of Isle of Wight County, conveying land in Southampton County, left him by his father, Arthur Applewhite.

Deed—1786 from Thomas Applewhite, of Southampton County, Mariner, son of Arthur Applewhite (whose will was dated 1766).

Marriage bonds of Henry Applewhite and Ann Harris, November 7, 1756.

Marriage bonds of Harry Applewhite and Charlotte Clopton, October 9, 1783—consent of Sarah Clopton and her daughter, Mary.

Marriage bonds of John Applewhite and Rebecca Moore, October 14, 1784.

Marriage bond of Henry Applewhite and Jane Harris, January 13, 1812.

There are many other interesting records regarding the family, too numerous for insertion in this brief sketch, but reference should also be made to some of the military records found in the Virginia State Library, Department of Archives. The name of John Applewhite appears as a private in the "pay roll of Captain Thomas Ridley's company of regulars under command of Colonel Thomas Aylett of the Fourth Virginia Battalion, from April 1, 1777, to the 1st day of May." The name John Applewhite as a soldier in the infantry also appears in a manuscript book in the Virginia State Library known as "War 4," which is a "list of soldiers of the Virginia Line on Continental Establishment who have received certificates for the balance of their full pay agreeable to an act of assembly passed November session in 1781." From another manuscript in the Virginia State Library, addressed to the governor and council of Virginia, is quoted the following: "I hereby respectfully submit for your consideration certain affidavits in proof of the Revolutionary services of Dr. John Applewhite as a surgeon in the State Navy of Virginia in the War of the Revolution on behalf of his one surviving heir and daughter, Miss Judith Cary Applewhite of Norfolk." The document goes on to urge that the case is one with very peculiar claims to consideration, the "proof of service begins in 1776 and terminates with the war, nay, extends beyond to the abolition of the navy."

STEPHEN SANDERS SIMMERMAN is an individual representative of a very prominent family of Southwestern Virginia. The Simmermans have long been prominently associated with the livestock industry. Mr. Simmerman is a son of the late Col. Stephen Sanders Simmerman, Sr., of Wythe County, who died October 9, 1928. An interesting record of the family activities and including many of the names in the different generations is presented on other pages of this publication.

Mr. Stephen Sanders Simmerman was born at Ivanhoe, Virginia, May 15, 1889. His mother was Louise Elizabeth (Painter) Simmerman. He was educated in private schools in Wytheville, and attended Virginia Polytechnic Institute and Hampden-Sidney College.

He left college in 1908 and joined his father in his extended farming and livestock business, and that has constituted his important work for twenty years. The Simmermans have handled thousands of cattle all over Virginia and the Southeast, and have been leading cattle exporters. Mr. Simmerman continues the business since the death of his father, and he also owns two large blue grass stock farms near Wytheville. He is a stockholder in the Bank of Speedwell, of which his father was president until his death.

Mr. Simmerman is a member of the Presbyterian Church. He married at Tupelo, Mississippi, September 8, 1920, Miss Virginia Preston Mitchell, of Tupelo. She comes of a family that is well known socially in Virginia. Mrs. Simmerman was educated in the Stonewall Jackson College of Abingdon, Virginia, and graduated in 1917 from Mary Baldwin Seminary at Staunton. She is a Presbyterian and a member of the Daughters of the American Revolution and United Daughters of the

Confederacy. Mrs. Simmerman is a daughter of George T. and Virginia Preston (Summers) Mitchell, of Tupelo, Mississippi. Her father is a graduate of the University of Mississippi and of the Michigan University, Ann Arbor, and is one of the outstanding criminal lawyers of Mississippi, maintaining offices at Tupelo, Atlanta, Georgia, Birmingham, Alabama, and Memphis, Tennessee. He was appointed by Governor Bibbs attorney-general of Mississippi. He lives on a Mississippi plantation and has been a cotton planter. He is one of the state's leading business men. He is a member of the Masonic fraternity and the S. A. E. Mrs. Mitchell is a very versatile and brilliant woman, highly educated, having attended Stonewall Jackson College and Mary Baldwin College in Virginia. She is a member of the Society of Colonial Dames, Daughters of the American Revolution, and the United Daughters of the Confederacy.

Mr. and Mrs. Simmerman have four children, Stephen Sanders Simmerman III, George Mitchell Simmerman, Virginia Preston Simmerman, students in private schools in Wytheville, and Louise Painter Simmerman.

Mr. Simmerman registered for service in the United States army May 13, 1917, and spent three months in training at Fort Myer, Virginia, was then transferred to the Aviation Corps at Camp Lee, Virginia, and finally to the Field Artillery Officers Training School at Camp Zachary Taylor, Kentucky. He was honorably discharged November 28, 1918.

EDWIN TRAVIS LAMB was born in the City of Richmond, Virginia, June 29, 1863. He died in the City of Birmingham, Alabama, November 9, 1919.

On his maternal side he was a direct descendant of Col. Edward Champion Travis, an officer in the American army during the Revolutionary war, for years a member of the Virginia House of Burgesses, and a man of much prominence in his native state. Colonel Travis, who married Susan Hutchinson, died in or about 1785. One of his sons, Edward Travis, a captain in the United States Navy, was wounded during the War of 1812. Another son, Champion Travis, married Katherine Bush, a daughter of Samuel Bush and a granddaughter of Maximilian Bush. The son of Champion Travis and Katherine Bush Travis, Samuel Bush Travis, married Elizabeth Bright. Their daughter, Elizabeth Travis, married Henry Edlowe. Of this marriage was born Harriet Edlowe, who married Junius Lamb. Among their children was Edwin Travis Lamb, the subject of this biographical note.

The railroads played a prominent part in the rebuilding and in the development of Virginia after the disastrous years of the Civil war. Early in life Edwin Travis Lamb was attracted to this service, first with the Chesapeake & Ohio Railroad, afterwards with the Southern Railway, becoming superintendent of one of the divisions of that line. Later he was made president of the Norfolk & Southern Railroad, and, in 1912, he became president of the Atlanta, Birmingham & Atlantic Railroad, which position he held at the time of his death. When the railroads were taken over for operation by the United States Government during the World war the services of Mr. Lamb were recognized by the administration, and he was made one of the regional directors.

Deeply interested in the promotion of the civic, industrial and commercial development of the City of Norfolk, in which city he resided for many years prior to his death, as well as of the City of Atlanta, in which city were located the offices of the Atlanta, Birmingham & Atlantic Railroad, he was always active in any well directed effort in that behalf. For many years he was vice president of the Norfolk National Bank of Commerce & Trusts.

He maintained memberships in several of the more prominent clubs both in Norfolk and in Atlanta, and his social contacts and business associations made for him a host of friends, who respected his ability, who admired his ideals and who revere his memory.

In the year 1888 he married Lucy Lane, daughter of Capt. Levin Winder Lane and Martha Spencer Lane. Lucy Lane Lamb, widow of Edwin Travis Lamb, is, through her maternal and paternal ancestors, a descendant of families which have long been prominent in the life of Virginia. Among these ancestors may be mentioned Gen. John Eaton Browne, prominent in the War of the Revolution; Sarah Cobb, daughter of Robert Cobb, of York, and Dudley Diggs. Martha, daughter of Gen. John Eaton Browne, married John Graves, son of Ralph Graves, a lieutenant in the navy in the War of the Revolution. To them were born two children, Caroline Dudley and Ralph II. Caroline Dudley Graves married Edward Dudley Richardson. To them was born Martha Richardson, who married William Spencer, the grandfather of Mrs. Lamb.

Three children were born of the marriage of Edwin Travis Lamb and Lucy Lane Lamb: Lucy Winder Lamb, wife of Commander Monroe Kelly, of the United States Navy, now with the United States Naval Mission to Brazil; Martha Lane Lamb, who married William Hunter Bell, a member of the firm of Dobie & Bell, insurance brokers of Norfolk; and Edwin Travis Lamb, Jr. Commander and Mrs. Kelly have two children, Monroe Kelly, Jr., and Lucy Lane Lamb Kelly, the latter of whom is a life member of the Historical Society of Virginia. Mr. and Mrs. Bell have two children also, Lucy Travis Bell and Martha Hunter Bell. Edwin Travis Lamb, Jr., is unmarried. After attending Yale University he returned to Norfolk, and is now with the Norfolk National Bank of Commerce & Trusts. He is a life member of the New England Historical Society, and is a member of the Colony Club, Brazillus Society and of the Norfolk Country Club, the Princess Anne Country Club and the Princess Anne Hunt Club.

JOHN SAMUEL MCCONNELL, of Radford, Virginia, is a business man and for thirty-five years has well expended his energies in merchandising and other lines, at present being engaged in real estate and insurance, with offices in the First National Bank Building, East Radford, Virginia.

He was born in Scott County, Virginia, April 7, 1875, a son of James M. and Mary (Quillin) McConnell, grandson of Samuel R. McConnell and great-grandson of George McConnell, Senior. The latter came to Scott County from Pennsylvania about the year 1800, serving the county as a member of the County Court and as first sheriff for the county. At the first meeting of the County Court for the organization of the government of the new County of Scott, at Moccasin Gap, in the fall of 1814, he was recommended to the governor of Virginia for appointment as a member of the County Court. Almost constantly since 1814 he or his descendants have held important county and district offices. He was also an active business man throughout his life as a merchant and farmer.

The family is one that has been long and favorably known in Southwestern Virginia. James M. McConnell was born and reared in Scott County, attended private schools and was in the Confederate army the latter months of the war. Since the war he has been a farmer and stock raiser, was for many years clerk of the school board for his district and deeply interested in the welfare and extension of school and church work there, the McConnell family being the pioneer Methodist leaders of that section.

His wife, Mary L. Quillin, was born and reared at Nickelsville, Virginia, attended private schools and was a member of the Methodist Church. She died in April, 1922, and is buried in the McConnell family cemetery, which is also the burial place of Samuel R. and George McConnell, Senior. Her father, James M. Quillin, was a merchant, contractor and surveyor at Nickelsville, Virginia. He was a fife major in the Confederate army, was captured at Cumberland Gap, Virginia, and confined in prison at Camp Chase until the war closed. He and his wife, whose maiden name was Tate, are buried in the cemetery at Nickelsville, Virginia.

Of the seven children of James M. McConnell and wife one, Tempie A., died in infancy, and Nannie E. died when a small child. Robert L. lives at Nickelsville, Virginia, and is surveyor for Scott County. Valice D. lives with her father, Wilburn M. is deceased, also his sister, Minnie E., who was the wife of C. E. Meade, of Nickelsville, Virginia.

John S. McConnell acquired a public school education in Scott County, taught one term in public schools and then spent four years in the store of his uncle, Wilburn Neeley, at Speers Ferry, Virginia. In 1900, in partnership with J. F. Ford, he established a mercantile business at Coeburn, Wise County, Virginia, and in 1910 they added another store at Appalachia, Wise County, Virginia, whither Mr. McConnell removed to take charge, the two stores becoming widely known as two of the leading mercantile establishments of the county. He was at Appalachia from 1900 to 1918, and after selling his mercantile interests removed to Radford, Virginia, and for ten years has carried on a business in real estate and insurance.

While located in Wise County he devoted his energies to business and took a large part in the commercial and mercantile enterprises of the county, was director of the First National Bank while living in Appalachia and has important connections with a large number of business firms and commercial institutions.

He has not confined his efforts and attentions to his own affairs, but has always taken a very active part in the development of the resources and the promotion of the business and financial interests of the section with which he has been identified.

He is a director of the First National Bank of East Radford, Virginia, and a director of the Shenandoah Life Insurance Company of Roanoke, Virginia. He has made a substantial success in business and is a recognized leader in community affairs. He is now secretary of the Radford Chamber of Commerce and treasurer and director of the Radford Rotary Club.

In the Masonic fraternity he is a member of Glencoe Lodge, Radford, Virginia, of Craig Royal Arch Chapter and Cyrene Commandery, Norton, Virginia, of Acca Temple and Dalcho Consistory, Richmond, Virginia. He is also a member of the Sons of Confederate Veterans, a Methodist and a Democrat.

He married at Baltimore, Maryland, September 12, 1910, Mae Virginia Woods, who was reared and educated there. She is a member of the Woman's Club, Music Club, Garden Club and First Baptist Church of Radford, Virginia, and is active in the educational, civic and religious work of Radford. Her father, William C. Woods, was for many years a merchant in Baltimore, and both parents are buried in that city. Mr. and Mrs. McConnell have three children, Lucile Virginia, Howard Johnson and Jean, the two elder attending Radford High School, while Jean is a grade pupil.

His family on both sides have for almost a century and a half been actively identified with the business, social and political life of Southwestern Virginia. His maternal family has had wide and influential connections and relationships in Southwestern Virginia from the earliest days of that section. Like the McConnell family it has been characterized by physical vigor, mental ability, courage, resourcefulness and enterprise in every field of activity.

HENRY CLEMENT TYLER, a son of the late Gov. J. Hoge Tyler, has long enjoyed public and professional honors and responsibilities quite apart from his high family connections. His home is at East Radford, and he is known throughout the state for his ability as a lawyer, and he has been given several proofs of the esteem of his fellow members of the bar in Southwest Virginia.

He was born at the old family homestead, Belle Hampton, in Pulaski County, December 10, 1878. His grandfather, George Tyler, a descendant of Richard Tyler, who came from London in 1674 and settled in what later became Caroline County, Virginia, was born in 1817, represented Caroline County in the Virginia House of Delegates a number of times, and married Eliza Hoge. Her father, Col. James Hoge, was a prominent planter of Pulaski County, and part of his estate became the property which Governor Tyler named Belle Hampton.

James Hoge Tyler was born in Caroline County August 11, 1846, and died January 3, 1925. He grew up in the home of Gen. James Hoge, inherited the family plantation, and named it Belle Hampton in honor of two of his daughters. He was educated in the Minor School in Albemarle County, and at the age of sixteen became a Confederate soldier. The greater part of his life was given to farming, and he was one of the master farmers of his generation in Virginia, and for many years was president of the Virginia Farmers Institute. He entered the State Senate in 1877, served as a member of the Board of Visitors and rector of the Virginia Polytechnic Institute, and belonged to nearly all the agricultural societies of the state. He was a member of the Virginia State Debt Commission. In 1897 he was elected governor by the largest plurality ever given up to that time a gubernatorial candidate. He was the fortieth governor of Virginia, and when he gave over the reins of administration he was able to retire with honor to private life, and thereafter devoted himself to the management of his farming

Edward P. Buford

interests and his activities in connection with the Virginia Farm Institute. Governor Tyler married, November 16, 1868, Sue Hammet, daughter of Col. Edward Hammet, of Montgomery County. She was born in 1845.

Henry Clement Tyler was next to the youngest of the seven children of his parents. He was liberally educated, attending St. Albans Academy, and in 1899 entered the law department of the University of Virginia. In July, 1901, he was admitted to the bar, and in the same year located at Radford, where he was soon established in a valuable general practice. In 1906 he was elected commonwealth's attorney for the City of Radford, and filled that office sixteen years, until 1922, when he was elected a member of the House of Delegates. For many years he has filled the office of city solicitor of Radford, and was largely instrumental in framing the new city manager form of government. Mr. Tyler is vice president of the Peoples Bank of Radford. He has been active in Democratic politics, and several years ago the local bar endorsed his candidacy for the Supreme Court of Appeals. Mr. Tyler is an elder in the Presbyterian Church and teaches a class in Sunday School. He is a member of the Rotary Club.

EDWARD P. BUFORD, of Lawrenceville, is a scholarly member of the Virginia bar, is the second son of Judge Francis E. Buford and is a member of a family that has long been distinguished for intellectual independence.

He was born at "Sherwood" in Brunswick County December 15, 1865, where he still resides. He was educated in public and private schools, studied under private tutors, spent one session in Col. Gordon McCabe's University School at Petersburg, and for one year studied law under the direction of his father. He took the law course at the University of Virginia in 1886-87, and on June 27, 1887, was admitted to the bar.

He has had more than forty years of working association with his profession. He argued his first case in the Supreme Court of Appeals of Virginia in 1890, and has practiced in that court regularly. In 1893 he was admitted to the bar of the Supreme Court of the United States. Mr. Buford was chosen commonwealth's attorney of Brunswick County in 1891, and held the office continuously until 1917, when he resigned, being unwilling to act officially under the prohibition law. He was elected a member of the House of Delegates in 1897 and was again elected to that office in 1919. In 1922 he was chosen president of the Virginia State Bar Association for the 1922-23 term.

Some of his discussions of legal questions and public problems have made his name familiar among lawyers and students outside the boundaries of Virginia. One such article was entitled "The Federal Employer's Liability Act," published in the *Harvard Law Review*, December, 1914. His three addresses delivered before the Virginia State Bar Association, entitled "Presumption of Malice in the Law of Murder," "Federal Encroachments Upon State Sovereignty," and "The Virginia Bill of Rights," were published in the reports of the association for the years 1922, 1923 and 1926 respectively. His article "The So-Called Eighteenth Amendment to the Constitution of the United States" was published in the April, 1928 number of the *Virginia Law Review*.

BRACKETT HENRY SNIDOW, of Pembroke, Giles County, is a veteran of two professions, the law and education. Probably his chief inclination has been for teaching, but he has used his knowledge of and skill in the law as valuable counsel both to himself and to his clients.

Mr. Snidow is a land holder, and his home at Pembroke occupies one of the most picturesque sites in Southwest Virginia, facing the famous Castle Rock on New River. "Castle Rock" was the name given to this towering precipice of stone by his grandfather, George Snidow.

Brackett H. Snidow was born at Pembroke, November 22, 1882, and represents a modern generation of one of the oldest families in the Middle New River settlement. The Snidows came originally from Germany, lived in the vicinity of Lancaster, Pennsylvania, for some years, and finally John Snidow and his wife, Elizabeth (Helm) Snidow, left Pennsylvania and started on the long journey to the New River settlement, where John Snidow had previously prospected and selected lands. He died on the journey, but his wife and family went on to the vicinity of what is now Pembroke, Virginia, where they have lived ever since. Simon Snidow, a nephew of John Snidow, was governor of Pennsylvania during the Colonial period.

John Snidow was the father of Philip Snidow, grandfather of Christian Snidow, who, in turn, was the father of George Snidow, grandfather of Brackett H. Snidow.

Brackett Snidow is a descendant from another branch of John Snidow's family (above mentioned), which is traced as follows: Captain Henry Walker, of Botetourt County, Virginia, married Martha Woods, youngest daughter of Andrew Woods. To this union were born eight sons and one daughter, one of whom was Major Henry Walker, who married Mary Burk Snidow, a daughter of Col. Christian Snidow. Martha A. Walker was the oldest daughter of Major Henry Walker, and on October 4, 1843, married George Snidow, who was the grandfather of Bracket H. Snidow. Capt. Henry Walker was an officer in the American Revolution under General Green for a period of three years in North and South Carolina. His son, Major Henry Walker, was an officer in the army during the War of 1812. Both Gen. Andrew Lewis and Gen. Samuel Houston were close relatives of this branch of the Walker and Woods families, and were reared in the same vicinity of Botetourt County. Gen. Andrew Lewis was a first cousin to Martha Woods, the wife of Capt. Henry Walker.

Brackett H. Snidow still has in his possession several heirlooms handed down to him from this branch of his ancestors, among them being two letters, one written by his great-great grandmother, Martha (Woods) Walker, on July 11, 1805, and another, written by her husband, Capt. Henry Walker, on February 13, 1793.

In order to eliminate confusion, it may be well to state that Brackett H. Snidow descends from two ancestors named, "Christian." Col. Christian Snidow was his great-great-grandfather and was of the branch to which his grandmother, Martha (Walker) Snidow, belongs. Christian Snidow, on the other side, was the son of Philip Snidow, and the nephew of Col. Christian Snidow. He was the father of George Snidow, who, in turn, was the father of Luther Snidow, the father of Brackett H. Snidow.

The old Snidow home occupied by the original settlers of that name was located on the north bank of New River, about two hundred and fifty yards below the mouth of Little Stony Creek, and within a few feet of the present residence of Arch D. Collins at Pembroke. The oldest residents of Pembroke now living remember this house as it stood years ago, but which has now been removed.

The old Snidow fort was built at the extreme upper end of the river bottom land on the Horse Shoe farm. At this fort several of the Snidow children were killed by the Indians and three others were captured, but later returned safely. The Horse Shoe Farm remained in the family possession for a number of generations, down to recent years. However, when the Snidows settled on New River, this farm was owned by Thomas Burk, and later was deeded to the Snidow family. Thomas Burk's home was located only a few feet directly in front of the old home now belonging to Mr. Albert Walker Snidow of Pembroke, Virginia. Mr. Albert W. Snidow is a great-great-grandson of Thomas Burk, and his mother, Mrs. Martha (Walker) Snidow, used the old Burk house for several years as a kitchen.

Col. Christian Snidow married Mary Burk, a daughter of Thomas Burk. He was an officer in the army of the American Revolution, and his commission is now preserved by Mr. William Bane Snidow, an attorney at Pearisburg, Virginia.

Thomas Burk was buried on the Horse Shoe Farm in 1808. Many members of the Burk family, as well as the Snidows, who descended from him, are buried in this cemetery. Much local history may be obtained from the monuments found in this burying ground.

W. Luther Snidow, father of Brackett H., was born and reared at Pembroke, attended private schools and spent his active life as a farmer and stock raiser. He is a member of the Lutheran Church and is now seventy-seven years of age. His first wife was Susan Abington, who was born and reared near Martinsville, Virginia, where she attended private schools; she was also of the Lutheran faith. She died in 1883 and is buried in the Horse Shoe Cemetery. Her only child was Brackett H. Snidow. The father subsequently married Mary Stiff, and the eight children of that union were Mabel, Martha, Geneva, Homer A., George S., W. Luther, Paul and Oren.

Brackett H. Snidow received his early educational advantages in a number of different localities, attending school in North and South Carolina and in Virginia. In 1906 he graduated A. B. from Roanoke College at Salem, and took his degree in law at the University of Virginia in 1909. Roanoke College bestowed upon him the M. A. degree in 1911. His teaching work has been done in high schools in Virginia, West Virginia and Kentucky. He was admitted to the bar in 1908; has affiliated with the Democratic party, is active in the Lutheran Church and superintendent of Sunday School.

He married, June 3, 1915, at Marion, Virginia, Miss Ethel Joyce Eller, of Marion. She attended and graduated from the high school there and the State Teachers College for Women at Farmville, Virginia. She was associated with Mr. Snidow in educational work for a number of years, teaching in Virginia, West Virginia and Kentucky.

Mrs. Snidow is a daughter of Junius A. and Georgia (Johnston) Eller, of Marion, Virginia. Her father owns several large grazing farms, and is one of the leading live-stock men in that

section of the state. He has been a member of the Board of
Supervisors of Smyth County for a number of years. More
extended reference is made to members of the Eller family on
other pages. Mr. and Mrs. Snidow have three children, Virginia
Joyce, Horace Eller and Martha Carolyn, all of whom are attending the public schools at Pembroke.

In connection with this immediate branch of the Snidows,
the several members of the family of George Snidow and his
wife, Martha (Walker) Snidow, are mentioned and their
descendants traced down to the present time. The oldest of the
family was Sarah Snidow, who never married. She had a very
brilliant mind and possessed a very cheerful disposition. Her
help and influence in the family will long be remembered by her
nieces and nephews, as she was very much interested in their
education. Elvira Snidow, second oldest of the family, married
James W. Snidow. Their only child is Herman Walker Snidow,
of Richmond, Virginia. Here he has been engaged as a sanitary
engineer for the Virginia State Board of Health for a number of
years. William Luther Snidow is the oldest son of George
Snidow, and he and his family have been mentioned above.
Alice Snidow married Rev. B. W. Cronk, a Lutheran minister,
who now serves a charge at Bluff City, Tennessee. Their only
son is Earle T. W. Cronk, of Richmond, Virginia, who married
Mary Elizabeth Eller, of Marion, Virginia, a daughter of Junius
A. Eller. Earle Cronk has two children: Shirley Cronk and
David Earle Cronk. The youngest son of George Snidow is
Albert W. Snidow (mentioned above). He married Miss Katherine Barrier, of Salisbury, North Carolina. Albert W. Snidow
now owns the old ancestral home which was built by Lewis
Peck in the year 1835, this farm and house having been purchased from Thomas Burk by Col. Christian Snidow and his
son-in-law, John Peck. At a later date Christian Snidow bought
this property from John Peck and willed it to his son, George
Snidow, in 1862. However, George Snidow had lived in this
house since March 10, 1845.

To Albert W. Snidow we are indebted for much of the data
and information concerning the Snidow family. He is a man
who has always taken much interest in the history of the early
settlement of New River, and whose unusual memory on such
subjects no one will question.

George Snidow (formerly known as "River George" to dis-
tinguish him from his uncle by that name) was born in 1816.
He was one of the leading, influential men of his day. He was a
man who took much interest in literature and education, as his
ample library will indicate. He was prominent in civic affairs
and especially interested in the work of his church, being a
member of the Pembroke Lutheran Church. He was often
appointed executor by the wills of many of the older Snidows.
He, in the same capacity, was appointed by the court to admin-
ister several estates of the Snidow family. Hence, as a personal
representative of many of his contemporaries, much data of
early history may be found among his papers.

His wife, Martha (Walker) Snidow, who lived to the old
age of eighty-nine, will long be remembered by the people of
her vicinity. She descended from a prominent ancestry, and
being a woman with a splendid memory, many people younger
than herself often sought information from her concerning the
early settlers of Botetourt, Craig and Giles counties. She was

born February 29, 1820, and reared at the old Walker home on the south side of Craig's Creek, opposite the mouth of Barber's Creek, in what is now Craig County, Virginia. She died December 29, 1908, and is buried beside her husband in the Horse Shoe Cemetery.

HON. LETCHER AMBROSE BRYANT, who entered the Virginia Legislature in 1928 as representative of Pittsylvania County, has for many years been prominently connected with the commercial and community interests of that section of the state. He is a resident of Dry Fork, and is associated with his brothers in some widely extended mercantile interests, including the Bryant & Graveley Automobile Company at Danville, Virginia.

Mr. Bryant was born at Spring Garden in Pittsylvania County, February 20, 1885, son of J. R. and Mary T. (Jackson) Bryant. His grandfather was "Buck" Bryant, a Pittsylvania County farmer and a prominent character in that locality. The press frequently reprints an old story of early courthouse days in which Buck Bryant figured as a witness in a murder trial. Two of his sons were Confederate soldiers, Charles and Matt, Charles having been killed in battle, while Matt went all through the war. He is buried near Ringgold, Virginia.

J. R. Bryant was born and reared at Kentuck, near Ringgold, had a private and public school education, and during the Civil war entered the Home Guard, helping guard bridges at Danville when about sixteen years old. His active life was spent as a farmer and tobacco raiser, and for several years he was road commissioner of his district. He died in December, 1922. His wife, Mary T. Jackson, was born and reared at Spring Garden, was educated privately and still occupies the old home place, at the age of seventy-seven. She is a member of the Primitive Baptist Church. Her father was Ambrose Jackson, a farmer, planter and slave owner, and this branch of the Jackson family is connected with that of which the immortal Stonewall Jackson was a representative. J. R. Bryant and wife had a family of thirteen children, one of whom died in infancy and a son, John, at the age of three years. The others were: Malissa, now deceased, was the wife of R. L. Shreve; Ella is the widow of R. E. Dallas; James W. is a merchant and farmer at Dry Fork; C. D. Bryant is a merchant, banker, farmer, tobacconist and warehouseman at Spring Garden and Danville; Christina is the wife of W. M. Bryant, who formerly was in the mercantile and farming business in the country and is now a Danville business man; Sallie is Mrs. W. G. Hall, of Dry Fork; Letcher A. is the next in age; Eugene F. is a farmer and tobacco warehouseman at Spring Garden; Mattie is Mrs. G. G. Barksdale, of Spring Garden; Myrtle is the wife of J. A. Nash, Southern Railway agent at Chatham; and Nettie is the wife of C. A. Abbott, a farmer at Spring Garden.

Letcher A. Bryant attended public and private schools in Pittsylvania County, and after completing a course in the Massey Business College at Richmond joined his brothers, J. W. and C. D. Bryant, in the general mercantile business at Chatham, in 1907. These brothers have since greatly extended their business connections and interests, owning and operating a chain of merchandise stores as well as the Bryant & Graveley Automobile Company at Danville, having the agency for the Hupmobile cars. They are interested in the Piedmont Tobacco Warehouse Company, of which C. D. Bryant is president. Letcher Bryant is secretary and treasurer of the Bryant & Graveley Company.

He was elected a member of the House of Delegates from Pittsylvania County in 1927, serving in the session of 1928, and was reelected for the 1930 session. He is affiliated with Carter Lodge No. 323, A. F. and A. M., Pittsylvania Chapter No. 24, Royal Arch Masons, at Chatham, Dove Commandery No. 7, Knights Templar, Acca Temple of the Mystic Shrine at Richmond, the Lodge of Perfection and Rose Croix Chapter of the Scottish Rite at Danville, and Dalco Consistory of the Scottish Rite at Richmond. Other fraternal affiliations are the Junior Order United American Mechanics, Improved Order of Red Men, and Lions Club. He is a Democrat and for a number of years was a steward and lay leader in the Mount Pleasant Methodist Episcopal Church, South.

Mr. Bryant married in Pittsylvania County in February, 1908, Miss Sudie E. Boaz, of Swansonville, where she grew up and attended school. She is a member of the Mount Pleasant Methodist Episcopal Church, South, and an officer in the Missionary Society. Her parents were George W. and Lula (Murrell) Boaz, of Swansonville. Her father, who died in 1927, was a farmer in that community. Her mother died in 1910. Mr. and Mrs. Bryant have two children, Cecile Douglas and Landon Ambrose. The daughter, Cecile, graduated in 1927 from the Spring Garden High School, then spent one year in Randolph-Macon Woman's College at Lynchburg, and is a member of the class of 1930 in William and Mary College. Landon Bryant is a senior in the Spring Garden High School.

Mr. Bryant has been very popular in business circles in Pittsylvania County and enjoys the fellowship of men in his lodges and in the Lions Club, and his work in the Legislature has done much to strengthen his hold on public confidence. He and his brothers as business men have been foremost in the support of schools and good roads in the county. During the World war Mr. Bryant was active in the Red Cross drives. For about twenty years he held the office of postmaster at Chestnut Level, resigning when elected a member of the House of Delegates.

POWHATAN FITZHUGH CONWAY. Because of the extent, importance and variety of his interests, as well as the willingness that he has evidenced in the support of constructive public movements, Powhatan Fitzhugh Conway is justly accounted one of the leading and most highly valued citizens of Danville, Virginia. Although he is probably best known for his activities in the lumber industry, with which he has been identified for about four decades, being now president of the Danville Lumber & Manufacturing Company, he has been a prominent figure in various other fields, and has been honored by election to a number of offices of responsibility and trust.

Mr. Conway was born near Danville, Pittsylvania County, Virginia, November 11, 1867, and is a son of Lysander B. and Elizabeth (Gouldin) Conway. The Conway family originated in England, and its coat-of-arms was presented to one of the early ancestors for valor shown in the Moorish wars and who received knighthood from the king. The first American ancestor came to this country in early Colonial days, settling in Virginia, whence Lieut. James Conway enlisted in the Sixth Virginia Regiment of the Continental army, and met his death on the battlefield near Trenton, New Jersey, December 28, 1776. Lieutenant Conway was the father of Christopher Conway, whose son, James Washington Conway, lived in Pittsylvania County, and was a land owner, planter, slaveholder and tobacco grower. He was distinguished by his high type of citizenship and for many years was a justice of the peace, in which capacity he was a wise counsellor and peacemaker out of court in preferment to foment or encourage litigation. He and his family are buried in the old Conway Cemetery in Pittsylvania County.

Lysander B. Conway, son of James Washington Conway, was born and reared in Pittsylvania County, where he attended private schools, and then secured a position as clerk in the State Treasury, Richmond, Virginia, later went into the banking business at Chatham, Virginia, and was cashier of the Bank of Pittsylvania, in which capacity he was acting at the time of the outbreak of the war between the states. He accepted an appointment as depositary for the Confederate government, later took up arms and served in the field until the close of the great struggle. When released from military service he moved from Chatham to Danville and entered the tobacco business. For a number of years he was chairman on the Danville School Board. He died August 25, 1912, and he and his wife are buried in the Green Hill Cemetery at Danville. Lysander B. Conway married Elizabeth Gouldin, who was born and reared in Caroline County, Virginia. She attended Rappahannock Academy, and during her life was an active worker in the Baptist Church, of which her husband was also a member. She died August 23, 1917, having been the mother of eight children: John, who died in infancy; Elizabeth, now Mrs. W. W. Holland; James W., deceased; Coleman B., of Washington, D. C.; Powhatan Fitzhugh, of this review; Lysander B., Jr., of Danville; Eustis R., of Henderson, Kentucky; and Brooke, who died in infancy.

Powhatan Fitzhugh Conway attended public schools until he was seventeen years of age, at which time he entered the employ of the Bass, Brown & Lee firm of lumber dealers at Danville, which later was acquired by the company of which Mr. Conway was the head. After working for four years as solicitor and collector Mr. Conway and F. L. Walker formed a partnership as dealers in coal, wood and lumber. The firm of Conway & Walker was conducted successfully for several years. About six years after its establishment they bought the business of Bass, Brown & Lee, subsequently consolidating with R. I. Anderson & Company, after which the business was incorporated as the Danville Lumber & Manufacturing Company, since which time Mr. Conway has been its chief executive and general manager. This is a large and prosperous organization, and employs between seventy-five and 100 men. The Danville plant manufactures an extensive line of millwork, including interior trim, sash, doors, frames, moldings, blinds and other materials. For some years the company operated lumber mills in North and South Carolina, but these plants have been sold and the business at present is concentrated at Danville. Mr. Conway has been prominent in the millwork business for over thirty years. He was one of the first members of the Southern Sash, Door and Millwork Manufacturers Association of Atlanta, Georgia, of which he was a member of the Board of Directors for a number of years, president from 1921 to 1925, and is still a member of the board. He likewise is a member of the Board

of Directors and vice president of the Millwork Cost Bureau of
Chicago.

One of the institutions to which he has given much of his
time and general helpfulness has been Averett College, of which
he has been a member of the Board of Trustees for a quarter of
a century. He is a member of Roman Eagle Lodge No. 122,
A. F. and A. M.; Euclid Chapter, R. A. M.; and Dove Commandery, K. T., of which he is a past commander, and is a
Shriner, being a member of Acca Temple. He is vice president
of the Masonic Building Corporation, which erected the handsome Masonic Temple at Danville. He likewise belongs to the
Tuscarora Club, and for a number of years was president of the
Danville Golf Club, during which time the course was laid out
and the clubhouse built. He became by invitation a charter
member of the Biltmore Forest Country Club of Asheville,
North Carolina. Politically he is a Democrat, and his religious
connection is with the Baptist Church, of which he was formerly
chairman of the board, has been on the Board of Deacons for
many years, and for fifteen years was superintendent of the
Sunday School. During the World war he served as a member
of the War Service Committee of the Millwork Industry at
Washington, D. C. During the war period he was chairman
of the drives of the American Red Cross in Danville.

On February 14, 1893, at Richmond, Virginia, Mr. Conway
was united in marriage with Miss Maggie Bradford Brown, of
Richmond. Her father, Capt. J. Thompson Brown, was a captain of volunteers in Parker's Battery, C. S. A., and later became
brigadier-general of the United Confederate Veterans. Mrs.
Conway was educated in Danville College for Young Women,
now a branch of Randolph-Macon Woman's College, and was
an active member of the Baptist Church. She died April 2,
1925, and is buried in Green Hill Cemetery. To this union
there was born one daughter, Mrs. Margaret Conway Moore,
who attended Averett College at Danville and Mary Baldwin
Seminary at Staunton, Virginia, and is a graduate of Emerson
College of Oratory at Boston, Massachusetts. She has one son,
Warner Moore. On November 18, 1928, at Hickory, North
Carolina, Mr. Conway married Mrs. Frances Marler Russell,
of Asheville, North Carolina, a daughter of Dr. William A. and
Sallie (Phillips) Marler, the former of whom was for many
years a prominent dental surgeon at Hickory. Mrs. Conway
completed her educational training in St. Mary's Episcopal
School at Raleigh, and is highly accomplished in music as an
instrumentalist and vocalist. Like Mr. Conway, she is greatly
interested in civic affairs, and is also active in religious and
charitable work, being a member of the Presbyterian Church.

ALEXANDER CARSON CONWAY in his interests and connections
with Danville business life has for a number of years been one
of the community's most constructive and substantial citizens.

Mr. Conway represents an old and distinguished Virginia
family. He stands in the eighth generation of at least three
Virginia immigrants. Edwin Conway (ca. 1610-1675) came
from England in 1640, settled in Lancaster County, where he
became a large landed proprietor. His first wife, Martha, was
a daughter of Richard Eltonhead. Lieut. James Conway, great-
grandson of Edwin (ca. 1752-1776), was a lieutenant in the
Sixth Virginia Continental Line and was killed near Trenton,
New Jersey, December 28, 1776. His son, Christopher (ca.

1774-1854) was married about 1795, and his wife, Anne, died about 1837. They were the parents of James Washington Conway (1805-87), grandfather of Alexander Carson. James Washington Conway married in 1824 Annie Brook Stamps (1807-44).

James Martin Conway (1827-98), father of the Danville business man, married in 1850 Emily Anderson (1831-1903). She was a descendant of Richard Anderson (descended from Sir Edward Anderson, chief justice of Northumberland County, England), who came to Virginia in the *Merchant's Hope*. His son, Thomas, settled at Gloucester Point, Virginia. Robert, son of Thomas, had a land grant in New Kent County, Virginia, in 1683. Richard, son of Robert, lived from about 1718 to 1796, and his second wife was Anne Foster. Their son, Thomas Anderson (1765-1815), married Polly Haley. Joseph Eggleston Anderson (1808-70), married in 1830 Minerva Caroline Terry (1812-94). Minerva Caroline Terry was descended from William Clopton, who settled in St. Peter's Parish, New Kent County, Virginia, and was a member of the council. He and his second wife, Frances, had a son, Robert, who married Ann, believed to be the daughter of Robert Wentworth of New Kent. Their son, Robert, born in 1728, lived in Pittsylvania County, and his wife's name was Frances. Robert Clopton, son of the latter (1755-1841), married Miss Pulliam. Their daughter, Mary, was the wife of Daniel Terry and the mother of Minerva Caroline Terry. Joseph Eggleston Anderson had his home at Spring Garden, where he was a merchant, postmaster and justice of the peace. His daughter, Emily (Anderson) Conway, was educated in private schools and she and her husband were leaders in the Baptist Church. James Martin Conway was for many years superintendent of the Sunday School and was a trustee of Roanoke Female College, now Averett College, of Danville. James Martin Conway was born and reared in Pittsylvania County, was a soldier of the Confederacy in the Army of Northern Virginia under General Lee, and was wounded in action just before the surrender at Appomattox. He was also captured, but made his escape and was on his way home when the final scenes were enacted. Before the war he had served as deputy treasurer of the county. The children of James Martin Conway and wife were: Ella (1852-1920), married H. E. Robertson; John Daniel (1855-62); Josephine (1857-97), married E. B. Moore; Caroline (1859-62); Alexander Carson; James Anderson, born in 1863; Joseph Mercer, born in 1865; Mary (1867-87); Abner Wentworth, born in 1870; and Charles Spurgeon, born in 1876.

Alexander Carson Conway was born at Spring Garden, Pittsylvania County, June 23, 1861, and was educated in private schools and in 1881 graduated from the Virginia Polytechnic Institute. He taught one year, was deputy county treasurer one year, and for over forty-five years has been identified with the commercial life of Danville, at first as a retail furniture man and since 1899 as a real estate operator and capitalist. He has had much to do with the promotion and financing of Danville theaters, owning the Rialto Theater Building, where he has his offices, and is president of the Danville Theaters, Incorporated, an operating company for the four local theaters, the Rialto, Broadway, Majestic and Capitol. Mr. Conway is also secretary and treasurer of the Home Building Loan & Investment Company. For some time he was a trustee of the Roanoke School, now Averett College, and was chairman of the committee which bought the grounds and a member of the building committee which erected the structure now used by the school. For twelve years he was a member of the public school board and since September, 1928, has been on the Danville City Council.

Mr. Conway owns one of the beautiful homes of Danville, located on West Main Street. He is a member of the Kiwanis Club, is a Democrat, and for years was a deacon of the board of the First Baptist Church. He is a member of the Society of the Cincinnati, the Danville Country, Danville Golf and Tuscarora Clubs.

Mr. Conway married, January 25, 1888, Lillian May Cardwell, who was born in 1867 and died in 1891, daughter of George Washington Cardwell, of Pittsylvania County. By this marriage there were three children, the second and third being twin boys, born August 20 and died September 8 and 21, respectively, in 1891. The surviving child, Annie Lillian, was born at Danville October 30, 1888, graduated from Randolph-Macon Institute in 1906 and was united in marriage, June 28, 1911, to Lee Averett Wilson. Mr. and Mrs. Wilson have three children, Lee Aiken, Jeanne Miller and Lillian Page.

Mr. Conway on June 5, 1901, married Corinne Gray, who was born at Baltimore, Maryland, February 25, 1880, daughter of Allen Eugene Gray, of Danville. By this marriage there were three children, all born at Danville. The daughter, Emily Corinne, born August 22, 1902, was married December 12, 1922, to Judge Archibald Murphey Aiken, of Danville, and they have a son, Archibald Murphey, Jr., born January 23, 1924. Mary Anderson Conway, the second daughter, was born January 16, 1906, and Alexander Carson Conway, Jr., was born January 12, 1909.

JAMES SKINKER GOLDSMITH is one of the veterans in the service of the Norfolk & Western Railway, with which he has been identified for thirty-nine years. During a large part of this time he has been agent for the company at Christiansburg.

Mr. Goldsmith was born at Leonardtown, Saint Marys County, Maryland, across the Potomac River from Stratford, the birthplace of Robert E. Lee. He was born November 16, 1870, son of Capt. John Mason and Mary Isham (Skinker) Goldsmith. His grandfather, Rev. Zachariah Goldsmith, was a minister of the Episcopal Church in Westmoreland County, Virginia, and was a descendant of Henry Goldsmith, a brother of the famous English poet, Oliver Goldsmith. Capt. John M. Goldsmith was born in Westmoreland County, Virginia, was educated in private schools at Charles Hall, Maryland, and during the Civil war was assigned special duties by General Lee in getting supplies across the Potomac River. A number of times he was captured but was released. The family prize very highly a pair of field glasses presented to him after the war by the people of Westmoreland County in token of appreciation for the assistance he rendered them in securing food and clothing from across the Potomac. His life after the war was spent as a farmer, and he died in 1903, being buried in the cemetery at Warrenton in Fauquier County, Virginia. His wife, Mary I. (Skinker) Goldsmith, now eighty-three years of age and living with her youngest son, Percy, at Denver, Colorado, was born in Fauquier County, Virginia, finished her education in Mary Baldwin Seminary at Staunton and has always taken a deep interest in the Episcopal Church. There were nine children in the fam-

R.W.Williams D.D.S.

ily: James; Elizabeth, wife of D. M. Waller; Marshall; Duval;
Miss Mildred; Minnie, deceased; John, deceased; Charles and
Percy.

James Goldsmith attended public schools in Fauquier County,
and Bethel Military Academy. Immediately after leaving school
in 1890 he went to work for the Norfolk & Northwestern Railway Company as a telegraph operator. His services as operator
and agent came to different points on the division, but for
twenty-one years he was a resident and representative of the
company at Salem, Virginia, and in 1923 was transferred to
Christiansburg as agent. Mr. Goldsmith has acquired property
interests in real estate at Roanoke and Christiansburg. He is
a past master of Taylor Lodge, No. 23, A. F. and A. M., at
Salem, a member of the Christiansburg Rotary Club, a member
of the Cohee Country Club of Blacksburg, the Christiansburg
Chamber of Commerce and the Order of Railway Telegraphers.
While living at Salem he served ten years in the City Council.
Mr. Goldsmith is a Democrat and a member of the Episcopal
Church.

He married at Bluefield, West Virginia, May 29, 1895, Miss
Mira L. Hammersley, of Lynchburg. Mr. and Mrs. Goldsmith
had a family of eleven children, two of whom died in infancy.
The others are: Elizabeth Eyre, Lee Hammersley, Rebecca
Marshall, Florida Graves, John Marshall, Duval Pope, Mary
Isham Skinker, Edward Livingston and Mercer Waller. Elizabeth is the wife of Frank E. Kelly, of New York City, and has
one daughter, Mira Lee. Miss Lee Hammersley Goldsmith at-
tended school at Salem and Columbia University in New York,
was a teacher, but now operates an employment bureau in New
York City. Miss Rebecca Marshall attended public schools and
Elizabeth College and is in her father's office. Florida Graves
married Charles W. Pumphrey, of New York City. John Marshall is a student of law at the University of Virginia. Duval
Pope is at the University of Virginia and Edward is at Virginia
Polytechnic Institute. Mary is a student in the Parsons Art
School in Paris, France and Mercer is in high school at Chris-
tiansburg.

ROGER WALTER WILLIAMS, Doctor of Dental Surgery at
Lynchburg, has practiced his profession in that city for eighteen
years.

He was born near Washington in Montgomery County,
Maryland, May 23, 1885, on the same farm where his father
and grandfather lived. Doctor Williams now owns this farm
and conducts it as a profitable hobby, raising live stock. He is
a son of Charles M. and Jane (Waters) Williams, both natives
of Maryland. His grandfather, Richard Walter Williams and
Doasey Waters, were both Maryland farmers. Charles M. Williams was a Democrat in politics, and for several terms was a
member of the Board of County Commissioners of Montgomery
County. He was a Baptist and his wife, a Methodist. In their
family of eight children Dr. Roger W. was the fifth in order of
birth.

Doctor Williams attended high school at Poolsville, Maryland,
and graduated with his degree in dentistry from the University
of Maryland at Baltimore in 1908. For eighteen months he
practiced at Buena Vista, Virginia, and in 1910 established
his permanent home at Lynchburg. He is a member of the
Piedmont and Virginia State Dental Societies. Doctor Williams

is a member of the Lynchburg Kiwanis Club, is a Mason, and has been a vestryman in the Episcopal Church.

He married, in 1910, Miss Mabel Stewart White, also a native of Maryland, who was educated in the Episcopal Female Institute at Winchester, Virginia. She died in 1920, leaving two children, Ella Whitmore, born in 1912, now a student in Sweet Briar College in West Virginia, and Roger Walter, Jr., born in 1915.

REV. WILLIAM CARSON TAYLOR, pastor of the Baptist Church at Blacksburg and one of the chaplains of Virginia Polytechnic Institute, is a native Virginian, has been in the Baptist ministry for over forty years, and has filled many prominent pulpits in the North and West.

He was born at Taylorsburg, now Mayo, in Henry County, Virginia, February 7, 1858, son of Rev. James I. and Ruth (Pratt) Taylor and a grandson of Reuben Taylor and a great-grandson of George Taylor, who came to America from Wales, served as an ensign in the Revolutionary war and became a large land owner and planter in Henry County, Virginia, operating his estate with the aid of numerous slaves. He and his family are buried at the Mayo Baptist Church Cemetery in that county. Rev. James I. Taylor was born April 13, 1831, was educated in private schools and in Patrick Henry Academy, and devoted many years to farming and tobacco growing. Later he was ordained in the Baptist ministry, preached in Henry County and after the Civil war moved out to Oregon, where he was active in the ministry until advanced years. He died March 17, 1911, at the age of eighty, and he and his wife are buried at Mount Newton, Oregon. His wife was born near Madison in Rockingham County, North Carolina, and died May 11, 1928. They had large family of children: William Carson; George Reuben; Nannie, wife of E. J. Hawkins; Joseph, who died at the age of three years; Jennie, wife of J. T. Vincent; Minnie, wife of J. L. Tate, of Chicago; Frank; Samuel C., who died at the age of two and a half years; and Jesse, of Silverton, Oregon.

William Carson Taylor was educated in private schools in Henry County and graduated with the B. A. degree from the University of Oregon in 1884. He took his M. A. degree there in 1890, and in the meantime had completed the course of study in the Rochester Theological Seminary with the class of 1887. In 1895 the Doctor of Divinity degree was conferred by Georgetown College of Kentucky. At that time Doctor Taylor gave up his ministerial work for an extended tour of Egypt, the Holy Land and Europe, and visited all the localities and communities most famous in Biblical history.

Doctor Taylor was ordained a Baptist minister July 11, 1887. His first work was in a city mission at Buffalo, resulting in the organization of what has since been known as the Filmore Avenue Church. He was pastor of the First Baptist Church at Frankfort, Kentucky, about seven years, pastor of the First Baptist Church at Jefferson City two years, at the College Avenue Baptist Church in Indianapolis four years, the First Baptist Church of Petersburg, Virginia, eight years, spent five years with the First Church at Clarksburg, West Virginia, five years in the First Church at Martinsburg, West Virginia, and in 1922 came to Blacksburg as pastor of the First Baptist Church and as one of the chaplains of the Virginia Polytechnic Institute. Doctor Taylor is also moderator of the Valley Baptist

Association, comprising sixty-four churches in Roanoke Valley. At different times he has served on a number of college boards, and has been identified with mission work. He is a Royal Arch Mason at Petersburg, Virginia, formerly was a member of the Knights of Pythias, and is an independent Democrat.

Doctor Taylor married at Rochester, New York, May 10, 1899, Miss Ida Meyer, daughter of Mr. and Mrs. C. C. Meyer, of Rochester. She was educated in Rochester and was very gifted as an artist. She was deeply interested with her husband in all matters connected with the church. She died at Indianapolis November 13, 1901. There were three children by this marriage: Ruth, wife of Harvey S. Gill, of Petersburg, Virginia; Esther, who died of influenza in 1918; and William C., Jr., of Falls Church, Virginia.

On May 15, 1903, at Suffolk, Virginia, Doctor Taylor married Miss Lillian Alice Jones, daughter of Henry and Alice (Holleman) Jones, of Suffolk. Her father was owner of one of the finest farms in Eastern Virginia, the Cedar Brook Farm. He died about 1905 and his wife, in 1893. Doctor and Mrs. Taylor have three children: Alice, a graduate of West Hampton College in 1926, now teaching in high school at Petersburg; Francis Taylor, a graduate of the University of Richmond with the class of 1927, now studying medicine at the University of Virginia; and Lucy, a student in West Hampton College.

NORVELL ELLIOTT WICKER, JR., B. D., pastor of Camden Parish of the Episcopal Church at Danville, is a young and inspiring church leader, and though he has been in the ministry only a few years some unusual honors and responsibilities have been conferred upon him in the Southern Virginia Diocese.

He was born at Petersburg, Virginia, April 24, 1897, son of Norvell Elliott and Catherine (Winfield) Wicker, grandson of William Elliott Wicker, and great-grandson of Robert Tate Wicker of Richmond. The Wicker family is of English ancestry and has been in Virginia for many generations. Norvell Elliott Wicker, Sr., was born and reared at Petersburg, has been a tradesman, and now operates a store and service station at Petersburg. He has held the office of justice of the peace since 1928. His wife, Catherine Winfield, is a daughter of George Winfield, a native of Greensville County, Virginia, who served in the Confederate army and after the war moved to Petersburg, Virginia, and for a number of years was on the police force. He and his wife and the paternal grandparents of Rev. Mr. Wicker are all buried in Blanford Cemetery at Petersburg. Mrs. Catherine Wicker was educated at Petersburg, and she and her husband are members of the Episcopal Church. Of their seven children three died in infancy. Rev. Mr. Wicker has two sisters: Alice Catherine, wife of H. A. Hawkins, of Petersburg, Virginia, and they have a daughter, Marjorie Dare Hawkins. Miss Virginia Dare Courtney Wicker is attending the Petersburg High School.

Rev. Norvell Elliott Wicker grew up at Petersburg, attended school there, continued his education in the College of William and Mary, completed his work in the Virginia Theological Seminary at Alexandria in 1922, where he received his Bachelor of Divinity degree. On June 9, 1922, he was ordained a deacon and in June, 1923, ordained a priest of the Southern Virginia Diocese. His first assignment of duties was in the Martins Brandon Parish in Prince George County and Southwark Parish in Surry County, where he remained from June, 1922, to April 15, 1925. At the latter date he accepted the call to the Camden Parish at Danville, and for the past four years has had a very busy routine of duties. Outside of his home parish he is chairman of the executive committee of the Board of Trustees of Chatham Hall, the Diocesan Episcopal School for Girls at Chatham. He is a member of the executive board of the Diocese of Southern Virginia. He is the type of citizen with many points of contact with his fellow men. He is a director of the Lions Club, is affiliated with Roman Eagle Lodge No. 122, A. F. and A. M., is a thirty-second degree Scottish Rite Mason, member of the Modern Woodmen of America, and an honorary member of the Danville Golf Club.

He married at Washington, D. C., April 24, 1923, Miss Marion Alta Bailey, of Washington. She attended grade and high schools in Washington, and specialized in music in the Washington College of Music. She is a member of the Wednesday Club, Shakespeare Study Club and Music Study Club. Her parents were Oliver Wilbert and Marion Elizabeth (Winfree) Bailey. Her father was born and reared in Washington, D. C., and for a number of years has been with the United States Railway Postal Service, with home at Washington. The Winfrees are an old family of Huguenot ancestry and settled in Chesterfield County, Virginia. Rev. Mr. Wicker and wife have one son, Norvell Elliott III, born in Danville, Virginia, December 5, 1927.

RORER A. JAMES, JR., publisher of the *Danville Register and Bee*, was associated with those two papers under the ownership of his father before he completed his education. He was educated for the law, but has given all his time since leaving college to his responsibilities as a newspaper man and as an official in a number of Danville business corporations.

Mr. James was born at Danville, January 24, 1897, son of Rorer A. and Annie (Wilson) James and a grandson of Dr. Bruce James, who for many years was a leading physician of Pittsylvania County. Rorer A. James was born and reared in Pittsylvania County, attended public school and Roanoke College, was a graduate of the Virginia Military Institute and of the law school of the University of Virginia. For many years he appeared regularly in connection with cases in all the courts of his district, and he represented the Thirteenth Senatorial District in the State Senate and in the closing years of his life was elected to succeed Judge E. W. Saunders in Congress from the Fifth Virginia District. He was reelected, and died during his second term, in 1921. In connection with his other interests he acquired the *Danville Register* in 1898 and in 1900 bought the *Bee*, consolidating them as the only daily newspaper published at Danville.

Annie Wilson James was born and reared in Pittsylvania County, was educated by private tutors, and has been a lifelong member of the Episcopal Church. She lives in Danville and still owns the old Wilson home in Pittsylvania County. Of her five children one died in infancy and the others are: Robert Wilson, a farmer and stock raiser at the old Wilson place, known as Dan's Hill, married Miss Irene Dwyer, of Washington, D. C.; Rorer A., Jr.; Annie, wife of James Covington, who is a representative of the Universal Tobacco Company interests at Shanghai, China; and John Bruce, now a medical student in

W. G. Cunningham

the Medical College of Virginia at Richmond, married Miss Helen Hodges, of Ringgold, Virginia.

Rorer A. James, Jr., was educated in private schools and Virginia Military Institute, and pursued his law course in the University of Virginia in 1918. Before completing his studies there he was assigned duties as civilian instructor in the Transportation Corps at Charlottesville, and was with the colors until after the armistice. On January 1, 1919, he returned home to become publisher of the *Register and Bee*, and on the death of his father in 1921 bought the other interests of the family in the newspaper and has since been sole owner. Mr. James is also president of the Piedmont Hardware Company, director of the Danville Street Car Company, director of the Danville Warehouse Company, director of the William M. Bassett Furniture Company. He is a charter member of the Danville Kiwanis Club, and for about two years had a prominent part in the organization. He is a member of the Danville Country Club, Danville Golf Club, the Delta Chi fraternity, is a Democrat and a member of the Episcopal Church.

He married in New York City, June 16, 1919, Miss Elizabeth Letcher Stuart, of Newport News. She attended public school at Newport and the Chatham Episcopal Institute. Mrs. James is a granddaughter of the famous Confederate cavalry leader, Gen. J. E. B. Stuart. Her own parents were J. E. B., Jr., and Joe (Phillips) Stuart, of Newport News. Her father for many years was connected with the Texas Oil Company, and was also under appointment from President Roosevelt collector of the port of Norfolk. Mr. and Mrs. James have two children, Elizabeth Stuart and Anne Wilson James, the former a student in the public schools of Danville.

WALTER G. CUNNINGHAM, who is the commissioner of revenue for Giles County, was born in that section of Southwest Virginia, and his experience comprises a number of years with the Norfolk & Western Railway Company, and he is also a practical farmer, his home being an attractive country place at Bluff City.

He was born at Poccahontas, in Tazewell County, Virginia, December 11, 1887, son of William G. and Sarah Jane (Keister) Cunningham. The annals of the Cunningham family run back to very early days in the Valley of Virginia. One of his ancestors was Capt. William Cunningham, a captain in the Revolutionary forces from Virginia and an early settler in Giles County. A son of Captain William was John M. Cunningham, who was born in Giles County and who on May 1, 1837, was appointed the first clerk of the first Crcuit Court for the county. For a number of years he was a merchant at Pearisburg, and he died October 14, 1864. His wife, who passed away April 9, 1860, was Louisa Jerrell, a name afterwards spelled Gerald. Her mother, Julia Pearis, was a daughter of Col. George N. Pearis, who gave the fifty acres of ground for the county seat of Giles County, and in his honor the town took the name of Pearisburg.

William G. Cunningham, father of the county official, was born and reared in Giles County, attended private schools and taught school for several years. His chief occupation was farming. He was a life long Democrat and a member of the Presbyterian Church. He died April 12, 1925, and is buried at the East Side Cemetery at Pearisburg. His wife, Sarah Jane Keister, was born in Montgomery County, Virginia, and died November

23, 1924. She was a member of the Methodist Episcopal Church. There were nine children: Effie, Walter G. and Mary (twins), Charles, who died in infancy, D. E. Cunningham, Jane Pearis, deceased, Nell, Ruth and W. L. W. L. Cunningham was a volunteer at the time of the World war, went overseas with Company F, One Hundred and Sixteenth Infantry, was in France seventeen months and was gassed during the Argonne campaign.

Walter G. Cunningham was educated in public schools, and after school spent two years in construction work for the Norfolk & Western Railway, and for three years had charge of the ware house of the company at Pearisburg, and for three years did clerical work for the company. For nine years he was the company's cashier. Mr. Cunningham on leaving the railroad service was in the wholesale produce business three years and in 1923 was elected deputy commissioner of revenue, and in 1927 was elected chief of that office and is giving a highly efficient and satisfactory administration of his duties.

His farm is a tract of blue grass land, where he has had his home since 1920. He is specializing in the raising of the Chinchilla rabbits. For some years he has been interested in the sand and gravel business. He has had affiliations with the Modern Woodmen of America, is a Democrat, member of the Methodist Episcopal Church, of which he is steward and teaches a men's Bible class.

He married at Bluff City, Virginia, June 6, 1917, Miss Lake Erie Carter, of Bluff City, where she was reared and educated. She takes much interest in Methodist church affairs. She is a daughter of Thomas M. and Dora (Marrs) Carter, of Falls Mills, Tazewell County, where Mrs. Cunningham was born. Her father was a merchant at Falls Mills in Tazewell County, and died in 1898. Her mother died in 1904. Mrs. Cunningham's grandparents, Daniel and Elizabeth (Owens) Carter, were early settlers in Tazewell County. Mr. and Mrs. Cunningham had three children, one of whom died in infancy, and the two living are Walter G., Jr., and Mary Jane, Walter being a student in the public schools of Pearisburg.

FRED B. GREEAR is an ex-service man of the World war, and for the past five years has been steadily building up his reputation and rendering a useful service in the profession of law at Saint Paul. He is mayor of that Wise County town.

He is a son of Dr. James N. Greear, who was born in Wise County February 27, 1859, a descendant of William Greear, a Colonial settler in Loudoun County, a grandson of Noah Greear and son of Francis B. Greear, who was born in Grayson County, Virginia, in 1819, and for many years was a successful teacher in Southwestern Virginia. Afterwards he engaged in farming, and during the Civil war was a Union Democrat and afterwards became a Republican. He died at his home in Wise County February 21, 1908. Francis B. Greer married, in 1851, Sarah Mullens, who died in 1852. His second wife, whom he married in 1854, was Priscilla Stallard, who was born in 1828 and died March 31, 1905.

Dr. James N. Greear was reared on a farm, attended public and private schools, graduated from the Abingdon District High School in 1880, and finished his medical course at the University of Virginia in 1883. He had further training in the New York Polyclinic, and first practiced at Castlewood until 1892, then at Toms Creek in Wise County, and in 1895 established his home and permanent interests at Saint Paul. He has been active in

Claude B. Talley

the medical societies, has been a member of the Town Council, is a Mason and has been a trustee of the Methodist Episcopal Church, South.

Dr. J. N. Greear married, June 17, 1886, Bessie E. Earnest, daughter of Isaac and Victoria (Burts) Earnest. She was educated in the Martha Washington College at Abingdon, Virginia, also attended a college at Asheville, North Carolina.

Fred B. Greear was one of a large family of ten children. He was born at Saint Paul May 26, 1899, graduated from high school there, attended Emory and Henry College, and in April, 1918, volunteered at Washington, D. C. He was sent to Gettysburg, Pennsylvania, for training with the Tank Corps, and in September, 1918, went overseas to France, passing through Liverpool to LaHavre. He had intensive training for four months at Langres, was stationed at Bordeaux for two months, and came home and received his honorable discharge May 25, 1919, at Camp Meade.

In the fall of 1919, Mr. Greear entered the University of Virginia and took his law diploma at that institution in 1923. He has been engaged in practice at Saint Paul, and besides a general practice acts as attorney for the Dickerson-McNeer Corporation, the Saint Paul Bottling Company, Saint Paul Baking Company and the Clinchfield Lumber and Supply Company.

He is a member of the Wise County Bar Association and is one of the leaders of the Democratic party in the county. He was elected mayor of Saint Paul in June, 1927. Mr. Greear is master of the Masonic Lodge, is vice president of the Civitan Club, and is a member of the Methodist Episcopal Church, South.

CLAUDE BARR TALLEY, certified public accountant, is a resident of Danville, and is secretary and treasurer of the Danville Traction & Power Company.

Mr. Talley was born in Pittsylvania County, Virginia, April 20, 1892, a son of John H. and Laura (Moss) Talley. His great-grandfather, Peyton Talley, represented a Virginia family of Halifax County, and he moved across the state line to Rockingham County, North Carolina, where he spent his life as a farmer. His son, John H. Talley, Sr., was a soldier of the Confederacy during the war between the states, and after the war followed farming in Rockingham County until his death, about 1870. His son, John H. Talley, Jr., was born in Rockingham County and was eight years of age when his father died. He attended public schools there, and is still active as a farmer in Pittsylvania County. His wife, Laura Moss, was born and reared at Cascade, Virginia, attended public schools and is a member of the Vandola Baptist Church. Her parents were Robert H. and Rebecca (Mize) Moss, of a family well known and prominent in Tazewell County. Robert Moss and five of his brothers were soldiers on the side of the Confederacy, all of them members of a company that went out from Stuart, Virginia, soon after the war began and participated at Gettysburg and many other great battles, but none of the brothers was killed in action. John H. and Laura (Moss) Talley were the parents of four children: Claude B.; Arnett P., of Brookneal, Virginia; John H. III, of Danville; and Margaret K., of Pittsylvania County. Arnett and John were soldiers in the World war, members of the One Hundred and Eleventh Field Artillery. Arnett was a first lieutenant and participated in the great Argonne offensive. John was also overseas.

Claude B. Talley attended public schools in Pittsylvania County and Danville, a private school at Danville, and as soon as he had concluded his school work in 1910 he became an employe of the Southern Railway Company as clerk in the office of the auditor of the Southern Short Lines department, and during the six years he was there he was promoted to assistant to the auditor. During 1916-17 he was assistant auditor of the City of Danville, and then went with A. M. Pullen & Company, certified public accountants at Richmond, with whom he remained until July, 1920. For the past nine years he has given all of his time to the Danville Traction & Power Company as secretary and treasurer. He is also secretary and treasurer of the Westbrook Elevator Manufacturing Company and holds a certificate from the State of Virginia as a certified public accountant.

Mr. Talley is active in Masonry, being affiliated with Roman Eagle Lodge No. 122, A. F. and A. M., Euclid Chapter, Royal Arch Masons, Danville Lodge of Perfection, Rose Croix, Dalcho Consistory of the Scottish Rite at Richmond, and Acca Temple of the Mystic Shrine in the capital city. He was formerly identified with Kiwanis Club work. He is a Democrat and a member of the Lee Street Baptist Church.

Mr. Talley married August 30, 1919, at Greensboro, North Carolina, Miss Mamie Etna Thornton, of Danville, Virginia, where she attended grade and high school and Averett College. She has an interested part in the Lee Street Baptist Church work and the Eastern Star. Her parents were John B. and Pattie (Atkins) Thornton, of Danville. Her father is a veteran printer and for a number of years has been associated with the Waddill Printing Company, Incorporated. Mrs. Talley is member of an old Virginia family.

ARTHUR LEE PLEASANTS. The late Arthur Lee Pleasants, of Arthur L. Pleasants & Company of Richmond, was one of the leading insurance men of his day, very popular with all classes, active in church and civic affairs, and notably charitable. His death, April 2, 1918, removed from Richmond one of its best citizens, and took from his family a devoted husband and father. Mr. Pleasants was born in Henrico County, Virginia, January 13, 1861, a son of George D. and Martha J. Pleasants, who had thirteen children. George D. Pleasants was in early life a surveyor, but later went into the insurance business, and continued in it for many years, being succeeded by his son. The Pleasants family was established in Curles Neck during the Colonial period in this country's history. This has always been one of the most distinguished and aristocratic families of the Old Dominion, and socially prominent from the earliest days.

The public schools of Richmond and Richmond College educated Arthur L. Pleasants, and when he had completed his college course he entered his father's business, which he later bought, and continued to operate it under the name of Arthur L. Pleasants & Company, general insurance, until he was claimed by death. For many years he was a zealous Mason, and he belonged to the Westmoreland Club and the American Underwriters Association. From his youth up a member of the First Baptist Church of Richmond, he was long one of its valued workers, and superintendent of the senior department of the Sunday School. His widow is active in that same work.

On October 11, 1899, Mr. Pleasants married Miss Edna Lee Shelton, a daughter of Harper W. and Rosalie P. Shelton, and the youngest of their six children. She was educated in Richmond schools and the Richmond Woman's College, now Westhampton College. Mr. Shelton was for many years engaged in the manufacture of coffee, spices and extracts in Richmond. The Shelton family was established at a very early day in Mecklenburg County, Virginia, and Doctor Shelton, grandfather of Mrs. Pleasants, was a son of the first settler of Buffalo Springs, Virginia, in which place he located prior to the American Revolution. Those bearing the name of Shelton served in that great conflict, as well as in the War of 1812, and, they with the Virginia troop to which they belonged, were with General Washington at the surrender at Yorktown.

The following children were born to Mr. and Mrs. Arthur Lee Pleasants: Arthur Lee II, who was graduated from the Annapolis Naval Academy, class of 1922, is a lieutenant in the United States Navy, married Phyllis Bagby, and they have two children, Arthur Lee III, and John Bagby; Snowden, who is assistant roadmaster of the Virginia Electric Power Company; Rosalie, who married John Morgan Applegate, of the David M. Lee Box Company of Richmond, has three children, Katrina, James Magill, Shelton Pleasants; and Martha Jane, Mary Adeline, Edna Shelton and Gertrude Allen Pleasants, all four of whom are living with their mother in their beautiful home at 4004 Dunston Road, and are prominent in the social life of Richmond.

GEORGE L. TAYLOR. Among the lawyers of Southwest Virginia who have traveled the weary and difficult self-made road to success, George L. Taylor, of Appalachia, is deserving of more than passing mention. While he has been a member of the Virginia bar for twelve years, he has practiced his profession independently for only a comparatively short period, but this has been sufficient to give him prestige as one of the rising men of his calling. At present he is the representative of varied and important interests, and in addition is a leader in the Democratic party in his section of the state and well known in fraternal circles.

Mr. Taylor was born January 5, 1887, in Lee County, Virginia, and is a son of E. R. and Sarah A. (Burkhart) Taylor. The family is of English origin and settled in North Carolina at an early date in the history of the colonies. The great-grandfather of Mr. Taylor was born in the Old North State, whence he removed to Scott County, Virginia. His son, William M. Taylor, the grandfather of George L. Taylor, was born at Rye Cove, Scott County, but prior to the war between the states moved to Lee County, where he passed the rest of his life as a farmer. He was a member of the Methodist Episcopal Church.

E. R. Taylor was born on his father's farm in Lee County, Virginia. He married Sarah A. Burkhart, the daughter of a pioneer minister of the Methodist Episcopal Church in Southwest Virginia, who belonged to the Holston Conference and filled many pulpits in this section. He was of German descent.

George L. Taylor received his early educational training in public schools in Lee County, following which he pursued a course in shorthand and typewriting at Shelbyville, Kentucky. He next entered the office of Maj. J. F. Bullitt, of Big Stone Gap, in the capacity of law clerk, and in 1916 took the examination and was admitted to the bar. At that time Mr. Taylor became associate counsel with the firm of Bullitt & Chalkley, with whom he remained until 1922, then forming a law partnership with J. F. Bullitt, Jr., with offices at Big Stone Gap and Appalachia. This connection was mutually severed in 1924, since which time Mr. Taylor has practiced alone at Appalachia, with offices in the Peoples Bank Building. He has built up a splendid practice, and is local attorney for the Standard Accident Insurance Company and other casualty companies, and a director in the Coal Field Motor Company. During his career Mr. Taylor has been identified with much important litigation, in which he has demonstrated a sound knowledge of legal principles, precedents and procedure, and a ready ability in their application. He is a member of the Wise County Bar Association, and the Virginia State Bar Association, and enjoys an excellent reputation among his fellow-practitioners as a valuable assistant and a worthy opponent. Mr. Taylor is a well known Mason, being a past high priest of the local chapter and a past district deputy grand master, and is also a member of the Modern Woodmen of America and the Kiwanis Club of Big Stone Gap. He is a friend of education, and for several years served as a member of the Virginia Normal School Board. Politically a Democrat, he is conceded to be a man of much influence in the ranks of his party in Southwest Virginia, although not an office-seeker. He belongs to the Episcopal Church in which he is very active, being vestryman, lay leader and superintendent of the Sunday School.

On September 16, 1908, Mr. Taylor was united in marriage with Miss Margaret Barron, of Lee County, a daughter of J. K. P. and Rebekah Anne (Scott) Barron, members of old and distinguished Virginia families. Mrs. Taylor was educated in public schools in Lee County, Jonesville Institute and Martha Washington College, and is active and popular in the social and club life of Big Stone Gap. She is a member of the Big Stone Gap Chapter of the United Daughters of the Confederacy, and has served the Virginia Division as Fourth Vice President and District Chairman. She is also a member of Sycamore Shoals Chapter, Daughters of the American Revolution of Bristol, Virginia. She also takes an active and constructive part in the work of the Federated Women's Clubs of Wise County, and the Episcopal Church of Big Stone Gap. To Mr. and Mrs. Taylor there have been born two children: James Polk, a student in the University of Kentucky at Lexington, Kentucky, and Anne Scott.

CAPT. ELIHU J. SUTHERLAND, commonwealth attorney of Dickenson County, was born in that county, and represents some of the oldest family names in this section of Southwestern Virginia.

He was born at the Sutherland homestead farm, a mile east of Tiny, December 22, 1885, son of William B. and Eliza Jane (Counts) Sutherland. His great-great-grandfather, James Sutherland, was born in Scotland, came to America when a boy, and the first record of him obtainable is a deed recorded in Bedford County, Virginia, dated February 24, 1783. From Bedford County he moved to Catawba Creek in Botetourt County, about 1800, and in 1810 settled in Russell County, where he was a planter and figured influentially in the early history of that locality. James Sutherland married Sarah Buchanan.

Their son, Daniel Sutherland, was born in Bedford County in 1793, gave most of the years of his long life to farming and planting, and died February 5, 1875. He was born only twelve years after the close of the Revolution, was a young man during the War of 1812, and later saw his country pass through the ordeals of the Mexican war and the war between the states. He married Phoebe Fuller, who was born in North Carolina in 1797, and died February 16, 1868.

William Sutherland, grandfather of Captain Sutherland, was born in Russell County, Virginia, March 25, 1822, and in 1847, moved to Dickenson County and established the old homestead near Tiny, where he lived for many years in the enjoyment of the returns of his labor and management as a planter. He took an active part in Democratic politics, serving as the first constable of that part of Russell County now in Dickenson County, and was supervisor in Dickenson County from 1880 to 1887, being chairman of the board from 1883 to 1887. The act of 1880, establishing Dickenson County, named him one of the commissioners to divide the county into magisterial districts, which work he assisted in accomplishing. He was an active member of the Primitive Baptist Church, and during the Civil war served as orderly sergeant of Company E of the twenty-first Virginia Cavalry, under Colonel Peters. William Sutherland died June 3, 1909, at the age of eighty-seven. He married Sylvia Counts, who was born October 5, 1826, and died December 25, 1916, being a daughter of Joshua Counts.

William B. Sutherland, father of Captain Sutherland, was born February 24, 1861, and gave all his active years to the management of the Sutherland homestead farm. He was for two years a justice of the peace and on the Board of Supervisors eighteen years, fourteen years of the time as chairman of the board. He represented Dickenson, Buchanan and Wise counties in the House of Delegates of Virginia in 1895-96. He has always been a Democrat, an elder in the Primitive Baptist Church, and has served as moderator of the Washington District Baptist Association since 1897.

He married Eliza Jane Counts, who was born in Dickenson County March 12, 1863, and was a first cousin of her husband. She was a descendant of John Counts, who settled at Hawkshill Creek in Page County, Virginia, purchasing a large tract of land in 1765. He died at Glade Hollow in Russell County about 1802. He and his wife, Magdaline Counts, were of German ancestry. Their son, John Counts, was born in Shenandoah County, was a planter in Russell County, Virginia, and died October 1, 1843. He married Margaret Kelly, who died July 6, 1835. Their son, Joshua Counts, was born August 27, 1801, was a planter living where the present town of Cleveland is located, in Russell County, was a staunch Primitive Baptist in religion and a Democrat in politics. He died February 15, 1883. He married Martha Kiser, who died October 18, 1839. Their son, Noah Counts, was born in Russell County, April 21, 1831, and died December 1, 1898. He was a planter, for many years a justice of the peace, was a supervisor in Buchanan County, and was a first lieutenant of Company E, Twenty-first Virginia Cavalry, in the Confederate Army. Noah Counts married Aily Amburgey, who was born February 12, 1832, and died December 12, 1918.

William B. Sutherland and wife had a large family of children, third among them being Elihu Jasper Sutherland.

Mr. Sutherland grew up on the home farm in Dickenson County, attended public schools, began teaching at the age of nineteen, and while teaching continued his higher education, graduating from the high school of Chattanooga, Tennessee, in 1911, and taking his A. B. degree at the University of Chattanooga in 1917. On May 8, 1917, he entered the Officers' Training Camp at Fort Oglethorpe, Georgia, was commissioned a second lieutenant August 15, 1917, was with Company D, Three Hundred and Sixteenth Machine Gun Battalion at Camp Jackson, South Carolina, until April 16, 1918, when he was transferred to the One Hundred and Fifty-sixth Depot Brigade, and was at Camp Sevier, South Carolina, from September 23, 1918, until January 4, 1919, when he returned to Camp Jackson. He was given his honorable discharge April 23, 1919, having been promoted to first lieutenant on June 20, 1918, and May 20, 1919, was commissioned a captain in the Reserve Corps.

Captain Sutherland graduated from the law department of Chattanooga University in 1920, and has since been engaged in the practice of law, with home and offices at Clintwood. He was elected on the Democratic ticket to the office of commonwealth attorney in 1923, and has also served as school trustee of the Clintwood District and clerk of the Town Council. Captain Sutherland is a member of the Independent Order of Odd Fellows, the Delta Chi social fraternity and the Delta Theta Phi legal fraternity.

ANDREW BEIRNE BLAIR, for thirty years a prominent figure in business at Richmond, was a member of a family that has been distinguished in the Presbyterian Church of America from early Colonial times. The late Mr. Blair was a first cousin of Prof. Walter Blair, who for forty years was a professor in Hampden-Sidney College. Like Professor Blair, he was a descendant of Rev. John Blair, who was ordained to the Presbyterian ministry in 1742, and for a time was professor of divinity in what is now Princeton Theological Seminary. He was a great-grandson of Rev. John D. Blair, better known as Parson Blair, pastor of the First Presbyterian Church in Richmond. Andrew Beirne Blair was born at Richmond in February, 1866, and died in that city January 22, 1922, being one of the five children of Adolphus and Ellen (Beirne) Blair. His father was a wholesale grocery merchant at Richmond. Andrew Beirne Blair attended the McGuire School in Richmond, finished his education at the University of Virginia, and as a young man took up the insurance business in the firm of Blair & Tabb, representing the Travelers Insurance Company. He was active in that business from 1889 until 1919, retiring after thirty years.

Mr. Blair had many prominent connections with the civic affairs of his home city. He was fuel administrator in Richmond during the World war, at the same time that the present governor, Harry F. Byrd, was state fuel administrator. He was an alderman of the city from 1903 to 1910. Mr. Blair was a vestryman in St. Paul's Episcopal Church, was a member of the Commonwealth Club, Sons of Colonial Wars, Country Club of Virginia, Richmond Chamber of Commerce. Mrs. Blair is a member of the Woman's Club, Country Club of Virginia, Society of Colonial Dames and Daughters of the American Revolution.

Mr. Blair married in November, 1894, Miss Bertha Small, who was reared and educated at Hagerstown, Maryland, a daughter of Albert and Alice (Newcomer) Small. Her father graduated in law from Princeton University and practiced for many years at the Hagerstown bar. The Small family came from Scotland and settled in Franklin County, Pennsylvania, about 1700, while the Newcomer family settled on a land grant in Washington County, Maryland, the date of the grant being 1730. Some of the descendants are still living on the land. Mrs. Blair had fourteen ancestors in the War of the Revolution and the War of 1812.

Mrs. Blair, who resided at High Acre, Rothesay Road in Richmond, died January 6, 1929. She was the mother of two children. Her daughter, Alice, married Robert Carter, a descendant of "King Carter." Robert Carter is manager of the Richmond Forging Corporation. Mrs. Carter was educated in the Oldfields School of Baltimore. She is the mother of four children, namely, Robert, Beirne, Noland and Maria. Mr. and Mrs. Blair's only son, Beirne, was a student in the University of Virginia when the war broke out, and at once enlisted, was trained in the Aviation Corps, and gave his life as a supreme sacrifice while in action in France.

JAMES THOMAS CATLIN, JR. No name is pronounced with more respect in the city of Danville than that of Catlin. The late James T. Catlin, Sr., had a close and intimate relationship with the business life of that community, and was even more notable for the constructive leadership he afforded in behalf of educational, religious and other institutions and movements that express the civic ideals of the city as much as its great industrial plants.

James T. Catlin, Sr., was born and reared in Richmond, Virginia, and was a son of William Catlin, of Richmond, who had two sons, E. A. Catlin and William Catlin, in the Confederate army. James T. Catlin, Sr., attended public schools in Richmnd and as a young man came to Danville about 1885 and bought from his brother, J. E. Catlin, an insurance agency. The Catlin Insurance Agency has been doing business at Danville for nearly half a century. James T. Catlin, Sr., passed away December 27, 1926. He headed the building campaign and was the first president of the Danville Y. M. C. A., and for many years was chairman of the Board of Stewards of the Methodist Episcopal Church, South. He married Elnora Grace Greenwood, who was born and reared at Norfolk, Virginia, where her father, C. F. Greenwood, owned and conducted a leading jewelry house. Mrs. Elnora Catlin attended public schools in Norfolk, the Murfreesboro Academy and, like her husband, was closely identified with the Main Street Methodist Episcopal Church, South, at Danville. She died May 26, 1923, and both are buried in Green Hill Cemetery. There were two sons, William Greenwood and James T., Jr. William Greenwood was born at Richmond December 20, 1877, was in the insurance business at Danville and was drowned in the Pee Dee River of South Carolina February 2, 1905.

James T. Catlin, Jr., was born at Richmond December 15, 1882, but has lived nearly all his life at Danville. He attended private schools there and the Danville Military Institute, also the Bryant & Stratton Business College at Baltimore. On leaving school in 1900 he became teller in the Citizens Bank of Danville, a bank that later was absorbed by the First National

Bank. On the death of his brother, in 1905, he joined his father in the insurance agency, and the name James T. Catlin & Son has been retained since his father's death. It is one of the leading organizations handling insurance in all branches in that part of the state. Mr. Catlin is also a director of the Commercial Bank and in the Danville Warehouse Company.

He showed the spirit of his father in his willingness to work for the general welfare and to organize movements. He is a past president and a director of the Danville Y. M. C. A., a past president and director of the Chamber of Commerce, served two terms as president and is still a director of the Kiwanis Club and is president of the Patrick Henry Council of Boy Scouts of America. He is a trustee of the Ferrum Training School, and is a trustee of the Randolph-Macon systems of colleges and academies. He is one of the leading laymen in Virginia of the Methodist Episcopal Church, South, being on the Board of Finance of the church in Virginia and is a steward of the Main Street Church and teacher of a young men's Bible class in Sunday School. He is a director of the Danville Golf Club, is president of the Danville Shrine Club and is a thirty-second degree Mason, affiliated with Roman Eagle Lodge No. 122, A. F. and A. M., Euclid Chapter, Royal Arch Masons, Dove Commandery, Knights Templar, Dalcho Consistory of Scottish Rite and the Mystic Shrine. He is a Democrat in politics.

Mr. Catlin married at Danville, April 11, 1911, India Mabel Robinson, member of a very prominent family of Southern Virginia. Her father, Dr. W. L. Robinson, was a physician and surgeon, and during the Civil war was in the Confederate army, having been wounded twice in action and for some time was a prisoner of war. After the war he continued the practice of his profession until his death, and both of Mrs. Catlin's parents are buried in Green Hill Cemetery at Danville. She was educated in Randolph-Macon Institute and Gunston Hall at Washington. She is a member of the Main Street Methodist Episcopal Church, South, the United Daughters of the Confederacy, Daughters of the American Revolution and Wednesday Club. Mr. and Mrs. Catlin have two children, Juliet Greenwood and James T. III. Juliet graduated in 1929 from Randolph-Macon Institute, and attended a finishing school, Gunston Hall, at Washington. The son is a student in public school at Danville.

ROBERT BURNS HALDANE BEGG, Virginia educator, holds the chair of civil engineering in the Virginia Polytechnic Institute at Blacksburg.

Professor Begg was born in Campbell County, Virginia, January 4, 1880, son of James Beveridge and Janet (Haldane) Begg. Both his parents were born in Scotland, his father at Kinross and his mother at Ayr. His father's grandmother was a sister of the immortal Scotch bard, Robert Burns. James B. Begg came to America in 1872, when he was forty years of age, and Janet Haldane came in 1873, and they were married at Norfolk, Virginia. He engaged in general farming and tobacco growing in Campbell County for many years. Both parents were active in the Episcopal Church. The father died in November, 1909, and is buried in the Good Shepherd Cemetery in Campbell County. The mother passed away in 1926 at Williamsburg, Virginia, where she had lived for many years and where she is buried. There were three children. Mary Haldane is the wife of George P. Coleman, former highway com-

CHARLES BERNARD PRITCHETT JR.

missioner of the State of Virginia, living at Williamsburg. Grace Isobel is the widow of B. W. Hubbard, of Williamsburg.

Robert Burns Haldane Begg, the only son, attended public schools in Campbell County, the New London Academy, and graduated from the Virginia Polytechnic Institute with the Bachelor of Science degree in 1899, and received the degree of Civil Engineer in 1901. He has given over twenty years of his life to educational work, and has been a member of the faculty of the Virginia Polytechnic Institute since 1913. He joined the institute as professor of civil engineering, and has held that chair for over fifteen years. He is also director of the Engineering Extension Division of the institute.

Professor Begg was formerly president of the Virginia section of the American Society of Civil Engineers. He is a director of Southwestern Virginia, Incorporated, is a member of the University Club, Hunters Lodge of Masons, Rotary Club and Cohee Country Club. He is an independent Democrat and a member of the Episcopal Church.

In May, 1917, he volunteered, was in training at Fort Myer, Virginia, and was commissioned a captain of engineers. In September, 1917, he went overseas as a casual with the rank of captain of engineers, and was assigned duty in the purchasing department of engineering supplies in London, and later was made officer in charge of water supplies and sewage, Base Section No. 3, in England. In March, 1919, he returned home and was honorably discharged at Washington March 15, 1919, with the rank of major of engineers, Officers Reserve Corps. He is now major of cavalry in the Officers Reserve Corps.

Professor Begg married in Albemarle County, Virginia, September 7, 1907, Miss Adah Mann, of Albemarle County. She is an active worker in the Episcopal Church. Mrs. Begg is a daughter of William and Eleanor (Atkinson) Mann. Her father was for many years a farmer, fruit grower and cattle raiser in Albemarle County, where he died in 1910, and is buried in the Grace Church Cemetery. Her mother now resides at Charleston, West Virginia. Professor and Mrs. Begg have one son, James Currie Begg, attending the Blacksburg public schools.

CHARLES WESLEY PRITCHETT, M. D., of Danville, has had more than a normal quota of the credits and distinctions that accompany a long and purposeful career as a physician and surgeon.

The Pritchetts are an old family of Virginia, and several branches of the family in different parts of the country have produced men of outstanding achievements in the professions. The Pritchetts on coming to America first settled near Petersburg. They were Scotch-Irish. Doctor Pritchett was born at Mount Cross in Pittsylvania County, July 1, 1864, son of Charles Wesley and Lydia A. (Robertson) Pritchett and grandson of William Pritchett, who was a fine example of good citizenship in the early days of Pittsylvania County, a teacher as well as a planter. He and his family are buried in a cemetery near Whitmell. Charles Wesley Pritchett was also born and reared in Pittsylvania County, was educated in private schools, and was a soldier of the Confederacy with the Thirty-eighth Virginia Infantry. He was in Lee's Army of Northern Virginia, and much of the time in General Pickett's famous division. After the war he conducted his farming and planting operations on an extensive scale until his death, in 1906. His wife, Lydia A.

Robertson, was a member of the well known Robertson family of Virginia and a daughter of Nathaniel and Priscilla Robertson. She was born and reared in Pittsylvania County, was educated in private schools, and she died in 1892, she and her husband being buried in the family cemetery. Both were members of the Sharon Baptist Church. Dr. Charles W. Pritchett was one of a family of four sons and four daughters. There were two sons named Charles Wesley, the first dying in infancy. His brother William Nathaniel died in 1916, at the age of sixty-two, and his sister Annie Gertrude, died in 1898, at forty, the wife of James R. Breedlove. Ida Virginia is a resident of Danville, widow of C. D. Ramsey. Emma Celeste is the widow of J. S. Reynolds and lives at Danville. Joshua Howard is a farmer and planter near Keeling, Virginia, and the daughter Rosa Lee died when five years old.

Dr. Charles W. Pritchett was educated in public schools in Pittsylvania, continued his literary education in Richmond College, and prepared for his profession in the College of Physicians and Surgeons of Baltimore, now affiliated with the University of Maryland. He was graduated M. D. in 1886 and had the training and experience of an interne in the Maternity Hospital at Baltimore and did post-graduate work in Johns Hopkins University. Since beginning practice he has several times taken special courses in the New York Polyclinic. Doctor Pritchett for twelve years practiced at Keeling in Pittsylvania County and in 1898 moved to Danville, where he has given the best of his talents to the community for over thirty years. In 1907 he built a very attractive home at 644 Main Street, part of which he specially planned and arranged for a suite of offices, and that has been the headquarters of his profesional work ever since. Doctor Pritchett is acknowledged to have one of the largest private practices in the city of Danville. He is a surgeon on the staff and chairman of the staff of the Memorial Hospital at Danville, and for many years was a member of the staff of surgeons and the governing staff of the Danville General Hospital.

Doctor Pritchett is interested in practically all the banking institutions in Danville. He is president of the Danville Laundry Company and of the Lea Lewis Furniture Company. For over twenty years he was president of the local Board of Health. Fraternally he is affiliated with Roman Eagle Lodge No. 122, A. F. and A. M., Euclid Chapter, Royal Arch Masons, is a past commander of Dove Commandery, Knights Templar, is a member of the Scottish Rite bodies at Danville and Richmond, and Acca Temple of the Mystic Shrine at Richmond. He also belongs to the B. P. O. Elks and is a member of the Pittsylvania County, the District and American Medical Associations, the Southern Medical Association, and the Association of Southern Railway Surgeons, is a past president of the Lions Club, member of the Tuscarora Club, Chamber of Commerce. Doctor Pritchett votes as a Democrat and is a member of the First Baptist Church at Danville.

He married at Keeling, Virginia, December 12, 1888, Miss Clay Keesee, of Keeling, daughter of Capt. P. C. and Sallie (Terry) Keesee. Her father owned and conducted a large plantation near Keeling and was an honored veteran of the Confederacy. He died in 1913 and his wife, in 1917, and they are buried near Keeling. Mrs. Pritchett was educated in public schools at Keeling, attended Roanoke College for Women, now

Averett College of Danville, and has always been deeply interested in the work of the Baptist Church. Doctor and Mrs. Pritchett have two children, Dr. Charles Bernard and Miss Eunice Clay. The son, Charles Bernard, is a man of splendid mind who has made a mark for himself in his chosen career. He graduated from Washington and Lee University in 1912 and took his M. D. degree at Johns Hopkins University School of Medicine in 1916. During the World war he was commissioned a first lieutenant in the United States Navy, part of the time being at Charleston, South Carolina, and later transferred to Washington with the Army and Navy Medical School. After the armistice he received his honorable discharge and was engaged in practice at Danville from 1919 until 1929, when he moved to Roanoke. He is a specialist in urology and diseases of the skin. Dr. Charles B. Pritchett married Miss Shepherd Leake, of Wadesboro, North Carolina, and they had a son, Charles Bernard, Jr., who at the age of three years died as a result of accidental burns.

The daughter, Miss Eunice Clay, was educated in Roanoke College, now Averett College, also attended Sweetbriar College in Virginia, studied art in the Washington Art School, in the Philadelphia School of Fine Arts, and abroad in France and Italy. She is now teacher of art in Averett College at Danville.

FRANK JAMES CRITZER is a native Virginian, and in his present profession as an educator has enjoyed an increasing range of responsibilities. He is now principal of the high school of Blackstone, Nottoway County.

He was born in Albemarle County, Virginia, June 12, 1900. His grandfather, James Critzer, was born and reared in Albemarle County, descended from a family that came to America about the time of the Revolution. James Critzer was an educator, and for many years conducted a private school. He married Elizabeth McCue, representative of an old Scotch-Irish family in Virginia. Chesterfield Critzer, father of Frank James Critzer, was born and reared in Albemarle County, attended his father's school, and has spent his active life as a farmer and orchardist and is also a member of the firm Critzer Brothers, operating a machine shop at Afton, Virginia. Chesterfield Critzer married Minnie Schultz, who was born and reared in Albemarle County and was educated in public and private schools there. Both parents are Presbyterians. There were six children: Nellie, wife of Rev. J. Hillis Miller, who is assistant to the distinguished divine, Rev. Harry Emerson Fosdick, of the Calvary Baptist Church of New York City; Frank James; Chesterfield C., Jr., a graduate of the University of Virginia, now an employe of the Chesapeake & Potomac Telephone Company at Baltimore; Miss Bessie, who finished her education in the Harrisonburg State Normal School and is now Mrs. George E. Brooks, wife of a professor at William and Mary College; Philmore, who died at the age of ten years; and Sheild, a member of the class of 1931 in Hampden-Sidney College.

Frank James Critzer was educated in public schools in Albemarle County and spent two years in Hampden-Sidney College. He was there at the time of the World war, and was a member of the Student Army Training Corps, from which he was honorably discharged December 8, 1918. After leaving Hampden-Sidney he taught one year at Madison, West Virginia. His studies were then resumed in the University of Virginia, where he graduated in 1925. After leaving the university he taught for two years in the Millers Industrial School at Crozet, Virginia, and in the fall of 1927 took up his duties as principal of the high school at Narrows. The enrollment in this school is over five hundred students, and he had charge of the work of a staff of seventeen teachers. In the fall of 1929 he was appointed to the place at Blackstone, a school of over seven hundred enrollment.

Mr. Critzer is a member of the Narrows Business Men's Club, is a Mason, a Theta Kappa Nu and member of the Phi Delta Kappa honorary fraternity. He is a Democrat, and teaches a class in the Sunday School of the Presbyterian Church.

He married at Springfield, Kentucky, August 6, 1927, Miss Mildred Lake. Mrs. Critzer is also a teacher of experience. She attended public schools at Springfield, was an art student in St. Catherine's Academy, attended Sullins College in Virginia, and continued her art studies in the Chicago Art Institute. She was art instructor in the high schools at Franklin and Springfield, Kentucky, and for two years had charge of the domestic art department of the Miller's School at Crozet. Mrs. Critzer is a member of the Presbyterian Church. Her parents are B. D. and Zelma (Thompson) Lake, residents of Springfield, Kentucky, where her father has been prominent in business for a number of years and where he is district representative of the R. J. Reynolds Tobacco Company. The Thompsons are an old family of Virginia and Kentucky, and Mrs. Critzer had several ancestors who were in the American Revolution. Mr. and Mrs. Critzer have one son, Ben Lake Critzer.

JOHN M. ORR, of Narrows, Giles County, is a past master of the tanning industry, a business he has followed since boyhood, and his experience has brought him contact with every phase of the industry. He has had a long succession of responsibilities in different localities and at the present time is superintendent of the Union Tanning Company at Narrows.

He was born at Mountaindale, Sullivan County, New York, August 10, 1868, son of Samuel and Elizabeth (Kennedy) Orr. His father was a native of Ireland, and shortly after his marriage came to America, first living at Mountaindale, New York, and then at Grahamsville in the same state, where he was in the tannery business. He died about 1880 and his wife about five years earlier. Their children were Mary, Annie, Margaret, James, John M., Louise and Edward Orr. All are deceased except John M. and Edward, the latter a resident of New York City.

John M. Orr attended public schools in New York State, had several years of experience as a farm boy, and then found employment in a tannery at Limestone, New York. At Reynolds, New York, he became identified with the Hall & Vaughn Tannery Company, and after a few years this company sent him to their plant at Middlesboro, Kentucky, where he remained eight years. For two years Mr. Orr was superintendent of the plant of the United States Leather Company at Davis, West Virginia. Following that he was superintendent of a tannery at Mineral Bluff, Georgia, and also in Wisconsin.

Narrows has been his business headquarters since 1911, and for seventeen years he has been the superintendent of the Union Tanning Company's plant there. He is one of the very popular and respected business men of his community. He is a Repub-

Jas H Wilson

lican in politics, a Methodist, is a Royal Arch Mason and member of the Independent Order of Odd Fellows.

He married at Keyser, West Virginia, September 18, 1908, Miss Ella Blanche Fisher, who was educated at Keyser and taught school in West Virginia before her marriage. She is an active worker in the Methodist Episcopal Church. Her father, Conrad Fisher, was a carpenter contractor and builder at Keyser, where he died in 1920, having survived his wife about five years. Mr. and Mrs. Orr have one daughter, Beulah Elizabeth, attending the Narrows High School.

JAMES HERBERT WILSON is a veteran South Virginia tobacconist, one of the oldest in the business at Danville, where he owns the Central Warehouse. Mr. Wilson on Christmas Day of 1928 was the object of a unique honor bestowed by the buyers of the various tobacco companies at Danville, when they presented him with a loving cup as a token of his long service as a tobacconist and of their collective and individual esteem for his business integrity and fair dealings.

Mr. Wilson was born in Charlotte County, Virginia, October 25, 1859, son of James H. and Mary (Price) Wilson. The Wilsons came from England and have been in Virginia since Colonial times, and the records of Charlotte County in particular indicate many important activities of the family there. James H. Wilson, Sr., was born at Red House in Charlotte County, was educated in private schools and entered the Confederate army soon after the war began. As the result of an accident at Richmond he died in 1865, about the close of the war. He is buried at Ruff Creek, about seven miles from Charlotte Court House. His wife, Mary Price, was born in a home that occupied the present site of the American National Bank Building at Danville. She finished her education at Winston-Salem, North Carolina, and was a life long member of the Presbyterian Church. By her first marriage, to James H. Wilson, she was the mother of five children, one of whom died in infancy. Lelia, now deceased, was the wife of Dr. Robert F. Grey, of Winston-Salem. James H. Wilson, the tobacconist, is the next in age. Mollie, of Danville, is the widow of W. P. Averett, whose father and uncle were prominent educators, and it is for them that Averett College was named. George N. Wilson, who died in March, 1929, at Dallas, Texas, had lived in that city for thirty years. Mrs. Mary Price Wilson after the death of her first husband was married to James W. Elliott, of Charlotte County, Virginia, and by that union there were also five children: Susie, wife of John Boswell, of New York City; Ella, widow of Hoffman Allen, of Baltimore; Willie R., who died at Oxford, North Carolina; Dr. Samuel T., of Phoenix, Virginia, who was with the Medical Corps overseas during the World war; and Mattie, now Mrs. Talbert Anderson, wife of a tobacco man with the Liggett & Meyers Company at Louisville, Kentucky.

Mr. James H. Wilson was six years of age when his father died. He grew up at Danville, attended private schools there, and was a student in the noted Bingham School at Mebane, North Carolina. His early life was spent as a farmer and tobacco grower, and since 1892 he has been in the tobacco warehouse business at Danville. He was prominent during all the years when the cooperatives were an important factor in the tobacco business. In 1908 he was made president of the Danville Warehouse Company, then almost a bankrupt concern, and when he retired from the presidency in 1925 the company owned over $400,000 worth of real estate. He still owns the largest individual interests in the company. Since 1925 he has operated the Central Warehouse, located on what was the garden of his grandfather Price at Danville. Mr. Wilson also owns the Independent Warehouse at South Boston, Virginia, and much valuable real estate in Pittsylvania County and in North Carolina.

For many years he has been deeply interested in Masonry, and is a member of Roman Eagle Lodge No. 122, A. F. and A. M., Euclid Chapter, Royal Arch Masons, Dove Commandery, Knights Templar, and Acca Temple of the Mystic Shrine at Richmond. He is a Democrat and a member of the First Baptist Church.

Mr. Wilson married at Danville, November 16, 1881, Miss Lelia Virginia Rosser, daughter of George G. and Betty (Miller) Rosser, and granddaughter of Samuel Thomas Miller, whose name is familiarly associated with educational interests in this section of Virginia. Mrs. Wilson is a graduate of the Roanoke Female College, now Averett College of Danville, has long had a prominent part in the Baptist Church and is a member of the Woman's Club, Garden Club and other woman's organizations. Mr. and Mrs. Wilson became the parents of seven children. Their daughter Miss Bessie Miller was educated in Averett College and is at home. James Herbert III was a graduate of the Virginia Polytechnic Institute, was a foreign representative of a large tobacco company, and died in Africa April 19, 1909. Mary Wilson, who was educated in the Lynchburg Woman's College and is a graduate of Randolph-Macon Institute at Danville, is the wife of Addison B. Freeman, of Samuel T. Freeman & Company of Philadelphia. Lee Aiken Wilson has charge of his father's tobacco warehouse at South Boston. Frances Temple married Albert B. Freeman, of Philadelphia. George Price Wilson, a graduate of Washington and Lee, is tobacco buyer for the export trade, spent several years in Mexico and was a soldier during the World war. He married Louise Smith, daughter of a well known Petersburg, Virginia, physician, and they reside at Raleigh, North Carolina. Page Gray Wilson, the youngest of the family, lives at Staunton, Virginia, and is a representative of the Fred D. Nolling Bond & Stock Brokers of Richmond, Virginia. He married Claudia Sentell, of Bunkie, Louisiana.

JAMES M. PAYNE is a well known member of the business and civic community of Newport, Giles County, where for a number of years he has handled the local agency and distribution of the products of the Standard Oil Company.

Mr. Payne was born at Newport, September 1, 1900, son of R. Y. and Flora C. (Puckett) Payne, and grandson of John R. Payne and great-grandson of Charles Payne. Charles Payne was a pioneer of Southwest Virginia, a farmer and hunter in the early days of Giles County. The Payne family have been in Virginia since early Colonial times. R. Y. Payne was born and reared in Giles County, received advantages in private schools and spent his early years as a farmer. In 1908 he moved to the coal fields of West Virginia, but in 1929 returned to Newport, where he and his wife reside. He has always voted the Republican ticket and is a member of the Masonic fraternity. His wife, Flora C. Puckett, was born in Giles County, grew up in Newport, where she attended public school and for about twenty

James A. Tilman Jr.

years held the office of postmaster there, serving until the advent of the Wilson administration. She is a member of the Methodist Episcopal Church, South. These parents had a family of seven children: W. C. Payne, now in the lumber business at Welch, West Virginia, was in training at Camp Lee during the World war, getting his honorable discharge December 1, 1918; Francis R., of Newport; Harry W., of Widemouth, West Virginia; James M., of Newport; Helen, who died at the age of nine years; Miss Grace, a teacher in the public schools of Narrows, Virginia; and Miss Tootsie, who is attending the State Teachers College at Harrisonburg.

James M. Payne was educated at Newport, attending the grade and high schools, and when he left school he went with the American Coal Company at Widemouth, West Virginia, and was clerk in the commissary there for about five years. This gave him a very thorough commercial training. In 1922 he returned to Newport and took the agency for handling the products of the Standard Oil Company for a territory comprising about half of Giles County. Besides this business he is associated with his brothers in the Newport Service Station. Mr. Payne is affiliated with Newport Lodge No. 261, A. F. and A. M., is a Republican and member of the Methodist Episcopal Church, South.

He married at Princeton, West Virginia, June 2, 1922, Miss Thelma Craig Reynolds, of Newcastle, Craig County, where she was reared and educated, attending high school. She was also a student in the University of Virginia and for three years before her marriage taught school, two years at Newcastle, and was a teacher for one year at Newport. She now conducts a class in the Methodist Sunday School. Mrs. Payne is a daughter of F. E. and Ella Maude (Carper) Reynolds, of Newcastle. Her mother died there April 17, 1923. Her father has spent the greater part of his life in the lumber business and is still active. Mr. and Mrs. Payne have one daughter, Elinor Marie, born April 28, 1923.

JAMES ASBURY TILMAN, JR., became deputy to his father, whom he later succeeded as county clerk of the Circuit Court in Powhatan County, and the combined service of father and son in public office makes a record of more than half a century of consecutive and faithful performance of duty.

James A. Tilman, Jr., was born in Powhatan County November 20, 1883, son of James A. and Mattie A. (Ligon) Tilman. His father was born in Fluvanna County, Virginia, and his mother in Powhatan County. His father was a private in the Confederate army, enlisting at the early age of sixteen, and was seriously wounded in one battle. After the war he was in the mercantile business at Pineville until 1877, when he was elected to the office of county treasurer. He served ten years and in 1887 was elected county clerk, and performed the duties of that office and that of circuit clerk continuously until 1920, when he voluntarily retired, declining to become a candidate for another term, since he had given forty-three years of his life to cares and responsibilities of public office. He was seventy-nine years of age when he died, May 21, 1924. The widowed mother now resides at Powhatan.

James A. Tilman, Jr., was reared and educated in Powhatan County, attending Oak Grove Academy and the College of William and Mary at Williamsburg. In 1906 he was made deputy clerk to his father, and when his father quit the office he was chosen his successor in 1919, and was reelected in 1927. He also has farming interests in Powhatan County. He is a Democrat, a Baptist, a Royal Arch and Scottish Rite Mason. He is a member of the old Powhatan Troop Association. Mrs. Tilman is treasurer of the Powhatan Chapter of the United Daughters of the Confederacy.

Mr. Tilman married, October 11, 1911, Miss Martha Novella Reynolds, daughter of Rev. James W. and May (Gibbs) Reynolds. Her father was born in Fluvanna County and her mother in Alleghany County, Virginia. Her father, who died August 8, 1928, at the age of sixty-eight, gave forty years of his life to the Baptist ministry. Her mother died May 24, 1907. Mr. and Mrs. Tilman became the parents of seven children: Martha May, born August 17, 1912, Courtney Virginia, born January 30, 1915, James Asbury III, born July 7, 1919, Nancy Byrd, born June 26, 1922, Samuel Cole, born August 1, 1924, Emma Jane, born January 9, 1926, and Mary Louise, born July 8, 1927.

GEORGE CLEVELAND SUTHERLAND, a graduate of the Law School of the University of Virginia, has practiced for eighteen years at Clintwood, Dickenson County, and is one of the outstanding representatives of a family which has been in Southwestern Virginia since pioneer times.

Mr. Sutherland was born sixteen miles west of Clintwood, in Dickenson County, in February, 1886, son of Jasper and Louise (Dyer) Sutherland.

He is a direct descendant of James Sutherland, who was born in Scotland, came to America when a boy, and the first record of him obtainable is a deed recorded in Bedford County, Virginia, dated February 24, 1783. From Bedford County he moved to Catawba Creek in Botetourt County, about 1800, and in 1810 settled in Russell County, where he was a planter and figured influentially in the early history of that locality. James Sutherland married Sarah Buchanan.

Their son, Daniel Sutherland, was born in Bedford County in 1793, gave most of the years of his long life to farming and planting, and died February 5, 1875. He was born only twelve years after the close of the Revolution, was a young man during the War of 1812, and later saw his country pass through the ordeals of the Mexican war and the war between the states. He married Phoebe Fuller, who was born in North Carolina in 1797 and died February 16, 1868.

William Sutherland, grandfather of Captain Sutherland, was born in Russell County, Virginia, March 25, 1822, and in 1847 moved to Dickenson County and established the old homestead near·Tiny, where he lived for many years in the enjoyment of the returns of his labor and management as a planter. He took an active part in Democratic politics, serving as the first constable of Dickenson County, and was supervisor from 1880 to 1887, being chairman of the board from 1883 to 1887. The act of 1880, establishing Dickenson County, named him one of the commissioners to divide the county unto magisterial districts. He was an active member of the Primitive Baptist Church, and during the Civil war served as orderly sergeant of Company E of the Twenty-first Virginia Cavalry, under Colonel Peters. William Sutherland died June 3, 1909, at the age of eighty-seven. He married Sylvia Counts, who was born October 5, 1826, and died December 25, 1916, a daughter of Joshua

Counts. Sylvia Counts was a descendant of John Counts, who
settled on Hawkshill Creek in Page County, Virginia, and bought
a large tract of land in 1765. He died at Glade Hollow, Russell
County, about 1802. His son, Joshua Counts, was born in Shenandoah County, Virginia, was a planter, and died October 1,
1843. Joshua Counts married Margaret Kelly, who died July 6,
1835. Their son, Juscobia Counts, born August 27, 1801, and
died February 15, 1853, married Martha Kiser, and one of their
children was Sylvia Counts.

Jasper Sutherland was born in Dickenson County February
1, 1845, and spent his active life as a farmer at Stratton. He
was a Confederate soldier during the last two years of the war,
and for eight years was supervisor of his township. He was a
Republican in politics. His wife, Louise Dyer, was born in
Dickenson County February 5, 1848.

George Cleveland Sutherland, the youngest of a family of
nine children, was reared on a farm, had the advantages of the
local schools, and from 1907 to 1910 was a student in the Law
School of the University of Virginia. He was admitted to the
bar in September, 1910, and has made the practice of law and
the interests of his large clientage the first call upon his consideration and talents and energies, with the result that he has become
one of the outstanding attorneys of Southwest Virginia.

He is a Republican in politics, is a member of the Phi Alpha
Delta legal fraternity, Clintwood Lodge No. 66, A. F. and A. M.,
and is a past grand of Chase Lodge No. 175, Independent Order
of Odd Fellows.

He married at Clintwood, May 1, 1912, Miss Bertha McFall,
daughter of Russell S. and Rosalie (Ratcliff) McFall. Her father
was a Dickenson County attorney. The children of Mr. and Mrs.
Sutherland are: Pauline Russell, born March 23, 1913, George
Foster, born January 19, 1916, Billie Mack, born February 7,
1918, and Edwin Morrow, born October 28, 1920.

William Edwin Neelett is of the third generation of the
Neblett family in Lunenburg County, each generation having
supplied lawyers who have filled the office of commonwealth's
attorney.

Mr. Neblett, now in his second term as commonwealth's
attorney, with offices at Lunenburg Courthouse, was born at
Hollydale in Lunenburg County June 1, 1896, son of William
Edwin and Rosa Cabel (Hite) Neblett and grandson of William
James Neblett. His grandfather was a Lunenburg County
lawyer and was elected and served one term as commonwealth's
attorney, resigning before filling out the term. He was also a
member of the House of Delegates from Lunenburg County, and
he practiced for many years at Lunenburg Court House and
Whittle's Mills in that county.

William Edwin Neblett, Sr., was born in Lunenburg County,
was graduated from the law department of Washington and
Lee University in 1881 and practiced at Lunenburg Court House
until 1884, when he was elected commonwealth's attorney. He
held that office altogether twenty-four years. Only once, in
1896, was he defeated as a candidate for the honor. During
the next four years he resumed his private law practice and in
1900 was again elected. His last term would have expired January 1, 1916, but he died in office December 11, 1911. He was
born January 13, 1854. He is survived by his widow, who resides with her son, William E., at Lunenburg Court House. There
were three other sons, all of whom are living in California,

Benjamin Haynie being a lawyer at Los Angeles, Norman Henry, an insurance man at Los Angeles, and Sydney Smith, in the oil business at Long Beach.

William Edwin Neblett was educated in Lunenburg County public schools, graduated from William and Mary Academy in 1915 and was a student in the College of William and Mary until 1917.

He answered the call to the colors as a private and served overseas twelve months with a regiment of infantry. He received his honorable discharge June 5, 1919, and soon afterward resumed his law studies in Washington and Lee University. He was granted the LL. B. degree in 1922, and in the same year engaged in practice at Lunenburg Court House. In 1923 the office which his father had so long held was bestowed upon him and in 1927 he was again elected commonwealth's attorney. Mr. Neblett is unmarried. He owns farming interests in Lunenburg County, is a member of the Virginia State and Lunenburg County Bar Associations, belongs to the American Legion, the Masonic fraternity, the Kappa Sigma College fraternity and the Kiwanis Club at Victoria. He is a Democrat and a vestryman in the Episcopal Church of Lunenburg.

RALPH MINTHORNE BROWN, librarian of the Virginia Polytechnic Institute at Blacksburg, has an interesting record not only as a librarian, but also as a World war veteran. Both of Mr. Brown's brothers were also in the World war.

Mr. Brown was born at Fort Shaw, Montana, August 27, 1878, a son of Major Paul R. and Anna Maria (Melius) Brown. He is a descendant of Jean De Bruynne, of Lorraine, France, who settled in New York in 1647.

Major Paul R. Brown was born and reared in New York City, was educated as a physician and surgeon in Wesleyan University in Massachusetts and Columbia University, New York. In 1874 he entered the Regular Army as a surgeon, and was soon sent to the Northwest, where he served under General Custer and General Cook. He was on active duty during Indian wars in the West, and in the routine of army life he was at many army posts in the Dakotas, Nebraska, Montana, Wyoming, Arkansas, Texas and New York. Major Brown died May 30, 1906, at Philipsburg, Pennsylvania, where he is buried. His wife, Anna Maria Melius, was born at Claverack, New York, in 1845, and was educated in private schools and academies. She died January 22, 1917, and is buried in the Rock Creek Cemetery at Washington, D. C. Of her five children two died in infancy. Of the three sons the oldest is Dr. Paul Richard Brown, a physician and surgeon at Tulsa, Oklahoma, who served with the rank of captain in the Medical Corps with the First American Division in 1918-19, and was overseas during the St. Mihiel and the Meuse-Argonne offensives. Ralph M. Brown is the second son.

Herbert Childs Brown, the third son, who was born March 1, 1882, joined an American Ambulance Corps for service with the French armies before America entered into the world struggle, and he was on duty behind the lines at Verdun, and was badly gassed there. After recovering he enlisted in the Thirty-seventh United States Engineers, First Division, and again went overseas, seeing service at Chateau Thierry, St. Mihiel and the Meuse-Argonne. Subsequently he was decorated with the Croix de Guerre by the French government. When he

first enlisted he gave up his position as cable and development
engineer with the Mountain States Telegraph & Telephone Company at Denver, and after the war he was made appraisal engineer with the Pacific States Telegraph & Telephone Company,
with headquarters at San Francisco. He lost his life in an automobile accident at Oakland, California, July 18, 1927.

Ralph Minthorne Brown acquired his early education in
schools maintained at the different army posts where his father
was on duty. He completed his academic training in the Brooklyn
Polytechnic Institute, after which he spent four years in Cornell
University of New York, graduating with the class of 1901.
During 1915-16 he took special work in George Washington Uni-
versity at Washington. Mr. Brown did his first library work in
1901, with the New York State Veterinary College. In 1902-03
he was desk assistant in the public library at Buffalo, New
York, from 1904 to 1906 was librarian for the United States
Department of Commerce at Washington, and from 1906 to 1917
acted as chief of the Division of Archives of the Library and
Archives of the United States Coast and Geodetic Survey at
Washington.

Mr. Brown on May 20, 1917, joined the colors, entering an
ambulance corps, and was on duty with Fourth and Fifth French
armies in the Champagne defensive, the Champagne-Marne,
Aisne and Oise-Aisne offensives, and remained overseas until
after the armistice. He was granted his honorable discharge
April 22, 1919. Mr. Brown then became geographical editor
for Redfield, Kendrick and Odell at New York, and from 1920
to 1923 was geographical editor for the Rand McNally Company
of Chicago. During 1923 he was book editor for the *Popular
Mechanics* Magazine, published at Chicago, and in 1924 was
assistant reference librarian in the Chicago Public Library, and
from September, 1924, to August, 1925, was librarian of the
State Teachers College at Minot, North Dakota.

Mr. Brown came to his present post in September, 1925.
In addition to being librarian he is secretary of the Virginia
Polytechnic Institute University Club and a member of the Board
of Directors. He belongs to the Blacksburg Lions Club, Harvey
Howe Post of the American Legion and the American Ambulance
Association. Mr. Brown is unmarried.

JOHN LeROY YATES. One of the chief claimants to the distinction of having had the longest consecutive service in one
county office is John L. Yates of Lunenburg County, who has
recently rounded out a half century of continuous service in
the office of county clerk and clerk of the Circuit Court.

Mr. Yates was born in Lunenburg County, September 21,
1854, son of Dr. Benjamin L. and Sophia M. (Ralls) Yates. His
father was born in Mecklenburg County and his mother in
Rockingham County, Virginia. Dr. Benjamin L. Yates was a
Confederate soldier, serving three years and three months with
the armies of the South. He was a private in Wise's Brigade
of the Thirty-fourth Virginia Regiment, and was wounded in
the battle of Hatcher's Run at Petersburg. He practiced the
profession of dentistry in Mecklenburg and Lunenburg counties
for many years after the war, and died in 1905. His wife
passed away in 1907.

John L. Yates was reared and educated in Lunenburg County.
He grew up on the farm of his father, remained there until
he was twenty years of age, and since that year has been at

Lunenburg Courthouse, for the first three years as deputy circuit clerk. For one year he clerked in a store and in 1878 was elected circuit clerk. He has been chosen at every successive election since that time, and the efficiency of his service needs no other comments than the fact that he has been only once opposed for reelection. The only time he ever encountered opposition was in 1888.

Mr. Yates married, April 7, 1881, Miss Mary F. Cooksey, daughter of Hartwell P. and Evelyn A. (Royal) Cooksey, both natives of Lunenburg County. Her father was with the Home Guard Regiment in the Civil war and spent his life as a farmer in Lunenburg County, where he died in May, 1901. Mrs. Yates' mother died in 1861. To the marriage of Mr. and Mrs. Yates were born three children. The daughter Mary McGuire is the wife of Dr. E. L. Kendig, of Victoria, Virginia, and the other daughter, Helen Murray, married Dr. W. D. Kendig, of Kenbridge, Virginia. These doctors are brothers. The only son of Mr. and Mrs. Yates was John Elliott, who died July 15, 1901, at the age of thirteen years, seven months, fifteen days.

Mr. Yates for many years has been interested in farming and owns about 2,200 acres of land in Lunenburg County. He is affiliated with the Masonic fraternity, the Sons of the Confederacy, is a Democrat and a steward in the Methodist Episcopal Church, South. Mrs. Yates is a member of the Daughters of the American Revolution and the United Daughters of the Confederacy.

JOHN WILLIAMSON MCGAVOCK, JR., county treasurer of Wythe County, was born in that county and is one of a family connection that has been prominently identified with the county for several generations.

Mr. McGavock is a descendant of James McGavock, who settled in the Marx Meadows locality of Southwestern Virginia some time between 1758 and 1765. During the Revolutionary war he helped supply the army of General Washington as a member of the Quartermaster's Department. The grandfather of the county treasurer was Ephraim McGavock, a Wythe County merchant, who carried on business before the Civil war.

John Williamson McGavock, Sr., was born at Wytheville, in a building which stood where the present postoffice is located. He is now eighty-two years of age and a man whose long life has brought him a wealth of esteem. He attended private school at Norwood in Nelson County, continuing his education in the Virginia Military Institute and the University of Virginia. He was one of the cadets called out from the military institute to take part in the battle of New Market, and remained with the Confederate forces during the last year of the war. After the war he entered the pig iron industry at Barren Springs, Virginia, but for the greater part of his active life has been a farmer and stock man, owning extensive tracts of land in the eastern part of Wythe County. He has some of the finest blue grass soil in that section. He is a Republican in politics and for a number of years was chairman of the Republican party of Wythe County, and also served on state committees. John Williamson McGavock, Sr., married Emily M. Graham, who was born and reared in Wythe County, daughter of David Graham, a farmer and cattle man. David Graham was also a manufacturer of iron, and after his death his son, with John W. Robinson and John W. McGavock, Sr., continued this pig iron industry for a number

A. S. Harrison Jr.

of years. Emily Graham was educated in private schools and in the Girls School of Staunton, was an active member of the Methodist Episcopal Church, South. She died July 28, 1889. Of her children two died in infancy, and the others are: D. G., John W., Jr., Ephraim, Martha Pierce, Mrs. A. Jouett Noyd, James H., Mrs. Margaret Robinson, Crockett and Miss Mary Belle. John W. McGavock's second wife was Miss Jane Byrd Pendleton, of Wytheville, and the children of this marriage were: Emily Graham, who married Olcott Neary, of Rochester, New York, and died at the age of twenty-eight; Byrd Page; Sara Jackson, now the wife of John Allison; Gurdon P.; Stephen; and Frank P.

John Williamson McGavock, Jr., was born in Wythe County, November 21, 1873, was educated in private schools and the Episcopal High School at Alexandria. In 1894, at the age of twenty-one, he went to work for the Wythe Lead & Zinc Company at Austinville, remaining with that industry for eight years. In 1902 he entered the mercantile business at Fries, continuing for three years, and then for three years was a brick manufacturer at Galax, and for one year was associated with the Richlands Brick Company at Richlands. Mr. McGavock in November, 1907, became a deputy internal revenue collector under Louis P. Summers, at Abingdon, Virginia, and was in that service until April 23, 1919, holding this position in the Federal Government during the World war period. When he retired from this service he was in the real estate business with the Pace Brothers at Roanoke until December, 1919, when he returned to Wythe County and accepted the appointment of deputy county treasurer. On December 31, 1927, he began his elected term as county treasurer.

Mr. McGavock is a member of the Masonic fraternity, is a Republican, a Presbyterian, and is superintendent of the Draper Valley Presbyterian Church Sunday School.

He married at Bedford City, Virginia, July 26, 1898, Miss Nannie Harrison Miller, of Bedford City, daughter of Alford H. and Rebecca (Ficklen) Miller, now deceased. Mrs. McGavock was educated in public schools at Saltville, attended Randolph-Macon Woman's College at Lynchburg, and for three years taught in the Orphan Girls School at Lynchburg. She is a member of the Presbyterian Church, Mr. and Mrs. McGavock have one son, Alford Miller McGavock, who attended the grade and high schools of Salem, and is now a member of the class of 1929 in the Virginia Polytechnic Institute, where he is specializing in chemistry.

ALBERTIS SYDNEY HARRISON, JR., is a member of a well known family of Brunswick County, and since graduating in law has practiced as junior member of the firm Hammack & Harrison in the Wesson Building at Lawrenceville.

He was born January 11, 1907, at the home of his parents near Lawrenceville, son of Albertis Sydney and Lizzie Thomas (Goodrich) Harrison. His mother was born at Petersburg, Virginia. His father has always lived in Brunswick County, and is a well known local tobacco grower, having a plantation of 400 acres near Lawrenceville.

Mr. Harrison, Jr., grew up on the home farm and attended the Brunswick County schools, graduating from high school at Lawrenceville in 1923. He took both the academic and law courses at the University of Virginia, and was graduated LL.B.

in June, 1928. In 1927 he passed the state bar examination. In the same month he formed a partnership with Lorenza J. Hammack for the practice of law.

Mr. Harrison, who is unmarried, is a member of the Virginia State Bar Association. He is a Delta Sigma Phi, a Democrat and an Episcopalian.

ANDREW W. GATEWOOD is an engineer who has spent many years building and maintaining railroads and in handling the technical operation of other industries. He is now manager of ore mines for the Pulaski Iron Company of Pulaski, Virginia.

Mr. Gatewood is a member of an old Virginia family. He was born at Big Spring, West Virginia. His grandfather, Samuel B. Gatewood, came with two brothers from England, one of whom later returned to the old country. Samuel B. Gatewood settled at Mountain Grove in Bath County, Virginia, and spent his active life as a farmer and stock man. His son, A. C. L. Gatewood, was born in Bath County, was educated in private schools and graduated from the Virginia Military Institute in 1861. He served as a first lieutenant in General Stuart's Eleventh Virginia Cavalry, and was all through the war, being twice wounded in battle. After the war he engaged in farming and stock raising at Big Spring, West Virginia, and lived there until his death in 1919. His wife, Mary Warwick, was born at Warwickton, Bath County, Virginia, three miles from Warm Springs. Warwickton was named for her family, who owned a large tract of land in that locality. Her father, Judge James W. Warwick, was a judge of the Circuit Court of Virginia for many years. Mary Warwick was educated in private schools at Lexington and attended the Mary Baldwin Seminary at Staunton. She and her husband were actively interested in the Presbyterian Church. She died in 1923. They had a family of seven children: Warwick, who died in infancy; Mary Preston, who died in 1915, wife of Dr. W. T. Cameron, of Mingo, West Virginia, leaving two children, Margaret and Gatewood; Eugene Samuel, farmer and cattle men at Big Spring, married Minnie Ray and has a daughter, Mary Elizabeth; William B. Gatewood, railroad contractor at Huntington, West Virginia, married Miss Goldie Yeager, who died leaving one surviving son, Charles Warwick, and his second wife was Eva Gardner, by whom he has two children, W. B., Jr., and Nancy; Massie C. Gatewood, an engineer with the State Highway Department of West Virginia; Andrew Warwick; and Elizabeth Pleasants, wife of John M. Dunlap, a farmer and stock raiser at Lexington, Virginia, their five children being named Elizabeth, Mary Warwick, Gatewood, Martha McKee, and J. M., Jr.

Andrew Warwick Gatewood was educated in schools in West Virginia, and had his training for the engineering profession through practical work. As a boy he spent a year and a half in the engineering department of the Chesapeake & Western Railroad Company, and for three years was with the Chesapeake & Ohio Railroad, engaged in construction work in Kentucky. For some months he was engaged in location work as a transit man from Marion, North Carolina, to Spartanburg, South Carolina, during the location of the Carolina, Clinchfield & Ohio Railroad. He then returned to the Chesapeake & Ohio Railway as resident engineer on maintenance of way work at Clifton Forge on the Clifton Forge Division for three years, and was then transferred

T. F. Chism

to the Huntington Division on construction work in the Guyandotte Valley District.

Mr. Gatewood during the past twenty years has been identified with mining industries. On October 15, 1908, he became superintendent of mines at Oriskany, Virginia, for the Oriskany Ore & Iron Corporation. In July, 1911, he was transferred to Gretna, Virginia, as superintendent of mines for the same corporation. He became a resident of Pulaski March 1, 1918, at which date he took up his duties as superintendent of ore mines for the Pulaski Iron Company, and since 1921, has been manager of mines for that company.

Mr. Gatewood is a Knight Templar Mason, member of Acca Temple of the Mystic Shrine at Richmond, is affiliated with Pulaski Lodge No. 1065, B. P. O. Elks, is a member of the Rotary Club, Pulaski Country Club, is a Democrat and a Methodist.

He married at Marlinton, West Virginia, March 30, 1910, Miss Brownie Elizabeth Yeager, who was educated at Marlinton and St. Hilda's Hall of Charles Town, West Virginia. She is a member of the Pulaski Methodist Episcopal Church and the Country Club. Mrs. Gatewood is a daughter of B. M. and Harriet Elizabeth (Arbogast) Yeager. Her father for many years was a timber dealer and real estate man at Marlinton, and served two terms in the West Virginia Legislature from Pocahontas County. Her mother died in 1917 and her father in 1924. Mr. and Mrs. Gatewood reared from infancy Charles Warwick Gatewood, son of William B. Gatewood, above mentioned. This foster son is now a student in Hampden-Sidney College.

THOMAS FLOURNOY CHISM had the rare good fortune to find his calling at an early age and take up the business which he has followed without important deviation. Mr. Chism is one of the oldest men in the commercial life of Danville, where for fifty-three years he has been with one firm in the furniture trade. He has had many associates and partners in that time, but the business today under its present title is a logical continuation of the firm with which he started during the 1870s.

Not only did he start out in his youth to make a success of the furniture business, but he has ever persevered and stuck to it, working hard and continuously, saving his earnings and keeping the same invested therein that the enterprise might flourish and grow. So after many long years, when the golden opportunity arrived, he was ready, able and willing to contribute to the building of the magnificent furniture home, the finest in the South, along with Danville's best hotel, theatre and other convenient places of business, which is proving to be a profitable investment and a monument to the city. He is a rare specimen of humanity, ever affable, kind and friendly, pleasant in all business and social transactions, always ready to consider the other fellow's opinion and interest, gladly willing to live and let live, generous in philanthropy. Those who know him best say that he has not an enemy on earth, makes friends and holds them. He claims that in all these more than fifty years in public business he does not believe there is a customer living whom he has ever sold that he cannot sell again should he desire to. Moreover there are few families within fifty miles of Danville with whom he has not had transactions. These attributes and this business capacity have largely contributed to his success in building up a clientele which will make this the leading furniture business of this section for many long years to come.

A great booster for organization and cooperation, Mr. Chism was a charter member of the "Tri-State Retail Furniture Dealers Association," Virginia, North and South Carolina, which has accomplished much in the betterment of the furniture business in the three states during the last fifteen years. So enthusiastic was he in its activities that he was once made president of the association, and for many years attended the annual conventions held consecutively rotating in the three states. This association is still flourishing, doing more and more for the best interest of the general retail furniture business. Mr. J. A. Gilmore, of Charlottesville, Virginia, is and has been its secretary-manager from the date of its organization.

Mr. Chism was born in Pittsylvania County, Virginia, November 11, 1858, a son of William P. and Caroline Williams (Poindexter) Chism. The Chism family came from France in the early Colonial period of Virginia. His grandfather, Jimmy Chism, was a planter in Pittsylvania County, and lived to the good old age of ninety-eight years. William P. Chism was born and reared in Pittsylvania County, his home community being near Kentuck Church. He attended private schools, was a farmer and tobacco planter and owned and worked a number of slaves. He was long active in the Kentuck Baptist Church and died in 1861. His wife, Caroline Poindexter, was born and reared at Catawba in Halifax County, Virginia, was educated in private schools, and throughout her life was a consecrated Christian woman, active in the Baptist Church. She died in 1880. There were four children: Mary Susan, who died April 21, 1927; Nannie Carr, who died in June, 1925; Thomas Flournoy; and William Armistead, who died in 1885.

Thomas Flournoy Chism attended public schools in Pittsylvania County and from the age of sixteen was gaining experience in a business way. From December, 1874, to January 7, 1877, he clerked in a grocery store at Danville, and on January 7, 1877, made his first connection with the furniture business. It had been his decision for several years that the line he would follow permanently was furniture. His first employer was Gustavus W. Crumpecker, for whom he clerked until he was twenty-one years of age, and was then taken into partnership, the firm being Crumpecker, Chism & Company until 1882. In that year Mr. William P. Hodnett bought the Crumpecker interests, and the business was conducted as the Hodnett-Chism Furniture Company until 1914. With the withdrawal of Mr. Hodnett in that year other associates came into the business, and the firm is now Clements, Chism & Parker, Incorporated, with Mr. Charles B. Clements and A. Rucker Parker active members, both of whom have been with the business for a number of years, Mr. Parker since 1898 and Mr. Clements since about 1904. The president of the corporation is Mr. M. O. Nelson, while Mr. Chism is vice president, Mr. A. Rucker Parker, second vice president, and Mr. Charles B. Clements secretary and treasurer. Mr. Chism is interested in other local industries at Danville.

Fraternally he is affiliated with Maratock Lodge No. 210 A. F. and A. M., with Euclid Chapter, Royal Arch Masons, and is a past regent of Dan River Council No. 1319, Royal Arcanum. He is a Democrat, and since the age of thirteen has been a devout Baptist. He first joined the Kentuck Baptist Church near his old home and immediately on moving the Danville united

with the First Baptist Church, where he has had his membership for over half a century.

Mr. Chism married at Danville, March 24, 1886, Miss Ella
May Bowles, who grew up in Danville and attended public school
there. She was a Baptist, but her life was really lived in her
home. She died October 1, 1928, and is buried in Green Hill
Cemetery. Her parents were Dr. R. C. and Mary Ann (Eggleston) Bowles. Her father spent some years in the Government
service at Washington, D. C., and after moving to Danville practiced medicine and surgery. Both her parents died in about
1890.

EARLE B. NORRIS, descended from a line of inventors and
industrial leaders, has made a distinguished record in the field
of engineering, and has held chairs in the engineering schools
of several prominent universities. At the present time he is
dean of the School of Engineering of the Virginia Polytechnic
Institute at Blacksburg.

He was born at Jamestown, New York, September 17, 1882.
He is a descendant of Nicholas Norris, who came from England
and settled at Salem, Massachusetts, in 1640, and later representatives of the family served in the war for independence. His
grandfather, Josiah H. Norris, was a Pennsylvania inventor and
manufacturer. Among other things he invented tools for fishing drills and other equipment for oil wells. He and his wife
are buried at Warren, Pennsylvania.

Harry E. Norris, father of Dean Norris, was born at Glens
Falls, New York, was educated in private schools, and during
most of his life has been engaged in the manufacture of electrical equipment. For over thirty years he conducted a factory
at North East, Pennsylvania, where he resides, having retired
from business about 1925. Some of the manufactured articles
produced by him were his own inventions. His wife, Belle
(Barker) Norris, was born and reared at Nunda, New York.
She and her husband are members of the Presbyterian Church.
Of their six children one daughter, Nina Belle, died very young,
and the five living children are: Edwin R., Earle B., Harry B.,
Donald G. and Walter L.

Earle B. Norris attended high school at Warren, Pennsyl-
vania, and received his technical training in Pennsylvania State
College, where he was graduated with the degree of Bachelor of
Science in mechanical engineering in 1904. On leaving college
he spent one year as assistant mechanical engineer with E.
Bement's Sons at Lansing, Michigan, and another year in the
same city as assistant superintendent of the Central Implement
Company. With this practical experience he returned to the
Pennsylvania State College as instructor of mechanical engineering for two years, and also carried on graduate work. Pennsylvania State College gave him the degree of Mechanical Engineer in 1908, and in the same year he entered the faculty of the
University of Wisconsin as assistant professor of mechanical
engineering, in 1912 was advanced to associate professor, and
in 1916 to professor of mechanical engineering. This post he
resigned to become industrial commissioner of the Saint Paul
Association of Commerce in Minnesota, but here his work was
interrupted by America's entrance into the World war.

In the summer of 1917 he joined the colors, with the United
States Army Ordnance Department, and with the rank of captain of ordnance. He was at Washington until December, 1917,

then ordered to France, and put in charge of the engineering
service on heavy howitzers in the A. E. F. In February, 1919,
he was promoted to major of ordnance, and in April of that year
returned to Washington. He was assigned to Rock Island, Illinois, as chief engineer of the Rock Island Arsenal, but resigned
from the service in September, 1919. At the close of the war
he was cited by General Pershing for "conspicuous and meritorious services."

At that time Mr. Norris went to the University of Montana
as dean of Engineering, and remained in the Northwest for nine
years. In August, 1928, he came to Blacksburg, Virginia, as
dean of the School of Engineering. He is a member of the
American Society of Mechanical Engineers and holds the rank of
lieutenant-colonel in the Ordnance Reserve Corps. He is a member of the Phi Gamma Delta, Phi Kappa Phi, Tau Beta Pi, is a
thirty-second degree Scottish Rite Mason, and a member of
Algeria Temple of the Mystic Shrine at Helena, Montana. He
is the author of several widely-used textbooks in the field of
engineering.

He married at Lansing, Michigan, Miss Faye Hurd, of that
city. She attended public schools there and the Michigan State
College. Her parents are Israel T. and Lillian (Tenny) Hurd,
of Lansing. Her father for many years has been Michigan sales
manager of the widely known manufacturing concern, Hunt,
Helm & Ferris of Harvard, Illinois. Mrs. Norris is a descendant in the paternal line of the Randolphs of Virginia.

ALLEN DOUGLAS LATANE, County and Circuit Court clerk of
Essex County, and owner and editor of the *Rappahannock
Times,* is a man who looms big before the people of this region,
for he not only is a most able and conscientious public official,
but he is also a newspaperman known all over his part of the
state as one who understands the details of his business and is
able to put out a live, readable and clean weekly that is supported
by the people of the Tappahannock and surrounding counties.
Mr. Latane was born on Meadow Farm twelve miles from Tappahannock, Essex County, August 30, 1876. He is a direct descendant of Parson Lewis Latane, one of the first French Huguenots who came to this country in 1700 to escape religious persecution, and brought his band of worshipers with him. Allen
D. Latane is also a nephew of Capt. William Latane, of Civil
war fame, who was the subject of the picture of "The Burial
of Latane," and the famous poem by Thompson under the same
caption, and Mr. Latane has in his possession a beautiful gold
watch which Captain Latane was wearing when he was killed.
Allen D. Latane is a son of Henry W. and Martha (Gordon) Latane. Both were born in Essex County, and in this county the
father was engaged in farming all of his mature years. He was
a Confederate veteran, and he served for two terms as county
treasurer. He died in August, 1892, aged sixty-two years, and
she died in January, 1919, aged eighty-three years.

Reared in Essex County, Allen Douglas Latane attended
Aberdeen Academy in King and Queen County, Virginia, after
which he went into the newspaper business and learned the
printer's trade and after two years' connection with the *Rappahannock Times* he bought it, in April, 1900, since which time
he has continued to issue it. The *Times* has a circulation of
1,200, and is recognized as an admirable medium for advertising by the merchants and other business men of the city and

Wm R. Rowe

county. Politically a Democrat, Mr. Latane is one of the local
party leaders, and for the past ten years has been town treasurer, and for eighteen years has been a member of the Town
Council. On June 15, 1928, Mr. Latane was appointed County
and Circuit Court clerk of Essex County to fill an unexpired
term. For four years he had charge of the custom house here,
or until 1915, when it was removed to Reedsville, thus taking
away from Tappahannock the distinction of being the port of
entry for over two hundred years.

On December 19, 1906, Mr. Latane married Miss Emma C.
Cauthorn, a daughter of Robert Thomas and Fanny (Brooke)
Cauthorn, natives of Essex County. For thirty or more years
the father was a merchant of Tappahannock, and here he died in
1921, and the mother in 1919. Three children have been born
to Mr. and Mrs. Latane: Alice Brooke, who was born August
19, 1908; Martha Gordon, who was born October 2, 1910; and
Emma Cauthorn, who was born June 1, 1912.

Mr. Latane is chairman of the Essex County Democratic
Committee. In earlier years he belonged to the Knights of
Pythias. For years he has been a stockholder in the South Side
Bank of Tappahannock and he owns jointly the old homestead
of his family, which is a valuable farming property of Essex
County, and one of the oldest residences in Tappahannock,
which was built in 1690, the walls of which are a yard in thick-
ness. It is one of the historic places of this part of Virginia,
and Mr. Latane is very proud of it. He has affiliations with the
Protestant Episcopal Church and is president of the local Laymen's Association, belongs to the Sons of the Confederate Veterans and his wife belongs to the United Daughters of the Confederacy.

WILLIAM R. ROWE, secretary-manager of the Northern Neck
Mutual Fire Association of Virginia, with home office in Irvington, Virginia, is one of the astute, energetic and experienced
insurance men of the state, and one who has traveled far on
the road that leads to permanent success. More and more each
year the general public is coming to realize the absolute necessity for protection, through insurance, from the ravages of
disastrous fires, and among the numerous companies writing
insurance none stands any higher than does the Northern Neck
Mutual Fire Association of Virginia, which confines its business
to the state in which its headquarters are located. The volume
of this company's business has steadily expanded until today it
has $22,000,000 in force. Thinking people insure in this com-
pany because its way of doing things appeals to them, especially
if they are business men, as being eminently sound and progressive.

The birth of William R. Rowe occurred in Irvington, Virginia, May 20, 1877, and he is a son of James W. and Mary E.
(Haydon) Rowe, also natives of Irvington. The father was the
first oyster packer on the Rappahannock River, and was a ship-
per of oysters and a dealer in all kinds of sea foods. He died
in February, 1886, aged thirty-eight years. The mother died
in August, 1927.

Reared in Irvington, William R. Rowe attended its public
schools until he was fifteen years old, at which time he went to
work in a printing office in Baltimore, Maryland, where he
remained for five years. Returning to his native place, he continued in the newspaper business for eighteen years as associ-

ate editor and manager of the local paper, and at the same time
was connected with his present company as director and
assistant secretary. In 1918 he became secretary and manager
of this company, and is making a record second to none in this
connection. The same spirit which has carried his company into
the fields of large business makes him a supporter of citizen-
building projects, as well as other business enterprises that aim
at the betterment of conditions in Irvington. He is vice president and chairman of the Board of Directors of the Lancaster
National Bank, a director of the Humphries Marine Railway,
Incorporated, and a director of the Standard Products Company,
Incorporated.

In February, 1923, Mr. Rowe married Miss Mary D. Seward,
of Baltimore, Maryland, a daughter of Elliott and Brooke
(Boughton) Seward, natives of Essex County, Virginia. Mr.
Seward was in the livestock business in Baltimore for many
years, and he died in that city in 1913. Mrs. Seward survives
and makes her home with Mr. and Mrs. Rowe. The latter have
one child, William R. Rowe, Junior, who was born August
23, 1924.

Mr. Rowe is a Mason and belongs to the Independent Order
of Odd Fellows, the local Rotary Club, and the Westmoreland
Club of Richmond, Virginia. In political faith he is a Democrat,
but is not active aside from exercising his right of suffrage.
The Baptist Church holds his membership, and he is senior
deacon and superintendent of the Sunday School. A man of
the highest personal character, Mr. Rowe's connection with his
company gives it added strength, and its outlook for the future
is very encouraging.

REV. OSCAR SMITH BUNTING, D. D., son of Jeremiah and
Mary Lindsay Bunting, was born in Williamsburg, Virginia,
April 18, 1853. He was the oldest of eight children, and was
educated during the stormy period of the Civil war in the schools
of his native town. Later he entered Richmond College, from
which he graduated with honor in 1874. While at Richmond
College he made his home with his grandparents, Mr. and Mrs.
Thomas Orlando Lindsay, who were devout Christians of fine
character, of Scotch-English ancestry, and zealous members of
the English church. As long as he lived he spoke of these years
with pleasure, the fine character and culture of his grandparents having greatly impressed him. In 1874 he entered the
Episcopal Theological Seminary at Alexandria, and finishing
the course was ordained a deacon in 1877 and entered the priesthood the following year, 1878.

Doctor Bunting was a man of splendid scholarship and great
spirituality. He was especially gifted as a pastor and a Bible
teacher. This gift of teaching he inherited from his mother,
who in turn inherited her cultured tastes from her parents.
Bishop Randolph of Virginia always spoke of his parents as
pioneer church people of Southwestern Virginia. His father
always took charge of the church services when there was no
rector, was senior warden, superintendent of the Sunday School,
and the family composed the choir.

Doctor Bunting during his career had four parishes. He first
did mountain work in Nelson and Amherst counties, going from
there to the church at Harrisonburg, Virginia. Later he was
rector of the old Colonial church, St. Michael's, Trenton, New
Jersey, and he died while rector of St. Paul's Petersburg, Vir-

ginia, February 24, 1905. He was greatly loved by the members of his congregations, and in three of the churches beautiful memorials have been placed to his memory.

He married Mary Plummer Harriss, daughter of Dr. Samuel Goode Harriss and Mary Alston Plummer, his wife, of Mecklenburg County. Of this marriage there are four children: Mary Dandridge, now Mrs. Bernard Rawl; Oscar Lindsay; Plummer Goode; and Anne Spotswood Bunting, who is now Mrs. Louis Bregy and lives in Canada, where her husband is a mining engineer. There is one grandson, Oscar Lindsay Bunting II.

CHARLES ROBERT ADAIR has developed one of the largest and most prosperous general insurance agencies in Giles County, located at Narrows. Mr. Adair is a business man with a wide and diversified experience. He represents one of the old families of this section of Western Virginia, though he is himself a native of Kansas, where his parents lived only a few years and then returned to the old home in Giles County.

Mr. Adair was born in Sumner County, Kansas, February 3, 1880, son of John A. and Jennie (McClaugherty) Adair. His grandfather, James Adair, was born in County Down, Ireland, June 4, 1807. In 1817, when he was ten years of age, the family left Ireland and on October 31, 1817, landed at Norfolk after a voyage of fifty-seven days by sailing vessel. The family went west to Greenbrier County, in what is now West Virginia, and subsequently James Adair moved to Giles County, where he lived out his life. John A. Adair was born at Bell Point in Giles County, was educated in private schools and devoted most of his years to farming. He died December 30, 1928, at the age of seventy-eight, at his home at Narrows. He was in Kansas a few years and then returned to Giles County. He served for a time as deputy sheriff. His wife, Jennie McClaugherty, was born and reared near Pearisburg, Virginia, was educated in private schools and in Humphreys Academy at White Gate. She died about 1893 and is buried near Pearisburg. She was a Methodist, while her husband was a Baptist. There were four children: James; Charles R.; Janie, wife of P. O. Ivery; and Miss Ellen Kyle Adair.

Charles Robert Adair received his early education in the public schools of Giles County, but his education has been severely practical and has come from his contact with men and affairs rather than from higher institutions of learning. Shortly after he left school he went west and saw a great deal of the real West before he came back to Virginia. For four years he was a cowboy on the cattle range, and spent several years in the gold, silver and coal mining districts of New Mexico and Colorado. He was also an employe of the Iron Mountain and Southern branch of the Missouri Pacific Railway System.

In 1904, at the time of the Saint Louis World's Fair, he returned east and settled in Giles County. For some years he was on the road as a commercial traveler and in 1916 started his insurance business at Narrows. He is sole owner of his agency and has made a splendid success of this business. His agency now represents about twenty companies, covering all lines of insurance. The service in life insurance is supplied by the Pilot Life Insurance Company. Other companies represented by him are the Fidelity and Casualty, the America Four, a group of fire companies, the National Liberty of New York, the Globe and Rutgers and others. He also handles real estate and is a director of the Cavalier Hosiery Mills and of the Giant Caverns Corporation.

Mr. Adair is active in the Masonic fraternity and is a member of Kazim Temple of the Mystic Shrine at Roanoke. He is secretary of the Narrows Business Men's Club, Incorporated, and secretary of the Giles County Fair Association. He has served as a police justice. He is a Democrat and a Presbyterian, being deacon of his church and for some time was superintendent of the Sunday School.

He married in Fluvanna County, Virginia, September 30, 1907, Miss Margaret Davis, who was reared and educated there, attending a girls' academy, and she taught before her marriage. She is a member of the Presbyterian Church, the Eastern Star and United Daughters of the Confederacy. Her father, Henry Davis, was for many years a farmer in Fluvanna County, and still lives there at the age of seventy-six. Her mother died in 1883. Henry Davis after the death of his first wife married Jessie Hughes, and by that marriage has three children: Allen; Edith, who is Mrs. W. W. Arnold; and Henry. Mr. and Mrs. Adair have had three children: Mary Davis graduated from the Narrows High School in 1926 and is a graduate of the class of 1929 from Averett College at Danville, Virginia; Frances Elizabeth died when fourteen months old; and Charles Robert, Jr., is in the class of 1930 in the Narrows High School.

CHARLES A. CRABTREE carries out the succession of three generations of the Crabtree family activities as farmers and stock raisers in Bland County. Mr. Crabtree is one of the leading men in the business at Ceres and is also a county supervisor.

He was born at Sharon, now Ceres, April 25, 1866, son of Reece and Polly (Foglesang) Crabtree and a grandson of John Crabtree, who about a century ago moved from Washington County, Virginia, to Bland County. He died about the close of the Civil war, and both he and his wife are buried in the Sharon Cemetery. Reece Crabtree was educated in private schools and was a soldier of the Confederacy under Gen. Jubal Early, participating in many of the battles in the Valley of Virginia and elsewhere. His active years after the war were devoted to farming and stock raising, and he died on Easter Sunday in 1908. His wife, Polly Foglesang, was born and reared at Ceres, like her husband was educated in private schools, and she taught for a time before her marriage. She was an active Lutheran, while her husband was a Methodist. She died in 1906, and both are buried in Sharon Cemetery. There were ten children: Susan Emiline, John Henry, Manda Eliza, Julia Ann, Charles Abraham, Elbert Smith, William Terry, Mary Louise, Cora Lee and Peter Estel.

Charles A. Crabtree attended public school at Ceres and for two years was a student in Roanoke College. After leaving college he returned home and took up the work of farming and stock raising on his father's place, and there has been no interruption to this business for over forty years. He has 500 acres of the fine blue grass land of Bland County, improved with one of the most attractive homes in any of the rural districts around Ceres. He also owns improved real estate in Wytheville. Mr. Crabtree for nine years has been a member of the Bland County Board of Supervisors, and although living in a Republican county he has been twice reelected on the Democratic ticket, a fact that is a striking testimonial to the general esteem in

which he is held and the confidence reposed in his judgment as a public official. Mr. Crabtree is a member of the Lutheran Church and for a number of years was superintendent of the Sunday School.

He married at Ceres, November 29, 1893, Miss Elberta Foglesang, who after the public schools attended Trinity College at Wytheville. She has always carried her share of work in the Lutheran Church. She is a daughter of H. S. and Mollie Ann (Rose) Foglesang, her father for many years a farmer and cattle raiser near Ceres. Her father was a soldier under General Breckenridge in the Confederate army, and was in many engagements, including Gettysburg and once was wounded in action. He died in 1886 and is buried in Sharon Cemetery. Her mother died in 1891. Mr. and Mrs. Crabtree had six children: Charles Alfred, Nellie Beatrice, Cora Lee, Willis Edgar, who died December 18, 1901, at the age of two years, Mary Clare and Robert Paul. Charles Alfred Crabtree was educated at Ceres and in the Collegiate Military Institute at Mount Pleasant, North Carolina, went to France, serving in the infantry for eighteen months, and is now a farmer and stock man at Ceres and also an undertaker and funeral director. He married Ruth Tilson and has two children, Alvin and Edwin. The daughter Nellie Beatrice was educated at Ceres, and in the Wytheville High School, and is the wife of T. O. Umbarger, of Wytheville, a farmer and stock man, and has three children, Barkley Crabtree, Owen Umbarger and Nellie Alline. Cora Lee Crabtree finished her education in the Wytheville High School, and is the wife of G. P. Hubble, a resident of Concord, North Carolina, and their children are Dorothy Jean, Gilbert Willis, Mary Gladys and Ralph Wayne. Mary Clare Crabtree attended school at Ceres, the high school at Rural Retreat and is the wife of J. B. Groseclose, a son of S. R. Groseclose, of Ceres, and they have three children, Joseph, Donald and Francis. The youngest child of Mr. Crabtree, Robert Paul, was educated in the grade and high schools at Ceres, and is working for his father on the farm.

COL. NATHANIEL JAMES PERKINS is president of the Fork Union Military Academy, a high class boys' preparatory school, which a great many Virginia men take pride in referring to as an important source of their early training. It is one of the older schools of its class in Virginia, and its equipment and standing and its facilities attract students from all over the state and other states.

Colonel Perkins has spent the greater part of his life in educational work. He was born at Carysbrook in Fluvanna County, Virginia, May 31, 1877, and the farm where he was born and reared is now owned by him. His parents were Isaac Otey and Lelia (Hughes) Perkins, both natives of Fluvanna County. His father at the age of sixteen entered the Confederate army and saw service of fourteen months before the end of the war. After the war he devoted his energies to the old farm in Fluvanna County, and died January 12, 1913, at the age of sixty-seven. For a number of years he was deputy treasurer of the county. His widow now resides at Palmyra, Virginia.

Nathaniel James Perkins received his elementary training while a boy on the farm, graduated from the Palmyra High School in May, 1897, and then went north to Ohio to take his college training in Denison University at Granville, Ohio, where he was graduated with the A. B. degree in the class of 1902.

Following his university career he taught one year at Nashville, Illinois, also at Aspen, Colorado, and for ten years was a school man in Florida. For two years he was principal of the Sanford High School and was then made city superintendent, holding that office for eight years. For several years Colonel Perkins lived on the home farm at Carysbrook and for two years of that time also acted as principal of a local school.

He first became identified with the Fork Union Military Academy as an instructor during the school year 1916-17. In the fall of 1917 he became president of the institution, and during the past twelve years has brought new fame to the school.

Colonel Perkins married, September 1, 1904, Miss Ethel Beard, daughter of John and Lena (Goodwin) Beard. Her parents were born in Amherst County, and her father for twenty years was sheriff of the county, holding that office when he died. He was accidentally killed by a train in 1908, and her mother died in 1911. Colonel and Mrs. Perkins have one daughter, Ethel Goodwin, born April 4, 1907.

Colonel Perkins is a real leader in the life and affairs of his native county. He is president of the Fluvanna Chamber of Commerce, is a York Rite Mason and Shriner, a Beta Theta Pi and Pi Gamma Mu, is a Democrat, and is a deacon in the Baptist Church and teaches a class in Sunday School. He is a member of the Sons of Confederate Veterans, and both he and his wife are eligible to membership in the sons and daughters of the American Revolution.

OLVERTON EVANS BOOKER, who represented a prominent old family of Amelia County, was for many years a business man in Richmond, and was widely known all over the state in the grain trade.

He was born in Amelia County August 30, 1857, and died at Richmond in November, 1918, at the age of sixty-one. The earliest records of the Booker family run back in Amelia County two hundred years or more, and the county records show that King Charles bestowed upon members of this family a grant of land there. Mr. Booker's father was William Lewis Booker, a lawyer by profession, who for several years before his death was commonwealth's attorney for Amelia County. William Lewis Booker married Lavinia Wilson Hobson, daughter of Joseph and Mary Hobson. Of their nine children, seven sons and two daughters, Olverton E. was the youngest son.

During his boyhood he attended school in Amelia County and also in Powhatan County, where his father lived for some years. He had several years of experience as a practical farmer, and on removing to Richmond entered the service of the Richmond Grain Exchange. That organization gave him practically his life work and for many years he was secretary and treasurer. From the Grain Exchange his business connections extended to other local financial organizations.

As a young man Mr. Booker was chosen a magistrate of Amelia County, but never qualified for the office. He was a Democrat and a member of the Episcopal Church, and Mrs. Booker, who survives him and resides at 3030 Grove Avenue, has always taken a deep interest in the church.

Mr. Booker married, May 7, 1884, Miss Sallie Evans, daughter of Dr. M. F. T. Evans, who came from Georgetown, South Carolina, and was a member of an old family of that state. Doctor Evans practiced medicine at Georgetown. He married

Wm F. Henderson. M.D.

Mary Rebecca Wiley, of Amelia County, Virginia, daughter of John and Mary Bolling (Branch) Wiley. Doctor Evans served with the rank of lieutenant-colonel in the Fourteenth Virginia Regiment in the Confederate army and participated in the battle of Seven Pines and the Peninsular campaign. Mrs. Booker had one brother, Thomas P. Evans, who married Anne Irwin, of Amelia County, and had one child, Frances.

Mr. and Mrs. Booker were the parents of eight children: Mrs. Mary Godwin, wife of a captain in the United States Army, and mother of one child, Marion Elizabeth; William Olverton, who is in the automobile business at Richmond; Yelverton Evans, connected with an investment banking house at Washington, D. C., married Cornelia Ellis, of Montgomery County; Marion Elizabeth, the wife of T. C. Williams, a merchandise broker at Richmond; Miss Mina, who lives in Richmond; Lawrence F., a resident of Richmond; Frank Stockton, a traveling salesman at Richmond; and Catherine, the youngest, the wife of Glover Wales, an insurance man at Norfolk, Virginia.

WILLIAM F. HENDERSON, physician and surgeon, began the practice of his profession more than half a century ago. His work has especially identified him with the Virginia Polytechnic Institute at Blacksburg. He was one of the first students of that institution, and was the official physician and surgeon for many years.

Doctor Henderson was born near Blacksburg, October 10, 1853, son of Francis and Nancy Ann (Brown) Henderson, and grandson of Jonas Henderson. Jonas Henderson came from Botetourt County, Virginia, and settled near Blacksburg early in the last century. He was a soldier in the War of 1812, and he cleared up and developed a fine farm in Montgomery County, owning many slaves. His old plantation is still owned by his family. He and many other members of the family are buried in the family cemetery. Jonas Henderson was of Scotch-Irish ancestry. Francis Henderson was born and reared in Montgomery County, attended private schools, was a member of the Home Guards during the Civil war, and followed farming and stock raising until his death. For a number of years he was sheriff of Montgomery County, and was also justice of the peace at a time when that office had the trial of many important local cases, so that he well deserved his title of judge. Judge Henderson died in 1893, at the age of eighty-two. His wife, Nancy Ann Brown, was born about eight miles from Blacksburg, daughter of Thomas Brown, an elder in the Presbyterian Church and a leading farmer and planter of Botetourt County. Judge Henderson and wife had seven children. The oldest, Thomas J., was a soldier of the Confederacy, participating in the battle of New Market, Virginia, and is still living, making his home with his son-in-law, Major Brodie. The other children were: James K., deceased; Dr. William F.; Joseph, deceased; Mary E., deceased; Elinor Ann, deceased, the wife of Charles L. Peck; and Rachael, deceased, the wife of Dr. W. D. Meeks.

William F. Henderson as a boy attended public school near Blacksburg and was a student in the Preston and Olden Institute, an old institution of learning whose traditions are now fused with those of the Virginia Polytechnic Institute. The Virginia Polytechnic Institute was organized and founded in 1871, and Doctor Henderson was one of the first students to enroll. He remained there three years, and in 1877 was graduated M. D.

from the University of Maryland. He at once returned to Blacksburg, opened his office, and has steadily given his services as a competent doctor in that community for over half a century. He was surgeon to the Virginia Polytechnic Institute from 1890 until he resigned in 1920, but still is consulting physician to the college. This office took a great deal of his time, but he had a large private practice besides. Doctor Henderson is a member of the Medical Society of Virginia and the Southwestern Virginia Medical Society. He is a member of the Masonic fraternity and Mystic Shrine, being affiliated with Hunters Lodge No. 56, A. F. and A. M., and Kazim Temple of the Mystic Shrine at Roanoke. He was formerly a member of the Knights of Pythias. Doctor Henderson is a Democrat, and for about thirty years was an elder in the Presbyterian Church.

He married at Christiansburg, Virginia, in October, 1888, Miss Maggie Lee Figgatt, who was educated in the Montgomery Female Institute at Christiansburg, and was a very interested member of the Presbyterian Church. She died in 1893. Her uncle, Dr. Guy L. Edie, was physician to President Grover Cleveland, later was on duty for the Government at Brest, France, during the World war, and is now a specialist at San Francisco, California. Doctor Henderson by his first marriage has two daughters, Aline W. and Miss Susie. Aline is the wife of Selden Heath, of Southampton, Massachusetts, now a resident of Blacksburg, and they have two sons, William F. and Selden, Jr.

Doctor Henderson married at Salem, Virginia, February 22, 1894, Miss Minnis C. Wiley, who was educated at Blacksburg and Salem. She is active in the Presbyterian Church. Her parents were William B. and Betty (Lawson) Wiley. Her father for many years was a merchant at Blacksburg, and both her parents are buried in the Blacksburg Cemetery. Doctor and Mrs. Henderson have a daughter, Betty Lawson, who graduated from the Blacksburg High School and spent two years finishing her education in the Mary Baldwin Seminary at Staunton.

J. LINDSAY COBB, clerk of the County and Circuit Courts of Nottoway County, was born on a farm in Dinwiddie County, Virginia, July 11, 1896. The Cobb family was established in Virginia in Colonial times by Col. Benjamin Cobb, who came from England. Mr. Cobb's grandfather, Jeremiah Cobb, was a Virginia lawyer and spent his active life in Southampton County. J. Lindsay Cobb is a son of Benjamin E. and Maggie (Westray) Cobb. His father was born in Southampton County in 1859, was a farmer and lumberman, and he and his wife had a family of eight children: Walter Westray, who was overseas during the World war with the rank of first lieutenant; Benjamin E., Jr., in the lumber business; Archer Lee, who trained with the Marines during the World war; John Lindsay; Horace W., formerly a professional ball player, who was in France for eighteen months with the Motor Transport Corps; Kenneth A., Margaret W. and Virginia.

J. Lindsay Cobb spent his early life at Blackstone, attended the Blackstone Military Academy, leaving there to volunteer during the World war. For a time he was in training with the Motor Corps at the University of Virginia, and on September 13, 1918, entered the Officers Training School at Camp Lee, remaining until discharged December 12, 1918. After the war Mr. Cobb was in the banking and insurance business, becoming cashier of the bank at Phenix in Charlotte County, until he was

E Blaine Lenox

elected clerk of the Circuit Court and county clerk of Nottoway County. He is a member of the Masonic fraternity, the American Legion and the Episcopal Church.

EPHRAIM B. LENOX from early manhood has been identified with the hard wood manufacturing industry, particularly furniture manufacture, in Western North Carolina and Western Virginia. He is a resident of Galax, an important center of the hard wood industries of Southwestern Virginia, and is one of the outstanding business men of that community.

Mr. Lenox was born at Mechanicsburg, Cumberland County, Pennsylvania, February 5, 1881. He was given one of his names in honor of the Pennsylvania statesman, James B. Blaine, at that time one of the most influential figures in our national life, and who in 1884 was nominated for the presidency by the Republican party. Mr. Lenox is a son of Richard Porter and Katie (Fenstermacher) Lenox. His father was born in Lancaster County, Pennsylvania, in 1855, son of Samuel Lenox, who gave up his life while serving as a Union soldier in the Civil war. The Lenox family of Lancaster County is closely related to a branch of the family for whom the Lenox Library of New York City was named. Richard Porter Lenox was educated in public schools and in the Normal High School of Pennsylvania, was a teacher in Lancaster County, leaving educational work on account of poor health and engaging in farming. Subsequently he moved south to Moore County, North Carolina, and later moved to Cumber'and County, North Carolina, where he followed farming until his death. His wife was born in Lancaster County and is still living there with her daughter, Mrs. Victor Kittner. She has been an active member of the Presbyterian Church. Her parents were Ephraim and Katie (Kilfaher) Fenstermacher. Richard Porter Lenox and wife had a family of ten children: Ephraim Blaine; Estell, born in 1883, is the wife of "Left" Caufman, of Lancaster, Pennsylvania, and mother of two sons and one daughter; Fannie, who was born in North Carolina, is now the wife of Edgar Shultz, of Lancaster, and has two daughters and one son; William Clarence and Rebecca, twins, born in North Carolina, Rebecca dying at the age of four years, while William, who died in 1927, married Kate Sluggerbach and was the father of five sons; Samuel Richard is married and lives in Lancaster County; Daniel is a resident of Lancaster County and has a family of five daughters; Joseph died in 1912; Katherine is the wife of Victor Kittner, a contractor and builder at Eden, Pennsylvania; and James Clinton is a resident of Lancaster County and has one son.

Ephraim Blaine Lenox attended public schools, and when twenty-one years of age went to work in one of the numerous furniture factories at High Point, North Carolina. He was employed by the Home Furniture Company there for two years, and left that concern to become machine room foreman with the Bassett Furniture Company at Bassett, Virginia. On October 14, 1914, he returned to North Carolina and was superintendent of the Forsythe Furniture Company at Winston-Salem until 1919.

Mr. Lenox has been associated with the Vaughan-Bassett Company at Galax since 1919, having had charge of the furniture plant of this business at Galax as superintendent for the past ten years. During that time he has become a stockholder and official in the group of industrial interests that give Galax an important place among the productive centers of Southwest Virginia. He has been a director of the Vaughan-Bassett Furniture Company since 1925, and also vice president of that company, which is operating on a capital of $300,000. Since 1923 he has also been a director of the Vaughan Furniture Company at Galax, a company with capitalization at half a million. Since 1926 he has been a director of the Webb Furniture Company, a $300,000 corporation, and is also a director and vice president of the Galax Knitting Company, an organization with $77,000 of capital and operating hosiery mills turning out about a thousand dozens daily. The furniture factories with which he is identified specialize in dining room and bedroom furniture. He is also vice president and a director in the Galax Mirror Company. Mr. Lenox since 1922 has been a director of the Peoples State Bank of Galax. He owns two farms in Henry County, Virginia, and also the "Old Rough and Ready Mill," situated on a seventeen acre tract in the same county.

His business responsibilities have been heavy, but none the less he has manifested a keen and loyal interest in his home community and has been elected three times a member of the Galax City Council, his first term being from September, 1922, to September, 1924, and in September, 1926, he was again elected and is now in his third term. He is a Democrat, a thirty-second degree Scottish Rite Mason, member of Kazim Temple of the Mystic Shrine at Roanoke, is a Rotarian and a deacon in the Primitive Baptist Church.

Mr. Lenox married in Henry County, Virginia, January 1, 1907, Miss Ella Bertha Wagoner, daughter of James Wagoner. She was born April 18, 1884, was educated in public schools, is a member of the Primitive Baptist Church, president of the Woman's Missionary Society, and also belongs to the Eastern Star.

THOMAS HENRY STARKE was a very popular business man of Richmond for many years, was known, liked by all, and he expressed his character through his business, earning a wealth of esteem that remains today.

He was born at Richmond, December 17, 1855, and died at the age of sixty, in 1915. His father, Thomas Jefferson Starke, of Hanover County, was also a business man in Richmond for some years. His mother was Sarah Hutchinson. There were six children: Ella, Ed, Laura, Sue, Thomas H. and Melville H.

Thomas H. Starke attended public schools in Richmond, finished his education in Richmond College, and as a young man went with the business to which he devoted practically all the years of his life. It was then a men's furnishing store conducted by Wilkerson, Withers & Wanamaker. The business was later acquired by McAdams and Berry, and after a few years reorganized and subsequently known as the O. H. Berry Company, one of the oldest and best known houses of the time in Virginia. About the time of the reorganization Mr. Starke was appointed manager, and in that capacity he remained with the business until his death.

He also enjoyed outside relationships, having served at one time as a first lieutenant of the Richmond Howitzers. He was an active member of the Second Baptist Church, member of the Knights of Pythias, and a Democrat in politics.

He married Miss Laura Curtis, of Hampton, Virginia, daughter of William H. Curtis, who was born in Gloucester County and moved to Richmond in 1871. Her father was a veteran in the service of the Southern Railway Company. William H. Curtis married Mothella Dobbins, of Hampton, and they had six children: R. H. Curtis, of Richmond, whose children are Claude, of New York, Ashton, of Pennsylvania, Mrs. Marsella Greenway, of Richmond, Mrs. Emily Conrad, Mrs. Endie Freeman, and Ernley; Mrs. Laura M. Starke; Hylha, now Mrs. Charleston, of Richmond, has a son, Curtis Charleton, of New York; Herbert, who as a boy was a page in the Virginia Legislature at Richmond; Marie; and John, deceased. R. H. Curtis married Miss Virginia Barham, of Baltimore. The father of these children was for many years a member of the Richmond City Council. Mr. and Mrs. Starke had no children of their own, but they reared an adopted son, Thomas Curtis, who married Phyllis Morrison, and has a daughter, Jane Starke Curtis.

HERBERT W. HALE is a farmer and banker at Narrows, and is member of a family that has had a prominent part in the social and business life of that community of Giles County for a great many years. Thousands of Virginians and visitors from out of the state also have a ready means of identifying Mr. Hale as owner of one of the interesting scenic wonders of Southwest Virginia, the Giant Caverns.

Mr. Hale was born at Narrows March 24, 1864, son of William H. and Rebecca (Bolton) Hale, and grandson of Charles Hale. Charles Hale a great many years ago put up a mill at Narrows, and that mill continued in operation until it was destroyed by fire. His son, William H. Hale, was born and reared at Narrows, learned the trade of miller and operated the mill and the adjoining farm until his death. During the Civil war the mill ground a great deal of meal and flour for the soldiers as well as the home people. William H. Hale was also a skilled surveyor, and served as county surveyor and ran a great number of important boundary lines in Southwestern Virginia. His wife, Rebecca Bolton, was born in County Cork, Ireland. She made two visits to America, and on the second visit met and married Mr. Hale. She was educated in public schools in Ireland and was reared in the Episcopal Church, but after her marriage became a member of the Methodist Episcopal Church, South. She died about 1870. There were four children: Alice, now deceased, wife of B. T. Johnson, Jr.; Herbert W.; Kate A., of Narrows, widow of Dr. A. G. Coburn; and Fred, who died when fifty-eight years old. After the death of the mother of these children William H. Hale married Miss Elizabeth Carpenter, and there is one child by this union, Custis Hale, who has been twice married and had a large family of children by his first wife and two by his second marriage.

Herbert W. Hale attended public schools in Giles County, and after completing his school work went to Bristol, Tennessee, spent three years clerking in a store, and in that way laid the foundation of a sound business training. He returned to Narrows to settle up the estate of his father, and after his marriage he lived for seven years at Forest Hill in Summers County, where he engaged in farming and stock raising. About 1897 he and his family returned to Narrows. He increased his own share in his father's estate by buying another interest. Through his efforts the land was cleared on possibly three-fourths of the site of the town of Narrows. In recent years his enterprise has done much to develop and make available to visitors the Giant Caverns, located on his property. The caverns have been electrically lighted and the improved State Highway No. 23 leads up to the entrance of the caverns.

Mr. Hale was one of the organizers and is now the oldest director of the First National Bank of Narrows, and is also a director of the Narrows Wholesale Grocery Company and a director of the Bland County Lumber Company. For a number of years he served on the Town Council, and is prominent in Masonry, having been for two years district grand master of District No. 41. He is a Methodist, and is on the Board of Trustees of the church.

He married at Forest Hill in Summers County, West Virginia, June 17, 1890, Miss Mary Margaret Symns, who was reared and attended school in Summers County and in Giles County, finishing in what is now the Virginia Intermont College. She is a member of the Methodist Episcopal Church, South, and the Eastern Star, and is a daughter of Lewis C. and Isabel (Nelson) Symns. Her father was a farmer and cattle raiser in Summers County. Both her parents are buried in Forest Hill Cemetery. The oldest of the children of Mr. and Mrs. Hale is Nell Symns Hale, who attended the Narrows High School, Sullins College, graduated from the Leland Powers School of Expression at Boston and also attended Columbia University, the Peabody Institute at Nashville, the University of California, and is now a member of the faculty of Stonewall Jackson College at Abingdon, Virginia. The son Percy Hale attended high school and Emory and Henry College of Virginia, and is now cashier of the First National Bank of Narrows. He married Grace Coburn, of Narrows, and has had two children, Harry Lyle and Pete, but the latter died aged twenty-one months. Lyda Kate Hale, educated in high school and Sullins College, is the wife of Cyrus Brown, a merchant at Narrows, and their children are Herbert Hale, Hamilton Wells, Mary Gray, Billie Bolton, Nancy and Sarah. Harold W. Hale, educated in high school and the Virginia Polytechnic Institute, is clerk in the First National Bank of Narrows. He married Louise Coburn and has a daughter, Charlotte Ann. Margaret Hale also attended the high school at Narrows, continued her education in Martha Washington College at Abingdon, and is the wife of Maxie Bailey, superintendent at Pearisburg for the Chesapeake & Potomac Telephone Company. They have one child, Don. Mary Helen Hale is a student in the Stonewall Jackson College at Abingdon, and the youngest of the family is Miss Armand Gardner, in the Narrows High School.

EMERSON DANIEL BAUGH is a native Virginian, a lawyer by profession, and has the active connections and the prestige of a capable member of his profession at Lawrenceville.

He was born in Dinwiddie County, Virginia, July 30, 1902, son of Arthur C. and Mollie (Daniel) Baugh. His father was born in Dinwiddie County and his mother in Prince George County, and she died October 29, 1906. His father for twenty years was in business as a merchant at Carson, and since that time has looked after his farming interests in Dinwiddie County.

Emerson D. Baugh grew up in Prince George County, graduated from the Carson High School in 1920, and studied law at

the University of Richmond and also under the direction of James M. Quick, Jr., at Petersburg, Virginia. He was admitted to the bar December 15, 1924. Mr. Baugh practiced at Petersburg and Prince George until July 1, 1928, at which date he located at Lawrenceville.

. He married, November 23, 1927, Miss Maggie Lee Matthews, of Brunswick County, daughter of Emmet and Maggie Lee (Abernathy) Matthews, both natives of the county. Her father was a well-to-do farmer of Brunswick. They have one son, Emerson Daniel Baugh, Jr., born July 2, 1929.

Mr. Baugh is a member of the Virginia State and Third Judicial Circuit Bar Associations. He is a Baptist, and has been very active in the Democratic party. While in college he was the first freshman to organize and be president of the First Democratic Club. He is also a thorough sportsman, loving all the activities of the athletic field as well as outdoor diversions of hunting and fishing and motoring. He is secretary of the Brunswick chapter of the Izaak Walton League of America.

JOHN EDWARD WILLIAMS, whose name stands in the front rank among Virginia educators, has for a quarter of a century held the chair of mathematics in the Virginia Polytechnic Institute at Blacksburg, and since 1924 has been dean of the college.

Doctor Williams was born in Charlotte County, Virginia, September 17, 1867, and represents a family which was among the first settlers of Lunenburg County and which has given a long list of worthy men to the state. He is a son of Albert Henry and Matilda Ann (Berkeley) Williams. His father was born in Lunenburg County, was privately educated, and served four years in the Confederate army as a member of Company K of the Twenty-third Virginia Regiment, under "Stonewall" Jackson. He was several times wounded. After the war he engaged in farming, and died August 16, 1925. His wife was born in Appomattox County. Both parents were active members of the Presbyterian Church. She died January 14, 1920, and both are buried in the Presbyterian Church cemetery at Charlotte Court House. They had six children: Walter G., treasurer of Charlotte County, John Edward, Robert W., a farmer in Charlotte County; Annie M., wife of Cabell Morton, of Charlotte County; Miss Ida Lee, of Charlotte County; and Miss Eula, a teacher at Cary, North Carolina.

John Edward Williams attended the grade and high schools of Charlotte Court House, and in 1892 received the Bachelor of Arts degree from Hampden-Sidney College. Hampden-Sidney in 1925, in recognition of his attainments as an educator and scholar, conferred upon him the Doctor of Laws degree. After teaching for some time he entered the University of Virginia for post-graduate work, and won the Doctor of Philosophy degree in 1899. In 1902 the university also gave him the Master of Arts degree.

Doctor Williams was principal of the high school at Boydton, Virginia, in 1892-94, assistant principal of the Commerce Street School at Roanoke in 1894-95, was principal of a private school owned by Col. Thomas F. Goode at Boydton in 1895-96, and in the fall of the latter year became a graduate student of the University of Virginia. While there he was licentiate instructor in mathematics from 1897 to 1903. Doctor Williams has been with the Virginia Polytechnic Institute at Blacksburg since 1903, at first as adjunct professor of mathematics, and since 1904 as professor of mathematics.

Doctor Williams since 1919 has been a member of the Virginia State Board of Education. He is a Phi Beta Kappa, Phi Kappa Phi, member of the Raven Society of the University of Virginia, and the Pi Gamma Mu honor society. He is a member of the American Mathematical Society, Mathematical Association of America, the Virginia Academy of Science, Association of Virginia Colleges, of which he was president in 1920, is a fellow of the American Association for the Advancement of Science, and a member of the National Council of the National Economic League. For over twenty years he has been a member of the Athletic Council of the Virginia Polytechnic Institute. Doctor Williams is a Royal Arch Mason, a member of the State Central Democratic Committee, and a Presbyterian.

He married, August 28, 1905, at Blacksburg, Miss Sallie Taylor Patton, daughter of Col. William M. and Annie Gertrude (Jordan) Patton. Her mother died September 10, 1921. Her father entered the Confederate army as a cadet from the Virginia Military Institute. After the war he was graduated from Virginia Military Institute as a civil engineer, became prominent in the practice of his profession, and for many years occupied the chair of civil engineering at his *alma mater*. In 1895 he was elected to a similar position at the Virginia Polytechnic Institute, holding this office until his death. He became, in 1904, the first dean of engineering in the history of Virginia Polytechnic Institute. As a tribute to his outstanding qualities as a teacher, a scholar and a man, the recently completed engineering building at the Virginia Polytechnic Institute has been named the Patton Engineering Hall. He died May 26, 1905, and is buried at Lexington. Mrs. Williams is a member of the Episcopal Church. Doctor and Mrs. Williams have three children: William Patton, Anne Berkeley and Margaret French. The daughters are attending public school at Blacksburg. The son finished his high school work here, graduated with the Bachelor of Arts degree from Hampden-Sidney College in 1927, and has had two years in the School of Architecture at the University of Virginia.

M. BLAIR DICKINSON has given the best years of his life to educational work in his native State of Virginia and in Alabama, and is now superintendent of schools in the City of Fredericksburg.

He was born near Hampden-Sidney College in Virginia, March 25, 1872, and was reared in that classic environment. His parents were Robert M. and Lelia (Cralle) Dickinson, both natives of Prince Edward County. His father was captain of a company in the Confederate army in Thornton's Regiment, was a lawyer by profession and practiced for many years at Farmville. He died May 28, 1898, and his wife, in August, 1880.

M. Blair Dickinson was reared and educated in his native county, attending Prince Edward Academy, graduated with the A. B. degree from Hampden-Sidney College, and in the intervals of teaching attended and pursued a course of study in the University of Virginia, where he was awarded the Master's degree in 1900. He also studied at Harvard, Columbia and Peabody, taking summer courses. Mr. Dickinson from 1900 to 1918 was co-principal of the University High School at Birmingham, Alabama. On returning to Virginia he became principal of the high school at Farmville, and in 1922 was elected superintendent of schools of Fredericksburg, and has been the able head of the school system of that historic city for the past six years.

J. W. Chase Morton

Mr. Dickinson is an elder in the Presbyterian Church, and while living at Birmingham taught a large Bible class in his church there. He is a past chancellor of the Knights of Pythias, Jefferson Valley Lodge No. 11, of Birmingham, is a member of the Kiwanis Club and a Democrat. His home is at 1313 Winchester Avenue in Fredericksburg. Mr. Dickinson married in June, 1902, Miss Mattie White, daughter of David Campbell and Ada (Brown) White. Her father was born in Kentucky and her mother in Alabama. David C. White was a captain in the Confederate army, was a planter, and died at Sumterville, Alabama, February 10, 1888, and Mrs. Dickinson's mother still resides at Sumterville. Mr. and Mrs. Dickinson had four children: Lelia B., born April 16, 1903, and died October 16, 1918; Mary Michaux, born February 23, 1906, now teaching in the Chancellor High School in Spotsylvania County; M. Blair, Jr., born January 2, 1915; and Alexander B., born July 20, 1916.

WILLIAM CHASE MORTON was a youthful soldier of the Confederacy, and Richmond was his life-long home.

For many years he held public office, and was known as a man of rare efficiency in the performance of all his duties, a Virginia gentleman and scholar of great talent and ability. He was educated in Bloomfield Academy in Albemarle County. He was a devoted member of St. Paul's Episcopal Church at Richmond, and was a Mason and a past master of Metropolitan Lodge No. 11. His love of Virginia, his native state, with all her wonderful traditions, was the ruling passion of his life.

Mr. Morton was born in Richmond in 1845, and died in that city August 16, 1921, a son of Jackson and Elizabeth (Archer) Morton, a grandson of William and Charlotte (Clarke) Archer, and a great-grandson of Major John Clarke and Elizabeth H. Moseley, his wife, and a great-great-grandson of Charles and Mary Anne (Salle) Clarke. The historical register of the Continental Army shows that John Clarke was a first lieutenant of the Eighth Virginia Regiment in January, 1777, and was taken prisoner at the battle of Germantown October 4, 1777. Major John Clarke was admitted to the Society of Cincinnati in 1778, his certificate of membership, now a prized possession of Mrs. William Chase Morton, being signed by George Washington, then president of the Society, and J. Knox, its secretary. A great-uncle of William Chase Morton was Branch T. Archer, who was a prominent figure in the history of Texas through the revolution of the Republic, and whose name is carried by a county of that great state.

Hon. Jackson Morton, father of William Chase Morton, served several terms as a member of the Florida State Senate. He numbered among his close friends, Webster, Clay and Calhoun. He was a large lumber merchant in Florida, and was beloved, revered and highly honored both in private and public life. Mrs. William Chase Morton has the original appointment of Mr. Morton as navy agent for the port of Pensacola, Florida, signed by President John Tyler. She also has the original appointment to rank of brigadier general of the First Brigade of the Florida Militia, signed by Governor W. D. Moseley of Florida. A brother of William Chase Morton, Howard Morton, of Richmond, was well known as a writer of verse, and graduated from the University of Virginia with high honors.

William Chase Morton was educated in private schools, attending a boys' school, the Bloomfield Academy, Abemarle

County, Virginia. He was seventeen years old when he entered the Confederate army with a Virginia regiment, and with a Florida regiment of artillery, and had one year of duty in the field before the close of hostilities. After the war ended he returned to Richmond to take charge of his mother and sisters during the illness of his father. Later he became a clerk in the second auditor's office, and remained at his official post of duty for forty years, at the time of his death being chief clerk. He was a Master Mason and a member of St. Paul's Episcopal Church. He was a member of the Society of the Sons of the Revolution in the state of Virginia, and served as president of that society for one term.

In every relation of life William Chase Morton was above praise, and it would be vain to search the pages of history for the record of a life more stainless. To a strong intellect, he united a heart of princely generosity and a character of unsullied integrity which commanded the respect of all who knew him, and the admiration and affectionate regard of his numerous friends. Beloved too for his social qualities, for general benevolence and every virtue, his surviving friends and his posterity may cherish his memory with a certain assurance that no blot or cloud rests upon his name. His kindly courtesy to all whether rich or poor gave a charm to his presence everywhere and at all times.

Mr. Morton married, April 25, 1894, Miss Mary Porterfield, of Charles Town, West Virginia. Mrs. Morton, whose home is in Richmond, is descended from a number of old families of Virginia Colonial ancestry. Mrs. Morton is a member of the Edgar Allan Poe Shrine and of the Confederate Memorial Literary Society, and was a member of the Richmond Woman's Club. Her father, Col. George A. Porterfield, was born in Berkeley County, in what is now West Virginia, and Mrs. Morton was the fifth of his seven children. Her brother, Charles Porterfield, is an author and publisher of New York City, who had three sons in the World war, one of them, Alexander, being now a resident of England, and who was gassed in action and was distinguished in saving an ammunition dump from fire, which would have killed many of the American troops in that vicinity. In recognition of this feat of valor he was awarded the Victorian Military Cross. A second son, Capt. Charles Porterfield, of the United States Army, was wounded in action, and the third soldier son was James Porterfield. Mrs. Morton's youngest sister, Serena Porterfield, married George Washington, youngest son of Col. John Augustine Washington, who was the last private owner of "Mount Vernon." George Washington was the last Washington born at "Mount Vernon."

The ancestry of Mrs. Morton in the paternal line also includes the Tabb family. Her grandmother, Mary Tabb, was a daughter of George Tabb, granddaughter of William Tabb, who in turn was a son of John Tabb, son of Thomas Tabb, son of Humphrey Tabb. Humphrey Tabb was a member of the Virginia House of Burgesses of 1742.

The mother of Mrs. Morton was Emily Terrill, a member of a great family which has adopted various spellings for the name, but which has been in Virginia since the middle of the seventeenth century and whose authenticated ancestry runs back through English history to the time of the Conqueror, and then into the annals of the Norman French to the century immediately following the time of Charlemagne. Of the Terrills it has been well said that in the wars of the borders of Virginia in Colonial times, at Guilford Court House, Kings Mountain and

Yorktown in the Revolution, in the Indian campaigns in the
West under Harmar, Wayne and Harrison, at Horseshoe Bend
and New Orleans under Jackson, and in the Civil war, at Perryville, Cold Harbor and Cedar Creek, both in the Federal and
Confederate armies, the American descendants of the name have
nobly sustained the chivalric record of their armour-clad forefathers in the middle ages. Mrs. Emily Terrill Porterfield,
mother of Mrs. Morton, was a sister of Brigadier-General William R. Terrill, a graduate of West Point, and who as chief of
artillery in McCook's Division at Shiloh, was credited with
saving the army of his friend and commander, General Grant,
and who later, at the battle of Perryville, October 8, 1862, gave
up his life in action. He was buried at West Point, New York.
Gen. William R. Terrill's brother, Gen. James B. Terrill, on the
Confederate side, fell while leading his brigade of Southern men
under Gen. A. P. Hill in the Thirteenth Virginia Regiment,
known as the bloody Thirteenth, at the battle of Bethesda
Church, Virginia, and was buried in Hanover County, Virginia,
near the spot where he was killed. His commission as General
was received just as he died. A few years ago a writer in the
National Geographic Magazine made the statement that the
heartbroken father of these two soldiers, Col. William H. Terrill
of Bath County, Virginia, inscribed on a stone to their memory
these words: "God alone knows which was right." Mrs. Emily
Terrill Porterfield's youngest brother, Philip Mallory Terrill,
was mortally wounded at the battle of Cedar Creek, near Winchester, Virginia, and died at the age of twenty-one years.

The father of these three gallant soldiers was Col. William
H. Terrill, for many years commonwealth's attorney for the
county of Bath. He had one brother, Dr. George Terrill, of
Newport, Rhode Island, a retired surgeon of the United States
Navy.

Mrs. Morton's father, Col. George Alexander Porterfield, died
at his home in Charles Town at the advanced age of ninety-
seven. He was the only son of George and Mary (Tabb) Porterfield, and was born in Berkeley County, West Virginia, November 24, 1822. He graduated from the Virginia Military Institute
in 1844, and was the oldest living graduate at the time of his
death. He taught school at Martinsburg, West Virginia, two
years, and when war was declared on Mexico he and two of
his former classmates, Edwin Carrington and Carlton Munford,
raised and organized a Richmond company of volunteer infantry.
He was appointed adjutant and served under Gen. John Wood
throughout the war, 1846-48. He was a charter member of the
Aztec Club of Washington, D. C., composed of veterans of the
Mexican war. After his return he was engaged under Prof.
Alexander Dallas Bache in the United States coast survey.
When the Civil war broke out he joined the Confederate army,
participating in operations in Western Virginia. In 1870 he
became the secretary of the Valley Fire Insurance Company of
Charles Town, West Virginia, and at his suggestion it was reorganized as the Bank of Charles Town, and for years he was
cashier of that institution. Colonel Porterfield was a kinsman
of Gen. Robert Porterfield and of Col. Charles Porterfield, of
Revolutionary fame.

Mrs. Morton has one daughter, Miss Elizabeth Jackson
Morton, who was educated in the school of Miss Virginia
Randolph Ellett and has since been engaged in secretarial work

at Richmond. Miss Morton is a member of the Confederate Memorial Literary Society and of the Little Theatre League of Richmond, Virginia, and of the Virginia Randolph Ellett Alumnae Association.

CLINTON H. PAINTER, cashier of the Bank of Draper, is a man whose natural abilities fit him for the responsible position he is holding, and these, combined with his courtesy, his understanding of the banking business in all its phases, and his wide acquaintance make him a valuable asset to his concern. He was born at Ivanhoe, Wythe County, Virginia, September 12, 1878, a son of Leicester E. and Virginia Margaret (Hatcher) Painter, he born, reared and educated in Wythe County, and she in Pulaski County. A soldier of the Confederacy during the war between the states, he served throughout the war period and participated in a number of the major engagements of the war. Captured, he was held in the Federal prison at Indianapolis, Indiana, for the last nine months of the war, and was not released in time to rejoin his regiment, the Forty-fifth Virginia Infantry, and take part in the closing scenes of the great conflict. After the war he devoted himself to farming and stock-raising until his retirement, and he died July 11, 1923, aged eighty-one years. His remains lie in the cemetery at Ivanhoe. The Painter family is of German origin, and came to the American colonies prior to the Revolution. Those bearing the name received grants of land in the beautiful and fertile Valley of Virginia, and were among the pioneers of this section of the Old Dominion. Mr. Painter of this review has in his possession some old documents and deeds dating back to the settlement here of the Painters, and some stock certificates of his grandfather Abraham Painter, of stock in the Virginia & Tennessee Railroad, bearing the date of July 9, 1852, all of which have an historical as well as sentimental value.

Mrs. Virginia Margaret (Hatcher) Painter was educated in a private school in Lexington, Virginia, and there she was married. All her life she has been an active member of the Methodist Episcopal Church, South. Still living, she is residing in Roanoke, Virginia, being now eighty years old. She and her husband had three children: Clinton H., whose name heads this review; Hattie Alma, who died about 1901, the wife of J. W. Miller, a contractor of Pulaski, Virginia, and mother of two children, one of whom died in infancy, and Leicester; and McTeer Painter, who resides in Roanoke, connected with the Norfolk & Western Railroad, married Miss Forrest Jones, and they have three children: Frederick, Kent, and Jean.

Clinton H. Painter is a well educated man, having received more than ordinary advantages, for following his completion of the courses in the public schools of Wythe County, he was a student of Emory and Henry College, and later took a commercial course in Bryant and Stratton's Business College, Baltimore, Maryland. On leaving college he farmed for a few years, and then went with the Colonial Coal & Coke Company of Dorchester, Virginia. Still later he was with the Ivanhoe Furnace Company for a year, and at the end of that period he began his banking career as assistant cashier of the Peoples National Bank of Pulaski, Virginia, and held that position for thirteen years. For eight years thereafter he was with the Empire Anthracite Coal Company, and then, in 1928, he became cashier of the Bank of Draper, entering upon his duties February 1.

H. D. Gardner

On July 13, 1902, Mr. Painter married Miss Nanye Pierce Porter, of Ivanhoe. Mrs. Painter was educated in the public schools of Ivanhoe and Martha Washington College, Abingdon, Virginia, and for a few years taught in the public schools of Wythe County. All her life she was active in the work of the Methodist Episcopal Church, South, and died firm in its faith January 28, 1928. In her passing her community lost a kind neighbor and devout Christian, and her family a loving and devoted wife and mother. She lies in Oakwood Cemetery, Pulaski. Her father, M. F. Porter, has been for many years one of the leading farmers of the Ivanhoe neighborhood. Mrs. Porter died some years ago and is buried in the cemetery at Ivanhoe. Mr. and Mrs. Painter had one child, Frances Virginia Painter. She attended the Pulaski High School and Randolph-Macon College, Danville, Virginia. She married Barker F. Warner, of High Point, North Carolina, where they now reside and where he is a successful furniture dealer and manufacturer, operating under the name of the Giant Furniture Manufacturing Company.

Mr. Painter belongs to the Benevolent and Protective Order of Elks. In political faith he is a Democrat, but has never cared to come before the public for office. For many years he has been an active member of the Methodist Episcopal Church, South. He has always made friends on every side and retains them, and is always willing to do everything within his power to advance their welfare and further develop his home community in which his interests are centered.

HENRY DANIEL GARDNER had a place and part in the citizenship of Louisa County in the State of Virginia which was well in keeping with the record of his honored ancestors in America.

It is a matter of historic record that the American founders of the Gardner family were three brothers who came from England to serve as instructors of Colonial Troops. One of them was Joseph, who came from England to Rhode Island some time between 1635 and 1640, and later his descendants moved to Virginia. John, aide de camp to his brother, Colonel George, in the British army, came to America and settled in New York. Colonel George settled at Boston in 1637. They were the sons of Sir Thomas Gardner, Knight, soliciter general to King Charles I, who died in October, 1632.

Daniel Gardner, who came from Charles City, Virginia, was the founder of the family in Louisa County. He settled at the point that is still known as Gardner's Cross Roads. His son, George Iverson Gardner, born in 1800, married Mary Ann Burnley, who was a daughter of Harry Burnley and Ann (Goodman) Burnley.

Henry Daniel Gardner, son of George Iverson Gardner and Mary Burnley, was born on April 1, 1844, in the County of Louisa and State of Virginia, at the old Gardner home near Gardner's Cross Roads. He died at Grace Hospital, Richmond, Virginia, December 24, 1915.

He received an excellent education from private tutors. At the age of nineteen he entered the Civil war and served as a gallant soldier until he bade farewell to his general, Robert E. Lee, at Appomattox on April 9, 1865.

After the war he returned to his home and spent his time with his father, brother and sisters trying to build up the shattered fortune of his beloved Southland.

November 1, 1870, he married Mrs. Clara Harris Kimbraugh, widow of Charles Y. Kimbraugh. The children of this union were: Mary Caroline, George Iverson, Margaret Morton, Henry Daniel, Jr., Frederick Overton, Clara Bacon, Lucy Nelson, Helen Campbell. Lucy Nelson married Thomas Edward Trotman, mentioned in the following sketch. They have one child, Helen Gardner. Mrs. Gardner was the daughter of Abner Nelson Harris, born in 1795, whose father, Nelson Harris, born in 1758, was a soldier in the Revolutionary army.

Mr. Gardner spent his whole life in his native county state, engaged principally in agricultural pursuits, although at different times he held several district and county offices, and was for a number of years, a member of the Board of Public School Trustees for his district of the county, all of which duties he discharged with marked fidelity and efficiency, that won the approbation of his fellow countrymen.

Mr. Gardner was a true type of the old fashioned Virginia gentleman, courteous and kind in manner, but resolute in deeds, with a generous charity, dispensed, wherever he saw its needs, among the less fortunate of his fellow-beings, and was regarded by them with a full measure of deference and respect. He was a devoted christian, and stood ready at all times to give his aid and support to every enterprise, private or public, whose object was to advance the cause of righteousness on the earth and the spread of the Messiah's kingdom among men.

Truly, it may be said of him:

"His life was gentle, and the elements
So mixed in him, that Nature might stand up,
And say to all the world, *This was a man.*"

　　　　　　　　　　　　　　—C. T. J.
　　　　　　　　　　　　　　Apple Grove Virginia

THOMAS EDWARD TROTMAN, who died at Portsmouth, Norfolk County, May 15, 1923, was in the most significant sense the architect of his own fortune. The success he achieved through his own ability and efforts marked him as one of the influential figures in the industrial and business life of the Old Dominion State, which was the stage of his activities from his early youth until the close of his earnest and worthy life.

Eldest in a family of eight children, Thomas Edward Trotman was born in North Carolina, November 9, 1854, and thus was sixty-eight years of age when he died. He was a son of James and Ann (Euer) Trotman. His father was a North Carolina farmer. The founder of the family in North Carolina was the paternal grandfather. Thomas Edward Trotman was reared to adult age under the depressed conditions that marked the South after the close of the Civil war. Consequently his early educational advantages were limited. His broader education was that gained by his close application and by his experience in connection with the practical affairs of life. As a youth of sixteen years he came to Virginia. For the first four years he was employed as clerk in stores in Nansemond County. He was not yet twenty when, in 1872, he set up as a merchant for himself at Churchland, Norfolk County. From that he soon turned to the line of enterprise in which he was to gain his chief success, truck farming. What he did in this field constituted a work that gave him national distinction. At one time he was known as the world's largest potato grower. His progressive policies and careful management expanded the scope and importance of his truck farms each successive year. He was a grower of green

vegetables as well as potatoes, and made shipments in carload lots to New York City, Boston, Baltimore, Chicago and other centers. His active connection with this business was uninterrupted until his death, and during that time he acquired 2,500 acres, all devoted to the growing of special crops for the Northern markets. The business was one that gave employment to several hundred men in the cultivation and harvesting of vegetables, and probably no other individual along the Atlantic Coast had a larger business under his direct control. He was vice president of the Southern Produce Company at the time of his death, and his interests extended much beyond the immediate field of planting and harvesting and marketing of crops. He was equally well known for his progressive citizenship. He was president of and the largest stockholder in the Planters Manufacturing Company of Norfolk County, was a fertilizer manufacturer as president and owner of the business conducted under the title of Trotman Manufacturing Company in Nansemond County. He was a director of the First National Bank and the American National Bank. Intrinsically he was a business man, and while always responsive to the obligations of citizenship and a staunch supporter of the Democratic party, he had no desire to enter the arena of political politics or become a candidate for public office. As one of the world's noble army of constructive workers he justified himself most fully in all of the relationships of his signally successful life.

His first wife was Mary B. Surles, who died in 1910. The two sons of this marriage are Percy E. and Harry L., both prominent in the produce and truck farming industry in Norfolk County.

On September 10, 1921, Mr. Trotman married Miss Lucy Nelson Gardner. She is a daughter of Henry Daniel Gardner, whose career is appropriately given in the preceding sketch. Mrs. Trotman, whose home in Norfolk is at 701 Baldwin Place, has one daughter, Helen Gardner Trotman, now six years of age. Mrs. Trotman has membership in the Woman's Club and the United Daughters of the Confederacy, besides which, on the maternal side, she is eligible for affiliation with the Daughters of the American Revolution.

REUBEN LEE HUMBERT, Virginia educator, now executive secretary of the Virginia Polytechnic Institute at Blacksburg, is a native of the Shenandoah Valley, born at Harrisonburg, August 22, 1900. His ancestors were a part of the early German colonization of the Valley of Virginia. He is a descendant of Philip Jacob Humbert, whose parents were German, of French ancestors who had lived in the Lorraine country. His great-grandfather, Jacques Humbert, was born in Nancy, France, May 11, 1641, and had three sons. His granduncle, Joseph Humbert, ancestor of the Humberts of Tonnoy, was created a nobleman by the Duke of Lorraine. His grandfather, Antoine Humbert, lived in the French colony at Frauenberg and later was recognized as one of the founders of Neu Kelsterbach.

Philip Jacob Humbert was twenty-three years of age when he came to this country in the ship "Janet," landing at Philadelphia, October 7, 1751, and later settling in the Shenandoah Valley of Virginia. He married Elizabeth Shingler. Their son, Jacob Humbert, Jr., was born January 22, 1786, and died January 11, 1852, and was the father of Reuben Holt Humbert, who was born in 1826 and died September 30, 1863. A son of the latter is Joseph Lee Humbert, born September 29, 1862, at Harrisonburg, where he has lived out his life as a farmer, postmaster, highway official and commissioner of revenue in his town and county, always an active Democrat. Joseph Lee Humbert married Fannie May Armentrout, daughter of Harrison B. Armentrout, a land owner near Harrisonburg, where she was born April 3, 1874.

Reuben Lee Humbert grew up at Harrisonburg, graduated from the Broadway High School, took his A. B. degree at Bridgewater College, was a graduate student of Columbia University, received the M. A. degree at the University of Michigan, and on October 1, 1918, enlisted for service in the World war and was in training in Washington and Lee University at Lexington until honorably discharged December 13, 1918.

Mr. Humbert was principal of the Timberville High School in 1922-24, two years, and in 1925 became a member of the staff of the Detroit Bureau of Governmental Research. After returning to Harrisonburg he was secretary of the Chamber of Commerce during 1926-27, and in 1928 moved to Blacksburg as executive secretary of the Virginia Polytechnic Institute.

Mr. Humbert is a Democrat, a member of the Methodist Episcopal Church, South, and is affiliated with Rockingham Union Lodge No. 27, A. F. and A. M., Kiwanis Club, honorary member of the Tau Kappa Alpha, and is a member of the Virginia Social Science Association and the Southern Commercial Secretaries Association.

Mr. Humbert married Louise White Swope on August 24, 1929, daughter of John M. Swope of Lexington, Virginia. John M. Swope was the eldest son of William L. Swope and Rebecca W. Alderson. Mrs. Humbert's mother is a member of the Templeton family of Virginia and descended from the Henleys who first settled in Virginia in 1661, of English ancestry. Mrs. Humbert was born at Union, West Virginia, April 22, 1906.

The Swope family of Monroe County, West Virginia, is descended from the ancient Swabian family which dates back to Julius Cæsar 60 years B. C. The Swabian family was noted for its bravery and skillfulness in warfare. It is known that the Swabians took part in the Crusades and were with Conradin, as is proved by the crest in their coat-of-arms, as no German who cannot trace his lineage back to the Crusades is allowed to wear red on their coat-of-arms.

The Swope family is a German family (Schwab or Swab, being the original German name for what is now known as Swope). Joseph Ulrich Swope was the first settler of Monroe County, West Virginia. He was the second son of Yost Swope and was born in the town of Leiman, in the Duchy of Baden, in 1707. His grandfather was mayor or burgomaster. His father, Yost Swope, was born in the same town on February 2, 1678, and owing to the persecutions of the Lutheran Church, of which he was an active member, he immigrated to the new world and settled in Lancaster County, Pennsylvania. Joseph Ulrich Swope left Pennsylvania and migrated into the Valley of Virginia, settling in Augusta County, near the site of the present Swope Depot on the Chesapeake and Ohio Railway. During the next three years he migrated to more westerly territory and settled in what was later Monroe County, West Virginia. Here his second son was born, Michael Swope, the first white male child born in the territory of Monroe County.

William L. Swope was born 1842 and was the youngest son of John and Nancy Swope of Monroe County, West Virginia. John

Swope was born September 29, 1753, the son of Michael Swope referred to above.

Louise Swope Humbert's great-grandfather was Col. George Alderson of Fayette County, West Virginia. Col. Alderson was a man of great prominence in his day. While serving in the Virginia Legislature and with the aid and cooperation of General Beckley the County of Raleigh was cut off from Fayette. Mrs. Humbert's grandmother was also the aunt of the late John D. Alderson who represented the Third District of West Virginia in Congress for two or more terms.

THOMAS COLEMAN ANDREWS, one of the representative business men of the younger generation of his native city of Richmond, is senior member of the firm of Pace, Gore & McLaren, certified public accountants. The well appointed executive office of the firm is established in the American Bank & Trust Company Building, and branch offices are maintained in the National Bank Building at Charlottesville, Virginia's educational center, and in the Stonewall Jackson Hotel at Staunton, the commercial and industrial center of the Valley of Virginia. Mr. Andrews is also a general partner, one of the managing partners, and special assistant to the executive partner of the international firm of Pace, Gore & McLaren, which maintains offices in forty-eight cities in the United States, eight cities in Canada and two cities in Cuba, and extensive connections through correspondents in Great Britain, Continental Europe and Australia.

Mr. Andrews was born in Richmond, on the 19th of February, 1899, and is a son of Cheatham William and Dora (Pittman) Andrews, representatives of old and honored Virginia families. His maternal grandfather, William Coleman Pittman, was a scion of the well known Coleman family of the Old Dominion State and a prominent educator of his day, having been highly regarded as an instructor in mathematics and the classical languages.

After his graduation from John Marshall High School of Richmond Mr. Andrews began a series of accounting employments with industrial and commercial houses in Richmond which culminated in his entering the accounting profession at the conclusion of service in the World war, during which he was connected with the Students Army Training Corps with the rank of sergeant-major and as special instructor in mathematics. His academic preparation for the accounting profession, begun shortly after entering business life, was made principally through the extension courses of Pace Institute of New York, one of the leading institutions in the teaching of accountancy, auditing, business law, applied economics and business administration.

After four years of training with another firm, having been licensed as a Certified Public Accountant in the meantime, Mr. Andrews began the general practice of accountancy on October 16, 1922, under the firm name of T. Coleman Andrews & Company. On January 1, 1926, Alvin Wright Burket, who had been with the firm since its inception, was admitted to partnership. On October 1, 1928, the practice of the firm was consolidated with that of Carlton George Van Emon, a prominent accountant of the western part of the state. On October 1, 1929, in order to meet the demands created by the tendency of industry and commerce toward centralized control, the firm

adopted the name of the international firm of Pace, Gore &
McLaren, with which it was already closely affiliated through
Mr. Andrews' previously mentioned connections therewith. The
firm maintains a large staff of skilled accountants, and numbers among its clients some of the largest industrial, commercial
and financial institutions in Richmond and Virginia. And in
addition to general accounting, auditing and tax service its offers
a business management service, with which it has been con-
spicuously successful.

In 1926 Mr. Andrews was appointed one of the delegates
of the American Society of Certified Public Accountants to the
International Accountants Congress held in Amsterdam, Holland, in July of that year. And at the Congress he had the distinction of being recognized as the head of the delegation of The
American Society of Certified Public Accountants by being
elected a member of the Presiding Council of the Congress. In
1927 he was elected treasurer and a member of the Board of
Directors of The American Society of Certified Public Accountants and the Virginia Society of Public Accountants, having
taken an active interest and served in various offices in the
latter.

From 1922 to 1925 Mr. Andrews served as an instructor of
accountancy and business administration in the Virginia Mechanics' Institute at Richmond, taking an important part in
developing this important department of the institution to its
present high standard of efficiency and in placing a number of
its graduates in important positions in Richmond and vicinity.

In the time-honored Masonic fraternity Mr. Andrews is a
past master of Lewis Ginter Lodge No. 317, A. F. and A. M.,
of Richmond, a member of the Ancient and Accepted Scottish
Rite of Freemasonry of the thirty-second degree, and a Shriner.
He is also an active member of the Kiwanis Club of Richmond.

Mr. Andrews wedded Miss Rae Wilson Reams at Richmond
on October 18, 1919, and their two children are: Thomas Coleman, Jr., born February 15, 1925; and Wilson Pittman, born
May 14, 1929. The family home is at 3811 Chamberlayne
Avenue.

MAITLAND H. BUSTARD is one of the younger members of the
Bar of Southside, Virginia, practicing at Danville, where he is
a member of the firm of Aiken, Benton & Bustard.

Mr. Bustard was born at Danville, April 9, 1898, and is a
son of John and Vina (Clarke) Bustard. His father, John
Bustard, a native of Canada, moved to Virginia in 1870, where
he identified himself with the tobacco industry. He was well
known in tobacco circles, and at the time of his death, in 1928,
he was secretary and treasurer of the Danville Tobacco
Association.

Vina Clarke Bustard, the mother of Maitland H. Bustard, was
a daughter of Eppa Hobson Clarke, of Halifax County. She was
born at Alchie, Halifax County, Virginia, and died in Danville
in 1917. Both John and Vina Bustard were members of the
Episcopal Church, and both are buried in Green Hill Cemetery
at Danville.

Maitland H. Bustard grew up at Danville, where he attended
the grade and high schools and the Danville School for Boys.
He attended Randolph Macon College at Ashland, and upon
completing his academic work there he entered the University
of Virginia law school. He graduated in 1924 with the degree

EDMOND S. MASSIE

of Bachelor of Laws. For the two years following he was connected with the law department of the Southern Railway Company at Washington, D. C. In 1927 he formed a partnership with Judge A. M. Aiken and Jesse W. Benton, with offices in the Masonic Temple Building, Danville, Virginia.

Mr. Bustard is a member of the Phi Delta Theta social fraternity, the Phi Delta Phi legal fraternity, Improved Order of Red Men, Lion's Club, Danville Golf Club, Tuscarora Club, the Danville, Virginia State and American Bar Associations. He is a member of the Episcopal Church. Mr. Bustard is the Democratic nominee for the Virginia House of Delegates from Danville and Pittsylvania County.

EDMOND SIMS MASSIE. The records of the Massie family run back in American and English history for about ten centuries. There was a Hamo de Masci who accompanied William the Conqueror to England, and according to an account in Ormond's *History of Cheshire County* was made overlord of some twenty towns in England. A duplicate of the family seal in Virginia accords with the Armorial Bearings of the family as described by Burke.

About 1680 records show the name of Peter Massie as a resident of New Kent County, Virginia. He was a surveyor. His three sons were John, Thomas and Charles. Of these Capt. Thomas Massie, who died prior to 1732, owned extensive lands situated in New Kent, Hanover and Goochland counties. He was a member of the House of Burgesses from New Kent County in 1723-26. He married Mary Walker, and their son, Capt. William Massie, whose will is dated October 23, 1749, was a member of the House of Burgesses from New Kent in 1748-49. He likewise owned lands situated in New Kent, Hanover and Goochland counties. Capt. William Massie married Martha Macon, and after his death she became the wife of Col. Richard Bland, who was a member of the Continental Congress at the same time as Patrick Henry. Colonel Bland and Martha Massie were married January 1, 1759, in the same week and in the same county when and where Mrs. Martha Custis and George Washington were married.

Major Thomas Massie, a son of Captain William, was born in 1747 and died in 1834. Besides his possessions in New Kent, Frederick and Nelson counties, Virginia, he owned lands over the mountains in Ohio and Kentucky. He was in the Revolution with the rank of major, and was given a land grant of 5333 acres for this service. At one time he was rector of George Washington's Church in Fairfax County, Virginia. Major Thomas Massie married Sarah Cocke.

One of the later representatives of this family was Edmond Sims Massie, who became a prominent lumberman in Kentucky. He was as a young man in business as a merchant at Trenton, Kentucky, and from that turned his attention to the buying of timber land, a business in which he continued until his death. He was a Democrat and a member of the Methodist Church, and belonged to the Masonic fraternity and Knights of Pythias.

Edmond Sims Massie married at Pulaski, Gates County, Tennessee, in 1898, Miss Sue Abernathy, who is a descendant of one of two Abernathy brothers who came to America in the Colonial period. Many of the Abernathys became business and professional men, and part of the family went over into Tennessee when it was a part of North Carolina. Mrs. Sue Massie, who resides in Richmond at 403 N. Belmont Street, was educated in Martin's College at Pulaski, Tennessee. Her father, Andrew J. Abernathy, was a lawyer, and served seventeen years as judge of the Seventh Chancery District of Tennessee and was a member of the American Bar Association. He served with a regiment of Tennessee infantry in the Confederate army, and failing strength caused him to be transferred to the cavalry, and he was in Kentucky and Georgia, and was killed at Charlotte, North Carolina, after General Johnston's surrender in April, 1865. Andrew J. Abernathy married Sarah Talley, of Clarksville, Montgomery County, Tennessee.

Mrs. Massie became the mother of four children. The son Andrew, now in the automobile supply business at Richmond, was a volunteer in the World war, serving with the Forty-second Division, and was in France eighteen months. He was gassed. Miss Sarah Abernathy Massie, the second child, graduated as a registered nurse from the Johnston Willis Hospital at Richmond. She received her early education at Marion, South Carolina. She is now connected with the Department of Medical Inspection with the Richmond public schools, and is a member of the United Daughters of the Confederacy and National Education Association. The second daughter, Miss Elizabeth Abernathy Massie, was educated at Marion, South Carolina, and is a private secretary in the State Planters & Trust Company at Richmond. She also belongs to the United Daughters of the Confederacy. The son Edmond Massie, Jr., graduated from the Marion schools, attended a university, and his scholastic honors brought him membership in the Phi Beta Kappa. He graduated in the civil engineering course and is now connected with the Bethlehem Steel Corporation.

WILLIAM HENRY THOMAS is proprietor of the Thomas Mercantile Company, a business he has built up through many years of experience as a merchant and which conducts two of the largest establishments of the kind in Giles County, one located at Bluff City and the other at Pearisburg.

Mr. Thomas was born in Campbell County, Virginia, September 17, 1866, son of La Fayette Henry and Mary (Traylor) Thomas, grandson of La Fayette Thomas and great grandson of Philip Thomas. Philip Thomas moved to Virginia from Pennsylvania. The Thomas family was originally Scotch, and in Great Britain they possessed a coat of arms. La Fayette Thomas, the grandfather, owned a farm in the vicinity of Long Island, Virginia. His son La Fayette was born and reared in Campbell County, was educated in private schools and at the outbreak of the Civil war joined the 37th Virginia Infantry in Stonewall Jackson's brigade. He took part in the battle of the Wilderness and in many other engagements, and before the war was over he was captured and was held a prisoner at Point Lookout, Maryland. The guards would not permit him to make communication with his family, and his bride, whom he had married during the war, mourned him as dead until he returned from prison at the close of the war. Seeking new opportunities in Southwestern Virginia, he settled at Big Lick, which later became the City of Roanoke, in 1870, and in 1872 he moved to Pulaski County, where he lived on a farm until 1911 and then moved to Giles County, where he died July 4, 1914. He was buried in the family cemetery at Bluff City. La Fayette Thomas, though he came out alive, made many sacrifices as a soldier of the South. A few years after the war he became completely deaf, and he had to go through life with that serious handicap. It was his faithful and ever loyal wife who gave him the inspiration for his work, and she in many ways assisted him in rearing and providing for their large family of children. On the death of La Fayette H. Thomas he had reached the age of seventy-three. They had celebrated their golden wedding anniversary at the home of their son William Henry in Bluff City. Mrs. Thomas survived him several years, passing away February 13, 1922. She was born in Campbell County, Virginia, April 5, 1845, daughter of Archer W. and Elizabeth Traylor and a granddaughter of Bosewell C. Traylor, a Baptist minister. The Traylor family have been in Virginia since early Colonial times. William and Judith Traylor owned 3,000 acres on Appomattox River as early as 1695. Mary Traylor was educated by a private governess and by her brother Marcellus, and was eighteen years of age when, on February 18, 1864, she became the bride of La Fayette Henry Thomas, then a soldier in the Southern army. She was a remarkable woman for her labors and her self-sacrificing devotion and also for the inner beauty of her character. She was a devoted member of the Baptist Church at Pulaski, and she lived for the best things in life, poetry, flowers and she exemplified the beautiful qualities of character. She is buried in Spring Hill Cemetery at Huntington, West Virginia. Of the twelve children born to her marriage three, Marcellus, Edward and Mollie, died in infancy. The nine who grew up were: William Henry, Laura, Lena C., J. F., Callie, R. B., A. C., Daisy and Georgia.

William Henry Thomas spent his boyhood days on the home farm in Pulaski County, was educated in public schools, assisted his parents on the home farm for several years and then took up construction work with Mills & Fairfax, a firm of railroad contractors, doing work for the Norfolk & Western Railway and building the Elkhorn Tunnel near Coopers, West Virginia. Mr. Thomas was the first to pass through the opening in that tunnel. In the spring of 1888 Mr. Thomas was foreman of the first force of men to begin grading streets and round house and shops for the Norfolk & Western Railway Company in the present town of Bluefield, West Virginia. During 1889-90 he was at Danville, Virginia, in the hardware business, and for a year and a half was in the lumber business in Clinch Valley. From 1891 to 1894 he was at Pocahontas, associated with J. L. Baber in the mercantile business, and in 1894 the firm of Baber & Thomas opened a general mercantile store at Keystone, West Virginia. Mr. Thomas in 1897 bought Mr. Baber's interest, and remained in business there until 1902, when he sold out.

It was in 1902 that he located at Bluff City, near Pearisburg buying a farm and also establishing a general store. That is the original business conducted by the Thomas Mercantile Company, and is one of the largest firms in this part of the state handling general hardware and also doing a large business as representative of the Dodge Brothers Motor Company. In July, 1926, Mr. Thomas and his oldest son, W. H., Jr., opened a hardware store at Pearisburg, and this store is managed by the son. The store carries a large stock of general hardware, furniture, radios, victrolas. Mr. Thomas is also interested in farming and stock raising, and he was the first man in Giles County to introduce pure bred horses, cattle and hogs. For a number of years he has been president of the Giles County Fair

Association. While at Keystone, West Virginia, he was recorder of the town and member of the school board.

He is a Knight Templar Mason, member of Beni Kedim Temple of the Mystic Shrine at Charleston, West Virginia, belongs to the Independent Order of Odd Fellows, B. P. O. Elks, Knights of Pythias and Royal Arcanum. In politics he votes as a Republican, and is a member of the Baptist Church.

Mr. Thomas married at Pocahontas, Virginia, June 5, 1895, Miss Orrie Olivia Dills, who was reared and educated in Giles County. Before her marriage she was a teacher of music. After the death of her parents she moved to Pocahontas and lived with her sister there. Mrs. Thomas is a steward of the Methodist Episcopal Church, South, and president of the Ladies' Aid Society, and is historian of the George Pearis Chapter of the Daughters of the American Revolution. Mr. and Mrs. Thomas built a beautiful home on the site occupied by the first courthouse of Giles County. The old log building was torn down only a few years ago, and the Thomas home rests on a part of the original foundation.

Mrs. Thomas is prominently related to old Virginia and Maryland families. She is a daughter of Granville Henderson and Susanna (Stafford) Dills. Her father was a son of William and Margaret (Hoppess) Dills and a grandson of Peter and Mary (Wysor) Dills. The Wysor name was originally spelled Weisor. Mary Wysor was a daughter of Henry and Barbara Ann (Ripseed) Wysor. Henry Wysor was a soldier in the American Revolution. Mrs. Thomas' grandfather, William Dills, married Margaret Hoppess a granddaughter of a German nobleman who came from Bavaria. This nobleman eloped against the wishes of his parents and was consequently disinherited, so that his American descendants never shared in the rich German estate.

Mrs. Thomas is also a descendant of the Cecil family of Maryland, related to the Lord Baltimore who was the founder of the colony. Mrs. Thomas' mother, Susanna Stafford, was a daughter of Capt. James Stafford, who married Vicy Cecil. Vicy Cecil was born May 18, 1792, daughter of John and Keziah Cecil. John Cecil, who was born January 24, 1751, and died August 5, 1832, was born in Cecil County, Maryland, and as the oldest son inherited the large estate of his father. He was a son of Samuel W. and Rebecca (White) Cecil. Samuel W. Cecil was a native of England, and on coming to America settled in the Province of Maryland. About 1760 he and his wife and children moved to the Southwestern part of Virginia, settling in what is now Pulaski County, where he acquired over 1,000 shares of land on the headwater of Neck Creek. He died about 1785, leaving a large property. His widow kept a public inn at what is now known as Dublin in Pulaski County, and was ninety-six years of age when she died in 1815. Thus the Cecils are one of the oldest families in Southwestern Virginia. John Cecil was a soldier in the American Revolution. The mother of Mrs. Thomas was educated in Hollins College, then known as Valley Union Seminary. Mrs. Thomas was one of a family of ten children: Maggie, James, Keziah, one that died in infancy; Sallie, Alberta, Rev. John Dills, a presiding elder in the State of Washington, Mrs. Thomas, William Dills, of Pearisburg, and Nowlin, who died in childhood.

To the marriage of Mr. and Mrs. Thomas were born five children, one of whom died young, the other four being Wanda

VIRGINIA 479

Olivia, William Henry, Jr., Mary Sue and Theodore Traylor. Wanda Olivia was educated in the grade and high schools of Giles County, graduating in 1918, also attended Sullins College, is a member of the Daughters of the American Revolution and is associated with her father in the mercantile business at Bluff City. The son William Henry, Jr., graduated from high school in 1918, spent one year in Washington and Lee University with the Students Army Training Corps during the war, and now has charge of the Thomas Mercantile Company at Pearisburg and is a member of the Business Men's Club of that city. Miss Mary Sue Thomas graduated from the Pearisburg High School in 1920, from the Virginia Intermont College at Bristol in 1922, and since taking a course in the National Business College at Roanoke has been assisting her father in the Mercantile Company. The youngest child, Theodore Traylor, graduated from the Pearisburg High School and is now attending Washington and Lee University.

GEORGE B. SETZLER, M. D. In the present century of expanding horizons in medical science, of marvelous discoveries and undreamed of surgical skill, the profession seems to have almost reached a time when its accomplishments are no less than miracles. The modern physician and surgeon, taking advantage of every opportunity for acquiring knowledge, must often realize with professional elation his great power over disease and disability, and be encouraged in his struggle to conquer the strongholds that have not yet been overcome. Possessing the steady nerve, the patience that never tires, the trained understanding gained through his long period of special study, he must yet possess, in order to be a successful surgeon, a courage that never quails, together with a superb technical manual skill. In every physician's life must come emergencies which make just such demands upon him, and he must be equal to them all. Virginia has her share of these noble, self-sacrificing men who are an honor to their profession and communities, and one of them who has attained to distinction as a surgeon is Dr. George B. Setzler, of Norton.

Doctor Setzler was born in Pomaria, South Carolina, December 17, 1895, a son of James P. and Mary Huff (Long) Setzler, both of whom survive and are still residing in Pomaria, where he is a merchant and planter. A man active in civic affairs, he served Pomaria as mayor and gave a very businesslike and satisfactory administration. The paternal grandfather, Dr. George A. Setzler, was engaged in the practice of medicine at Pomaria for more than half a century, and is still remembered with affectionate regard by those who benefited because of his skill and kindly charities. He was a graduate of the medical department of the University of South Carolina, and a close student all his life. Like his son, father of Doctor Setzler of this review, he was a Lutheran, but the Longs were Baptists, and the maternal grandfather belonged to the Baptist Church of Greenville, South Carolina, where he lived, but his large plantation was outside the city. The Setzler family was one of the earliest ones of South Carolina, and is of aristocratic origin.

Growing up in a normal way, surrounded by a happy home atmosphere, Dr. George B. Setzler attended the schools of Pomaria and later Newberry College, and was graduated from the latter in 1913, with the degree of Bachelor of Arts. For one year thereafter he took post-graduate work in the University of

Virginia, and then entered its medical department and was graduated therefrom in 1918 with the degree of Doctor of Medicine. At the time of his graduation he was placed in the United States Reserve Medical Corps and assigned to interne work in the University Hospital for the war period, and he continued there as an interne until 1921. From 1921 to 1922 he was a student physician and assistant in medicine in the same hospital. In 1922 he came to Norton as chief surgeon of Norton Hospital, and has since built up a reputation as a surgeon second to none in all this part of the state. A man who takes pride in keeping abreast of his profession, he has attended different clinics, including that of the Mayo Brothers, Rochester, Minnesota, in May, 1924. He is a member of the Wise County Medical Society, the Clinch Valley Medical Society, the Virginia State Medical Society and the American Medical Association, and is now president of the first named. High in Masonry, he has been advanced through the bodies of the York Rite to the Commandery, and he is now serving as junior warden of the Norton Blue Lodge. He belongs to the Norton Kiwanis Club, Phi Beta Kappa, Alpha Omega Alpha, Phi Beta Pi and the Raven Society. At different times he lectures before the Kiwanis Club and similar bodies upon different subjects, and is a popular speaker, being able to impress his hearers with the force of his statements and the sincerity of his own belief in them. In religious belief he is a Presbyterian, and his wife is of the same faith as he.

Doctor Setzler married Miss Caroline Gaujot in 1920, and she is a daughter of Claude L. and Annie (Fluorney) Gaujot, the latter of whom survives and resides in Huntington, West Virginia, but the former is deceased. During his lifetime he was a mine engineer of some prestige. Mrs. Setzler was graduated from the Huntington High School, and is a cultured lady, a member of the Woman's Civic League, active in it, in society and in church work. The one child born to Doctor and Mrs. Setzler, Mary Jane, died in infancy.

LAURENS D. HANDY, of Danville, has an interesting record of service both in the field of education and in business. He is a member of a family that has been distinguished through the professional, military and other services of its members.

Mr. Handy was the practical educator and business executive chosen as the first superintendent of the Hughes Memorial Home and School. The late John E. Hughes, of Danville, was a very wealthy tobacconist. At his death he left a legacy, valued at about $1,500,000, for the purpose of establishing a home for destitute white children from the states of Virginia and North Carolina. The provisions of the legacy were made public in 1922, and several years later Superintendent Handy began the actual work of establishing the home in line with the provisions. The site, located four miles north of Danville, comprises 256 acres, was specified in the will. The actual laying out of the grounds was done in October, 1925, and the first building construction was started soon afterward. The first building was the Administration, followed by a group of three cottages, for boys, for girls and for infants. After that came a home for the superintendent, pumping station, central heating plant, sewage disposal system and necessary farm buildings and shelter for farm equipment and homes for employes. Later was erected a chapel for religious services and public assemblages, a modern six-room school building, a gymnasium and swimming pool and also an additional cottage for boys. This construction was completed at an outlay of about $500,000. All the buildings are of brick and fireproof construction. The system of administration is on what is known as the Cottage Plan, with a maximum of thirty children to each cottage. The children who become wards of the home must be between the ages of two and twelve years at the time of admission, and may remain until reaching the age of eighteen. The first children were accepted in July, 1927, and the institution now houses about one hundred from the two states.

Mr. Handy was born at Cleveland, Tennessee, June 19, 1896, son of Rev. Thomas R. and Carrie (Ball) Handy. His grandfather was John Handy, a soldier of the Confederacy, who died of smallpox during the war. The Handy family is of English descent. Rev. Thomas R. Handy was born near Jefferson, North Carolina, had a private school education, and at the age of nineteen entered the ministry of the Methodist Episcopal Church, South, and later took four years of Conference training. He was superannuated after many years of earnest toil in 1914, and is now living retired at Waugh, Alabama. He was with the Holston Conference of Virginia and Tennessee, and among other places was pastor at Cleveland, Spring City and Chattanooga, and for fifteen years was presiding elder. He is now nearly eighty years of age. His wife, Carrie Hall, was born and reared in Montgomery, Alabama, and was educated in Miss Fallansbee's Private School there. She was a member of the Methodist Protestant Church before her marriage. She is now seventy-five years of age. Seven of her brothers were soldiers in the Confederate army, including: Bowling Hall, who was wounded in action; Capt. Crenshaw Hall, who was also wounded; John Hall; Capt. James, who lost a leg in battle; Tom Brown, who was killed in the first battle; Hines Hall.

Rev. Thomas R. Handy and wife were the parents of six children. One of them is Bowling H. Handy, who served as a member of the Industrial Commission of Virginia until April 15, 1929, having previously practiced law at Bristol, Virginia, and is now a resident of Richmond. Major Tom Troy Handy was one of the first American soldiers decorated in France, going overseas and serving with the Rainbow Division and received three citations, being decorated with the Croix de Guerre, the distinguished service medal and one other decoration. He is now in the Regular Army and was recently ordered to the Philippines. Stuart Handy, of Waugh, Alabama, was a private overseas during the World war. Dr. Frank Handy, of Coeburn, Virginia, physician and surgeon, was a lieutenant in the field artillery. The youngest of the family is Jean Handy, of Waugh, Alabama.

Laurens D. Handy was educated in private schools and graduated from Emory and Henry College of Virginia in 1917. The same year he joined the colors and for several months was in training at Fort Myer, Virginia. After being honorably discharged he served about a year as commandant of cadets at the Bingham Military School at Asheville, North Carolina, and the following two years was athletic director and teacher of English and history in that famous preparatory school. He left there in 1920 and for three years was connected with S. E. Massengill Company of Bristol, manufacturers of pharmaceuticals.

Mr. Handy became a resident of Danville as business manager of Randolph-Macon Institute. After a year he resigned to become the first superintendent of the Hughes Memorial Home and School.

Mr. Handy is a Royal Arch Mason, being affiliated with Roman Eagle Lodge No. 122, A. F. and A. M., and Euclid Chapter Royal Arch Masons. He is a member of the Rotary Club, and he and his wife are active members of the Mt. Vernon Methodist Episcopal Church, South.

He married at Danville, June 18, 1921, Miss Margaret Temple. She attended private school at Danville and Randolph-Macon Institute, Converse College in South Carolina, and Sweetbriar College of West Virginia. She is eligible to membership in the Daughters of the American Revolution, but her chief interest is her home and the work of the splendid institution over which Mr. Handy presides. The only child born to Mr. and Mrs. Handy died in infancy. Mrs. Handy is a daughter of George G. and Amine (Hamner) Temple, of Danville, where her father for years has been in the real estate and insurance business.

HARRY WOODING is known all over Virginia because of his long and consecutive and capable service as mayor of the City of Danville, an office he has held for nearly forty years. He is also held in high honor as one of the surviving veterans of the Confederacy.

He was born at Danville, April 27, 1844, son of William H. and Jane White (Grasty) Wooding, and grandson of Thomas H. Wooding, a pioneer of Pittsylvania County. William H. Wooding was born near Chatham, Virginia, was educated in private schools, graduated from the University of North Carolina, was a farmer and for several years represented his county in both Houses of the Legislature and was mayor of Danville for several terms. He died in 1872. His wife, Jane White Grasty, was born and reared in Pittsylvania County, and was an active member of the Presbyterian Church. She died November 11, 1858. Her father was Phillip Grasty. William H. Wooding and wife had eight children, three of the sons becoming soldiers of the Confederacy. The oldest, George W., was killed in the battle of Fredericksburg in 1862. Thomas G., who also served the Confederacy, died in Louisiana in 1874. Harry Wooding was the third child. The others were: Naticia, J. Henry, Sharshall, Jane and James.

Harry Wooding attended private schools, and was not yet seventeen years of age when he joined the Danville Greys and served with that organization one year. He was then transferred to Company C of the Fifth Virginia Cavalry, and was with that unit of the Confederate army until the close of the war. He participated in the first battle of Manassas and the seven days fighting around Richmond, at Gettysburg and many other hard fought campaigns. Mr. Wooding after the war became a merchant at Danville, and was in business consecutively for thirty years, until 1895.

In 1892 he was elected mayor of Danville, and has been re-elected to that office for twelve terms, and at the last election was given the largest majority he has ever received. For over thirty-seven years he has enjoyed not only the dignity, but has exemplified a high sense of responsibility in handling the affairs of one of Virginia's leading cities. He is also chairman of the Board of Police Commissioners. Mr. Wooding is a Democrat, is a member of the Independent Order of Odd Fellows, a past grand chancellor of the Knights of Pythias, and is affiliated with the Improved Order of Red Men, Junior Order of United American Mechanics, and is a trustee of the Presbyterian Church.

He married at Danville, January 9, 1873, Miss Mary E. Coleman, of Danville, where she was reared and educated. She was also a Presbyterian. Mrs. Wooding died March 14, 1929. Her parents were Capt. Daniel and Margaret (Ayres) Coleman. Her father was before the Civil war captain of a military company, and he was in the service of the Confederacy. For many years he carried on a business as a tobacconist at Danville. Mr. and Mrs. Wooding had a family of three children: Empsie, Toksie and Harry, Jr. Both daughters were educated in public schools and in Roanoke College. Empsie married Frank Spencer and has a son, Harry Wooding Spencer, Toksie is the wife of J. O. Boatwright, of Danville. Harry Wooding, Jr., a prominent Danville attorney, was educated in public schools at Danville, in the Danville Military Institute, and the University of Virginia, and was admitted to the bar in 1905. For a quarter of a century he has enjoyed a splendid law practice, his offices being in the Masonic Temple Building. He is a director of the Atlantic Building and Loan Association, and is a member of the Knights of Pythias, Junior Order of United American Mechanics, Sons and Daughters of Liberty, Lions Club, Wildwood Club, and is an elder in the Presbyterian Church.

Harry Wooding, Jr., married at Danville, June 19, 1912, Miss Elnora May Waller, daughter of W. E. and Vidillia (Mays) Waller. Mrs. Harry Wooding, Jr., attended public schools at Danville, Roanoke College and Hardin College at Mexico, Missouri. She is active in the Woman's Auxiliary, First Presbyterian Church, a member of the Wednesday Club, and is a past president of the local chapter of the United Daughters of the Confederacy and recording secretary of the Virginia Division. Mr. and Mrs. Harry Wooding, Jr., had two children, both of whom died in infancy.

WILLIAM POTTER STERNE, commonwealth's attorney of Dinwiddie County, began the practice of law about the same time that he received his honorable discharge from the navy. He made a fine record of service in the navy during the World war. Mr. Sterne is a native Virginian and is a graduate in law from the University of Virginia.

He was born at Dinwiddie December 12, 1894, son of William M. and Arabelle (Ettenborough) Sterne, his mother being a native of Dinwiddie County, while his father was born in Lunenberg County, and spent the greater part of his life in business as a lumberman and merchant at Dinwiddie, and for several terms served as chairman of the Dinwiddie County Road Board. He died March 17, 1920, and the widowed mother still resides in Dinwiddie.

W. Potter Sterne was reared and educated in his native community, graduating from high school in 1910. He prepared for university at Randolph-Macon Academy at Bedford and in 1916 took his A. B. degree at the University of Virginia. He was a law student at the university when America declared war, and on August 14, 1917, he enlisted in the navy as a third class fireman. His merit and efficiency brought him rapid promotions and he reached the rank of ensign, and at the end of the war was in command of a submarine chaser. He received his honorable discharge August 17, 1921, but in the meantime, on being released from active duty, he resumed his studies at the Univer-

sity of Virginia and completed the law course. He has since
been engaged in practice at Dinwiddie, and on April 8, 1921, was
appointed commonwealth's attorney to fill out an unexpired
term, and in 1923 was elected for a full term and reelected in
1927. He is also a commissioner in chancery.

Mr. Sterne married, July 11, 1918, Miss Helen Cornell Russell, daughter of John M. and Emma T. (Wilson) Russell. Her
parents were born in Michigan. Her father was a lawyer by
profession, at one time served as prosecuting attorney at Flint,
Michigan, where he became interested in the lumber industry,
and that brought him to Virginia. He located at Dinwiddie,
and in his later years he conducted a drug store at Petersburg.
He died in 1923 and her mother in 1927. Mr. and Mrs. Sterne
have two daughters, Frances Virginia, born January 25, 1922,
and Martha Ettenborough, born January 20th, 1929.

Mr. Sterns is a director of the Planters Bank of Dinwiddie.
He owns farm lands and operates some of them under his personal supervision. He is a member of the Virginia State Bar
Association, is master of his Masonic lodge, is a member of the
Pi Kappa Alpha national fraternity and the Skull and Keys
Society of the University of Virginia. Mr. Sterne is a Democrat
and a member of the Episcopal Church. He belongs to the
American Legion. During the war he was awarded a gold chev-
ron by the Government for duty in the war zone, and received
special commendation for rescuing a soldier lost overboard
at sea.

JOSEPH DU PUY EGGLESTON achieved his enduring fame as
one of the men contributing to and responsible for the great
educational revival in the South beginning in the closing years
of the previous century, a movement fully as important if not
prerequisite to the new industrialism which has distributed
among the people of the South a prosperity and economic independence unprecedented. Doctor Eggleston's work and influence as an educator belongs to the South as a whole, and at
least two states have directly benefited from his activities,
North Carolina and his native commonwealth of Virginia.

Virginia has raised up many notable sons for the service of
the modern era, and none is more closely linked with the famous
names of the Colonial and Revolutionary period of the old dominion than Joseph Du Puy Eggleston. Doctor Eggleston was
born at "Marble Hill," Prince Edward County, Virginia, November 13, 1867, and is in the eighth generation from Richard
Eggleston, who came from England in 1635 and settled in James
City County, becoming a planter. Either he or his son Richard
participated in the Indian battle of Bloody Run. This son,
Richard, of the second generation, was the father of Joseph
Eggleston, who served as a burgess from James City County in
1728-30. He married Anne Pettus, daughter of Dabney Pettus,
granddaughter of Thomas Pettus, Jr., a burgess, and great-
granddaughter of Col. Thomas Pettus, a burgess and member of
the governor's council. Their son, Richard Eggleston, who was
a member of the Committee of Safety of Cumberland County,
married Rebekah Clough. Their son, Edmund Eggleston, a
Virginia planter, married Jane Segar Langhorne, daughter of
Major Maurice Langhorne, of the War of the Revolution, and
granddaughter of John Langhorne, a burgess. The sixth generation was represented by Richard Beverley Eggleston, a
planter, at the age of fifteen becoming a corporal during the

War of 1812, and who married Elvira Du Puy. Her father, Capt. James Du Puy, was of French Huguenot ancestry and a soldier of the War of the Revolution.

Joseph Du Puy Eggleston, father of Doctor Eggleston, was born at "Cedar Grove," Nottoway County, Virginia, October 28, 1831, was educated in a private academy, studied medicine at the University of Virginia, graduated from the Jefferson Medical College of Philadelphia, and was a surgeon in the War of 1861-65. He was a deacon in the Presbyterian Church, and among other activities in behalf of education founded an academy. He married Anne Carrington Booker, who was born at Charlotte Court House February 3, 1836, daughter of a family connecting with many distinguished names, including the Bookers, Carringtons, Elliotts, and Reades. Her mother was a daughter of Dr. Thomas Colgate and Margaret (Jameson) Elliott, Doctor Elliott being a son of Col. George Elliott, of the War of the Revolution, whose father, George Elliott, came from England. Margaret Jameson was a daughter of Capt. William Jameson, of the Revolution, who had come from Scotland. Captain Jameson's wife, Nancy Reade, was a daughter of Clement Reade, an officer in the French and Indian war, a burgess and clerk of court of Lunenburg County from the establishment of that county.

Joseph Du Puy Eggleston II had the advantages conferred by a home environment where culture was traditional, and his boyhood was enriched by many things that wealth could not bestow. He attended home schools from the age of three to eight. From eight to fourteen he was a student in Prince Edward Academy, and from fourteen to eighteen in Hampden-Sydney College, where he graduated with the degree Bachelor of Arts. That was the foundation. Since then he has had forty years of intimate contact wth schools, with young people, and with many great and inspiring educators in the South. Doctor Eggleston has had one great vocation, education, but has also cultivated many avocations, contacts with men and life, or, as he expressed the answer to what most interested him: "Whatever touches life and improves it; and literature, which is an interpretation of life." From 1886 to 1889 he taught in public schools in Virginia, Georgia and North Carolina. He was a real teacher, though in a few years was called to the broader phases of educational administration. He was one of the first teachers in the South to vitalize instruction in geography by introducing pupils to a knowledge of the outside world through their immediate environment. The first important chapter of his educational work was the nine years he was connected with the schools of Asheville, North Carolina, going there as a teacher, but was soon elected principal, and after two years was made superintendent of the city schools. He was superintendent of Asheville from 1893-1900. Subsequently at the University of Tennessee Doctor Eggleston organized and conducted the Bureau of Publicity and Information of the Southern Education Board, a movement organized to arouse the South to the need of better schools. He personally prepared and distributed an immense amount of information in the form of news items, editorials and other statistical matter, which was published in hundreds of southern newspapers and did a great deal to prepare the way for the educational revival. He had to give up his work on account of failing eyesight, and for a time it seemed that his career as an educator was at an end. After returning to Virginia he worked his farm, and was county superintendent of schools of Prince

Edward County during 1903-05. Under the new constitution of
Virginia a change had been made in the method of selecting a
state superintendent of public instruction. In 1905 that office
was to be filled by popular vote. A great campaign was put on
to arouse the attention of the people of the state to the importance of emphasizing popular education as the outstanding
opportunity presented by the inauguration of the new system
of government. Doctor Eggleston after failing to persuade several prominent men in educational affairs to became candidates
for state superintendent offered himself as a candidate on a
platform declaring for longer terms, sanitary and properly
lighted school houses, consolidated schools and transportation of
children and other reforms. In the election he carried eighty-
two out of a hundred counties.

Doctor Eggleston was state superintendent of public instruction from February, 1906, to January 1, 1913. The outstanding
features of his work in that office are best described in Heat-
wole's *A History of Education in Virginia.* (1) the state department of education was systematized so that its influence was
strong and effective as an educational force in the state; (2) the
various educational activities of the state were unified and
coalesced into one great educational effort, directed toward the
goal of popular decision; (3) a series of constructive legislative
acts, providing for, (a) a state system of high schools, (b) a
loan fund by which the trustees in the counties might borrow
money from the literary fund for the purpose of erecting school
buildings; (c) the control by the state board of education of the
systems of heating, lighting and ventilating of school buildings,
(d) a scheme by which the division superintendents' salaries
could be increased so as to secure expert supervision of the
schools, (e) an appropriation to encourage the consolidation of
one-room schools into two or three room schools, (f) the establishing and maintaining of normal training high schools and
agricultural high schools, (g) compulsory education, (h) retirement fund for teachers, (i) establishment of three state normal
schools for women; (j) the control of the sanitary and health
conditions about the schools; (k) a system of medical inspection
of school children; (4) a system of demonstration and extension
work by which agriculture and kindred subjects could be taught
through the organization of boys' corn clubs and girls' canning
and poultry clubs.

Largely out of his experience as state superintendent Doctor
Eggleston in collaboration with R. W. Bruere wrote "The Work
of the Rural School," which for a number of years has been regarded as a standard authority on the subject. Through all the
years of his busy life he has been constantly writing and using
newspapers, magazines and bulletins to carry on the campaign
for general enlightenment in the South.

During the first six months of 1913 Doctor Eggleston acted
as chief of field service in rural education under the United
States Bureau of Education. Since 1913 two splendid institutions of higher education in Virginia have benefited and made
progress under the able, high-minded guidance of Doctor Eggleston. The first of these was the Virginia Polytechnic Institute at Blacksburg, of which he was president from 1913 to 1919.
On July 1, 1919, he returned to his alma mater, Hampden-
Sydney College, as president. His election as president of
Hampden-Sydney coincided with the taking over of that institution by the Presbyterian Synod.

Doctor Eggleston's name is an honored one on the rolls of membership of many patriotic, civic, educational, religious and scholastic organizations, but a recounting of them would add nothing to his fame and solid distinctions as one of the South's able leaders in his generation.

Doctor Eggleston married at Farmville, Virginia, December 18, 1895, Julia Jane Johnson. She is a graduate of the State Normal School at Farmville. Mrs. Eggleston likewise has many noted Colonial and Revolutionary ancestors, and she and Doctor Eggleston have their ancestry coalescing in one line, their common ancestor being Col. Clement Reade, a burgess and officer in the French and Indian war, and clerk of court in Lunenberg County. Her ancestors also include Richard Cocke, a burgess, Col. Walter Aston, burgess, Abraham Venable, burgess, Capt. Samuel Woodson Venable, and officer of the War of the Revolution, and Nathaniel Venable, a Revolutionary officer, also a burgess, and in whose office the plan for the founding of Hampden-Sydney College was formulated in 1775, the college first opening its doors on January 1, 1776. Mrs. Eggleston's father, William Thomas Johnson, was a soldier in the War of 1861-65, was of Quaker and French Huguenot ancestry and had four Revolutionary ancestors. Her mother, Elizabeth Cabell Carrington, was a daughter of Tucker Carrington, lawyer and planter, whose father was Gen. George Carrington, of the Revolution, and whose grandfather was Judge Paul Carrington, a Supreme Court judge of Virginia and a prominent leader in the war for independence. Judge Paul Carrington's wife was Margaret Reade, a daughter of Col. Clement Reade, already named.

Doctor and Mrs. Eggleston have two children. Their daughter, Elizabeth Carrington Eggleston, was born at Asheville, North Carolina, graduated from the Blacksburg High School, Sweet Briar College, took the Master of Arts degree at Syracuse University, and graduated with honors and the A. B. degree from Oxford University in England. The son, Joseph Du Puy Eggleston III, born October 11, 1903, at "the Oaks" in Prince Edward County, attended the Blacksburg High School and Hampden-Sydney College. He has been connected with the Export Leaf Tobacco Company, and is now a student at the University of Virginia.

DR. HENRY A. WISEMAN, JR., physician and surgeon at Danville, is a native of that city, where his family have lived for over one hundred years. Doctor Wiseman has had in his life experience a record of participation in two wars, and has had a fruitful round of duties in the practice of his profession.

He was born at Danville, August 24, 1877, a son of Henry A. and Willie Anna (Yager) Wiseman. His grandfather, John Wiseman, came to America from England in the early part of the last century and settled at Danville. On other sides Doctor Wiseman is descended from Colonial and Revolutionary ancestors. His great-great-grandfather was Col. William Downs, a Revolutionary war officer, a brother of Henry Downs, signer of the famous Mecklenburg Declaration of Independence in North Carolina. Doctor Wiseman's father was born and reared at Danville, attended schools there, and was a student in the medical college of Virginia at Richmond. He served in the Civil war and joined the Virginia State Troops, at first with the Ringgold Artillery in Longstreet's Brigade and afterward was transferred to the Medical Corps. He was all through the war, and when it was ended instead of resuming his medical studies he engaged in the drug business at Danville. He owned and conducted two fine stores in that city and for a time had another store at Asheville, North Carolina. He was one of five of the first executive committees that founded the Virginia Pharmaceutical Association. He was one of Danville's most highly esteemed citizens and for some time served as town treasurer, was an elder in the First Presbyterian Church and for years was treasurer of Roman Eagle Lodge No. 122, A. F. and A. M. He died December 27, 1902, and is buried in the Greenhill Cemetery. His wife, Willie Anna Yager, wos born in Orange County, Virginia, December 20, 1847, and at the age of eighty-two lives with her son, Doctor Wiseman. Her education was acquired in private schools and in the Roanoke Seminary that is now Averitt College. All her life she has been much interested in the work of the Presbyterian Church. Her parents were William B. and Elizabeth C. (Whitelaw) Yager. Her grandfather was Eli Yager and her mother's father was a doctor. The Yagers were planters and were of remote German ancestry. The old home of Dr. David Whitelaw is still standing in Orange County. The Whitelaws came from Scotland. Henry A. Wiseman, Sr., and wife had four children. Mary Whitelaw, now Mrs. Henry E. Kendall, of Shelby, North Carolina; Dr. Henry A. Plumer Wiseman, of Danville; and Willie Anna, now Mrs. Lee B. Weathers, of Shelby, North Carolina.

Dr. Henry A. Wiseman grew up at Danville, attended a private school and the Danville Military Institute, and in 1901 took his medical degree at the University of Virginia. His interne work was done in the New York Polyclinic and in the Dr. Joseph Price Hospital at Philadelphia. About the time he graduated he went to South Africa and served with the rank of captain in the Medical Corps of the English army during the Boer war. After returning home he settled at Danville, and except for the World war period has been steadily engaged in the general routine of a medical and surgical practice. In July, 1917, he organized Battery E. First Virginia Field Artillery, and commanded the same until transferred to the Medical Corps of the Twenty-ninth Division at Camp McClellan, Alabama, in May, 1918, and later was transferred to the 113th Infantry as medical officer and went overseas with that regiment as acting regimental surgeon. He did field hospital work, first aid work at the front and was in the Alsace sector and later in several battles in the Argonne Forest. A citation given him for distinguished service reads as follows: "Headquarters Blue and Grey Division. Captain Henry A. Wiseman, Medical Corps, U. S. A. 'I have read with much pride the report of Commanding Officer 113th Infantry regarding your courage and devotion to duty October 10, 1918, north of Verdun, when with utter disregard for personal safety you remained in a position of great danger in order to care for the wounded, and have ordered your name and deed inscribed upon the record book kept at these headquarters for that purpose.' C. G. Morton, Major General, commanding 29th Division."

Doctor Wiseman received his honorable discharge at Camp Dix, New Jersey, in May, 1919, and soon after reorganized the Virginia Hospital Company, which he commanded for a number of years as major. During the past ten years he has pursued his professional routine without special interruption. He enjoys a very large practice over Danville, and some years ago he erected a beautiful home at 842 Main Street, where he also has his offices. He is a member of the Danville Academy of Medicine, the Pittsylvania County, Virginia State and American Medical Associations, and on the staff of the Memorial Hospital. He is affiliated with Roman Eagle Lodge No. 122, A. F. and A. M., is a member of the Danville Golf Club, and for some years was active in the Tuscarora Club and other organizations. He is now chairman of the City Democratic Executive Committee and is a deacon in the First Presbyterian Church.

Doctor Wiseman married at Danville, December 12, 1916, Miss Annie Laurie Burton, of Danville. She attended the Roanoke Seminary now Averitt College, and is also a member of the Presbyterian Church. Her parents are William T. and Maud (Jennings) Burton. Her father for many years was a leading tobacco warehouseman at Danville, but he and his wife for some years have lived retired, with a home on Holbrook Avenue. Of the four children born to Doctor and Mrs. Wiseman one died in infancy. The son Henry A. III, born February 10, 1920, is a pupil in the public schools of Danville. The two younger children are Annie Burton, born May 4, 1923, and Plumer Whitelaw, born October 19, 1926.

HERMAN W. BOAZ. In but few departments of human endeavor have there been greater strides made during recent years than in the art of photography. The individual who succeeded a decade or so ago would find himself hopelessly in the background should he, without modern equipment and accessories, attempt to cope with conditions of this time. Photographic portraiture is an art which admits of infinite conception, and requires versatile knowledge and great capacity for painstaking and careful work in its development. The individuals who maintain its highest artistic development must necessarily have a thorough knowledge of human nature and be scholarly and scientific in their inclinations. To this class belongs Herman Boaz, proprietor of the Boaz Studio, the only enterprise of its nature at Galax, Grayson County.

Mr. Boaz was born at Woodlawn, Virginia, March 25, 1891, and is a son of James Robert and Amanda I. (Morris) Boaz. His great-grandfather was Robert Boaz, who was born in Patrick County, Virginia, and reared in the eastern part of the state, but during the latter part of his life lived with his son Abraham near Martinsville, Virginia, where he died, as also did his wife, who had been Patsy Sandifer. Abraham Sandifer Boaz, the grandfather of Herman W. Boaz, was born in 1823, and throughout his life followed agricultural pursuits in Henry County, where he was a large land holder. He died in 1909, at the age of eighty-six years, and was buried in the family cemetery near the Smith River, about ten miles south of Martinsville. He served in the Confederate army during the war between the states, and was captured and imprisoned by the Federal troops for about eleven months prior to the close of the struggle. His service was as a wagonmaster. His wife bore the maiden name of Annie Nunn.

James Robert Boaz was born March 1, 1862, near Martinsville, Henry County, Virginia, and on attaining manhood moved to Drenn, Carroll County, this state, where he purchased land and engaged in sawmilling and the raising of live stock. He became well and widely known as a substantial citizen, and remained in that community until 1900, at which time he removed for a short period to Cranberry Church. In December, 1921, Mr. Boaz located at Galax, where he established the mercantile firm of J. R. Boaz & Son, the junior member of which is his son William E. Boaz. Mr. Boaz married Miss Amanda I. Morris, a daughter of William Pendleton and Caroline (Smith) Morris, the former of whom was a prominent stock raiser and farmer of Carroll County. He volunteered for service at the start of the war between the states, and served until captured about one year prior to its close, until which he was confined in a Federal prison. To James R. and Amanda I. Boaz there were born the following children: Herman W., is the subject of this review, Marvin Abraham, registered May 17, 1917, in Carroll County, was drafted about September 5, 1917, with the first five boys then called, sent to camp at Petersburg as cook for a detachment company until receiving a medical discharge a few days before the signing of the armistice, married Cora Sceliga, of Carroll County, and has two daughters, Jessie Ruth and Marie. Ida Mabel, attended Woodlawn High School, married Roby T. Manning, of near Galax, and has two sons, Buford and Herman, William E. attended Woodlawn High School and assisted his father in sawmilling and farming until 1921, since when he has been associated with his father at Galax. He married Hope Cole, daughter of Wylie Cole, of Carroll County, who died May 23, 1920, and was buried at Gladeville Cemetery, near Galax, and after her death married, September 19, 1923, Zula Edwards, who died March 23, 1928, and was also buried in Gladeville Cemetery. He is an Odd Fellow and a member of the Chamber of Commerce; Vaughtie Carroll; fifth child, attended high school at Woodlawn, and is now the wife of B. C. Cole, of Galax, and has one child, Alma. Walter Robert attended Woodlawn High School and is now an employe of J. R. Boaz & Son. He married, in 1928, Mary Landreth, daughter of Orville Landreth, of Carroll County. Charlie Alfred attended Woodlawn High School.

Herman Winford Boaz attended the high school at Woodlawn, and May 5, 1918, enlisted for the World war at Hillsville, Virginia. He was sent to Lehigh University, South Bethlehem, Pennsylvania, for a sixty-day course in locomotive engineering, and was then transferred to a detachment company at Washington, D. C. Two weeks later he was transferred to Fort Myer, Virginia, and attached to Company C, Seventy-sixth Engineers, subsequently being sent to the American University at Washington, D. C., where he received his honorable discharge December 10, 1918.

Returning home, Mr. Boaz engaged in the photographic business for two years, and then attended the Illinois College of Photography, one of the foremost schools of photography in the world. Returning again to Galax, he bought out the interest of his former partner and reestablished a modern business, which he has since conducted with great success at the Boaz Studio, this being the only enterprise of its kind at Galax. His studio is light, airy and artistic, and in its furnishings and equipment permits the most satisfactory results possible with present-day knowledge of photography. Mr. Boaz is a prominent Mason and a member of Kazim Shrine, A. A. O. N. M. S., of Roanoke; also belonging to the United Commercial Travelers No. 174, Roanoke; the Independent Order of Odd Fellows and the Modern Woodmen of America at Galax; American Legion Post No. 145, of which he is a commander; the Rotary Club and the

L.W. Vermillion M. D.

Brotherhood of American Yeomen. He is a republican in his political allegiance, and a member of the First Christian Church of Galax, of which he is an elder and superintendent of the Sunday School.

Mr. Boaz married Miss Thelma Howlett, daughter of Mr. and Mrs. Ben Howlett, of Galax.

LEVI WOODBURY VERMILLION, M. D., was a very fine doctor, capable in his profession, which he made a source of service to a large community in Giles County. His home during the greater part of his life was at Poplar Hill.

Doctor Vermillion was born near Dublin in Pulaski County, May 2, 1850, and was the second son of Uriah and Nancy (Morehead) Vermillion. The Vermillion family is of French-Huguenot and Scotch-Irish ancestry. Uriah Vermillion was a farmer and stock raiser, owning one of the best blue grass farms in Pulaski County, at Haws Springs. He served as a Home Guard during the Civil war and participated in the battle of Cloyd's Mountain. His wife, Nancy Morehead, who was born and reared near Dublin, was a direct descendant of Lord Baltimore. Both were members of the Presbyterian Church. She died May 6, 1906. Of their ten children nine grew to mature years: Joseph, Dr. Levi W., Thomas, Rena, Elizabeth, Lessie, Mollie, James H. and Nannie.

Levi W. Vermillion had the advantage of good schools in his youth, took a course in the University of Virginia, and afterwards was graduated from the Richmond Medical College in 1874. In the same year he located at Poplar Hill and at once secured a large practice. His professional life for over thirty years was one steady chapter of successes. There he devoted his time and abilities to his work until his death on August 15, 1906. He is buried in the Grove Church Cemetery at Poplar Hill. At the time of his marriage he joined the Presbyterian Church, was made an elder a few days later and proved himself a useful and esteemed official. He was a member of the Masonic fraternity and was a lifelong Democrat.

Nature had endowed him with superior mental faculties which had been carefully cultured in youth, and he preserved in manhood the tastes he then acquired. He was a man of genuine culture. It was apparent to those who knew him that he had read much, and remembered what he had read. He was well grounded in materia medica, and a physician of fine ability. In all points in which personal merit can be viewed, in science, in learning, in taste, in honor, in generosity, in humanity, in every liberal sentiment, and every conservative accomplishment, he had few if any superiors in Southwest Virginia. He was a man of warm impulses.

In the words of appreciation written at the time of his death —"His cordial manners and tender emotions contributed the most beautiful traits of his character. He had a word of good cheer for all, and was among the first to lend the assuring hand and offer the encouraging word to his fellow beings. Those of us who knew him best cannot forget his accustomed kindly greetings, and his cheerful, inspiring pleasantries."

Doctor Vermillion married at Poplar Hill, September 27, 1876, Miss Sallie Ann Allen, daughter of William Allen and of Scotch-Irish descent. She was educated in private schools, attending the girls' school at Pearisburg and later at Christiansburg, where she won distinction. She was endowed with a bril-

liant mind. For several years before her marriage she taught
in Giles County. She was a Methodist and taught a class in Sunday School for a number of years. Her death occurred June 25,
1923. Her father, William B. Allen, who married Hannah King,
owned a large amount of land and operated farms and raised
stock at Poplar Hill, and before the war owned a large number
of slaves. He was a generous and hospitable Virginia gentleman, and was remembered for his kindness to the soldiers at the
time of the Civil war, keeping open house for men in uniform
who passed his way. He died in 1878 and his wife, on January
17, 1890.

Doctor and Mrs. Vermillion had six children: Dr. Vance A.,
a physician at White Gate; Miss Mary Statira; Elizabeth, wife
of Dr. D. P. Cannaday, of Roanoke, whose children are Sarah
Elizabeth, Henry Lee, Mary Frances, Dexter Edgerton and Jack
Vermillion; Miss Nannie Louise, who died at the age of twenty-
seven; Sidney Uriah; and Annie Lee, wife of Elmer L. Ayres, of
Lynchburg.

Miss Mary Statira and her brother, Sidney Uriah, occupy
the old home place at Poplar Hill, where Sidney U. is engaged in
farming and stock raising. He is a World war veteran, having
been a member of the Headquarters Company in the Three Hundred and Seventeenth Infantry, Eightieth Division, and was
overseas in France from May, 1918, to April, 1919. Miss Mary
Statira Vermillion attended public schools and Sullins College
and the State Teachers College at Radford, also the University
of Virginia, and spent several years in teaching in Giles County.

HARVEY G. JOHNSTON. This is one of the most honored
names in Giles County, carrying associations with fine abilities
and splendid service in the medical profession and representing
the best ideals of citizenship and manhood.

The founder of the family in America was David Johnston,
who came from Annandale, Scotland, and settled in Eastern
Virginia. His son, Andrew Johnston, was one of the early settlers of Giles County, and became the father of several men
of high character and eminent position in their locality and
state. One of them was Capt. James D. Johnston, a great Virginia lawyer who lived at Pearisburg until a few years before
his death and had his law office there. James D. Johnston was
a member of the House of Delegates of Virginia and was one
of the men who met at the Exchange Hotel in Richmond, December 31, 1868, and appointed a committee of nine to confer
with General Grant, recently elected President, for the purpose
of having submitted to popular referendum certain clauses of
the Underwood Constitution separately. As a result of this
referendum these clauses, held to be highly obnoxious to the
welfare of reconstruction, were practically eliminated from the
constitution.

Another noted member of the family in Southwest Virginia was Judge David E. Johnston, a nephew of the Andrew
Johnston previously referred to. This David E. Johnston served
as a member of Congress, but the work for which he is chiefly
remembered is his authorship of the History of the New River
Settlements, one of the most important source books of material
bearing on the history of that section of the state.

One of the sons of Andrew Johnston, the pioneer, was Dr.
Harvey G. Johnston, Sr., who was born and reared in Giles
County, was educated in private schools, attended Emory and

Henry College and continued his higher education in the University of Virginia and Jefferson Medical College at Philadelphia. He spent all his mature years in the practice of medicine in Giles County and died in 1881. His first wife was Anna Marie Snidow, of Giles County, and the children of this marriage were: Dr. Will A. Johnston, of Roanoke; Carrie, deceased wife of Rev. J. E. Triplet, a Presbyterian minister; Miss Ada, of Norfolk; and Jennie, widow of W. E. Black, of Norfolk. The second wife of Dr. Harvey G. Johnston, Sr., was Mary Priscilla Fowler, who was born and reared at Sevierville, Tennessee, attended private schools and the Moravian School for Girls at Salem, North Carolina. Her first husband was Captain Halsey, of Lynchburg. She was a loyal Presbyterian. She died in 1910, the mother of four children: Lula J., wife of B. E. Bransford, of Pittsburgh, Pennsylvania; Fowler Johnston, who died at the age of thirteen; Dr. Harvey G.; and Vivian D., of Roanoke.

The present representative of the family in the medical profession at Pearisburg is Dr. Harvey G. Johnston, Jr., who was born in Giles County November 18, 1875. He attended public schools, the institution now known as the Tennessee Military Institute at Sweetwater, and in 1899 graduated from the University of Medicine at Richmond. He was an interne in St. Luke's Hospital, practiced five years at Elkhorn, West Virginia, and in 1905 returned to Pearisburg and opened his office in the building which his father had used for the same purpose and which stands in the yard of the substantial brick home of the Johnston family, a structure that was erected in 1820 by Doctor Johnston's grandfather. This home had the very unusual distinction of having sheltered three Presidents of the United States. After the battle of Cloyd's Mountain in Virginia the office at different times was used by General Hayes, General Garfield and Capt. William McKinley, all of whom were officers in the Ohio troops that had a prominent part in this Western Virginia campaign, and all of whom subsequently served in the White House. Doctor Johnston for over twenty years has been very busy with his practice as a physician and surgeon at Pearisburg. He is local surgeon for the Norfolk & Western and Virginia Railway companies and is a member of the County and Southwestern State Medical Societies.

In addition to his professional work he owns and manages a commercial orchard of a hundred acres, planted to Stark Delicious and Stamans Winesap apples. He is member of the Masonic fraternity, and was commissioned a lieutenant in the Army Medical Corps during the World war, and was at Fort Oglethorpe, Georgia, when the armistice was signed. He is a Democrat and a member of the Presbyterian Church.

He married at Roanoke, November 15, 1915, Miss Myra O. Woolwine, of Roanoke, daughter of C. C. and Emma (Burke) Woolwine. Her father was an undertaker and funeral director at Roanoke and died about 1908. Her mother resides at New Market. Myra Woolwine graduated from the Roanoke High School, was a member of the Methodist Episcopal Church, but after her marriage became a Presbyterian. She died in February, 1922, leaving two sons: Harvey G. III and Fowler Woolwine Johnston, both of whom are attending public schools at Pearisburg. Doctor Johnston on February 27, 1924, married at Mount Airy, North Carolina, Miss Marjorie D. Johnson, of Mount Airy, where she was educated in the grade and high schools, and also attended the Vrginia State Teachers College at Radford, and was a teacher in the high school at Pearisburg before her marriage. She is a working member of the Presbyterian Church. Her parents were J. W. and Ella (Banks) Johnston, of Mount Airy, where her father was a farmer and cattle raiser. Doctor and Mrs. Johnston had one daughter, Mary Jane, who died February 1, 1927, at the age of three years.

BOYD E. P. DICKERSON, M. D. With the exception of a few months each in Tennessee and Texas, practically the entire professional career of Dr. Boyd E. P. Dickerson has been passed at Abingdon, where he is now in the enjoyment of a large and lucrative practice. His career has been one of ambition, energy, and industry, combined with native and acquired talent, all of which have led to splendid accomplishments and a recognized position among the leaders of his calling in Southwestern Virginia. Doctor Dickerson has won success through none of the wiles of the charlatan, but by steady work and by due attention to the developments made in his profession, to the ethics of which he devotes himself in every way.

Doctor Dickerson was born at Bedford, Virginia, May 30, 1884, and is a son of John Clay and Virginia F. (Jeter) Dickerson, both of whom are now deceased. His grandfather Dickerson was a man of broad education and a noted Baptist minister, filling many pulpits throughout Virginia, where he was highly esteemed and respected because of his great zeal and piety and for the immense amount of good he accomplished during his long and useful life. His son, John Clay Dickerson, was also a prominent man in his community, where he served as a justice of the peace or "squire" for many years, and was also active in the work of the Baptist Church. The maternal grandfather of Doctor Dickerson was born at Bedford, Virginia, in which community he was well known for a long period of years. He reared a large family of boys, several of whom went to Texas, where they became wealthy and prominent factors in the history of their adopted state and where many of the Jeter family still reside. To John Clay and Virginia F. (Jeter) Dickerson there were born four sons and two daughters: Dr. Boyd E. P., of this review; James H., who is manager of a lumber company at Richmond, Virginia; W. P., who is a machinist at Dinton, Virginia; Harry W., who is the proprietor of a pharmacy at Bellaire, Ohio; Lula, who is the wife of R. H. St. Clair, of Roanoke, this state; and Minnie, who is single and a resident of Dinton.

Boyd E. P. Dickerson received his earliest educational training in a public school at Bedford, this state, following which he pursued a course in a high school at Richmond. He then enrolled as a student in the medical department of the University of Virginia, from which he was graduated as a member of the class of 1908, receiving the degree of Doctor of Medicine. Doctor Dickerson commenced his practice at Alto, Tennessee, where he resided for eight months, and then went to Prattsville, Texas. The great Southwest, however, did not appeal to him, either in a personal or professional way, and he returned to his native state and settled permanently at Abingdon, where he has since made his home and built up a professional standing and reputation. He is equally familiar with all branches of his calling, and therefore specializes in none, and has had great success in general medicine and surgery, being known as a capable diagnostican, a skilled practitioner and a reliable and steady handed surgeon. His well appointed and perfectly equipped offices are situated in

THE REV. ALEXANDER WATSON WEDDELL D. D.

the First National Bank Building. Doctor Dickerson is a thorough student of his calling and has done much post-graduate work, each year visiting clinics or educational institutions in Chicago, Baltimore, Richmond, or other large cities. He is a member of the Washington County Medical Society, the Virginia Medical Society and the American Medical Association and has several fraternal and business connections. His religious faith is that of the Baptist Church. During the World war Doctor Dickerson tendered his services to the United States Government, and was all ready to leave with a contingent of the Medical Corps when the armistice was signed. Doctor Dickerson is unmarried.

ALEXANDER WILBOURNE WEDDELL, who was for nearly a quarter of a century in the American Foreign Service, retired from the office of consul general at Mexico City in October, 1928. Mr. Weddell is a native Virginian and his family record contains many notable names in Virginia and Carolina history.

His paternal great-grandparents were John and Henrietta Laurie Weddell, of Scotland. James Weddell, their son, came to America with a family friend, Alexander Watson, and settled in North Carolina. He was a planter and president of the Tarboro branch of the Bank of the State of North Carolina. He married Margaret Ward of Edgecombe County, North Carolina, whose father, of a distinguished family of Virginia, had moved to that state and was one of the largest land owners of Edgecombe County. The Weddells later moved to Petersburg, Virginia, where their home on Sycamore Street still stands, an interesting historical landmark. James Weddell became prominent in the social and religious life of Petersburg, as well as business circles. He died in 1865 near Warrenton, North Carolina. He was a Mason and also a vestryman of St. Paul's Church of Petersburg in 1854 and 1855, and in 1855, when the cornerstone of the new St. Paul's was laid, his name was on the parchment deposited in it with those of the vestry. One of his sons was Capt. Virginius Loraine, who died at his home in Petersburg, Virginia, June 23, 1862, as the result of wounds from an exploding shell at the close of the battle of Frazier's Farm near Richmond, Virginia. He belonged to Company E, Forty-first Virginia Regiment, and was an alumnus of the University of Virginia. Another son was Capt. John Archibald, of Company G of the Forty-first Virginia Regiment, who was killed in the battle of Chancellorsville, Friday, May 1, 1863. He was an alumnus of the University of Virginia and Hampden-Sidney College.

Rev. Alexander Watson Weddell, D. D., father of Alexander Wilbourne Weddell, was born at Tarboro, Edgecombe County, North Carolina, May 20, 1841, and died in Richmond, December 6, 1883. He was taught by Charles Campbell, the distinguished historian, at Petersburg, later attended Hampden-Sidney College, studied law at the University of Virginia and attended the Theological Seminary at Alexandria, Virginia. In 1878 the degree of Doctor of Divinity was conferred on him by the old College of William and Mary. With the outbreak of the war between the States he left the university to enter the Confederate army, being commissioned a first lieutenant and assigned to Company G, Forty-first Virginia Infantry, Mahone's Brigade, Huger's Division. In June, 1862, he resigned his commission and was honorably discharged, and during the remainder of the war was in the Secret Service under Judah P. Benjamin, Secretary of War in Jefferson Davis' Cabinet.

The eighteen years that remained to him of life after the war were spent as a clergyman of the Protestant Episcopal Church and in religious educational work. He was a noted missionary preacher and pulpit orator. "After 1865 a Sunday school of colored people was organized in Grace Church, Petersburg, and sustained by Alexander W. Weddell and Robert A. Gibson, candidate for Orders." "In 1877 Alexander Weddell organized the first Episcopal Congregation of colored people in Petersburg and ministered to them in the chapel in connection with a day school numbering four hundred or more." "The children were instructed in the Bible and Prayer Book," says Slaughter, in his *History of Bristol Parish*. Later the church known as St. Stephen's Church was built for this congregation. Alexander W. Weddell was ordained to the priesthood in the chapel of the Seminary at Alexandria in 1871. June 23, 1871, he became rector of Emmanuel Church, Harrisonburg, Virginia, having served his diaconate there. He started several missions in the surrounding country which are now churches. In September, 1875, he became rector of the historic St. John's Episcopal Church at Richmond, where he remained until his death. His ministry there was a notable one, and the congregation and Sunday School became one of the largest in the state. For a short time after the war he practiced law, engaged in business and was associated with the *Petersburg Index Appeal*, but he had always been an active layman of the Episcopal Church. After entering the ministry amid all of his other activities he was the founder and one of the editors of *Our Diocesan Work*, the organ of the Episcopal Diocese of Virginia (now called *The Virginia Churchman*). He was a pioneer in all lines of Christian philanthropy or social service, and active in civic work and was a member of the public school board for years. The Weddell Memorial Episcopal Church, Fulton, Richmond, Virginia, was named in his honor. It was erected by the St. John's Congregation near the site of Doctor Weddell's first missionary effort among the poor people of the community, one of the lots on which it stands having been presented by Peter H. Mayo in 1885. He was a member of the Beta Theta Pi fraternity, Omicron Chapter, and was a Mason.

Doctor Weddell was buried in the old graveyard of historic St. John's Church, where "the morning shadows of the church fall on his grave," as he requested, and his wife is interred by him. On a large monument erected by his devoted congregation is an inscription which gives his traits of character and makes one realize why he was one of the beloved ministers of his day. It reads: "Large hearted, large minded; a lover of truth and of manhood; bold, untiring, faithful in the service of the Master; tender, watchful and unceasing in the care of his flock; his people loved and revered him." In the *Centennial History of the University of Virginia* by Dr. Philip Alexander Bruce, Doctor Weddell is spoken of "as the beloved pastor of a city church." Only three other Episcopal ministers were mentioned and this is quite a tribute when we consider the large number of alumni who have entered the Episcopal ministry. A marble tablet to his memory erected by the Vestry of St. John's Church, is in St. John's Church, Richmond.

Rev. Alexander Watson Weddell married, January 31, 1866, Penelope Margaret Wright at "Ashburn Hall," Greenville

County, North Carolina. She was eldest daughter of Dr. David Minton and Penelope Margaret (Creecy) Wright, and was born in Edenton, North Carolina, February 29, 1840. She was educated in the Norfolk Female Institute, where she specialized in French and music. She was a brilliant musician and taught music at St. Mary's School, Raleigh, during the war, when the tragic death of her father broke up the home. One of her maternal ancestors was Sir Christopher Gale, born in York, England, in 1680 and immigrated to North Carolina in 1734, becoming chief justice of the colony in 1742-47. He was one of those from North Carolina to lay the dividing line between Virginia and that state, with William Byrd from Virginia, and was attorney-general, collector of customs and major of the military. A tablet to his memory is in the old court house at Edenton, North Carolina. Another prominent figure in the ancestry was Thomas Benbury, whose home was "Benbury Hall," a plantation near Edenton, North Carolina, and who was a member of the First Provincial Congress from the Edenton District on August 25, 1774, served as a member of the committee on safety, as paymaster of the Fifth Regiment of North Carolina Militia, appointed April 22, 1776, was a member of the Constitutional Convention at Halifax, North Carolina, November 12, 1776, was elected speaker of the General Assembly April 14, 1778, and twice reelected, and was a vestryman in St. Paul's Church, Edenton. A tablet to his memory hangs in this Colonial church.

David Minton Wright was a son of David and Mary (Armistead) Wright, a grandson of Nathaniel Wright and a descendant of William Wright, the burgess of Nansemond County. Doctor Wright was a native of Nansemond County, Virginia, attended the famous Bingham School at Hillsboro, North Carolina, graduated from medicine at the University of Pennsylvania, practiced his profession in Edenton, North Carolina, later, and became a citizen of Norfolk, earning the special love and respect of that community because of his unselfish services during the yellow fever epidemic of 1857. He was a great nature lover and an authority on the Virginia and North Carolina flora and fauna. Two of his sons were in the Confederate army. One of them, Minton A. Wright, was numbered among the missing after the battle of Gettysburg. When the Federal troops occupied Norfolk, May 10, 1862, Doctor Wright was allowed to go about his professional duties as a non-combatant, many of his patients being Union families and Federal soldiers. On July 10, 1863, while on Main Street, he protested against the unruly conduct of a troop of negro soldiers, the first of this race in uniform to enter the captured city, and who were occupying the entire pavement, jostling the women and children into the gutter. A white lieutenant, A. L. Sanborn, advanced toward him with drawn sword. He was unarmed then and all who knew him also knew that he never even owned a pistol. A friend thrust a pistol into the hands of Doctor Wright, who called upon the lieutenant to stand off, but continuing to advance Doctor Wright fired a shot, striking the officer in the hand. He at once rendered the officer medical aid and was deeply distressed. Doctor Wright was arrested by the negro troops and in the melee which followed, Lieutenant Sanborn was killed and Doctor Wright was charged with his murder. For eight days he was led in chains to the farcical trial and at its conclusion was sentenced to death. Letters and telegrams and a paper pleading for Doctor Wright's life, signed by hundreds of citizens of all walks of life, were sent President Lincoln, who granted a reprieve of one week, but further influences to secure a mitigation of the harsh decree proved unavailing and Doctor Wright was executed. His memory is held in great reverence in the South, where he is regarded as a patriot and martyr. The great honor was done him of having his body lie in state in Christ Church and watched over by his professional friends until burial.

From the war diary of Penelope M. Wright, afterwards Mrs. Alexander Watson Weddell, of Thursday, April 18, 1861, at Norfolk, is taken the following item: "A meeting was held last night of the men over forty-five, or, in fact, those who from age would be exempt by law from military service, but these gentlemen all too patriotic in this time of need and probable danger to withhold their services from their state, so they resolved to form themselves into a Home Guard. Mr. Cincinnatus Newton was elected captain and Father (Dr. David Minton Wright) first lieutenant. A great many put their names on the list as members and 'twill probably be the largest company in town." Dr. Wright like many Virginians had been a strong Union man until Virginia seceded.

Mrs. Wright, widow of the murdered man—as he has ever since been regarded—came through the lines to Petersburg by the kindness of General Barnes, U. S. A., in February, 1864, and was a resident of that city until it was infested by the Federal troops, when she moved her family to Chapel Hill, North Carolina. The General Assembly of Virginia on March 10, 1864, put on record resolutions which read:

"Whereas, the arrival within Confederate lines of the distressed family of the deceased, established beyond question the newspaper announcements of the execution by the Federal authorities, in obedience to the sentence of a military commission, of Dr. David M. Wright in the city of Norfolk, on the twenty-third day of October, 1863; and

"Whereas, it is fit and proper that Virginia should place upon permanent record her high appreciation of a son whose courage, zeal and devotion marked with blood the first effort to establish upon her soil an equality of races, and to introduce in our midst the leveling dogmas of a false and pretended civilization:

"Be it resolved by the General Assembly of Virginia, that in the death of Dr. Wright this Commonwealth recognizes another addition to the long and illustrious catalogue of martyrs whose stern, inflexible devotion to liberty have rendered heroic the history of her people in the present struggle.

"That as the proudest tribute which Virginia can offer to his memory, she would earnestly invoke her children, whether within or beyond the enemy's lines, to imitate his example and emulate his high resolves."

Rev. Alexander Watson Weddell and wife were the parents of six children. The oldest, James Wright, born in Petersburg, is deceased. Miss Margaret Ward Weddell, a graduate of John B. Powell's Richmond Female Seminary, is a member of the Colonial Dames of America, Virginia Society, the Woman's Club, Richmond, the United Daughters of the Confederacy, Confederate Memorial Literary Society (Confederate Museum), and the Association for the Preservation of Virginia Antiquities. Penelope ("Pencie") Wright Weddell, who died in 1925, was the wife of St. George Mason Anderson and left three children, Penelope Weddell, Mary Mason and Margaret Ward. She was a member of the Society of the Colonial Dames of America, Virginia Society, the James River Garden Club, the Woman's Club of Richmond, and the Musician's Club, Richmond.

William Sparrow Weddell attended private and public schools in Richmond and the Virginia Military Institute at Lexington and is a member of the Sons of the Revolution, Sons of Confederate Veterans, Confederate Memorial Literary Society (Confederate Museum), Commonwealth Club, Country Club of Virginia, and the Association for the Preservation of Virginia Antiquities. He married Elizabeth Fletcher Parrish of Richmond.

Alexander Wilbourne Weddell, the fifth of his parent's children, was born at Richmond April 6, 1876. After his early schooling he was with various banking and traction enterprises until 1904, when he went to Washington and for three years was an assistant in the Library of Congress, specializing in copyright law. He continued his education in George Washington University from 1904 to 1907, receiving the degree of LL. B. from that institution. Mr. Weddell was private secretary to Maurice Francis Egan, United States minister to Denmark at Copenhagen from 1908 to 1910. He served as consul at Zanzibar, Africa, in 1910-12, and as consul at Catania, Italy, 1912-14. He was a student in the University of Catania during 1912-13. He was appointed consul general of Athens, Greece, April 24, 1914, appointed consul general of Beirut, Syria, in December, 1916, was attached to the American Diplomatic Agency at Cairo from January to May, 1917, and in May, 1917, was reappointed consul general at Athens. His foreign service brought him in close touch with American interests during the war, and he was commercial delegate of the United States on the Inter-Allied Bureau of Commercial Attaches at Athens in May, 1917; was delegate of the American War Trade Board at Athens in January, 1918; was permanent delegate on the Commission Financière Inter-Alliée at Athens, and provisional delegate on the Commission Militaire Inter-Alliée, at Athens, in February, 1918. Mr. Weddell was Charge d' Affaires from September to October, 1918, and during 1920-24 was consul general at Calcutta, India. Then came his appointment as consul general at Mexico City.

His war services brought him several awards including the Cross of Commander of George I from the King of Greece, the Collar of Commendatore della Corona d'Italia from King Victor Emmanuel, the Medal of Solidariedad of Panama, and the Order of Mercy from Serbia.

Mr. Weddell has always had his home address in Richmond, and he resides at "Virginia House," just beyond the city named. Virginia and the Nation feel under a special debt of gratitude to Mr. and Mrs. Weddell for having brought from England the material from ancient Warwick Priory, then under demolition, and erecting therewith the lovely Tudor mansion which they now occupy. One wing of "Virginia House" is a replica of Sulgrave Manor, the home in England of George Washington's ancestors. Recently Mr. and Mrs. Weddell have deeded the entire property to the Virginia Historical Society, retaining only a life interest therein.

Mr. Weddell is a member of the Association for the Preservation of Virginia Antiquities, the Virginia Historical Society, the Confederate Memorial Literary Society (Confederate Museum), the Sons of Confederate Veterans, Sons of the Revolu-

tion, Society of Colonial Wars, is a Phi Beta Kappa, the Society
of Cincinnati, the Century Club of New York, Metropolitan Club
of Washington, Bengal Club of Calcutta, St. James Club of
London, and the University Club of Richmond. He has several
times been a contributor to the *National Geographic Magazine*
and an article entitled "The Glory That Was Greece" has been
favorably commended on by many scholars and critics.

Mr. A. W. Weddell married on May 31, 1923, in the Cathedral of St. John the Divine, New York, Mrs. Virginia Chase
Steedman, widow of James Harrison Steedman of St. Louis, Missouri.

The youngest of the children of Rev. Alexander W. Weddell
and wife is Miss Elizabeth Wright Weddell, who was educated
in John H. Powell's Richmond Female Seminary. She is a
member of the board of directors of the Association for the
Preservation of Virginia Antiquities, member of the Confederate Memorial Literary Society (Confederate Museum) the
Woman's Club of Richmond, United Daughters of the Confederacy, and during the World war was active in the Woman's
Munition Reserve Corps at Seven Pines.

The ancestry of the present generation of Weddells includes
also the Armistead family. William Armistead, the first of the
name in Virginia, who lived in Elizabeth City County, was the
father of Anthony Armistead, who served as an officer under
Berkeley in Bacon's rebellion, was a member of the House of
Burgesses, 1693-96, and again in 1699. He married Hannah
Ellyson, daughter of Robert Ellyson of James City County,
and was a member of the House of Burgesses from 1656 to
1663. Anthony Armistead, son of William Armistead, married
Elizabeth Westwood, and their son, Anthony, married Mary
Tucker, daughter of Anthony Tucker. There was also an Anthony Armistead in the next generation, and he married Sarah
Archer and moved to North Carolina. The son, William Armistead, born September 19, 1730, and died in January, 1791, married Sarah Jordan, a descendant of Thomas Jordan of the James
River plantation. Thomas Jordan was a member of the House
of Burgesses from Warrosquioake (Isle of Wight) 1629-1631½.
Their daughter Mary became the wife of David Wright and they
were the parents of Dr. David Minton Wright.

J. VALENTINE WEBB, for many years identified with the furniture business, both as a manufacturer and dealer, is one of
the men responsible for the growing prestige of Galax as one
of the large industrial centers of Southwest Virginia. Mr. Webb
is president and treasurer of the Webb Furniture Company
there.

He was born near Madison in Rockingham County, North
Carolina, February 14, 1884, son of Thomas Walter and Laura
(Coadwell) Webb. His grandfather Webb moved from Floyd
County, Virginia, to Rockingham, North Carolina, and was a
planter and slave owner there. Thomas Walter Webb was born
in Rockingham County in 1854, and spent his active career as a
grower of tobacco and live stock. He was a Democrat, but became a Republican during the Cleveland leadership of the party.
He died in 1918, at the age of sixty-four. His wife, Laura Coadwell, was born in Rockingham County, daughter of a tobacco
planter and stock raiser. She and her husband had a family of

ten children: Anna Lula, born in 1878, is the wife of John F. Grogan, of Rockingham County; Nannie Elizabeth, born in 1880, is the wife of J. W. Dodson, of Stokes County, North Carolina; Henry Clay, born in 1882, died at the age of twenty; J. Valentine; Bell, born in 1886, is the wife of Pomp Smith, of Stokes County; Walter G., born in 1888, superintendent of coal mines at Anawalt, West Virginia, married Hester Herd; Fletcher L., born in 1890, lives at Leaksville, North Carolina, and married Daisy Darnigan; Naomi J., born in 1892, is the wife of Arthur Middleton, of Stokesdale, North Carolina; Mrs. Ruth Middleton, born in 1894, is the widow of a brother of Arthur Middleton; and Della, born in 1896, is the wife of John White, of Winston-Salem, North Carolina.

J. Valentine Webb attended public schools in his native county, and when twenty years of age went to work for the Bassett Furniture Company at Bassett, Virginia. He was with that company from September, 1904, to September, 1911, as a general machine man. Following that he was associated with C. C. Bassett as a partner in a lumber business at Bassett in Henry County, and managed the business until 1914. He then bought the Hotel Bassett, conducted a general store, and was in the retail furniture and undertaking business at Bassett until 1918. In that year he resumed his active connections with lumber manufacturing, with J. D. Bassett as a partner. Mr. Webb on the death of his wife in 1920 sold his lumber interests, and subsequently organized the Valley Veneer Company, Incorporated, of Bassett, being president, director and stockholder. This business was sold in 1925 to Frank English and J. W. Jones, Jr., of Martinsville, Virginia, and at that time Mr. Webb removed to Galax and organized the Webb Furniture Company, Incorporated, which is operating on $225,000 of paid up capital. It is one of the important furniture manufacturing industries of Galax. Mr. Webb is president, treasurer and director of the company.

In politics he is a Republican. He is a thirty-second degree Scottish Rite Mason, member of Kazim Temple of the Mystic Shrine at Roanoke, belongs to the United Commercial Travelers of Roanoke, is a member of the Country Club and the Missionary Baptist Church.

His first wife was Hattie Vaughan, daughter of G. T. and Mary (Turner) Vaughan. She was born in 1885, was a graduate of the high school of Henry County, and taught there until her marriage. Mrs. Webb died March 24, 1920, and is buried at Bassett. Mr. Webb by his first wife had three children: J. Herman, born May 15, 1908, graduated from the Randolph-Macon Academy of Bedford, Virginia, received a diploma in commercial law at Lincoln Memorial University in Tennessee, when nineteen years of age, and is now associated with his father in business, being one of the directors of the Webb Furniture Company; Rachel, born in October, 1910, died November 2, 1916; and Julia Vaughan, born March 12, 1912, is a student in the Galax High School.

Mr. Webb married, May 15, 1921, Miss Myrtle L. Wood, daughter of Daniel C. and Maggie (Jackson) Wood, of Roanoke, where her father is a contractor and builder. Mrs. Webb graduated from the Roanoke High School, also had a commercial course and was employed by the Liberty National Bank and the Colonial National Bank until her marriage. Mr. and Mrs. Webb have one son, born in 1923.

HON. WALTER H. ROBERTSON. It has always been a disputed question how far temperament goes in the determination of personal destiny, but it is an accepted fact that where education, training and experience run parallel with individual inclination, the combination is irresistible in its impetus. Neither does it require keen observation to recognize intellectual temperament when the general personality is large and strong. During the more than a quarter of a century that he has been a member of the Virginia bar Hon. Walter H. Robertson has demonstrated that he possesses in a marked degree the true legal temperament, particularly in the broad and prolific field of civil law, in which branch of his profession he has gained a substantial and lasting reputation.

Mr. Robertson was born near Saltville, Washington County, Virginia, February 22, 1879, a son of Wyndham Bolling and Florence (Henderson) Robertson. This branch of the Robertson family is of Scotch origin, tracing in direct descent from William Robertson, merchant and bailie, of the City of Edinburgh, Scotland, and a cousin of Alexander Robertson, of Struan, who was the prototype of Baron Bradwardine in Sir Walter Scott's "Waverly." Alexander Robertson, the famous Jacobite chief and poet, born about 1670, was of the Clan Donnachaidh, or Duncan, or Robertson. He was a son of Duncan, King of Scotland, oldest son of Malcolm III. This fact supports the statement concerning the Robertsons made in the *Caledonian* of March, 1918 (p. 503), that "the MacGregors are not the only Scottish clan entitled to the proud boast, 'My race is royal.' " From the Clan Donnachaidh, or Duncan, sprang many learned men and warriors famous in the annals of Scotland. It is said that the great historian and divine, William Robertson, the great statesman, William E. Gladstone and Lord Brougham, and the great American orator, Patrick Henry, were all of the Clan of Struan.

William Robertson, bailie of Edinburgh, married Christian Ferguson, and they became the parents of six sons and one daughter: John; William; Arthur, who was chamberlain of Glasgow in 1766; Robert; Patrick; Archibald; and Agnes, who died young and unmarried. Patrick and Archibald Robertson immigrated to America, the former settling in Connecticut and the latter in Prince George County, Virginia.

Archibald Robertson, son of William and Christian (Ferguson) Robertson, married in 1748 Elizabeth Fitzgerald, daughter of John Fitzgerald, an Irish gentleman and patriot of the American Revolution. To this union there were born three sons and two daughters: William, Archibald, John, Christian and Elizabeth.

William Robertson, son of Archibald and Elizabeth (Fitzgerald) Robertson, was born February 5, 1750, and in 1775 married Elizabeth Bolling, daughter of Col. Thomas and Elizabeth (Gay) Bolling, of "Cobbs." It is interesting to note in this connection that Thomas Bolling was the son of John Bolling and Elizabeth (Blair) Bolling, the latter a niece of Commissary James Blair, founder of the College of William and Mary. John Bolling was a son of Col. John Bolling of "Cobbs" and Mary (Kennon) Bolling. Col. John Bolling was the son of Col. Robert Bolling and Jane (Rolfe) Bolling. Jane Rolfe was the only child of Thomas and Jane (Poythress) Rolfe, and Thomas Rolfe was the son of John Rolfe and Pocahontas. Thus, Elizabeth Bolling, who married William Robertson, was sixth in descent from Pocahontas. In writing of the descendants of Pocahontas, many of whom were Robertsons, Wyndham Robertson, in 1887, noted this observation: "In disposition, they seem to have been mild, but firm; brave, but not aggressive; unambitious, but public-spirited; affectionate with one another and just to all. In character, upright and unreproached." (*Pocahontas and Her Descendants*, pp. 73-74.)

William Robertson was vestryman, warden and deputy of Bristol parish, Virginia, 1779-89, and a member of the Virginia Council. He was a merchant at Petersburg, but took up the practice of law and later became a member of the Council. He raised a large and distinguished family, there being in a.l twelve children, eight of whom survived, as follows: Archibald, who married a cousin, Elizabeth Bolling, and died without issue. Thomas Bolling, born February 27, 1778, who married in April, 1821, Lelia Skipwith. He studied law under the distinguished John Thompson of Virginia, and became a member of the House of Delegates from Dinwiddie County, Virginia, in 1805-06. In 1807 he was appointed by Thomas Jefferson as secretary of the territory of Orleans, and was a member of Congress from Louisiana from 1812 to 1818. After serving as attorney general of that state he was elected governor of Louisiana in 1820, and was appointed United States judge for the District of Louisiana in 1825, holding that position until his death October 5, 1828, without issue, at White Sulphur Springs (now West Virginia), where he was buried. The third child, William Robertson, married Christian Williams, and was a member of the Virginia Assembly. The fourth child, John Robertson, was born in 1788, and had a distinguished career, being at various times attorney general of Virginia, member of the State Assembly and chancellor, and member of Congress from Richmond for more than a half a century. He died in 1873. He and his wife, Anne Trent, left issue. Anne Robertson, the fifth child, married Dr. Henry Skipwith and left issue. Jane Gay Robertson, the sixth child, married John H. Bernard, member of the State Senate, who lived at Gaymont, Caroline County, Virginia, and left issue. Wyndham Robertson was the other child to grow to maturity. Wyndham Robertson, son of William and Elizabeth (Bolling) Robertson, was born January 26, 1803, in Chesterfield County, Virginia, and in his youth attended private schools at Richmond, following which he pursued a course at William and Mary College, from which noted institution he was graduated as a member of the class of 1821. After studying law and being admitted to the bar in 1824 he practiced until 1827, which year he spent traveling in Europe, during which he visited London and Paris. Returning to the United States, in 1833 he was elected a member of the Council of State, and in 1836 became senior member of the Council and as such lieutenant-governor, and, in the same year, on the resignation of Gov. Tasewell Wyndham Robertson, became governor of Virginia. He advocated the building of a railroad to the West to take the place of the old James River and Kanawha Canal, and although his plans were defeated at the time their wisdom was later shown in the successful operation of the present Norfolk & Western Railway. He was opposed to Secession and untiring in his efforts to avert war, but when Virginia seceded from the Union he stood with his native state. A sketch of Wyndham Robertson, published in the *Richmond Evening Dispatch* of December 11, 1920, concludes thus: "Robertson was a man of letters, and his *Poca-*

hontas, alias Matoaka, and Her Descendants ranked almost as a classic." He died February 11, 1888.

Wyndham Robertson married Mary Frances Trigg Smith, the only child of Capt. Francis Smith, of Washington County, Virginia, who lived about a mile south of Abingdon. In his daughter's honor he named his home "Mary's Meadows," and to the present day it is known far and wide as "The Meadows." Col. Thomas L. Preston, in his *Historical Sketches and Reminiscences of an Octogenarian,* published in 1900, in speaking of the descendants of Capt. Francis Smith, says "they are among the most refined and cultivated of the present generation." (See p. 161.) The only descendants of Capt. Francis Smith are the descendants of Wyndham and Mary (Smith) Robertson, who were the parents of five children. The first of these, Mary, deceased, was the wife of the late Colonel Blackford, and they had four children: Elizabeth, who married Rev. A. S. Lloyd, now Bishop Lloyd of New York, and have children and grandchildren living in New York, Virginia and Tennessee; Gay Robertson, who never has married; Pelham, of Richmond, Virginia, who married Evelyn Baylor and has three sons; and Wyndham Robertson, who died at Baltimore, Maryland, was twice married and had no children. The second child of Wyndham and Mary (Smith) Robertson, Frank S. Robertson, who was a gallant soldier of the Confederacy during the war between the states, married Miss Stella Wheeler, of Baltimore, and following the war lived at "The Meadows" until his death in August, 1926. Successful in his business affairs, charming in his home life and socially, he was loved by thousands, but never sought and therefore never held public office. His oldest daughter, Mary, affectionately known as "Mamie," brilliant and charming, married Prof. Willoughby Reade, and resided at the Episcopal High School, Alexandria, Virginia, until her death a few years ago. Mr. and Mrs. Reade had several children, all but one of whom are married. The next daughter, Kate Markham, married W. T. Booker, a civil engineer and farmer of Abingdon, where they reside without issue. For many years Miss Katy Robertson was superintendent of the George Ben Johnston Memorial Hospital at Abingdon, Virginia. She was capable and efficient and greatly admired and respected, and her unselfish disposition, her gentle manners, her tender sympathy and her careful attention for the welfare of all who came under her care have given her an abiding place in the hearts of the entire people of Southwest Virginia. The youngest daughter, Stella (Nellie) Wheeler, married Dr. J. Coleman Motley, physician and surgeon of the George Ben Johnston Hospital, Abingdon, where they with three attractive children now reside. The third child of Wyndham and Mary (Smith) Robertson, Kate Markham Robertson, married James L. White, of Abingdon, who served with the rank of captain in the war between the states, in the Confederate army. After the war he settled at Abingdon, where before his death he became known as one of the most able legists in the state. He was a man of fine physique, tall, erect and handsome, and his sincere and courtly manners endeared him to all. He lived and died one of the most popular men of his generation. Kate (Robertson) White, his wife, was one of the loveliest characters of her time. Vivacious, well read, possessing a sense of humor, she yet had one of the tenderest and most sympathetic of hearts and spent her time assisting others. She was a devoted member of the Episcopal Church and her faith was as strong as it was beautiful. To James L. and Kate R. White eight children were born, all of whom survive: Annie C. and Madge C., of Abingdon; Wyndham R., of Roanoke, Virginia, who married his cousin, Mary Clifton White, daughter of Capt. John C. and Mary (Preston) White, of Abingdon, and has three children, "Wyndy" White, famous Virginia Military Institute football star and now coach and teacher at Virginia Episcopal School, Lynchburg, Virginia; and Mary and Anne, both of Roanoke; and W. C. Y., of Abingdon, clerk of the Circuit Court of Washington County, Virginia, and ex-member of the House of Delegates of Virginia, who married Miss Hattie Harris and has six children, all residents of Abingdon with the exception of James, a graduate of the Virginia Military Institute; Pocahontas Trigg, who married Judge Harry Sergent, of Norfolk, Virginia, and has no children; Kathleen Robertson, who married Clarence B. Penn, an attorney of Los Angeles, California, and has no children; and Frank Robertson, who married Miss Anita Clark, and resides at Kennewick, Washington, without issue, and Gay Robertson, seventh in order of birth, who married Thomas Preston Trigg, of Los Angeles, California, and has no children. Ann Pocahontas Robertson, the fourth child of Wyndham and Kate (Smith) Robertson, married Connally F. Trigg, a prominent lawyer of Abingdon, who was commonwealth's attorney and member of Congress from the Ninth Virginia District. Both Mr. and Mrs. Trigg were charming people and greatly beloved at Abingdon, where they passed their lives and died without issue. The fifth child of Wyndham and Kate (Smith) Robertson was Wyndham Bolling Robertson.

Wyndham Bolling Robertson, the youngest son and child of Wyndham and Mary Frances (Trigg) Robertson, was born at Richmond, Virginia, January 17, 1850, and died at Abingdon, July 24, 1923. His father, at the time of Wyndham Bolling's birth, was in the custom of spending the winter months at Richmond and the summers at his country home, "The Meadows," in Washington County. Thus Wyndham Bolling Robertson's childhood was divided between the eastern part of the state, at Richmond, and the southwestern part, at and about Abingdon. His education was acquired at Hanover Academy, Belleview High School and the University of Virginia, but when still quite young had the misfortune to lose the sight in one eye, and for that reason his education was not completed as planned. In early manhood Mr. Robertson went into business at Richmond, where for a short time he was superintendent of the Vulcan Iron Works. This enterprise did not prove successful and in the early part of 1875 he moved to Washington County and became superintendent of the Buena Vista Plaster Company, a mining corporation, and the Buena Vista Farms, near Saltville. Here he resided until his death. In 1910 the Buena Vista Plaster Company leased its mining operations to the United States Gypsum Company and thereafter Mr. Robertson continued to manage the farm, also holding a position with the Mathieson Alkali Works, which he held until his death.

Mr. Robertson was a man of public spirit, but never cared for public office. He was appointed by Governor Tyler a member of the Board of Visitors of Virginia Polytechnic Institute and took great interest in the work and progress of the institution. He was a typical Southern gentleman of the old school, and among his outstanding characteristics were courtly manners, a genial disposition, warm hospitality, a laugh that was contagious, a big and sympathetic heart, devotion to his family, loyalty to his friends and fidelity to every trust. Honor, truth, charity and justice were always uppermost in his mind and heart, and he was a friend to widows and orphans and to all who were in trouble or distress. In his reverence for God and love for humanity he was obedient in the noblest sense of the highest law. His days were spent in doing good. "Life may be given in many ways, and loyalty to truth be sealed, as bravely in the closet as the field, so bountiful is fate." And to no one are these lines more appropriate than to Wyndham Bolling Robertson. He was said to have been one of the most loved and lovable men who ever lived in Washington County. On one occasion his son, Walter H. Robertson, who was at the time a member of the Virginia House of Delegates, went to Washington with Lieut.-Gov. B. F. Buchanan to see U. S. Sen. Carter Glass. Mr. Buchanan introduced young Robertson to Senator Glass, saying: "I suppose you know his father, Mr. Wyndham Robertson?" Senator Glass replied: "Oh, yes, I know him well. I doubt if there is a man in Virginia who is better known than Wyndham Robertson."

In 1870 Wyndham Bolling Robertson was united in marriage with Miss Florence Henderson, of Lynchburg, Virginia, and eight children were born to them, of whom three died in infancy. Eliza Holcombe, the oldest, married L. Norvell Lee, and she and her husband now live at Alpooa, West Virginia, the parents of two married sons and an unmarried daughter. Mrs. Lee is a delightful conversationalist, with a fine sense of humor, and her conversation sparkles with wit and friendly repartee. She is a member of the Episcopal Church and is outstanding in her Christian faith and character. Wyndham Bolling, the next child, is a physician and lives near Charleston, West Virginia. He married Miss Saida Claiborne, and they have two sons: Bolling and Archibald. Doctor Robertson, although exempt from the draft and in other ways, volunteered and for three years gave patriotic and distinguished service overseas to his country and the allies in the World war. Mary Smith, the third child, died in 1917 as the wife of George E. Worden and the mother of seven small children. The fourth child is Walter H. Robertson, of this review. The next three children, William, Charles Bolling and John Rolfe, died in infancy. Pocahontas Trigg Robertson, the last child, is unmarried.

Walter H. Robertson, the youngest surviving son of Wyndham Bolling and Florence (Henderson) Robertson, was fourteen years of age when he entered the College of William and Mary, where he spent two sessions. After working for one year he spent a year in study at Roanoke College, Salem, Virginia, and then entered the service of the Mathieson Alkali Works at Niagara Falls, New York. In the fall of 1899 he became a student in the University of Virginia, where he took a one-year academic course and two years in law, and received his degree of Bachelor of Laws in June, 1902. Admitted to the bar in the same year, he began the general practice of his profession at Bristol in January, 1903, but in 1905 went to Wise Court House, where he spent two years. In 1907 he removed to Johnson City, where he became general counsel of the Carolina, Clinchfield & Ohio Railway and the Clinchfield Coal Corporation, and resided in that community for seven years. In 1915 Mr. Robertson formed a partnership with H. C. and A. K. Morison, under the style of Morison, Morison & Robertson, and moved to Big

Stone Gap, where he resided for two years, and the firm then changed its headquarters to Bristol, where they have offices in the Dominion National Bank Building. Mr. Robertson is known as one of the most capable and resourceful members of his profession in the state, and is particularly prominent in the field of civil law, of which he makes a specialty. He is a member of the Washington County Bar Association, the Virginia Bar Association and the American Bar Association, the Phi Kappa Alpha fraternity, the Benevolent and Protective Order of Elks and the Civitan Club. He is an ardent Democrat, but has little taste for politics, although he was a member of the Virginia House of Delegates in the session of 1920, and in 1923 was elected a member of the Bristol City Council. He is an elder of the Central Presbyterian Church.

On October 12, 1905, Mr. Robertson was united in marriage with a member of an old distinguished Virginia family, Miss Bessie Wilson White, a daughter of Capt. John G. White. Captain White earned his title as a gallant Confederate soldier during the war between the states, in which he was wounded, and after the war was engaged in agricultural pursuits during the rest of his life. He also was prominent and influential in public life, and served as postmaster of Abingdon during the administrations of President Cleveland. To Mr. and Mrs. Robertson there have come two daughters: Margaret White, a student in Sophie Newcomb Memorial Hospital College at New Orleans, Louisiana; and Florence Henderson, who is attending Virginia Intermont College at Bristol.

MAJ. WILLIAM R. NICHOLS, an officer of the Regular Army, is a native Virginian, born at Petersburg, July 25, 1885.

His grandfather was Capt. James N. Nichols, an officer in Lee's army in the Civil war, and died shortly after the close of the war. He was a co-partner in the ownership and president of the gas works at Petersburg. Major Nichols' father, William R. Nichols, Sr., was born and reared in Petersburg, was in business in that city and died in 1892, at the age of thirty-seven. His wife, Nora Préot, was born and reared at Farmville, Virginia, attended Buckingham Institute, where her father was one of the professors, and she died in 1911. She was a member of St. Paul's Episcopal Church at Petersburg and of the United Daughters of the Confederacy. Her father, George Arnaud Préot, was a distinguished musician and scholar. Among his many musical compositions is the music for that beautiful poem, "Thou Art Crumbling to the Dust," for the old Blanford Church at Petersburg, one of the oldest churches in America. Major Nichols was the fourth in a family of six children. His sister, Ann Lillian, is now the wife of James M. Ruffin, a descendant of Thomas Jefferson. A brother is James N. Nichols. Nora Page, now deceased, was the wife of Alexander W. Bryant. Marie Conway is Mrs. William H. Worth, of Petersburg, and Elizabeth married J. Thurman Clark, of Bedford, Virginia.

Major Nichols attended public schools in Petersburg, graduated Bachelor of Science and second Jackson-Hope medalist in 1906 from the Virginia Military Institute, and after one year of engineering work returned to the institute as assistant professor of mathematics. He spent one semester in the Massachusetts Institute of Technology at Boston, and in the spring of 1909 was commissioned a second lieutenant in the Coast Artillery Corps of the United States Army. He was promoted to first lieutenant in 1911, and in 1916 to captain. From June, 1917, to September, 1918, he was on duty with the army organization for the World war as commanding officer of the Torpedo Depot at Fort Totten, New York. Early in 1918 he was promoted to major and later to lieutenant colonel in the National Army, but in April, 1920, resumed his regular army rank of captain, and in July of that year was promoted to major, the rank he still holds. Major Nichols has been professor of military science and tactics and commandant of cadets at the Virginia Polytechnic Institute since the fall of 1924.

He is an honor graduate of the Coast Artillery School of 1914 at Fort Monroe. He was detailed as an instructor of the Coast Artillery School, assigned for a special course of study, to the Massachusetts Institute of Technology during the sessions of 1915-16. He graduated from a course in the Command and General Staff School at Fort Leavenworth, Kansas, in 1924, and is under orders to attend the War College at Washington with the class of 1929-30. Major Nichols is a member of Mountain City Lodge No. 67, A. F. and A. M., at Lexington, is a member of the Phi Kappa Phi honor fraternity and the Kappa Alpha social fraternity, the Army, Navy and Marine Corps Country Club, and is an independent in politics. He is a member of the Episcopal Church.

He married at Savannah, Georgia, January 10, 1912, Miss Josephine Stoney Stevens. She attended private school at Savannah and studied music abroad, specializing in violin. She is a member of the Episcopal Church and of the Society of Colonial Dames. Her parents are Henry Dana and Josephine (Stoney) Stevens, of Savannah. Her father for many years was a cotton factor and otherwise prominent in the business life of Savannah, and is now retired. Major Nichols and wife have two children, Nora Préot and William Robert, Jr. Préot is a graduate of the Mary Baldwin Seminary at Staunton, Virginia, and Robert is in a private school at Savannah, Georgia.

HARVEY LEE PRICE, dean of agriculture at Virginia Polytechnic Institute, is an outstanding authority on horticulture and other phases of agricultural science, and has been connected with the faculty of instruction at Blacksburg since 1900.

He was born at Prices Fork, Virginia, March 18, 1874, son of William Taylor and Margaret (Hawley) Price. His great-great-grandfather, Michael Price, came from Germany to America in 1738, and from Philadelphia moved into Southwestern Virginia, settling on New River, near the mouth of Strubles Creek, in Montgomery County. He built a block house, and it served as a place of muster during the Revolutionary war. He and his family are buried at old St. Peter's Lutheran Church near Prices Fork. Professor Price's grandfather was David Price. William Taylor Price was born and reared in Prices Fork community, served as a private in the Confederate army, in General Horton's brigade, and after the war engaged in farming and stock raising until his death in 1914. His wife, Margaret Hawley, was born near Vickers Switch in Montgomery County, was educated in private schools and was a member of the Christian Church. She died in 1900.

Harvey Lee Price, only son of his parents, attended public school in Montgomery County, grew up in the environment of a farm and learned the fundamentals of agricultural science by practical experience. He graduated from Virginia Polytechnic

Institute with the Bachelor of Science degree in 1898 and Master of Science in 1900, and in the latter year became instructor in horticulture at the institute. From 1903 to 1908 he was horticulturist and professor of horticulture and since 1908 has been dean of the department of agriculture. Mr. Price owns two farms in Montgomery County, where he has the opportunity of carrying out some of his ideas, one a general farming proposition and the other devoted to orchard crops.

He is a member of the Phi Kappa Phi honor fraternity, American Association for the Advancement of Science, American Pomological Society, American Genetic Association, is a charter member of the Society for Horticultural Science, member of the Virginia Academy of Science and Virginia State Horticultural Society. For many years he has been interested in Masonry and is affiliated with Hunters Lodge No. 156, A. F. and A. M.; Blacksburg Royal Arch Chapter, Blacksburg Commandery of the Knights Templar, and is a charter member of Kazim Temple of the Mystic Shrine. Formerly he belonged to the Knights of Pythias. Professor Price is an independent Democrat in politics and is a member of the Christian Church.

He married at Blacksburg, September 21, 1904, Miss Daisy Conway, who grew up and attended public school at Blacksburg, graduated in 1896 from the Farmville State Normal College, and prior to her marriage taught school on the eastern shore of Virginia, in Lancaster and Montgomery counties and at Roanoke and in the State Teachers College at Athens, Georgia. Since her marriage she has kept in close touch with educational movements. She is a member of the Daughters of the American Revolution. Readers of poetry all over the country are familiar with the name of Mrs. Price, who has written verse for many years, and some of her offerings have been published in such magazines as *Ainslies, American, Poetry* and the *American Magazine of Verse*. Mrs. Price is a daughter of Dr. William B. and Julia (Thomas) Conway. Her father for a number of years was college physician at the Polytechnic Institute, and in the later years of his life he engaged in general practice at Athens, Georgia. He served as a soldier in the Confederate army under Gen. J. E. B. Stuart. Doctor Conway died in 1920 and his wife in 1917, and both are buried at Blacksburg. Dean Price and wife had six children, one of whom died in infancy. William Conway was educated in public schools of Blacksburg, graduated from the Virginia Polytechnic Institute in 1927 and is now a research student in Boyce Thompson Institute at Yonkers, New York. The other children are: Harvey Lee, Jr., a sophomore in Virginia Polytechnic Institute; Margaret Hawley, who died at the age of four and one-half years; Mary Luster, now a first year student in high school; and Jule, in the grade school.

B. STANLEY STEVENS. For many years one of the old established concerns in Pulaski County has been the furniture and undertaking business now carried on as the M. W. Stevens estate, of which B. Stanley Stevens is active manager.

Mr. Stevens was born in Pulaski July 9, 1895, son of M. W. and Lucretia (Kirby) Stevens. His grandfather, Capt. Robert Stevens, was for many years in the service of the old Virginia & Tennessee Railroad Company as a conductor, and was killed in a railroad accident. M. W. Stevens was born at Cambria, Virginia, attended public schools there, and began his business career in Pulaski as clerk in a general store. Later he became

associated with Dr. John Darst in the furniture and undertaking
business. The business for some years was known as M. W.
Stevens & Company. About 1900 he acquired the interest of his
partner and continued under his individual name as M. W. Stevens until his death on March 1, 1913. Since then the business
has been a part of the M. W. Stevens estate. Lucretia Kirby,
widow of M. W. Stevens, was born in Pulaski County and attended public schools there and at Christiansburg. She is a member
of the Presbyterian Church. Of her two children the only survivor is B. Stanley. A daughter, Frances Elizabeth, died at the
age of nine months.

B. Stanley Stevens attended public schools, graduating from
the Pulaski High School in 1913. He had just finished his high
school course when the death of his father threw upon him unusual responsibilities as manager of the M. W. Stevens estate,
and he has given his time and energy to that with few outside
interests or diversions during the past fifteen years. The business
is now conducted in a two-story brick building at the corner of
Washington Avenue and Third Street. The furniture department
includes a full line of house furnishings, also phonographs and
radios, and the funeral and embalming department is one of the
most completely equipped in this section of the state.

Mr. Stevens is a Knight Templar Mason and member of the
B. P. O. Elks, Rotary Club, is a Democrat in politics and a deacon in the Presbyterian Church.

He married at Dublin, Virginia, July 23, 1924, Miss Helen
Buford, of Dublin, daughter of John and Mary (Whaling) Bu-
ford. Her father for many years was a farmer and cattle man at
Dublin. Mr. and Mrs. Stevens have one son, Robert Whitfield
Stevens.

COLIN ELWOOD RICHARDSON is a native of Carroll County,
Virginia, a comparatively young man who in a brief period of
years has accumulated business interests and connections that
make him one of the outstanding figures in the commercial affairs of Pulaski, where he has his home.

Mr. Richardson was born at Sylvatus in Carroll County,
July 16, 1890 son of Floyd I. and Orlena (Davis) Richardson.
The Richardsons came to America in Colonial times, first set-
tling in Maryland, and from there moved to Southwestern Virginia in pioneer times. Mr. Richardson's grandfather, Lorenzo
Dow Richardson, was the son of the pioneer of the family in
Carroll County. Floyd I. Richardson was born and reared in
Carroll County, and spent his active life as a farmer and stock
raiser. For about twenty years he has been postmaster of Syl-
vatus. His wife, Orlena Davis, was born and reared in Carroll
County. She is an active worker in the Baptist Church. They
had a family of twelve children: Colin E.; Maggie Mae, wife
of George Halsey; Dexter J., who died when twenty-one years
old; Amanda, wife of C. J. Sears; Ramsey, Stephen H. and
D. Gratton, all of whom reside at Stone, Kentucky; Joseph, of
Sylvatus, Virginia; Martin, of Stone, Kentucky; Aaron and
Troy, both residents of Sylvatus.

Colin Richardson attended the public schools of Carroll
County and for three years assisted his father in the post office
at Sylvatus. This was followed by a course in the National
Business College at Roanoke, and on leaving there he went to
Welch, West Virginia, and for nine years was junior partner
in a general mercantile business known as C. D. Brewster &

Company. On returning to Virginia, Mr. Richardson located at Honaker in Russell County, where he organized a wholesale grocery, and for several months was associated with this business, known as Bradshaw & Richardson. He sold out to his partner, J. H. Bradshaw, and in 1920 established his home at Pulaski. At Pulaski, associated with Currell Dalton and Sexton Dalton, he built the Dalton Theater Building, and had the active management of the theater for one year. He then organized the Dix-Richardson Wholesale Dry Goods & Notions Company, and for four years gave most of his time to that business as secretary and treasurer of the company, and is still financially interested and a director. Since 1926 he has been secretary, treasurer and manager of the Pulaski Veneer Corporation, and also secretary and treasurer of the Virginia Panel Corporation. These are important industries utilizing the hardwood timber resources of Southwestern Virginia, and turning out veneers and panels which are sold and worked up by many of the leading furniture maufacturers of the country. Mr. Richardson helped organize the Pulaski Veneer Corporation. The company built a three-story building covering about two acres and has complete equipment of modern machinery for veneer manufacture. Mr. Richardson is a director in the Peoples National Bank and in the Pulaski Trust Company, and has also found opportunity to express his public spirited interest in the community by memberships in a number of social and civic organizations. He is affiliated with Lodge No. 112, A. F. and A. M., is a thirty-second degree Scottish Rite Mason, member of Kazim Temple of the Mystic Shrine at Roanoke, is affiliated with the B. P. O. Elks, Pulaski Rotary Club, of which he is a charter member and former president, member of the Pulaski Country Club. He is a Republican and a Baptist.

Mr. Richardson married November 3, 1913, in Carroll County, Miss Stella Dalton, who was reared and educated there. She is a member of the Baptist Church, the Woman's Civic Club and the Pulaski Country Club. Her parents were Currell and Ladeski (Martin) Dalton. Her father was a farmer and stock raiser, merchant and wholesaler in Carroll and Pulaski counties. He died December 30, 1919, and her mother passed away in July, 1920. Mr. and Mrs. Richardson's only child died in infancy.

JULIAN ASHBY BURRUSS, president of the Virginia Polytechnic Institute, has given thirty years to educational work as teacher and administrator, having been president of the State Normal School at Harrisonburg prior to coming to Blacksburg.

Doctor Burruss, one of the leading authorities on education in the state, was born at Richmond, Virginia, August 16, 1876, son of Woodson Cheadle and Cora Emmett (McDowell) Burruss. The Burruss family came from England to Virginia about two centuries ago. Doctor Burruss had two ancestors in the War of the Revolution, Jacob Gann Burruss and his son, William Burruss. A son of William Burrus was Pleasant Burruss, who was the father of Jacob Burruss, grandfather of Julian A. Woodson Cheadle Burruss was born in Caroline County, Virginia, attended the old field schools of the state and served as a private all through the Civil War in the Confederate Army, in the Bowling Green Grays, which was a part of General Pickett's Division. After the war he became a building contractor at Richmond, and died in 1908. His wife was born and reared in Hanover

County, Virginia. She died in 1905, and they are buried in Riverview Cemetery at Richmond. Doctor Burruss has one sister, Eva May, wife of Albert H. Gillock, of Lexington, Virginia.

Julian Ashby Burruss had his early advantages in the schools of Richmond, and in 1898 graduated from the Virginia Polytechnic Institute with the degree Bachelor of Science in civil engineering. In the intervals of his school work he has carried on his studies in various institutions, including Richmond College and Harvard University, was scholar in 1905-06 and fellow in education in 1906-07 at Columbia University, which gave him the Master of Arts degree in 1906. His Doctor of Philosophy degree was conferred by the University of Chicago in 1921.

Doctor Burruss was instructor in the Normal College at Waleska, Georgia, in 1899-1900, in the Searcy Female Institute in Arkansas and the Speers-Langford Military Academy in 1900-01, and was principal of the Leigh School at Richmond from 1901 to 1904. He then became director of Manual Arts in the Richmond public schools, holding that office in 1904-05, and after returning from Columbia University, again in 1907-08. Doctor Burruss became president of the State Normal School for Women at Harrisonburg when it was founded in 1908, and served until 1919. He has been president of the Virginia Polytechnic Institute since July 1, 1919. He was an instructor in the summer quarters of the University of Chicago School of Education in 1919, 1920 and 1921.

Doctor Burruss is author of numerous addresses and reports, and a volume published in 1921, entitled "The Business Administration of Colleges." He is a member of the State Board of Agriculture, the Virginia Truck Experiment Station Board, the Commission on Medical Education in Virginia, Commission on Simplification and Economy of State and Local Government in Virginia, and State Agricultural Commission. He was president in 1912-13 of the Virginia State Teachers Association, president during the same year of the Virginia Association of Colleges and Schools for Girls, is a member of the National Society for Vocational Education, National Education Association, Association of Land Grant Colleges. He is a Phi Kappa Phi and Pi Gamma Mu, member of the Sons of the American Revolution, the Masonic fraternity, Westmoreland Club of Richmond, and is a Presbyterian.

He married, June 18, 1907, Miss Rachel Cleveland Ebbert, of Covington, Kentucky. They have two children, Julian Ashby and Jean McDowell.

CHARLES ROSS HUDDLE, a chemical and metallurgical engineer, who has been associated with a number of mining and manufacturing enterprises in Southwestern Virginia, is now superintendent of the Ivanhoe Mining & Smithing Corporation at Ivanhoe in Wythe County.

He comes of a family of engineers. He was born on Frances Mill Creek, near Cripple Creek, in Wythe County, Virginia, in 1885, son of John Foster and Katharine Elizabeth (Ross) Huddle. His grandfather Huddle was one of the pioneer men in the iron industry of the Alleghany Mountains, and at one time operated a chain of iron mines in the coal regions of Pennsylvania. Immediately after the Civil war he established a furnace and forge for the manufacture of cutlery, chiefly axes, near Ivanhoe, on Cripple Creek, at a place now called Catron. He was buried near Ivanhoe. John Foster Huddle was born in Lehigh County,

Pennsylvania, in 1841, and was sent abroad for his technical education, which he completed at Freiburg University in Saxony, Germany. After returning to the United States he had an extensive experience in the mining industry of both the East and the West. He and Charles H. Nimpson formed the firm of Nimpson & Huddle, consulting metallurgical engineers. He had charge of the furnaces and mines for the Eastern Tennessee & Western North Carolina Railroad, managing these properties from 1885 to 1905. He also engaged in a large private practice, examining mines in Virginia, Kentucky and Tennessee. During the Civil war he was drafted for service with the Confederate government at Lynchburg and was put in charge of a gunplant near Wytheville, where the old flint lock guns were changed to equipment with percussion caps. John Foster Huddle died in 1908 and is buried at Ivanhoe, Virginia. His wife, Kathrine Elizabeth Ross, was born in the Shenandoah Valley of Virginia, daughter of Alfred Ross, who came from Nova Scotia and became a planter in the Valley of Virginia. John Foster Huddle and wife had five children: Charles R.; William Boyd, born in 1888, a metallurgical engineer now living in California; Nora Bell, who died at the age of fourteen; Minnieola, born in 1887 and died in 1893; and Agnes Bertha, who died at the age of six months.

Charles Ross Huddle graduated from high school at Bristol, Virginia, and has had the benefit of both a thorough technical and practical training in his line of work as a metallurgical engineer. Mr. Huddle is a Republican in politics and a member of the Episcopal Church.

He married at Ivanhoe, Virginia, November 25, 1909, Miss Ida Lawson, of Ivanhoe. She attended public schools and Martha Washington College at Abingdon, Virginia. Mrs. Huddle is a daughter of James Columbus and Louenna (Branscomb) Lawson. Her father was a merchant at Ivanhoe, and her grandfather Branscomb was for many years a merchant in Carroll, near Hillsville, Virginia. Mr. and Mrs. Huddle have one son, Charles Richard, born January 2, 1911. He graduated from the Ivanhoe High School in 1928 and is now associated with his father in chemical laboratory work.

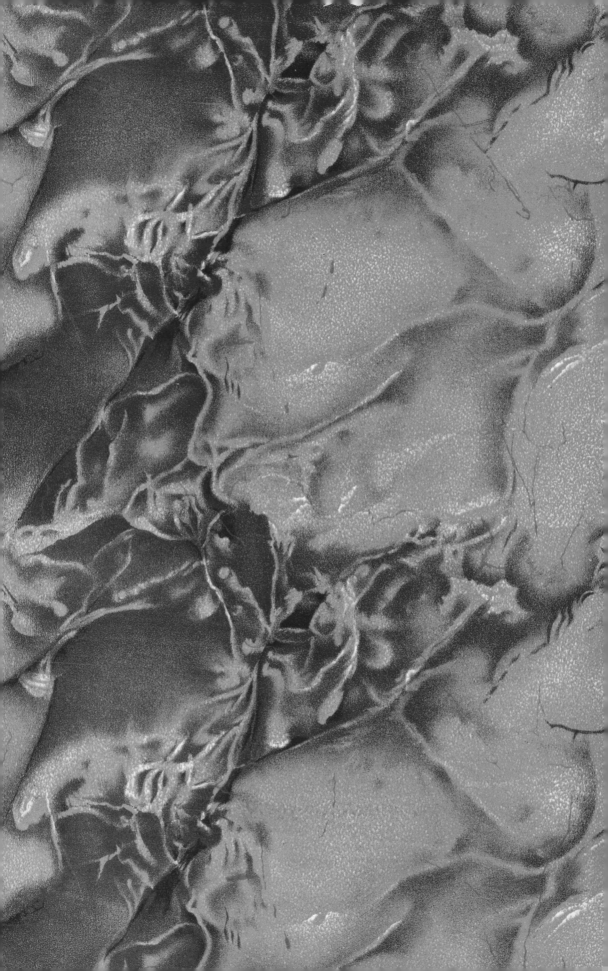